Professional Biztalk

Stephen Mohr

Scott Woodgate

Wrox Press Ltd.

Professional Biztalk

Published by Wrox Press Ltd,
Arden House, 1102 Warwick Road, Acocks Green,
Birmingham, B27 6BH, UK
Printed in Canada
ISBN 1861003293

Trademark Acknowledgements

Wrox has endeavored to provide trademark information about all the companies and products mentioned in this book by the appropriate use of capitals. However, Wrox cannot guarantee the accuracy of this information.

Credits

Authors
Stephen Mohr
Scott Woodgate

Additional Material
Michael Kay

Technical Reviewers
David Balisles
Jeff Becraft
Maxime Bombardier
Michael Corning
Joe Haines
Mark Harrison
Wilfred Jansoone
Brian Loesgen
Oleg Ovaneysan
Jordan Milushev
Fredrik Normen
Phil Powers-DeGeorge
David West

Technical Architect
Jon Duckett

Technical Editors
Christian Peak
Helen Callaghan
Matthew Moodie

Category Manager
Viv Emery

Author Agent
Tony Berry

Project Manager
Nicola Phillips

Production Manager
Simon hardware

Production Project Coordinator
Mark Burdett

Illustrations
Shabnam Hussain

Cover
Shelley Frazier

Proof Reader
Chris Smith

Indexing
Michael Brinkman
Andrew Criddle

About the Authors

Stephen Mohr

Stephen Mohr is a software systems architect with Omicron Consulting, Philadelphia, USA. He has more than ten years' experience working with a variety of platforms and component technologies. His research interests include distributed computing and artificial intelligence. Stephen holds BS and MS degrees in computer science from Rensselaer Polytechnic Institute.

> *For my wife, for her support and understanding as always; for Jos, Celeste, and the other relatives for their help; for James, who just wants to be a "computer workman" like his Dad, and Matthew, who's going to figure it all out and bend it to his will.*

Scott Woodward

Scott Woodgate, a Microsoft Certified Solution Developer, is a Technical Product Manager for Microsoft BizTalk Server 2000. His interest in computers was sparked as a teenager in the mid-80's when he wrote commercial computer assisted learning software, and accounting/inventory software running under MSDOS. Scott spent far too long at university ignoring his passion for computing and in the process obtaining five pieces of paper in nine years including a PhD in Organometallic Chemistry, a Commerce Degree, and finally a Computer Science diploma. Before immigrating to Redmond with his girlfriend, Scott was an e-commerce project manager at Datacom in New Zealand where he was responsible for building complex web solutions using all aspects of Windows DNA, Site Server Commerce Edition and occasionally Java 2 Enterprise Edition.

> *To Artemiza for all her patience during long weekends of writing that could have been spent playing.*

Table of Contents

Table of Contents

Table of Contents

Table of Contents

Table of Contents

Table of Contents

Introduction

The increasing sophistication of web applications brings new challenges to programmers. As we expose more applications to run over the Web, we have to make use of existing legacy applications. For example, if you think about an e-commerce site, much of the data that supports it will come from legacy back-office systems. Efficient inventory checking and order fulfilment requires an automated link to the firm's supply-chain software. Within an organization, there is increasing interest in linking applications that were formerly run as stand-alone islands. The manual links in business processes are being replaced by automation. These are examples of **Enterprise Application Integration** or (**EAI**). EAI is the ability to directly link separate applications to work cooperatively as part of a larger system. Application integration requires the exchange of structured data, so that data can be moved through the different applications that make up part of a larger system in a meaningful way.

The trend toward **Business-to-Business** (**B2B**) integration takes EAI to a new dimension. Organizations want to forge tight links with their suppliers and customers so that goods may move quickly and efficiently, reducing the need to maintain an inventory or wait for delivery. These partners want to be able to trade electronically, tying one partner's enterprise resource program (ERP) to their partner's ERP system. This is EAI on a grand scale, spanning organizational boundaries and computing platforms. Though issues of network interoperability, security, and data exchange loom large over B2B, the rewards of successful B2B integration are so great as to make the effort worthwhile.

Our task as programmers is to find effective and reliable solutions for passing this information. This can be especially challenging when dealing with legacy or mission-critical systems. A company's inventory management system or financial system is probably well-established, proven, and absolutely essential to the operation of the company. Unlike a departmental application or utility program, programmers can seldom modify these systems, and certainly must not bring them down. In traditional integration projects, the integration layer required to bind applications together is embedded in the applications themselves. This means that changes to the larger system require modifications to the source code of the applications that make it up; since integration code is distributed across a number of applications, this kind of integration requires great care to maintain.

In the illustration below, a new application – a web-based gateway to internal system – has been grafted onto two existing systems, the organization's financial application and its inventory application. The latter applications are mission-critical and may not be changed. They were originally developed in isolation, and use different means of communications and data formats. The financial application uses COM and exchanges data in fixed positional file formats, while the inventory application uses MSMQ to transport data in comma separated variables (CSV) file format. The gateway uses HTTP and passes data in the form of XML documents. In the center, controlling the flow of data between these applications, is an **integration server**, another application that will be the focus of this book.

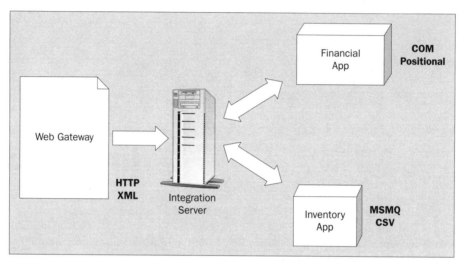

We mentioned that legacy applications are often used for mission-critical tasks, so modification of the source code is usually not permitted. This means that these applications cannot be integrated using traditional techniques. Instead, we have to integrate these applications using the programmatic interfaces or I/O mechanisms they use in normal operation.

There are, however, benefits to integrating applications in this manner. It largely removes integration from an application's code and makes it a matter of configuration instead. When programming is required, it is generally in the form of components or scripts invoked by integration software. Workflow integrators look at the flow of data between the applications that make up a system, and write code that coordinates the movement of data between the applications in order to implement the desired workflow. When the workflow changes, the data, or the coordinating pattern, or both, must change. If these are located on a central integration server, the task of modifying the workflow is much easier. In many cases, it is largely a matter of reconfiguring the data that runs the integration server.

In the following schematic, the central flowchart represents the desired behavior of some distributed system – the **workflow** of the business. Each activity in the flowchart is implemented by an application. The three applications must be coordinated by some central application that understands the workflow and can orchestrate the actions of the three applications. Ideally, the coordinating application is a general-purpose application initialized by some body of data describing the desired workflow. Additionally, the coordinating application must have some mechanism for communicating with the three applications using the communications protocols and data formats they support.

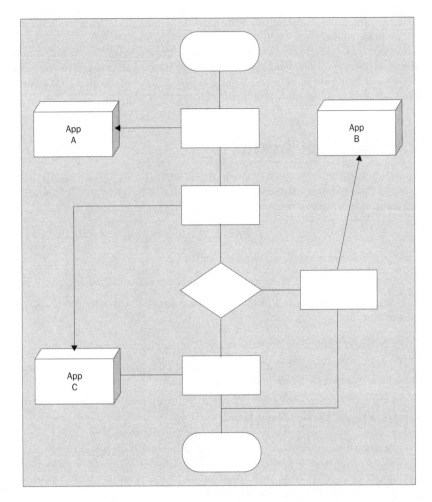

This is where **Microsoft BizTalk Server** comes into the picture. It gives us a central integration server that is data-driven, and a set of tools for performing application integration. Although it makes extensive use of the proprietary features of Windows 2000 for its implementation, it is capable of integrating applications across platforms. It is completely capable of accomplishing integration solely through the use of open Internet-related standards. Programmers can:

❑   design the flow of information through a system

❑   use BizTalk and its interfaces as the glue to perform the actual integration

❑   track the flow of information through the resulting system

BizTalk Server permits you to take advantage of your existing, proven applications to rapidly develop business systems for EAI and B2B e-commerce. BizTalk Server is equally useful tying together internal systems or linking business partners over the Internet. In fact, it may be considered whenever you need to connect important applications without making major code modifications.

Indeed, in many situations, you may not just be dealing with applications that are in your own company; you may often need to integrate with partners' applications for a truly automated system. For example, taking the e-commerce example further, you might need to integrate with a supplier's system for just-in-time ordering, so that you can maintain lower stock levels. Or you might need to integrate with an order fulfillment house to send the products that have been ordered to the customer. At all of these stages you will also want to know what the state of play is – to be able to **track** records. BizTalk Server can provide you with the ability to do all of these things.

What This Book is About

This book introduces BizTalk Server and how to deal with issues in Enterprise Application Integration, in particular rapid development of e-commerce systems (both B2B and B2C). It helps you learn how to use BizTalk Server to tie together separate applications to create a larger system.

We will learn about the various tools that BizTalk provides to help you with the tasks of:

❑   Planning the flow of data between applications

❑   Defining the structure of the data that will flow between applications

❑   Transforming disparate message formats so that data can work between applications that use different formats

❑   Tracking messages in the system

It will show you how you can use BizTalk Server to create integrated solutions that make use of – both you own and trading partners – existing applications.

Who Should Use This Book?

This book is for programmers who are embarking on all sorts of Enterprise Application Integration projects, especially e-commerce systems. It will teach you how BizTalk Server can be used to aid these tasks. Some experience of developing web applications on the Windows platform would be helpful (including messaging using MSMQ, although this is not essential).

If you need to integrate applications, whether you are looking to use BizTalk Server, or you want to be able to integrate with someone who uses BizTalk Server, this book will teach you to work with this exciting new product.

Technologies Used in the Book

Being about integrating different types of system, this book makes use of a variety of technologies. These include XML, Windows 2000 running IIS and ASP, SQL Server, MSMQ, and Visual Basic. It also features examples of integrating with delimited and positional flatfile formats (although you do not need experience of working with these).

Many of the sample applications have been developed using Visual Basic, and while you don't need to know this to get a lot from the book, if you want to run all of the examples, you will need at least VB 6. We also make extensive use of XML, and familiarity with it would be helpful, but is not a prerequisite.

Conventions

We have used a number of different styles of text and layout in this book to help differentiate between the different kinds of information. Here are examples of the styles we use and an explanation of what they mean:

Code has several fonts. If it's a word that we're talking about in the text – for example, when discussing a For...Next loop, it's in this font. If it's a block of code that you can type as a program and run, then it's also in a gray box:

```
<?xml version 1.0?>
```

Sometimes you'll see code in a mixture of styles, like this:

```
<?xml version 1.0?>
<Invoice>
   <part>
      <name>Widget</name>
      <price>$10.00</price>
   </part>
</invoice>
```

In cases like this, the code with a white background is code we are already familiar with, while the line highlighted in grey is a new addition to the code since we last looked at it.

Advice, hints, and background information come in this type of font.

> **Important pieces of information come in boxes like this.**

Bullets appear indented, with each new bullet marked as follows:

- ❑ **Important Words** are in a bold type font
- ❑ Words that appear on the screen, in menus like the File or Window, are in a similar font to that you would see on a Windows desktop
- ❑ Keys that you press on the keyboard like *Ctrl* and *Enter*, are in italics

Customer Support

We've tried to make this book as accurate and enjoyable as possible, but what really matters is what the book actually does for you. Please let us know your views, either by returning the reply card in the back of the book, or by contacting us via e-mail at feedback@wrox.com.

Source Code and Updates

As you work through the examples in this book, you may decide that you prefer to type in all the code by hand. Many readers prefer this because it's a good way to get familiar with the coding techniques that are being used.

Whether you want to type the code in or not, we have made all the source code for this book available at our web site at the following address:

http://www.wrox.com/

If you're one of those readers who likes to type in the code, you can use our files to check the results you should be getting – they should be your first stop if you think you might have typed in an error. If you're one of those readers who doesn't like typing, then downloading the source code from our web site is a must!

Either way, it'll help you with updates and debugging.

Errata

We've made every effort to make sure that there are no errors in the text or the code. However, to err is human, and as such we recognize the need to keep you informed of any mistakes as they're spotted and corrected. Errata sheets are available for all our books at http://www.wrox.com. If you find an error that hasn't already been reported, please let us know.

Our web site acts as a focus for other information and support, including the code from all our books, sample chapters, previews of forthcoming titles, and articles and opinion on related topics.

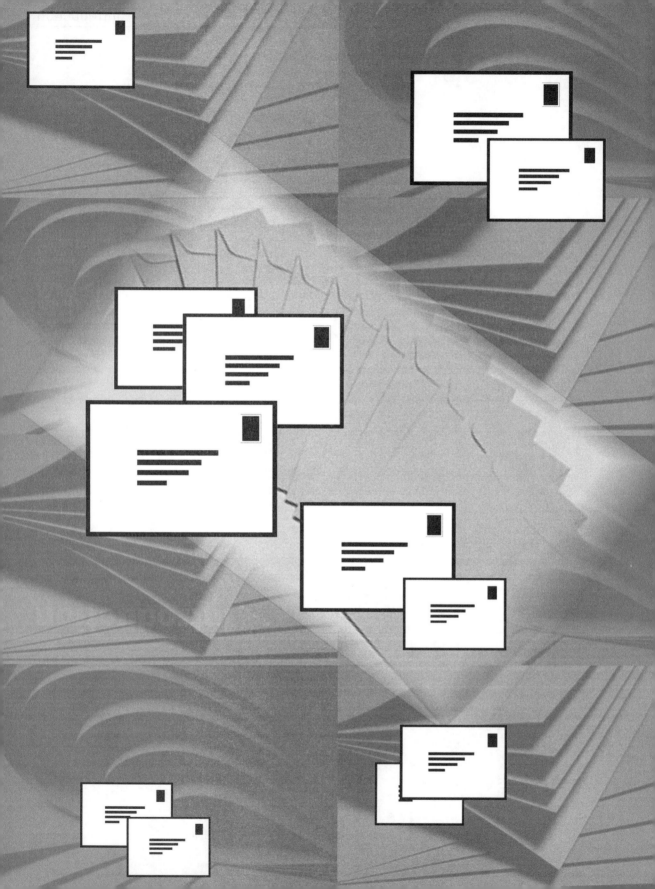

1

BizTalk and Application Integration

In the Introduction, we discussed how BizTalk Server enables you to integrate separate applications together to create a larger system. Whether the applications are your own, or those of your business partners, BizTalk Server allows you to keep integration code on a central server rather than writing integration code into the applications themselves.

This chapter will provide you with a general overview of the application integration process, and the benefits of BizTalk Server in regard to this process. We will start by looking at some common situations that require application integration, and identify some common problems that BizTalk Server can solve for us. We'll survey the major features and tools made available to us by BizTalk Server, and orient ourselves for the rest of our journey through this book.

When you have finished this chapter, you will have an understanding of the role and features of BizTalk Server. In particular, you will appreciate the following:

❑ The increasing need for application integration tools in corporate development

❑ The role that open standards for information interchange can play in application integration

❑ The features and scope of Microsoft BizTalk Server

❑ How BizTalk Server uses a data-driven mechanism for coordinating application integration

❑ The interprocess and internetworking protocols that are essential to application integration with BizTalk Server

Benefits of Enterprise Application Integration

Let's remind ourselves of why we should want to perform **Enterprise Application Integration** (**EAI**). Applications, in particular mission-critical applications that are used to run the enterprise, represent chunks of proven functionality. At the highest levels, they perform the functions that represent what the organization does in the business sense. They represent ordering supplies, scheduling manufacturing, fulfilling customer orders, and reconciling the finances of the company.

These business applications work in isolation in many companies. Since, in reality, the business processes do not occur in isolation, manual steps exist to integrate the applications. These steps introduce delay and add cost to the end product or service of the organization. Anything that can be done to replace manual integration with interprocess coordination is likely to speed up the company and reduce overhead. We want to go from the industrial revolution to Internet time.

Carrying this idea a step further, companies are themselves steps in a complete process. Few companies do everything to move a product from raw materials to finished goods. Companies operate in a web of business relationships, with one supplying the other with what they need. Here, as with processing within a single organization, companies mostly interact through manual processes. However, if an inventory application in one company can place an order directly with the order entry process of a trusted supplier, the entire process can be streamlined. Essentially, this is EAI carried out between companies, and it is often referred to as **Business-to-Business** e-commerce (**B2B**).

Finding a way to carry out EAI without having to rewrite mission-critical applications is the goal of this book. Microsoft BizTalk Server is a product that can perform this task for you, by coordinating the flow of message document files between applications. This is illustrated below:

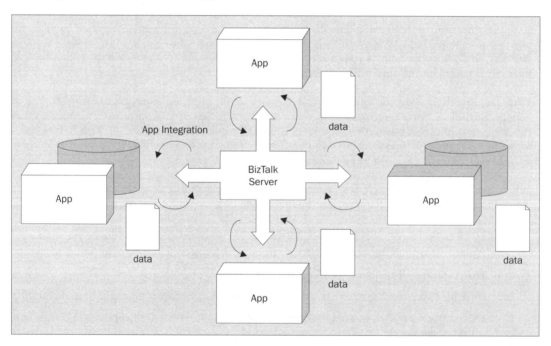

> **Microsoft BizTalk Server is a product that performs application integration, using messaging.**

Data from one application can be transmitted to BizTalk Server over some communications protocol, such as HTTP, and BizTalk can forward it to another application in another data format over another protocol. It does this based on internal configurations supplied by business analysts and programmers. It is a general-purpose server customized to a particular task through the provision of data configurations.

However, the presence of multiple data formats and communications protocols in such a system suggests some challenges that BizTalk Server must overcome before it can implement application integration. Let us turn now to take a look at those challenges.

Challenges of Enterprise Application Integration

In this section we are going to look at some of the inherent problems we encounter if we wish to integrate applications within a business process. First, let's compare and contrast a typical multi-application business system with the simple client-server model with which we are all familiar.

Simple Client-Server Model

If you have ever programmed a client-server system, you have actually performed application integration. Neither of the applications can fulfill the requirements of the system by itself; they must be able to exchange data. The two programs must be made to share data reliably. Without a predictable, efficient, and robust protocol for exchanging data, the client-server system cannot be made to work.

The simplicity of the client-server model produces some distinct advantages in comparison with the sort of application integration we will focus on in this book. Client-server has just two entities sending data back and forth. Although one entity – the server – can communicate with one or more clients concurrently, there are only two roles in the system. A party is either a client or a server. A single interprocess communication technology is embedded into both applications in the client-server model. The two programs are designed from the start around a protocol suited to the overall system. Typically, both applications are programmed by the same people, or at the very least, the two programming teams are in close communication. In short, the client and server applications were intended to work together, so application integration is relatively simple.

Distributed Business Systems

Contrast the client-server model with the problem of building a distributed business system involving multi-part data flow (known as **workflow**). Information comes into the system through some client interface, and one or more applications perform processing on the data. These programs may act directly on the data, or they may perform supporting functions as a side effect of the data passing through the system.

Often, many of the applications are in existence before the distributed system is implemented. In one way, this is a desirable situation, as we are then dealing with well-tested building blocks. However, integrating these applications poses several challenges:

❑   Incompatible protocols and data formats

- ❏ Workflow design and error handling
- ❏ Monitoring the workflow

Let's take a look at each of these potential problem areas.

Incompatible Protocols and Data Formats

First, we have the problem of incompatible protocols. If the applications were built independently, it is highly unlikely that they will use the same technology for interprocess communication. An application enabled for DCOM cannot speak directly to another application designed for HTTP. Some older applications may not be equipped for direct interprocess communication at all – they may expect to find a data file on a local disk.

We also encounter the problem of incompatible data formats. This may be a question of mismatched low-level data type representation between dissimilar computers, or a higher-level issue of mismatched data structures.

Mismatched data types may arise because one computer uses a different binary representation for some data type – numeric types are particularly troublesome – from another computer. Structures that are logically identical will be physically different at a low level of representation.

Dissimilar data structures involve two programming teams choosing different data structures to represent the same body of data. For example, one program might use a hierarchical structure well suited to programmatic use. Another might serialize its data in fixed length fields, a system oriented to saving data to disk or performing bulk data exchanges through files. Whatever the case, application integration usually needs some facility for translating between data formats. This facility must correctly **map** one item of data into another and back again if two programs are to communicate.

Workflow Design and Error Handling

Application integration is not complete when two programs are made to communicate with one another. We have to deal with data flow and error handling. Implementing a non-trivial process usually requires the connection of multiple applications in an appropriate sequence. The architect of such a system must also consider how the process can fail and provide for alternative paths through the system.

Consider a simple retail purchase at a web site:

1. The site searches and displays a catalog

2. The user selects purchase

3. The site accesses an inventory control system to confirm availability and mark the product for selection

4. An order price is calculated (this may involve shipping costs, sales taxes, and promotional discounts)

5. An e-mail acknowledgement is formatted and sent

6. A shipping invoice is generated so that warehouse fulfillment workers can complete and check the order

If you have the luxury of starting this business from scratch and have to write custom systems to support it you have little need for extra application integration. If, on the other hand, you are enabling web solutions for an existing business, you will probably have to coordinate the activities of several programs.

Also, the path I have just described is the path the process will take if everything works correctly. If the site is to be robust, though, the architect will have to consider various contingencies, such as:

❑   What if the product is back ordered, or perhaps discontinued?

❑   Is the product compatible with all forms of shipping?

❑   What happens if the acknowledgement is bounced at the receiving domain?

Different applications may have to be invoked in different sequences to account for all the contingencies that are possible in the system, as shown in the diagram below:

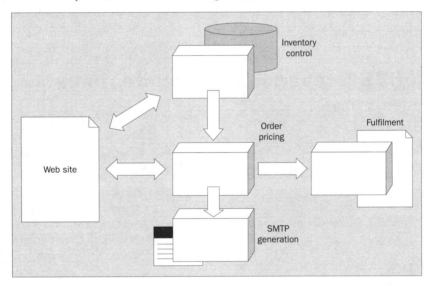

In other words, we need an integrated system that is flexible, and has built-in error-handling.

Monitoring the Workflow

Even when all the individual applications have been stitched together to implement the desired workflow, system administrators must be able to monitor the process during run-time, to manually verify the status of any particular item of work and intervene if necessary. They should also be able to adjust the parameters governing each step in the workflow. Considerations include:

❑   Should some steps be processed in batches, and if so, at what intervals?

❑   How long should one process wait for a reply from another before raising an error?

In other words, it is not enough to build an integrated system. We must be able to monitor and control it, as well.

Summarizing the Challenges of Enterprise Application Integration

The task of application integration poses several challenges. Efficiently overcoming them requires a set of tools and technologies. The challenges include:

- ❑ Defining one or more data formats for the exchange of data

- ❑ Defining the logical exchange of data between two applications

- ❑ Implementing the physical exchange of data, accounting for dissimilar protocols and asynchronous exchanges

- ❑ Defining ideal workflow processes

- ❑ Identifying error conditions and processing exceptions, and defining workflow to handle these cases

- ❑ Monitoring and operating the integrated system effectively and efficiently

These are the challenges that BizTalk Server is designed to overcome. When we discuss the various parts of the product later, you will see that there are different tools and services that address each of these areas. Before we get into that, however, let's look at some scenarios that use EAI so that you can see some ways in which these challenges arise.

EAI and B2B Scenarios and Architectures

Enterprise Application Integration can occur in any type of project. Some classes of project involve integration by their very nature. But what are these projects and what kind of integration is involved?

In this section I'm going to briefly describe four types of projects, focusing particularly on those that you might encounter in enterprise-scale web applications. These project classes are:

- ❑ Business process integration

- ❑ Trading partner integration

- ❑ Automated procurement

- ❑ Business to Business (B2B) aggregation

All four of these classes can involve web technology, but not necessarily like the retail e-commerce sites with which we are all familiar. Business process integration, in particular, is almost exclusively conducted via an intranet; but it also happens that internet technologies – protocols and servers – are well suited to implementing this kind of integration as well. The reason for this stems largely from the fact that the Web is inherently **loosely coupled**. In other words, servers and clients have little (or no) prior knowledge of one another, so each has provisions for dealing with a failure on the part of the other. They all speak HTTP, but there is a great deal of flexibility in data formats (HTML and other MIME types). A **tightly coupled** system, by contrast, has explicit and closely-integrated data formats and communications. It is easier to add reliability to loosely coupled systems than to break apart tightly coupled systems to gain the flexibility and responsiveness we will need.

Business Process Integration

Application integration is important even when we stay inside the boundaries of a single company. Each functional or organizational unit begins by automating its core process: Human Relations might roll out a benefits application or personnel directory; the Sales organization tracks orders and leads; Inventory control and supply chain systems are introduced.

Before long, *islands of automation* have appeared throughout the company. Each contains some valuable store of data focused on some process of compelling interest to the company. Quite simply, the company could not function competitively without these systems.

This has been the pattern throughout companies for some years. It does have the advantage of permitting a company to focus its efforts on getting one important function right, instead of trying to automate every process at once. But a company shouldn't be a collection of islands; it should be an integrated and interrelated set of people and processes, which work together to achieve a goal.

Business Process Integration is the task of connecting these isolated applications in such a way that it mirrors the idealized workflow of a company. It is typically used to gain some competitive advantage by cutting costs and the time needed to move an order from placement to completion (the **cycle time**).

At first sight, you might have thought that integrating processes *within* a business should be a great deal easier than integrating the systems of two distinct companies. After all, it should be much easier for integration teams within the same company to work together, to share source code, and reach consensus. In practice, however, we actually encounter the same problems of dissimilar data formats and technologies when integrating within companies as we do when integrating applications owned by different businesses. Why should this be so? There are several reasons:

1. Different approaches to the same data from different organizations

2. Different data processing needs for different organizations

3. Documentation can also be lost, or even never created, so programmers cannot count on crossing boundaries to fix applications

Because each organization within the company has its own goals and focus, this focus is reflected in the software and hardware it selects. This means that data tends to be specialized to the tasks demanded of the organization, even when that information is broadly applicable throughout the company.

For instance, any effective company is interested in tracking its customer from pre-sales to post-sales customer support. But the view of the customer held by the Sales Force is often quite different from that held by the Customer Support or Manufacturing divisions, so specialized information of interest only to Sales gets mixed together with general information about the customer, which is also of interest to Customer Support and Manufacturing.

The way data is processed may differ as well. For example, a Sales Force automation system will typically perform bulk synchronization once a day, when individual salesmen connect from their remote locations. Service representatives in a customer support call center, by contrast, need to be able to update customer records as they receive information from individual customers. Programmers assigned to integrate dissimilar systems will therefore also have to overcome these differences.

Strangely enough, these integration problems may also be beneficial to the development process, as they force programmers to deal with interfaces in a rigorous way. The discipline of designing, documenting, and implementing interfaces leads to more robust systems. Assumptions are tested with running code instead of paper models and anecdotes.

Business process integration sometimes has a reputation for involving a lot of legacy systems. Although probably true for established companies that adopted automation early on, modern applications are increasingly built using web-based intranet applications: these are easier to access throughout the company, and require less coordination and support to distribute. Every employee who possesses a web browser is a potential user of the application, while the details of technology and hardware platforms are hidden by the intranet.

We can expect business process integration to increasingly become a matter of harnessing internal web applications, which is good news for programmers seeking new technical challenges. Their companies benefit, as well: although web applications do not eliminate the problems of application integration, they do diminish the cost of solving them. Web applications are inherently distributed across a network and loosely coupled, meaning that integration programming teams can work independently, crafting and exploiting interfaces between business organizations.

Trading Partner Integration

It is becoming increasingly common in business for two or more companies to share information more closely, and at a higher level of trust than they would with other firms. These companies are known as **trading partners** because they have established a mutually trustworthy reputation by regularly doing business with one another. As a result, they share more information, require fewer formal contracts, and link their internal systems more closely than usual, for mutual benefit. The process of connecting the two electronically is called trading partner integration.

Trading partners may have regular agreements in place for recurring orders, or may simply place orders as needed. The benefits from a trading partners scheme are low overheads and rapid response, due to the close integration of the partners' systems. The tighter the integration, the lower the cost of doing business.

Trading partners must be able to express their needs in a recognizable format, and their partners must be able to respond appropriately. There must also be accountability at each step. The identity of the trading partners must be securely verified, with agreements in place so that each partner can be confident that they will get paid. One effort to put this discovery process on a formal basis is the proposed UDDI standard. UDDI, which stands for Universal Description, Discovery, and Integration of Business for the Web, is a coordinated set of XML data structures, SOAP messages, and APIs for describing and discovering goods and services offered for commerce over the Web.

> *UDDI's formal structure is described in documents hosted at www.uddi.org. You may also register there as a potential trading partner and describe your offerings and interests.*

Electronic Data Interchange (EDI)

EDI is an existing message standard used by trading partners. It comes in two forms, both of which specify long lists of message types designed to facilitate business-to-business e-commerce:

❑ United Nations Electronic Data Interchange for Administration, Commerce, and Transport (UN/EDIFACT)

❑ ANSI X12 (used largely in North America)

However, two problems have largely hampered widespread adoption of these standards:

❑ EDI has classically involved the use of proprietary wide-area networks.

❑ The formats used to exchange data were proprietary and difficult to read.

Both of these factors increased the cost of implementing an EDI system.

In recent years however, an effort to implement EDI on the public Internet, using XML as the basis for developing message formats has sprung up. By using common network transport, enabled by open protocols for security and reliability, the hardware cost of EDI is greatly diminished. The use of XML decreases the cost of software because XML tools are readily available from third parties, and the self-describing nature of XML makes it easier to develop and debug software for specific EDI message vocabularies.

While we can expect to see more and more XML implementations of EDI, particularly in smaller businesses, we must still expect to have to integrate X12, EDIFACT, XML EDI, and other proprietary formats when dealing with trading partner integration. We will therefore still need to map data from one format to another.

Thus, while trading partner integration offers exciting opportunities for programmers to reshape entire businesses, it still means that many of the classic problems of application integration must be overcome. In fact, the challenge is greater than for business process integration, because in this case the two parties exchanging information are distinct legal and organizational entities (and they may be geographically distant as well). Integration must occur at the interfaces between the partners (we cannot rely on being able to get inside the source code for the partner's respective systems).

Automated Procurement

This is a variation on the trading partner integration scenario. Here, the relationship is formalized and so close that the partners involved are sometimes said to form a **virtual company**. A company may entirely outsource some critical function to a procurement partner because it is cheaper or more reliable to do so.

Obviously, integration like this has to be close and effective. A partner's systems must seem like an extension of one's own systems; this often involves integrating some internal systems so that information may flow directly from one partner's system to another.

The problems of trading partner integration exist here in magnified form. We are no longer talking about one partner among several, but about a partner that may be a company's sole source for a critical good or service. The benefits, however, are vast: a company that can quickly satisfy a prospective partner's concerns about the reliability and speed with which it can integrate systems can lock in a substantial volume of business on a recurring basis. The cost of obtaining follow-on business then drops markedly.

Systems integrators are crucial to the success of automated procurement. An effective set of methods and technology for implementing integration is a critical differentiating factor for would-be partners. Poor integration, by contrast, can sink one or more businesses.

Just-In-Time Ordering

Consider the following process, which is a classic example of automated procurement known as **just-in-time** ordering.

A large manufacturing company negotiates special terms with a limited number of suppliers. When supplies fall below a predetermined level, the inventory system at the manufacturing company automatically places an order with the appropriate supplier. The order goes *directly* into the scheduling system of the supplier, thereby saving time and money for the supplier.

Because the process is completely automated, the supplier can offer lower rates as well as a guaranteed, prompt delivery time. The manufacturing firm also benefits, because it can count on having supplies arrive as they are needed, avoiding the need to carry large inventories and therefore lowering costs.

The entire process relies on several things. First, both partners have to have a comprehensive supply chain system: they need to track their inventories and orders automatically and in real time. Second, the systems must be closely integrated. The benefits of trading partner integration will be lost if manual intervention is needed to convert an order from the manufacturer's system into an order in the supplier's system. This means that the two partners must be connected via some network.

Finally, issues of security and workflow must be agreed upon ahead of time. Both partners must know who can approve orders and how orders are to flow between the partners. These issues will be settled offline prior to implementing the partnership, but the details must be captured online so that the integrated system can respond appropriately at every step.

Business to Business Aggregation

Until recently, integration between distinct businesses, in terms of automated procurement or trading partner integration, has largely been a matter of large, established firms engaging in long-duration integration projects. This has limited the benefits of business-to-business electronic commerce to large, wealthy companies. However, as application integration becomes more routine, and particularly as Internet technologies come to the fore, smaller companies should increasingly be able to take advantage of electronic commerce.

The problem of finding a suitable supplier or partner has long been a big problem for smaller companies, since they do not have wide experience in finding and dealing with vendors outside their immediate area. This is a business problem that cries out for a technical solution. The result is the emergence of **business-to-business portals**, or **B2B** aggregators.

A B2B aggregator acts as a trusted intermediary, helping partners to:

❏   find one another

❏   establish trading agreements

❏   integrate their trading processes

These are challenges that the previously mentioned UDDI proposal seeks to address. Regardless of how you go about it, however, you must establish some common mechanism for trading. By establishing a high profile in the business community, aggregators draw potential partners to a common ground. These partners are then able to verify the credentials of the aggregator and examine their processes, before deciding whether the aggregator can be trusted to certify other vendors. Aggregators frequently specialize in a particular vertical market, further helping to focus their trading community.

If aggregators simply provided a partner-finding service, leaving agreements and integration details to be worked out offline, they would be of little real value to businesses. Instead, they provide common mechanisms for publishing product and service catalogs. They also provide standard mechanisms that allow partners to establish agreements and exchange messages that implement some commercial workflow between the two partners. The relationship between business partners and an aggregator is illustrated opposite above.

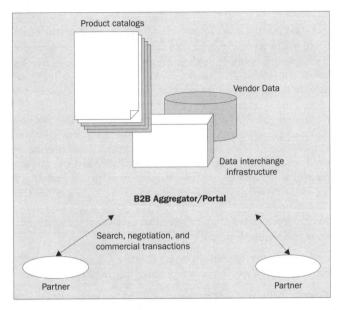

By taking on some of the infrastructure of trading partner integration or automated procurement, the aggregator facilitates electronic commerce for small- and medium-sized businesses. In return, an aggregator charges some fee for its service, typically a per-transaction charge. An aggregator web site typically takes the form of a portal, providing information and services to a vertical market. Its service to market participants may be as simple as offering a library of message formats, or as complex as hosting e-commerce fulfillment and settlement software.

Aggregators have an interest in open (public) protocols and internet technologies, and push for standard protocols and Web-enabled commerce systems. This is because the businesses most likely to seek their services cannot afford custom solutions and networks. These businesses are likely to be equipped with third party, packaged software operating over the public Internet; they resort to custom arrangements only when they cannot avoid it – usually when it involves some unique facet of their business.

Before we get into the details of BizTalk Server, let's take a look at the BizTalk Framework initiative. The Framework is one effort to address some of the issues we have just seen. Looking at this will give us a better appreciation of what must take place to do B2B integration and prepare us for the specifics of BizTalk Server.

The BizTalk Framework Initiative

In previous sections, we discussed the problems faced by businesses that wish to integrate their applications. We also discussed the advantages and disadvantages of established schemes for implementing application integration. We saw that integration was hindered by a multitude of different proprietary message formats that were difficult to translate into other formats. Messages are the chunks of structured data that flow between applications. They are the heart of EAI because they are the glue that connects applications. Although the EDI message standards have been implemented, they are very complex, and expensive for businesses to implement. Furthermore, business systems may use different communication protocols to send messages, bringing compatibility problems. All-in-all, such problems have meant that, until very recently, only big business has taken a real interest in application integration.

What is really needed is a framework for developing standard industry message schemas. Servers like BizTalk server could then use these schemas as the basis for configuring their messaging system. Using this framework should mean that we can build a message format that complies to a relatively simple set of standard rules, but is also flexible enough to allow for collaboration during schema development. We also need to be able to implement this framework relatively inexpensively, which will allow small businesses to participate in application integration.

This was the motivation for the **BizTalk Framework Initiative**. The Framework was initiated by Microsoft, but it is explicitly designed to be open to everyone. It does not presuppose any specific operating system or software. It is a schema repository, and a set of messaging specifications, that can be implemented by some middleware server. Microsoft BizTalk Server is one such implementation, although it can also deal with messages outside the Framework. The schema repository has attracted dozens of partners and well over one hundred schemas. The initiative has three main thrusts:

- ❑ **BizTalk Framework**: a set of guidelines that enables reliable message exchange between organizations and applications

- ❑ **BizTalk.org**: a community web site that provides information about message exchange and its associated technologies, as well as a repository for message schemas

- ❑ **BizTalk Server**: software that processes BizTalk-compliant message documents

For the remainder of this chapter, we will take an introductory tour of the BizTalk Initiative, focusing especially on the Microsoft BizTalk Server 2000 software. But let's begin our tour with a look at the BizTalk Framework.

BizTalk Framework

The BizTalk Framework comprises rules for creating message schemas for document exchange. It is based upon two open standards:

- ❑ Extensible Markup Language (**XML**)
- ❑ Simple Object Access Protocol (**SOAP**)

Let's have a closer look at these standards, because it will help us to understand the structure of the BizTalk Framework.

XML

Although the "M" in "XML" is short for "Markup", XML is not just a markup language as you may think. Confused? Let me explain.

A markup language is one that allows us to *mark up* data; in other words the language allows us to add meta data that describes the data. An example is HTML, the universal language for the display of information, where we place data between simple tags, which label the data in some way.

XML is different; it is not really a "language" at all, but a standard syntax that allows us to create markup languages. It enables you to create a clear, human-legible, custom markup language that is well suited to your needs. Therefore, an XML-based framework for messages is ideal, since it is flexible yet descriptive and clear.

SOAP

We have already mentioned the problems associated with exchanging messages between systems with different protocols. A message may invoke a method on an object on one system or platform, but it will probably have trouble doing so on a system that uses a different communication protocol.

To work around these platform-specific data-accessing problems, the **Simple Object Access Protocol** was proposed. SOAP is an XML-based syntax that defines an *electronic envelope* into which you put data. It enables us to produce applications that can remotely invoke methods. A SOAP package consists of a SOAP client and server, which are used in the following way:

1. The SOAP client creates and submits a SOAP request document (over HTTP) to a SOAP server at another site.

2. The SOAP server grabs the message, parses the SOAP document, and invokes a method on a remote object on its domain.

3. The remote object returns information to the server, which places it in a SOAP document and sends it on to the SOAP client.

Therefore a SOAP server acts as an interpreter, and the SOAP package itself provides an interface between two incompatible protocols.

BizTalk Messages

So, where does the BizTalk Framework fit in? Well, a BizTalk document is an extension of a SOAP document, incorporating extra BizTalk-specific XML tags (**BizTags**). A server that implements BizTalk Framework is expected to recognize and act on the BizTags in the manner prescribed by the Framework. The BizTalk Framework is also largely based upon the SOAP standard, and so BizTalk messages have the advantages we have just discussed of both XML and SOAP: extensibility, clarity, and platform-independence.

Of course, developers at many companies will have to independently adopt the framework's conventions if it is to be generally useful as a messaging protocol for ad hoc and open electronic commerce. The message schemas themselves could be used outside of the BizTalk Framework, but the processing implied by the BizTags requires implementation of the messaging laid out in the Framework. Even assuming developers do embrace the framework as a useful approach, the success of B2B efforts using BizTalk is not assured. The first three types of business integration – business process integration, trading partner integration, and automated procurement – can occur between small numbers of participants. This has been the history of EDI to date. A few participants willing to commit to a long process can manually establish agreements on technology and data interchange formats. The result is a large potential benefit to the participants, but no guarantee that the benefits will spread to the business community at large.

Business to business aggregation is required to promote B2B electronic commerce for the multitude of small and medium–sized businesses. Such businesses cannot afford proprietary networks and lengthy development efforts. They seek widely adopted frameworks running on commodity systems that make use of open protocols. This is what the BizTalk Initiative will provide.

BizTalk.org

To promote the use of BizTalk Framework documents and XML-based messaging in general, the BizTalk.org web site (www.biztalk.org) was created. This site, which is hosted and managed by Microsoft, provides information on the BizTalk Framework, BizTalk community news and forums, and tools to help with application integration.

The site also contains a repository of XML schemas representing message formats designed by companies embarking on implementing the BizTalk Framework. There are, for example, schemas for ordering food services or building maintenance services. The repository provides open access for anyone who wishes to publish a new message schema, or find useful schemas already published. It also serves to educate developers by providing examples of well-designed interchange formats. A developer can be assured that any schema published in the repository has been tested and is technically valid.

Long-term, however, the repository could be the cornerstone in a B2B aggregator portal; potential partners could obtain the schemas of vendors and initiate integration efforts. As BizTalk Server comes into wider use within the corporate world, BizTalk Framework can leverage the community formed around the educational mission, to create a B2B aggregator portal compatible with BizTalk Server. Although the framework does not require the use of BizTalk Server, so any third party can develop to the its conventions, developers who have learned to use BizTalk Server effectively will have a distinct advantage over newcomers to the Framework.

BizTalk Schema Repository

If application integration between trading partners relied on formal coordination, business-to-business integration would be slow to take off. To be successful, a prospective partner must first locate a suitable partner and then find out what sort of schemas they use. Next, the partner must either adopt those schemas or specify a mapping between their own schemas and the new partners. As we shall shortly see, BizTalk Server provides tools for the final step. A central repository of e-commerce schemas is needed to address the first two steps.

The BizTalk.org web site hosts just such a library. Prospective trading partners can go to the site and search by schema keywords or industry categories. The latter are defined in terms of the North American Industry Classification System (NAICS), a system of classification codes that progressively refine a business in terms of the industry groups or categories to which it belongs. By using a combination of the two, a prospective customer of the published partner can identify a small number of schemas and inspect them to see if they are relevant to its needs.

Upon finding relevant schemas, a trading partner can download and inspect detailed information. Each schema listed on the site has three documents: the schema itself, HTML-based programming documentation, and a sample message that complies with the schema. The sample is especially important as it communicates a sample of what the schema developer meant when they devised the schema. This helps a prospective trading partner decide if the schema is relevant, and if so, helps its programmers understand the schema.

Developers can rapidly perform integration with little intervention from a prospective partner by writing software that speaks to the partner's published schemas. If the developers are building an electronic commerce capability from scratch, they can adopt the vendor's published message formats as their own, writing internal software to the published schemas. If, however, they have an existing capability, they will need to design mappings between their own formats and those of the prospective partner. This is a task supported by the tools in BizTalk Server. Intervention by the prospective trading partner is required only when the two companies negotiate a workflow agreement.

The repository helps in another way. Schemas may be expected to evolve over time. Users of schemas should not have to rely on the schema originator for update notifications; after all, the whole point of a central repository is to get away from one-to-one coordination. When a trading partner finds a relevant schema, it can register its interest in the schema with BizTalk.org. When a new version of the schema is uploaded to the repository, the partner receives an e-mail notification. In addition, schema interest registrations are used to provide feedback to the original designer and to rank schema searches in order of their popularity. This ranking will reflect the rate of adoption of a particular schema, helping the trading community to coalesce around emerging standards.

Other Message Schema Repositories

BizTalk.org is not the only e-commerce message schema repository. A number of organizations are joining the repository effort. Although most focus on XML as the basis for exchanging business information, some use other techniques as well. It is far too early to predict how the market for repositories will evolve: it may organize itself around the portals of vertical market communities, or it may coalesce around the software used to implement e-commerce. There may be a few dominant repositories, or so many that every new trading relationship involves the exploration of a new repository. It is worth taking note of the pioneer repository efforts so that we can see where BizTalk's competition lies, and how other organizations view business-to-business data interchange.

OASIS

The Organization for the Advancement of Structured Information Standards (OASIS) is a non-profit organization that hosts www.xml.org. This site seeks to become a reference repository for industrial and commercial vocabularies expressed in XML. As of this writing (December 2000), OASIS is beginning to host XML message schemas and DTDs for e-commerce. A committee is in the process of defining the process by which a searchable repository will operate.

OASIS is also participating in an international effort, the Electronic Business XML Initiative, along with the United Nations Body for Trade Facilitation and Electronic Business (UN/CEFACT). The initiative seeks to develop a consistent framework for developing XML vocabularies for e-commerce.

The repository may be found at www.xml.org, *while OASIS itself resides at* www.oasis-open.org

RosettaNet

This is another repository effort that takes a layered approach to developing e-commerce vocabularies. RosettaNet is an industry consortium of diverse businesses seeking to develop a common e-commerce framework. RosettaNet sees three layers supporting commerce:

- ❑   dictionaries
- ❑   frameworks
- ❑   Partner Interface Processes (PIP)

A **dictionary**, in their view, is a collection of words or properties that can be used to describe business transactions. RosettaNet is engaged in writing two data dictionaries. The first is intended to describe product properties. The other will provide properties describing catalogs, partners, and transactions. Next, these words and properties will be combined through interchange protocols to form a grammar.

RosettaNet's **framework** will consist of XML DTDs that describe e-commerce protocols.

The real focus of RosettaNet, however, is their **PIP** concept. They see a PIP as a dialog between two business partners. A PIP consists of some collection of XML interchange documents and a business model that describes how trading partners interact. A PIP also provides a mechanism for validating individual documents.

RosettaNet imposes more structure on would-be partners than BizTalk does. Where BizTalk provides a loose framework for message vocabularies, and some placeholders for information of interest to consuming applications, PIPs impose a protocol for the exchange of messages. This is useful if you desire a complete and tested protocol for your integration. Unfortunately, it also limits the reach of the project by excluding any integration projects for which a PIP has not been specified. It is consequently more focused on particular markets and business flows than BizTalk.

RosettaNet is found at www.rosettanet.org

CommerceNet

Like RosettaNet, CommerceNet is a consortium. It casts a wide net, involving over 500 businesses and organizations and embracing a variety of e-commerce protocols. CommerceNet was founded in 1994, so it is somewhat more developed than the other efforts. Its principal focus is on bringing together partners to engage in particular opportunities.

CommerceNet's most significant effort from the standpoint of this book is the **eCo Framework**. This framework seeks to provide a common structure for all e-commerce specifications, including EDI, Open Buying on the Internet (OBI), and a variety of XML-based vertical market vocabularies.

CommerceNet's site is found at www.commerce.net

BizTalk Servers

In order to be able to use the BizTalk Framework to integrate applications, we need software that can process the message documents and do something useful with them. The BizTalk Framework can be implemented by any software, as long as it conforms to the guidelines laid out in the Framework. In fact, several companies are working on servers that will process BizTalk documents. One of the most-heralded products is Microsoft's BizTalk Server 2000, which we will now investigate.

Introducing Microsoft BizTalk Server 2000

This product is what we will be talking about for the rest of this book. Microsoft BizTalk Server 2000 is a collection of tools and server software that enables us to implement application integration efficiently. It runs on the Microsoft Windows environment, but it is important to note that the Server is not restricted to integrating Windows applications; it is sufficiently open to work with data coming from or going to other platforms. In the next chapter we'll introduce a hypothetical business devoted to the installation and upkeep of residential services – for example, pool care. We'll use this example over the course of several chapters and build a sample system to illustrate the core services and tools of BizTalk Server.

BizTalk Server Features

So just what do we want from a BizTalk Server? Obviously we want an ability to understand and process BizTalk message documents. But we need to think about what application integration really involves beyond this if we are to understand the features included in Microsoft BizTalk Server.

Lets start at the top. We have a business process consisting of separate applications (or *islands of automation* as they were described earlier in the chapter), which may span across internal organizations, or across businesses. Each of these applications needs to communicate information to the others via network messages. This implies that our Server needs to provide tools to perform at least three functions related to the management of the full business process (the workflow):

- ❑   Define the workflow
- ❑   Control the flow of messages throughout the workflow
- ❑   Monitor the workflow

Now let's consider the messages themselves. We need tools to control the format and movement of messages by:

- ❑   Defining message specifications
- ❑   Defining translations from one message specification to another
- ❑   Controlling message exchange and translation
- ❑   Monitoring message content

With these requirements in mind, lets get an overview of the tools available to us in Microsoft BizTalk Server.

BizTalk Server Tools: An Overview

The product itself consists of eight tools, most of which are graphical user interfaces:

- ❑   **Orchestration Designer** is a Visio-based graphical tool for defining workflows into files called **XLANG schedules** (pronounced *slang*). The runtime process that hosts instances of these workflow schedules is called the **XLANG Scheduler**.

- ❑   **Editor** is a graphical tool for defining message formats (BizTalk Framework-compliant and otherwise), termed **specifications** that are used to initialize the parts of the messaging system that read and write messages.

- ❑   **Mapper** is a graphical tool for designating how messages are mapped from one message format to another, so that BizTalk Server can translate between formats automatically.

- ❑   **Messaging Manager** is a graphical management tool used to configure BizTalk Messaging Services to exchange documents between organizations. **Messaging Services** is a runtime server process that implements message exchange and data transformation as specified in Messaging Manager.

- ❑   **Document Tracking** is a browser-hosted interface which provides the ability to query for reports on messages passing through Messaging Services.

- ❑   **Server Administration** is a snap-in for the Microsoft Management Console that allows system administrators to manage the properties of servers and server groups, as well as message queues and receive functions (more about these topics later in the chapter).

You should be able to see that we have tools to fulfill every requirement stated in the previous section. Having whetted your appetite, we'll now finish the chapter with a tour of most of these tools. We'll also examine how BizTalk Server implements messaging, which will help us to understand the significance of the configuration options available to us through BizTalk Server's tools.

BizTalk Messaging Services

Many of the low-level messaging services performed by BizTalk Server, such as sending, receiving, parsing, and tracking message documents; and data mapping, are grouped together and termed (unsurprisingly) **BizTalk Messaging Services**. In this section we are going to learn more about how BizTalk Server implements messaging.

As we progress through this section, bear in mind that in order to achieve application integration, all messages must pass through BizTalk Server before they reach their destination. Remember that BizTalk Server is a centralized means of routing and translating documents. Therefore a message transfer actually consists of two steps:

1. A message is sent to BizTalk Server

2. BizTalk Server sends the message on to another application

We shall start this section by introducing a few BizTalk Server-specific definitions associated with messaging. These will be used in later chapters. Then we will look at how BizTalk Server actually sends and receives messages, and we will finish by discussing the advantages of queueing messages.

Organizations

An **organization** in BizTalk is a fairly broad concept. It can encompass a whole business, or a distinct entity within a business. Remember that earlier in the chapter we described a business process (workflow) as a series of *islands of automation* linked by the exchange of documents? If we continue with this theme, then each island will be represented in BizTalk as an organization.

The **Home organization** is the object that represents your business in BizTalk; it is created for you by BizTalk Server automatically. You can rename it to the actual name of your business to make it easy to identify in the workflow.

In a simple model where a company is sending a document to a trading partner, the partners and organizations exactly correspond. In more complex situations involving multiple applications within a single company, it is better to think of each entity in control of each application as an organization.

BizTalk can select a **channel** (explained below) for message delivery based on the organizations involved, together with the type of the document being sent. You must be sure that your definition of each organization is sufficiently detailed to uniquely identify the proper receiving party. The organization is therefore the point of contact for the exchange of messages.

Document Definitions

The **document definition** refers to the type of message document that is processed by BizTalk Server. It provides a pointer to a particular document **specification**, which is data about what the file can contain – hence it is meta data (data about data). Note that any particular specification can be used in any number of document definitions, and any particular document definition can be used in any number of channels.

BizTalk supports a variety of message types, such as XML and EDI. We shall see later that the navigation pane of the Document definitions section of Messaging Manager contains a listing of all the document specifications known to a particular BizTalk Server installation. This information is maintained in the BizTalk database.

Envelopes

Envelopes are conceptually similar to real-world, paper postal envelopes. When you want to send a document to a partner, you will specify an envelope in which the document travels. Unlike real-world envelopes however, BizTalk associates a particular envelope with a particular type of document.

You should note that envelopes are not strictly required for XML-format messages. Because we tag data in XML, BizTalk can look at the root-level tag to determine document type. However, they are critical in flatfile formats: the envelope contains information about the document that BizTalk needs to route the message. If you submit a message with routing information based on the sending and receiving organizations, Messaging Services must find a channel to use based on the organizations and the document type. Without an envelope, BizTalk would be unable to determine the document type for non-XML formats.

The Envelopes section of Messaging Manager permits management and creation of envelopes for BizTalk documents.

Ports and Distribution Lists

A **port** is a set of properties that directs how documents are enveloped, secured, and transported to a designated destination organization or application.

By specifying a port to use, two applications can exchange a message without either of them needing to know how the message is transmitted (protocol) or where the message is delivered to (the end location). The applications do not need to involve themselves in actual message delivery either; that is the responsibility of Messaging Services. At runtime, Messaging Services consults the properties of the named port to determine how and where to send the message it has been given. By removing responsibility for message transmission from the applications themselves, the applications can remain unchanged even when the end location or protocol changes.

For example, an application might start out using MSMQ – naming a specific queue in the process – and later move to HTTP when it is web-enabled. The application's port would initially specify MSMQ and the designated port, then would shift to HTTP and, say, a particular ASP page on a particular server as the new endpoint. So long as the port definition is updated in the Messaging Manager, the sending application would not notice the change.

There will be occasions when we need to broadcast a particular message to several applications. Each application or organization that should receive a message needs a port designated for message delivery. It would be unwieldy to have to configure one-to-one relationships with each recipient, so Messaging Manager allows you to select a collection of ports and give them a name. This named collection is known as a **distribution list.**

*Distribution lists are also termed **port groups** in the configuration object model that we will explore later in this book.*

At runtime, Messaging Services notes the use of a distribution list and sends the submitted message to each port in the list. Note that each port may potentially use a different protocol, so sending a message to a distribution list can result in multiple transmissions over differing protocols.

Channels

A **channel** is a set of properties that designates the source of documents, and also defines specific processing steps that must be performed by BizTalk Messaging Services before a document is delivered to the destination.

The destination is designated by the messaging port. By themselves, ports and message specifications are not specific to any particular message exchange in the workflow, and so they can be reused whenever necessary. By contrast, when associated with a particular port and message specification, channels can be used to implement a specific message exchange within the workflow.

Channels are an important link between the low-level configuration details of Messaging Services, and the high-level workflows of the XLANG Scheduler. Specific actions within a XLANG schedule are designated by naming a channel. At runtime, when XLANG Scheduler attempts to execute a particular action, it invokes the channel, thereby bringing Messaging Services into play to actually send the message.

Transactions

A **transaction** is a set of actions that are grouped together into one discrete unit. When the transaction is implemented at runtime, if all the actions are carried out successfully, the transaction succeeds. If any of the actions cannot be carried out, the transaction fails and the data flow is "rolled back" to the beginning of the transaction.

Why should we need to employ such a system? Well, there are many occasions where the failure of one action has an important knock-on effect to other actions. For example, say we had a system where money was being transferred from one bank account to another. Here we would need (a minimum of) two actions:

1. Debit the original account

2. Credit the new account

We could place these actions in the workflow, but consider what would happen if the attempt to credit the new account failed. We would be left with a situation where the original account had been debited but the new account has not been credited: money is lost because of the error.

On the other hand, if we tie the two actions together in a transaction, the transfer will only occur if both actions are successful; otherwise the workflow will be rolled back to the start of the transaction. In both cases no money is lost. We will learn more about transactions in Chapter 2.

Message Transfer

BizTalk Server uses two techniques for transferring messages between applications:

❑   Open Internet protocols

❑   Windows-specific communications

Let's now explore both of these options more closely.

Open Protocols

The Web relies on open (public) protocols for communication between applications. Any product interested in performing application integration over the public Internet, therefore, must support these protocols in order to support common strategies for implementing Internet applications. Intranet applications are becoming common in business process integration situations, and they often use these protocols too.

It should not be surprising, therefore, that BizTalk Server supports the major web protocols for the transport of data interchange documents between applications. These are the protocols BizTalk Server supports for communications:

- ❑ Simple Mail Transport Protocol (**SMTP**) – communications via e-mail
- ❑ Hypertext Transfer Protocol (**HTTP**) – the communications mechanism used by web pages and applications (ASP, CGI, and so on)
- ❑ Secure Hypertext Transfer Protocol (**HTTPS**)– a version of HTTP that uses the Secure Sockets Layer (SSL) to encrypt traffic passing between the client and server

Of the three, HTTP and HTTPS permit the most interactive form of communication. It is possible to implement an application as an ASP page or CGI script and connect it directly to BizTalk Server. When a message is received for the HTTP-based application, BizTalk Server makes a request of the designated page or script. The results of executing the script can, in turn, be a reply message sent through BizTalk Server to the sender.

SMTP requires that a script be run upon receipt of the e-mail message. This script can perform the desired application functions or use other mechanisms to invoke applications. Because of the nature of e-mail, SMTP communications may not be immediately responsive.

Message Security: Active Directory

The **Active Directory** is a directory service that Windows 2000 uses as a central, hierarchical store of system configuration information. This information includes security principles as well as **digital certificates**. Certificates are used to authenticate message interchanges, as well as optionally performing encryption on the message contents. BizTalk Server also supports the use of secure Internet protocols such as HTTPS, SSL, and secure Multipurpose Internet Mail Extensions (S/MIME), which can be used for the encryption of messages passing between partners. As mentioned above HTTPS and SSL work together to protect HTTP transfers and form the basis for most commercial Internet purchasing pages. All of these use digital certificates to authenticate the partners to a conversation and perform encryption.

Active Directory is accessible through a variety of administrative tools and is capable of communicating with any client that supports the Lightweight Directory Access Protocol (LDAP), an open standard protocol for directory access.

Windows-Specific Communications

There will be times when you want to use communications that are specific to the Windows operating system. BizTalk supports the following proprietary protocols:

- ❑ Microsoft Message Queue (MSMQ)
- ❑ Reading and writing files to the local file system (file transport)
- ❑ COM+

MSMQ is a feature of the operating system that implements messaging middleware. You can use MSMQ to transfer chunks of data, termed messages, to other computers using a queuing system. The queues implemented in MSMQ provide various levels of reliability and recovery. The entire queuing system, in addition, includes features designed to work around partial communications outages in the network. There are also products that enable MSMQ to communicate with IBM MQ Series messaging middleware.

Many legacy applications exchange data with the outside world solely through files on disk. They take in data by reading a file and send data to other programs by writing a file. BizTalk treats such files as messages by providing a service that can monitor a designated folder for the arrival of files, then read those files and submit them to Messaging Services, where they may be handled like any other message. This provides a valuable link to a wide range of applications that have no other communications protocol.

COM+ is the core implementation technology for Windows. Major subsystems and supporting services are implemented and exposed to applications through COM components. The recommended application design philosophy for Windows applications has long been component software using COM or COM+ as the component technology. It should not be surprising, then, that BizTalk Server is implemented using COM+, and applications often integrate most closely with BizTalk Server using COM+ interfaces.

Even when you integrate two applications using some other protocol, for example HTTP, you will end up using COM+ at some point in the process. BizTalk Server provides COM+ components to look for inbound documents on other protocols, and complementary components for forwarding documents on other protocols. Integration using non-COM+ protocols is a matter of configuring receive and transport COM+ components through the Messaging Manager tool we discuss later on in the chapter. Core Messaging Services deals with these COM+ interfaces.

You can extend BizTalk's capabilities by building custom COM+ components or using BizTalk-related COM+ interfaces. For example, you can use the COM+ interfaces offered by BizTalk to perform all the management tasks you can perform manually through the Messaging Manager. You can also take advantage of BizTalk COM+ interfaces to monitor and dynamically manipulate XLANG schedule files (which describe the workflow of a business process).

If an application is written with BizTalk in mind, a tighter degree of integration than using open protocols can be performed. Applications that that wish to exchange BizTalk messages can directly invoke methods that belong to COM+ interfaces. Let's take a closer look at the COM+ interfaces most commonly encountered in BizTalk messaging.

Sending Messages to BizTalk Server

Documents are sent to BizTalk Server by invoking the `Submit()` or `SubmitSync()` methods of the `IInterchange` COM+ interface.

An application can call either the `Submit()` or `SubmitSync()` method directly, passing the document or the file path across to the method. However, this direct form of messaging is only available if the application is designed to support direct calls to BizTalk Server.

If the application is not capable of invoking COM+ methods on BizTalk Server directly, there is another option available. We can use **receive functions** to submit messages to BizTalk Server. Receive functions are configured to monitor specific directories on a server where message documents are placed. When it detects a new message, the receive function submits it to BizTalk Server. Receive functions can also be configured to monitor message queues (we will discuss these later) and submit messages from the queue to BizTalk Server.

Receiving Messages from BizTalk Server

BizTalk Server uses COM+ components known as **Application Integration Components** (**AICs**) to deliver data to an application. BizTalk Server calls, and passes the message data to, the AIC, which in turn passes the data on to the receiving application. The first question that springs to mind is: why bother? Why not just let BizTalk Server send the data directly to the application?

The answer is that, by doing this, we remove the need for BizTalk Server to understand how to communicate with the application. There are many applications that can only be communicated with using a non-standard proprietary protocol. So, by placing an AIC between the Server and the application, we can let BizTalk Server communicate with the AIC using a standard protocol, and let the AIC worry about how to transfer the message data to the application. If we need to communicate with a system that doesn't use a standard protocol, instead of having to add functionality to BizTalk Server, we produce a custom AIC that can talk to the application. This concept is illustrated below:

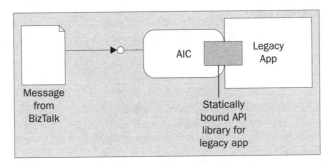

For example, SAP is a (non-XML based) Enterprise Resource Management System, which is used to manage the supply chain and inventory of very large companies. SAP provides an AIC that allows documents from BizTalk to flow directly into SAP's server.

For BizTalk to communicate with the AIC, the AIC needs to implement one of two interfaces:

- ❑   IBTSAppIntegration
- ❑   IPipelineComponent

Components that implement IBTSAppIntegration are known as "lightweight", because the interface does not allow BizTalk to configure the AIC. This interface contains a single method, ProcessMessage() through which a message document is passed to the interface.

A different approach is to create what is known as a **pipeline** COM+ component to communicate with the application. The idea of a pipeline derives from Microsoft Commerce Server, where a pipeline is a chain of custom COM+ components arranged by the site designer to execute in a particular order. A pipeline is designed to implement some multi-step task, for example purchasing goods. Each component is responsible for implementing a single step – sales tax calculations on purchases for instance. Commerce Server passes a Dictionary object holding the information built up during prior steps in a pipeline to the component. In this way, Commerce Server is able to support the construction and execution of arbitrary functionality.

> *For more on Commerce Server and pipelines, see* Professional Site Server 3.0 Commerce Edition *(Wrox Press, ISBN 1-861002-50-5).*

The point of pipeline components is to be able to produce custom COM+ functionality. On the other hand, all pipeline components must have a common framework so that the Server knows how to communicate with them. Therefore all pipeline components must implement an interface called `IPipelineComponent`, which contains several methods, one of which, `Execute()`, enables the functionality of the component. The `Dictionary` object is one of the parameters passed to `Execute()`. The `IPipelineComponent` interface permits properties whose nature is not known until runtime to be passed to the component.

BizTalk Server also supports pipeline components; it invokes the `Execute()` method to pass the data to the component. Using pipeline components, BizTalk can configure and invoke arbitrary custom pipeline processing, and Commerce Server can make use of BizTalk to enhance the capabilities of commerce pipelines. It also gives BizTalk Server a potential pool of custom developers in the existing community of Commerce Server component builders.

Message Queueing

BizTalk Server places messages in **queues**. Message queuing is important for two main reasons:

❑   reliability

❑   scalability

Messages are buffered in queues on the sending and receiving machines. This promotes **reliability** because loss of connectivity between the sending and receiving machines will not lead to loss of a message. Queued messages are then delivered when connectivity is restored.

Queuing also promotes **scalability** because receiving applications do not have to process the peak volume of message traffic, only the average volume. The sending application can send a message and then go about other tasks even if the receiving application is experiencing a backlog. The message is not lost; it remains in a queue until the receiving application can clear the backlog.

The default messaging middleware product for BizTalk Server is **Microsoft Message Queue** (**MSMQ**), which allows applications to send messages between queues on one or more machines. In addition to the features we mentioned earlier in passing – queuing, buffering, network reliability – MSMQ can also perform message routing, encryption/decryption, and all of the other services needed for proper delivery of messages. In a sense, MSMQ is "e-mail for applications".

Note that although MSMQ is a major messaging middleware product for the Windows platform, it is far from being the only one. Messaging middleware has a long history in mainframe processing. For example. IBM MQSeries is another product with a long history of use on various platforms. MSMQ supports MQSeries on Windows via the MSMQ-MQSeries Bridge from Level 8 Systems, and MQSeries on other platforms via Level 8's FalconMQ product.

> *Obviously, this is a tremendous simplification of messaging middleware in general and MSMQ in particular. MSMQ is covered in depth in* Professional MTS & MSMQ Programming with VB and ASP *(Wrox Press, ISBN 1-861001-46-0). More details on MSMQ and MQSeries interoperability may be found at* www.level8.com/falcon.htm.

BizTalk Server Tools: Introductory Tour

We now conclude this chapter with a closer look at the tools which BizTalk Server provides for implementing application integration. The idea of this section is to give you a taste of each tool, before we use them extensively in later chapters.

Defining the Business Workflow: Orchestration Designer

The whole point of BizTalk Server is application integration, and the reason why we want to integrate applications in the first place is to implement some workflow. A business supply chain is an example, specifying the interrelationships of customer orders, manufacturing scheduling, inventory management and purchasing software.

Consider how workflows are usually designed. They are designed at the highest level, which a manager or business analyst understands, although at a deeper level they involve specific technical issues such as transactions. Ideally, such a system is implemented by starting at the highest level too, drawing a flowchart of the individual activities needed to define and implement the workflow. Then the specific details of integrating each activity are added in.

Note that the activities themselves, however, are accomplished by the applications you wish to integrate. It may be necessary to write the odd utility or component, but by and large the idea is to integrate existing applications.

The process of designing and implementing a workflow is known as **orchestration**. Orchestration Designer is the tool provided by BizTalk Server for accomplishing the design task. It is highly graphical – in fact, it consists of VBA on top of Microsoft Visio (a package used for business diagram creation).

Analysts and programmers start the workflow design by drawing a flowchart of the business process. Systems in BizTalk are built by exchanging messages between applications, so the next step is to specify the messages to be sent or received at each step, and the locations from which messages are received or to which they are sent.

Finally, a designer provides Orchestration Designer with a high-level view of the workflow through the system. This is more important than it sounds at first. Since BizTalk Server uses a messaging model for applications, the workflow itself is viewed by BizTalk as a series of transformations or modifications of data. The flow of data, then, *is* the application. An example workflow flowchart is shown below. The data flow, not visible in the view below, details how data enters the system in a message, then flows to other messages which are sent out.

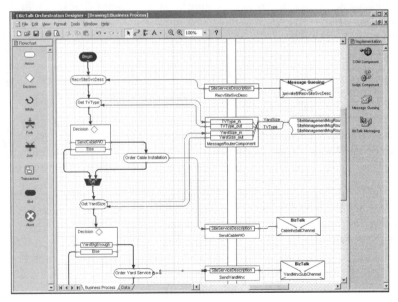

In fact, you will see a variation of the flowchart above in the next chapter when we begin our sample application. This flowchart will explain how a field agent sends a message describing a residential property back to a BizTalk Server at the home office. Rules in the flowchart are applied to the message to determine whether certain services should be ordered on behalf of the homeowner. If they are to be ordered, the flowchart directs messages be sent to the business partners whose supply those services.

Orchestration Designer permits you to specify message exchanges with Microsoft Message Queue, COM or script components, or its own Messaging Services. It supports transactions (several actions that must succeed or fail as a whole) and concurrency (two or more processes occurring at the same time). These features are so important to building systems with orchestration that we come back to them later, devoting Chapter 6 to their study.

When you have finished specifying a workflow, Orchestration Designer exports an XML document that defines the workflow. This document, termed a **XLANG schedule**, is later used by XLANG Scheduler to run your distributed system by controlling how and when your applications are sent messages.

It should be stressed that Orchestration Designer only specifies the high-level semantics of workflows. It orchestrates the activities of lower-level functions, chiefly Messaging Services and your individual applications and components, to compose a complete, distributed business application.

Orchestration Designer and the fundamentals of XLANG schedules are covered in Chapter 2, while advanced features of schedules are discussed in Chapter 6.

XLANG Scheduler

BizTalk Server installs a default COM+ application called **XLANG Scheduler**. Its function is to host the running instances of **XLANG Scheduler Engine**. In turn, this Engine is a service that manages and runs instances of XLANG schedules.

This somewhat confusing dichotomy – a COM+ application and a service with a similar name – allows any new COM+ application to host the Scheduler Engine. This permits great flexibility in how BizTalk systems are deployed, managed, and run, because writing a custom COM+ application that hosts the scheduling services allows you to take control of various aspects of scheduling. However, in general, and in this book, you will be using default XLANG Scheduler and its default support for the scheduling services.

The XLANG Scheduler Engine loads XLANG schedules – the XML documents produced by Orchestration Designer – and executes them. At its most basic, this involves calling Messaging Services in response to actions specified in the schedule.

There is a less obvious function of the Scheduler, however, and that is managing the resource utilization of schedules. Schedules can require a comparatively long time to execute. For example, executing the standard protocols of the Web over the public Internet can often require seconds or minutes to complete an operation. BizTalk schedules can wait for the arrival of a message, but since these messages are coming from other applications, even other organizations across the Internet, there is the potential to wait minutes, hours, or even days for a message. You might also be running hundreds of schedules in a production environment. Clearly, the scheduling services must ensure system resources are not consumed by schedules that are not actively executing a scheduled action.

To do this, XLANG Scheduler uses a process called **hydration**. A schedule is *dehydrated* when it is blocked waiting for an incoming message. The current state of the entire schedule is serialized to a database. When the Scheduler Engine detects the arrival of the message, unblocking the schedule, the schedule is *rehydrated*. Its serialized state is read and the schedule resumes where it left off.

An application causes XLANG Scheduler to load an XLANG schedule file by passing it a **moniker**. The moniker is a name that represents a particular schedule file or schedule instance. A moniker may be thought of roughly (very roughly) as being analogous to a URL. It is a sometimes arcane-looking string that locates a resource in the COM+ system. Here is a sample of a schedule moniker used by XLANG Scheduler:

```
sked://ibex!XLANG Scheduler/{770C13A4-AB4C-4470-821F-D1FAE5235AE0}/WaitForReply
```

XLANG Scheduler passes this off to the Scheduler Engine, which then produces an instance of the schedule. Since a schedule can be instantiated many times, on different servers, the moniker syntax not only identifies the schedule document but also the location and instance of the running schedule. This allows programmers to access any particular instance of the schedule for custom purposes.

Defining Message Specifications: BizTalk Editor

The process of providing the low-level details needed to implement a workflow starts at the bottom. Remember, the key to application integration using BizTalk is the exchange of structured messages. Whether those messages use XML or some other parsed text scheme, programmers must be able to specify the structure of a message file – the **specification**. This is the function of **BizTalk Editor**.

The Editor is a graphical tool that uses a tree-structure metaphor to build message specification files, or simply the specifications themselves. Editor is influenced by database terminology, which is a reasonable approach given that much of the information used to compose messages will come from databases anyway. Database programmers work with *records* and *fields*. A record corresponds to an object or entity, while fields are equivalent to the properties of the object. This works nicely with a database-style table structure in which the rows are individual objects, and the objects are described by the values contained in the row's fields.

Unlike a relational table, however, a specification can nest records within other records. This allows us to describe parent-child relationships like those represented by a database join. The tree that represents a specification in Editor is also analogous to a file directory structure, with records standing in for directories and fields replacing files.

In the Editor window shown below, the name of the specification is SiteServiceDescription. The pane on the left shows the tree structure of the specification, while the pane on the right displays some properties of SiteServiceDescription.

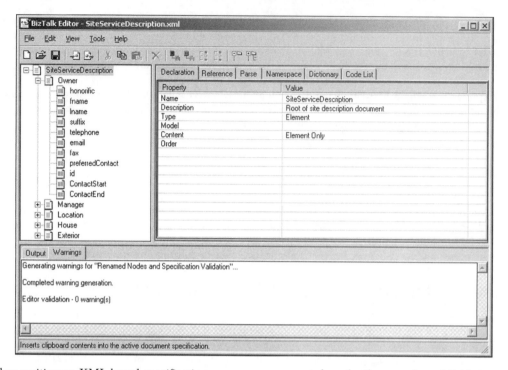

When writing an XML-based specification, a programmer may describe the records and fields in terms of the basic XML data types, as well as the derived types permitted under the XML – Data Reduced (XML-DR) Schemas technology implemented in the XML parser supplied with Internet Explorer 5.0. All the options available in a schema are available to specification builders. This includes being able to specify the cardinality (repetition) of specific records and fields.

In Chapter 3, we will use Editor to create three message specifications for our sample application. One will be XML. The other two, simulating legacy formats, will be non-XML in nature. These specifications will be used by BizTalk to tell the Server how to read our messages.

XML appears to be replacing other text formats for a variety of reasons. Editor permits programmers to take full advantage of XML without forcing them to become XML experts. Because Editor allows the use of formats other than XML, the interface is carefully constructed so that XML terminology does not dominate.

> *A complete discussion of XML, including its advantages with respect to other text file formats, is found in* Professional XML *(Wrox Press, 2000, ISBN 1-861003-11-0).*

Right out of the box, BizTalk Server and Editor can handle the following text formats:

❑   XML

❑   Delimited flatfiles

❑   Positional flatfiles

❑   Hybrid delimited and positional flatfiles

❑   EDI (X12 and UN/EDIFACT)

With some custom coding, BizTalk can be made to understand your own custom formats. This may potentially include binary formats.

Using XML does not force programmers to start from scratch when defining specifications. For example, there are initiatives underway to transform EDI commerce message formats and Health Level 7 medical message formats to XML. BizTalk Server includes a collection of basic XML template specifications for common business messages such as purchase orders and invoices. ADO, the mainstream Microsoft database access technology, now allows database recordsets to be persisted as XML. Programmers can use this feature to model their specifications on existing database table schemas.

Many legacy message formats are in forms other than XML. Both EDI formats, X12 and EDIFACT, use delimited message formats. Versions of Health Level 7 prior to version three also used non-XML formats. Messages built around mainframe systems are frequently written in character delimited or fixed position formats. Editor supports the use of these formats; indeed, BizTalk includes specifications for both X12 and EDIFACT. A programmer can load these specifications and modify them as needed. When working with EDI formats, the Code List tab in the right-hand pane of the Editor window contains a list of all possible fields and records in the type of EDI message that is loaded.

More importantly, Editor permits programmers to specify all aspects of delimited and positional flatfile formats. Programmers may specify how to handle end-of-record delimiters in such files. Delimiting characters may be specified. Field sizes may be specified for positional files. This information is retained and used by BizTalk server to properly parse an incoming message.

The primary file format of a specification produced by Editor is an XML document that includes an XML-DR schema, but also has elements added by the Editor to record specification-specific information. These extra elements are especially important when working with non-XML specifications. For example, XML-DR schemas cannot capture delimiter and field position information. It is the extra elements that capture this information, and they are proprietary to BizTalk.

The BizTalk Framework schema repository works with XML-DR schemas, not BizTalk specifications. For this reason, Editor can export XML-DR schemas. A programmer can design a specification in the Editor, then export a schema and submit it to a repository. Going in the other direction, Editor can import an instance of a well-formed XML message and build a specification and schema from it.

The capabilities of BizTalk Editor, along with the specific syntax of BizTalk Server message specifications, are described in depth in Chapter 3. Microsoft has pledged to migrate to W3C standard XML schemas when they are approved as a formal W3C Recommendation. Schemas have now reached Candidate Recommendation status, one step away from formal approval.

WebDAV

Web Distributed Authoring and Versioning (**WebDAV**) is a standard of the Internet Engineering Task Force (IETF) for collaborative document editing over the Web. It permits someone to retrieve and work with a document, and then submit it to a repository using extensions to HTTP. BizTalk Editor and Mapper use WebDAV to allow administrators to create, edit, and save document specifications and maps.

Why should we want to store documents in the WebDAV repository? Well, if you are working with BizTalk tools running on the BizTalk Server machine, you could use normal file access to open, save, and close documents. However, to do so from another computer, you would need security privileges to the folders where BizTalk keeps its documents. Obviously, you would not want to do implement this scheme – it would permit almost anyone to manipulate or delete files without going through Messaging Manager.

WebDAV, by contrast, exposes your documents and folders through HTTP. If you are working with document specifications through WebDAV, the BizTalk Editor will only show you folders devoted to document specifications. These are actually folders on the server, but this information is not exposed and you cannot navigate away from the specification repository. There is also a XLANG schedule file repository.

By using WebDAV, BizTalk lets administrators edit documents from any computer with web access to the BizTalk Server. Users do not need to be aware of the folder structure of the repository to find the documents they need. WebDAV also locks documents to prevent users from accidentally overwriting each other's changes. As well as this, it enables users to share and work with server-based documents, regardless of their authoring tools, platforms, or the type of web servers on which the files are stored.

Translating Between Message Specifications: BizTalk Mapper

Defining how one message format translates – or **maps** – to another, is a critical task in application integration, as we have seen. The Mapper tool is supplied with BizTalk Server to help programmers perform this task. It is a graphical editor that displays two specifications, the *source* and the *destination*, and then permits a programmer to specify how the records and fields map to one another. Mapper allows not only one-to-one mapping relationships, but also one-to-many, or many-to-one relationships. It even facilitates data processing during mapping   for example, you might wanted to multiply a source field value by a number before mapping it to the destination field. As we will see, some of the processing that can occur during a mapping is quite complicated, potentially including iteration through similar fields, or database access.

The Mapper interface, an example of which is shown below, consists of two regions.

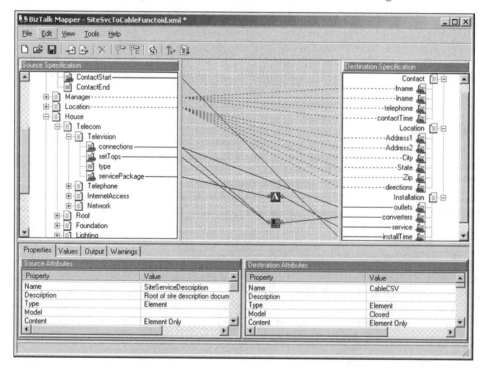

At the top we have a mapping diagram showing three panes: the left and right panes contain tree representations of the source and destination message specifications respectively, while the middle pane is a **mapping grid**, which displays lines linking source fields to destination fields. Simple relationships between fields are mapped by dragging a record or field in one specification to the appropriate record or field in the other, thereby establishing a **link**. In such cases, BizTalk Server performs the translation by simply copying the content of a record or field in the incoming message into the mapped record or field in the other message specification.

Sometimes, though, there is no simple translation. The contents of several source fields may need to be combined to form the contents of a destination field, or some data processing may need to be performed on the contents of the source specification field to produce the required contents of the destination field. In Mapper, there are two ways to introduce intermediate data processing during the mapping process:

❑ **Functoids**: functional objects that perform simple predefined operations (for example, string manipulation, or mathematical operations)

❑ **Scripts**: Short user-written scripts, executed by the script functoid, which allow for more complex data processing.

If you look again at the screenshot of the Mapper, you will see that the grid contains icons, like the box containing **A**. This is how functoids and scriptlets are represented in the mapping grid.

When the desired mapping is complete, a programmer compiles the map using the Mapper. This results in an XML transformation (**XSLT**) **stylesheet**. Then, when mapping between message specifications is required, the runtime server process can apply the appropriate stylesheet to perform the appropriate message mapping. This process, for mapping between different XML specifications, is depicted in the diagram below:

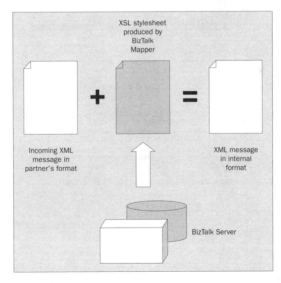

You should note that the transformation process for mappings involving flatfile formats has several additional steps.

The region at the bottom of the Mapper interface contains useful information, such as lists of attributes of the fields/records selected in each specification, and any compilation errors.

We will discuss the Mapper in greater detail in Chapter 4.

In the sample Site Managers application that we will develop throughout the book, we will need two maps. Each will take the message format describing the site and translate a subset of its information into one of the other message formats. That way, we use our own message format, and use BizTalk mapping to send out messages in the formats used by our business partners. One of the maps will use a functoid that we will create specially for this purpose. We will examine this more closely in Chapter 4.

Configuring Messaging Services: BizTalk Messaging Manager

Messaging Manager is an application that allows you to configure and manage how messages are passed through BizTalk Messaging Services. It can be used to specify the organizations and applications that are the components of your workflow. From there, you define how they are integrated by specifying the format of messages that pass between organizations, and what should happen when a message arrives at the server from a particular source, bound for a particular destination. In short, Messaging Manager lets you manage the business processing relationships that define message exchange.

Messaging Manager consists of two main panes: a **navigation** pane on the left that outlines the different items under management, and a **detail** pane to the right in which search results are presented. Editing an item in the detail pane invokes a wizard, that guides you through the steps required to fully configure that item. A sample Messaging Manager window is shown below, which details the channels under management:

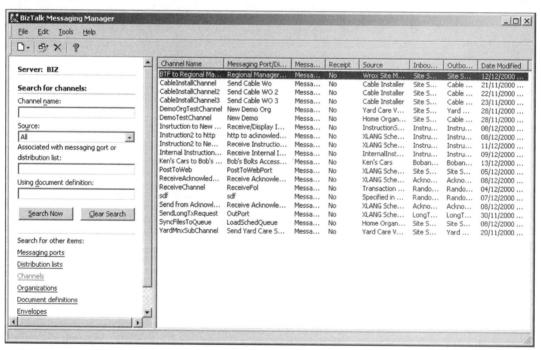

BizTalk message transfer is completely defined by the major entities managed through Messaging Manager. These areas are:

- Ports
- Distribution Lists
- Channels
- Organizations
- Document Definitions
- Envelopes

You should be familiar with these terms from our earlier discussion of BizTalk messaging. Application integration with BizTalk involves configuring message documents, organizations, ports, and channels. Only a thin layer of code is required, in most cases, to make an application BizTalk-aware. In some cases, no custom code is written at all. The Messaging Manager is therefore fundamental to using BizTalk. You cannot use any runtime aspect of BizTalk Server (except, perhaps, an extremely limited example of orchestration) without configuring some entities in the Messaging Manager.

We will cover Messaging Manager and messaging configuration in depth in Chapter 5, although we will also be seeing different aspects of using Messaging Manager throughout this book as we configure our sample applications.

When we cover the Messaging Manager in detail, we'll put it to practical use by configuring the details of the messaging that must take place in the orchestration schedule we build for our sample application. In other words, in Chapter 2 we will produce a sample schedule – a high-level view of the process. Then the low-level messaging functions that make it work will be specified through Messaging Manager in Chapter 5, to complete the sample application.

Viewing Run-time Messages: Document Tracking

Once you have a BizTalk Server installation up and running, it becomes important to be able to track individual messages transiting the messaging system. Recall that Orchestration Designer and XLANG Scheduler view systems in terms of the flow of messages. Viewing the status of messages, therefore, is viewing the state of the system. Without the ability to track messages, you cannot monitor and troubleshoot the system as a whole. In the absence of message tracking, you could only study individual applications and guess at the problem; if you were exchanging messages with an external partner, you couldn't even do that.

Thankfully, BizTalk Server does have the ability to track messages. Every message interchange that passes through Messaging Services is recorded by default in the Document Tracking and Activity (DTA) database. When you configure messaging, you can change these defaults. You can even record specific fields from particular classes of messages, fields that play an important role in your system.

For example, one of our applications might assign a tracking number to an order. This number might be used throughout the business to monitor the status of the order. Since this datum has no meaning to BizTalk, it would not be retained by default. Since it is of critical importance to our business, however, we can direct the tracking process to record it in the DTA database so that we can readily report on messaging according to this number. Clearly, there is a lot of message information available for you to mine.

While you could access the underlying SQL Server database directly, it is convenient to have a default interface that understands the layout of the DTA database. This is the function of the **Document Tracking** application that comes with BizTalk. Document Tracking is a web-based application. It makes extensive use of ActiveX controls, however, so don't expect to use it in practice to provide self-help tracking information to external partners. This is, practically speaking, an internal troubleshooting tool.

The basic controls allow you to filter messages based on:

❑ Date Range (the date and time the message transited Messaging Services)
❑ Message Source
❑ Message Destination
❑ Message Type

For example, say you send a particular type of message document to several partners, but one of them requires a transformation. You could single out documents bound for that partner by filtering based on the destination organization. Actually, this is a common scenario. If there is a fault in the message map, that partner would be the only one to experience difficulty. Looking at the status of the messages intended for that partner would help you track down the problem.

You can further refine your criteria when dealing with messages sent within the Home Organization, because you can look inside the Organization and track the messages sent between applications.

As you can see from the screenshot below, the document definitions known to BizTalk are displayed in the list box in the lower right corner of the Document Tracking query window, which makes it relatively simple to filter on message type. In addition to filtering, you can sort your results based on the same criteria by which you were able to filter. You may specify up to six levels of sorting.

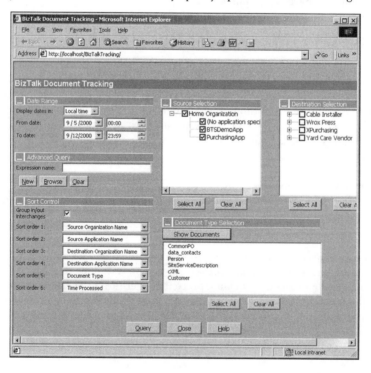

By default, BizTalk Server does not single out any fields in your messages for retention. You can tell it to retain copies of all original messages through the Server Administration MMC snap-in, or you can use the Messaging Manager to be more selective in retaining information. If you want to track messages based on specific fields, you can tell BizTalk to capture the values of those fields in the database and then write queries using expressions based on those values.

In the Messaging Manager, you can select fields in either Document Definitions properties or Channel properties. The former captures the designated fields for every instance of that message type seen. The latter captures the fields when a message of that type transits BizTalk Server as part of the specific channel selected.

Once you have fields captured in the database, you can use the **Advanced Query** group in Document Tracking to build expression-based queries. Clicking **New** in that group leads you to a dialog that permits you to select a captured field and build a logical expression around it. This expression becomes part of the selection criteria for your search.

Regardless of your query parameters, the results of a query are displayed in a new browser window that looks like this:

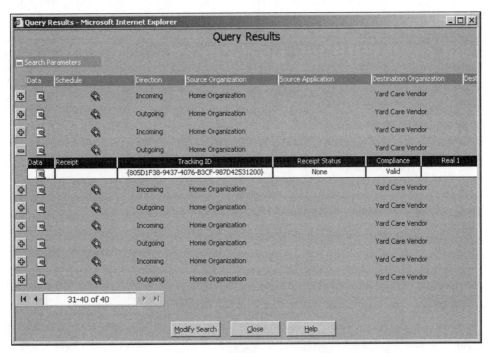

Note that you can expand any single document instance to view its status information. Any fields you have asked BizTalk to save to the DTA database will be displayed. Clicking the icon in the **Data** column pops up a window showing the body of the message, assuming you configured Messaging Services to log message bodies when you configured the channel for this interchange. Clicking on the **Schedule** icon displays any available information for the schedule (if any) that executed the interchange. While basic, the Document Tracking application is a good first stop for troubleshooting and tracking. It enables someone unfamiliar with the DTA schema to query the database and obtain reports on BizTalk messaging activity.

Document Tracking is discussed in detail in Chapter 12.

Managing BizTalk Server: Server Administration

Not surprisingly, all administration of BizTalk Server is performed through the Microsoft Management Console (MMC). BizTalk Server instances are organized into **BizTalk Server Groups** for scalability. A Server Group is a collection of identically configured BizTalk Servers that share a common view of administrative configuration and document interchange. This means that any server in the group can be used to process a particular interchange of documents. They all share the same view of organizations, documents, and agreements. This is accomplished by having all the Servers in a group share several things:

- ❑ the Shared Queue (SQ) SQL database
- ❑ the Document Tracking and Activity (DTA) SQL database
- ❑ receive functions for file or MSMQ message transport
- ❑ parsers and serializers for message processing

These concepts, and how we manage them, are the topic of Chapter 9. A typical Server Administration window is shown below:

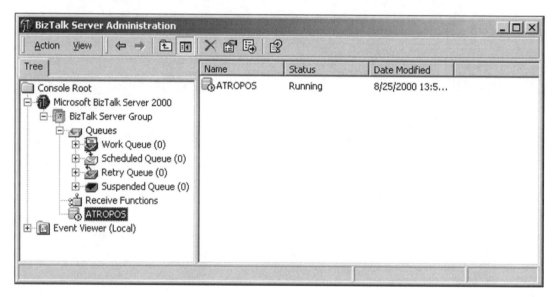

The **SQ database** is where incoming and outgoing messages are stored as they pass through the Server. The database consists of the following logical queues:

- ❑ Work – messages currently in process
- ❑ Scheduled – messages processed and awaiting delivery to a distribution list
- ❑ Retry – messages that have failed transmission and are queued awaiting a retransmission attempt
- ❑ Suspended – messages that could not be transmitted

The DTA database logs message interchange activity for the server group. Administrators use it to run reports on activity within the group using the Document Tracking application, as we have just seen.

The BizTalk Server Administration MMC snap-in allows an administrator to add new groups to the enterprise and configure them in terms of their shared resources. Administrators can also use the MMC to add a server to a group. Within a server group, the MMC provides a view of messages in the various queues.

It also lists the receive functions configured for that group. These are specific MSMQ queues or directory folders that Messaging Services will monitor for incoming messages.

If you open the **Properties** dialog for the Server group, you can also configure the tracking behavior and database location for message activity on that group. Each group also shares a collection of parsers that BizTalk uses to handle various message formats. Under certain circumstances, an administrator may wish to change the order in which BizTalk tries these components on an unknown incoming message. This occurs mainly when programmers have created custom parsers to extend BizTalk's features and the administrator wants to ensure the custom parser is tried first.

Note that the WebDAV repository is treated differently from the other resources we have discussed so far. It is shared among all BizTalk Server groups in an enterprise. This is reasonable on several counts:

❑ Document specifications and maps are likely to be common to the entire organization, not just one working group.

❑ Access to the WebDAV repository is going to occur much less frequently than message interchanges.

Clearly, you develop a specification and then use it repeatedly in the course of normal processing. The WebDAV repository, then, has much lower demands on scalability than the shared queues and DTA databases.

The Server Administration MMC snap-in focuses on the maintenance of the servers and the components they require. Maintenance of the business logic embedded in the workflow is handled through the Messaging Manager and Orchestration Designer. These tools are complementary in terms of managing a BizTalk installation.

Server Administration and Configuration is taken up in Chapters 9 and 13.

Summary

We've defined application integration and the need for it in electronic commerce. Common problems of interoperability between technologies and data exchange formats are common to most implementations of application integration. BizTalk, both the Framework and the BizTalk Server product, are a formal attempt to provide programmers with robust tools with which to overcome these problems. More than that, BizTalk attempts to provide a common approach that will enable potential business-to-business partners to rapidly integrate their commerce system applications effectively. In this chapter we've explored the following:

❑ The role of open standards for information interchange in application integration

❑ The scope of Microsoft BizTalk Server, its tools, and its features

❑ The common interprocess and internetworking protocols BizTalk Server uses to accomplish application integration

❑ The relationship between BizTalk Server and the BizTalk Framework

In the chapters to come, we will explore each of the tools provided by BizTalk Server in depth. Once you have an understanding of how to use each tool, we will use them to perform some integration tasks. In addition to understanding how to use the individual parts of BizTalk Server, you will see how to effectively build support for BizTalk Server and BizTalk Framework into your applications.

The first step in building a complete, integrated system using BizTalk Server is to design the business process using Orchestration Designer. This becomes the framework for BizTalk messaging and dictates the capabilities and constraints of your system. In the next chapter, we'll discuss this process and introduce you to the sample Site Managers application. Over the course of the next few chapters, you'll learn how to use BizTalk Server by building and configuring this sample application.

2

Applications and Schedules

Virtually all real-world distributed systems will require the exchange of more than one message. Many of these messages will require some sort of response. More complicated systems are implemented by collections of messages, and the selection and sequencing of these messages depends on some set of rules that collectively define the business process, or **workflow**, of the system.

In the past, application integration involved adding code to the applications themselves to implement the workflow. If the system consists of only two applications, this can be managed. A system involving many applications, however, makes this particular approach difficult to implement and manage. It is hard to effectively manage the sequencing of operations for the whole system from any particular application. Factor in Internet e-commerce as well, and it falls apart, because your side of the workflow may look very different from your partner's. What is needed is a central entity outside all of the applications that make up the system, to manage the state of the system and coordinate the activities of the individual applications. BizTalk Server provides this mechanism; the application integration code is pulled out of individual applications, and into the server in a way that is totally visible to administrators.

The mechanism for coordinating all the application-to-application exchanges in a system is called **orchestration**. BizTalk orchestration tools provide a way to specify the workflow in a special document called a **schedule**. This schedule then drives a runtime engine that implements the workflow and performs the needed coordination. You visually specify the workflow in a special Visio diagram, then export it as a schedule, in an XML form that the runtime engine can read. Applications cause the BizTalk scheduling engine to load individual schedules. This engine then coordinates, or orchestrates – hence the name – the actions of BizTalk Messaging Services, as well as any COM components or MSMQ messaging that may be involved in the overall system.

Orchestration is a big subject, and we'll cover the more advanced topics in a later chapter. However, orchestration is a good place to begin our study of BizTalk Server. In this chapter, you'll be introduced to the main concepts that the messaging server implements, and you'll also get a good idea of how to design BizTalk-enabled applications using the design-time tool, the **BizTalk Orchestration Designer**. We'll also design the sample application that we will be implementing over the next few chapters. When you are finished with this chapter, you should know how to do the following:

- ❏ Work with the basic flowcharting shapes used to design BizTalk Server-based applications
- ❏ Understand the tools provided by the BizTalk Orchestration Designer to represent transactions, concurrency, and decision making
- ❏ Connect schedules with applications and components outside BizTalk Server
- ❏ Access individual fields in messages, and methods and properties in COM components through BizTalk Server
- ❏ Designate the flow of data through a schedule
- ❏ Export a schedule for use with the BizTalk Scheduler

Actually implementing the BizTalk messaging functions and services that the scheduling server orchestrates requires tasks we shall take up in the next three chapters, so we will not actually load and execute the schedule we build in this chapter. Nevertheless, the schedule will orient you to BizTalk Server in general and our sample application in particular.

The Need for Orchestration

Application integration consists of single message exchanges between applications. A distributed system, in contrast, is composed of many such interchanges coordinated to form a logical sequence. Therefore, the purpose of BizTalk orchestration is to integrate a complex system, by defining and coordinating the flow of messages within it. This involves issues of system state, and decision-making, which are above individual applications.

Consider a web site that sells a broad array of consumer items. The consumer places an order with the site, triggering several activities. First, credit authorization must be obtained. If that succeeds, the ERP (Enterprise Resource Planning) system must be updated, and a shipping list must be generated at the warehouse so that the order can be assembled. A confirmation e-mail must also be sent to the customer. Depending on inventory levels, orders to suppliers may be generated to keep the warehouse stocked. Alternatively, some companies do not keep any inventory at all, in which case orders for items may be passed to a vendor for shipment from their stocks. The diagram below provides details of the implementation of this process:

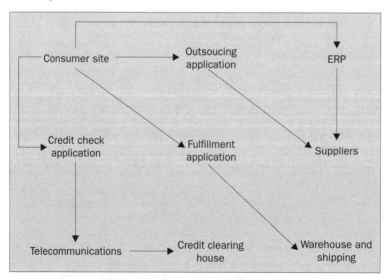

In this overly simplified diagram, the consumer site relies on four applications:

❏ The *credit check* application encapsulates the protocols and logic of communicating with the credit card clearing house.

❏ The *fulfillment* application translates a shopping cart into a fulfilment list and shipping slip at the warehouse.

❏ The *outsourcing* application handles the ordering of any items that are shipped directly from the manufacturer or vendor. It is able to determine the appropriate source of supply, update internal databases to reflect the status of the order, and communicate with the vendor.

❏ The *ERP system* manages inventory and purchasing for the e-commerce company.

These may be full-blown applications or components called from scripts on the site, but each delivers specific functions to the site. The complexity of integrating these functions – orchestration – presents some problems. Let's briefly look at these problems, and see how BizTalk Server helps solve them.

Each application executes a specific, well-defined function. The overall system, however, has its own processing to do in order to implement the workflow. Code is needed to **coordinate** the constituent applications, and the coordinating application will require some knowledge of the applications. For a web site, we might opt to use Microsoft Commerce Server pipelines, although this would not work in general since not every system is a web application. Pipelines, moreover, tie execution to the web servers, which is bad for scalability. After the consumer executes the order, we'd like to push the execution of the system off to some other group of servers and free the web server farm for new orders.

Another aspect of integration to consider is how the applications **communicate**. Web sites have to handle high volumes of traffic, which generally means they will use asynchronous communication, which in turn implies some sort of messaging solution. The system will be integrated by sending and receiving messages to and from the applications that implement the system. The process that coordinates the applications must understand messaging, and be closely tied to some messaging middleware technology. We could use COM – indeed, BizTalk supports COM interchanges – but asynchronous messaging is much more scalable and resistant to temporary network outages.

Orchestration: The Solution

In order to address these concerns, a common form of integration has to be found. As seen above, distributed systems found in business environments are composed of individual applications that focus on one task, which makes implementation and testing easier. This means that separate teams can program the applications, and their task will be simpler because they are only trying to do one thing. In addressing problems of communication and coordination, the separation of systems is actually an advantage, because we can treat these separate applications as black boxes and coordinate them through the exchange of messages. We don't actually want to put the code that implements the integration into any particular application because we'd have to modify the application whenever any of the other applications changed. The system workflow is itself an application and one whose behavior should be visible to the system designers and administrators. This process is handled by BizTalk, and is what is termed orchestration.

Implementing Orchestration

Orchestration in BizTalk Server comprises a runtime engine and a design-time tool. The tool, a Visio-based program called **Orchestration Designer**, allows programmers to specify the business process in terms of a sequence of message exchanges. Designers draw a flowchart in which specific actions are related to ports, and to messages that pass through those ports. Data items in the associated document interchanges are related so that information flows from one field in a message to another field in a subsequent message. As a result, the flowchart, termed a **schedule**, dictates how data flows through the business process from message to message.

Once the schedule is completed, the designer exports it, producing an XML schedule document in a vocabulary called XLANG (often pronounced *slang*). It is this document that the runtime engine, known as the **XLANG Scheduler**, uses to load schedules into memory for execution. This does not happen automatically. Programmers write applications that control when schedules are initially loaded into memory. After that, the Scheduler manages how and when the schedule is loaded, unloaded, and generally managed. Because the execution of a schedule may span long periods of inactivity, say, when a schedule is waiting for an incoming message, the XLANG scheduler is able to write out the state of the schedule to a SQL Server database while taking note of the event for which it is waiting. When the event occurs, the schedule is returned to memory and the flow of control continues.

A more accurate definition of orchestration, then, is a layer of application-level logic over BizTalk's lower-level messaging functions. A message interchange, optionally including the data and protocol translation features we mentioned in the last chapter, describes a single event in a larger application. While this is useful and important, it is insufficient to implement an application or system. If BizTalk did not include orchestration, the higher-level functions of application integration would be left to the applications themselves.

Since the purpose of BizTalk is to remove application integration code from individual applications, orchestration is an important piece of the overall solution. Orchestration gives designers and analysts a way of describing business processes that is readily visible to managers. Such managers can look at a schedule's flowchart and decide if the requirements of the application are met, even though they have little programming expertise.

Configuring BizTalk orchestration, then, is a matter of a visual file for human users and an equivalent representation in XML for the orchestration engine. While both of these files are often referred to as a BizTalk schedule, it is sometimes useful to distinguish them by referring to the logical diagram as the **business process diagram,** and describing the XML document as a **XLANG schedule**. Let's look at business process diagrams in general to see what they do for us; then we will take a brief look at XLANG to see how the runtime engine is configured.

Business Process Diagrams

We've said that a schedule is designed by drawing a flowchart that represents the workflow in Orchestration Designer. This flowchart is known in BizTalk as a business process diagram. Although flowcharts are losing their appeal as a formal programming methodology, you have probably encountered flowcharts somewhere in your education as a programmer. The symbols and concepts of schedules and their graphical business process diagrams will therefore be somewhat familiar, although there are some important distinctions to understand.

Like classic programming flowchart business process diagrams have symbols to mark the *beginning* and *end* of the process. There are also symbols that denote *actions* to perform, and *decision* symbols that direct the flow of control through the flowchart. There are symbols representing common *programming constructs* such as loops and transactions too. We'll cover all the available symbols and their meanings in a later section.

The action symbol is where business process diagrams differ most markedly from classic flowcharts:

❑   First, they are represented by ovals, instead of the rectangles used in a flowchart. Flowcharts use ovals for modules, and a process diagram action encapsulates a number of things, so there is some logic in this selection.

❑   Second, in a flowchart, the action symbol refers to some body of code that performs a particular task. Action symbols in a process diagram refer exclusively to a message interchange.

When the diagram reaches an action it must send a message to another application, or wait for the arrival of a message from another application. Such messages will typically pass through the document interchange side of BizTalk Server, but this may also include Microsoft Message Queue messages as well as method calls on COM components or scripted components. Given that this is the only construct in a BizTalk schedule that can perform an action other than flowing control, it should be clearer now that BizTalk orchestration is dedicated strictly to coordinating message flows. It is up to the applications connected to those message flows (including method calls on components in which a message is passed) to implement the specific features of the overall business process.

When you add an action symbol to a business process diagram, you will specify the direction of the message, but that alone is obviously not enough to connect the action to some document interchange in BizTalk's Messaging Services. To do that, you create an implementation port and **bind** the action to it. The port denotes a connection between something in the schedule and a message in the outside world. To implement the binding, you must indicate what sort of message the port binds to, and provide other configuration information using a wizard. Each type of communication – BizTalk messaging, MSMQ, and so on, has its own wizard and we'll discuss these in detail later.

To be useful and efficient, BizTalk schedules also need symbols to control the flow of execution within the schedule. To this end, Orchestration Designer includes symbols for decisions, concurrent execution, and while loops. Decision symbols permit the designer to enter VBScript expressions that evaluate to True or False, but they usually operate on some value passed in a message field rather than provide significant logic of their own. Their purpose is to direct the schedule down one branch or another. We will discuss the individual symbols used in schedules shortly, together with their limitations and conditions.

Defining the Data Flow Between Messages

There is another way of looking at the movement of information throughout the workflow, in addition to the business process diagram. Actions are associated with messages, so one way to approach the problem of defining the workflow is to consider how data flows from one message to the next – the **data flow**. Orchestration Designer provides a view of the data flow between messages, in the Data tab. As you build your business process diagram, you will link fields in one message to those in another to tell BizTalk how data should be passed between the messages. This tab will be illustrated and discussed in more detail later when we take up the task of using Orchestration Designer.

XLANG Schedules

Once you have a graphical depiction of your business process, you need to translate that diagram into something the BizTalk Scheduler can read. Orchestration Designer takes care of this for you, writing out the information contained in a business process diagram as an XML document. Given the extent to which Microsoft has embraced XML, you may not be surprised to learn that the BizTalk development team has devised an XML vocabulary to model schedules. That vocabulary, called **XLANG**, contains elements and attributes that define the parts of a schedule together with the data flows and message bindings.

A XLANG document describes the state machine for your schedule. The XLANG Scheduler is a blank slate, completely driven by the XLANG document derived from your Visio process diagram. The XLANG document is the chunk of data that communicates your orchestration logic and implements your orchestration through the Scheduler. Since schedules involve communications between applications, a XLANG document records the nature of the communications, as well as information about the ports that allow Scheduler to take in data from other applications and send data out to them.

The steps where a schedule sends or receives data are called actions. Any process has to include constructs to control the flow of the process, and XLANG includes these in the form of a starting point, one or more end points, decision points, a while loop, and a pair of constructs for handling concurrent threads of execution. XLANG Scheduler is the executable code that can implement the flow of activity, and maintain the state of the schedule, but without the XLANG version of the schedule, the Scheduler Engine has no knowledge of your desired process.

Orchestration Designer reads the contents of the business process document, saved in Visio-format, before converting them into the form of a XLANG document. As you might imagine, tinkering with native XLANG data is dangerous – rather like opening an executable file and modifying the machine code in a hex editor. BizTalk does expose a COM API to let you dynamically modify a schedule, so you can do some very sophisticated things with schedules without ever learning XML. Still, XLANG is XML and XML is text, so some of you will want to get your hands dirty and pull XLANG documents apart. However, you should remember that the safest (and therefore the recommended) way to produce and modify XLANG schedules is using the BizTalk Orchestration Designer tool. Let's turn to this tool now, and see how to use it to develop schedules for BizTalk.

BizTalk Orchestration Designer

Orchestration Designer is the tool that takes your knowledge of the business process, uses its knowledge of the XLANG syntax, and generates schedules that the XLANG Scheduler can execute. It is based on Microsoft Visio 2000 with knowledge of the requirements and syntax of XLANG schedules programmed into it. If you have used Visio you will find the visual interface somewhat familiar. Here's what a typical business process diagram looks like in Orchestration Designer:

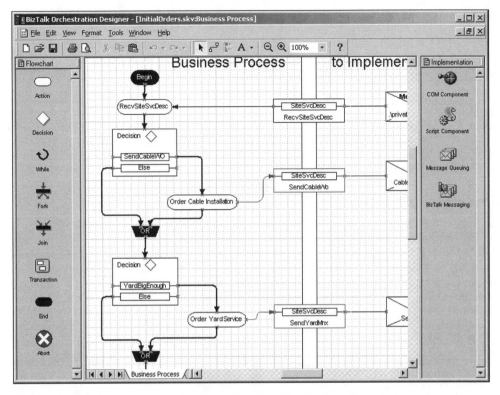

Your choice of symbols is constrained to those that describe the flow of control and messaging implementations of schedules, but most of the tasks involved in specifying a schedule are accomplished by drawing a flowchart. There is also some data field mapping required to tell the scheduler how message data will flow through your application, but it too is specified with a diagram.

Once you have drawn up a schedule, Orchestration Designer translates the schedule into a XLANG document. This is sufficient to instruct the XLANG Scheduler how to execute a BizTalk application, but not enough to completely implement the messaging functions that make up such an application. Orchestration Designer lets you build schedules, but schedules only orchestrate the messaging building blocks. In this chapter, we'll go ahead and construct a schedule for a sample business process. In subsequent chapters, we'll learn the messaging tasks needed to fully implement the messaging functions in the schedule.

In order to get to grips with the Orchestration Designer, we will first look at its user interface and the two views it provides, and then go on to look at how we actually design a schedule using it.

Orchestration Designer User Interface

When you first start Orchestration Designer a new schedule is created by default. This document consists of two views, a business process diagram and a data flow. The two views are Visio documents accessed by clicking the tabs labeled Business Process and Data. The views are flanked by two Visio stencils, which contain the shapes (symbols) for the business process diagram. Orchestration Designer generates the symbols in the Data view for you as you construct the business process diagram, so your sole interaction with the Data view will be to indicate the flow of message data through the system by linking fields in one message with fields in the next.

Four types of messaging are permitted in Orchestration Designer:

❑ **BizTalk messaging**

❑ **MSMQ**

❑ **COM components**

❑ **Script-based COM components**

Each has a configuration wizard associated with it, and there is also a wizard for configuring the ports that links message implementations to flow chart shapes. Message implementation will be covered more comprehensively in Chapter 5. Meanwhile, in this chapter we'll see how to design schedules using Orchestration Designer. Let's start by looking at each of the views.

Business Process View

The Business Process tab, shown in the previous screenshot, is where you will be spending the majority of your time when designing BizTalk Schedules. This view is shown below. The left-most pane, by default, is the Visio stencil containing the flow chart shapes. The right-most pane contains the four messaging implementation shapes. These template panes are dockable, so you can detach them to float over the business process diagram or move them about to dock with either side or the top or bottom of the main window. A dockable toolbar containing standard Windows application and Visio-specific tasks is normally found at the top of the window.

Take another look at the top of the Business Process view:

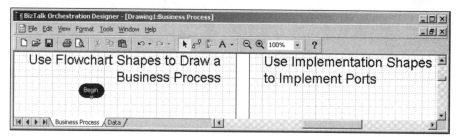

The main pane of the business process view is a Visio document with a double line bisecting it. To the left, in the area titled Use Flowchart Shapes to Draw a Business Process, you will draw the flow chart portion of the business process diagram. To the right, in the area entitled Use Implementation Shapes to Implement Ports, you will place the messaging implementations that your schedule orchestrates. As each messaging implementation shape is placed, a port shape appears on the double line boundary. After the port and messaging implementation wizards are finished, you have only to connect the flow chart shape on the left with the port on the boundary. Ports are created connected to the messaging implementation that instantiated them.

If the titles are in your way, or you simply find them as annoying as I do, you will be glad to know that you can select them with a mouse click and delete them with the Delete key.

Microsoft's philosophy is that a business analyst knowledgeable in the underlying business function will draw the flowchart, and a developer conversant with BizTalk messaging and the organizations applications will specify the messaging implementations. This may be true to some extent. The flowchart, however, adopts the conventions of programming flowcharts, and some constructs, especially the while loop and the decision symbol, rely on the analyst having some familiarity with these concepts. Generally speaking, developers can expect to participate in both parts of the business process diagram, although a business analyst will have primary responsibility for the business flowchart.

Data View

As you work through the business process diagram, Orchestration Designer is busily creating shapes on the Data view. These are very important to your application. Nothing happens in the schedule itself except the movement and transformation of data. You hand the data out to other applications and components and take in modified data by sending and receiving messages. The messages you send and receive are analogous to data structures in a conventional program. Scheduler has to know what the discrete messages are and how data moves from one to another. This is what enables Scheduler to know what data to send when you tell it to send a message.

Each message and port you create in the business process diagram results in a shape in the Data view. The diagram below shows a Data view for a sample schedule. Note especially the contents of each box. Each box represents the data in a single message. The arrows between data fields depict the flow of information from one message to another over the course of the schedule's execution. How and when the data flows take place, however, cannot be seen in this view. For that, you have to refer back to the Business Process tab.

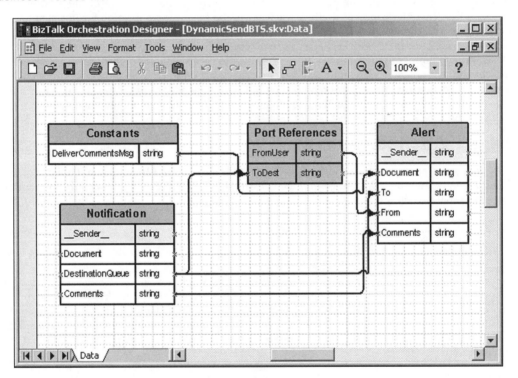

Consider the data flow depicted above. This is taken from an actual schedule we will build in Chapter 6. It is not important that you follow all the details of the data flow now (we'll cover that later); it is used here to give you an idea of what the Data view is used for.

The top banner of each box indicates the name of some body of data in the schedule. Directed links between them depict how data moves from one item to another over the course of the schedule's execution. The boxes labeled Alert and Notification denote messages. Constants are hard-coded values we provide to the schedule for later use. Port References lists all the messaging ports in the schedule and provides identifying information about them.

The rows in each message box are the field names and types for designated fields. Orchestration Designer always provides the __Sender__ and Document fields. The former denotes who is sending the message, while the Document field represents the entire body of the message as a string. As long as we have a formal message specification file available to us to describe the contents of the message (which is the topic of the next chapter), Orchestration Designer allows us to pick individual fields within the message for display in the Data View. That, in turn, allows us to establish a link that will take a piece of information from one message and insert it into the body of a subsequent message.

Now consider the links in the diagram above. While it is not apparent from the Data View, the schedule receives the Notification message and sends the Alert message, with addressing and message contents drawn from various sources within the schedule. The body of the Alert message is drawn from a constant string to start. Various fields, however, are overwritten with information from other sources. The Comments field, for example, is copied from the Notification message that was received. The From field is taken from the port that received the Notification message.

It is important to realize that the flow of information depicted in the Data View is the flow with which the XLANG Scheduler concerns itself. As we'll see in the schedule we develop for this chapter, Orchestration Designer and XLANG Scheduler have no interest in any data manipulation that occurs within BizTalk Messaging Services. The links you establish in the Data View tell Orchestration Designer, and through it the XLANG Scheduler, how to move data around within a schedule. This idea may be difficult for some programmers to grasp. We are accustomed to writing procedural code to accomplish data manipulation. In orchestration however, you tell Orchestration Designer what pieces of data should move where and XLANG Scheduler worries about how to implement that flow.

Designing Schedules

Now that you are oriented to the idea of schedules and the views in Orchestration Designer, it is time to go into detail about the tasks that go into the construction of schedules. This is chiefly a matter of learning about two things:

- ❑ flowchart shapes – of which there are nine
- ❑ message implementations – which involve a port shape, and four shapes for messages

Since we can do nothing without a flowchart, and because Orchestration Designer will generate any shapes in the Data View from what you add to the flowchart, let's start with that side of the business process diagram. We have to draw a flowchart using the flowchart shapes, and then we can attach some message implementations to them. Specifying data flow is then essentially a matter of connecting the generated fields, and the connection of these fields is best learned by example so we'll do that later in this chapter.

So that we can see how we design these schedules we need to familiarize ourselves with the nine flowchart shapes, and four message implementation shapes and their accompanying port shape.

Flowchart Shapes

All flowcharts in BizTalk are constructed using just nine shapes. These are visible in the template on the left side of the Orchestration Designer. The shapes are:

Shape	Description
Action	Message interchange, either sending or receiving a message
Decision	One or more conditional expressions; analogous to an `if-then-else` statement
While	Loop construct that executes so long as a condition is True
Fork	Branches the flow of control into multiple concurrent threads
Join	Joins threads created by a fork shape, or code paths created by a decision shape
Transaction	Encloses multiple shapes to denote transactional boundaries
End	Schedule terminator
Abort	Triggers the termination of an enclosing transaction so that corrective action may be taken
Begin	Denotes the starting point of a schedule; it does not appear on the stencil, but is instead provided automatically by Orchestration Designer

Begin and End Schedule

The Begin and End terminal symbols denote the starting and ending points of a schedule. They are shown here:

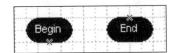

Every schedule has exactly one Begin symbol; created for you when you create a new schedule. The tool will not allow you to add a Begin symbol to the business process drawing yourself. There can, however, be more than one End symbol in a diagram. This may occur in diagrams containing decision or fork symbols. These symbols introduce multiple code branches and you can terminate these paths directly with an End symbol. The Begin and End symbols take no action themselves. The symbols are just logical bounds on the schedule depicted in the business process diagram, so no initialization or termination routines are called.

Although code is not called from either shape, the Begin shape has several properties of interest to you. If you double-click on the Begin shape or right-click and select the Edit Properties menu item you will see the Begin Properties dialog box. It looks like this:

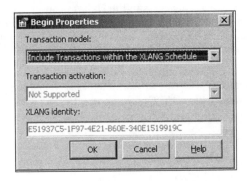

The GUID listed for the **XLANG Identity** property uniquely identifies this schedule's Visio file. Note we are referring to the schedule in general. You may run multiple instances of the same schedule concurrently (as we will discuss in Chapter 6), and there is a different mechanism for identifying specific schedule instances. The XLANG identity GUID is recorded in the XLANG schedule that Orchestration Designer exports from the business process diagram. This value can be used to associate exported schedules with the version of the diagram used to create them.

Of the remaining two properties, **Transaction Model** is the only one you may set. This property can take on one of two values:

❑ **Include transactions within the schedule** is chosen when you wish to use transaction shapes.

❑ **Treat the XLANG schedule as COM+ component** is chosen if you will be calling the schedule from a COM+ transaction.

The former lets you use the transaction mechanisms built into BizTalk orchestration. We will discuss these in detail in Chapter 6. For now, you should know that orchestration provides transactional mechanisms that cover situations that cannot be addressed through traditional methods, like long transactions, or transactions that span transactional and non-transactional resources. The latter property value (COM+), lets you make use of a transactional context passed in from a COM+ component using normal COM+ transaction mechanisms. In that case, the **Transaction Activation** property is set to **Not Supported** by Orchestration Designer, and it will not export a schedule that includes transaction shapes.

In summary then, orchestration transaction mechanisms – the first option – lets you handle things COM+ transactions cannot, but treating the schedule as a COM+ component provides closer integration with COM+ applications and gives you tighter control over transactions.

Actions

Action shapes indicate a message interchange: either sending messages out from the schedule or receiving them from some external source. They look like this:

(Action 1)

It is a good idea to label each action symbol with a name that describes what the interchange accomplishes, but do not be fooled into thinking that the action symbol somehow accomplishes an action by itself. Before a schedule can be compiled, loaded, and executed you must bind each action to a port and port implementation. We'll go into that process shortly. For now, just understand that actions are how BizTalk Scheduler coordinates messaging in the execution of a schedule.

Action symbols have a name property that you can configure. You access a properties dialog box by double clicking on the symbol or by right clicking on the symbol and selecting the **Edit Properties...** menu item. This dialog only gives you access to the **Name** property. This property is a string that is used in the business process diagram as a label inside the symbol. By default, action symbols are given a name that begins **Action** and ends with a sequential number. You should always replace this with something more descriptive.

Action symbols have additional properties associated with the communications they implement. These properties are set through the XML Communication Wizard, which we shall discuss when we come to message binding.

Decisions

Decisions allow a schedule to look at a field within the body of a message and alter the flow of control within the schedule. This might mean choosing between two action shapes based on the contents of a field. For example, you might want to send an approval for a purchase order message if the dollar amount is below a certain amount and the originator is a certain person, or send a rejection if it is above a certain amount for the same person. The Decision shape looks like this:

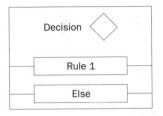

Note the box containing Rule 1. A **rule** consists of a VBScript expression that evaluates to either True or False. Generally, a rule examines the value of a message field. As we shall see when we come to implementing a messaging port, you can designate a message specification file for the message. The specification is the formal document describing the contents of the message, which we will learn to define in the next chapter. When you use such a specification, Orchestration Designer lets you add fields defined in the message specification to the message reference in the Data View. You must add all the fields you wish to use in rules to the Data View before you can use them in a rule. Fields are addressed in the format message.field where message is the message name that appears in the Data View and field is one of the fields that appears in the message.

> *XLANG scheduler adds three fields, two of which do not appear in the data view, including one that checks to see if the message exists. These fields may be referenced in rules. The field names are __Sender__, indicating the originator of the message, __Exists__, indicating whether or not the message exists in the schedule, and __Status__, which is the HRESULT returned from a COM call.*

Imagine that you've made a call to a COM component's method named Perimeter. The Data View will show a compound message shape with Perimeter_in and Perimeter_out. The method takes a document describing some arbitrary shape and returns the perimeter of the enclosed area as an eight byte double value named dPerimeter. The data view will show the field dPerimeter under Perimeter_out. If you wanted to send different messages depending on whether the perimeter was longer than 1000 meters, you could add a rule that contained the expression Perimeter_out.dPerimeter > 1000. Decision shapes automatically include an Else rule when they are created, so you don't have to define a rule to cover shorter perimeters. You can then attach one action to the rule and another to the Else rule, thereby causing the schedule to branch.

Decision shapes may contain more than one rule. When a schedule encounters a decision shape with more than one rule, it begins to examine them sequentially. The first rule to evaluate to TRUE determines which branch the schedule follows. If none evaluate this way, the Else branch is followed.

Rules may be added to decision shapes in one of two ways. If you select the shape and right-click on it, you can select the Add Rule menu item. Alternately, you can reach the shape's properties dialog by double-clicking on it or right clicking and selecting Edit Properties. The latter method (double-clicking or Edit Properties) results in the following dialog:

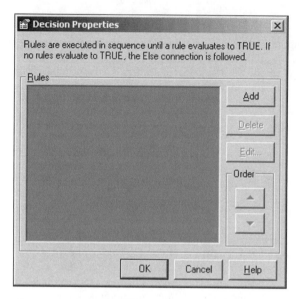

Clicking the Add button allows you to name and specify a new rule. Delete removes the selected rule, and Edit calls up the Rule Properties dialog, which is also used to create new rules. That dialog (which also appears when you use the Add Rule menu item on the Decision shape's context menu) looks like this:

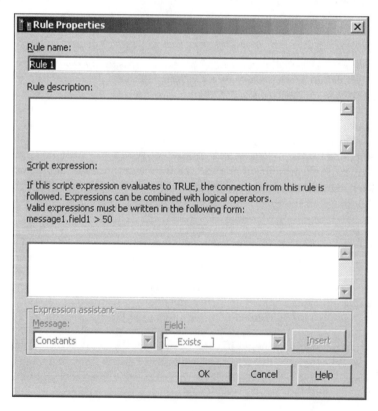

The Rule name is used throughout the schedule. If you have defined a rule and subsequently add a new decision shape, you will see the name of the existing rule in the Decision Properties dialog.

> *Even if a rule is no longer used in any decision shape on the schedule flowchart, the rule will still exist and may be referenced in a future decision shape. To permanently remove it from the schedule, you must select the Delete Unused Rules item on the Tools menu.*

Since rules are evaluated sequentially, it may be important to you to have the correct order to the rules in a decision shape. If there is a chance that a given field may cause more than one rule to evaluate TRUE and one rule is more important than the others, you will need to ensure that the rules appear in the order in which you want them evaluated. You can move a rule up or down in the list by selecting it in the Decision Properties dialog and clicking the up and down arrow keys in the Order group.

Concurrency: Fork and Join

Many systems will require **concurrent** (simultaneous) threads of execution. This is especially true of messaging applications where there may be a delay of seconds or minutes. For example, you might have an action shape waiting to receive a message, with several other messages waiting to be sent. XLANG Scheduler supports concurrency through the fork and join shapes, shown below:

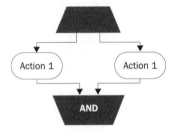

To create a branch in the code path, drag the fork shape (shown at the left as the topmost black polygon). The sequential thread of execution is connected to it. With the fork in place, you may connect up to 64 other shapes to it and each will execute concurrently. In the schedule fragment above, Action 1 might be sending a message while Action 2 is receiving. With a little care, you can realize great efficiencies in your applications using concurrency. A comparatively long-running action shape – a message sent over HTTP, say – could be on one thread while several short actions such as COM method calls to local components occupy another.

In contrast, the purpose of the join shape is to bring all the branches back together. The join shape is depicted in the diagram above as the bottom-most black polygon. A join accepts up to 64 incoming connections and one outgoing connection, restoring the flow of control to a single, sequential thread. All the threads coming out of a fork shape must be brought back together by a single join. You cannot join one subset with one join shape and the rest with another. If you attempt this, Orchestration Designer will fail to compile the schedule. You may also use the join shape in conjunction with the branches coming out of a decision shape. Such joins follow the same rules as joins in conjunction with fork shapes.

Join shapes have a single property, the Join Type. You can set this in the Join Properties dialog, which is opened by double-clicking on the shape or right-clicking and selecting the Properties... menu item. Join Type can be set to one of two values, each a logical operation: AND or OR. Once set, the value is displayed in the Join shape on the business process diagram. The Join Type property controls whether the XLANG Scheduler will synchronize the concurrent threads.

The Join Type value has some very important implications for the flow of control in the schedule. If you want the actions following a join to wait until all threads coming into the join have completed, set Join Type to AND. If, however, Join Type is set to OR, XLANG Scheduler will allow execution to proceed whenever a thread is completed. The implication of this, which is not immediately obvious, is that the actions following the join – the entire sequential thread coming out of the join – will execute once for every thread coming into the join. Consequently, if you want the actions that follow the join shape to execute once, you must synchronize the threads by setting Join Type to AND.

Transactions

Transactions are an important part of real-world applications. Having originated in databases, transactions have moved out into other operations in Windows, such as COM components and message queue operations. A transaction permits you to group several operations together and ensure that then succeed or fail as a block as seen from operations outside the transaction. That is, if one operation fails and the rest succeed, the effects of the successful operations are rolled back before the transaction completes. The classic example is transferring money from one bank account to another. Either you want the debit and the credit operations to succeed, or you want the accounts to remain the same. You certainly don't want the debit to succeed and the credit to fail, losing you money, and the bank doesn't want the credit to succeed and the debit to fail, losing them money.

XLANG Schedules support three kinds of transactions: *timed*, *short*, and *long*. We'll discuss the types in more detail shortly. For right now, think of short transactions as those to which you may be accustomed from database or Windows programming: a series of local, short-lived operations wholly under the control of a single process. Messaging, though, brings about potentially lengthy operations. Your message to an external partner might take minutes to arrive via the Internet. Worse, the response may be held pending manual intervention (for example an approval). We cannot manage long transactions with the same mechanisms used by short transactions, but we want equivalent semantics. Timed transactions work just the way the name suggests: if all the operations included within the transaction do not complete within the interval you specify, the transaction aborts.

All of these cases are accommodated by the transaction shape in a schedule:

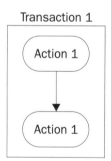

Drag a transaction shape onto the flowchart and size it so that it encloses the shapes you wish to make part of a transaction. Any shapes that fall within the shape are included in the transaction. You may add or remove shapes from the transaction by dragging and resizing the transaction shape so that it encloses or does not enclose the shape you wish to add or remove. Next, you will want to configure the properties of the transaction. Double-click on the transaction shape or right-click and select the Properties... menu item. The Transaction Properties dialog looks like this:

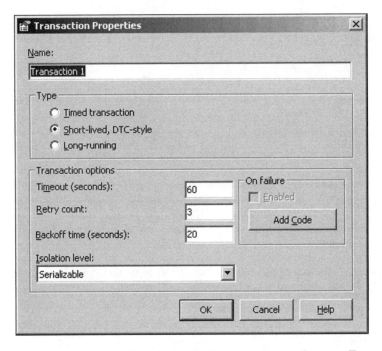

The **Name** property is the label that will appear in the business process diagram. **Type** allows you to select between timed, short, and long transactions. For any type of transaction, there are a number of options that must be configured. **Timeout** is the number of seconds to wait for a transaction to complete before timing out and failing. You may specify an integer for the **Retry Count** property to indicate how many times a transaction commit should be attempted before failing. **Backoff Time**, the interval between retry attempts, is expressed in seconds, like the timeout value. **Isolation Level** pertains to how concurrently running transactions view the same data. Since this requires a deeper understanding of transactions, we'll put off discussing this for the moment until we revisit transactions in greater depth later on in this chapter.

An important consideration in transactions is how failure is handled. After all, one of the main purposes of transactions is to provide a defined and reliable mechanism for restoring the state of a system to its status prior to the start of the transaction, in the event of a failed action within the transaction. Short transactions use the standard recovery mechanisms of the DTC, but long and timed transactions must provide recovery measures of their own. This is accomplished through the **On failure** group of controls. If you click on the **Add Code** button, a new page is created with the name **On Failure of Transaction**, where **Transaction** is replaced with the name you give the transaction. You can then draw a new business process diagram that is executed when the transaction aborts. To make use of this feature, you must check the **Enabled** checkbox. Once an **On Failure** page has been created, the button in the **Transaction Properties** dialog is renamed **Delete Code**. Clicking it deletes the On Failure page associated with the transaction.

The capabilities and calling sequence of On Failure pages can be quite involved. We'll take up the topic at length in Chapter 6, providing multiple sample schedules with transactions.

While Loops

The While shape, below, allows you to perform iterative looping within a schedule by adding a rule.

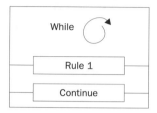

When this rule evaluates to `True`, the code branch leaving the rule will be executed. Unlike a classic flowchart While symbol, you do not connect the code path back to the while shape. Instead, the path ends in an End shape. XLANG Scheduler takes care of returning control to the While shape. When the rule evaluates `False`, the code path connected to the **Continue** rule is executed.

> **Take care that you have performed some activity to update the value tested by the rule, or you will place your schedule into an endless loop.**

The single rule in a While shape is added in the same way and using the same **Rule Properties** dialog as for the Decision shape.

There is an additional dialog associated with the While shape, and that is the **While Properties** dialog depicted below

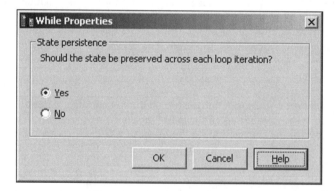

It is opened by double-clicking the While shape or right-clicking and selecting **Properties...** from the context menu. The question to be answered in this dialog is how messages sent and received within a While loop should be saved. If you select the **Yes** option, each message instance is saved and preserved across loop iterations. By contrast, if you select the **No** option, XLANG Scheduler will only save the messages from the latest iteration. Remember, these messages are the source of data in your schedule. If an iteration generates data you wish to have available outside the While loop, you must select **Yes**.

Abort Shape

The Abort shape is used within a transaction when you wish to trigger a failure condition. It is shown here:

You can end a code path and abort the transaction simply by terminating the path with an abort shape. This shape has no properties to set. When execution reaches this shape, any On Failure pages provided and enabled for the transaction will be invoked.

We have now looked at the nine flowchart shapes, so let's move on to look at the other type of shapes we need to learn – messaging implementation shapes.

Messaging Implementation Shapes

The flowchart in a XLANG schedule is only a specification of the flow of control through the schedule. Without messaging implementations, the schedule can accomplish nothing. Messages are the basic operations through which a schedule implements its behavior. There are two kinds of shapes in the messaging implementation pane (which is the right side of the business process diagram to the right of the double line):

❑   the port shape

❑   the four message implementation shapes:

  ❑   COM component

  ❑   Script component

  ❑   MSMQ messaging

  ❑   BizTalk messaging

To implement a messaging operation, you drag one of the four message implementation shapes onto the business process diagram, and then a wizard appears to guide you through the messaging implementation process – the wizard varies slightly depending on which message implementation shape you choose.

In order to fully understand how messaging shapes work with business process diagrams, we have to get into the details of the flowchart shapes, the capabilities associated with them, and the information they convey to a programmer. We will look further at the shapes Orchestration Designer uses. As part of this, we will give you more detail on using transactions, then return to messaging implementations.

Ports

Every message implementation has a port that serves to connect it to an action. Port shapes are generated for you by the message implementation wizard and are always placed on the double line separating the flowchart from message implementations. They look like this:

A port shape, as can be seen above, consists of one or more boxes within a box. The concept here is that one or more message types are passed through the port on the way to or from an application. The name of each message type is given in an inner box, while the port name is given outside this box but within the outer box. In the sample above, SiteServiceDescription messages flow through a port named RecvSiteSvcDesc.

Actions in the flowchart are connected to the left-hand side of the port where the line connects the outer and inner boxes. The message implementation similarly connects the port shape's right-hand side to the message implementation shape. Double-clicking on a port shape, or right-clicking and selecting Edit Properties... results in a simple Port Properties dialog. The port shape's Name property can be set in this dialog. Changing the message type requires that you edit the properties of the message implementation through the wizard.

Message Implementations

Dragging a message shape, like the one below, onto the business process diagram triggers the process of message implementation configuration.

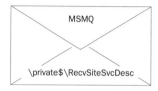

This process is what ties the theory of a schedule to some practical implementation in the real world. The practical implementation may be an MSMQ queue, a BizTalk messaging channel, a COM component, or a scripted component.

> *Don't worry too much about the term channel with respect to BizTalk messaging at this time. We will touch on this topic lightly when we discuss implementing BizTalk messages in schedules and cover it in detail in Chapter 5.*

The four shapes give information relevant to their implementation. For example, the MSMQ queue shape shown above displays the MSMQ label at the top center, and the name of the queue to use at the bottom center. Here is a list of the message implementation shapes and the information they display.

Message Implementation Shape	Information displayed
MSMQ	Queue name
BizTalk	Channel name
Script component	Name of the file implementing the component, the interface description, and the component moniker or progID
COM component	Names of the interfaces exposed by the component

There is a great deal of information associated with a message implementation. A wizard is provided for each implementation shape. We will discuss these options in detail shortly, in the section *Binding Message Implementations.*

Transactions

Schedules coordinate the activities of multiple resources, usually applications. The integrity of a schedule depends on the successful operation of each resource. Since failure is always an option in distributed systems, we need a formal mechanism to deal with it. Transactions, as noted earlier, are that mechanism.

Transactions grew out of research into multi-user databases. They offer strong protection with respect to the integrity of data. Because they are such a useful and powerful concept, transactional semantics have gradually been extended through the Windows platform. A message queue, for example, may be thought of as a sort of database table composed of message records. If multiple applications try to remove messages from the queue and read their contents, the queue must be transactional to ensure one application does not remove a message another application has just located and is about to read.

Transactions have been extended to non-database technologies on Windows through COM interfaces such as ITransaction and ITransactionDispenser. The COM+ runtimes incorporate the **distributed transaction coordinator** (DTC) that uses these interfaces to implement a transaction. The DTC originated with SQL Server several years ago and has migrated through Microsoft Transaction Server (MTS) to its current status within the COM+ runtimes. So long as you implement the prescribed interfaces with the proper semantics, you can write COM components that can take part in transactions, committing their data or rolling back at the direction of the DTC.

The XLANG Scheduler does not introduce any new transactional capability. It relies on the DTC for proper transaction handling. The Scheduler also does not enforce the use of transactional components in a transaction shape. If you call non-transactional components within a XLANG transaction, you cannot guarantee proper transactional behavior. MSMQ and BizTalk messaging components are transactional, so the risk here is limited to COM component messaging.

The potential for XLANG schedules to do messaging over the Internet introduces new challenges for transactions. In addition to traditional transactions using local resources (within the bounds of a LAN totally under the control of local software), we now have widely distributed resources that are not necessarily under central control – indeed, they usually will not be under the control of one entity – as well as actions that may involve manual intervention. Even when manual intervention is not required, the connectivity outages and routing delays inherent in a network the scale of the Internet mean that transactions are not as simple as in the days of client-server database technology. Because of this, XLANG schedules borrow a relatively recent distinction from transaction theory: the notion of **short** and **long transactions**. The nature of these transactions, how they may be isolated from one another, and how to recover from a failed transaction are important issues in designing and implementing robust schedules.

Short Transactions

Short transactions are also simple transactions. They consist of a simple sequence of shapes that do not include a transaction nested within them, nor can they be part of another transaction. Because of this, they are relatively easy to rollback. Another feature of short transactions is that they should involve operations that complete or fail within a short span of time – seconds or fractions of seconds – which means that BizTalk messages using Internet protocols are not usually found in a short transaction. Short transactions are more likely to involve local COM calls or an MSMQ message. The latency of the Internet and asynchronous protocols involves lengthy delays that make short transactions difficult to implement.

> **Remember, the Scheduler will call on the DTC for commits and rollbacks; it is up to you to ensure all the actions within the transaction support transactional behavior. For example, if you are using MSMQ, be sure you have configured a transactional queue.**

There is another caution involved in using transaction shapes. As you will see when we get to our sample application, you can bind many action shapes to the same message port, and you will frequently do this with COM components. The message implementation wizard presents you with all the methods exposed by a given component, so, if you know you will be using more than one method in the course of your schedule, it is simpler to select all of the methods first time you deal with the component, and then connect the different action shapes to the port created by the wizard. If you do this, you must be careful about transaction boundaries. All action shapes bound to a single port must be in the same transaction, or none of them can be in a transaction. Ports cannot span transaction boundaries.

Long Transactions

Long transactions, known in the BizTalk documentation as **long-running business processes**, are very different in many ways from short transactions. Every schedule is itself a long transaction. The first difference is the duration of such a transaction. A short transaction succeeds or fails at the speed of locally managed operations. They work in seconds or fractions of a second. Even a DCOM timeout is measured in a small handful of minutes. The time span of a long transaction alone complicates retries and timeouts. How long do you wait to see if an SMTP message arrived? You know fairly quickly if your server sent it, but you really want to know if it arrived at its destination. Do you keep a COM component in an uncommitted state waiting for an Internet operation to succeed, or do you shut off a lengthy operation so as to conserve resources held by quickly completed local operations? Even a local operation, like a message queue retrieval, can cause timing problems when you are receiving the message within the schedule. The action shape receiving the message will block waiting for the message. If the sending process doesn't generate the message for a long time, the transaction is going to be a lengthy one even if the ultimate retrieval operation takes a fraction of a second.

Another difference between long and short transactions is the fact that there is no single point of control over all the actions in a long transaction. A short transaction can call on the DTC to manage its transactional behavior. Who can rollback a message sent to a server on the other side of the globe running under a different operating system? This difference is the key to understanding recovery from a long transaction. You cannot rely on a transaction coordinator. All you can do is take independent steps designed to restore your system to the state it was in prior to the beginning of the transaction. This takes some careful planning. There are two mechanisms available to you in schedules for dealing with aborted long transactions. These are the On Failure and Compensation pages. We'll take these up in a few moments.

Timed Transactions

Timed transactions are a variation on long transactions. Unlike an ordinary long transaction, timed transactions have an explicit timeout period which, if exceeded, causes the transaction to fail. All the actions in the transaction that completed prior to the timeout may have completed successfully, but since the timeout is exceeded, the transaction is aborted and recovery measures like the On Failure page are invoked. You can use this type of transaction when you are waiting for a response from a partner, for example, and you want to place an upper limit on how long the system will wait for a reply.

Isolation Levels

Transactions are defined by four characteristics: **atomicity**, **consistency**, **isolation**, and **durability**. While a rigorous discussion of these characteristics is beyond the scope of this book, they work together to ensure that code outside the bounds of a transaction, especially another transaction executing concurrently, views the multiple actions within a transaction as an all or nothing proposition.

These properties, frequently referred to via the acronym **ACID**, arose in connection with database transactions. A transaction is **atomic** if it completes as a single unit of processing. That is, the multiple actions grouped as a transaction complete as a whole or not at all. **Consistency** relates to the overall integrity of the system. A transaction is consistent if it leaves the system in a consistent state regardless of the success or failure of the transaction. If the transaction completes successfully, the system is in a state that reflects the success of the transaction; all the relationships within the transaction maintain their integrity and no rules are violated. If the transaction fails, any partial actions must be rolled back to restore the system to the state in effect prior to the start of the transaction

A transaction meets the requirements of being **isolated** if the sum of the effects of the individual actions of the transaction is the same as if those actions had occurred in series. The transactional system may execute some actions in parallel, but it must guarantee that their effect appears to the outside observer as if they had occurred one at a time. Finally, a transaction is **durable** if the effects of a transaction survive a system failure. Normally, this means that some persistent state is written to disk before the transaction reports success. As a practical matter, transactional system usually implements some sort of log file so that transactions interrupted by a system fault may be replayed upon recovery.

One characteristic we should discuss in more detail because of its immediate relevance to schedules is isolation. The SQL-92 standard defined **isolation levels** to describe how concurrent transactions could be isolated from one another. In essence, the problem is this: what updates are transactions allowed to see? Complete isolation such that the updates might as well have been applied in sequence offers the most protection but greatly diminishes performance. This is the ideal form of isolation set forth under the ACID concept. In practice, programmers have some idea how their applications will access data and so can safely relax the isolation level. This holds true for XLANG schedules. The four isolation levels supported by schedule transaction shapes are:

- ❑ **Serializable** – the highest level of isolation. All concurrent transactions are executed so that their results are the same as if they had been sequentially issued to a single user transactional system. As you might imagine, this isolation level requires the most effort and greatest caution on the part of the DTC and is therefore the slowest to execute.

- ❑ **Read uncommitted** – the weakest isolation level and so executes fastest. Transactions executing at this level may see data updates made by other transactions that have yet to be committed. The only protection afforded by this level is protection from physically corrupt data such as disk media faults.

- ❑ **Read committed** – a transaction may only see changes that have been committed by another transaction.

- ❑ **Repeatable read** – this is a bit more difficult to understand. A transaction executing at this level acquires shared locks on the resources it is using. It sees committed data, but data it has read that is subsequently changed by another transaction becomes invisible to it. The transaction making the change takes hold of the lock, and bars the first transaction from accessing the data again. This guarantees that the first transaction does not see an inconsistent form of the data while allowing the second transaction to execute without the overhead of having the first transaction re-read data.

Dealing with Failures – On Failure and Compensation Pages

While you were looking at the Transaction Properties dialog, you may have noticed a group we have not yet discussed: On failure. This deals with recovery from an aborted transaction. Should one of the components in a transaction return an error, the transaction aborts.

Let's consider the basic case first: a single transaction. If you are not using transactional components which the DTC can control, you need to specify what actions the scheduler must take to restore your system to the proper state. You do this with the On Failure page.

In the Transaction Properties dialog box, click on the Add Code button found in the On failure group. When you do this, the Enabled check box becomes available to you and the button label changes to Delete Code.

After you click OK to dismiss the dialog box, something very interesting takes place: Orchestration Designer adds a new page to the Visio document with a tab labeled On Failure of Transaction. The word Transaction is replaced with the name you gave the transaction, so in the case shown below, the page would be called On Failure of Fail Tx:

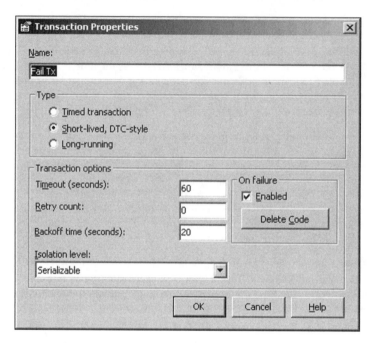

This allows you to create a schedule that will be called if the transaction aborts. The purpose of this schedule is to roll back the effects of the failed transaction. To cause this to happen, you need to check the Enabled box. Since the intent is to give you a way to recover from an aborted transaction in the main schedule, the On Failure page has access to the ports and message implementations you created on the business process diagram. You may also include transactions on the On Failure page, each of which in turn can trigger its own On Failure page.

If you wish to prevent XLANG Scheduler from calling the On Failure page while still retaining the diagram in the Visio document, uncheck the Enabled box and export the schedule again. You might wish to do this if you were temporarily withdrawing failure actions because actions or applications they require are temporarily unavailable in your network, or when you wish to save interim versions of a schedule with an incomplete On Failure page. If you wish to permanently delete an On Failure page, click on the Delete Code button.

Transactions are a complex topic, and there are advanced features we have not covered here. The topic of transactions is so important that we have devoted most of Chapter 6 to their study. Not only will you learn more about transactions there, you will find practical examples of each transactional feature available to schedules.

Binding Message Implementations

Now that we know all the pieces used to build a business process diagram – the flowchart and message implementation shapes – we can get to the business of connecting a schedule to the real world. This is the process of binding a message implementation to an action in the business diagram.

When you first drag a message implementation shape onto the diagram, the message binding wizard opens. You may edit a message implementation's configuration later by double-clicking on the message shape or right-clicking and selecting the Edit Properties... menu item. The first dialog shown by the wizard involves the port the implementation will use. Each message implementation leads you through a slightly different binding wizard. Now let's consider each message implementation in turn: MSMQ messaging, COM Components, Script Components, and BizTalk messaging.

MSMQ Messaging

The first dialog of the Message Queuing Binding Wizard asks you to Create a new port or use an Existing unbound port:

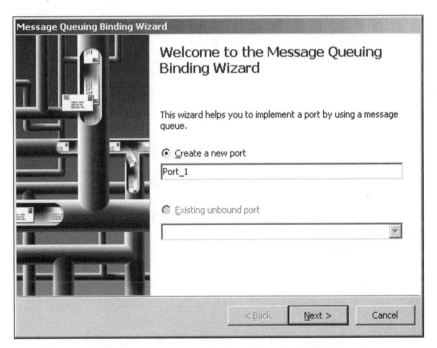

Next, you need to connect the port to a queue. XLANG Scheduler is very accommodating in this regard. In addition to the obvious choice of explicitly specifying a queue, it will let you dynamically choose a queue when a message comes through the messaging system. If you choose the latter, you will have to connect a field in a message on the Data View with the port reference for this message. Either way, here is the second dialog in the MSMQ Message Binding Wizard:

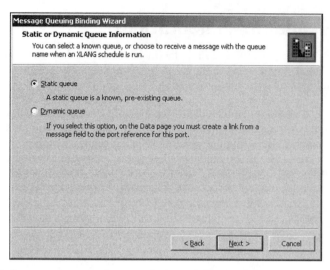

If you choose the Static queue option, the next dialog asks you for the name of the queue. Besides providing a name, though, you have a choice to make. XLANG Scheduler will happily create a new queue for each instance of a XLANG schedule. If you will be using this implementation repeatedly throughout the schedule, this is a simple way to tell the difference between different instances of the same schedule. Of course, the application on the other end of this implementation will have a hard time knowing what queue to use, but it is effective if you are buffering messages for latter consumption elsewhere within the same schedule instance that creates them. If you opt for this method, the name you provide will be used as a prefix for the actual queue name and Scheduler will generate the rest of the name when it creates the queue. When a schedule terminates, all queues dynamically created under this option for the schedule instance are automatically destroyed.

In most cases, however, you will want to set up a queue for use by another application and have that queue used by any instance of the schedule. In that case, finding the name of the queue is easy. It must not matter which instance of the schedule generates the message, however, or you must provide some mechanism for associating a schedule with the messages it generates. Here is the dialog in which you provide a queue name:

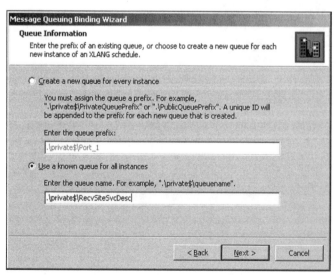

There is one final dialog to contend with before completing an MSMQ message binding. Since queues, like all Windows resources, are subject to the security system, you can require that Scheduler obeys some restrictions. You have several properties you can specify: the effort Scheduler puts into identifying the message sender, what group or user account to use for writing to the queue, and, since MSMQ supports transactions, you may indicate whether or not you are using a transactional queue:

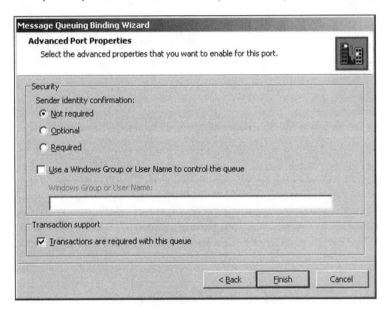

Your choices for the effort to put into determining identity are:

❑ **Not required** – Scheduler will not try to identify the message sender. The __Sender__ field on the data view will always be blank.

❑ **Optional** – XLANG Scheduler will attempt to authenticate the sender. If successful, the __Sender__ field on the data view will contain the value of the MSMQ message's SenderID property.

❑ **Required** – Scheduler will make the same effort it did in the previous case, but if it fails to obtain the identity the message will be ignored. If authenticated, the __Sender__ field in the data view will have the message's SenderID value.

If you wish to control write access to the queue, check the **Uses a Windows Group or User Name** checkbox in the dialog and enter the name of the account Scheduler should use when writing to the queue. If the queue you specified on the **Queue Information** page is transactional, you must check the **Transactions are required with this queue** checkbox. This causes XLANG Scheduler to implement the proper MSMQ API calls when sending a message through this port.

Once you click **Finish**, a port will appear on the double line border of the business process diagram and it will be connected to the message shape. You will be required to connect any action shapes that use this port to the port shape. Doing so invokes the XML Communication Wizard, which we'll discuss later. If you click on the **Data** tab, you will see a new port shape has been created. However, you will not have a new message shape yet, because that is deferred until you fill out the XML Communication Wizard.

COM Components

Binding a message implementation to a COM component will be similar to the process described above. Just remember that BizTalk Server doesn't think in terms of components with methods and properties. Instead, it treats each method as if it were a message in two parts: the call into the method and a message coming back.

The first dialog in the COM Binding Wizard is almost identical to the one from the MSMQ Binding Wizard. The only differences are that the title reflects COM and not MSMQ, and that you *must* specify a new port. There is no option for referring to an existing port.

The next dialog is very important. The Scheduler must know how you want to instantiate the component. You have three options:

- ❑ Static – let the XLANG Scheduler create an instance of the component.

- ❑ Dynamic – let some other application instantiate it. In that case, you must pass an interface pointer into the Scheduler so the method can be called. The message shape Orchestration Designer will create for this case will include a field for this pointer. You must create a link from some other field containing a valid pointer to this field.

- ❑ No instantiation – used only when the port will be receiving a message. A method on an outside component is accessing XLANG Scheduler to pass information in. The Scheduler itself is neither instantiating the component nor executing the method call.

This dialog looks like this:

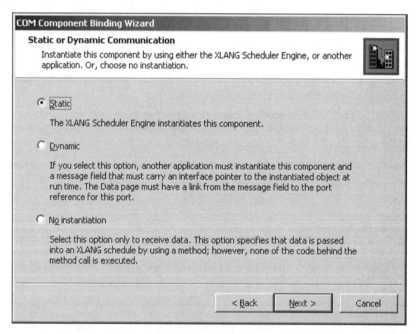

If you chose one of the latter two choices in the previous dialog, you will skip over the next step. If, however, you elected to have the Scheduler instantiate the component for you, you must now tell it what component you want. The third dialog in the COM Binding Wizard gives you two options: selecting from a list of all components known to the system, or specifying a **moniker**.

Normally, you would use a registered component, but monikers offer a few benefits that such references do not. For example, some components, notably those implementing the Microsoft Excel spreadsheet model, will allow you to reference a location within a document when you use a moniker. You either select from the list or type in a moniker in the edit control.

This third dialog is depicted below:

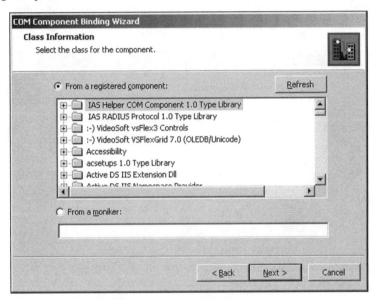

If an external application is instantiating the component for you, or if you are receiving a message from an externally created component, you must specify the interface XLANG Scheduler will be working with. You will see the following dialog if you made either of these choices; if you chose to instantiate the component from the Scheduler, you will skip over this step:

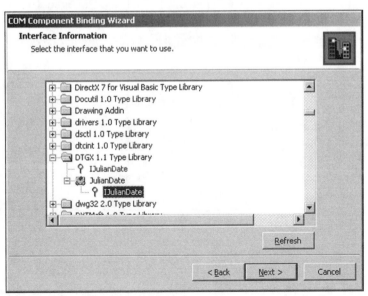

This dialog lists all the COM interfaces known to the local system. You select the interface in which you are interested and click Next.

Now, finally, all the different choices come back together. If you elected to have XLANG Scheduler instantiate the component, you picked the component. If you selected one of the other choices, you selected an interface. There is one remaining task before you can address security issues, and that is to select the method(s) you will use in your schedule. The wizard presents you with a list, shown below, of every method of the interface. You must check all the methods you wish to use. Buttons for Check All and Uncheck All are provided as a convenience.

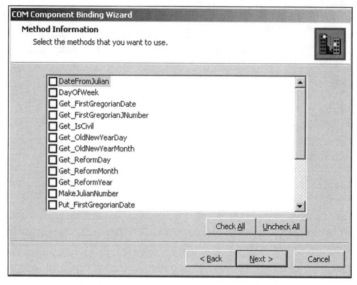

There are just a few choices remaining. The first concerns security. As you did with MSMQ messaging binding, you need to tell XLANG Scheduler how must effort to put into determining the identity of the sender. Recall that your choices are Not required, Optional, and Required. Here's what the dialog looks like:

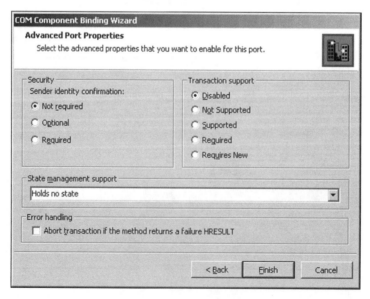

Transaction support in the chosen component will affect the next choice. The choices in the **Transaction support** group are similar to those COM programmers used to see in Microsoft Transaction Server. Your choices are:

- ❑ **Disabled** – disable transaction support when using this component
- ❑ **Not supported** – the component does not support transactions
- ❑ **Supported** – the component supports transactions
- ❑ **Required** – the COM+ component requires a transaction, and may use an existing transaction or a new transaction
- ❑ **Requires new** – the COM+ component requires a new transaction

The next choice you have to make concerns *state*. When we discuss the more advanced parts of schedules and BizTalk applications in Chapter 6, we'll see how XLANG Scheduler is able to move long running schedules in and out of memory while they wait for a message to come in. When that happens, the Scheduler has to persist the current state of the schedule and all its components to disk. If you are using a COM component, the Scheduler must know what to do with the component.

Most components built for high volume systems will be stateless and have no information that must be retained from one method call to another. If that is the case with your component, select **Holds no state** in the list box labeled **State management support** and Scheduler will ignore your component.

However, if you want the current state of your component persisted, you will have to implement the `IpersistStream` or `IPersistStreamInit` interface in your component. Once you have done this, you may select **Holds state, and does support persistence**. This will cause XLANG Scheduler to use that interface to stream your component's information to disk. If the component holds state but does not support one of those interfaces, you must select **Holds state, but does not support persistence**, in which case XLANG Scheduler will hold the component in memory. This will have an adverse impact on performance.

Every COM component has a single return value, which is an `HRESULT`. Programmers accustomed to C++ will recognize the `HRESULT` type as the standard COM return value. Visual Basic consumes this value for you and uses it to decide whether to throw an error. An `HRESULT` is COM's standard mechanism for indicating the error status of a method call. There is a formal way to break down the `HRESULT` to locate the error code and the subsystem throwing the error. XLANG Scheduler will see this `HRESULT`, though, and you can examine it to do detailed error trapping much as you would from a C++ program. The next choice in the dialog, the checkbox in the **Error handling** group, permits you to automatically abort a transaction if the value of the `HRESULT` indicates an error.

> *Our scripting and Visual Basic programmers should know that this is not quite so dramatic as it might seem. HRESULT is set up so that there is one value for success, and an elaborate system for designating failures. Every value except the one for success, though, indicates failure.*

When you have finished with this dialog, click **Finish** to complete the COM binding message implementation.

Script Components

Binding to a script component is very similar to binding to a COM component, as you might expect. A script component is treated like a COM component, although all you have is a script source file in a particular format. The difference is that it uses the operating system's script engine to turn a script in a particular form into a COM component.

For more on writing and using script components, see the Windows Script Components area beginning at msdn.microsoft.com/scripting/scriptlets/default.htm.

The first two dialogs of the Script Component Binding Wizard are identical to those used by the COM Binding Wizard except for the dialog titles. First you name a new port to use, then you make a choice about how to instantiate the component. Your choices for the latter remain Use the XLANG Scheduler Engine, Use another application, and No instantiation. Unlike the COM Binding Wizard, however, all three choices lead to the same dialog box. This is the dialog in which you tell the Scheduler which file contains the script code for the component. You may either enter the path and filename directly, or access a file open dialog to browse for it. This dialog in the wizard looks like this:

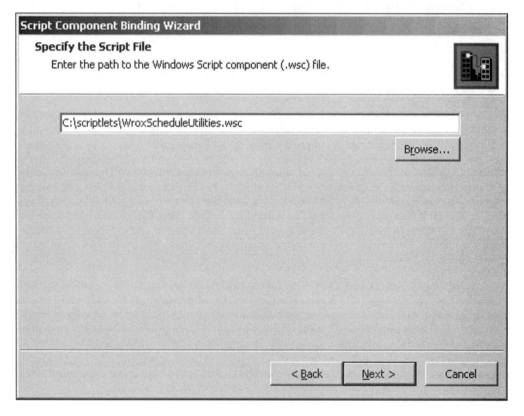

At this point, you will branch off in one of two directions based on your choice of component instantiation methods.

If you chose to have XLANG Scheduler instantiate the component, you will need to decide whether to use a moniker to instantiate the component, or the progID. The moniker for script components begins with the word Script and a colon, followed by the fully qualified pathname of the script source file (.wsc extension). The progID for the component should be displayed in the dialog itself, as the wizard is able to examine the file you picked in the preceding step for registration information. This is the same information you would see in the system registry for this component. If you do not see a progID in the binding wizard's dialog, check the script file and make sure it is correctly constructed. This is what the dialog looks like:

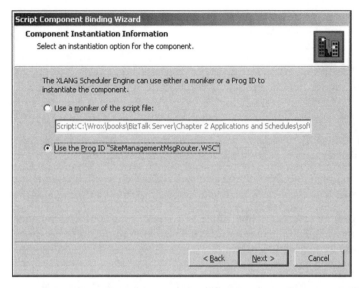

If you chose one of the other options for instantiating the component, you will skip this dialog. No matter what option you selected for component instantiation, the next dialog in the Script Component Binding Wizard is the one for selecting the component methods you wish to use in the schedule. This is the same dialog we saw in the COM binding situation except for a change in the dialog's title to reflect scripting components.

The final step in the Script Component Binding Wizard is the **Advanced** dialog. Like the COM Component Binding Wizard, it has the sections for security, transaction support, and error handling. Unlike the COM component wizard, though, the script components wizard omits the **State Management** group. Script components only have a dispatch interface, so there is no possibility of implementing the IPersistStream interface for component persistence. XLANG Scheduler will assume that your component is stateless, so ensure that this is the case or you may have some nasty run-time surprises when using script components in a long running schedule. The dialog looks like this:

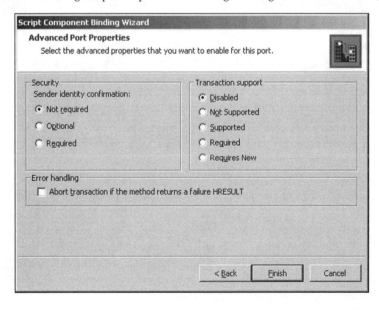

Make your selections regarding identity confirmation, transaction rollback, and error handling, then click Finish to complete the binding.

BizTalk Messaging

The binding process for BizTalk messaging will take us into new territory. We'll cover the details of configuring BizTalk messaging in Chapter 5, but you must know a little bit about the topic now for the binding to make sense. BizTalk messaging uses two concepts, **ports** and **channels**:

❑ A port in BizTalk messaging encapsulates the destination and transport protocol for a particular message type for a particular organization.

❑ A channel identifies the source organization, as well as additional details regarding message processing that are specific to the exchange between the two organizations.

We cover **mapping** in Chapter 4, but suffice to say that this is a process by which data in one message format can be transformed into another message format. Mapping offers us great flexibility in connecting to partners and applications, as we can retain our preferred formats and our partners can do the same.

The BizTalk Message Binding Wizard begins much as the MSMQ wizard did by asking us to either name a new port or select an existing one. These ports are only the ports used in the schedule and need not correspond to a port in the BizTalk messaging system. Make a selection and click Next.

Your next selection comes in the Message Direction dialog box and is very important. Like the instantiation options in the component wizards, the choice of message direction will cause the wizard to take one of two branches. If you are sending a message, select Send. Otherwise, if you want the schedule to wait for an incoming BizTalk message, select Receive. As the dialog itself notes, however, BizTalk messaging will only receive via HTTP. If you need to receive messages from protocols other than HTTP, you must find some way to get them into an MSMQ message queue, and then use the MSMQ Binding Wizard. The dialog box is shown below:

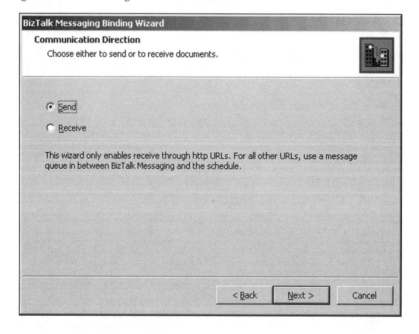

If you selected Send, you now need to tell Scheduler how to find a BizTalk channel to use to send the message. The simplest way is to directly specify one by name. Since we haven't learned how to configure channels yet, take it for granted that you are dealing with a simple name. This must be the name of a channel configured through the Messaging Manager.

You can also see, from the Channel Information dialog shown below, that BizTalk messaging is sufficiently flexible as to permit **dynamic routing** options as well. This extends to finding the name of the channel to use in a field within the message itself, at run time. Using this facility, two message instances might go to different places in different formats because they use different channels. Messaging Services receives this information from the Scheduler, which, in turn, looks at the message. This information is passed into this message shape from a field in a preceding message shape.

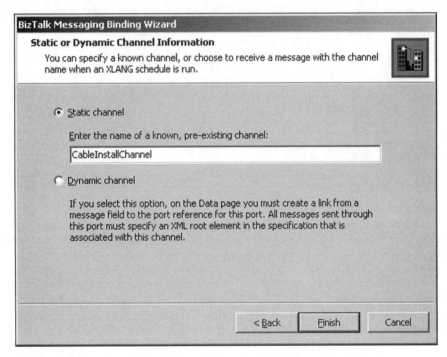

You should note that if you select the Dynamic channel option, your message must be XML-based. This enables BizTalk to be able to locate the field in which the channel information is found.

At that point, you would be finished with an implementation for sending a message out of the schedule. Now we'll look at the configuration for receiving a message. If you selected Receive in the Communication Direction dialog, you would see the following dialog:

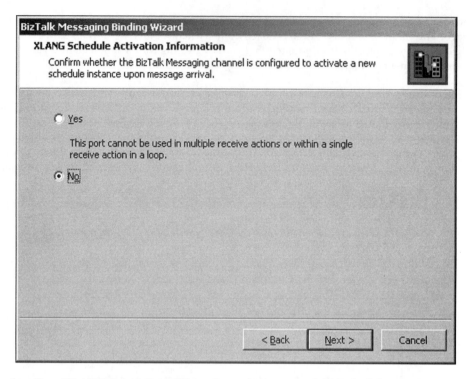

If you select Yes, XLANG Scheduler will launch a new instance of this schedule when a message is received. This is a very convenient feature, because it allows you to easily create a schedule that responds to events. Such schedules start with a message receive action. Selecting Yes here takes care of launching the schedule for you – XLANG Scheduler does it for you and automatically places the incoming message into the initial receive action. If you do select Yes, however, you must observe the restrictions noted in this dialog. This port cannot be used in multiple receive actions, nor can you use it inside a loop. XLANG Scheduler has to unambiguously know where to begin. That means a single port associated with a single action outside a loop. If the receive action were within a loop, Scheduler would have no way of knowing what iteration of the loop to begin with.

Next, you specify the channel information. As with an outbound BizTalk messaging port, you specify the name of the channel BizTalk Messaging Services should use in processing the message. The receive function for HTTP in BizTalk must be a resource that can execute scripts (for instance an ASP) and you must also provide the URL of this resource.

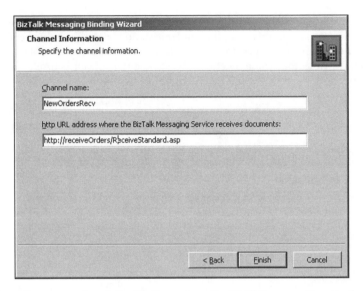

Click Finish and you have completed the configuration of a BizTalk messaging implementation.

So, now we've seen how to configure port implementations in schedules. But there is one crucial problem. None of these implementations is connected to an action shape. For that, we need to use the XML Communication Wizard or the Method Communication Wizard. These wizards are automatically invoked by Orchestration Designer when you connect a handle on an action shape to a handle on a port implementation.

Connecting Actions to BizTalk or MSMQ Implementations

After you have an action shape, and a port implementation for it, you will want to connect the two. Drag a link from the action shape to the handle of the port on the flowchart side of the business process diagram. When you do this you for BizTalk or MSMQ messaging, you will see the first page of the XML Communication Wizard:

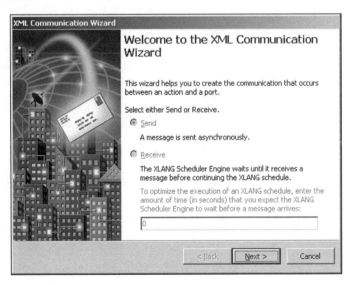

Note that the controls are disabled in the illustration. This wizard picks up information from the messaging implementation. In this case, the implementation is configured to send a message. If it had been configured to receive messages, the edit control would have been enabled and you would be able to enter an average value that you expect XLANG Scheduler to wait before a message arrives at the port. This information is used to help XLANG optimize hydration.

The next page of the wizard (for both directions of message flow) is the Message Information page. This is where you tell Orchestration Designer what kind of message will flow through this port.

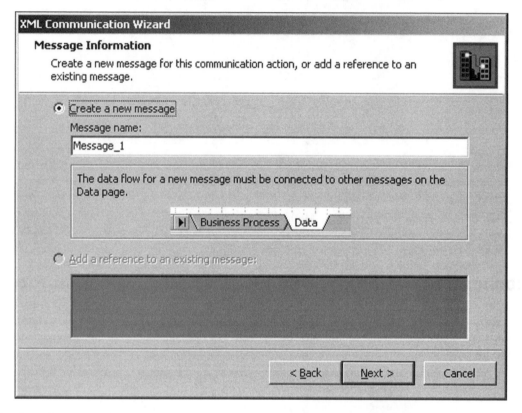

You have the option of creating a new message or referring to a message that you previously created for the schedule. If you have existing messages defined, they will appear in a list in the lower list box. Remember, these messages will have shapes associated with them on the Data View. In order to move data between messages and through the schedule, you will need to establish links between message fields. We'll explain that when we get to the practical example later in this chapter.

The flow of the wizard branches at this point. If the message implementation sends a message, you see the XML Translation Information page:

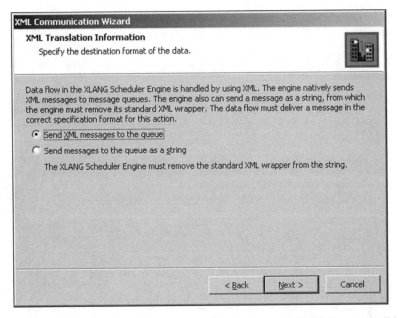

XLANG Scheduler deals exclusively with XML. If your message is a flatfile type, it will be wrapped by the Scheduler in XML. If you have an XML-based message, click Send XML messages to the queue. This gives you flexibility in selecting fields in the message so that they will be available to the schedule for making decisions or for passing to other messages. If you have a flatfile message, you must check the other radio button and you will be unable to select fields within the message. The message will be treated as an opaque whole (the StringData field in the message shape on the Data view) and you will need to use COM components if you have to extract field-level information.

Clicking Next takes you to the Message Type Information page:

The sole item of information you enter here is a label. If you are dealing with an MSMQ implementation, the label should match the label of the message on the queue. If you are dealing with BizTalk, the Scheduler will try to match the label against the document element of the message itself. If you are dealing with a flatfile format message, this label will be part of the XML wrapper Scheduler adds (but which you never see).

If you sent the message as a string in the XML Translation page, you would see a button labeled Finish, and you would be done with the wizard. Otherwise, you have the ability to go into greater detail and select message fields in the Message Specification Information page:

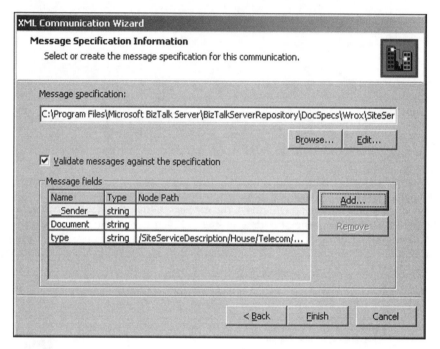

You browse to the message specification file you created with BizTalk Editor (the topic of the next chapter) and select it. This file tells Scheduler about the internal structure of the XML message. You have the option of validating outgoing messages against the specification. If you need to gather information from message instances for use with the rest of the schedule (for example to make decisions and select different code paths), click Add. You will see a tree view of the message structure from which you may select fields. These fields will appear in the Message fields list box of the dialog. Click Finish to save the information you have specified.

> We will see the process of selecting fields in detail in the practical example at the end of this chapter.

That's the process you would use if you were sending a message. What about receiving messages? After the Message Information page, you would proceed directly to the XML Translation Information page, with the difference that it would talk about *receiving* XML or string data rather than *sending* XML or string data. You then proceed to the Message Type Information page and so on as with sending messages.

Connecting Actions to COM and Script Implementations

Dragging a link between an action shape and a COM or Script component implementation invokes the Method Communication Wizard:

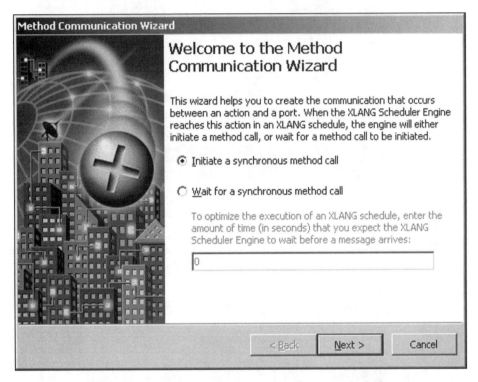

The first choice, Initiate a synchronous method call, should make perfect sense to a programmer who has experience using COM components. You are telling the Scheduler that you want to call one of the methods of the component you selected while setting up the COM or script component implementation. The second choice should cause alarm bells to go off in the head of such a programmer. Wait for a synchronous method call? Suffice to say, for now, that schedules may be called from the outside using COM, and that takes the form of a COM interface of your choosing with methods. We will return to this topic in detail, with samples, in Chapter 6. For now, let's assume we are calling the COM component and click Next.

The Message Information page, shown overleaf, allows you to create a message in the schedule that is tied to the method you will be invoking. Remember, schedules deal in messages, not methods, so Orchestration Designer will be creating a pair of messages: one for the inbound method call and one for the return of the call.

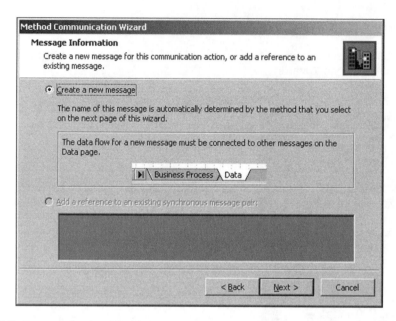

As with the XML Communication Wizard, you may create a new message or refer to an existing one. If you create a new message, its name will be based on the method you select in the Message Specification page:

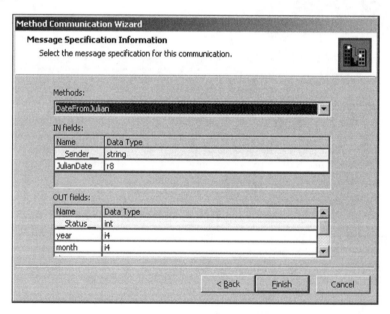

The Methods list box contains all the methods you selected while you were creating the port implementation. Select the one you wish to work with in this action. You will see the IN and OUT fields of the method, and their types. These fields will appear on the Data view, and may be referenced elsewhere in the schedule. Once you have selected the method, click Finish to save your information to the schedule.

The Wrox Site Managers Application

We'll be writing some code over the next few chapters to implement a sample BizTalk-enabled system. The practical examples will be tied in some way to a fictitious company called Wrox Site Managers. Before designing our first schedule, then, I'd like to introduce you to its business.

Imagine you own a house but don't like doing your own care and general maintenance. If you are like me, you aren't particularly handy with home repair. Since houses are prone to their problems, you quickly become involved in scheduling various contractor visits. If you are really lazy, you might like to have someone come and take care of the lawn for you, or clean your swimming pool. If you've just moved in, you need to arrange for telephone service. Since you like technology, you might have other services like broadband Internet access, a premium television service, or a home network.

So, you contact *Wrox Site Managers*, to act as representatives for organizing all your household maintenance needs. You tell Wrox Site Managers what recurring services you want, or what repairs you need, and it works with contractors to accomplish the task. You have a single point of contact – Wrox – and in turn it gains an application integration problem: integrating with the contractors.

> *We'll assume for the purposes of this book that all these contractors and service providers have applications that schedule or order the services desired. This is presently the case with large organizations like telephone companies or cable TV operators. If B2B implementation becomes sufficiently inexpensive, smaller companies will benefit from adopting this approach. Even if they rely on manual processes, they can be integrated with using e-mail.*

The first task Wrox Site Managers faces is describing a residential site. When you sign up for their service, a representative is sent to your home to survey the site. Equipped with a laptop or Pocket PC, the site manager records the details of your home and yard using a Visual Basic application. The end result of using the application is an XML document called a **Site Service Description**. This message is sent back to a BizTalk Server at the Wrox Site Managers home office, using Microsoft Message Queue. If the representative is within range of a cellular provider, the message is sent immediately. If not, the message is queued up for transmission when the representative is within range. From there, the data from the Site Service Description will be redistributed, as messages, to contractors. This whole setup is shown in the illustration below:

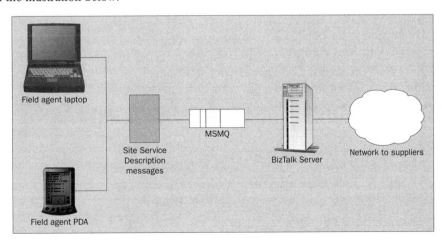

The Workflow

The Site Service Description message sent by the field agent represents a description of the residential site, and the services for which the homeowner has contracted. When the message is received, it needs to be analyzed to determine which subcontractors require notification so that they can provide the services. Doing so will require a schedule that can analyze the incoming messages and send out appropriate messages to the subcontractors.

Over the next few chapters we're going to focus on a subset of the requirements, specifically those for ordering a new cable TV installation and subscribing to a lawn maintenance service. These two vendors require messages in formats that differ from the Site Service Description. In fact, just to motivate specific issues in Chapters 3 and 4, we'll assume that these vendors use legacy formats that are flatfiles, and Site Service Descriptions are XML documents. The workflow, then, needs to orchestrate the following tasks:

1. Receive a Site Service Description from an MSMQ queue

2. Check to see if a cable TV installation is required

3. If required, cause a message to be sent to the cable installer in the appropriate format

4. Check to see if yard maintenance service is required

5. If required, send a message to the landscaper ordering periodic lawn care

6. Ensure a schedule instance is always available to handle incoming new Site Service Description messages

Here's what the finished flowchart will look like when we have finished building it. Don't worry too much about the details right now. Try to get a general feel for the flow of the schedule so that you will be in a better position to understand the role of each step as we get to it.

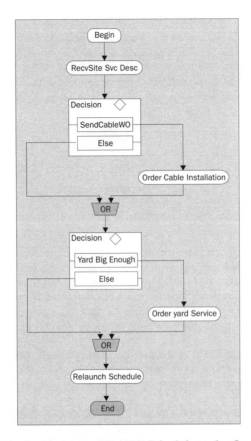

Let's design this application by building up a XLANG Schedule in the Orchestration Designer. We can gloss over the details of each message implementation for now. We'll use the wizards for binding and communicating, but the low-level messaging configurations will have to wait for Chapter 5. The end result of this sample will be a fully configured schedule, complete with the links needed in the Data view. Over the next three chapters, we'll build up the configurations and components needed by the BizTalk messaging system. At the end of Chapter 5, all the pieces will be in place and we can see the schedule work from start to finish. What goes on in this chapter, then, will be a bit more detailed than a pure design effort but will leave out important details needed by the final application.

Waiting for Message Arrival

The first task is to create a new business process diagram, and add an action for receiving the Site Service Description (sent from the field by a Wrox Site Managers representative) from an MSMQ queue.

To this end, start up Orchestration Designer. A business process diagram with a Begin shape on it appears. Just to get off on the right foot, save the diagram under the name InitialOrder.skv. The name reflects the fact that we are dealing with a brand new customer and are sending the initial customer information to the subcontractors.

Now drag an Action shape onto the flowchart grid and drop it so that it is directly beneath the Begin shape. This is going to be the action that waits for an incoming message to appear in the queue. Edit its properties and give it the name RecvSiteSvcDesc.

Next you need to connect it to the **Begin** shape, to indicate that this is the first action to be executed by the schedule upon startup. Select the **Begin** shape, then position your cursor over the bottom control handle. The cursor should change to indicate a Move pointer (on most systems this is four arrows emanating from a center out to the four compass points). Drag from that control handle to the top control handle of the Action shape. A directed line from the **Begin** shape to the Action shape should appear. Your flowchart should now look like this:

Binding to MSMQ

An Action shape is no use until it is bound to a message implementation. We've told the schedule that we want to take an action, but without a messaging implementation the schedule does not know that we want to receive a message from an MSMQ queue. Let's bind our new shape to an incoming MSMQ message. Drag a Message Queuing shape from the **Implementation** template to the right side of the business process diagram. The Message Queuing Binding Wizard should start. On the initial dialog, specify the creation of a new port and give it the name `RecvSiteSvcDesc`.

On the **Static or Dynamic Queue Information** dialog, check **Static Queue**. We're going to have a single queue to receive all messages, and we're going to create it outside the schedule. We will eventually write a client application that sends a message to this queue, so we will have to configure that manually.

On the next dialog, check **Use a known queue for all instances**. Enter the queue name `.\private$\RecvSiteSvcDesc`. This is MSMQ's way of specifying a private queue on the local machine with the name `RecvSiteSvcDesc`. On the **Advanced** dialog, leave the settings on their defaults (ensuring this includes **Transactions are required with this queue**) and click **Finish**.

Now look again at the business process diagram. The Message Queuing shape you dropped on the diagram now bears the name of the queue you provided in the binding wizard. A port shape with the name of the port, and a placeholder for the message name was created on the double line border separating the flowchart from the message implementations.

We need to connect the implementation to the Action shape now. Drag the cursor from the action shape's control handle to the port. This starts the XML Communication Wizard. On the initial page, check **Receive** and provide **300** as the number of seconds to expect to wait. Click **Next**. On the **Message Information** page, create a new message and name it `SiteSvcDesc`. Click **Next** and tell Orchestration Designer to **Receive XML messages from the queue** on the **XML Translation Information** page.

On the **Message Type Information** page, enter `SiteServiceDescription` as the message type. This is the name of the document element of the message we will be creating in the next chapter. Click **Next** to go to the **Message Specification Information** page.

The decision to send a message to the cable installer depends on the type of TV service the homeowner wishes to order. Obviously, we only need to inform the cable installer if the homeowner wants cable television service. Similarly, we will only send a message to the lawn care service if the yard is big enough. Both conditions require access to information in the Site Service Description messages.

To perform the next step, you need to have the message specification file. Since we have not created it as yet, copy the file `SiteServiceDescription.xml` *into the BizTalk document repository. We suggest creating a folder under* **DocSpecs** *named* **Wrox** *and putting the file there.*

Browse to the message specification file and select it. Check the Validate messages against the specification box. Now click the Add... button. You will see the following Field Selection dialog box:

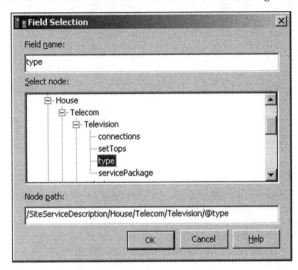

Navigate to the `type` field under `House/Telecom/Television` and select it. Click **OK**. Then click **Add...** in the Message Specification Information dialog again, and repeat the process for the `size` field under `Exterior/Yard`. Here is what the Message Specification Information dialog should look like when you are done:

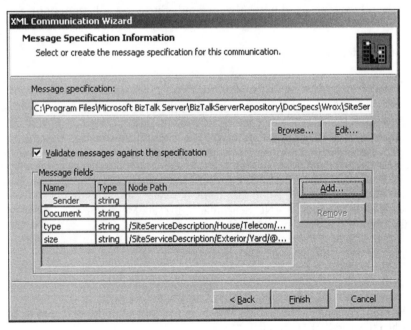

What you've just done is introduce some information into the system. If you peek ahead to the Data view, you will see a message reference shape with the fields shown here. The __Sender__ and Document fields are created automatically by XLANG Scheduler at run time and contain the sender's identity (if known) and the text of the message as a string, respectively. What is somewhat more useful for our present purposes is the presence of type and size. Since they are now known to the schedule, we will be able to refer to them in a decision shape rule, and other messages. At run time, they will contain the values of these fields as found in the message the schedule received.

Now that we've configured the port for use with this action, click Finish to save the information. A directed line will appear on the business process diagram, which will now look like this:

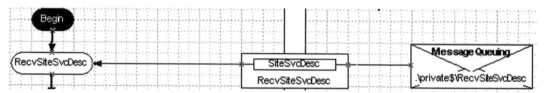

Delivery Decisions

Now we're ready to determine whether we need to send a cable installation message or not. Remember, this decision is based on the values we just added to the schedule from the incoming message. Perform the following actions:

1. Drop a Decision shape onto the flowchart side of the business process diagram.

2. Right-click on it and select Add Rule.

3. We'll name the rule SendCableWO (for "work order"). For the script expression, we need to reference the type value of the SiteSvcDesc message (which is the message we added to the schedule to stand in for the incoming Site Service Description). Such fields are referred to like a property of a Visual Basic object: SiteSvcDesc.type, in this case.

4. Enter the following text for the expression:

```
SiteSvcDesc.type = "cable"
```

When the incoming message has the value cable in the type field this expression returns True, and False otherwise. If the value is True, we want to send a BizTalk message to the cable installer. To accomplish this, we need to add another action that sends the Site Service Description out to the cable installer. Note that we are not sending some other type of message. In Chapter 4, we'll develop a **map** to translate the Site Service Description to the format the cable installer requires, and we'll use that map in Chapter 5 to perform the translation at run time when the schedule invokes the messaging implementation. As far as the schedule is concerned, though, it is sending the Site Service Description; the translation occurs outside XLANG Scheduler in BizTalk Messaging Services. To accomplish all this, do the following:

5. Add an Action shape to the flowchart.

6. Give it the name Order Cable Installation.

Leaving the message implementation aside for a moment, we want this action to be in the path that executes when the SendCableWO rule is True.

7. Connect the rule to the Action shape by dragging from either control handle on the rule within the Decision shape, to the control handle on the top of the new Action shape.

Regardless of whether the cable installation message is sent or not, we want the divergent paths coming out of the Decision shape to come back together before we decide whether we need to send a yard care subscription message. In other words, the decision to order yard care service should be independent of the decision to order cable TV service. To reflect this:

8. Add a Join shape to the flowchart, beneath the decision shape where you want the paths to come together.

9. Drag a connection from the `Else` shape within the Decision shape to the Join shape, then drag a connection from the `Order Cable Installation` shape to the Join shape.

10. Since only one of the two code paths will be executed for any given instance of the Site Service Description message (you can't order cable TV and also *not* order cable TV), double-click on the Join shape and set the **Join Type** property to OR.

11. Finally, connect the `RecvSiteSvcDesc` Action shape to the Decision shape.

The decision portion of the flowchart should look like this when you are finished:

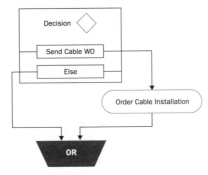

Leave the port and message implementations aside for a moment. We still have another decision to make: the decision regarding whether or not we need a yard care contract. This follows the same pattern as the one you just saw. Our business decision will be to order this service whenever the total yard area is greater than 1000 square feet. The total area will be given by the `size` field of the `Yard` record in the Site Service Description message. The value is in the schedule since we extracted this field when we defined the message. Here is the process:

12. Create another Decision shape and connect it to the outbound side of the Join shape.

13. Add a rule to it named `YardBigEnough` and give it the following expression:

```
SiteSvcDesc.size > 1000
```

This checks the value in the message to see whether it complies with our business rule.

14. Add an Action shape named `Order Yard Service`, as well as a Join shape, and connect them to the Decision shape in the manner of the cable TV decision. Again, the low-level messaging implementation will be defined in a later chapter, but we will be creating a port implementation for this action shortly.

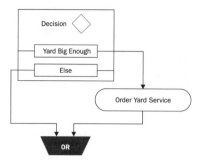

Now we've diagrammed our two decision making tasks, and associated them with BizTalk messaging actions. Let's go back now and provide implementations for those messages.

Binding to BizTalk Messaging

The messages sent to the cable installer and the yard maintenance service are Site Service Descriptions. However, the individual vendors actually only want a subset of the overall site information. To make matters worse, we're also assuming that each is using a non-XML format that is very different from the message we have. Fortunately, we can rely on the data transformation capabilities of BizTalk Messaging Services to handle this for us at the time we send the messages. We'll go into this in detail in Chapter 4. As far as we are concerned right now, though, all we have to do is send the Site Service Description message on to each interested party. We start by configuring the cable installation message implementation:

1. Drag a BizTalk Messaging shape onto the right side of the business process diagram.

2. Specify a new port and give it the name `SendCableWO`. This will be the port to the cable installer.

3. In the second dialog, specify the message direction as **Send**.

To keep our example simple, we'll assume we are dealing with a single cable TV installer. In the real world, with vendors covering different service regions, we'd want to use dynamic communication and select a channel on the basis of the message's content. Since we're dealing with a single vendor for the purposes of illustration (and because we won't go into dynamic routing until Chapter 10), however, we'll go ahead and select a channel now. As you will learn in Chapter 5, a channel is the highest level of messaging configuration in BizTalk Messaging Services. By naming it here, we are telling the schedule what messaging configuration to invoke to process this action.

4. Enter the channel name `CableInstallChannel`. We'll get around to specifying it in Chapter 5. When you've entered the name, click **Finish**.

5. Now connect the `Order Cable Installation` Action shape to the newly created port.

6. In the **Message Information** page of the XML Communication Wizard, select the `SiteSvcDesc` message from the list in the lower list box.

7. In the **XML Translation Information** page, select **Send XML messages to the queue**.

8. In the **Message Type Information** page, enter `SiteServiceDescription`. This is the top-level record (in BizTalk terminology) or document element (in XML terms) of the message.

9. On the final page, note that the fields you selected earlier are present and click **Finish**.

Now we'll configure the message implementation for the yard service:

10. Once again, add a BizTalk Messaging shape to the business process diagram.

11. Create a new port named `SendYardMnx`, and specify the direction as **Send**.

12. Enter `SendYardCare` for the channel name and click **Finish** to complete the implementation.

13. Connect the `Order Yard Service` shape to the new port.

14. In the XML Communication Wizard, add a reference to the existing `SiteSvcDesc` message. Select **Send XML messages to the queue.**

15. Enter `SiteServiceDescription` as the message type in the **Message Type Information** page.

16. On the final page, note the fields are present and then click **Finish**.

With these message implementations, we have almost everything we need to specify the flow of messages through our schedule.

The business process diagram, with the ports, now looks like this:

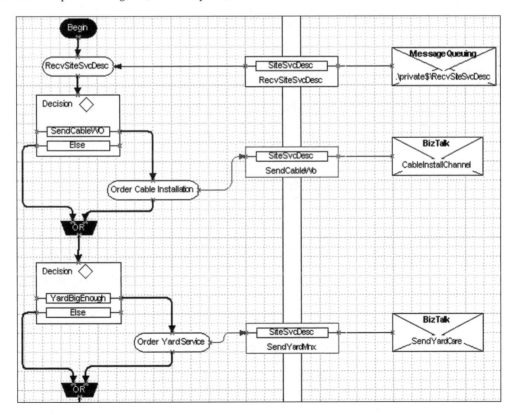

The next task is to show Orchestration Designer how we expect data to flow from one message field to another. For that, we turn our attention to the Data view.

Configuring the Data Flow through the Schedule

The starting point for our data flow is the Document field in the SiteSvcDesc (Site Service Description) message shape. In fact, it is also the end of our data flow. Recall that we said that the translation to the other formats will take place using a map in Messaging Services, and that from the schedule's point of view we are merely sending the same Site Service Description out to the cable installer and the yard care service. This data flowed into the schedule and stopped. We are sending messages out, but no data moves out of this message. The Data View looks like this:

Constants		Port References	
		RecvSiteSvcDesc	string
		SendCableAb	string
SiteSvcDesc		SendYardMhx	string
__Sender__	string	SchedUtilComponent	object
Document	string		
type	enumeration		
size	number		

The Constants shape is added automatically and is not used in this schedule. We'll see more of it in Chapter 6. Orchestration Designer added the Port References shape and populated it as we added port implementations.

> The SchedUtilComponent port will be created in the next section.

If the text of the SiteSvcDesc message flowed to another message format, we would draw a connection between the Document field in the SiteSvcDesc shape and the other shape. If the value of type or size needed to go somewhere, we could draw the connection with those fields too.

> If you are disappointed that you don't get to connect data fields to each other in this example, rest assured we will be giving the Data view quite a workout in Chapter 6, as we move data through some advanced schedules in complicated ways.

There is one final task in our schedule, and that is to ensure that there is always a schedule resident in the XLANG Scheduler to process a new incoming Site Service Description message from a field agent. We've chosen to launch the schedule independent of incoming messages, perhaps using some batch process when the server starts up. Now we need to launch a replacement instance of the schedule when the current instance terminates.

Loading a Schedule

If we stopped here, the schedule would pick one message off the queue, do its work, and stop. We'd rather have the schedule hang around, processing messages as they come into the queue. It turns out that using the existing schedule to launch a new instance of itself, as its final action, is fairly easy.

Launching a new schedule instance is a matter of making a call to the system operating system function `GetObject()` using a file moniker that points to the schedule file. XLANG Scheduler is registered as the application that is associated with schedule files, so the COM+ runtime hands the moniker off to Scheduler to process. Scheduler simply finds the schedule file and loads it.

In its simplest form, the moniker for a schedule is `sked:///schedule_filename`, where `schedule_filename` points to the `.skx` file that is created by exporting a schedule in Orchestration Designer. For example, the moniker for this schedule could be:

```
Sked:///myfiles\InitialOrders.skx
```

Here `myfiles` is a placeholder for the fully qualified pathname of the file. The moniker syntax can get more complicated, but we don't need the additional capabilities here. Therefore we will cover them in Chapter 6. Now, a schedule file can't make `GetObject()` call itself, but there is nothing to keep us from writing a script component to do that for us. To that end, I created `WroxScheduleUtilities.wsc`.

The scripting section of MSDN has a utility to help create script component shells. You can find the scripting section at msdn.microsoft.com/scripting/default.htm.

It has a single method, `LaunchSchedule()`, that takes no parameters. It is implemented in the following way in Javascript:

```
function LaunchSchedule()
{
  var objSked;

  objSked = GetObject(" sked:///c:\\myschedulefiles\\initialorders.skx" );
  return objSked;
}
```

`InitialOrders.skx` is the schedule file we'll export from the business process diagram in our next step. You should, of course, substitute the correct drive and path (in place of `myschedulefiles`) for your installation before trying to run this schedule. We don't have to worry about the life cycle of the object returned from the `GetObject()` call. That is managed by XLANG Scheduler, which loads the schedule when a moniker is received. When the End shape is encountered, the schedule terminates. Even though we haven't set the `objSked` variable to Null in our code, BizTalk Server is fairly aggressive about taking objects out of memory.

To call this method and relaunch the schedule:

1. Add a new Action shape named **Relaunch Schedule** following the final Join shape.

2. Choose a Script component implementation, creating the port `SchedUtilComponent` and **Static Instantiation** of the component.

3. Point to the file `WroxScheduleUtitilities.wsc` in the **Specify the script file** page.

4. In the Component Instantiation Information page, select Use the Prog ID "WroxScheduleUtilities.WSC".

5. Accept the defaults on the final page and click Finish.

6. Connect the Action shape to the port, and specify Initiate a synchronous method call.

7. Select the LaunchSchedule() method as your message and click Finish.

We will discuss how the schedule is initially launched in Chapter 5 when we have all the pieces in place to actually run the schedule.

We aren't passing any data into the message – the moniker is hard-coded and therefore we don't have to pass in a message – so there is no need to revisit the Data view. The final step is to drag an End shape onto the page. When you have connected the output of the Action shape to the End shape, the flowchart should look like the diagram we showed at the beginning of this *Wrox Site Managers* section.

Exporting the Schedule for Production Use

As you worked through the schedule you probably used File | Save or File | Save As... to preserve your schedule. This made a file with the extension .skv. If you opened that file in a text editor expecting to find XML, you'd be sorely disappointed. As noted earlier, these files are in Visio's binary format. They are all about diagrams and pictures and nothing at all about schedules, messages, and processes. Fortunately, Orchestration Designer speaks both languages.

I saved my business process diagram under the name InitialOrders.skv. If you select File | Make XLANG InitialOrders.skx, Orchestration Designer will go off into a moderately lengthy process, during which it turns a Visio diagram into a XLANG schedule. If the export fails for any reason, you will get a dialog box advising you that the schedule failed to export.

If the export does fail, there is probably an error in the layout and connectivity of your diagram. Check the business process diagram to make sure everything is connected, and that you have obeyed the various rules for the different shapes. Don't forget to turn to the Data view to make sure that you remembered to specify the flow of data through the schedule.

The error messages given by Orchestration Designer are extremely cryptic, so don't expect much help here. You will be better off stepping back and reviewing the schedule from start to finish, as if you were a computer trying to execute the flowchart.

Summary

Orchestration is a very different way to design and think about systems and application integration. As programmers, we are accustomed to specifying our intentions as lengthy stretches of code. Even if you have experience implementing finite state machines, you are used to thinking in code. Orchestration abstracts the code and lets us design systems from the standpoint of the flow of data through the system. So long as our basic building blocks are present in the form of applications and application components, building a system through orchestration is a matter of specification, not programming.

In this chapter, you learned the basics of orchestration. You learned how to use a design tool called Orchestration Designer to define schedules both visually, as a **business process diagram**, and as an XLANG document, that BizTalk Server can use to implement orchestration.

You saw how a **business process diagram** consists of a flowchart side and a messaging implementation side. On the flowchart, you learned about the basic shapes used to specify schedule semantics and how to configure and connect them. On the messaging implementation side, you learned how to implement each of the four types of communications supported by orchestration.

A schedule also consists of a **Data View** in which the flow of data through a schedule is specified in terms of links between messages. You learned that specific messages introduce data into schedules, and data flow is implemented by drawing connections between message fields.

You were introduced to the requirements of the hypothetical **Wrox Site Managers** business. This business forms the basis of a system we will progressively develop over the next few chapters. You built the XLANG schedule that connects the business with two service suppliers to whom the business outsources specific functions.

What you did not do was implement the low-level details of the messaging functions that our schedule will orchestrate. This may be frustrating to you as a programmer – all that work and no running code. Before you can send a structured message, though, you must specify how it is laid out. Our schedule involves one message that is transformed into two other message formats, the cable installation and yard maintenance subscription messages. That means three message specifications, which is the topic for our next chapter. BizTalk supports powerful features for data transformation, and that will be the topic for Chapter 4. Executing messaging functions involves some configuration, a step we will take up in Chapter 5 when we bring everything together and send messages through our schedule.

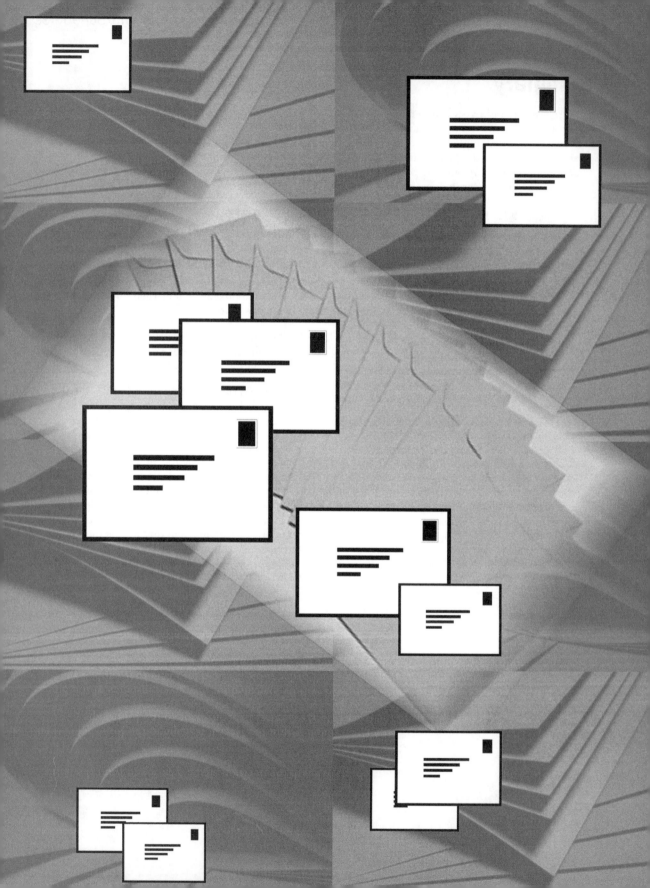

3

Specifications

As we saw in the last chapter, BizTalk-enabled workflows are data-driven processes built around structured text messages. All messages passed by BizTalk Server are structured text messages. However, simply passing messages is not enough; BizTalk Server often needs to be able to process (parse) a message document, in order to extract important information from the document. To do this, the Server must understand the format of the message. In BizTalk Server, message format information is stored in a file called a **specification**.

Actually, if BizTalk restricted itself to XML-based messages, there would be no need for these special message specifications, because schemas like those used by Microsoft's XML products contain enough information to describe the structure of BizTalk XML messages. However, BizTalk Server is not limited to just XML message formats; it can work with delimited text flatfiles, and positional text flatfiles as well. Flatfile messages can't be completely described by an XML schema as schemas have no notion of delimiters or field positions. Therefore, specifying a flatfile format requires tools beyond schemas; this is why we need message specifications.

BizTalk borrows techniques from XML for the specification of BizTalk messages, which allows BizTalk Server to take advantage of existing XML tools. However, the good news is that you don't need to be an XML expert to understand BizTalk message specifications. Indeed, BizTalk's message specification model takes some pains to move message designers away from XML theory, and toward a model that should be more familiar to working corporate programmers. BizTalk also provides us with an easy-to-use graphical tool for the creation of specifications: **BizTalk Editor**, which we will use extensively in this chapter.

Having introduced you to the Editor, we will return to our case study, Wrox Site Managers, in which a hypothetical business wishes to use BizTalk Server as the foundation for electronically integrating its business processes. If you recall the schedule we developed in the last chapter, you'll remember that BizTalk Server first received a message describing a residential site. Then it sent messages containing data from the site description to the Cable Installer and the Yard Care Service.

In this chapter, we will introduce a typical business application integration problem into our case study: that the message formats the service providers require are *not* the same as the message format of the original site description. The original site description is an XML message, but the Cable Installer requires a delimited flatfile message, while the Yard Care service needs a positional flatfile. Towards the end of the chapter, we will show you how to use the Editor to produce the message specifications that describe each of the message formats used in our case study. These specifications will then be used in the next chapter, where we will show you how to specify the translation between the message formats.

We'll round off the chapter with a brief look at BizTalk Server's support for EDI. We'll see that BizTalk Server includes some EDI specifications for use out of the box. BizTalk Editor also has some helpful tool support for message designers who need to modify EDI formats to fit their applications. True to its objective of integrating applications and e-commerce partners, BizTalk Server draws existing formats into its world and encourages their use alongside newer specifications.

So, as you can see, in this chapter we are going to cover message specifications in depth. As you read through it, you will:

❑ learn what message specifications are and what forms they can declare

❑ learn how to write message specifications for use with BizTalk Server

❑ learn some issues of data modeling associated with good message specification design

❑ and most importantly, be introduced to the BizTalk Editor, a tool provided by BizTalk Server for the creation of message specifications

By the time you have worked through this chapter, you should begin to see your business less in terms of programming language data structures, more in terms of structured message flow. This chapter describes the main BizTalk tools you need to create these messages.

What is a Specification?

As we have seen, BizTalk makes extensive use of XML in sending messages between different parts of a system. This enables it to orchestrate the different parts of the application integration from a central server, removing integration code from the application itself. Of course, BizTalk Server must be able to understand these messages, so that it can parse them, retrieve appropriate information from them, and then generate new messages for other systems. Understanding a message is not as simple as it sounds; BizTalk can receive a message in a variety of formats, so if we don't describe the information that each message can contain, the Server will not be able to understand the message.

The mechanism for defining what information a message can contain and the structure and format of that message is called a **specification**. BizTalk Server makes use of XML Data Reduced (XDR), a schema language (see below) for XML, in its specifications. A BizTalk message specification, however, is actually more than just an XDR schema: a specification is an XML document with an XDR schema embedded in it. The information that cannot be conveyed in a schema alone is contained in the other elements and attributes of the specification document.

Rather than having to write these XML-based specifications by hand, BizTalk provides a tool called the **Editor**, with its graphical interface to make the creation of them much easier.

> **A message specification is a formal document that describes the allowable structure and contents of a message processed by BizTalk Server. It is machine-readable and intended to be used by BizTalk Messaging Services to validate message structure and perform translation between message formats.**

The Role of XDR Schemas in BizTalk Server

A **schema** is a template defining the way information should be structured within a document, as well as the vocabulary which can be used within the document. XML file schemas come in two main forms: Document Type Definitions (DTDs), and schemas, which (unlike DTDs) are also written in XML. Such XML-based schemas have several advantages over DTDs, including the ability to make use of the multitude of XML tools on offer.

Microsoft's implementation of an XML-based schema syntax is called XML-Data Reduced, or **XDR**. It also includes support for XML features such as namespaces and datatyping (more on these later) beyond what is provided in the W3C XML 1.0 Recommendation (the base specification upon which the XML family is built).

The **W3C** (the World Wide Web Consortium, which produces standards for the Web) has its own standard XML Schema effort too, and the Microsoft *XML Data* proposal upon which XDR is based was but one input to that effort. Microsoft proceeded with its proprietary approach, to provide running code support for schemas prior to the approval of the W3C effort. Indeed, while XDR support has been available for nearly two years, the W3C Schema effort is only now (December 2000) nearing the end of its standardization process. Microsoft is, however, committed to supporting the W3C XML Schemas proposal when it becomes a recommendation.

As we have said, BizTalk Server can handle different types of message, including delimited and positional flatfile formats as well as XML documents. However, since the core processors of BizTalk Server are XML based, we must describe the contents of all message formats, including flatfiles, using XDR schemas. In order to do this, some extensions must be added to the XDR syntax to accommodate flatfiles. These extensions are the main difference between a message *schema* and a message *specification* in BizTalk.

We'll take up the specifics of these extensions in a bit, but let's first look at which formats BizTalk can accommodate through message specifications.

Message Formats

The universe of messages BizTalk Server can process consists of both XML and flatfile text formats. Flatfile types are quite varied, but are usefully categorized further into "delimited" or "positional".

- ❏ **XML files** – these can be any XML message that obeys the rules of the XML 1.0 Recommendation and the XML Namespaces Recommendation.

- ❏ **Delimited flatfiles** – where data fields appear separated   delimited   by some predefined character (one that is not expected to appear in any of the data fields). Common delimiters are commas, colons, tab characters, and pipe characters. Each record is typically terminated by a hard return (a line feed-carriage return pair).

- ❏ **Positional flatfiles** – also known as **fixed-width** files, allocate a particular number of bytes to each data field. When a piece of data is shorter than the space allocated, *padding* characters are inserted into the field space until the appropriate number of characters has been used. There is often (although not always) a hard return stored at the end of every record.

Whichever message type is used, the message specification must contain sufficient information for BizTalk's parsers to correctly interpret the contents of the message. The BizTalk team could not possibly know every message format that BizTalk users can or will dream up, so BizTalk also relies on data-driven parsing. This meant that the team had to write general-purpose parsers that use specifications to indicate how messages are to be parsed.

A flatfile parser component, for example, can recognize a flatfile format message, but it must turn to a message specification to obtain the specific details (field positions, say) needed to effectively parse the message for BizTalk. BizTalk will even let you write your own specialized parsers to handle unusual formats that cannot be handled by the standard parsers included with the product.

We should have a closer look at the characteristics of each of these basic message formats now, so that we know how we are going to describe them when we come to writing a specification.

XML Files

BizTalk Server can handle any vocabulary that can be written under the rules laid out in the W3C XML 1.0 Recommendation, with extensions defined in the XML Namespaces Recommendation. But what is XML, and what does it look like?

In Chapter 1, we briefly discussed XML, and noted that it is a *meta-markup language*; in other words it describes a syntax that you use to create your own markup languages. It will be useful to take a moment to study XML syntax more closely, which will aid our understanding of XML specifications.

> *XML, although conceptually quite concise, is much richer than the following discussion might suggest. If you are new to XML you might like to pick up a copy of* Beginning XML *(ISBN 1-861003-41-2) from Wrox Press. Or if you are familiar with the basics and want a more comprehensive treatment, try* Professional XML *(Wrox, ISBN 1-861003-11-0). The text of the W3C XML Recommendation is found at http://www.w3.org/TR/REC-xml.*

Generally speaking, you do not need to master XML to use BizTalk. We will discuss some approaches to encapsulating the use of XML in applications later in the book. For now, only a general knowledge of the broad features of XML is necessary. Let's take a look.

Elements and Attributes

Very simply, XML is a text format in which data is delimited before and after by **tags**. These tags are produced by surrounding a name by a pair of angle brackets, for example `<FirstName>`. Each such instance of a tag pair and its data is known as an **element**. Elements can contain text, other elements, or a combination of the two. Here is a brief sample of XML:

```
<? xml version="1.0" ?>
<Person>
  <Name>
    <Given>John</Given>
    <Family>Doe</Family>
  </Name>
</Person>
```

The first line consists of a special construction called the **XML declaration**, which tells a processing application that the contents of the file are XML. The remaining content consists of elements. Note how elements are closed: by repeating the tag with a slash (/) preceding the tag name.

XML also provides the notion of **attributes**. These are simple properties associated with an element, much in the way that Visual Basic objects have associated simple properties. Let's use an attribute to add the person's age to our simple document:

```
<? xml version="1.0" ?>
<Person age="40">
  <Name>
   <Given>John</Given>
   <Family>Doe</Family>
  </Name>
</Person>
```

Attributes consist of name-value pairs in which the name of the attribute is assigned a value delimited by quotation marks. In our example, age is the attribute name and "40" is its value.

Namespaces

From our earlier discussion of schemas, we know XML supports any *document type* (any particular vocabulary and way of structuring data in a document) that adheres to the XML 1.0 Recommendation. This is all well and good, but what happens if we want to use XML elements from different document types? In some cases, we will get elements that have exactly the same name but derive from different document types, which would confuse an XML parser. For example, an element called <title> might refer to the title of a book in one document type, and the title of a person in another.

The most obvious way to get around this problem is to make sure all of the elements in a document have different names. This is achieved in XML through the use of **namespaces.** In this system, we assign a unique namespace to each vocabulary, which is added to the front of the name of any element from that vocabulary. Since a namespace must be unique, a URL is often used (which also frequently points to the relevant schema or DTD). However, URLs are often long and unwieldy strings, so XML also allows us to associate a short *prefix* with the namespace, as a substitute for it within the document.

For example, we could create an XML vocabulary containing an element <sites>, and give the vocabulary the namespace "http://jonnykool.com/koolstuff" in another XML document. The namespace is represented in the document by the prefix kool:

```
<kool:sites xlmns:kool="http//jonnykool.com/koolstuff"/>
```

Note the use of the reserved attribute xmlns to declare a namespace, and the use of a colon to associate an element with a namespace. Therefore, we may infer that the following two elements are from different vocabularies:

```
<kool:sites>
<sites>
```

The second element derives from the **default namespace** for the document. Obviously, only one namespace in a document can be the default, and it has no prefix defined for it. Therefore, any elements lacking a prefix are assumed to be drawn from this namespace.

Now that we understand what XML is about a bit more clearly, let's turn to look at the flatfile formats handled by BizTalk.

Delimited Flatfiles

You may have noticed that, technically, XML is a delimited format. In XML items are delimited by names wrapped in angle brackets. More commonly, though, we'll use the term "delimited" to refer to a file format in which items of data are separated by a known character or sequence of characters known as the **delimiter**. For example, database dumps in comma separated variable (**CSV**) format use commas to delimit individual columns, and the line feed, carriage return pair to delimit records:

```
John,Doe,39
Mary,Smith,28
Lazarus,,438
```

In this example, we have no trouble seeing that John Doe, Mary Smith, and Lazarus (no last name) are individual people – or at least, records describing people – and we can tell where the first name ends and the last name begins even though these columns are of varying length.

CSV isn't the only delimited format, of course, so BizTalk message specifications must have the capability to specify arbitrary delimiters for each record and column (or item) of data. A further problem is that delimiters sometimes appear within valid data – for example, we might need to handle data that contains commas. In that case, the specification needs to provide an **escape character**. If you are writing a string in Visual Basic, you can enclose a quotation mark in a string literal by escaping it with an apostrophe. BizTalk will let us do much the same thing with delimiters. For example, we might provide the slash (\) as the escape character. Consider this record:

```
John, Doe, Director\,Programming Division, 39
```

In the record, we've inserted a field for job title between the last name and the age. John Doe's title is Director, Programming Division. When the parser sees the escape character, it knows to overlook the comma that follows. When escaped, the comma is a part of the field, not a delimiter.

In all our CSV examples so far, the field delimiter has always occurred between fields, and there isn't a delimiter following the last field of a record (although there is a newline character delimiting the record). This is an example of *infix* notation. We can also specify *prefix* (delimiter preceding every field) or *postfix* (delimiter after every field). Our delimiters have also been printable ASCII characters, except for the end of record delimiter. As you might suspect from our use of the end-of-record delimiter, we can use any hexadecimal character as a field or record delimiter, and combining these different choices results in many possible delimited formats.

BizTalk message specifications for delimited files will have to capture all this information so that the parsers invoked at run time can handle delimited messages properly. This is the sort of information that cannot be contained in just an XDR schema, and forces BizTalk to use special message specifications that are a superset of schemas.

Positional Flatfiles

Positional flatfile formats take a different approach to data from delimited formats. In positional files, only records use delimiters, typically a carriage return-line feed pair. In fact, records may not be delimited at all, in which case the entire file is one long stream of characters. Each field, by contrast, occupies a fixed position – a range of characters – in the record. The parser should always find the contents of the field in the specified positions.

Data items that are shorter than the field width are padded with a known character. This **pad character** must be specified similar to the way that delimiters are in specifications for delimited files, so that BizTalk's parsers can tell the difference between data and padding. Like delimited files, positional files may also have a known character or sequence of characters to indicate an end-of-record condition. This character or set of characters is known as the **record terminator**.

Here's our delimited example converted to a positional format:

```
JohnxxxxxxDoexxxxxxxxxxxxx39x
MaryxxxxxxSmithxxxxxxxxxx28x
Lazarusxxxxxxxxxxxxxxxxxx438
```

We've used the carriage return, line feed pair as the record terminator in our example. The lower case character x is our pad character, although in reality space characters are more frequently used. In the case of Lazarus, the entire second item (last name) is filled with the pad character.

Closer inspection of the example raises another question: if some item is shorter than the allowed field length, do the pad characters precede the item or follow it? In our case, obviously, we've left-justified the fields. This is not a requirement of all positional formats however, so BizTalk message specifications will have to have some way of indicating how fields are **justified**. Now what would happen if Mr. Doe were named Nebuchanezzar instead of John — we've only left ten characters for the first name field? In that case, the first name item is **truncated** to fit into the fixed field:

```
NebuchanezDoexxxxxxxxxxxxx39x
```

Because the field is fixed length, the parser has no difficulty determining that the D in Doe starts a new field.

That concludes our brief tour of the different message file formats we will encounter in BizTalk. We now move on to look at how we can produce XML specifications for any type of format, even flatfiles, by adding extensions to XDR schemas.

Extending Schemas into Specifications

Message specifications for XML-based messages can be described entirely by an XDR schema. However, the universe of applications we'd like to integrate includes many – perhaps mostly — systems that use flatfiles. So, how can we capture the kind of information we've discussed in flatfile formats without losing the ability to use the tools XML provides? The answer is to create some extensions that will allow us to describe special properties of flatfiles (for example, delimiters) within XDR schemas.

Ordinarily, adding proprietary extensions to an open standard like XDR, for use with open systems is a spectacularly bad idea. The exceptions, of course, are:

❑ when all users support the extensions (in other words, the system is not open)

❑ when the extensions are hidden from the users of the system.

The whole point of BizTalk Server is to achieve open systems across platform boundaries by using open protocols and standards, so the first point does not apply here. The second point does though: message specifications are only used by BizTalk Server. You will use the Editor to create specifications, Messaging Services will read the specifications, but the specifications are *never* passed between systems. In this case, the use of extensions is perfectly harmless, because these extensions are never exposed to any software or user outside BizTalk Server.

Actually, this means that BizTalk could use any format it wants, even to the point of abandoning schemas entirely. However, the BizTalk programming team realized that using schemas with XML extensions allows them to leverage existing XML tools. The extensions were carefully segregated from the standard schema information through the use of namespaces, so it is always clear when viewing a specification in a text file what is standard and what is a proprietary extension.

What happens, though, when a trading partner wants to obtain a message specification from a repository like BizTalk.org's schema library   must they support the extensions used by BizTalk Server? If the partners are dealing with flatfile formats and need an explicit format specification, yes. Although we expect most new message specifications to be XML, we should not make BizTalk completely reliant on the proprietary extensions to schemas used in message specifications. Therefore, one of the features of BizTalk Editor is that it allows a user to import an XDR schema or DTD and construct a message specification from that. This is a case of putting the extended elements with default values into the schema to produce a message specification. It will also allow you to import a message instance – a sample of the document type – and create a message specification from that.

Message Specifications for XML-Based Messages

Although the Server is the only entity that should ever see a message specification generated by the Editor, it will be worthwhile for us to take a look at a sample specification to get a sense of what is going on. Here is a portion of a message specification for an XML document:

```
<Schema name="SiteServiceDescription" b:BizTalkServerEditorTool_Version="1.0"
    b:root_reference="SiteServiceDescription"
    b:schema_type="SiteServiceDescription" b:standard="XML"
    b:standards_version="1.0"
    xmlns="urn:schemas-microsoft-com:xml-data"
    xmlns:b="urn:schemas-microsoft-com:BizTalkServer"
    xmlns:d="urn:schemas-microsoft-com:datatypes">
  <b:SelectionFields/>

  <ElementType name="Yard" content="empty" model="closed">
  <b:RecordInfo/>
  <AttributeType name="size" d:type="number">
    <description>yard area</description>
    <b:FieldInfo/>
  </AttributeType>
  <AttributeType name="grassType" d:type="string">
    <description>type of grass planted</description>
    <b:FieldInfo/>
  </AttributeType>
    . . .
```

The root element is <Schema>. Three namespaces are also declared:

❑   The namespace for XDR schemas (the default since it has no namespace prefix)

❑   Microsoft's namespace for data types beyond the XML Recommendation is given the prefix d

❑   The namespace for concepts specific to BizTalk Server is declared with the prefix b

Since most of our elements come from the XDR namespace, it is useful to be able to use them without qualifying the name with a prefix. The attributes of the BizTalk namespace element identify the creating tool, the root record of the document, and indicate that we are dealing with an XML 1.0 document. The <Schema> element is the root of an XDR schema for this message, with elements from the data-types and BizTalk namespaces added.

Notice that the developers of BizTalk Server, while extending XDR for their purposes, have followed sound XML procedures for extending a document type. Rather than recreating the XDR schema with additions, they have separately declared their additions and mixed them with the XDR schema to create the message specification vocabulary. An application without knowledge of the Microsoft extensions could still parse this document and understand the standard information simply by ignoring the namespace-qualified elements and attributes.

Also note that each `ElementType` and `AttributeType` element (from the default XDR namespace) is followed by either a `RecordInfo` or `FieldInfo` element. These are the extensions provided for BizTalk Server, as indicated by the b namespace prefix. In this example, these extensions add nothing to our knowledge of the message structure. The Editor tool generates empty elements when additional information is not needed. This should not be surprising. BizTalk Server is designed to operate on XML messages. It is only when we turn to flatfile format messages that we need to provide additional information.

Message Specifications for Flatfile Formats

Let's now turn to a message specification for a flatfile format message and see what information changes from the specification for an XML message. Here is a sample delimited message:

```
C,Jacques,Sprat,610-555-1212,08:00:00
L,123 Chestnut Ave,Division 6,Philadelphia,PA,19100,First house on left
I,4,4,PREMIUM,12:00:00
```

And here is a portion of the XML message specification BizTalk produced for it:

Do not spend much time worrying about the specific details of the extensions in the following specification. The Editor hides the XML syntax of message specifications from you. What we are trying to accomplish here is to get you thinking about how BizTalk messaging uses information beyond that which XML schemas convey.

```
<Schema name="CableCSV" b:BizTalkServerEditorTool_Version="1.0"
        b:root_reference="CableCSV" b:schema_type="data_contacts" b:version="1.0"
        b:codepage="0x4e4" b:is_envelope="no" b:standard="FlatFile"
        xmlns="urn:schemas-microsoft-com:xml-data"
        xmlns:b="urn:schemas-microsoft-com:BizTalkServer"
        xmlns:d="urn:schemas-microsoft-com:datatypes">
    <b:SelectionFields/>

    <ElementType name="Location" content="empty" model="closed">
        <b:RecordInfo tag_name="L" structure="delimited" delimiter_type="char"
            delimiter_value=","/>
        <AttributeType name="directions" d:type="string">
          <b:FieldInfo/>
        </AttributeType>
        <AttributeType name="Zip" d:type="string">
            <description>Zip code of the party</description>
            <b:FieldInfo/>
        </AttributeType>
    ...
```

Now we see a few interesting changes. The namespace declarations remain the same as for the specification for an XML message, but now the <Schema> element's attributes tell us we are dealing with a FlatFile whose root is CableCSV.

Take a look at the RecordInfo element that is immediately under the ElementType element bearing name="Location". The RecordInfo element provides extension information about the Location record. Now we have a tag_name attribute whose value is a record delimiter that will appear in the document. Every time the record appears, as it does in the second line of the sample message, the character L starts the line to indicate that we are starting a new Location record. Note, however, that we've also got an attribute named structure that tells us this record is delimited. The attribute delimiter_type tells us we are using a printable character, and the attribute delimiter_value tells us a comma will be used to separate fields within the record.

Now you can begin to see why BizTalk adds extensions to schemas when they make message specifications. These extensions give BizTalk places to store all the information needed to correctly process flatfiles at run time.

> *These examples are certainly not intended to be an exhaustive description of the message specification file format. As noted, these files are intended for use exclusively by BizTalk Server. As such, the format is subject to change without notice.*
>
> *More importantly for programmers, manually altering a message specification file can break BizTalk-integrated applications in ways that are hard to diagnose. These examples are intended purely for background knowledge and to help you understand how BizTalk Server works.*

In the next section, we'll discuss good specification design, and give you a few handy hints to help you when you need to design specifications of your own.

Designing Specifications

The success of a system integrated by BizTalk Server rests in large measure on the quality of the message specifications used to exchange data between applications. Specifications need to encapsulate all of the items of information needed by the applications that are placed in communication.

Less obvious, however, is the need for flexibility. Message designers must anticipate that some information may not always be available, while other information may occur many times within a single exchange. BizTalk message specifications require the same sort of analysis and thought that go into the design of relational database schemas or class designs in object-oriented programming. Message specifications are essentially XML schemas with some proprietary extensions, so the task of designing a message specification is really one of modeling data in XML.

While the construction of effective XML schemas could easily consume an entire book, there are no hard and fast rules to follow. A variety of guidelines and rules of thumb are to be found in the archives of XML newsgroups and mailing lists   success requires a certain amount of analytical talent and even more experience. In short, I suggest that you dive in and write some specifications. Write sample messages that conform to the specifications and think through how they might work with – or against – an application.

Having said this, however, I think it is important to offer some help in the form of an introduction to some design techniques that are common in the BizTalk community.

To that end, we will:

- look briefly at how to adapt legacy formats to BizTalk specifications
- discuss a fairly conventional approach that builds **hierarchical** structures to represent objects in XML
- review a formal technique, the **canonical style**, promoted by the BizTalk Framework site

Adapting Legacy Formats

The easiest way to get hold of a specification, as you might expect, is to adopt an existing schema. Indeed, that's the whole idea behind the BizTalk Framework repository. If you can't find a schema that exactly fits your project requirements in the repository, the next thing you might try is to modify an existing format. If a schema appears to be similar to what you need, you'll generally find that most of the schema will work well in your application. You can keep the well-tested parts that work, delete what doesn't fit, and add what you need.

BizTalk Editor honors a time-tested programming tradition of adapting existing information to new situations, by permitting you to import data into Editor to start a specification. You can import a schema or DTD into the Editor, modify it, and save it as a message specification. More than that, though, the creators of the Editor realize that some common business functions have already been described in detail   this is the reason why BizTalk includes message specifications for X12 and EDIFACT EDI messages. These messages cover business constructs like purchase orders, order acknowledgements, and shipping information.

Even if you have no legacy of EDI, you can of course exchange the same kind of business data in XML; there is no need to drag flatfile formats into a brand new system. BizTalk Server ships with XML templates for purchase orders, price catalogs, and invoices, among other business constructs. You can select XML or EDI templates, then remove fields you will not use or restrict allowable values within fields to reflect your particular business needs.

Building a Hierarchical Form

There is a simple but useful principle used by many schema designers, including myself:

Objects are equivalent to elements, while properties are equivalent to attributes.

This principle seems to cover everything – at least until you are way into your first serious schema. At some point, you will encounter an object that has a property possessing objects of its own. For example, suppose we want to model a corporate campus. We might begin as follows:

```
<Campus id="A104" buildingCount="10" />
```

Consider the buildings on the campus. These properties will be impossible to model as attributes – each campus can have a different number of buildings   although we do know there will probably be more than one building per campus. That's easy enough to resolve, however; buildings are obviously objects in their own right, so we go ahead and model them as elements:

```
<Campus id="A104" buildingCount="10" >
  <Building … />
  <Building … />
```

XML allows us to repeat elements if we wish, so we have one <Building> element for every building on the campus. The buildingCount attribute of the <Campus> element gives us the number of buildings on this specific campus.

Before we turn to the representation of an individual building, let's turn our attention back to the campus to see if we've missed any properties. What about the address of the campus – should it be modeled as an element or an attribute? It is a property rather than an object, so we might expect that we should use an attribute.

However, an address has a structure of its own that cannot be easily represented as an attribute – one or two lines of street location, a city, a state, and so on. We might therefore argue for making it an element with child elements nested within, to model the individual elements of the address. Although this is simply a practical compromise, there is also a sound theoretical reason for making it an element. You might start out using a single address for the campus (the main mailing address, say) but later you begin to include multiple addresses (the addresses of all the entrances for instance). Therefore, the concept of address or location is not a simple property, but has complex structure of its own. This leads us to amend our basic principle:

> Objects are equivalent to elements, **simple** properties are equivalent to attributes.

But what's the rule for a complex property like an address? At this point, a veteran of several real-world schema design efforts will usually add: "...*and for complex properties, you are on your own!*" There is no rule for complex properties; you must consider the problem and the concept you wish to capture. First consider what sort of processing might be performed. This includes what kind of parser you will be using, and how you will be navigating and using the information in the document. With that consideration in mind, make a pragmatic decision about whether you want to use an element or an attribute.

The approach to schema design that we have discussed above is what I term the **hierarchical form,** as it leads to XML documents that are highly nested, with emphasis on the use of elements rather than attributes.

> *In Chapter 4 of* Designing Distributed Applications *(Wrox Press, ISBN 1-861002-27-0), I use the hierarchical form in XML to represent collections, specialization of objects in a manner similar to inheritance, and even multiple versions of the data format for a single object. These follow from some simple rules. I have found the hierarchical form to be highly versatile.*

Hierarchical form documents can lead to many levels of nested elements, and this can lead to complexity in navigating the document tree and obtaining properties that reside at lower levels. This can be managed to some extent by hiding the details of parsing the XML within a component that represents the business object that the document is intended to express.

For example, a common expression of a Customer object might look like this:

```
<Customer>
  <Person>
   <Name>
     <FirstName>Adam</FirstName>
     <LastName>Smith</LastName>
   </Name>
   <Address>
```

```
        <Street1>1 Wall Street</Street1>
        <City>New York</City>
        <State>New York</State>
      </Address>
    </Person>
    <PurchaseInformation>
    <CreditCard type="Amex">
      <Number>1234567890</Number>
      <Expires>Jan-2002</Expires>
    </CreditCard>
    <PurchaseHistory>
      <Order date="12-Dec-1999">
       <Amount>100.25</Amount>
       <ItemList>
         <Item>
           <SKU>9781861002273</SKU>
           . . .
         </Item>
       </ItemList>
      </Order>
    </PurchaseHistory>
    </PurchaseInformation>
</Customer>
```

The `Item` element is five levels down from the root element. Retrieving details about a particular item purchased involves diving down through a considerable amount of information. The document, moreover, goes to varying depths depending on the element. Code written to navigate the entire tree must always check for child elements before moving on to the next item on any particular level. Still, it is worth the extra processing because hierarchy lets us examine the `Customer` object in increasing detail, peeling away layers to reach the core, simple properties. If we write a business component to represent a `Customer`, we might have code like the following:

```
Order = Customer.PurchaseHistory(0);
Item = Order.Items(2);
Response.Write("The SKU for the third item is " + Item.SKU + ".");
```

This is actually a good deal simpler than writing special-purpose code to access the information through the W3C Document Object Model. The code must still be written, but it is written once in the business object and hidden away from application programmers.

The BizTalk Server SDK includes a code generator for building Visual Basic COM components of this type, given an XDR schema.

BizTalk Framework Canonical Form

Several members of the Microsoft XML team came to the conclusion that a common technique for expressing information in XML would be useful. Such a form would need to be easy to read, and should be able to generate an XML document representing any collection of objects and their properties by following a few simple rules. Since XML can be readily transformed from one form to another, this mechanical representation would serve as a common, or **canonical form** for data.

In contrast to the hierarchical form, the canonical form results in XML which makes heavy use of attributes to express its properties. General-purpose utilities can be written to take information in a known form (such as relational database tables) and automatically generate XML from that. Such utilities could greatly reduce the amount of custom code that would need to be written embodying implicit knowledge of the structure of the objects represented.

> *The method to achieve this is documented in the white paper* Serializing Graphs of Data in XML, *by Adam Bosworth, Andrew Layman, and Michael Rys, and is available on the BizTalk.org site in the Resources section www.biztalk.org/Resources/canonical.asp.*

> *It follows a formal model in which objects, their properties, and the relationships between objects are expressed as a collection of nodes, connected by edges. This collection of connected object nodes and properties forms a mathematical construct called a **graph**. Graph theory is proven to be able to represent all such object collections.*

> *Some efforts in the XML community, notably the Resource Definition Framework (RDF) for expressing meta-data, use the same underlying model. I'll take a more relaxed approach to the canonical form, as my intent is to suggest some useful techniques, not turn you into theoreticians!*

Objects and Properties

To start with, in the canonical form, objects are represented as XML elements. This is straightforward – you need something to represent objects, and objects stand on their own, unlike attributes. Simple properties of objects are represented as attributes of those elements. Attribute names are the names of properties, and their values are the values of the properties.

The top-level element is the name of a package of objects or a message. For example, if we modeled a catalog, the top-level element would be the catalog itself. All the objects in the package are children of the top-level element, with one exception. If one object can only belong to another object, and cannot exist independently of that object, it may be expressed as a child of either the top-level element or the element to which it is related. This commonly occurs in the case of ownership of one object by another, or when the subordinate object is an integral part of the superior object.

> *Practitioners of UML will find this similar to the types of containment supported by that method.*

Consider a team of people:

```
<Team>
  <Person firstname="John" lastname="Doe" age="46" title="leader"/>
  <Person firstname="Sue" lastname="Smith" age="34" title="coach"/>
  <Person firstname="Andrew" lastname="Fredericks" age="24" title="lackey"/>
</Team>
```

This attribute-heavy style might seem a little odd at first, particularly if you are used to writing XML vocabularies with hierarchical structure. Still, it has the attraction of keeping all the properties of the object close to the object itself. If you have an element representing an object, you can get the object's properties by iterating through its elements. That is, you iterate through the Person elements to understand the Team, then iterate through any given Person element's attributes to understand the properties of that Person object. A hierarchical structure will require, in the general case, that you walk the subtree, looking for attributes and nested elements at each step.

Expressing Relationships Between Objects

Objects are frequently bound to one another in relationships, so one goal of the canonical form is to easily express relational data. That goal, by itself, requires that we be able to express one-to-one, one-to-many, and many-to-many relationships. Fortunately, XML 1.0 has the following ID/IDREF/IDREFS data types that make this possible, and which are used extensively in the canonical form.

XML attributes can be typed as **ID** or **IDREF**, among others. Let's see how this works. An attribute typed as an ID takes a unique string value. Another attribute, belonging to another element, is given data type IDREF. Say there is a relationship between the elements supporting each of these attributes. This relationship may be expressed if the IDREF attribute of one element takes the value of the ID attribute of the other element. In other words we have linked the two elements with a cross-reference.

We can illustrate this with an example. Say we have two employees, each represented by a <Person> element. companyNumber is the ID attribute and supervisor is the IDREF attribute of a <Person> element. The two XML declarations that follow declare these companyNumber and supervisor attributes as ID and IDREF respectively (note the dt:type attributes on the declarations):

```
<AttributeType name = "companyNumber" dt:type = "id"/>
<AttributeType name = "supervisor" dt:type = "idref"/>
```

The next two lines of XML are the elements for each employee:

```
<Person companyNumber="A21" supervisor="A1" firstName="Bigge" lastName="Mann"/>
<Person companyNumber="L414" supervisor="A21" firstName="John" lastName="Doe"/>
```

The element for John Doe is related to the element for Bigge Mann, because the supervisor value for John Doe is the same as the companyNumber value for Bigge Mann, and we have declared that values for supervisor reference values for companyNumber. Common sense tells us that John Doe works for Bigge Mann.

There is also an **IDREFS** type, which permits one element to be related to multiple elements. An attribute whose type is IDREFS will have as a value a series of ID values separated by whitespace. For example, let's introduce a supervises attribute, and declare it as IDREFS:

```
<AttributeType name = "supervises" dt:type = "idrefs"/>
```

We now look at the element for another employee, Lucretia Borgia, who supervises four employees:

```
<Person supervises="L414 L512 C31 B18" firstName="Lucretia" lastName="Borgia"/>
```

According to this element, Lucretia Borgia is related to the elements whose IDs are L414, L512, C31, and B18.

This ID/IDREF/IDREFS system works for relationships between different types of elements too. Here is the relationship between a Customer element and a bank Account element, assuming the customer can only have one account:

```
<Customer id="C128a" account="A12"/>
<Account number="A12" holder="C218a"/>
```

119

In this example, the attributes id and number are declared as ID, while account and holder are IDREF attributes. Note that in this example, we've expressed the relationship in both directions (customer to account and account to customer) to make it easy to follow the relationship regardless of what element we are examining.

Of course, in reality customers *can* have more than one account, so we can change our example by replacing account with an IDREFS attribute named accounts:

```
<Customer id="C128a" accounts="A12 B8180 S14"/>
<Account number="A12" holder="C218a"/>
<Account number="B8180" holder="C218a"/>
<Account number="S14" holder="C218a"/>
```

The canonical form gets a bit more complicated in the case of many-to-many relationships. If the relationship has no attributes of its own, we can get away with modeling the relationship with an IDREFS type attribute on each element that participates in the relationship:

```
<Crime designation="robbery-1" suspects="Alias-2 Alias-3"/>
<Crime designation="robbery-2" suspects="Alias-2 Alias-3"/>
<Crime designation="robbery-2" suspects="Alias-2"/>
<Crime designation="assault-1" suspects="Alias-3"/>
<Crime designation="vandalism-1" suspects="Alias-1"/>

<Criminal id="Alias-1" crimes="vandalism-1" />
<Criminal id="Alias-2" crimes="robbery-1 robbery-2 robbery-3" />
<Criminal id="Alias-3" crimes="robbery-1 robbery-2 assault-1" />
```

In our little world of mayhem, the criminal known by Alias-3 participated in three different crimes, and the crime known by robbery-1 is believed to have been the work of the hardened criminals Alias-2 and Alias-3. The canonical form lets us assign properties to relationships by promoting the properties to the status of elements. Each pair of related objects in the many-to-many relationship gets an element. This relationship element has a series of IDREF attributes to identify the related objects, then as many attributes of other types as are needed to express the properties of the relationship. This is less complicated than it sounds; a simple example should make this plain. I like a tidy world, so let's revisit our crime example and introduce some punishment:

```
<Crime designation="robbery-1" suspects="Alias-2 Alias-3"/>
<Crime designation="robbery-2" suspects="Alias-2 Alias-3"/>
<Crime designation="robbery-2" suspects="Alias-2"/>
<Crime designation="assault-1" suspects="Alias-3"/>
<Crime designation="vandalism-1" suspects="Alias-1"/>

<Criminal id="Alias-1"crimes="vandalism-1" />
<Criminal id="Alias-2" crimes="robbery-1 robbery-2 robbery-3" />
<Criminal id="Alias-3" crimes="robbery-1 robbery-2 assault-1" />

<Trial case="J1" defendant="Alias-2" crime="robbery-1" outcome="conviction"/>
<Trial case="J2" defendant="Alias-3" crime="robbery-1" outcome="conviction"/>
. . .
```

We've brought our offenders to justice by introducing Trial elements to represent the relationship of a single criminal to a single crime. There is still a many-to-many relationship between crimes and criminals, but we need to express the outcome of the trial for each part of the relationship. The Trial element has attributes named defendant and crime, which are typed as IDREF attributes. Outcome is an attribute used to express a property of the relationship, in this case the verdict of the trial. As long as we didn't have any properties of the relationships themselves, we could express the overall many-to-many relationship through the use of attributes on the elements modeling the objects in our little world. When we needed to talk about the relationship itself, that is, express properties of the relationship between the objects, we had to add an element to which we could attach an attribute capturing the value of the property.

An Assessment of the Canonical Form

The canonical form has a number of advantages:

❑ It requires no features that do not already exist in W3C Recommendations related to XML

❑ Code to serialize objects according to the canonical form is easy to write as it is completely expressed in some simple rules

❑ It is well-suited to expressing objects from a variety of methods or data forms common to computing

From our examination of relationships, it should be apparent that relational tables could be mapped to the canonical form rather easily. The canonical form is based on the mathematical graph model mentioned in passing above, so any structure that uses graphs or their derivatives can be expressed in the canonical form. Graphs appear more frequently than you might imagine – trees are a specific form of graphs, as are lists, and ordered sequences of processing, such as workflow, can be expressed as graphs as well. The canonical form is well suited to the problem of serializing objects for persistent storage. Objects are commonly modeled using UML, and the canonical form has enough features to express class instances and associations, as well as other features of that method.

There are a few drawbacks to the canonical form, however:

❑ Lines can get very long, since elements can contain long lists of attributes

❑ Some complex properties do not lend themselves to expression as attributes very well

The values of these complex properties (like addresses, as we have discussed) may contain spaces, yet spaces are permitted only in attributes formally typed as IDREFS, not in ID or IDREF attributes. (Untyped attributes, however, may have spaces without causing a parsing error.) If the property you wish to serialize as XML contains spaces, it must be expressed as an element or broken into its constituent parts. The former – expressing the property as an element – breaks with the simple canonical form, while breaking the property into its parts is an awkward representation of the property value, to say the least.

The principle value of the canonical form is that it is well suited to the implementation of XML schema generators that must operate on arbitrary objects, as you can implement such utilities by encoding the formal rules of the canonical form. A secondary use is as an example of one technique for modeling data. Consider when it can be used instead of the hierarchical form – there will be occasions in your practice when it seems more natural to express properties as attributes. Relationships can be modeled relationships effectively whether you use the canonical or hierarchical forms, and even if you totally reject the canonical form, you will have considered an alternative approach to modeling business objects in XML. This can only improve your skills as a data modeler and give you confidence in the schemas you create for use with BizTalk.

BizTalk Editor

Hopefully you are more than ready by this point to dive in and start writing some message specifications. The BizTalk Editor is the tool used to specify how messages may be written.

User Interface

Open up the BizTalk Editor using the shortcut icon present in the Microsoft BizTalk Server 2000 folder.

On launching the Editor, you will see a window similar to that shown below, containing three panes. Note that your panes will be blank until you have opened a specification file (the specification shown in the screenshot is `SiteServiceDescription.xml`).

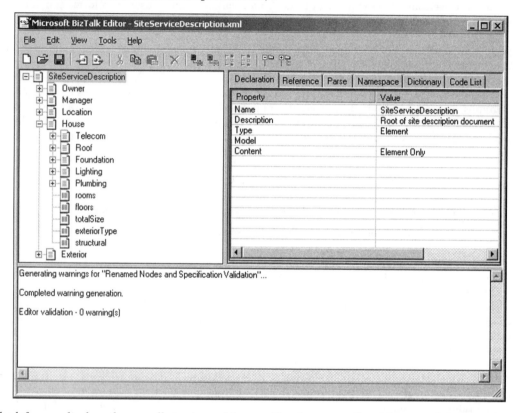

The left pane displays the overall structure of the specification as a collapsible tree, while the right-hand pane consists of six tabs for specifying various parameters of the specification. Within the right pane, you can see the names of the various options for the selected node of the specification tree in the left-most column, while the right-hand column contains a variety of controls to specify the values of the parameters named on the left. In some cases you will enter a value directly, in others, you will select a value from a drop-down list box   the nature of the control used to specify a value becomes apparent when you click in the cell.

Underneath these two panes is another pane, for recording the status of various tests, much as an IDE for a programming language informs you of warnings and errors found during compilation.

To fully understand how to build a message specification we will need to understand the basic concepts BizTalk uses to refer to specifications. You will find in the next section that we have encountered many of these concepts before. BizTalk has drawn common concepts from related areas; areas that provide the sort of data we might commonly want to exchange.

A Quick Recap...

Let's pull everything together and recap the concepts we've learned so far. Central to understanding BizTalk Server is understanding the relationship between **messages** (or business documents) and **specifications**. A message is generally a single instance of a document that is exchanged between applications. A specification, on the other hand, describes the permissible form of an entire class of messages. It names all the component parts and their cardinality, and specifies the type and range of values of those parts.

Specifications

Specifications are not simply XDR schemas. As we saw when we were discussing the types of message format BizTalk Server can process, XML schemas are insufficient to describe flatfile formats completely. BizTalk Server is certainly dominated by XML, but it is unlikely to ever abandon flatfiles. Consequently, specifications remain a superset of XML schemas.

Schemas

Schemas are insufficient to completely describe flatfile BizTalk messages, but they remain a very powerful tool. BizTalk may accommodate flatfiles, but it is designed for XML – it certainly makes sense to leverage the tools XML provides. In fact, all messages pass through BizTalk Server in XML form, even when they begin and end as a flatfile format. This will become apparent in the next chapter when we consider how BizTalk Server maps a message written to one specification to the form dictated by another specification. An intervening XML format is used so that the core of BizTalk Server can use XML tools.

Records and Fields

Given the central part XML schemas play in BizTalk Server messages, you might expect the Editor to use more XML terminology. You might expect to learn and use elements and attributes. However, the BizTalk team has made an effort to mask implementation details from users, and rather than make everyone learn XML before they can become productive in using BizTalk Server, Microsoft has chosen to use generic terms to describe the component parts of specifications. In discussing the canonical and hierarchical forms we repeatedly referred to relational database sources, which was natural because they happen to be a source that commonly underlies the exchange of information. Such tables contain records, which in turn contain fields, and it is this structure that Microsoft has adopted for message specifications.

A BizTalk message **record** is a named collection of fields. A **field** is an item of information possessing a unique name, data type, and constraints. A record may also contain other records. As a result, we can represent structure to any arbitrary level of nesting. This is extremely difficult to do with relational databases.

Records and fields are represented in the Editor's left-hand pane by document icons. Records have horizontal green lines representing text rows, while fields have vertical teal lines suggesting columns (another reference to the relational world). In the illustration opposite, House is a record, while rooms is a field within it. House also nests some child records, such as Telecom and Roof.

When dealing with XML format messages, records translate directly into XML elements. It might be easy to assume that fields are always attributes, but this is not the case. As we saw in our discussion of the canonical and hierarchical forms, you sometimes need to use elements to express complex fields. Specification authors can indicate which they want to use.

Working with Specifications

Now we will get down to the specifics of working with BizTalk specifications. In this section, we'll learn how to work with XML-based message specifications. Actually, we will cover all of the core tasks common to the three message types (XML, delimited, and positional) so even if you are eager to get started on a flatfile format, read this section, as you will need it to specify the core elements of any message specification. Flatfile formats add features, but they do not take away anything that you will learn here.

Saving and Retrieving Specifications

BizTalk Editor uses two distinct areas to store message specification files:

- ❑ A local or networked hard disk
- ❑ WebDAV

WebDAV stands for Web Distributed Authoring and Versioning. It is an attempt, broadly speaking, to make the Web a read-write medium. It is a set of extensions to the HTTP protocol, which allows users to remotely edit and manage collaborative files on remote web servers. Importantly, a WebDAV repository features documents with overwrite protection.

If you are working locally or wish to work with a file to which you have access through normal networked access, you may use the File | Open menu item to invoke a standard file dialog. Usually, however, you will not have access to the folder where the BizTalk Server Repository is found unless you are physically working on the server – that folder and its subfolders should be secured to prevent tampering. If you are not physically working on the server access should be through WebDAV.

To open an existing specification from the repository through WebDAV, use the File | Retrieve from WebDAV... menu item. Select the server holding the repository where the desired specification is found, then select the message specification file itself and click OK. You may also enter the URL for the server, for instance http://MyBTServer/, then select the specification file.

When using WebDAV with a BizTalk Server installation, the retrieval dialog in BizTalk Editor will point directly at the message specification folder within the repository. You may establish subfolders to organize your specifications, but there is no need to navigate to the specifications folder from the root of the repository.

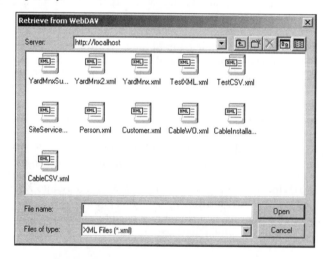

Creating New Specifications

You're just getting started, however, so you are probably more interested in creating new specifications. There are several ways to go about this. You can, of course, build your own from scratch. We'll do three of those later in the chapter. There are also a couple of short-cuts that should be particularly interesting to XML novices. Here are the options for creating new specifications:

- ❑ Write your own from scratch
- ❑ Use a standard
- ❑ Work from some other existing specification
- ❑ Import an instance of an XML document

BizTalk Server ships with specifications for the X12 and UN/EDIFACT EDI messages. There are specifications for the 2040, 3010, 3060, and 4010 X12 releases. UN/EDIFACT is represented through the D93A, D95A, D95B, D97B, D98A, and D98B folders. These are all flatfile format specifications.

The value in using these comes when you need to represent some information covered by a standard, but you are not using the standard itself. For example, nearly all businesses use invoices, so it is highly likely that you will need to represent an invoice. If you are not presently using EDI, there is no pressing need to embrace one of the standards as is – you may have data fields unique to your business that you want to include. At the same time, the concept of an invoice has been thoroughly covered and reviewed by experts, so you can peruse the X12 and UN/EDIFACT takes on invoices and modify an existing one. Not only does modifying a specification take less time then writing one from the beginning, but it makes it less likely that you will miss something important, so you benefit from someone else's design work.

BizTalk has not forgotten XML, however – the product also ships with a set of pure XML specifications covering much the same ground as the EDI specifications. All the common, low level constructs a business might use are there: invoices, purchase orders, purchase order acknowledgements, inventory advice, and many more.

To design a new message specification based on an **existing specification**, select the File | New... menu item. You will be presented with a New Document Specification dialog box offering you a choice of Blank Specification, EDIFACT, X12, and XML. Double-clicking on the Blank Specification icon, or selecting it and clicking OK returns you to the Editor with a new template containing a record named Blank Specification. You can proceed from there using procedures we will discuss shortly. Choosing one of the other options leads you to folders containing their message specifications. When you select a particular specification file, you are returned to the Editor with the specification loaded. At that point, you are ready to modify the specification and save it under a name of your own choosing.

There will be times when you need to work not from an existing specification, but from an instance document or some formal specification that did not come with BizTalk, such as a DTD. You may have legacy flatfile formats, or a well-formed XML message from a pilot project. You may simply find it easier to think in terms of sample messages and work back to a specification.

If you would rather start with an **instance document** rather than a specification, you can click on the Tools | Import ... menu item. This gives you a dialog box titled Select Import Module that asks you to choose between a Well Formed XML Instance, Document Type Definition, and XDR Schema. Each of the choices leads to a file selection dialog initialized to the appropriate file extension. When you pick a document, BizTalk Editor tries to reverse engineer a message specification using the document instance, DTD, or schema as an example, which makes for an excellent starting point.

If a well-formed document is truly representative of the type of message you want to exchange, your work as a designer will be limited to specifying the information that does not appear in the example. Obviously, this would include optional records or fields not found in the example. More subtle is the matter of cardinality – how often something can appear. This may not be obvious to BizTalk Editor from the example. Data types, also, are very difficult to infer from an instance document and may be unreliable. You should comb through the generated specification and check it carefully against your knowledge of the business process the message is trying to represent.

Even better than having an instance of an XML document is having an actual XDR schema or DTD. With this in hand you need not worry about cardinality being correct after an import, and all constraints are explicitly stated, too. If your organization is focused on XML – perhaps from pilot projects begun before BizTalk or because of a dedication to formal methods – you will need to go from a schema to a message specification, and this is readily done in the Editor. BizTalk Server expects to find a message specification, not a schema, for every message it processes regardless of whether it is based on XML or a flatfile format.

Adding Records and Fields to a Specification

The real work begins once you have created a new message specification. You need to create the records (think rows) and fields (think properties or columns) that define your message, then specify constraints that govern their appearance and permissible values. You can use the Edit | New Record and Edit | New Field menu items to create records and fields that are immediate children of the currently selected record. The toolbar provides icon-based alternatives. The green icon with a single child is the equivalent of Edit | New Record, while the blue icon next to it provides the same service as Edit | New Field. If you wish to create a new record or field at the same level as the currently selected record or field, you can click on the insert record or insert field icons on the toolbar or select Edit | Insert Record or Edit | Insert Field.

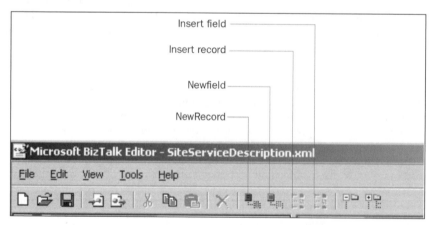

Remember, only records can act as containers. You cannot use Edit | New Record *or* Edit | New Field *when a field is selected. Similarly, since a message can have only one record at the top-most level,* Insert Record *and* Insert Field *are disabled when the document's root is selected.*

When a new record or field is created, it is given a default name. This name is selected for editing in the left-hand pane. You may also change the name from the Declaration tab in the right-hand pane. This tab is discussed in the next section.

You can manipulate the specification in other ways from the left-hand pane:

- You can copy records and their children, or fields, by selecting a record or field and using the Edit | Copy command.
- You can move a record (and its subtree) or a field by cutting and pasting, or clicking and dragging.
- You can delete records and fields, again using menu commands from either the main Edit menu or the context menu.
- You can rename a record or field. Select the item to be renamed, select the Name property of the Declaration tab, and start typing.

You will find it useful to create a dummy specification and practice manipulating it through actions taken in the tree view pane.

An interesting and underused technique is reusing a record or field in several places – once you have created an item and specified it, you can reuse it by creating a new item of the same type (record or field) and typing the existing name for the name of the new item. BizTalk Editor will recognize that this is an existing item and reflect the previously specified properties, even down to child records and fields for a record.

Using Tabs to Configure Records and Fields

You will need to specify constraints once you have your records and fields, and this is done through the tabs in the right-hand pane. Specifications for XML format messages are completely defined in the Declaration, Namespace, and Reference tabs. Flatfile format message specifications require that additional information is provided in some of the remaining tabs as well. Since whichever message specification you build you will need to enter information into the Declaration, Namespace, and Reference tabs, we will concentrate on just these three for now. Later, when we build some sample flatfile format specifications, we'll cover the remaining tabs in the Editor's right-hand pane.

The Declaration Tab

We saw the Declaration tab when we took our first look at the Editor's user interface. The illustration below shows the properties for the Owner record. Note that the properties you will see, and be able to specify, will depend on whether you are dealing with the root record, a record at a lower level, or a field. You can even create and specify custom properties.

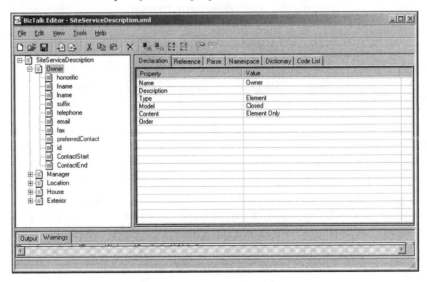

127

Here are the properties you can specify for **records** in a BizTalk document specification:

Property	Value
Name	Name of the record (or specification for the root element)
Description	Text describing the nature and purpose of the record
Type	Type of record (restricted to element for records)
Model	The degree of conformance between a document and the specification. Options: ❏ Open – a document may add fields and records to this record, but any specified fields and records in the specification must be conformed to in the document ❏ Closed – record content must match the specification exactly
Content	Describes what the record may contain. Options: ❏ Element Only – may contain only XML elements (records or element-type fields) ❏ Empty – may contain only attribute-type fields ❏ Text Only – may contain only text (no records or fields)
Order	Describes how child records and fields appear. Options: ❏ Many – zero or more of the children may appear, in any order ❏ One – one and only one of the children may appear (a choice) ❏ Sequence – each child must appear, and in the order listed

Matters are more complicated for fields. Records convey structure; fields convey detailed properties. Here are the properties you can specify for **fields** in the Declaration tab:

Property	Value
Name	Name of the field
Description	Text describing the purpose of the field
Type	Field type (Element or Attribute) – note warnings below
Data Type	A valid data type (see below)
Data Type Values	Applies to enumeration type fields; enter the enumerated values, separated by spaces
Min Length	The minimum number of characters a field value can use (valid only with fields of type String, Number, Binary(base64), and Binary(hex))
Max Length	The maximum number of characters the field can use (valid only with fields of type String, Number, Binary(base64), and Binary(hex))
Default Value	Default value provided for the field if the document does not explicitly contain this field (attribute-type fields only)

Warning! You should be aware of the hidden perils associated with **Type**:

❏ First, if you change from **Element** to **Attribute** or vice versa, BizTalk Editor will warn you that you may **lose information**. This is because the schema syntax for each type differs and you will lose type-specific property values in a switch.

❏ Second, if you are dealing with a specification based on the X12 EDI standard, some fields may have **codes** associated with them. Fields that use codes must be typed as attributes.

You should also note that element-type fields also have **Model** and **Content** properties, similar to those for records.

One of the great advantages of XML-based schemas over DTDs is the wider range of data types you can use for fields. Here are the data types supported for **fields** in message specifications:

Data type	Meaning and lexical form
Character	single character string
String	text string
Number	numeric type consisting of some number of digits and optional leading sign, fractional digits, and an exponent; for instance 16, 3.14159, -273.15, 6.02E23 (English punctuation marks are used)
Integer (int)	integer numeric with an optional leading sign (for example 4, -1)
Float	A number with no limit on the number of digits; may have a leading sign, exponent, or fractional digits
Fixed point (14.4)	A number type with the following additional constraints: no more than 14 digits to the left of the decimal point, and no more than four digits to the right (for example 3.1415, 24.1234, 8.2)
Boolean	logical True/False (the keywords **True** or **False**, or -1 or 0, respectively)
Date	ISO 8601 format date with no time or time zone information (like 2000-12-31)
Date Time	ISO 8601 subset date with optional time information and fractional seconds down to nanoseconds (for example 2000-12-31T18:30:10.2)
Date Time.tz	A Date Time type with the addition of optional time zone information, for example, 2000-12-31T18:00:00-5:00 (same example as for **Date Time**, but GMT -5 hours is the specified time zone)
Time	ISO 8601 subset time with no date information, like 18:00:12.4
Time.tz	A time type with the addition of optional time zone information (for example 18:00:12.4-05:00)
Byte (i1)	Single byte integer with optional leading sign
Word (i2)	Two byte integer with optional leading sign
Integer (i4)	Four byte integer with optional leading sign

Table continued on following page

129

Data type	Meaning and lexical form
Double Integer (i8)	Eight byte integer with optional leading sign
Unsigned Byte (ui1)	Unsigned single byte integer
Unsigned Word (ui2)	Unsigned two byte integer
Unsigned Integer (ui4)	Unsigned four byte integer
Double Unsigned Integer (ui8)	Unsigned eight byte integer
Real (r4)	Four byte floating point type from the range $\pm 1.17549435\text{E-}38$ to $\pm 3.40282347\text{E}38$, inclusive (for example 2.99E8)
Double Real (r8)	Eight byte floating point type in the range $\pm 2.2250738585072014\text{E-}308$ to $\pm 1.7976931348623157\text{E}308$, inclusive
Universal Unique Identifier (uuid)	Universally unique ID; a series of hexadecimal numbers representing octets with optional embedded hyphens (for example 214244AE-C207-11DA-3356-001924387956)
Uniform Resource Identifier (uri)	Internet uniform resource identifier (unique name)
Binary (base64)	Binary encoded as text (in other words, ASCII armored); used to transmit binary information as a text stream
Binary (hex)	Hexadecimal digits representing octets, such as 0x0FFAA
ID	XML ID type attribute
IDREF	XML ID reference type attribute
IDREFS	XML IDREFS (multiple ID references) type attribute
Enumeration	a series of enumerated names, like: apples oranges pears

You may also specify custom properties for application-specific purposes. You might use these when writing a custom parser to contain information you wish the parser to have when processing a message. To add a custom property, right-click the first blank cell in the Property column and select Add from the context menu. You then type a name for the custom property and press Enter. While BizTalk Editor permits you to duplicate names when naming two or more custom properties, you should use unique names for clarity.

Reference Tab

The Declaration tab lets you create a new record or property and specify a minimal set of constraints. Message specifications allow you to be more specific, and the Reference tab is where you do this. As with the Declaration tab, the properties you can set differ for root-level records, child records, and fields. The differences between root and child records are somewhat greater in the Reference tab, however. Similarly, the nature of the properties you can specify changes between element-type fields and attribute-type fields because XML treats the two types differently. In the illustration opposite, we see the Reference tab for the Owner record. The contents of the tab indicate that this record must appear exactly once.

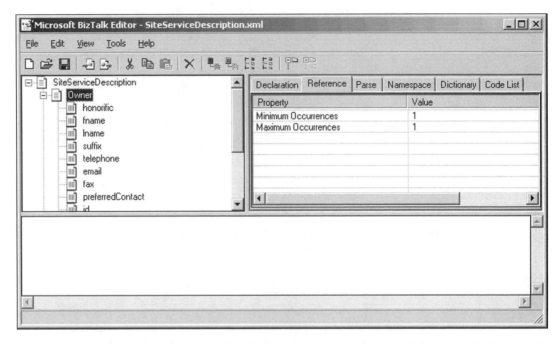

Here are the properties for **root-level records** that you can specify in the Reference tab. You should note that not all properties are available for all standards:

Property	Value
Specification Name	Name of the specification
Standard	Industry standard used to create the specification (XML, X12, EDIFACT, or CUSTOM)
Standards Version	Version number of the specification
Document Type	Document type of the specification (the root-level record name)
Version	Version number of the standard used to create the document (for instance 1.0 for XML)
Default Record Delimiter	The character used to delimit records. BizTalk allows this to differ from record to record (does not apply to EDI specifications)
Default Field Delimiter	Character used to delimit fields within this record (does not apply to EDI specifications)
Default Subfield Delimiter	Character used to delimit subfields (does not apply to EDI)
Default Escape Character	Character used to indicate that the following character is to be used literally and not read as a delimiter (does not apply to EDI)
Code Page	Indicates the character code page used to write the document

Table continued on following page

Property	Value
Receipt	Indicates whether a recipient acknowledgement is desired. Options: ❏ Yes – you desire a receipt indicating that the message has arrived ❏ No – you desire a functional receipt that includes system information gathered after validity checks are performed on the message
Envelope	Indicates whether this specification is an envelope or not (Yes or No); envelope specifications may be used to contain multiple messages (see Chapter 10 on Routing)
Target Namespace	Namespace of the body of the document (used with documents that conform to the BizTalk Framework)

Child records have just two configurable properties, associated with cardinality:

Property	Value
Minimum Occurrences	The minimum number of times this record can appear in the selected position in the document (0 or 1)
Maximum Occurrences	The maximum number of times this record can appear at this position in the document (1 or *, denoting many)

Note that **Minimum Occurrences** and **Maximum Occurrences** may vary for the same record at different places in the document. That is, if some element Stuff is a child of both MyStuff and YourStuff elements, its cardinality can be different when it appears under MyStuff from when it appears under YourStuff. The tab also shows **Start Position** and **End Position** properties, but these are only used with fields.

Fields use the following properties:

Property	Value
Required	Yes if the field is required, No otherwise
Start Position	The starting position of the field within a positional record
End Position	The ending position of the field within a positional record

The Namespace Tab

This tab allows you to record the XML namespaces you use within your specification. The three namespaces used by BizTalk appear automatically, as shown in the screenshot opposite. If you right-click and select **Add** from the context menu, a new entry is added. You can specify a prefix and fill in the URN (Uniform Resource Name) that identifies the namespace, then use the prefix in the document to avoid conflicts between identically named records or fields from different namespaces. This is used in conjunction with specifications written using the XML standard.

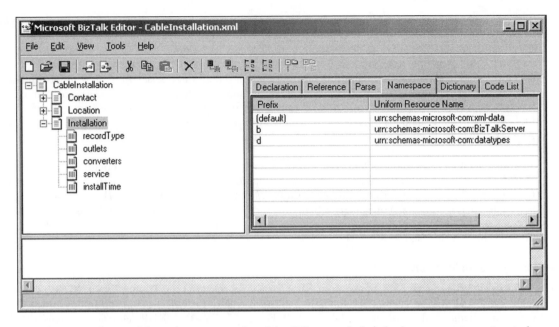

Now that we understand how the various tabs of the Editor work, let's look at some supporting tasks you can perform with the Editor. Specifically, let's see how we can interoperate with standard, non-proprietary specifications in a pure XML environment.

Validating and Exporting Specifications

The only tasks remaining before we roll up our sleeves and go to work on a practical example are those of checking our work and interoperating with the pure XML world. Specifically, we need to perform the following tasks:

❑ Validate the specification

❑ Validate a document instance against a specification

❑ Create an XML instance document conforming to the specification

❑ Export message specifications as XDR schemas with their extensions

Validation

The first thing to do is validate the specification against the syntax of BizTalk specifications itself using the Tools | Validate Specification menu item or the F5 key. This causes Editor to check the specification for completeness, internal consistency, and validity. Any errors in the specification will be listed in the result pane at the bottom of the application window.

> **Editor only refers to "warnings". Developers accustomed to compiled language IDEs should not think of these as just warnings, but as errors, since they indicate a specification that cannot be used.**

You can validate an instance of a message against a specification from the Tools menu with the Validate Instance menu item. Why validate a single instance? Sometimes it is easier to work up a sample message based on an intuitive understanding of the business problem you are trying to model, and validating such a sample against a newly created specification is a good check on your formal specification. If the message conveys the information you intend but doesn't validate, you have made an error in the specification. Conversely, when you are writing code to generate messages, you can use this feature periodically to test the correctness of your application. When you select the Tools | Validate Instance item, a file dialog is presented allowing you to select the instance document you wish to check. Any errors will be listed in the results pane as warnings.

You may want to work in the other direction. In other words, you may define a document specification then decide to view a sample message instance that conforms to that specification to see if it is what you had in mind. This is done with the Tools | Create XML Instance… menu item. When you select this item, a file dialog appears. You specify a filename and location, then click OK. At that time the Editor will generate a sample document using placeholders for the field values and save it using the file information you supplied.

Exporting a Specification

You can export a message specification in XDR format by selecting the Tools | Export XDR Schema menu item. You will be given a file dialog box allowing you to provide a name and folder for the exported schema, and upon clicking OK, BizTalk Editor generates the XDR schema and saves it to disk.

Now you have all the tools you need to build message specifications for use with BizTalk Server. Let's put this to use by creating the specifications we need to for the example schedule we produced in the last chapter. This will give you practical experience with both XML and flatfile message formats.

Specification for the Wrox Site Managers Sample

We started to build a sample application in the last chapter for the fictional Wrox Site Managers. The sample, like all BizTalk applications, relied heavily on the exchange of messages. Defining the specifications that describe those messages is the first step to configuring BizTalk for those exchanges.

Recall that we started by receiving a Site Service Description from site managers in the field. Based on some conditional logic, we may need to re-send that message to the Cable TV Installer and a Yard Care Vendor. But those outsourcing vendors don't really care about every detail of the residence, and the homeowner certainly doesn't want every detail going to every vendor.

We mentioned that BizTalk Messaging Services would be responsible for performing a transformation *en route* that would extract the relevant details. The need for this mapping between message formats implies that the two vendors each utilize different document formats.

Now, from the implementation of the script component in the last chapter, we know the Site Service Description uses the XML standard. The component used an XPath retrieval, and that is an XML technology. Since the purpose of the samples is to illustrate the use of BizTalk's various features, let's keep things interesting and have the two vendors using non-XML flatfile formats. In fact, we'll let the Cable TV Installer use a delimited format, and the Yard Care Vendor use a positional format. Those two specifications require that we learn a few more things about the BizTalk Editor, however, so let's start with the XML specification for the Site Service Description.

Site Service Description: A Sample Specification

The first task Wrox Site Managers faces is describing a residential site. When you sign up for their service, a representative is sent to your home to survey the site. Equipped with a laptop or PocketPC, the site manager records the details of your home and yard using a Visual Basic application. The message goes into an MSMQ queue for transmission. If the representative is within range of a wireless provider, an XML message is sent to the Wrox Site Managers' server immediately, and if not, the message is queued up for transmission when he is within range.

Since this is a new company free of legacy applications and formats, we'll design an XML message specification to accomplish this task. The structure of the document is depicted below – each box represents a record. Stacked boxes represent records that may appear multiple times. There are quite a few fields in the specification, so for simplicity they have not been included in the diagram. Don't worry about this missing information at the moment; what is important here is to gain a sense of the structure of the message and what it may contain.

Complete source code, including message specifications, for all samples in this book may be downloaded from www.wrox.com.

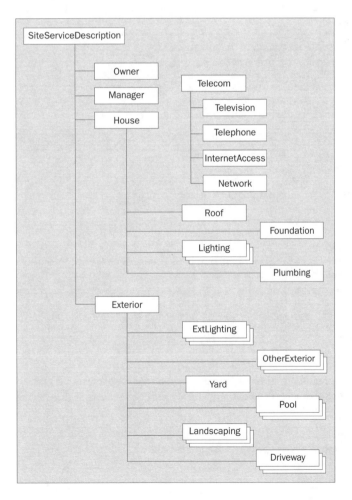

A sample document written to this specification should make this somewhat clearer, as well as showing the available fields. In the example below (`siteservicesample.xml` in the download), a home owned by Lucretia Borgia is under the management of Jacques Sprat of Wrox Site Managers. It is an elaborate home with many fixtures that need to be serviced. This is an example of the kind of document that will be created by field agents using a utility application, then transmitted to BizTalk Server at the home office.

```xml
<SiteServiceDescription>
    <Owner honorific="Dr." fname="Lucretia" lname="Borgia"
           telephone="610-555-1221" id="lborgiaII" preferredContact="phone"
           fax="610-555-0011" email="lborgia@poisons.org" >
        <ContactStart>12:00:00</ContactStart>
        <ContactEnd>23:00:00</ContactEnd>
    </Owner>
    <Manager honorific="Mr." fname="Jacques" lname="Sprat" suffix="Jr."
             telephone="610-555-1212" id="jsprat" preferredContact="email"
             fax="610-555-0001" email="jsprat@wroxmgrs.com" >
        <ContactStart>08:00:00</ContactStart>
        <ContactEnd>17:00:00</ContactEnd>
        <ManagementCompany>Wrox Site Managers</ManagementCompany>
    </Manager>
    <Location>
        <Street1>123 Chestnut Ave</Street1>
        <Street2>Division 6</Street2>
        <City>Philadelphia</City>
        <PoliticalRegion>PA</PoliticalRegion>
        <PostalCode>19100</PostalCode>
        <Directions>First house on left</Directions>
    </Location>
    <House rooms="14" floors="2" totalSize="20000" exteriorType="stone"
           structural="other">
        <Telecom>
            <Television connections="4" setTops="4" type="cable"
                        servicePackage="premium" />
            <Telephone jacks="4" lines="2"/>
            <InternetAccess type="DSL" datarate="1000" provider="GoFast"/>
            <Network cableType="Cat5UTP" hubCount="1" jacks="4" datarate="100"/>
        </Telecom>
        <Roof pitch="1" type="shingle" size="1000"/>
        <Foundation sump="1"/>
        <Lighting type="halogen" power="200" room="utility" />
        <Lighting type="track" power="60" room="library" />
        <Lighting type="highhat" power="60" room="living" />
        <Plumbing type="copper" />
    </House>
    <Exterior>
        <ExtLighting type="post" power="60"/>
        <OtherExterior type="gazebo" size="100"/>
        <OtherExterior type="shed" size="200"/>
        <Yard size="10000" grassType="rye"/>
        <Pool type="inground" size="80" cleaning="megachlorine"/>
        <Landscaping type="garden"/>
        <Driveway type="gravel" length="200" />
    </Exterior>
</SiteServiceDescription>
```

The Owner and Manager records are strongly influenced by the canonical form, with many fields consisting of XML attributes on the element representing the record. The Location record is a notable exception. We cannot continue to use the canonical form here as the street address is a complex field that will almost always include spaces, and these are not generally permitted in an attribute value. This is where flexibility is necessary; rigid adherence to a theoretical form would frustrate us.

Some records in this message require immediate action. For example, the Television record denotes a request for a connection to a commercial cable television service, and the Pool record (under the Exterior record) refers to an existing swimming pool that requires periodic maintenance. Wrox Site Managers does not provide these services, so instead, it forwards service requests to its affiliated suppliers.

Other records describe items that require neither periodic maintenance nor installation, but might need fixing in the future – the Roof, Lighting, and ExtLighting records are examples of this category. When the message arrives at the Wrox Site Managers communications server, an application on the server will examine the message, and items to be noted for possible future service will be recorded in a database. If a service call comes in later, the background information can be sent to the contractor sent out to fix the problem. That way, a homeowner can tell the site manager, "My roof has a leak", and the roofer can be informed of the particulars of the roof. Thus, after the initial site survey, the homeowner need never repeat herself.

You can determine the cardinality of the various records and fields from the diagram above. Remember that cardinality describes how often something may appear. Most data types should be obvious from the example, with a few exceptions. The honorific attribute of Owner and Manager is an enumeration, as are the preferrredContact, exteriorType, structuralType, and type attributes for the InternetAccess, Television, Lighting, ExtLighting, OtherExterior, Pool, Landscaping, and Driveway records. The ContactStart and ContactEnd elements are typed as Time.

Now let's open BizTalk Editor and begin to create this message specification starting from scratch:

1. Create a new XML document specification

2. Rename the root record as SiteServiceDescription

3. Select the root record, and create a new record through the menu or the toolbar

4. Rename this record Owner

5. Continue and create the structure of records depicted in the diagram in a similar way

6. Using the table overleaf, create the fields in the sample message

Note that all of the fields are also listed in the table below. Unless otherwise noted, all fields are attributes of data type string. You can check your work by referring to the specification file in the download (SiteServiceDescription.xml). Remember, any node that has child nodes must be a record and any leaf node (in other words, a node with no children) is a field. Most of the fields are attributes, but some, like Street1, Street2, ContactStart, and ContactEnd are elements. The street address fields are elements, which allows us to include whitespace within them.

Record	Fields
Owner	honorific, fname, lname, suffix, telephone, email, fax, preferredContact (enumeration – phone, email, fax), id, ContactStart (time), ContactEnd (time)
Manager	honorific, fname, lname, suffix, telephone, email, fax, preferredContact (enumeration – phone, email, fax), id, ContactStart (time), ContactEnd (time), ManagementCompany
Location	Street1 (element), Street2 (element), City (element), PoliticalRegion (element), PostalCode (element), Directions (element)
House	rooms (number), floors (number), totalSize (number), exteriorType (enumeration – siding, shingle, frame, stone, brick, other), structural (enumeration – wood, steel, stone, brick, other)
Telecom	(no fields)
Television	connections (number), setTops (number), type (enumeration – cable, satellite, antenna), servicePackage
Telephone	lines (number), jacks (number)
InternetAccess	type (enumeration – cable, DSL, wireless, satellite, other), datarate (number), provider
Network	cableType, hubCount (number), jacks (number), datarate (number)
Roof	type, size (number), pitch (Boolean)
Foundation	sump (Boolean)
Lighting	type, room, power (number)
Plumbing	type
Exterior	(no fields)
ExtLighting	type, power (number)
OtherExterior	type (enumeration – garage, patio, porch, deck, shed, gazebo, carport, other), size (number)
Yard	size (number), grassType
Pool	type (enumeration – aboveground, inground), size (number), cleaning
Landscaping	type
Driveway	type (enumeration – paved, dirt, gravel, other), length (number)

Next we should validate the specification, and if you have downloaded the sample code for this chapter, we should check the specification against the file `siteservicesample.xml`:

7. Use the Tools | Validate Specification menu item (or press *F5*) to validate your specification

8. Use Tools | Validate Instance... to check the specification against `siteservicesample.xml`

Ordinarily it is the instance document you are checking, but in this case you are using a known good document to check your specification. When you are finished, leave the Editor for a moment, and:

9. Create a folder named Wrox under the BizTalkServerRepository\DocSpecs folder

While BizTalk does not force you to use this repository it is a good idea to do so. BizTalk Editor saves specifications with the extension .xml, so keeping all your specifications in the repository will help you distinguish them from data documents. This folder is immediately under the folder in which you installed BizTalk Server. Now, returning to the Editor:

10. Select the File | Store to WebDAV... menu item

The Wrox folder will appear alongside the default Microsoft folder. Select that folder and save your specification as SiteServiceDescription.xml. You have now fully specified the Site Service Description document for the sample system.

Positional and Delimited Specifications

It is all well and good to specify a new message format in XML, but part of what motivates Wrox Site Managers to use BizTalk is the multitude of message formats their vendors require – some of these are flatfile formats. This is convenient, as it is now time to consider how to produce specifications for such messages in the BizTalk Editor.

Referring to the schedule in the last chapter, you'll remember that we will be sending site service messages to the cable vendor and the yard care service. A translation mechanism we'll discuss in the next chapter will convert a relevant subset of the information in the message into flat file format messages, one for each partner. We need to specify those message formats.

You specify a flatfile format by first filling out the information on the Declaration and Reference tabs as before. The delimiter information on the Declaration Tab for the root record, and the start and end position properties on the Reference tab (which we ignored for XML messages) now become important, as we shall see in the examples to come. For flatfiles, we also have to provide information for the Parse tab.

The Parse Tab

The next tab you need to worry about is the Parse tab. This tab lets you specify delimiter information, as well as instructions that will control how messages governed by this specification are parsed. The contents of this tab are depicted in the screenshot overleaf:

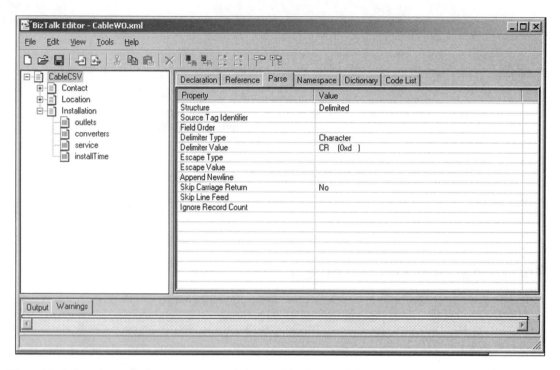

The table below contains the properties and their values for **records** in a flatfile format message. After we have seen which properties we can set, we will look at which ones we need to specify in greater depth. Note that any of these properties can be cleared, once set, by right-clicking on the property value and selecting Clear Property from the context menu.

Property	Value
Structure	Denotes the format of the message. Options are : Delimited or Positional (Delimited only for the root record). If you will be using a mix of delimited and positional structures (as in the Yard Care sample), choose Delimited.
Source Tag Identifier	Optional name identifying the record (if used, this name must appear at the start of the record in the document)
Source Tag Position	Number indicating the starting position of the source tag (positional type only)
Field Order	One of the following options for the ordering of fields (delimited documents only): ❑ Prefix: delimiter appears before field ❑ Infix: delimiter appears between fields (used by EDI) ❑ Postfix: delimiter appears following fields ❑ (Blank): field order is unknown

Property	Value
Delimiter Type	One of the following options to denote the type of delimiter (applies only to delimited files):
	❑ **Default Record Delimiter**: delimiter type of previous record is continued
	❑ **Default Field Delimiter**: delimiter type of previous field is continued
	❑ **Default Subfield Delimiter**: delimiter type of previous subfield is continued
	❑ **Character**: a character is specified for use as the delimiter
Delimiter Value	A character value used as the delimiter within the record; set only if Delimiter Type is Character (delimited files only)
Escape Type	One of the following values (delimited documents only):
	❑ **Character**: escapes the character that would otherwise be read as a delimiter
	❑ **Default Escape Character**: record inherits escape character from parent
Escape Value	The character value used to escape characters that would otherwise be read as delimiters (delimited files with a Character escape type only)
Append New Line	Yes if the next record begins on a new line, No if the next record continues on the current line
Skip Carriage Return	Yes if the carriage return character is to be skipped following a delimiter, No otherwise
Skip Line Feed	Yes if the line feed character is to be skipped following a delimiter, No otherwise
Ignore Record Count	Yes if carriage return and line feed characters are to be skipped when counting characters, No otherwise

The Structure property of the root record is fundamental and requires little design thought on our part. We will generally prefer XML as the structure, because of the flexibility it affords and the tools we already possess. BizTalk applications will use a flatfile form chiefly when an existing application or trading partner forces its use. Here, too, little thought is required on our part, as the form – delimited or positional – is usually determined for us. Delimited forms tend to be easier to read, but custom parsing code is simpler to write for fixed positional formats. We generally have no preference, though, because BizTalk is going to take care of the parsing for us as soon as we can provide a message specification.

The Type and Value of the Delimiter is a more difficult choice   we are not restricted to a single delimiter for everything. A common choice is to pick a carriage return line feed combination for the top-level record so that subsequent records appear on lines of their own. The comma character is a common choice for the field delimiter within a record (for separating fields), but is of course a bad choice when you expect to have commas within the data fields.

The **Escape Character** allows us to deal with situations where a delimiter character is found within a field. If, say, a comma is the delimiter and we occasionally expect a comma within a field, we can precede it with the escape character to tell the parser to ignore the character immediately following the escape character.

To refresh your memory, a positional format message consists of fixed position records that may or may not be delimited by a record terminator: Therefore, the Source Tag Identifier and Source Tag Position properties seem wholly unnecessary in these flatfile formats. However, as we shall see in the next chapter, BizTalk Server's parsing components use these for an intermediate XML format when mapping one file format to another. The Editor will usually take care of these for us, but it is a good practice to check that the identifier reflects the record name when changing this manually.

The properties for **fields** in a flatfile format message are as follows:

Property	Value
Custom Data Type	Set to indicate a custom data type for the field (EDI codes in brackets): ❑ String (AN): alphanumeric ❑ Binary Hexadecimal (B): binary fields ❑ Date (CY): four digit date field ❑ Number (D0 through D4): numeric, where the digit in the code indicates the number of places to the right of the decimal point ❑ Date (DT): Date fields ❑ String (ID): ID fields ❑ Number (N): integer numeric ❑ Number (N0 through N9): implied decimal numerics; the decimal point does not appear, so the digit in the code indicates how many decimal places are represented in the data ❑ Number (R): real number ❑ Number (R0 through R9): real numbers, where the digit in the code denotes the number of decimal places ❑ Time (TM): time fields
Custom Date/Time Format	If the Custom Data Type property was set to Date (DT) or Time (TM), select a format string from the list provided
Justification	Used to align data when it fails to meet the maximum field length (positional files) or the minimum field length (delimited files), takes either Left or Right as its value
Pad Character	Specifies a character used to pad fields of less than the maximum field length
Wrap Character	A character used to enclose a field value when it contains the character specified as the field delimiter
Minimum Length with Pad Character	The minimum permissible length of a field including any pad characters; this value must be greater than the minimum length property if set, or greater than one if not

Note that if you set a value for the Custom Data Type property, the Data Type property on the Declaration tab is reset. The same holds true in the other direction, setting a Data Type in the Declaration tab resets any previously set Custom Data Type value.

The Wrap Character is used in situations where the field delimiter is included in data. For example, if your delimiter is a comma and you wish to include a comma within the text of a field, you specify a wrap character and place it at the beginning and end of the field: Boolean, "yes,no" – this consists of two fields, where yes,no is a single field value, the fields are delimited by commas, and the wrap character is the quotation mark.

The Justification and Pad Character properties come into play when a field in a positional message is shorter than the field size. We can specify whether the text should be aligned to the Left or Right. The drop-down list for Pad Character has a long list of printable characters, but you may also type any character you wish. If you do so, Editor supplies the hexadecimal value of the character.

Advanced Properties

There are two more tabs in the right-hand pane of the Editor window:

- ❑ Dictionary
- ❑ Code List

These are more advanced topics and are not required in order to build a basic document. The somewhat obscurely named Dictionary tab sets up a document for **self-routing**. BizTalk's Messaging Services allows you to specify the routing of a document in the messaging configuration itself, or in fields within the document. While we'll go into this topic in more detail in Chapter 10, you should note that a self-routing document allows the same messaging configuration to apply to a number of different endpoint locations. Of course, if the document is going to be providing information to Messaging Services, it has to know where to look within the document. Explaining the fields of a document is the job of the specification, hence the presence of the Dictionary tab in the Editor. We'll take a closer look at the Dictionary tab in just a moment.

X12 and EDIFACT EDI documents have code values defined for various fields. When implementing an EDI document, you may wish to allow particular codes to be associated with a particular field to convey specific information to the recipient, and this is where the Code List tab comes in. If your specification is based on one of the EDI standards, the possible code values for the selected field are displayed for you. We'll cover the Code List tab after we have discussed the Dictionary tab in more depth.

The Dictionary Tab

The properties on this tab have little to do with the structure of the document and everything to do with self-routing.

BizTalk's Messaging Services needs to know the source and destination organizations and the document type in order to select the proper channel for processing the document. In a basic messaging configuration, this information will be hard-coded in the configuration itself. In a self-routing configuration however, the configuration tells Messaging Services to look to the document for this information.

We cover hard-coded routing in Chapter 5, where we show you how to configure it through the Messaging Manager tool or provide this information through parameters in code. In Chapter 10, we cover self-routing, in which specified fields in the message itself provide the information needed to get it to its destination. You may arbitrarily select which fields contain this information, so the Dictionary tab exists to allow the document designer to tell BizTalk where to look for routing information.

143

The Dictionary tab is divided into two columns:

❏ A list of selectable properties on the left

❏ A Node Path column on the right

Checking a property indicates that the field (or record) that is currently selected in the tree view is the field (or record) that will contain the value to be used for that particular property. When you select a property, Editor fills in the Node Path entry with an XPath expression that uniquely locates that field or record. At run time, when Messaging Services needs routing information, it will turn to the message specification to determine the locations to check for that information. The XPath expressions allow the parser to go to those records and fields and extract the values needed.

In addition to clicking the check box for the property, you can set or clear the property by right-clicking on a property and selecting the Set Routing Information or Clear Routing Information menu items, respectively.

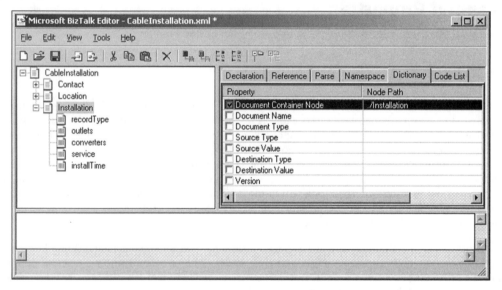

The Document Container Node property is the only property that may be selected for a record. It indicates which record contains the document itself. You might think this superfluous; surely the root record will always be the document container. In fact, it is convenient to be able to convey header information that is separate from the body of the document itself – this is exactly the approach taken by BizTalk Framework. Routing and state information is contained in a header section, with the business document itself contained in a lower-level record. Locating the record that begins the business document is what the Document Container Node property is all about.

The remaining properties on the Dictionary tab pertain to fields. Their names and meanings are given below:

Property	Meaning
Document Container Node	Path to the record that denotes the start of the business document. This will usually be the root record. In some cases, however, a business document can have an envelope wrapped around one or more business documents for the purposes of bundling messages or providing routing information.

Property	Meaning
Document Name	Path to the field naming the document
Source Type	Path to the field whose value denotes the type of organizational identifier for the message's source organization – in other words a standard identifier such as a Dun & Bradstreet or Federal Maritime Commision ID, or a custom identifier
Source Value	Path to the field whose value is the organizational identifier
Destination Type	Path to the field denoting the destination's organizational identifier type
Destination Value	Path to the field denoting the destination's organizational identifier

The Code List Tab

ANSI X12 EDI specifications have codes associated with various fields. There are many codes available, and not all codes can be used with all fields. The BizTalk Editor helps manage the confusion by providing a list of all available codes for a particular field in the Code List tab. Whenever a field with codes is selected in the tree view pane, the Code List tab will show a list of available codes.

You may constrain the list of codes for a message specification based on an EDI standard by selecting the subset of codes you want to use with the selected field. You identify code values for use with a particular field by clicking the check box for that value or right-clicking on the code value and selecting the Set Code(s) menu item. Clicking again or selecting the Clear Code(s) menu item resets the selection. The EDI example depicted below is a message specification created by selecting X12 as the specification type in the New Document dialog, then drilling down through the 3010 folder to the 810 specification. This specification is part of the X12 EDI standard. You would follow this procedure if you wished to create extensions or modifications to the standard for your own purposes.

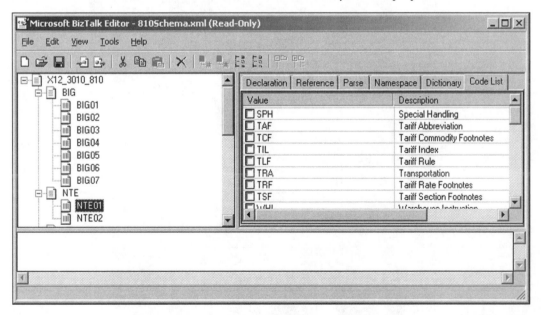

Cable Installation: A Delimited File Specification

For the sake of illustration, it is assumed that the Cable Television Vendor used by Wrox Site Managers (at least in the area of our sample customer) uses a legacy system for scheduling residential installations. This application is capable of taking CSV files that provide the details of an installation.

Since the Cable Company has no concept of a residential site manager, it uses a *single record* for the customer contact. They are also less cooperative in terms of scheduling contact calls and installation, using only a *single time* to denote the earliest time the installer will arrive, and they use the *telephone only* for contacting the customer. Of course, for our purposes, Wrox Site Managers wants to insert the Site Manager as the contact the Cable Company will use.

The site Location record in this specification is similar in content to the Location record in the previous message specification. The Installation record is also similar to its counterpart in the site description specification, except of course it has no type field since this installer only handles Cable TV installations. The Wrox Site Managers' communications server has to check the value of the type field and route those whose value is cable to this vendor.

Here is the schematic layout of the message specification, down to the field level, for the message we will be forwarding to the cable company. Records are rectangles, while fields are rounded corner boxes. All fields are strings, except cut and area, which are numeric types.

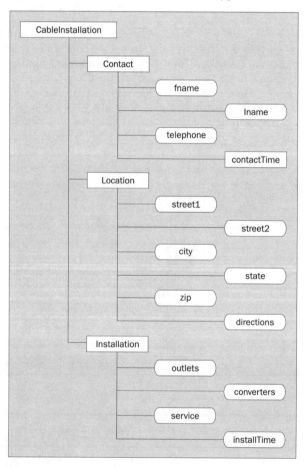

Shown below is what the message to the cable vendor should look like based on the sample site description we saw earlier. Note that the Site Manager has been inserted as the contact person. Also note that the first line is empty. This is caused by the fact that the root record – which exists to be a container for the rest – has no identifying character and no fields. The C, L, and I characters represent Contact, Location, and Installation respectively.

```
C,Jacques,Sprat,610-555-1212,08:00:00
L,123 Chestnut Ave,Division 6,Philadelphia,PA,19100,First house on left
I,4,4,PREMIUM,12:00:00
```

To create this specification, create a new blank specification and select the root record.

- ❏ On the **Reference** tab, set the **Standard** to **FlatFile**. This will have to be typed in manually as it does not feature in the dropdown list provided in the field.

- ❏ Change the root record's name to **CableCSV**.

- ❏ On the **Parse** tab, set the **Structure** property to **Delimited** to tell the editor that we are specifying a delimited, rather than positional, flatfile. This affects validity checks in the Editor.

- ❏ Leave the **Source Tag Identifier** blank, as all we want to appear is the data for the contact, location, and installation records.

- ❏ For clarity, let's put each record on its own line. The Messaging Service won't mind, but if a human user looks at the document it will be a lot easier to read. To do this, set the **Delimiter Type** property to **Character** and the **Delimiter Value** to **CR (0xd)**. What this means is that the root record's children – the three records we want to appear – will be delimited with a carriage return character.

- ❏ Set **Skip Carriage Return** to **No**. Since we have explicitly set the delimiter value, it must be included by the parser or the parser will lose track of its location and indicate a parse-time error.

- ❏ Add Contact, Location, and Installation records as children of the root record, setting their **Minimum Occurrences** and **Maximum Occurrences** properties to 1 on the **Reference** tag.

- ❏ On the **Parse** tab, set their **Structure** properties to **Delimited**, then specify a character type delimiter whose value is the comma (0x2c).

- ❏ Give them **Source Tag Identifier** properties of C, L, and I, (Contact, Location, and Installation) respectively on the **Parse** tag.

The remaining nodes in the tree diagram above are created as fields. They are typed as strings with the following exceptions:

- ❏ outlets (Integer)
- ❏ converters (Integer I4)
- ❏ installTime (Time)

After validating the specification, save it to the Wrox folder of the WebDAV repository under the name cablewo.xml.

Yard Work: A Positional File Specification

When a customer signs on with Wrox Site Managers, he also signs up for routine yard care. The contractor that handles this task needs to know the *area* of the yard, how often it needs to be *cut*, and what *type of grass* was used to plant the lawn. The frequency is a guideline; Wrox automatically takes a frequency of one week. The grass type helps the yard care contractor determine the proper care for the yard; based on observation and the yard type, they can apply fertilizers and herbicides as needed.

The Yard Care contractor uses a positional format for their new subscription information. For clarity, each record under the document record appears as a separate line. In other words, the top-level record is delimited with a new line character.

Within those records, however, the fields appear in a strict positional format. Since this is not XML, we do not have element names to indicate the start of each record, and, strictly speaking, we could do without this, but it is common in positional files to have a record identifier. So, for the `Owner`, `Address`, and `Yard` records depicted in the illustration below, we will use a single character record identifier of `O`, `A`, and `Y`, respectively. Each field is left-justified and padded with a space character. The contractor recognizes the concept of a time window for contacting the owner, and Wrox, as in the cable installation example, will substitute the name and contact information of the residential Site Manager into the Owner record.

All fields are strings with a few exceptions:

❑ The fields that bound the contact time window are Times.

❑ The fields for the frequency of cutting the yard and for indicating the area of the yard are Numerics.

❑ The field cut indicates how many weeks elapse between cuttings   Wrox will insert the value 1 automatically.

❑ Similarly, the field for denoting the type of agent, for example fertilizer or herbicide, will be filled with the string eval, indicating that the Yard Care vendor should assess the yard and select an agent.

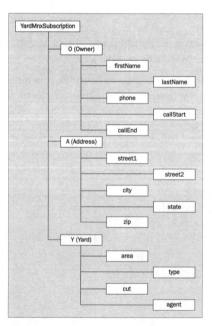

For our site example, here is what the message initiating yard care should look like:

```
OJacques  Sprat    610-555-121208:00:0017:00:00
A123 Chestnut AvDivision 6   Philadelphia  PA19100
Y10000 rye    1eval
```

We begin as with the cable installation example, creating a blank specification based on the FlatFile standard as before.

1. Rename the root record `YardMnxSubscription`.

2. Make it a delimited record with a carriage return delimiter.

At this point you may be wondering if you are reading the right section. Isn't this a positional example? In fact, it is, but a purely positional example is hard for human readers to view. Since you are likely to be troubleshooting things at some point, you want to make life easy for yourself. Therefore, this document is positional within the three records we wish to see, but delimited at the root record level. Actual messages sent through BizTalk will have this structure, which is an aid to troubleshooting.

3. Create child records named O, A, and Y.

4. Set their **Structure** properties to **Positional** and set their **Source Tag Identifier** properties to match.

5. The **Source Tag Position** property for each is set to 1   that means the BizTalk flatfile parser will expect to find the source tag value in the first position of each record.

The remaining nodes from the tree above are fields. All are left-justified and use whitespace for the pad character. For your convenience, the positional and required properties for these fields are shown in the following table.

Field Name	Required	Start Position	End Position
firstName	Yes	2	11
lastName	Yes	12	21
phone	Yes	22	33
callStart	Yes	34	41
callEnd	Yes	42	49
street1	Yes	2	16
street2	No	17	31
city	Yes	32	46
state	Yes	47	48
zip	Yes	49	53
area	Yes	2	7
type	Yes	8	17
cut	Yes	18	18
agent	No	19	33

Once you are satisfied with the specification and it validates without warnings, save it to the Wrox WebDAV folder under the name `yardmnxsubscription.xml`.

This completes our construction of message specifications for the case study. They are now ready to be used in the next chapter, where you will learn how to define a translation from one specification to another.

We finish off this chapter by taking a look at the BizTalk Server approach to EDI specifications.

EDI Specifications

EDI remains an important format for exchanging business documents. While there are efforts afoot to devise XML equivalents for EDI messages, and BizTalk and its competitors will surely begin to displace EDI, EDI itself is firmly established in some companies. Rather than attempt to avoid EDI, BizTalk embraces it. As we have seen, BizTalk is capable of dealing with messages in flatfile formats like those EDI uses, and the Editor even supports EDI through the Code List tab. Rather than make specification designers start with a blank message template and the EDI documents, BizTalk Server ships with a large number of EDI message specification templates.

Templates Provided with the Editor

BizTalk Editor comes with templates for both UN/EDIFACT and ANSI X12 EDI messages. Specifically, BizTalk Editor provides templates for the messages in the EDIFACT D93A, D95A, D95B, D97B, D98A, and D98B versions, while ANSI X12 is supported in its 2040, 3010, 3060, and 4010 versions.

It is not uncommon to start with an EDI message specification template and modify it to suit your particular business. You may prune the available records and fields of unneeded items. You will almost certainly constrain the codes used for the fields to more closely suit your business. The provision of message specification templates for EDI jumpstarts this process by doing the tedious work of translating the formal EDI documents for you.

Microsoft XML Versions

BizTalk Editor also comes equipped with specification templates that are similar to the EDI messages, but written in XML format. BizTalk certainly favors XML, yet the EDI messages do address common low-level business constructs. The result is the creation of some message specification templates that cover the same ground as EDI, but in XML form. The templates you will find available to you in the Microsoft folder of the WebDAV repository are:

- ❑ Canonical Receipt
- ❑ Common Advanced Ship Notice
- ❑ Common Inventory Advice
- ❑ Common Invoice
- ❑ Common Partner Profile
- ❑ Common Purchase Order
- ❑ Common Purchase Order Acknowledgement
- ❑ Common Price Catalog
- ❑ Common Shipping Advice
- ❑ Common Shipping Order

Why use XML to recode EDI? The usual advantages, touched on in this book but expanded upon elsewhere, apply. Certainly, parsers for XML documents are more readily available than EDI parsers. Also, it is easier for two partners to modify an XML version in the absence of a standard. The XML parser has no particular preconceptions; it works entirely based on the document specification. So, you may agree to add an item, taking advantage of the fact that element and attribute names are descriptive strings. An EDI parser may be hard-coded to expect a particular format.

> *Further information on using XML as the format for EDI is available from the XML/EDI Group's web site, www.xmledi.com.*

Summary

Structured messages are the heart of BizTalk, and the performance and effectiveness of a system integrated with BizTalk Server depends on the quality of the message specifications. We've seen how BizTalk is designed for XML, but also allows us to work with messages in flatfile formats.

BizTalk Server offers particularly strong support for EDI – message specification templates for X12 and EDIFACT are included, as are templates for XML equivalents. How BizTalk makes use of this information will become clear in the next chapter when we take up the topic of how to translate messages from one format to another. You will see that the effort BizTalk Editor went to in capturing flatfile information was not wasted, as the proprietary elements added to XML schemas will be read by components in a multi-step parsing sequence.

You were introduced to the BizTalk Editor, the primary tool for working with BizTalk message specifications. BizTalk tries to get away from XML-specific terms, using the more familiar database-style record and field model used in many applications today. You toured around the Editor at some length. We even created three message specifications to support our fictional site management application, and your patience in bearing with all this specification and design is about to be rewarded. In the next chapter, we will take up the task of specifying translations between formats.

I hope you have reached the end of this chapter with the idea that there is more to effective message design than simply learning how to use the Editor. I've included some theory in this chapter – the hierarchical and canonical forms – to help you as you go forth and write your own specifications for production applications. However, there is no substitute for experimentation and experience. Fortunately, the BizTalk Editor makes it relatively painless to get this experience.

Mapping BizTalk Messages

4

Let's consider what we have achieved so far. We first defined the business workflow using a BizTalk schedule. Then, noting that the schedule essentially describes the flow of messages, we described how to write a message specification. This is fine if we wish to transfer messages between organizations that use exactly the same message specification. Unfortunately, in reality, organizations rarely agree on document specifications, even when message content is very similar.

Before the BizTalk Framework was proposed, businesses were often left to define the specifications of their own messages themselves, resulting in competing specifications to describe the same thing. Actually, even if we *do* have a centrally imposed conformity we can get competing specifications, as EDI shows. The EDI world has two versions – X12 in North America and UN/EDIFACT in Europe. The trend away from specialized networks, towards applications built to run on the public Internet, also accelerates the diversity of message specifications. We got a hint of this in the last chapter when we created three specifications that overlap in their content yet differ radically in their form. As we will see in a moment, there are also other perfectly valid reasons to have a range of message specifications that contain similar content.

Whether this diversity is good or bad depends on who is authoring specifications and the nature of your business requirements. What is certain, however, is that we need to dynamically translate from one specification to another: a process known as **mapping**.

BizTalk Server supports mapping by translating messages as they are received or sent. Part of the business agreement (trading profile) between two partners or applications is a statement of the specification of the sent message and the specification of the format in which the recipient would like to receive it. Given this information, BizTalk Server is able to select an appropriate message map and convert the message into the desired form.

In this chapter, we are going to explore BizTalk message maps by going through the following steps:

❑ First, in order to understand the various parameters that go into a message map, we will need to understand how BizTalk Server parses and translates documents.

❑ From there, we'll be introduced to the **BizTalk Mapper**, the tool we will use to specify the translation between two document specifications. Not only will we learn our way around the Mapper, but we'll get a feel for how message maps are built, and also how BizTalk Server uses message maps to perform translations.

❑ Then we'll use what we have learned: we will build on our evolving sample application by specifying maps between the Site Service Description specification and both the Cable Installer and Yard Care specifications. The Site Service message is the one sent to us by the field agents, if you recall. Once in receipt of that, the schedule we designed in Chapter 2 sends the same message out to the cable installer and the yard care service. Since they want to receive messages in different formats, a map is required.

❑ BizTalk Server is also capable of processing data *as* it is mapped from one specification to another. This intermediate processing is performed by reusable components called **functoids**, which we will also consider.

❑ We'll finish off the chapter by building a custom functoid, which we can use in our sample application.

Why Does BizTalk Need Mapping?

There are lots of reasons for the message specification diversity we have today. As we have already noted, without a specification standard each organisation will tend to produce its own message specification; indeed it is this issue that prompted the production of the BizTalk Framework. However, while we should encourage the use of specification standards wherever possible, there are actually many scenarios where it is useful (or necessary) to write many specifications that describe the same concept yet differ in form. Let's now consider some of the most important.

❑ Trading partners may commit to standards other than the ones you select for institutional reasons.

This scenario is most commonly encountered when dealing with a large organization that has an investment in EDI. While such efforts are often kept separate from XML-based messaging on the Internet, I believe organizations will merge their EDI and non-EDI efforts over time, arriving eventually at a single internal standard. Supporting EDI and XML is effective only so long as the non-EDI effort is a pilot program. Once the volume of such integration grows to production levels, there is a tendency to want to bring everything under central coordination.

❑ Legacy systems generally use non-XML formats.

Flatfile formats are often encountered as export/import formats. Comma-delimited and fixed format text were the "near-universal" formats that preceded XML, and so are commonly used with legacy applications. These applications may be core to the running of a business. It is therefore not uncommon to encounter such file formats in export and import utilities for line of business applications. If an important application supports such a format, it is often easier (and safer) to use the application and translate its messages in BizTalk than it is to try to modify the application.

❑ Different businesses may view the same concept in different ways, placing different emphasis on items or adding details peculiar to their situation.

This problem should be familiar to you after the design discussions of the last chapter. Equally smart people can disagree on how to model a particular concept. When that happens, translation is more effective than site-by-site persuasion of the whole development team.

Equally important is the emphasis that an organization places on an item of data. If your organization uses a postal address solely to generate mailing labels while my organization does validity checks and targeted marketing based on zip codes, you can bet that my XML vocabulary covering addresses contains more structure than yours. Here again, rather than attempt to persuade you to see it my way, it is easier to translate my detailed structure into your less detailed structure. With run-time mapping available to us, everyone gets to keep their preferred data formats. Of course, throughput is higher when mapping is not required, but the flexibility in formats is a highly desirable feature.

❑   Different applications use the same concept differently, so a message specification might be tuned to yield better performance on commonly used portions of the message.

From what we have discussed so far, you might have assumed that message specifications are driven solely by theoretical issues of data modeling. However, processing performance also plays a part in the construction of message specifications. The canonical form is a particularly flat form that requires less manipulation to iterate through. It also tends to result in smaller documents than the hierarchical form, although hierarchical models can generally be compressed to a greater extent than their canonical equivalent.

This means that message specifications for high-volume systems may be modified to gain a performance advantage. So, if two trading partners use the same data in different ways, their optimization process may result in different specifications. Both forms model the same business concept, both are efficient in terms of their organization's needs, yet each has a different structure. Here again, document mapping is the bridge that lets these two organizations communicate.

❑   Work flow may involve *problem decomposition*, in which one large document is translated into several overlapping smaller documents. Some messages may be a subset of larger messages. In either case, some data must be extracted from the larger document.

You've already seen an example of message decomposition in the last chapter. Our residential site description is composed of many parts, each of which deals with a different aspect of the site. Therefore, each part relates to a different service provider, yet from the point of view of Wrox Site Managers, the document is an indivisible whole. Why should we take this approach, rather than having separate files for each aspect of the site?

For one thing, it is easier to map the relevant information from the site description into a message for each vendor, than it is to manage lots of files. This also makes it easier to switch providers: if I can get just one provider who handles all of the services previously handled by several providers, I can reduce the complexity of my business. Then, since the message decomposition is handled at run-time by mapping my site description into the service provider's message format, switching providers is a matter of changing just one set of message maps.

Also, since each provider only requires a subset of the data in the site description, decomposition also provides the means to avoid sending unnecessary data to each provider. In other words, decomposition allows us to reduce *data redundancy* in messages.

Run-time Message Translation

In the previous section we showed that there are a multitude of reasons why we would want to translate between message specification formats. We are going to move on now and discuss how BizTalk Server implements this mapping process.

Knowing how BizTalk Server maps are constructed will give you some insight into the kinds of translations the server is capable of performing. If you look at the source of a BizTalk message map, you'll see some structures that make little sense until you understand how the run-time engine processes incoming and outgoing messages. This section will provide you with a look "under the covers" at how BizTalk Server translates between message specifications.

> **You should note that you don't need to know any of the information in the following section in order to use BizTalk and map message specifications. However, it does provide an insight into the product's implementation and capabilities, and is also useful for very advanced troubleshooting situations. But, if you are eager to start mapping, you should skip ahead to the section entitled *BizTalk Mapper*.**

The Mapping Process

We'll start off by taking a brief look at the general process of moving a BizTalk message between specifications. First, we'll deal with the basic case of an XML to XML translation, then broaden our view to include flat file specifications.

XML to XML

Suppose we are sending a BizTalk document that uses an XML message specification to a recipient who expects it to be in another XML format. In this case, the processing of the run-time engine is relatively simple:

1. Once the initial XML message reaches BizTalk Server, BizTalk locates the proper channel to use based on the source, destination, and message types.

2. The messaging configuration calls for a translation to another XML specification, so BizTalk Server locates the applicable mapping file and uses it to produce the final message form.

3. The final document is then transmitted to the recipient according to the information contained in the agreement.

This process is illustrated below:

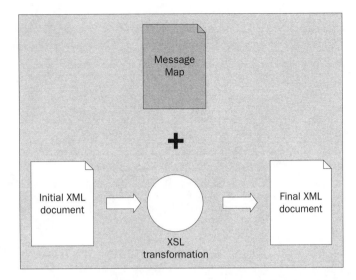

The important step is obviously the XML-to-XML translation, labelled "XSL transformation" on the diagram. Extensible Stylesheet Language (XSL) Transformations, or **XSLT**, is a rule-based mechanism for taking one XML document and converting it to another XML form, based on the rules set forth in an XSL stylesheet document. Bear in mind that BizTalk Server invokes an XSL processor to perform message mapping. We will return to this topic in a short while.

Flatfiles

The mapping process becomes a good deal more complicated when we bring flatfile message formats into the picture. Note that flatfiles include the various EDI formats as a special case. For one thing, you can't use an XML parser to read a flatfile document, and you can't use an XSL processor to perform flatfile-to-flatfile translation. The XSL processor can convert XML to a flatfile format, but it requires an XML document as its starting input. The workflow of the run-time engine for a mapping from a flatfile to another flatfile can be approximated to the following steps:

1. Translation of the initial flatfile to XML

2. XSL translation of the XML to an intermediate XML format

3. Translation of the intermediate XML into the final flatfile form

This process is shown in more detail below:

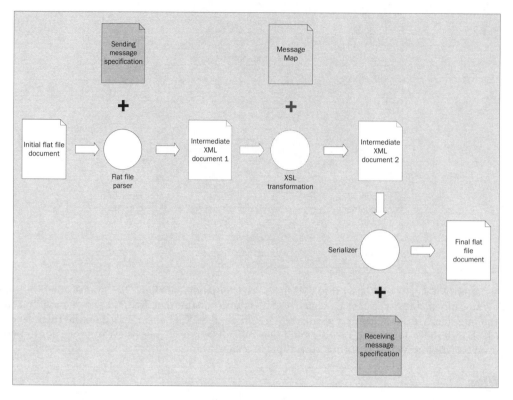

There are several points you should note here. First, we need a flatfile **parser** to process the initial flatfile so that we can convert it into an XML form that the XSL processor will understand. Second, note that exactly the same workflow shown in the preceding XML-to-XML example appears here as a central step. Finally, we need a component called a **serializer** to translate the intermediate XML document to the final flatfile form. Let's now take a closer look at these aspects of the mapping process.

XSLT

Clearly, the core BizTalk XML-to-XML translation step is a critical piece of the workflow. Without it, no message transformation could be performed. BizTalk goes to a lot of trouble to get flatfile formats in and out of XML form. There is a good reason for this. The XML community has the standard XLST rule-based mechanism for taking one form of XML document and converting it to another XML form. Each rule consists of a pattern and some output instructions. When an XSL processor finds some markup that matches the pattern, it applies the output instructions to convert the markup. Since Microsoft's XML parser also implements the XSLT recommendation, BizTalk has XSLT capabilities close at hand.

The XML parser BizTalk uses is the MSXML 3.0 component used throughout Windows 2000. This version fully supports XSLT, but it was developed in parallel with BizTalk Server. As a result, the stylesheets we'll examine shortly actually conform to the earlier draft, which was all that was available when BizTalk was being developed. Microsoft's stated intention is to migrate to the final W3C Recommendation over time.

Under the Hood

So what does a map file actually look like? In this section, we're going to take a quick peek at a typical map file.

> I am deliberately avoiding a detailed discussion of the map file structure because it may change in the future. This discussion of XSLT is provided solely to give you a better understanding of the map files and the XML tools that make translation work. In any case, you should not be working with raw map files; while it is interesting to see "under the hood", the BizTalk Mapper graphical tool has been provided to insulate you from the complexity of having to write XSLT script yourself.

A BizTalk message map file is an XML file that can be divided into sections, depending upon the information content:

❑ Specification information for the original and final documents – these are the specifications in XML-DR schema format; the source document is held in a `srctree` element, while the output file is contained in a `sinktree` element

❑ Links between fields in the original document and fields in the final document held in the `link` element

❑ An XSL stylesheet that accomplishes the transformation from the original to the final document

❑ A section containing script functions provided for intermediate processing in the course of a link

Here's an example of a map file. This is the map file we will use to translate a site service description message into a work order for the cable installer. It extracts the information the cable installer needs and converts from XML to a comma-delimited flatfile format:

```
<mapsource
 name="http://w2ktest/BizTalkServerRepository/Maps/Wrox/SiteSvcToCableWO2"
 version="1" xrange="100" yrange="420">

<srctree>
 <Schema name="SiteServiceDescription" b:root_reference="SiteServiceDescription"
 b:schema_type="SiteServiceDescription" b:standard="XML"
 b:standards_version="1.0" xmlns="urn:schemas-microsoft-com:xml-data"
 xmlns:d="urn:schemas-microsoft-com:datatypes"
 xmlns:b="urn:schemas-microsoft-com:BizTalkServer">
  <b:SelectionFields/>
  <ElementType name="Yard" content="empty" model="closed">
   <b:RecordInfo/>
   . . .
  </ElementType>
  . . .
 </Schema>
</srctree>
<Values>
 <TestValues/>
 <ConstantValues/>
```

```
  </Values>
  <sinktree>
   <Schema name="CableCSV" b:root_reference="CableCSV" b:schema_type="data_contacts"
    b:version="1.0" b:is_unicode="no" b:is_envelope="no" b:standard="FlatFile"
    xmlns="urn:schemas-microsoft-com:xml-data"
    xmlns:d="urn:schemas-microsoft-com:datatypes"
    xmlns:b="urn:schemas-microsoft-com:BizTalkServer">
    <b:SelectionFields/>
    . . .
   </Schema>
  </sinktree>
```

The `srctree` and `sinktree` elements contain the XML-DR schemas that the BizTalk Mapper found in the message specifications provided to it. This gives the parsers and serializers a convenient place to look to find the schema information they need.

```
  <links>
   <link linkid="1" linkfrom="/SiteServiceDescription/Owner/ContactStart"
    linkto="/CableCSV/Installation/@installTime"/>
   <link linkid="2" linkfrom="2" linkto="/CableCSV/Installation/@converters"/>
   <link linkid="3"
    linkfrom="/SiteServiceDescription/House/Telecom/Television/@setTops"
    linkto="2"/>
    . . .
  </links>
```

The `link` element consists of one or more links between fields in the source and fields in the sink. Since fields can be combined and passed through functions that manipulate their values, the `link` element has attributes that specify what type of link is involved, what fields are being mapped, and a numerical identifier for the link. This assists the Mapper in graphically depicting the links.

```
  <functions>
   <function functionid="1" xcell="59" ycell="220" funcfuncid="110"
     funcversion="1" isscripter="no">
    <inputparams>
     <param type="link" value="6"/>
    </inputparams>
   </function>
   <function functionid="2" xcell="57" ycell="218" funcfuncid="260"
     funcversion="1" isscripter="yes"
     script="Function MyFunction2( p_strConnections, p_strSetTops )
      if CInt(p_strConnections) &gt;= CInt(p_strSetTops)
       then
        MyFunction2 = p_strSetTops
       else
        MyFunction2 = p_strConnections
       end if
       End Function">
    <inputparams>
     <param type="link" value="4"/>
     <param type="link" value="3"/>
    </inputparams>
   </function>
  </functions>
```

The `functions` element is where the bodies of the script functions for intermediate processing will be found. They come from reusable components that will we examine in detail later in this chapter and are called from within the XSL stylesheet. The `inputparams` element contains some test values that we provided in the Mapper that let us check the intermediate processing from within that tool.

```
<CompiledXSL>
 <xsl:stylesheet xmlns:xsl="http://www.w3.org/1999/XSL/Transform"
     xmlns:msxsl="urn:schemas-microsoft-com:xslt"
     xmlns:var="urn:var" xmlns:user="urn:user" version="1.0">
  <xsl:output method="xml" indent="yes" omit-xml-declaration="yes"/>
  <xsl:template match="/">
   <xsl:apply-templates select="SiteServiceDescription"/>
  </xsl:template>
  <xsl:template match="SiteServiceDescription">
   <CableCSV>
    <xsl:for-each select="Manager">
     <Contact>
      <xsl:attribute name="fname">
       <xsl:value-of select="@fname"/>
      </xsl:attribute>
      <xsl:attribute name="lname">
       <xsl:value-of select="@lname"/>
      </xsl:attribute>
       . . .
     </Contact>
    </xsl:for-each>
    . . .
   </CableCSV>
  </xsl:template>
<msxsl:script language="VBScript" implements-prefix="user">
  <![CDATA[
  Function FctStringUCase( p_strA )
   FctStringUCase = Ucase( p_strA )
  End Function

  Function MyFunction2( p_strConnections, p_strSetTops )
   if CInt(p_strConnections) >= CInt(p_strSetTops) then
    MyFunction2 = p_strSetTops
   else
    MyFunction2 = p_strConnections
   end if
  End Function
  ]]>
  </msxsl:script>
 </xsl:stylesheet>
</CompiledXSL>
</mapsource>
```

The XSL stylesheet is generated by the Mapper and is wholly contained within the `CompiledXSL` element, which in turn is contained within the map file. As you can see, three files – two specifications and a stylesheet – and some supporting information are combined to create a single BizTalk map file. The fact that the message specifications of the source and destination documents are embedded within the map requires you to take care to update your map whenever you modify one or both of the message specifications.

The Intermediate XML Form

Let's now take a closer look at XSL translation to the intermediate XML form. We'll begin by constructing a simple XML message for a person consisting of name and address information. Then we'll construct a similar but distinct XML message, and a map between these two XML forms. This will demonstrate the basic mapping process. Although XSL is able to handle this by itself, BizTalk uses the full process, skipping the parsing and serializing steps because the configuration does not call for any flatfile formats. With that in hand, we'll move on to the more difficult case of mapping from XML to a delimited format.

Since the XSL stylesheet is embedded in a message map, we can manually extract it and apply it to a sample message written according to the originating specification. That way, we can see what a map file does for us without having to wait until the next chapter when we learn how to use the messaging service. Here's a sample of the XML message format:

```
<Person>
 <Name first="John" last="Doe"/>
 <Address>
  <Street1>1100 Main Street</Street1>
  <Street2>Suite A</Street2>
  <City>Philadelphia</City>
  <State>PA</State>
  <PostalCode>19100</PostalCode>
 </Address>
</Person>
```

I've used a canonical form for the name, but a hierarchical form for the address to allow for whitespace in the address lines. I've also followed my usual convention of using lowercase names for attributes, and names that begin with uppercase letters for elements.

To test the XML to XML mapping, I took the original specification, changed PostalCode to Zip, then made the first and last attributes into child elements of Name called FirstName and LastName. XSL should be able to handle this transformation directly. If we inspect the XSL (included in the sample code for this chapter as persontoperson2.xsl), you will see what the Mapper generates. If you apply the transformation through MSXML and script code or some XSL tool, you get the expected result, a finished XML document that complies with the receiving message specification:

```
<Person>
 <Name>
  <FirstName>John</FirstName>
  <LastName>Doe</LastName>
 </Name>
 <Address>
  <Street1>1100 Main Street</Street1>
  <Street2>Suite A</Street2>
  <City>Philadelphia</City>
  <State>PA</State>
  <Zip>19100</Zip>
 </Address>
</Person>
```

As you will see when we discuss BizTalk Mapper in a later section, you can test XML-to-XML transformations within the tool itself. You can also test flatfile translations, but you will only see the intermediate form – Intermediate XML document 2 in the diagram earlier in this chapter – that emerges from the XSL transformation.

Next, I devised a delimited flatfile specification for the same information. Here's what the message should look like after translation to the CSV format:

```
PersonCSV
Name,John,Doe
Address,1100 Main Street,Suite A,Philadelphia,PA,19100
```

All fields in the delimited specification are attributes. I changed some field names to make it easy to differentiate between the two specifications. All field names are lowercase, the root record is named `PersonCSV`, and the `PostalCode` field in the XML specification is named `zip` in the delimited specification. If you apply the XSL stylesheet embedded in the map file to the XML test data, the result is as follows. This is not the desired flatfile form, but rather an XML document. In fact, this is the intermediate form that emerges from the XSL step in the mapping process. The flatfile form is created from this XML document by the serializer component:

```
<PersonCSV>
<Name first="John" last="Doe" />
<Address street1="1100 Main Street" street2="Suite A" city="Philadelphia"
state="PA"
   zip="19100" />
</PersonCSV>
```

There are three important things to notice here. First, the resultant message is XML, not comma delimited. Second, all record and field names are drawn from the desired end specification (delimited). Finally, the form is entirely canonical and maps well to the desired flatfile format.

BizTalk can get away with whitespace in XML attributes because it is not validating the content. This is well-formed XML; the whitespace in the attribute values is permissible if the attributes are of type IDREFS. Since the actual data types are not available for validation, however, the XML processor used by BizTalk will not flag an error.

The intermediate form generated in a translation involving flatfile formats is always canonical. This means that the flatfile post-processing parsers will consistently locate field values for any given record. Once located, they can use the record and field names to locate additional information in the desired message specification to apply the proper delimiters. This segregation of translation tasks allows BizTalk to make maximum use of XSL support in the Microsoft parser. Flatfile parser components can be that much simpler while still generating the correct results.

Performing such tests for yourself is an effective aid in debugging maps as well as a great way to understand how BizTalk works. A good tool, which is available for free, is the XSL Tester from the open source VBXML site (http://www.vbxml.com/xsltester). Not only does it permit you to perform these tests for yourself, but you can interactively develop XSL stylesheets. Although you won't typically edit BizTalk maps manually, you may wish to be able to do this if you encounter especially tricky translation challenges.

Parsers and Serializers

BizTalk Server leverages the XML parser, MSXML, that comes with the operating system. Unfortunately for BizTalk, this parser (in common with all XML processors) is completely unable to parse flatfile formats, including EDI. BizTalk, therefore, requires some additional parser components.

A minimum requirement is a general-purpose parser that can look at delimited and positional messages and parse them into their component parts, given a message specification. As we shall see, BizTalk Server includes just such a parser in the form of a COM component. In fact, BizTalk also includes parsers specialized for X12 and UN/EDIFACT too.

As we have seen, the purpose of these pre-processing parsers is to extract the records and fields of a flatfile document and write them out in an equivalent XML form, so that the core (XML-based) functions of BizTalk Server can be brought to bear on them. The parsers use the record and field names provided by the message specification to provide meaningful element and attribute names in the XML form. Of course, application programmers may make mistakes. There is no guarantee that the document actually submitted to BizTalk conforms to the specification listed in the agreement. Consequently, the parsers perform the additional function of verifying that the document that arrives in BizTalk's queue conforms to the specification indicated.

On the other hand, we also have an intermediate XML message that needs to be written in the flatfile format specified in the agreement as the outgoing document type. BizTalk uses a process known as **serialization** to perform this conversion. Serialization components can read the known XML intermediate form and use the values found to write out a document that conforms to the outgoing type specified in the agreement.

By having specialized interfaces for parsers and serializers, and known general forms for conversion to and from flatfile formats, BizTalk makes sure that the core translation function receives XML and translates it into a form serialization components can read. All the components are able to do their piece of the conversion process without worrying about preceding or succeeding steps.

Although BizTalk needs to support a number of distinct parsers and serializers, these components fit into the same places in the workflow. That is, whether you are dealing with an X12 EDI document or a delimited file on the originating side, BizTalk loads the appropriate parser or serializer at the appropriate point in the translation sequence. A parser or serializer is needed at these steps, and BizTalk will select the right one and plug it in. Therefore, it is natural to define some COM interfaces to handle parsing and serializing before providing an implementation for each of the supported types.

This architecture has the happy consequence of making parser support in BizTalk open-ended. It would not be difficult for BizTalk to support a new document type by developing a new parser component. Indeed, we will discuss the documented interfaces for this task in Chapter 10.

> *Writing custom parsers and serializers is an exceptional case. The chief benefits of writing a specialized implementation of a parser instead of using one of the parsers that ship with BizTalk Server are to take advantage of domain-specific information to improve the performance or validation of the parser, or to handle a type, for example, binary, that is not handled by the standard components.*

Supplied Parsers and Serializers

The BizTalk snap-in for the Microsoft Management Console (MMC), which is accessible through the menu item entitled BizTalk Server Administration, gives you access to a list of installed parsers and the order in which they are tried against an incoming message. To view this information, expand the Microsoft BizTalk Server 2000 node, select the BizTalk Server Group node under it, then right-click and select the Properties menu item on the context menu. You will see the following dialog. The information we seek is on the Parsers tab:

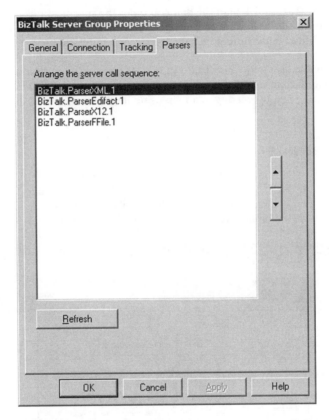

The standard parsers, which are listed above, are included as part of BizTalk Server and handle the following formats:

- ❑ XML – custom XML formats
- ❑ UN/EDIFACT – European EDI documents
- ❑ ANSI X12 – North American EDI documents
- ❑ Flatfile – delimited and positional documents

The administrative console does not expose the serializers, but if you wade through the type libraries, you will find implementations for UN/EDIFACT, ANSI X12, and flatfiles. You can view these by using OLE View, a tool provided with Microsoft's Visual Studio. Serializers are complementary to parsers, as shown in the flatfile-to-flatfile schematic we presented earlier, so you must have a serializer for every format other than XML that you wish to handle in BizTalk Server. Of course, XML documents do not require serialization as they are in final form following the XSL transformation step of the mapping workflow.

BizTalk Mapper

We have seen the processes involved in mapping between two formats, and looked at a sample map, now let's look at the tool that helps us write the map files: BizTalk Mapper. This is a graphical tool that allows you to select two specifications, and then specify a translation from one to the other. It not only allows you to map a field in one specification to a field in another, but gives you the option to perform en route data processing as well, using special components called **functoids**.

The end result is a BizTalk XSLT **map file** that combines the specifications with the rules used to translate between them. This stand-alone file can then be used to tell the run-time BizTalk Server engine how to transform a message document into the form required by the recipient.

In this section we will take a tour of BizTalk Mapper. We are going to start off by looking at how to use the Mapper user interface to map fields between specifications. Then we'll take a look at how to introduce intermediate data processing to a map using functoids. We'll finish off by compiling and testing a map.

The User Interface

When you start up the Mapper, you are presented with a blank mapping window, consisting of two specification panes (for the Source document and the Destination document) detailing records and fields, and a central grid, which is used to show the details of the mapping. If you were to open an existing map file using the Mapper, you would see something similar to the following:

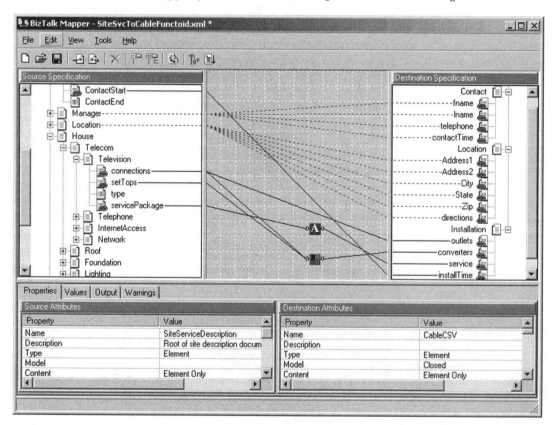

There are several items worth noting here. The most obvious is that mapped fields are linked by lines across the grid. You should also note the icons present in the grid; these are examples of functoids. The pane at the bottom of the window shows attributes of each specification, and of the translation, in a tabbed form.

Source and Destination Panes

The panes for the source and destination specifications are similar to panes you saw in BizTalk Editor. They are the tree-view controls that summarize the record and file structure of each specification. In the illustration above, the `connections` and `settops` fields of the `SiteDescription` specification are combined (via a functoid) to map to the `converters` field of the destination specification, `CableCSV`. Note also that fields use the standard field icon also used in the Editor, although linked fields have an icon that includes a pair of chain links that indicate that they are part of a link.

Source and Destination Attributes

The attributes of the selected field or record, for example the name, are displayed in the bottom pane. Attributes of the source specification are shown on the left, and destination attributes on the right. The format is similar to a property sheet in Visual Basic. Due to limited space, the contents of what are individual tabs in the attributes pane of BizTalk Editor are instead concatenated to form a single sheet in BizTalk Mapper. The contents of the Declaration and Reference tabs in BizTalk Editor are displayed in Mapper. When a specification is positional or delimited, the contents of the Parse tab are appended, as well.

The attributes pane is context sensitive. If you select a field or record in either the source or destination panes, the corresponding attribute sheet changes to reflect the selection.

Functoid Grid

The central grid shows the links established between items in the specifications as lines. It allows you to view links and select them for deletion as needed. It serves another purpose, too: the grid is where you can place functoids to provide intermediate data processing if you wish. You can see which fields provide the data input to the functoid, and which field receives the results from the functoid. You select a functoid, then move it on the grid or open a dialog to view its properties. To provide inputs, connect one or more fields from the source document to the functoid icon. The output of the functoid is then linked to one or more fields of the destination document.

Results Pane

A tabbed property page pane appears at the bottom of the Mapper window. It has tabs labelled Properties, Values, Output, and Warnings. The Properties tab displays properties of the selected source field or record and the destination field or record, as noted earlier. These are the properties you entered in the message specification when you created it in the Editor. The Output tab works like the output of a compiler's IDE. When you have constructed your map using the Mapper, you will need to **compile** it to produce the XSLT map file. We will discuss this in more detail later on. The results of compilation, especially any errors that crop up, will be displayed in the Output tab. When you test a map, the results of the transformation are displayed in the Output page and the warnings and status of the map are found on the Warnings page.

The Values tab allows you to test values for the source message. We will talk more about testing compiled maps later. The Values tab also permits you to enter constant values for the destination message. For instance, you may need to generate a constant value for a destination field that has no corresponding field in the source specification.

To set a constant, first select the destination field you want to feed a constant value to. Then, note that the Values tab has two edit controls, one labelled Source test value and one labelled Destination constant value. Ignore the first one for now as it applies to testing maps. Enter the constant value into the Destination constant value control; this value will be copied into the destination field when an incoming message is mapped. In other words, if you want the literal value XYZ to appear in the destination field, enter that value in the Destination constant value control.

Constructing Maps

BizTalk Mapper handles documents in a similar way to the Editor. A BizTalk map, as we have seen, is an XML document, so all the information collected in a session with the Mapper is written to a text file on disk. Both the native file system and WebDAV are supported. Once open, a map is abstracted away from its nature as an XML document through an interface that deals with records and fields, as well as links.

A **link** is what tells the run-time server process how to convert information in one form into the same information in another form; in other words it makes sure that data from a field in the source document is copied to the correct field in the destination document (or to a functoid). Before we can discuss links in greater depth though, we need to know how to create maps and designate links. This is the process that generates the XSL stylesheet and the extension information that Mapper puts in a map file.

Creating Maps

You begin a new BizTalk map by selecting the File | New... menu option, or by clicking on the standard new document toolbar button (the first button on the toolbar). You are immediately presented with the Select Source Specification Type dialog. This dialog is similar to a file selection dialog but initially gives three choices. These choices tell the Mapper where to look for the specifications for the source and destination documents:

❑ local files – message specification files in the local file system

❑ templates – use the standards-based templates (Microsoft XML, X12, EDIFACT)

❑ WebDAV files – use WebDAV to access the server's document repository

The first and last options work as you might expect; having selected the specification type, you must now Select Source Specification. You must navigate through the local file system or WebDAV repository and select an existing message specification for the source.

The template option, however, supports the mapping of standard documents such as EDI. If you select this option, the Select Source Specification dialog displays three folders. The first two, X12 and EDIFACT, pertain to templates for the various messages of the two Electronic Data Interchange (EDI) dialects. The last folder, labelled XML, contains templates created by Microsoft that represent common business documents, such as purchase orders or price catalogs. Unlike EDI messages, which use non-XML flatfile formats, these templates are XML in syntax. They are intended for business users who do not have an EDI legacy, but who nonetheless are looking for off-the-shelf representations of common business entities.

> As you may recall from the last chapter, the Editor permitted you to modify the templates to fit your needs. The Mapper, however, does not permit editing of either the source or the destination specifications. If you want to work with a specification that is a variation on one of these templates, you will have to open the template in the Editor and save your changed version to another folder or under another name.

Once you select a source specification, you are again presented with a file selection dialog, this one termed Select Destination Specification Type. You again have the choice of local files, templates, and WebDAV. The selection process is the same as for the source specification.

Once you have successfully picked source and destination specifications, they appear in their respective panes. You are now ready to begin specifying your message map.

Mapping Records and Fields

To establish a link between fields in the source and destination documents, you can simply drag the mouse from the source field to a field in the destination specification. Provided the data types of the two fields are compatible, a line appears between the two fields.

If linking was always as simple as that, though, this book would be a bit shorter. You have a number of options at this point. If you click on the Tools | Options... menu item, you will see the following dialog box:

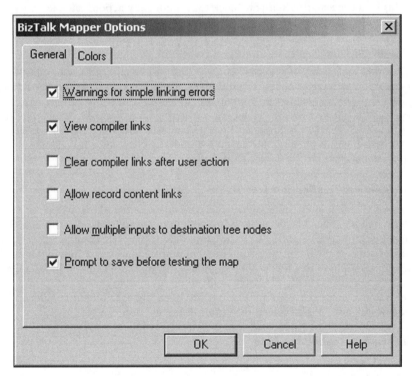

These are BizTalk Mapper's default settings for links. The options in this dialog require some explanation in the sections that follow.

Warnings for Simple Linking Errors

When this option is checked (the default), a warning is generated whenever you try to link two fields of conflicting data types.

View Compiler Links

A **compiler link** is an association between two records that is introduced as a result of your other links. In other words, when the map is compiled, Mapper detects that a record that is a parent, at some level, is now tied to a record that is a parent, again not necessarily the immediate parent, of the destination field. For example, in the map between the site service description and the cable installation order, fields from the `Television` record in the site service description are linked to fields in the cable message's `Installation` record. Although no link was explicitly created, Mapper knows these records are now related because it must locate them to implement the links between the child fields we explicitly specified. As you gain more experience and attempt increasingly more challenging maps, it is useful to see these relationships. The Mapper will have to generate an XSL element to select the source parent, so an abundance of compiler links will result in longer XSL in the map and consequently more time to map a source document instance at run time. Similarly, if you are not getting the results you expect (we will discuss how to test maps in a later section), you should inspect the compiler links to see if they match the behavior you expect. This is useful mainly when the source and destination records can repeat. For the beginner, however, it can be disconcerting to see links suddenly appear after you compile a map. This is perfectly normal behavior.

Clear Compiler Links After User Action

By default this is not selected. When you check this option, any action you take in Mapper will clear previously generated compiler links.

Allow Record Content Links

The next option to look at involves record content links. Remember that while the Mapper displays message specifications in terms of records and fields, a specification based on XML involves elements and attributes. However, elements can contain text as well. If this is the case in your source specification and the text value is one you want to include in the map, you will need to check the Allow record content links option, otherwise Mapper will not let you establish a link from a source record. In general, though, XML vocabularies intended for business-to-business exchange use elements as containers, so the default (an unchecked box) is a reasonable one.

Allow Multiple Inputs to Destination Tree Nodes

The next option you should consider right now is the one labelled Allow multiple inputs to destination tree nodes. In general, once you establish a link to a destination field, you cannot establish another link into the same field. Indeed, even if your destination field is properly composed of information from several source fields, you will typically combine the information using a functoid and not through a direct link from multiple source fields. You might use this option when you have content that can appear in one of several mutually exclusive fields in the source. In such a case, you would link all the possible fields to the single destination field in order to ensure the content you desire is picked up and placed in the destination. Nevertheless, the option is there if you need it.

Prompt to Save Before Testing the Map

When this item is checked, Mapper will prompt you to save the map file whenever you select the Tools Test Map menu item.

Functoids

Simple links from the source to the destination will cover most of what you want to do in a map. Sometimes, though, simply moving data from one document to another is insufficient. You may need to perform some intermediate processing to ensure that the data BizTalk puts into the destination document instance is in the form you require. This functionality is provided in BizTalk Mapper by functoids. Functoids accept data from one or more fields, process the data, and then output the result to a destination field.

Cascading Functoids

In fact, you can also *cascade* functoids in other words you can use the output from one functoid as the input of another. Why is this useful? Well, just as we break complicated programs into smaller subroutines, it is sometimes useful to be able to divide the intermediate processing between several functoids. You can continue cascading to whatever depth is required to implement the desired processing.

As a general rule, you might want to question your map if you have more than two or three layers of functoids between the source and the destination. You may be introducing so much logic that an application would be a better idea. Maps are intended to provide translation services for messages. While translation may, on occasion, require conditional logic or complex processing, in general the translation should be relatively straightforward. Cascading logic may be a sign that you are introducing procedural logic through the back door, logic which properly belongs in a schedule or application. If you have a lot of logic, you have the choice of either reducing the performance of the overall system with lots of script code during the mapping process, or short-changing the application logic by leaving out some functions.

Functoids Provided by BizTalk

BizTalk Mapper comes with an assortment of pre-built functoids which provide a wide range of functionality. For example, there are mathematical functoids to, say, multiply two fields together. There are also database functoids that can access a database and return data. One of the functoids even permits users to enter their own custom scripts, giving ultimate flexibility if you need non-standard functionality, you can write your own functoid!

> **You may even create your own custom functoids by creating a COM component. We will discuss custom functoids, and then build an example, later in this chapter.**

When you open the functoid palette, either through the View menu, or by clicking the toolbar button with the paint palette icon, you will find the stock functoids organized by category on nine different tabs.

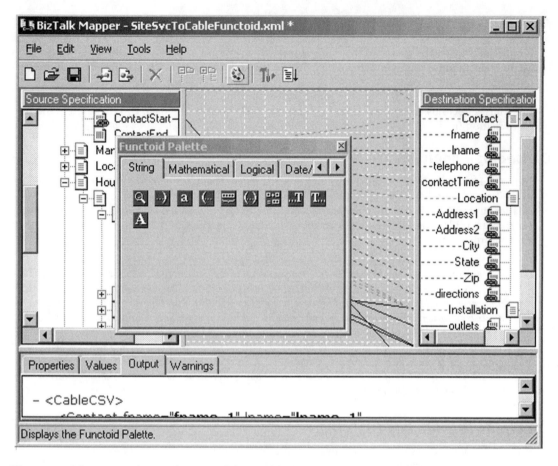

You may add a custom functoid to one of these tabbed property sheets, as well. The standard categories are:

- ❏ String
- ❏ Mathematical
- ❏ Logical
- ❏ Date and Time
- ❏ Conversion
- ❏ Scientific
- ❏ Cumulative
- ❏ Database
- ❏ Advanced

The most common mapping tasks, and many of the not-so-common ones too, can be handled with the functoids provided by BizTalk. Since you have not encountered any practical tasks as yet, the utility of a few of these functoids may not be clear to you. Skim the tables that follow for now to get a sense of what is available. Later, you can come back to them as a reference.

String Functoids

Functoid	Meaning
String Find	Returns the position in a string at which a second string begins, for example, looking for b in abc returns 2.
String Left	Returns a specified number of characters from a string, beginning from the left. Behaves like (and uses) the VBScript Left function.
Lowercase	Converts a string to lowercase, for example, ABC becomes abc.
String Right	Returns a specified number of characters from a string, beginning from the end of the string. Uses the VBScript Right function.
String Length	Returns the length of a string excluding pad characters. Uses the len function after converting the argument to a string.
String Extract	Returns a specified number of characters beginning at a specified location within a string. Works like the VBScript mid function.
Concatenate	Concatenates an arbitrary list of strings, for example, "ab","cd","xyz" becomes "abcdxyz".
String Left Trim	Removes leading spaces from a string.
String Right Trim	Removes trailing spaces from a string.
Uppercase	Converts a string to all uppercase characters, for example abc becomes ABC.

String functoids are most useful to you when the target field is either a subset of a source field, or a combination of several source fields. In those cases, you need to be able to perform some string manipulation to get the target results you want.

The ability to remove leading and trailing whitespace, and the ability to force a string to one case or the other, is useful when dealing with legacy systems. In such cases, you may find the target application performing string comparisons. The original data source the application was designed for may have been more restrictive in its input than the application you are now using. This is certainly the case when the source of data entry has moved from dedicated terminals to PCs. Being able to trim the incoming string during mapping, or force the case before the destination application receives it, can help you avoid difficulties.

Mathematical Functoids

Functoid	Meaning
Absolute value	Finds the absolute value of a number
Integer	Finds the integral portion of a real number
Maximum value	Returns the greatest value in a series of numeric values
Minimum value	Returns the smallest value in a series of numeric values
Modulo	Returns the modulus after dividing a number by an integer

Table continued on following page

Functoid	Meaning
Round	Rounds a number to a specific number of decimal places, or to the nearest whole number if none are specified
Square root	Returns the square root of the given number
Addition	Returns the sum of a series of numbers
Subtraction	Subtracts a series of numbers from the first number in the series
Multiplication	Multiplies a series of numbers
Division	Divides one number by another

The name of this functoid category is slightly misleading. The more advanced mathematical functoids are actually found in the Scientific functoids category. The functoids in this tab are the more pedestrian operators such as max, min, and sums. All the messages BizTalk is designed to handle will be textual in nature, and handling numbers expressed as strings in your target application can be annoying. The mathematical functoids do the appropriate conversions for you, allowing you to do some simple math during the mapping process, thereby avoiding conversion in your own code.

Logical Functoids

Functoid	Meaning
Greater than	True if the first parameter is greater than the second
Greater than or equal	True if the first parameter is greater than or equal to the second
Less than	True if the first parameter is less than the second parameter
Less than or equal to	True if the first parameter is less than or equal to the second parameter
Equal	True if the first parameter is equal to the second
Not equal	True if the parameters are not equal
Logical String	True if the parameter is a string
Logical Date	True if the parameter value can be interpreted as a date
Logical Numeric	True if the parameter value can be interpreted as a numeric type
Logical OR	Performs a logical OR on a series of input parameters
Logical AND	Performs a logical AND on a series of input parameters

You may have thought that the ability to generate a `true` or `false` value in the target document, based on a condition in the source message, is something that won't be needed very often. You are absolutely correct.

Logical functoids are actually mainly used in cascading functoids. Checking source message conditions in order to decide whether to perform a particular action (via another functoid) is extremely useful. Therefore, you will typically use logical functoids as the first stage of a cascaded functoid link, with one or more functoids from other categories as the next stage or stages. You might use a Boolean value from a logical functoid as an input to a script functoid.

Let's have an example. The "Value If True" functoid in the Advanced functoid category takes two input parameters. The first input is a Boolean; if this is `true`, the functoid outputs the value of the second parameter to the target document. This functoid is therefore tailored for use as the second step of a cascaded functoid mapping, in which the first step uses a Logical functoid.

Building on this idea, suppose I have a source message that is a store item requisition. One source field has the value of the requested item. Another source field contains the cost limit above which the requisition requires special approval processing (this limit varies between different departments). The target document, by contrast, has a single field holding the name of the approver. If the field is empty, the requisition is fulfilled without further approval. If it has a name in it, the message must be sent to the approver for review.

You could map the two source fields into a Greater Than functoid, and then link the output from this into the first input of the Value Mapping Advanced functoid. The second parameter of this functoid could either be a constant value (if all approval comes from the same source), or a link to another field in the source document that lists the name of the department head. These cascaded functoids are illustrated below:

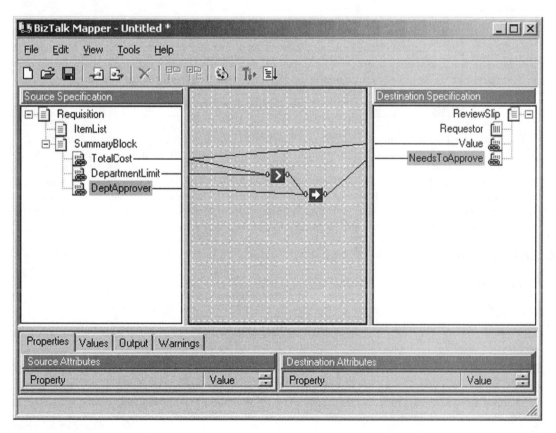

Date and Time Functoids

Functoid	Meaning
Add days	Adds the number of days specified in the second parameter to a date given in the first parameter, returning the date as a string value in ISO 8601 format (YYYY-MM-DD)
Date	Returns the current date as a string in ISO 8601 format
Time	Returns the current time as an ISO 8601 format string (hh:mm:ss)
Date and Time	Returns the current date and time as an IDO 8601 string (YYYY-MM-DDThh:mm:ss)

These functoids are useful for timestamping messages that do not have timestamps of their own. Many purchase order formats, for example, require the date and time of the purchase order as one of their field values. A source application might not record this information. Adding the timestamp during mapping is convenient. Similarly, the "Add days" functoid is a useful way to establish a deadline when you are given a "within x days" criterion. Since the dates and times in the messages we are dealing with are text strings, not binary types, performing this arithmetic yourself can be tedious.

Conversion Functoids

Functoid	Meaning
ASCII from Character	Returns the ASCII value for the given character
Character from ASCII	Returns the character represented by the given value
Hexadecimal	Converts the decimal input to a hexidecimal output
Octal	Converts the decimal input to an octal output

These functoids provide numeric conversions to and from various data types useful in computing. However, again bear in mind that they deal with string representations of numeric types, and the output they produce is also a string representation of numeric data. So, although these functoids relieve you of the necessity of doing their own type conversions to and from text, their results cannot be used as numerics in your own scripts. If you wish to perform further calculations, you will have to perform your own conversions. We will describe later (in the section about *Configuring Functoids*) how you can study the functoids' scripts to see how you can perform your own conversions.

Scientific Functoids

Functoid	Meaning
Arc tangent	Calculates the arc tangent of the input parameter
Cosine	Cosine of the input parameter
Sine	Sine of the input parameter
Tangent	Tangent of the input parameter
Natural Exponent Function	Calculates the value of e raised to the given power

Table continued on following page

Functoid	Meaning
Natural logarithm	Calculates the natural (base e) logarithm of the parameter
10^X	Raises ten to the given power
Common Logarithm	Calculates the base ten logarithm of the given number
X^Y	Raises the first parameter to the power specified in the second parameter
Base-Specified Logarithm	Calculates the logarithm of the first parameter in the base specified by the second parameter

Like the Conversion and Math functoids, this category offers numeric functions for source document content that represents numeric types. The same warning about text to numeric conversions we made under the Conversion category holds for this category as well.

Cumulative Functoids

Functoid	Meaning
Cumulative sum	Sums all the values of the given field by iterating over all occurrences of the field's parent
Cumulative average	Calculates the average value of the given field as it appears in all instances of the field's parent record
Cumulative minimum	Returns the minimum value of all occurrences of the input field
Cumulative maximum	Returns the maximum value of all occurrences of the input field
Cumulative string	Returns the string formed by concatenating the values obtained by iterating over all occurrences of the field's parent

To understand the functions in this functoid category, and also the ones that follow, we require a bit more understanding of the mapping process.

As you look at the source and destination specifications in Mapper, you see a single appearance of each unique field and record. In truth, though, some of these records may appear lots of times in a particular message instance. Our SiteServiceDescription specification from the last chapter, for example, allows the Lighting record to appear zero or many times in instances of this message. You may need to work with all instances of a record or field as a group to accomplish the mapping you desire.

The Cumulative category's functoids work by retrieving the value of a field each time its parent appears. Continuing with our Lighting example, for instance, we can map the Lighting element's power attribute into the Cumulative sum functoid. If we do so, we will get the sum of all the power attributes. The functoid is called once for each instance of the Lighting element and is passed the value of the element's power attribute each time.

Database

Functoid	Meaning
Fetch column value from row (Lookup)	Returns the value of the specified column from a row retrieved by the database extractor functoid
Fetch row by column value (Database Extractor)	Searches the specified table by the value
Error return	Returns the error string, if any, returned by executing the database extractor

There may be times when a field value is a key that references something in a database. In such a case, the data you want to map into the destination may not be explicitly listed in the source message; you have to access a database to retrieve the relevant data.

An example might be using some identifier code like a Social Security Number or employee code to reference a person. The source field contains the employee code, while you want to fill the name and telephone number of that employee, present in a database, into your destination fields. That is where the database functoids come in.

> *In a narrow, theoretical sense this is a bad design. XML vocabularies should be self-contained with regard to the data they contain. Even the efforts toward a linking technology for XML (such as, XLink, XPointer) generally deal with links to other XML sources rather than databases, although they do not preclude them. In practice, however, you may need to join data from a variety of sources using different storage mechanisms. If you can be sure the recipient of your messages (in this case BizTalk Server as it works to translate your message into the outgoing format) will have access to the referenced database and will understand the reference, this sort of design is a pragmatic and acceptable technique. A discussion of linking dissimilar data stores using XML may be found on ASPToday at http://www.asptoday.com/articles/20000830.htm.*

Database functoids are always cascaded. The first stage functoid will always be the database Extractor. This is connected to a field whose value is used as a SQL key to retrieve a particular row from a relational table. The rest of the parameters for the Extractor functoid are constants used to identify the table, connect to it, and identify the column on which to search.

The output of the Extractor functoid is a recordset containing the retrieved row. This output must go into either the Lookup functoid, the Error return functoid, or both. The output of the Lookup functoid is the value of the specified column within the row retrieved by the Extractor, while the output of the Error return functoid is the text of the error message (if any) resulting from the extractor's database retrieval. Let's say you need a series of names for customers living in a particular postal code. You would use the Extractor functoid to get the recordset containing customer records for the postal code, then the Lookup functoid to retrieve the names. Of course, if the postal code is in error or there is something wrong with the query, you would get an error, so you would also link the Extractor's output to the Error functoid. The output of the Lookup functoid would go to one field and the output of the Error functoid would go to another. If the recipient found an empty field where the lookup was to go, the recipient's application could examine the value of the error field to determine the problem. The output from whichever functoid is used is linked to a field in the destination document.

The ability to embed scripts in an XSL stylesheet is a Microsoft extension. XSLT uses a script-like capability that relies on XSLT elements rather than script code. Although the stylesheets the Mapper generates conform to the XSLT Recommendation, they retain the wholly proprietary Microsoft script extensions to that standard. This is what permits functoids to instantiate and call COM components from a stylesheet. Therefore stylesheets using functoids will not work in any XSLT processor other than Microsoft's MSXML. This is not a problem within BizTalk, as that is the XSLT processor it uses, but do not expect the XSL generated by Mapper to be independently useful with other XSLT processors.

Advanced

Functoid	Meaning
Scripting	Allows the user to enter a custom script for manipulating the input parameters
Record count	Returns the number of times the given record appears in the source document
Index	Returns the value of a specific record or field at a specified index
Iteration	Returns the iteration number (in a loop) of a source record
Value mapping	Generates code for the second parameter if the first parameter is `true`
Value mapping (Flattening)	Value maps, and flattens the source document hierarchy
Looping	Inserts an `xsl:for-each` element into the map, so that each time the source field or record appears, an instance of the destination record is generated

As the category name implies, these functoids provide advanced capabilities, such as you might provide if you were writing your own document object model (DOM) code or XSLT templates.

The Scripting functoid lets you write your own custom script code. The script you provide is inserted within an instance of the Microsoft-proprietary `script` element. The routine provided is invoked in the body of the map, via an instance of the `eval` element, which is also a proprietary extension of the XSLT schema.

Unlike almost all of the other functoids, the remaining functoids in this category do not result in script functions that are called from `eval` elements in the body of the map. Instead, they use XSLT elements to accomplish their function within the body of the map's stylesheet.

The Index and Iteration functoids provide you with the kind of information you would have if you were performing the translation in custom document object model code. You would have access to loop counters in such code, but you do not have this in XSLT stylesheets. That is what these functoids expose. The Index functoid returns the value of a particular instance of a repeating field given the index of the desired field, while the Iteration functoid returns the value of the loop iterator (telling you where you are in the iteration) as the mapping functoid works its way through each instance of the source field.

These two functoids are implemented with the XSLT functions count and position, respectively.

The Value mapping functoid is also used when you expect to have multiple occurrences of the source field or record. This functoid takes a source field as its first parameter and an integer index as its second parameter. Its output is the value of the nth occurrence of the field, where n is the value of the second parameter of the functoid.

For example, suppose you are mapping a field that can occur multiple times into a field that can appear exactly once. The source field might be a list of ID numbers for all the employees on a project, while the destination field could be the ID for the project leader. In our example, suppose we know that the project leader's ID will always be the first one. In our map, we want to copy the first ID we find, and ignore the rest. This functoid uses zero-based indices, so you would enter the index 0 for the second parameter of the functoid.

The value mapping functoid and its flattening version take a source field as their first parameter and a field or constant value as their second parameter. If the first parameter evaluates to true, then the second value is copied to the destination. If it is false, nothing is copied.

Finally, the Looping functoid inserts an xsl:for-each element into the map in which the argument of the for-each is the input parameter record. The xsl:for-each element works like a loop in a programming language. For each occurrence of the source, something will be generated in the destination. In this case, that something is an instance of the destination record. Note that we say 'record' and not 'field'. A field can be an XML attribute, which can appear only once per parent element, while a record is an element and elements can occur as often as you wish. Every time the source record appears, the multiple output records functoid will insert an instance of the record to which it is linked into the destination document. Think of a parts list in a requisition. The specification file for the source will have a single record named, say, Item with one or many cardinality to contain each part. You might end up linking this record to a similar record, Part, in the destination through the looping functoid. When a message instance is mapped, the output will have as many Part records as the source had Item records.

Configuring Functoids

Once you have selected a functoid and placed it on the grid, it is time to configure it. You establish links from the source into the functoid by dragging the mouse cursor from the source field (or record) to the functoid. Similarly, to link the functoid output to a destination field, record, or functoid, drag the cursor from the functoid to the destination.

There may be other properties of the functoid that require configuration. To do this, open the Functoid Properties dialog by double-clicking on the functoid, or by selecting the View | Functoid Properties... menu item. The dialog, which consists of two tabbed property pages General and Script, looks something like this:

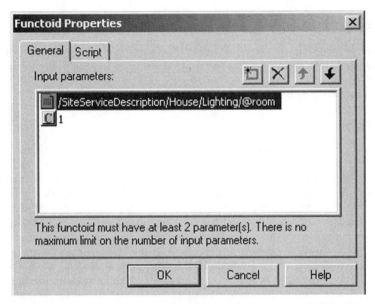

If you have created any incoming links, they will appear in the parameter list in the property page tabbed **General**. This is also where you can enter constant parameters.

For example, the screenshot above shows properties for a Value functoid (Advanced category), which takes two parameters. The first is a link from some repeating record or field for which you wish to map a particular occurrence. The second is the instance index of the field you wish to map; this parameter is a constant value. In the instance depicted above, we've indicated that we want to map the second occurrence of the room attribute (the Lighting element repeats). To configure this:

❑ link the desired attribute to the functoid

❑ open the **Properties** dialog

❑ add a constant by clicking on the left-most toolbar button (with a gold-colored rectangle icon)

❑ the constant appears with a red "C" icon; click on the value and enter your constant value (here 1)

The remaining toolbar buttons handle the deletion, promotion, and demotion of parameters within the parameter list. The button with the stylized X icon deletes the selected property. Since functoids are implemented with script code, the order in which parameters appear in the list matters. To change the order, select a parameter and click the promotion button (up arrow icon) to move it up in the list, or click the demotion button (down arrow icon) to move it down in the list.

In most cases, the **Script** property page is only useful for studying what the functoid is doing. It displays the actual VBScript code that will be inserted into the XSLT map file's stylesheet section. The Scripting functoid (Advanced category), however, is an exception. The **Edit** control on its property page is read-write, allowing you to enter your own script code.

If you inspect the script of the stock functoids, you may notice an apparent discrepancy between the stated number of parameters that Looping functoids and the database extractor functoid take, and the actual number of parameters given in the script. This is because these functoids require an index for various reasons. Mapper will insert these into the xsl:eval element that calls the functoid's script implementation. The remaining parameters in the script correspond to the parameters referenced on the *General* property page.

Compiling and Testing Maps

Once you have all your links in place (including links with functoids) you must compile the map before BizTalk Server can use it in production. You may also wish to test your map without going to the trouble of configuring BizTalk Server and submitting sample messages to it. You can accomplish both activities from BizTalk Mapper.

Compiling Maps

Compiling a map refers to the process of generating all the XSLT that is implied by the links and functoids, as well as copying the source and destination specifications into the map file in the form that BizTalk Server expects to find them at run time. All this information existed in memory in Mapper, but now it is written to a map file. A specification is automatically compiled when you save it to disk, or you may explicitly call for a compilation. The result of the compilation is an XML document, following the vocabulary devised by Microsoft for use with BizTalk Server's run-time mapping function.

There are a variety of ways to compile a map. You can select the Tools | Compile Map menu option, or press F5. You can also click on the Compile Map toolbar button, which has an icon that looks like a hammer, screwdriver, and right-facing arrow. The result of the compilation remains in memory, not disk, although the stylesheet portion of the compiled map is displayed in the Output tab of the pane at the bottom of the Mapper, as seen in the illustration below:

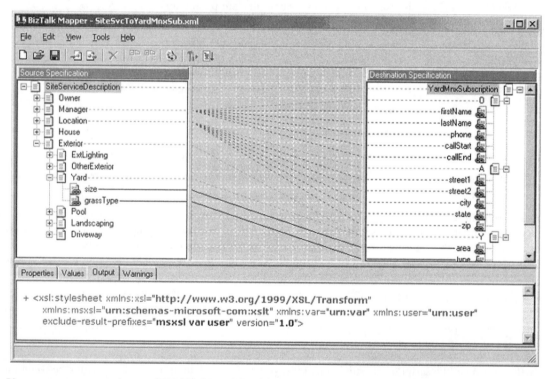

If you are accustomed to an IDE like Visual Studio, you should know that warnings in Mapper are not like warnings in an IDE for a compiled language. You should not ignore them because they are really critical errors in your map. Until you have corrected all the conditions flagged as warnings, you will not be able to use your map with BizTalk Server. The map below is contrived to generate a list of warnings, which you see in the Warnings tab:

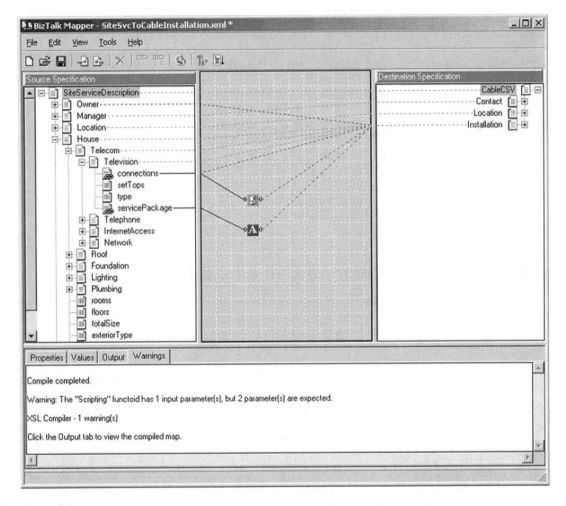

Testing Maps

If you look at the Tools menu, you will see a Test Map menu item. You can also invoke this feature with *Ctrl-F5* or by clicking on the toolbar button displaying the icon that resembles a page with a downward pointing arrow. If you do so with a map loaded into the Mapper, it will generate some test output in the Output tab of the bottom pane. If the map in the Mapper has not been compiled, you will be prompted to save your work; doing so compiles the map prior to saving it to disk.

Simply running the Test Map feature will be unsatisfying. The output will consist of a minimal shell of an output document. The Mapper has no source document instance, so it is unable to put any content into the destination document instance.

This is where the Values tab comes into play. Recall that earlier we saw how to set up a constant value for a field in the destination document using the Destination constant value edit control on the Values tab. At that time, we skipped over the other edit control on the tab, the one labelled Source test value. You can use this to provide a source value by selecting a field and entering a sample value. Do this for every field for which you want to test the map's processing. Then, when you use the Test Map feature, these values will be used to provide sample content for the map and will appear, after mapping, in the destination document instance displayed in the Output tab.

183

Of course, there is a limit to what you can do with these test values. You cannot use them to provide multiple instances of a source field. If the input is a non-XML flatfile, you cannot test delimiter processing. Still, this is a good way to test the broad outlines of your map, particularly any functoid processing. You can enter values that really test the boundaries of your scripts or functoids and see if the map works properly.

Mapping for Wrox Site Managers

The best way to really drive home the lessons of the preceding sections is to create a few maps. Our sample from the last chapter left us with three document specifications: a master Site Service Description, and two documents that are derived from it, the Cable Installation Order and the Yard Care message. Developing maps from the Site Service Description to each of the other specifications will not only show you how to create a map, but also give you an insight into the finer points of mapping to flatfile formats, as well.

Site Service Description to Cable Installation

The chief differences between the Site Service Description and the Cable Installation specifications are three:

❑ Site Service Description is XML while Cable Installation is a CSV flatfile

The conversion between formats is handled for us behind the scenes. The mapping process will convert the Site Service message into the intermediate XML form, then the delimited file serializer will use the Cable Installation specification to write out the data in the proper format.

❑ Cable Installation contains a subset of the information in Site Service Description

Mapping will handle this point. We will establish links between the information we need from Site Service and the final fields in Cable Installation and ignore the rest. Fields that are not linked will not be copied to the destination document.

❑ Site Service Description distinguishes between the owner and the site manager, while Cable Installation uses a single contact person

Here we are imposing a business rule. If the cable installation company needs to contact someone to clarify the order, we want them to contact the Site Manager not the owner (this is part of the benefit of having the site management service). When it comes to scheduling the physical installation, however, we must concern ourselves with the owner's availability   they have to be present to let the installer in.

We'll accommodate both of these conditions by mapping the owner's contact start time to the installation time field, thereby scheduling the earliest possible installation. We'll also map the manager's contact start time to the installation contact time field so that the cable company will call the manager at a convenient time (and leaving the home owner in peace!).

In order to illustrate the use of functoids, we'll introduce two more business rules. First, let's assume that the cable company requires that every cable outlet be paired with a set-top converter box, because the televisions cannot be connected directly to the cable outlet. This means that we must screen installation orders to ensure that cable connections can only be ordered in conjunction with a set-top box. We'll do this using a custom Script functoid. Second, we'll assume that a legacy application handles installation scheduling at the cable company; this application expects uppercase letters in the field describing the service plan. We'll enforce this during mapping with an Uppercase functoid.

To create this map file (`SiteServiceToCableInstallation.xml` in the download), create a new map with `SiteServiceDescription.xml` as the source and `CableWO.xml` as the destination specification. Next create the links listed below. You will need to open the functoid palette and drop a Scripting functoid and an Uppercase functoid onto the grid to accommodate the links that implement our business rules. The links you must create are summarized in the following table:

Source field	Destination field
Owner/ContactStart	Installation/installTime
Manager/fname	Contact/fname
Manager/lname	Contact/lname
Manager/telephone	Contact/telephone
Manager/ContactStart	Contact/contactTime
Location/Street1	Location/Address1
Location/Street2	Location/Address2
Location/City	Location/City
Location/PoliticalRegion	Location/State
Location/PostalCode	Location/Zip
Location/Directions	Location/directions
House/Telecom/Television/connections	Installation/outlets
House/Telecom/Television/connections	Script functoid (parameter 1)
House/Telecom/Television/setTops	Script functoid (parameter 2)
Script functoid	Installation/converters
House/Telecom/Television/servicePackage	Uppercase functoid
Uppercase functoid	Installation/service

The only detail remaining is the configuration of the functoids. The Uppercase functoid configures itself once the links are established. The Script functoid, however, needs us to provide some code. If the links are established in the order they are listed in the table above, the first parameter will be a text string denoting the number of cable outlets, and the second will be a string denoting the number of set-top boxes ordered. We need to compare the two parameters and check that there are at least as many set-tops ordered as there are cable outlets to be installed.

Here's the simple VBScript that implements this:

```
Function MyFunction2( p_strConnections, p_strSetTops )
  If CInt(p_strConnections) >= CInt(p_strSetTops) then
  MyFunction2 = p_strConnections
  Else
  MyFunction2 = p_strSetTops
  End If
End Function
```

The first thing the script does is convert the input strings into integers, and check to see if we have a set-top for each outlet. If not, we return the number of outlets as the output of this function. From the table above, you see that this functoid's output will be used as the value of the converters field, which is the number of set-tops to bring and install in the house. The number of outlets is also output if the number of set-tops exactly matches the number of connections.

If we've ordered more set-tops than cable outlets, we assume there is a reason for this and pass the number of set-tops along unchanged. Perhaps the owner is connecting a single outlet to both a VCR and a television so that they can watch and record two different premium channels at the same time.

Here's what the Mapper should look like when you have finished with the links:

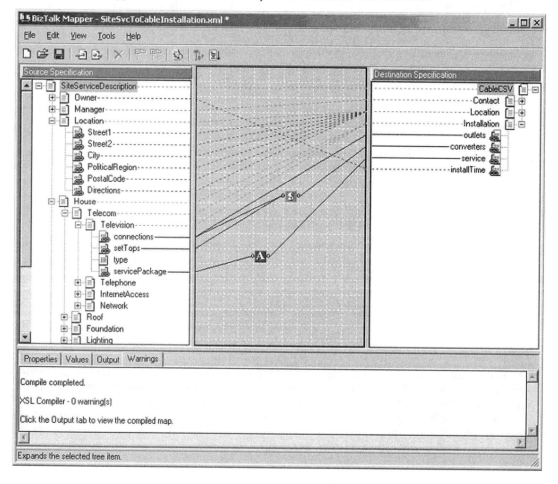

To finish, compile the map and save it to the WebDAV repository under the name `SiteSvcToCableInstallation.xml`. If you want to test the script functoid, enter different source test values for the `connections` and `setTops` fields in the source document and test the map. The output should reflect the business rule we've described.

Site Description to Yard Care

The map for converting Site Service Descriptions into Yard Care subscriptions is not an XML specification. This is a trait it shares with the Cable Installation map. The mapping process will use the positional file serializer component, driven by the Yard Care specification, to output the desired file format. Like the previous map, we will be dropping the fields in the Site Service Description that do not pertain to Yard Care. Start by creating a new map with `SiteServiceDescription.xml` as the source and `YardMnxSubscription.xml` as the destination. Next, create the links listed in the table below:

Source field	Destination field
Manager/fname	O/firstName
Manager/lname	O/lastName
Manager/telephone	O/phone
Manager/ContactStart	O/callStart
Manager/ContactEnd	O/callEnd
Location/Street1	A/street1
Location/Street2	A/street2
Location/City	A/city
Location/PoliticalRegion	A/state
Location/PostalCode	A/zip
Exterior/Yard/size	Y/area
Exterior/Yard/grassType	Y/type

Note that we didn't need any functoids to implement business rules or complicated processing. We do, however, need to enter some information that isn't present in the Site Service Description.

Firstly, Wrox Site Managers assumes that yards will be cut once a week. The Yard Care vendor, however, is a bit more flexible, permitting customers to specify the desired frequency in terms of the number of times a yard should be cut in one month.

Additionally, since Wrox Site Managers is not itself a Yard Care vendor, it makes no recommendations as to what fertilizer or herbicide to use. Instead, it wants the Yard Care vendor to make a recommendation.

These items are communicated to the Yard Care subscription order during the mapping process by specifying some constants for two destination fields in the Y record. The cut field, denoting how often the yard should be mowed per month, will take the constant value "4" (once per week). The `agent` field, denoting the type of fertilizer or herbicide to use, will be given the constant value `eval`, meaning that the service should evaluate the yard and make a recommendation to the site manager.

Here is a condensed version of what the map looks like after compiling it and saving it as `SiteSvcToYardMnxSub.xml`:

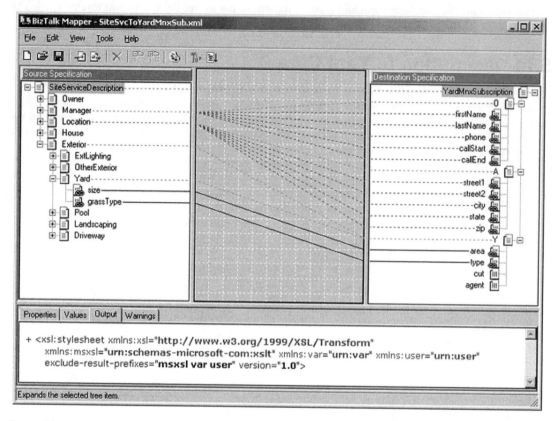

Functoids are even more useful than you might imagine based on the discussion above. Like so many things in Windows, they are implemented as COM components, which means we get to have some fun writing our own and adding them to the functoid palette. This is the next task we take up.

Developing Your Own Functoid

Functoids exist to provide map designers with reusable packages of processing useful in the creation of maps. Although BizTalk Mapper comes with a wide variety of ready-made functoids, it cannot anticipate every useful mapping function. For example, some markets may need specialized functions, which are commonly used in their industry, but not outside it. For this reason, BizTalk Mapper has a mechanism that allows programmers to create their own functoids.

Functoids are implemented as COM components that expose the `IFunctoid` interface. We'll discuss this interface in a moment. Then we'll demonstrate how to implement it, by packaging the custom script we have just used with a Scripting functoid on the Site Service to Cable Installation map, as a custom functoid.

How Functoids Work

If Mapper is going to be able to use a third party functoid, it needs to do three things:

- ❑   Locate all functoid components on the local system
- ❑   Query the functoid for its properties
- ❑   Serialize the functoid's behavior into a map file

Locating Functoid Components

COM includes a mechanism called **component categories**, whereby component developers are able to declare a category and then designate a component as belonging to it. These categories are identified with a GUID; a component belonging to the category provides the GUID as an entry in the registry, under the key Implemented Categories. This means that programs can find a desired category in the registry, and enumerate the class IDs of all the components that implement the category. With a class ID in hand, it is an easy matter for the application to locate the component's implementation, and then instantiate it.

If you look at the registry with the OLE View utility (included with Visual Studio) you will see an entry near the top of the tree labelled Grouped by Component Category. This is the first child of the root Object Classes node. Under this entry, you will find a node named MapEdit Functoids.

Expand this node and you will see an entry for CannedFunctoid Class. This is the component that comes with BizTalk Server, and which implements all the functoids you see in BizTalk Mapper.

If you do not have Visual Studio, you can inspect the registry with the Registry Editor, a utility that comes with the operating system. This utility is found in regedt32.exe under the operating system's system32 folder. However, it does not organize the registry's information as nicely as OLE View, so linking all the pieces we've just discussed can be a laborious process.

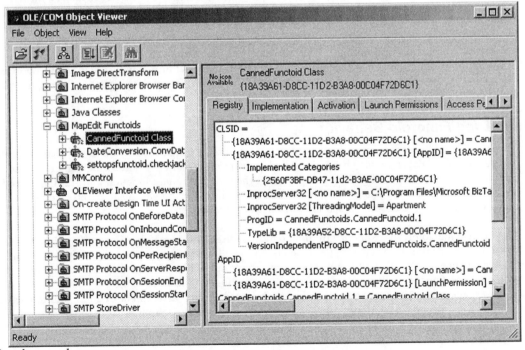

In other words:

> **Making a custom functoid known to BizTalk Mapper involves adding the appropriate key to the component's registry information.**

We'll do this a little later on in our sample by creating a **registry file** and merging it into the registry. A registry file is simply a text file in a particular format, so we can create it with Notepad or any other text editor.

Querying Functoid Properties

Custom functoids have to provide a lot of information to BizTalk Mapper. Just getting plugged into the functoid palette requires numerous properties:

- ❏ The palette is divided into tabbed pages, so the functoid has to indicate where it wants to go

- ❏ The functoid is represented on the palette by a bitmap you include in the resources of the implementing DLL; it must give Mapper the ID of the bitmap so that Mapper can retrieve it

- ❏ The palette includes tooltips, so the functoid must supply that information too

- ❏ The number of input parameters to the functoid, and their types, must be supplied to Mapper

This last requirement helps Mapper enforce proper linking. If you experiment with functoids, you'll find that there are occasions when you will try to establish a link from a field to a functoid and Mapper prohibits it, changing the cursor to the circle and slash icon. If you open the Properties dialog for a functoid, the first tab (General) tells you how many incoming parameters the functoid can take.

Retrieving Functoid Script Code

So far, all this reporting has only served to connect a functoid to the development environment. The whole point of a functoid is to provide some processing when the run-time server maps a message. This processing has to come in a form that is compatible with XSLT. Not surprisingly, all functoids implement their processing behavior through script code.

When you place a functoid onto the grid, Mapper retrieves most of the functoid's properties. One of the most important properties retrieved is the script source code that implements the functoid's processing behavior. Mapper is then able to display this code in the script tab of the properties dialog, or write the code out to a map file.

Serializing Functoid Behavior

Clearly, having the script source is an important part of serializing the functoid to the stylesheet portion of the map file. That script also has to be called appropriately from the non-script elements. In most cases, this is just a matter of grabbing the name of the functoid's main function and stuffing it inside an `msxsl:eval` element. If you go back to the reference tables for the various functoid categories, however, you'll find that some functoids work a bit differently.

The logical functoids, for example, are intended to be used with the Value If True functoid. Drop one of these functoids onto the grid, compile the map, and you'll find Mapper has wrapped the call inside an `xsl:if` element. The element is not closed until the Value If True functoid is added. Similarly, the last two database functoids rely on the Database Extractor functoid for one of their inputs. Clearly, Mapper makes special exceptions for some of its known functoids, so the assignment of a functoid to a category will have an effect on how Mapper serializes the functoid into the map file.

IFunctoid Interface

The predefined, COM interface IFunctoid is the mechanism by which Mapper queries a functoid. It has two properties (FunctionsCount and Version) and three methods (GetFunctionParameter, GetFunctionDescripter, and GetScriptBuffer), so we should have a functoid implemented in short order. There are a number of enumerated values involved with one of the properties and two parameters of the method, and this will take a bit of sorting out.

IFunctoid Properties

A functoid component is an in-process COM DLL. A component can implement one or more functoids (as we have come to understand the term so far) using Mapper's functoid palette. In terms of the IFunctoid interface, the functoids in the palette are **functions**, so each functoid component can put one or more functions into the palette. The properties of the IFunctoid interface, therefore, have to be able to tell the Mapper about the functoid component as well as the functions it implements.

The properties FunctionsCount and Version pertain strictly to the component, reporting the number of individual functions implemented and the version of the component, respectively.

Property Name	Meaning
FunctionsCount	Read-only. A long value indicating how many functoids are implemented by the component DLL.
Version	Read-only. A long value denoting the version of the component DLL.

The ScriptBuffer property retrieves the script source code that Mapper must insert into the map file to implement the functoid function. On the basis of what we have just discussed, you might expect that the function identifier is the only parameter needed. Mapper, however, permits functoid functions with variable parameter lists. The ScriptBuffer property, therefore, takes a second parameter indicating how many input links are connecting to the function. This allows the ScriptBuffer property implementation to make any changes to the script that may be needed. Mapper will generate a call to the script that reflects the number of incoming links, so the body of the script function must agree in the number of parameters.

GetFunctionParameter Method

The GetFunctionParameter method retrieves a bit pattern that indicates what types of connections are permitted for a given functoid function and parameter. It returns a long value containing a bit pattern composed of CONNECTION_TYPE enumerated values. This is what enables Mapper to give users a visual cue as to when a link is permissible, and to disallow any attempts to make a link that would give the function an illegal input. Mapper, though, also gives similar warnings on the output side, so we must have a way of interrogating the functoid about its output. The first parameter of this method, a long value named lFuncID, identifies which functoid in the component is being interrogated, and the second parameter is a long value, lParamIndex, which is a zero-based index of the parameter for which information is desired. If lParamIndex = -1, the connection type pattern for the functoid output is desired.

GetScriptBuffer Method

The GetScriptBuffer method retrieves the text of the script code that implements the behavior of the functoid. It takes as parameters a long value, lFuncID, denoting the functoid's ID, and a long value, lInputs, indicating how many input parameters are used.

GetFunctionDescripter Method

We're still missing a mechanism for providing quite a few items that we discussed in the introductory comments to this section. Some of these items are the functoid palette tab on which this functoid's icon should be placed, the bitmap resource of that icon, and the tooltip text for the functoid. The `GetFunctionDescripter` method provides this mechanism. Its first parameter is the identifier of the functoid function to interrogate. The remaining seven parameters of the method, however, are variables that will be filled by the functoid with the needed information. They are passed by reference to permit this to happen.

The function category (see table below) parameter helps Mapper put the functoid function on the proper tab of the palette and generate the proper XSLT elements to use the function when the map is serialized. The script category parameter tells Mapper what kind of script language is in use. The function type tells Mapper whether this function has a fixed or variable number of input parameters, or whether it allows the user to enter her own script code.

Parameter Name	Type	Meaning
lIdentifier	Long	Zero-based identifier of the functoid function
pFuncCategory	FUNC_CATEGORY enumeration (ByRef)	Variable for storing the value of the functoid's function category
pScriptCategory	SCRIPT_CATEGORY enumeration (ByRef)	Variable for storing the value of the functoid's script category
pFuncType	FUNC_TYPE enumeration (ByRef)	Variable for storing the value of the functoid's type
pbstrName	String (ByRef)	Retrieves the value of the functoid's name
pbstrToolTip	String (ByRef)	Retrieves the tooltip text for the functoid
plBitmapID	Long (ByRef)	Retrieves the ID of the bitmap resource for the functoid's icon
plParmCount	Long (ByRef)	Retrieves the number of input parameters accepted by the functoid

The next three parameters (`pbstrName`, `pbstrToolTip`, and `plBitmapID`) allow the functoid to communicate information needed for the user interface. These are the function name, tooltip text, and the identifier of the bitmap resource in the DLL that provides the functoid function icon for the functoid palette. The final parameter communicates how many input parameters the function can accommodate.

The Enumerations

The preceding discussion highlighted that there are some very important enumerations related to `IFunctoid`. In this section we're going to review them briefly. Recall that an *enumeration* is simply a set of defined identifier values which a field can take. In the context of functoids, each enumeration describes a particular aspect of a given functoid.

For example, the FUNC_CATEGORY enumeration (that you will see in a moment) relates to the category a functoid belongs to. The category of any particular functoid is described by one of one of the member values from the FUNC_CATEGORY enumeration set. This value is passed to functions and applications if they need to know about the category of the functoid.

Some of the IFunctoid enumerations have only a few member values, while others have lots of defined values. Most should be clear from the reference tables below, although several may not be completely clear to you until you have seen the sample functoid implementation that follows.

FUNC_CATEGORY enumeration

As we have already discussed, this enumeration is used to designate the category of the functoid. It is used to place the functoid's icon on one of the existing tabs of the palette. It is also used by Mapper to determine what sort of XSLT to generate to properly use the functoid in the stylesheet. Usually, this takes the form of an xsl:eval element calling the appropriate script. In a few cases where functoids must be cascaded or where XSLT functions are used directly, however, different XSLT will be generated.

Identifier	Value	Comments
FUNC_CATEGORY_STRING	3	String functoids
FUNC_CATEGORY_MATH	4	Math conversions
FUNC_CATEGORY_DATACONV	5	Data conversions
FUNC_CATEGORY_DATETIME_FMT	6	Datetime formatting functoids
FUNC_CATEGORY_SCIENTIFIC	7	Scientific functoids
FUNC_CATEGORY_BOOLEAN	8	Logical functoids
FUNC_CATEGORY_SCRIPTER	9	Script functoid (advanced tab)
FUNC_CATEGORY_COUNT	10	Record count functoid
FUNC_CATEGORY_INDEX	11	Functoid returning the value of a record or field at a particular index
FUNC_CATEGORY_CUMULATIVE	12	Cumulative functoids
FUNC_CATEGORY_VALUE_MAPPING	13	Value mapping functoid
FUNC_CATEGORY_LOOPING	14	Looping functoid
FUNC_CATEGORY_ITERATION	15	Iterative functoids
FUNC_CATEGORY_DBLOOKUP	16	Retrieve column from row
FUNC_CATEGORY_DBEXTRACT	17	Database extractor
FUNC_CATEGORY_UNKNOWN	31	Reserved

SCRIPT_CATEGORY enumeration

This enumeration denotes the script language used for the functoid's implementation.

Identifier	Value	Comments
SCRIPT_CATEGORY_VBSCRIPT	0	VBScript language
SCRIPT_CATEGORY_JSCRIPT	1	Javascript
SCRIPT_CATEGORY_XSLSCRIPT	2	XSLT scripts

FUNC_TYPE enumeration

The FUNC_TYPE enumeration is used by Mapper to set up the functoid **Properties** dialog. The first two values are used to correctly handle inputs, while the last indicates whether the Mapper should expect to receive script source code from the user.

Identifier	Value	Comments
FUNC_TYPE_STD	1	Standard, fixed input functoid
FUNC_TYPE_VARIABLEINPUT	2	Functoid supporting a variable number of inputs
FUNC_TYPE_SCRIPTOR	3	Functoid that accepts script from the user

CONNECTION_TYPE enumeration

The values in this enumeration are used by Mapper to control what types of links, both input and output, are legitimate for use with the functoid. Note that the values progress as powers of two. This permits the values to be added together, to obtain a bit pattern which combines several member values.

Identifier	Value	Comments
CONNECT_TYPE_NONE	0	Connections disallowed
CONNECT_TYPE_FIELD	1	Connect to fields
CONNECT_TYPE_RECORD	2	Connect to records
CONNECT_TYPE_RECORD_CONTENT	4	Content to record content, for example, XML element text
CONNECT_TYPE_FUNC_STRING	8	Connect to the string functoids
CONNECT_TYPE_FUNC_MATH	16	Connect to math functoids
CONNECT_TYPE_FUNC_DATACONV	32	Connect to dataconversion functoids
CONNECT_TYPE_FUNC_DATETIME_FMT	64	Connect to date and time functoids

Table continued on following page

Identifier	Value	Comments
CONNECT_TYPE_FUNC_SCIENTIFIC	128	Connect to scientific functoids
CONNECT_TYPE_FUNC_BOOLEAN	256	Connect to logical functoids
CONNECT_TYPE_FUNC_SCRIPTER	512	Connect to script functoids
CONNECT_TYPE_FUNC_COUNT	1024	Connect to the functoid providing a count of record or field occurences
CONNECT_TYPE_FUNC_INDEX	2048	Connect to the functoid that returns the value of a field at a specific index position
CONNECT_TYPE_FUNC_CUMULATIVE	4096	Connect to a functoid in the cumulative category
CONNECT_TYPE_FUNC_VALUE_MAPPING	8192	Connect to the value mapping functoid
CONNECT_TYPE_FUNC_LOOPING	16384	Connect to the looping functoid
CONNECT_TYPE_FUNC_ITERATION	32768	Connect to the functoid that provides an iteration count
CONNECT_TYPE_FUNC_DBLOOKUP	65536	Connect to the database lookup functoid
CONNECT_TYPE_FUNC_DBEXTRACT	131072	Connect to the database extractor
CONNECT_TYPE_ALL	-1	All connection types permitted
CONNECT_TYPE_ALL_EXCEPT_RECORD	-3	Any connection except records

Implementing Cable Business Rule as a Functoid

That's a lot of reference material for functoids, and some of it may not be entirely clear to you right now. The best way to illustrate the material above is to create a functoid of our own. The mapping between the Site Service Description document and the Cable Installation document used a script functoid to handle a bit of business logic. We'll now recreate that same logic as a custom functoid and test it by replacing the script functoid in that map with our new one.

To begin the implementation:

1. Create an ActiveX DLL project in Visual Basic

2. Give the project the name settopsfunctoid

3. Add a class module named checkjacks

This class module will implement IFunctoid, giving us a COM component with the progID settopsfunctoid.checkjacks that exposes IFunctoid and IDispatch.

4. To implement `IFunctoid`, we must add a reference to the Microsoft BizTalk Server Canned Functoids 1.0 Type Library:

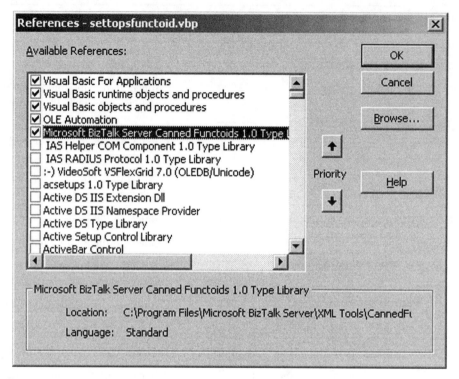

5. This will allow you to add the following line at the top of the class module file:

```
Implements CannedFunctoid
```

Now that we have declared our intentions, the hard work of implementing the interface begins.

Globals

There are a few constants that will be useful to us later on.

❑ Go ahead and make the following entries at the start of the class module:

```
Option Explicit
Implements CannedFunctoid

Const PROGID = "settopsfunctoid.checkjacks"
Const VERSION = 1          ' Version is 1
Const MAX_PARAMS = 2       ' Max number of input parameters

Const FUNCTOID_COUNT = 1   ' Total number of functoid functions in the DLL

Const FUNCID_CHECKJACKS = 0
Const BITMAP_CHECKJACKS = 101
```

`Option Explicit` is a good idea as it enforces rigorous type checking in the development environment. The `Implements` entry tells Visual Basic to check your class module entries against the `IFunctoid` interface type library to ensure a complete implementation. The constants are items we will be using to describe the functoid in parts of the code.

The FUNCTOIDINFO Structure

Since we're only implementing one function within our functoid component we could get away with burying the configuration information BizTalk Mapper needs in the property and method implementations. However, this does not make for clean code, and would get in the way if we were to add new functions.

The best way to handle extensibility is to create a data structure to contain configuration information and populate an array with these structures, one for each function implemented in the component. Our structure will be called the `FUNCTOIDINFO` structure. We'll make it private to the class.

❑   Add the following declaration to your class module:

```
Private Type FUNCTOIDINFO
 funcType As FUNC_TYPE
 funcCategory As FUNC_CATEGORY
 scriptCategory As SCRIPT_CATEGORY
 funcId As Long
 funcName As String
 tooltip As String
 bitmapID As Long
 scriptBuffer As String
 outparamConn As Long
 cInput As Long
 inputparamConn(MAX_PARAMS) As Long
End Type
```

Most of the members of this structure should be familiar to you, from the preceding sections on the interface and its enumerations. These are all items that Mapper will want to know about and which we will have to offer through the interface.

One item that bears discussion is the array `inputparamConn`. We've declared its size to be that of the greatest number of parameters used by any function in the functoid component. Since we are only creating one functoid function, in our case this is not really a problem. Actually, in most cases this won't be a cause for concern because functions will have similar numbers of parameters. However, if you ever find yourself implementing a functoid in which one function takes a large number of parameters and the rest have comparatively few, you might wish to refine this declaration a bit. As it stands, though, it keeps our code fairly simple. We have an array of known size through which we can iterate or into which we can index. We can declare and populate an array of these structures when the class is initialized.

Initializing the Component

Before Mapper can use the functoid, we have to make sure the `FUNCTOIDINFO` structure gets initialized. The best place to do this is in the private subroutine `Class_Initialize()`, which is called when an instance of the component is created.

1. Create the `Class_Initialize()` subroutine as below:

```
Private rFunctoidStruct() As FUNCTOIDINFO
Private mvarFunctionsCount As Long
Private mvarVersion As Long

Private Sub Class_Initialize()

 mvarFunctionsCount = FUNCTOID_COUNT
 mvarVersion = VERSION

 Call InitStruct(rFunctoidStruct())

End Sub
```

The variable `mvarFunctionsCount` acts to control the array of `FUNCTOIDINFO` structures. We use it to properly dimension the array when we initialize it, and to provide a boundary for loops and index checks subsequently.

The core work of the initialization occurs in the private subroutine `InitStruct()`. Ideally, we'd like to set up some sort of loop, but each function could be different, so we'll have to settle for a series of assignments. In this sample it doesn't matter since we only have one function, but it is always a good idea to plan ahead and write code that will extend well in the future.

2. Here's how we start the `InitStruct()` routine:

```
Private Sub InitStruct(rFunctoidInfo() As FUNCTOIDINFO)

 ReDim rFunctoidStruct(mvarFunctionsCount)

 rFunctoidInfo(0).funcType = FUNC_TYPE_STD
 rFunctoidInfo(0).funcCategory = FUNC_CATEGORY_MATH
 rFunctoidInfo(0).scriptCategory = SCRIPT_CATEGORY_VBSCRIPT
 rFunctoidInfo(0).funcId = FUNCID_CHECKJACKS
 rFunctoidInfo(0).funcName = "ReconcileSettops"
 rFunctoidInfo(0).tooltip = "Enforces business rule regarding jack, settop count"
 rFunctoidInfo(0).bitmapID = BITMAP_CHECKJACKS
```

The function has a fixed number of inputs and fixed source code, which we indicate with the assignment of `FUNC_TYPE_STD` to the `funcType` member. Also note that we've elected to place the functoid on the **Mathematical** tab of the palette. This isn't completely arbitrary on our part. The function takes numeric inputs and generates a numeric output. The **Logical** tab would be another candidate, but the functoids in that tab are called with XSLT elements that won't work with this function.

We're going to carry over our source code from the script functoid without much change, so we assign the value `SCRIPT_CATEGORY_VBSCRIPT` to indicate the implementation language. The next value to set is the function ID, and here we've established a useful convention. Mapper must treat function IDs as arbitrary values, unique *within* the functoid component, but not necessarily unique across *all* functoids. This is demonstrated by the fact that the function ID is a long value and not a GUID. Consequently, we're going to use the index of the function within the `FUNCTOIDINFO` array as the function ID. That way, we can go directly to the correct structure after performing basic bounds checking. If we did not observe this convention, we would have to iterate through the entire array inspecting the `funcId` member until we found the desired value.

Following that, we have assigned an arbitrary name and tooltip text for the function. The value BITMAP_CHECKJACKS, assigned as the bitmap ID, refers to the identifier of a 16 x 16 pixel bitmap resource. You can add this by creating such a bitmap through the system Paint utility, then using Visual Basic's Resource Editor to add the resource to the project and assign it an ID. The value of the ID is up to you, but it must be unique within the scope of the project's resources. The Resource Editor is found on the Tools menu. If it does not appear there, check the Add-Ins menu.

The heart of the functoid implementation is the script. This is assigned to the scriptBuffer member. Since we already have the text of this following our first map, this is an easy step. Take the entire script source and copy it into the project as a string literal. We've added some new line constants for visual clarity in the functoid property dialog, and there are some line continuation characters to make the text easier to read in the Visual Basic editor. The only substantive change over the script functoid version is that we've substituted a descriptive name, ReconcileOutletsAndSettops(), for the arbitrary one Mapper generated in the script functoid.

3. Create the assignment as shown below:

```
rFunctoidInfo(0).scriptBuffer = "Function ReconcileOutletsAndSettops(
p_strConnections,
 p_strSetTops )" & vbNewLine & _
 " If CInt(p_strConnections) >= CInt(p_strSetTops) Then " & vbNewLine & _
 "  ReconcileOutletsAndSettops = p_strConnections" & vbNewLine & _
 " Else" & vbNewLine & _
 "  ReconcileOutletsAndSettops = p_strSetTops" & vbNewLine & _
 " End If" & vbNewLine & "End Function"
```

All that remains is to specify connection types and link information. We'll allow this functoid's output to go to anything other than a record, and accept inputs from any field or the content of a record.

4. This functoid accepts exactly two inputs:

```
rFunctoidInfo(0).outparamConn = CONNECT_TYPE_ALL_EXCEPT_RECORD
rFunctoidInfo(0).cInput = 2
rFunctoidInfo(0).inputparamConn(0) = CONNECT_TYPE_FIELD + _
  CONNECT_TYPE_RECORD_CONTENT
rFunctoidInfo(0).inputparamConn(1) = CONNECT_TYPE_FIELD + _
  CONNECT_TYPE_RECORD_CONTENT
End Sub
```

Note the assignments for the two inputparamConn members. We've created the bit pattern by adding the two values we need together.

Implementing the Interface

Everything we've done so far goes to preparing our internal structures. Implementing the interface will require that we expose this information to Mapper through the IFunctoid interface.

1. The two properties are very brief:

```
Public Property Get CannedFunctoid_Version() As Long
  CannedFunctoid_Version = mvarVersion
End Property

Public Property Get CannedFunctoid_FunctionsCount() As Long
  CannedFunctoid_FunctionsCount = mvarFunctionsCount
End Property
```

The version, and the count of functions, in the functoid component are implemented by passing back the value of the private member variables that contain this information.

Implementing the methods is only slightly more complicated.

2. Let's start with the GetScriptBuffer() method:

```
Public Function CannedFunctoid_GetScriptBuffer(ByVal cFuncId As Long, ByVal _
                                    lInputParameters As Long) As String

  If cFuncId < 0 Or cFuncId >= FUNCTOID_COUNT Then
    CannedFunctoid_GetScriptBuffer = ""
    Err.Raise 5
  Else
    CannedFunctoid_GetScriptBuffer = rFunctoidStruct(cFuncId).scriptBuffer
  End If
End Function
```

The second parameter, lInputParameters, can be ignored as we have a fixed number of inputs. The script source code is static in consequence. All we need to do is some bounds checking to ensure we do not underrun - or overrun the array of FUNCTOIDINFO structures. If we meet those conditions, we can index directly into the array and pass back the scriptBuffer member's value.

Let's turn our attention to the GetFunctionParameter() method. Recall that the purpose of this method is to retrieve the connection type for a particular input or output parameter.

3. Implement GetFunctionParameter() as follows:

```
Public Function CannedFunctoid_GetFunctionParameter(ByVal funcId As Long, _
                      ByVal lParameter As Long) As Long

  If lParameter < -1 Or lParameter > MAX_PARAMS - 1 Then
    CannedFunctoid_GetFunctionParameter = CONNECT_TYPE_NONE
    Err.Raise 5
  Else
    CannedFunctoid_GetFunctionParameter = GetConnectType(funcId, lParameter)
  End If
End Function
```

The method is passed the function's ID and the index of the desired property. We do bounds checking on the parameter index to make sure we are looking for something within the bounds of the parameter array within the FUNCTOIDINFO structure. If that parameter passes the check, we delegate processing to a private function called GetConnectType().

4. Go ahead and implement the function below:

```
Private Function GetConnectType(ByVal ind As Long, ByVal lParameter As _
        Long) As Long
  If lParameter = -1 Then    ' -1 indicates an output param
   GetConnectType = rFunctoidStruct(ind).outparamConn
  Else
   GetConnectType = rFunctoidStruct(ind).inputparamConn(lParameter)
  End If
End Function
```

Remember that if the value of lParameter is –1, Mapper wants the connection type of the functoid's *output* instead. Otherwise, the value is an index we can use with the inputparamConn array. As with the GetScriptBuffer() method, the first parameter is an identifier, which, because of our internal convention, we can also use as an index into the array of FUNCTOIDINFO structures.

That leaves the GetFunctionDescripter() method. This is the one that passes the functoid an index as a list of by reference parameters that the method must fill with the appropriate values.

5. We start by performing a bounds check to ensure the function identifier, passed as the first parameter, is within the bounds of our array of structures:

```
Public Function CannedFunctoid_GetFunctionDescripter( _
  ByVal lIndex As Long, pFuncCategory As FUNC_CATEGORY, _
  pScriptCategory As SCRIPT_CATEGORY, _
  pFuncType As FUNC_TYPE, pbstrName As String, _
  pbstrTooltip As String, plBitmapID As Long, _
  plParmCount As Long) As Long

  If lIndex < 0 Or lIndex >= mvarFunctionsCount Then
   Err.Raise 5
   Exit Function
  End If
```

6. If the index is good, we retrieve the proper structure and assign values to the parameters that were passed by reference:

```
pFuncCategory = rFunctoidStruct(lIndex).funcCategory
 pScriptCategory = rFunctoidStruct(lIndex).scriptCategory
 pFuncType = rFunctoidStruct(lIndex).funcType
 pbstrName = rFunctoidStruct(lIndex).funcName
 pbstrTooltip = rFunctoidStruct(lIndex).tooltip
 plBitmapID = rFunctoidStruct(lIndex).bitmapID
 plParmCount = rFunctoidStruct(lIndex).cInput
```

7. Finally, we return the function ID as the return value of the method:

```
CannedFunctoid_GetFunctionDescripter = rFunctoidStruct(lIndex).funcId
End Function
```

8. With this in place, you should be able to successfully compile the component.

9. Then go to Project | settopsfunctoid Properties...

10. Choose the **Component Tab**, and click **Binary Compatibility**. `checkjacks.dll` should be present in the box below.

The final step is necessary to keep Visual Basic from changing the CLSID for the component every time it compiles the project. After you have done that, though, there is one final step you must take before Mapper will be able to recognize your component as a functoid library.

Registering the Component

Now that we have a working component – as we shall prove in a moment – we must register it.

1. Building the DLL in Visual Basic will register it with Windows. Otherwise, if you are deploying a previously built component, you can use `regsvr32.exe`, a utility that comes with the operating system.

There is one final thing to do. When we discussed how functoids work, we noted that Mapper finds functoid components by enumerating all the COM components that have indicated that they implement the **MapEdit Functoids** component category. Registering the component will not take care of this for us. We have to create a *registry file* and merge it with the system registry.

2. In Notepad or some other text editor, create the following file:

```
REGEDIT4
[HKEY_CLASSES_ROOT\CLSID\{4454D0DD-715E-445C-8A99-F0A0C01DD414}\Implemented
Categories\{2560F3BF-DB47-11d2-B3AE-00C04F72D6C1}]
```

Be sure to change the CLSID value in the first set braces to match the value Visual Basic generated for you. You can find this in the registry (try the OLE View tool) after you have built the component. This slightly formidable bit of code isn't as bad as it looks at first encounter. We are adding a key to the registry information for the component. If you have ever looked at the registry through an editor like `regedt32`, you know that the heart of a component's registry information is found under the CLSID that uniquely identifies the component. The CLSID entries for the system are found in the registry under `HKEY_CLASSES_ROOT`.

We need to identify our new component by its CLSID, then create a new sub-key under the component's `Implemented Categories` key. You can find the CLSID for the component by using OLE View after registering the DLL. In our case, the value is `4454D0DD-715E-445C-8A99-F0A0C01DD414`. If you build the component yourself, you will have a different value.

The other GUID that appears in our registry file is the GUID for the **MapEdit Functoids** component category. This is found in OLE View under the **Grouped by Component Category** entry. It will always be `2560F3BF-DB47-11d2-B3AE-00C04F72D6C1`.

3. After you have created this file, save it with the extension .reg, then locate the file with the Windows Explorer.

4. Right mouse click on it and select **Merge** from the context menu.

Windows will merge the new key with the existing information in the registry.

Testing and Using the Component

By this time you should be wondering if any of this really works. Start BizTalk Mapper and open the Site Service Description to Cable Install map file.

The map files for our sample application, along with all the other source code, may be downloaded from our site at http://www.wrox.com

1. Select the script functoid in the functoid grid and delete it.

2. Next, open the functoid palette and select the **Mathematical** tab.

The icon for our new functoid component should appear as the last entry on the tab.

3. Drag it to the functoid grid and create links from the connections and setTops fields to the functoid.

4. Open the properties dialog for the functoid and make sure that the parameters appear in the proper order (connections, then setTops).

5. Next, click on the **Script** tab. You should see the source code that we provided in the scriptBuffer field of the FUNCTOIDINFO structure.

6. Close the properties dialog, then create a link from the functoid to the converters field of the destination document.

If you test the map at this point, you should get the same result as you did when we used the script functoid. If you compile the map and look at the output, you will see that the script source from the functoid has been embedded in the stylesheet. Finally, you should try to create links to and from the functoid and various records and fields. Mapper will indicate which links are allowed by displaying a circle with a line through it when you attempt to create a link that conflicts with the connection types specified in the functoid DLL.

Summary

Mapping is one of the most fundamental tasks BizTalk Server provides. Without it, we would be restricted to e-commerce with partners using the same framework of message formats that we adopted. It is unlikely that such a situation would appeal to the mass of small and medium-sized businesses who have not embraced earlier initiatives. It would be like being restricted to trading in your own home town. Having mapping at our disposal is like expanding our trading horizons to the world.

BizTalk Server's mapping engine is powerful, providing the capability to establish maps between all textual data representations right out of the box. It makes clever use of XSLT, limiting specialized processing to the edges of the mapping process. While it is built on XML tools and clearly favors them, you can map to positional and delimited files as well. Pre-built support is provided for the two EDI dialects, and XML representations of common business functions are offered as starter templates.

The design tool for mapping, BizTalk Mapper, is extensible through functoids. It offers a wide range of pre-built functoids, but also exposes a COM interface permitting programmers to write and deploy their own functoids. In fact, the run-time engine is also extensible. As we shall see in Chapter 10, BizTalk Server permits you to write your own parsers and serializers, thereby allowing you to handle message types not handled by BizTalk's standard components.

Our overview of BizTalk Server in Chapter 1 trumpeted the fact that BizTalk makes application integration a matter of configuration rather than programming. It is now time to take the final step that allows us to send and receive messages through BizTalk Server. We have specified message formats and maps between message formats. These are important building blocks, but alone they are not enough to let us actually use BizTalk. In the next chapter we will tie together both specifications and maps, and send our first message through BizTalk Server.

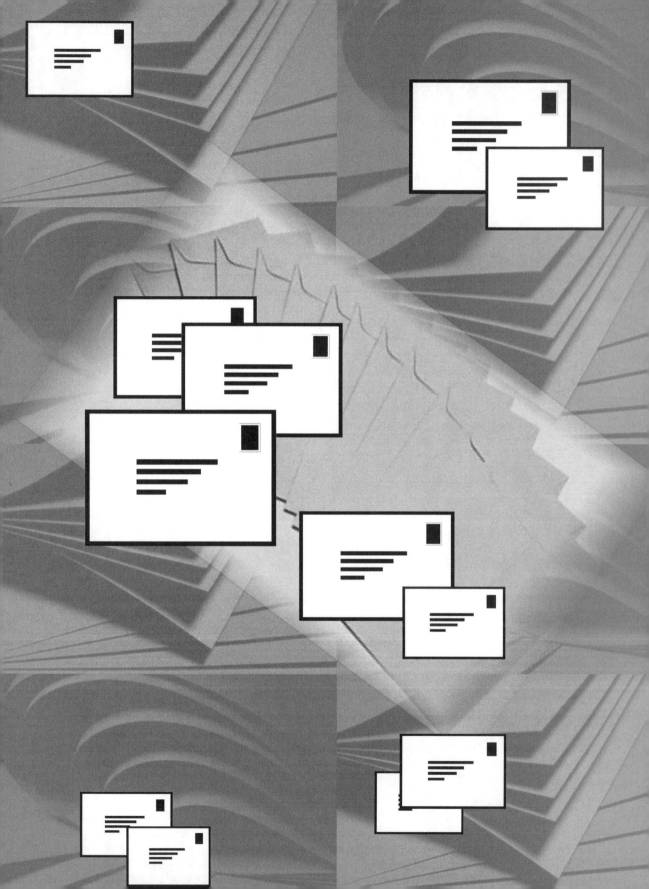

5

Managing BizTalk Messaging

In the preceding chapters, we defined a schedule for a system – but we had no implementation behind it; we defined document specifications but had no way to move actual documents; we then took those documents and specified how to transform the Site Service Description into Cable Installation and Yard Maintenance Subscription documents – but we still didn't have any way to exercise either the messaging engine or the Scheduler. In short, we're entering the fifth chapter of this book and we haven't run any of our own code. But, all the preparation has been building to a glorious finish at the end of this chapter, we will exercise everything.

Managing BizTalk's messaging engine is a matter of tying together all the various specifications and maps and explaining to BizTalk how a document of a particular type gets from sender to recipient.

The flexibility of the messaging engine means that we have to specify a lot of details we have to pick documents, transmission protocols, and locations. Happily, BizTalk has a tool for that called the BizTalk Messaging Manager, and like the Orchestration Designer, all the configuration tasks in Messaging Manager are driven by wizards as we shall see.

Once you have configured the messaging system, you still need to get documents into and out of BizTalk. Somehow, messages have to be presented to the messaging engine. So, in this chapter we will also see the ways to make BizTalk listen to various protocols and to receive messages (receiving messages is something we will discuss in more detail later); but there is also a COM interface for submitting documents directly to BizTalk, which we will cover. This interface not only lets you tie your applications to BizTalk messaging, but also allows you to write listeners for protocols such as HTTP. We will also build a small utility to test our configurations.

By the end of this chapter, you'll not only have running code but you'll also understand:

❑   How messaging is more configuration than programming

❑   The basic logical concepts involved in BizTalk messaging

❑   How BizTalk interfaces with standard transmission protocols

❑   How to configure BizTalk Server to send and receive documents

❑   The `IInterchange` COM interface for submitting messages to BizTalk messaging

We've demonstrated how BizTalk messaging is flexible in the options and methods it offers system architects for integrating applications through messaging. The beauty of BizTalk messaging is that implementing this integration is largely a matter of configuration. As much as we pride ourselves on our programming skills, we can appreciate getting the job done without writing code. Less time spent on integration leaves more time for building our own applications.

Configuration, Not Programming

Traditionally, programmers integrated applications procedurally. You wrote lots of code that made applications do very specific things. When the nature of the integration changed – changes in protocol, perhaps, or data structures – more code was written. Programmers had complete control over the integration process, but at the cost of having lots of highly specialized code.

BizTalk Server is designed to be data-driven. It consists of a general-purpose messaging engine and a general-purpose workflow scheduling engine. Programmers submit information to these engines that causes them to perform the desired integration automatically. Business data enters and leaves applications through the interchange of structured messages. Where does the data that drives the engines come from? From the programmers and architects by way of disk files and databases, or indeed any kind of data file. When you configure BizTalk messaging, you are generating instructions that will drive the run-time messaging engine. Not only does this make changes easy – you change configuration by pointing and clicking rather than editing and compiling – but it makes bits and pieces of the integration reusable.

Interchanges   specific messaging configurations   can be built up from definitions of documents, organizations, and receive locations. Specifying them for storage in a database means that the same information can be reused as often as we wish. Every interchange that involves the same class of documents will use the same definition, for example, just as every interchange that sends a message to the same location will use that bit of configuration.

BizTalk Messaging and Transmission Protocols

It's all well and good to say integration is configuration, not programming, in BizTalk Server, but if we're going to move messages between applications someone has to be working the transmission protocols. I can tell BizTalk to send a document over HTTP to *this* URL and wait for a document to arrive in *that* message queue, but if my partner doesn't understand HTTP and the MSMQ API, life is going to be very quiet for my application.

If you wrote an application that needed to communicate via HTTP, you probably bought a component or library that implemented HTTP. If you were in school or supremely unlucky, you wrote code to implement the protocol. Someone, somewhere, had to write code.

BizTalk is no different, in that it has its own components and offers its own API for message transmission. The mechanisms by which BizTalk implements messaging are extensible, so new protocols can be added. They're also well hidden behind the "configuration, not programming" scheme, so the vast majority of BizTalk programmers will never have to worry about them. Before we spend an entire chapter learning to configure BizTalk messaging, we should spend some time learning what goes on behind the messaging curtain. For some protocols, configuration does everything. For others, you'll have to make a call or two to hook into BizTalk.

Direct Communication with BizTalk

Like virtually all of Microsoft's server products, BizTalk exposes a COM API. In fact, a good portion of this book is devoted to working with the various object models exposed by BizTalk. When it comes to getting messages into BizTalk, though, the API is very simple. There is a single COM interface, `IInterchange`, with two methods, named `Submit()` and `SubmitSync()`. We'll cover this interface later in this chapter and build a little utility that takes advantage of it.

Notice that I said "getting messages into BizTalk". There are no methods to get messages out of BizTalk. This is a conscious and correct design decision. The focus in BizTalk messaging is on communications via existing and standard transmission protocols. You will get all your messages coming from BizTalk via one of them using the standard methods of the protocol. Nothing of worth would be added by offering an interface that grabbed messages from BizTalk's internal queue. Such calls would quickly become specialized legacy code needing maintenance over the years. That is exactly the problem BizTalk is supposed to avoid. Applications requiring queued behavior are better served with the robust features of MSMQ.

The messaging configuration tasks we will study in this chapter allow you to direct messages to an endpoint. That endpoint is a communications protocol-appropriate URL or queuename. Once a message is in BizTalk, you don't have to worry about getting it out – BizTalk sends it to the URL or queue. You deal with it using whatever API is appropriate to the protocol. Now, if you receive a message and wish to process it with BizTalk on your end – say, to route it internally so that your partners cannot see your internal configuration – you will need to get it into BizTalk on your side. That is where `IInterchange` comes in. So, for example, if you receive a message via HTTP, you can use `IInterchange` in an ASP script to submit the message to the BizTalk messaging service.

Generic Protocol Communcations

Now that the focus is off proprietary messaging APIs for moving messages between partners, we are left with the problem of working with the standard transmission protocols themselves. How is it that a middleware server like BizTalk can arbitrarily plug in to a variety of standard and proprietary protocols? In many cases, you want BizTalk to sit and wait for the arrival of a document from an application or external partner. You might have hundreds or thousands of concurrent messages in both directions, so whatever scheme BizTalk uses has to be efficient.

Receive Functions

Inbound messages travelling over MSMQ or as files dropped into a local directory are intercepted by BizTalk Server via **receive functions**. These are named configurations set up in the Messaging Manager that instruct BizTalk messaging to monitor the named queue or folder for arriving documents. When a message is found, BizTalk takes it off the queue or out of the folder and processes it. We will be looking more closely at receive functions in Chapter 9.

Transport Services

If you examine the registry (preferably via a tool such as OLE View, which comes with the Visual Studio tools), you will find a component category called BizTalk Component:

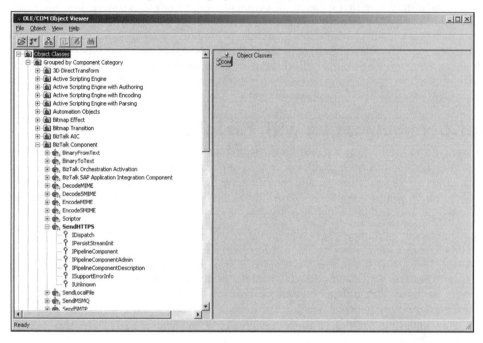

There are a number of components listed, but four are relevant to the topic at hand. These are called SendHTTPS, SendLocalFile, SendMSMQ, and SendSMTP. These components are used to enable the **transport service** that BizTalk messaging uses to send documents to other applications and partners. Transport services are protocol implementations. BizTalk supports the Internet protocols HTTP and SMTP, as well as local file copying (such as writing a document to a specified disk file in a specified location), and MSMQ. When you submit a document to be sent through BizTalk messaging, the messaging engine determines the transport service to use from the configuration. It then hands the document off to the service, which forwards the document via the appropriate protocol.

In Chapter 1, we said BizTalk also supports sending messages via COM. In fact, we used a version of this in Chapter 2, sending messages to a utility component to determine further actions. In Chapter 7 we'll see other ways to use COM messaging. So, why isn't there a transport service for COM? In effect the COM "protocol" is part of the operating system via the COM+ runtimes. BizTalk doesn't need a COM protocol implementation as it does for HTTP and SMTP. It can call a COM component directly using system calls. Your BizTalk configuration specifies the component progID to call when sending a message, and BizTalk constrains you to using IDispatch or one of its specialized interfaces (which are the topics of Chapter 7).

What About HTTP, SMTP, and FTP Reception?

HTTP is explicitly supported, but while we saw a transport component for that protocol, we did not see a receive function for it. FTP isn't officially supported by BizTalk Server, but it is a major Internet protocol. Why isn't it supported? SMTP transmission is supported, but there is no receive function for that protocol. In fact, you can receive documents via FTP and get them into BizTalk, and you can do the same via HTTP and SMTP.

The answer, in the case of HTTP and SMTP, is in writing scripts that leverage IInterchange. ASP (or other HTTP extensions like CGI or ISAPI) in Internet Information Server, and Exchange Server scripts for SMTP let you receive a message from some source – whether that source is using BizTalk or not – and submit it to your messaging service. MSMQ and local file reception, however, lack default applications   you have to send an application out to pick up your messages. When you specify a URL for HTTP or SMTP, something is already waiting on the other end of that URL – IIS or Exchange Server with the script code you've written. If you want to bring a message into BizTalk via HTTP, just write an ASP and give your partner or application its URL. Inside the ASP, you extract the document from the object you are using to receive. From there, you can use IInterchange to drop the document into the messaging engine. Things are only slightly harder for SMTP. E-mail wasn't originally intended as an automated solution. With Exchange, however, you can write scripts to process messages (for more information in devising scripts for Exchange, look in *Professional CDO Programming* Wrox Press Ltd, ISBN 1-861002-06-8). These scripts understand COM. Exchange Server acts as the receiving entity, and your script can call IInterchange to put the message into BizTalk.

But what about FTP? The receive function for local files should work just as well for FTP. This is, after all, the *File* Transfer Protocol. If you configure a file receive function that monitors the folder you've designated for FTP reception, BizTalk will take care of the rest.

BizTalk Management Concepts

That background is all well and good, but you have problems to solve and messages to move. It is time to go about the task of configuring the BizTalk messaging service. The first thing you need to do is understand how BizTalk messaging is organized.

BizTalk messaging is all about moving documents between applications or organizations. BizTalk therefore defines some concepts to help us think about (and therefore be better able to configure) messaging. These concepts are:

❏   Organizations – the entities that send and receive messages

❏   Document Definitions – the formal definition of the structure and content of messages – this is slightly different from the specifications we wrote in Chapter 3 – a document defintion points to a document specification file

❏   Envelopes – wrappers for routing non-XML messages

❏   Messaging Ports – locations to which messages are sent, such as protocol-specific URLs or queuenames

❏   Distribution Lists – groups of locations permitting multicasting of messages

❏   Channels – a set of parameters that collectively describe how the message must be processed

The Messaging Manager has wizards for configuring each of these. There are some dependencies between the different concepts, which will become apparent as we get into their details.

Organizations

The people who want to send and receive documents via BizTalk are **organizations**. Organizations have **names** or **identifiers** in the BizTalk configuration database. It is this information that helps the messaging engine determine what configuration to use to process a document.

Identifiers can be one of two kinds: **custom** and **standard**. A custom name is just a string you provide. A standard name refers to some industry standard code, tag, or identifier that uniquely names a corporate organization. BizTalk supports quite a few standards including Dun & Bradstreet numbers (DUNS) and Federal Maritime Commission identifiers. Standard names are useful when you are acquiring partners via an automatic process or when you want to verify the existence of an organization. They provide a tie into an external source of naming and information, and incidentally, an organization may have more than one identifier. For instance, an organization in the United States might be known to some domestic partners by a Federal Maritime Commission identifier, while overseas partners might find more meaning in a DUNS number. Different partners may use different identifiers, and internal organizations may be more comfortable using a custom name. Create as many identifiers as you need to uniquely identify a party to a document exchange under the different circumstances and cases that occur in your systems.

Given this, you might think that organizations have to be companies. If you use custom names, however, they can be any arbitrary body you want. BizTalk's only interest in organizations is in organizing configuration information. You can use organizations to define departments, workgroups, or any entity you want to have available for defining messaging configurations. BizTalk installs a default organization named the **Home Organization**. The Home Organization is special. It refers to the organization hosting the BizTalk Server installation.

Since the Home Organization is, by definition, local, it makes more information visible. Whereas other organizations are viewed as black boxes that take in messages for unseen processing and emit messages from unseen originating sources, the Home Organization is permitted to define "**applications**".

These applications can be, but are not necessarily, analogous with your real, internal systems applications. They may simply be names that you use to keep different configurations straight in your mind. Normally, you'll define these conceptual applications to correspond to real, executable applications. Since you don't *have* to tie an application to an executable program, however, you can use an application to refer to some script or process that handles a document. In the case of SMTP or file delivery, that process can be manual. BizTalk only cares about the name you provide for the application. It uses these names to differentiate two otherwise identical configurations within the organization, and it is this feature that allows you to use the same protocol and endpoint within the organization but deliver messages to different applications.

BizTalk treats these "applications" like black boxes, much the way Orchestration Designer and XLANG Scheduler treat documents. Applications, in this sense, are arbitrary named entities that are endpoints for documents. These conceptual applications are handy when you are integrating your own real applications and processes. You might define `OrderEntry` and `Scheduling` applications even though a single ASP receives the messages. Similarly, you can create names to represent the underlying business task but actually deliver the messages to applications with obscure names. Applications in the BizTalk sense are organizing names, not running programs. The messages you would use to integrate these applications all originate within the Home Organization and terminate within the Home Organization. Naming applications gives BizTalk a means of differentiating the configuration for messaging between one set of applications from the configuration for messaging between other applications.

Document Definitions

Document definitions are references to the specifications you learned to write in Chapter 3. They are not the specification files themselves, but rather pointers in the messaging configuration to the physical specification files. As you'll recall, the specification files drive the parsers and serializers that make the messaging engine work, so they must be accessible to BizTalk whenever a message comes in. After referencing the processing configuration, BizTalk is able to go to the WebDAV repository and use the document definition to locate and load the document definition it needs to process the message.

As with almost everything else in BizTalk, you'll give this reference to a message specification an alias. Since document definitions are one of the most basic things you'll configure through the Messaging Manager, you'll be using this alias in a number of different places. In fact, document definitions are taken together with organizations by BizTalk to help determine what configuration to load in processing a message presented to BizTalk. Consequently, there are many dependencies on document definitions.

Envelopes

If you try to mail a letter in the real world, you'd better have an envelope. It encloses the document inside and gives the postal service the information it needs to send the document on its way. A BizTalk **envelope** is similar. An envelope is necessary to send outbound messages and to open inbound messages, unless the messages are XML-based, in which case an envelope is optional. It is a collection of information that tells the messaging engine what to expect from the document it carries.

Envelopes can come in six formats, according to the standard of the document to be transmitted within:

- ❑ XML
- ❑ ANSI X12 (EDI)
- ❑ EDIFACT (EDI)
- ❑ Flatfile
- ❑ Reliable (BizTalk Framework 2.0)
- ❑ Custom

The point of specifying the format is to help the BizTalk messaging engine select the proper parser. By default, BizTalk chooses XML, so you can receive an XML document without an envelope in certain circumstances, rather like a postcard – the content is obvious. In other cases, notably a flatfile, BizTalk would have no way of knowing the standard without trying out each one. By specifying this information, you improve the performance of messaging. BizTalk can go right to the appropriate parser.

Of course, the standards listed do not completely specify the structure and permissible content of a document written using those standards. Consequently, one of the things you will specify with respect to an envelope is the message specification of the document associated with the envelope. Unlike a postal letter's envelope, each envelope can only contain one type of document, and it must match the envelope's specification.

The two EDI formats and the BizTalk Framework format specify header information for the documents within. Rather than make you recreate this information for every document you specify with these standards, BizTalk incorporates knowledge of the structure of these header formats. When using any of these formats, there is no need to point to a specific message specification.

If XML and flatfile formats permit custom structure, what purpose does the Custom envelope format serve? It enables you to create your own specialized headers in envelopes much in the way X12, EDIFACT, and BizTalk Framework do. If you go this way, you will need to create a custom parser to process the message, and you will need to refer to an envelope specification file. The advantage is that you can create a specification that contains the header and reuse it for every document meant to travel under that sort of envelope.

Messaging Ports

Organizations tell us "who". Document definitions tell us "what". "Where" is the purpose of **messaging ports**. A messaging port is a location surrounded by a set of rules governing how a document bound for a partner or application is transmitted and routed.

The first thing to specify for a port is location. You can specify a fixed destination organization and routing information, or you can configure an open port. An open port is one in which documents arriving at the port are routed based on information contained in the message itself. Open ports use the same transport for all messages, the only variable is the destination organization's endpoint URL. Open ports may only be used with ports to an application. All ports to applications are fixed and must specify the destination application explicitly. When you specify routing for a port, you select a primary transport, including the queue name, URL, or file location to which to send the document. You may optionally select a secondary transport to be tried in the event the primary transport fails.

Open ports and open routing are covered in depth in Chapter 10.

This might seem to finish the question of "where". However, you will also need to specify an envelope so that the messaging engine will know what sort of parsers and serializers to select and how to open the document to get routing information in the event of an open port. If you stick to XML, you can skip specifying the envelope (except for open ports) as BizTalk implicitly understands XML.

Just like a physical envelope is used to enclose a letter in the real world, a BizTalk envelope can also be used to enclose and protect a document. You can specify MIME encoding for document transmission, or even custom encoding provided you create and register a custom encoding component. You may also select S/MIME encryption if you wish to protect documents passing through this port with the Secure Multipurpose Internet Mail Extensions. Similarly, you can use S/MIME to digitally sign a document passing through this port. This allows the recipient to authenticate the message as coming from you.

Distribution Lists

There may be times when you want to send the same message to more than one recipient. Rather than repeat yourself, duplicating the configuration of each message exchange just so that you can change the transport and location, you can create a **distribution list**. This is a collection of ports that share the same inbound document type (inbound in the sense of what is submitted to BizTalk) and processing configuration.

Distribution lists are also known as port groups in some places in the documentation.

Open ports cannot be used with distribution lists, and this is not as arbitrary as it might seem at first. An open port directs BizTalk to change the transport and location based on the message's content. Since there is only one message, there can only be one destination contained within it in the case of open ports. If you need multiple locations, you can simply add multiple ports to the list.

All the ports in distribution lists share the same processing configuration (termed a channel) that we will discuss next. Suffice to say that this configuration is normally tied to a port in a one-to-one relationship. If any of the ports in the distribution list have a channel connected with them, the channel is ignored. Only the channel explicitly linked to the distribution list as a whole is used. The intent is to provide the same processing to one copy of the message while routing that message to multiple locations.

Channels

Channels are the processing agreements that tie the rest of the configuration together to completely specify the required processing for a particular message exchange using BizTalk Server. The term is a concise name for all the data stored in a SQL Server database that ties together all the lower-level concepts to produce a complete messaging configuration. A channel is dependent on the following:

- ❑ Messaging port or distribution list

- ❑ Source document definition

- ❑ Destination document definition

There are some implicit dependencies, as well. Because a channel depends on a port or distribution list, it is dependent on the organization(s) to which the port(s) are tied. If the source and destination document definitions differ, you will have to specify a map. Because of all these dependencies, a channel is the last thing you will configure before using a messaging implementation and the first thing you will delete when tearing down an unneeded implementation – in fact you will not be allowed to delete ports, envelopes, or document definitions if they are still referenced within an active channel.

Channels also specify some information that doesn't reside in any of the entities on which they depend. You can override the transport settings specified in the port used by the channel, for one thing. You can tell BizTalk what fields of the message to save to the tracking database and in what form to save it for later tracking. You can request a receipt for an outbound document or generate a receipt for an arriving message. If your partner used encryption or digital signatures, you can direct BizTalk to decrypt the document or verify the signature. In short, a channel tells BizTalk's messaging engine everything it needs to execute a specific message exchange. Everything up to this point has been an isolated and reusable part of the messaging configuration. You will reuse document definitions, and you may reuse ports, and you will probably reuse envelopes. A channel, however, is a very specific configuration and can be used for one specific type of document exchange between two organizations or applications. This relationship is depicted in the conceptual schematic below. All the individual configuration items are bound together by the channel to implement the transmission of the submitted document instance to its final destination and form.

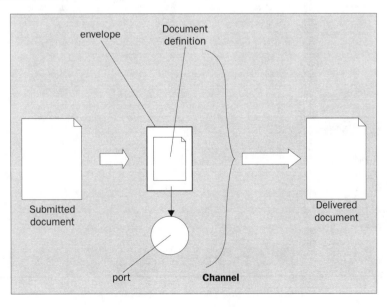

BizTalk Messaging Manager

The BizTalk Messaging Manager is the last tool you need to learn to use in order to configure message implementations in BizTalk. The specifications and maps you built with Editor and Mapper become the raw material for configuring message interchanges using the BizTalk messaging engine. It uses a DHTML interface in an embedded browser control to tie together the different messaging wizards that guide you through the configuration tasks. You can use it to configure messaging for a local or remote BizTalk Server installation to which you have administrative privileges.

User Interface

Messaging Manager uses a very utilitarian Web interface. The application window is divided into two frames. The one on the left acts as a sort of navigation console, and it displays the name of the BizTalk Server to which you are connected, followed by a series of form controls used to search the BizTalk configuration database for the various entities requiring management. At the bottom of this frame are a series of simple hypertext links that control what you are managing. When you click on one of the links, the search controls change to reflect the search parameters for that class of entities. For example, in the illustration below we see the Messaging Manager pointed at channels.

Search results are displayed in the right-hand frame. Summary properties are displayed for each result. Double-clicking on any row or right-clicking and selecting the Edit menu item on the context menu initiates the wizard for that item.

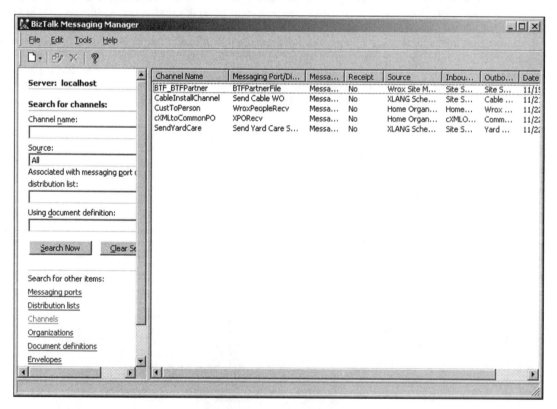

Now that you've seen the Messaging Manager, let's step closer and see how to use it in detail. In the sections that follow, we'll see how to use the Messaging Manager to properly configure all the logical entities of the BizTalk Messaging service.

Configuring Server Options

Before you can manage anything, you have to connect Messaging Manager to the BizTalk Server you wish to manage. You do this through the server Options dialog. This is invoked through the Tools | Options... menu item. The Options dialog permits you to set three things: the name of the server to be managed, the maximum number of search results to display in the results frame, and the timeout interval for communicating with the server.

Conducting Searches

Each of the six classes of management objects has its own search form. The illustration opposite shows the form for a channel search (in the left-hand pane of the Messaging Manager). The following table summarizes your search options:

Object or search field	Search constraint options
Messaging Ports	
Messaging Port Name	Name of the port
Destination	Type of destination represented by the port:
	All – all ports
	Organization – ports for delivery to organizations
	Open Destination– open ports
	Application – ports for delivery to applications
	XLANG Schedule – ports used to invoke XLANG schedules
Distribution Lists	
Distribution list name	Name of the distribution list
Containing messaging port	Name of a port contained in the desired list
Channels	
Channel name	Name of the channel
Source	Type of entity originating the message processed by the desired channel:
	All – all channels
	Organization – channels for messages from organizations
	Open Destination – channels with open ports
	Application – channels for messages from an application
	XLANG Schedule – channels governing messages originating with an XLANG schedule

Table continued on following page

Object or search field	Search constraint options
Source (depending on source type chosen above)	Changes with the source type selection:
	All – control disappears
	Organization – control is named Source Organization Name and takes the identifier of an organization
	Open Destination– control disappears
	Application – control is named Source Application Name and takes the name of an application
	XLANG Schedule – control disappears
Associated with port or distribution list	Name of the port or distribution list which uses this channel
Using document definition	Name of the document definition involved in the channel
Organizations	
Organization name	Name of the organization
Home organization (checkbox)	Check to search for the server group's home organization; when checked, the Organization name field is cleared of any existing entry and disabled
Document Definitions	
Document definition name	Name of the document definition
Envelopes	
Envelope name	Name of the envelope
Format	Name of the standard used to write the document to which the envelope applies:
	All – all standards
	Custom XML – user-defined XML
	X12 – ANSI X12 EDI formats
	EDIFACT – UN/EDIFACT EDI formats
	Flatfile – user-defined flatfile
	Custom – custom format
	Reliable – BizTalk Framework 2.0 envelopes

In all cases, clicking on Search Now executes the search using the parameters you've entered. Clicking the Clear Search button clears all search criteria. Searches on names, for example document definition or organization name, permit you to enter an incomplete name and search for all matching names. For example, I might enter site to search for my Site Service Description.

Configuring Organizations

The task of configuring organizations consists of a single dialog box with three property tabs. This is because you are basically providing names and an identifier or reference to some external entity. The Organizations Properties dialog is accessed by double-clicking an organization listed in the search results pane of the main Messaging Manager window, or selecting an organization in that pane and selecting the File | Edit menu item.

The Organization Properties dialog comes in two variations. All organizations have tabs labeled General and Identifiers. The Home Organization is unique because it allows the definition of applications. When you are editing the Home Organization, you see a third tab, labeled Applications, as seen below. All other organizations have only the two common tabs.

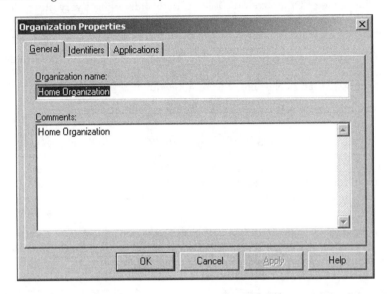

General

The General tab allows you to provide a name and some descriptive comments. Note that you can rename the Home Organization with any name you wish.

Identifiers

The Identifiers tab lists all the identifiers you have provided for the organization:

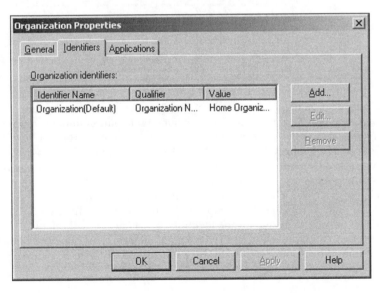

Note the three columns. You have the:

❑ The Identifier Name, which denotes the type of identifier you are providing. The first identifier you provide must be an organization name. Messaging Manager assigns the Identifier name of Organization (Default) to this identifier. Every other identifier receives as its identifier name the name of the type of identifier. An identifier which is a Dun & Bradstreet number gets an identifier name of DUNS (Dun & Bradstreet), for example.

❑ The Qualifier property is really an index. The qualifier value for the default – an organization name, remember – takes the value Organization Name for this property. After that, Messaging Manager assigns an integer index beginning with 1.

❑ The Value property is the value of the identifier you provide.

You add a new identifier by clicking the Add... button, or edit an existing identifier by selecting it and clicking the Edit... button. Either action presents you with a dialog known variously as the Identifier Properties or New Identifier dialog, depicted below. Selecting an identifier entry and clicking the Remove button permanently removes that identifier from the configuration information for the organization. The default organization identifier cannot be deleted.

The Home Organization also has an identifier named Reliable Messaging SMTP From Address that is the e-mail URL for receiving message acknowledgements when using BizTalk Framework 2.0 messages. This topic is taken up in Chapter 10 when we discuss routing.

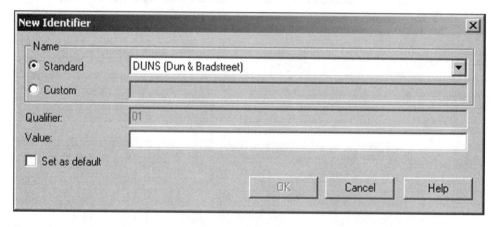

Regardless of whether you are adding or editing an identifier, you have the same options. First, you must select either the Standard name or Custom name radio button to indicate which type of identifier you are configuring. When Standard is selected, the top drop-down list box is enabled and you may select one of a host of identifiers such as DUNS or Federal Maritime Commission as the type of identifier. If you select Custom, the edit field directly below the standards list box is enabled and you may enter a string value for the identifier. The Qualifier and Custom name fields are enabled only if you are working with a custom name. When working with a standard name, Messaging Manager will assign the integer index for the qualifier property. In either case, the Identifier Value field is enabled. This is where you provide the value for the identifier by which you will refer to this organization throughout the other configuration tasks in Messaging Manager. Checking the Set as default checkbox makes this identifier the default identifier for the organization. If the user selects no default, Organization is the default identifier.

Applications (Home Organization)

If you are configuring the home organization, you may designate one or more applications – in this sense, we mean the "logical" applications that are part of the conceptual tools BizTalk uses to organize messaging arrangements, as described above, though obviously these can be analogous to real applications. This allows you to organize your channels by application as well as by external organization.

The Applications tab looks like this:

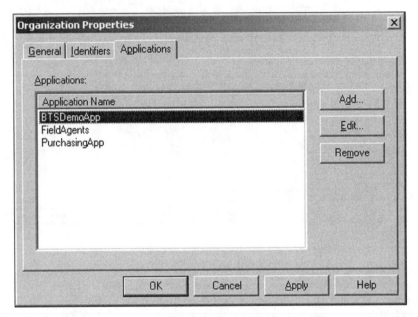

It functions much as the Identifiers tab did, allowing you to add, edit, and delete applications. Specifying an application is much simpler than configuring an identifier. The dialog for that, the Application Properties dialog, offers a single edit field where you provide a name for the application. BizTalk Server knows nothing more about the application than this. There is no reference to an executable program on disk, for example. An application in BizTalk is merely a logical entity. This allows you to be very creative, referring to executable applications, components, and processes as applications for BizTalk messaging purposes.

Configuring Document Definitions

Document definitions are like organizations in that they are configurable through a single dialog with multiple property tabs. Double-clicking a document definition in the results pane or selecting it and selecting the File | Edit menu item opens the Document Definition Properties dialog. Right-clicking in the results pane and selecting New Document Definition, or selecting the File | New Document Definition menu item opens same dialog under the name New Document Definition.

The Document Definition Properties dialog looks like this:

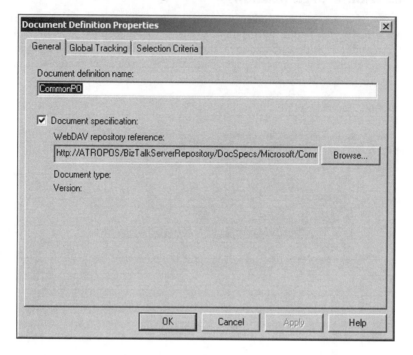

General

In most cases, you will only need to use the General tab. In that tab, seen above, you provide a common name by which to refer to the document definition in other configuration tasks. BizTalk needs a reference to a document specification file generated by BizTalk Editor. You provide this reference by clicking the Browse... button and navigating through the WebDAV dialog to select the desired file. The WebDAV URL appears in a label in the dialog.

> *Although BizTalk Editor can save to either WebDAV or the local file system, Messaging Manager will only look for documents in the WebDAV repository. This is appropriate as the messaging service uses WebDAV to retrieve specifications. Any specification you wish to put into production must be in the repository.*

Global Tracking

As we will see in Chapter 12, BizTalk provides a message tracking capability. Certain basic information is stored by default, but you can extend this to include fields of your own selection. The Global Tracking tab is used to do this. The settings you make here will apply to all instances of this document type unless specifically overridden in a channel configuration, as we shall see later. Using the controls on this tab, you may designate a limited number of fields to retain in the document tracking and auditing database when you send a document of this type from BizTalk Server. This will allow you to improve the reporting capabilities of your server installation.

> *If you attempt to go to this tab before you have selected a document specification for this definition, Messaging Manager will warn you that you must select a definition before using global tracking features.*

Let's take a look at that tab now:

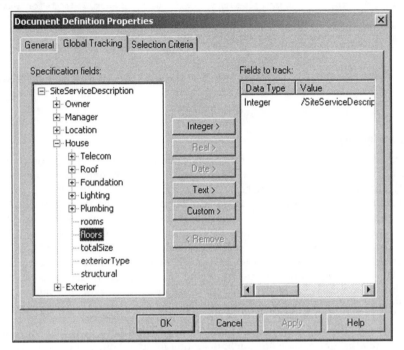

In the left-hand window you see a tree-view representation of the document definition. When you select a field for which a data type has been declared in the message specification, the buttons between the windows that correspond to similar types are enabled. Clicking on one of these buttons adds an entry in the right-hand window that consists of the data type you selected and an XPath expression that locates the chosen field. You may select as many as two fields for tracking under any one data type. Clicking the Remove button removes the selected entry from the Fields to track window.

If you reach the maximum number of selections for a particular type and select a similarly typed field in the Specification fields window, only those related types that have not filled their quota of selections will be enabled. For example, if you select the rooms and floors fields in the Site Service Description document for tracking, then select the totalSize field, only the Text and Custom buttons will be enabled even though that field is typed as a Number in the document specification. In such a case, you must either make room in the type desired or store the field as another type.

The Integer, Real, Date, and Text buttons are self-explanatory. The Custom button, however, requires a bit of explanation. You may select more than two fields for storage using the custom type, but they are not stored individually. Instead, all your custom selections are concatenated as a single string of XML, with each value delimited by tags representing the field name. For example, I'll randomly select some fields from the Site Service Description for tracking as custom fields and run the schedule from Chapter 2. The result (with whitespace and line breaks added for clarity) looks like this in the document tracking database:

```
<CustomSearch>
  <totalSize path="/SiteServiceDescription/House/@totalSize">20000</totalSize>
  <type path="/SiteServiceDescription/House/Plumbing/@type">copper</type>
  <connections
      path="/SiteServiceDescription/House/Telecom/Television/@connections">
  4
```

```
      </connections>
      <setTops path="/SiteServiceDescription/House/Telecom/Television/@setTops">
         4
      </setTops>
      <type path="/SiteServiceDescription/House/Telecom/Television/@type">
         cable
      </type>
      <servicePackage
            path="/SiteServiceDescription/House/Telecom/Television/@servicePackage">
         premium
      </servicePackage>
   </CustomSearch>
```

Selection Criteria

The Selection Criteria tab is only used for EDI documents. The information you configure here is needed to allow the messaging engine to determine the document definition of an inbound document. In an XML document, BizTalk can refer to the document element of the message itself. For other types, the information might be passed as a parameter of the call to submit the document. Also, information identifying the document type might be contained within a field within the message itself. X12 and EDIFACT messages present a problem for BizTalk. Identifying information for inbound EDI documents is found in the functional group header (GS header for X12 or UNG for EDIFACT), if functional groups are present, or the interchange header for EDIFACT interchanges without functional groups. Since multiple EDI documents can be contained in a single interchange and multiple document types can be mixed within an interchange, there is no way for BizTalk to resolve the document definition for any single document when it is presented for processing.

The Selection Criteria tab allows you to specify a list of name-value pairs that will allow BizTalk to uniquely identify the appropriate document definition for an inbound document. The tab's UI is fairly sparse, as you can see below. Clicking the Add... or Edit... button evokes an even more spartan dialog, one consisting solely of two edit fields, one for the name and the other for the value.

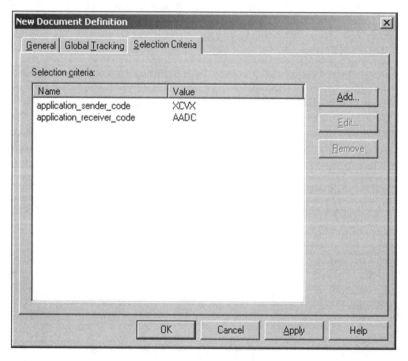

This dialog does not check the names you input. BizTalk's messaging engine, however, only understands certain names, and then only in certain combinations. These name combinations are shown in the table below and are cross-referenced by the EDI standard used to create the document specification. The values you enter are the values BizTalk must match within the document instance presented for processing. When BizTalk receives an inbound document, it checks the names for each document definition. When the values of the named fields match the selection criteria you provided, BizTalk selects that document definition for use in processing the document instance. The list of name-value pairs you provide for a document definition must be unique across all your document definitions because BizTalk must be able to unambiguously select a definition for processing.

Name	ANSI X12	UN/EDIFACT
application_sender_code	Required	Required
application_receiver_code	Required	Required
functional_identifier	Required	Required
standards_version	Required	Not required
standards_version_type	Not required	Required
standards_version_value	Not required	Required

The foregoing applied to inbound messages arriving at BizTalk Server from the outside   what about EDI messages that are ready for transmission to their recipient? BizTalk uses selection criteria to construct the envelope used to send the message. This time, instead of trying to match a name-value pair from a functional group header, BizTalk is taking the name-value pairs in the document definition to write the field and its corresponding value in the functional group header. BizTalk uses the same list of required field names listed in the table above to construct a valid header.

Envelope Configuration

Envelopes are needed whenever you are using non-XML documents. Configuring them is a matter of informing BizTalk of the standard format (XML for example), used to create the document that will travel within the envelope and pointing BizTalk to the document specification file for the document. You configure envelopes with the aid of the **Envelope Properties** dialog. You can reach this dialog by double-clicking on an envelope listed in the search results pane of the Messaging Manager, or by selecting an envelope's listing and selecting the **File | Edit** menu item or the **Edit** menu item on the right mouse-click menu. The same dialog is used under the caption **New Envelope** to create new envelopes. This may be done from the **File | New Envelope** menu item off the main Messaging Manager menu, or by right-clicking in the search results pane and selecting the **New Envelope** menu item from the context menu.

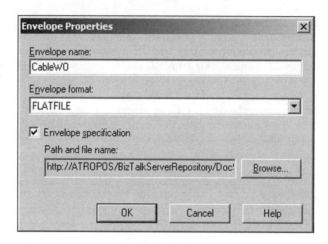

The Envelope name field takes a descriptive name string. This is the name by which you will refer to the envelope during other configuration tasks. The Envelope format list box lists the permissible standards on which document specifications may be based. The choices are CUSTOM XML, X12, EDIFACT, FLATFILE, CUSTOM, and RELIABLE. The first three are plain and direct. FLATFILE refers to any delimited or positional flatfile format you might specify. CUSTOM refers to documents that rely on a custom-built parser and serializer. RELIABLE pertains to documents that use the BizTalk Framework 2.0 specification, outlined in Appendix C.

When you select CUSTOM XML, FLATFILE, or CUSTOM, you must select an "envelope specification", which in this context will actually be a document specification (in the other cases, where an envelope specification is not required, the Browse... button is disabled). Clicking the Browse... button opens the WebDAV dialog used throughout the BizTalk configuration tools to the document specifications repository folder. Select the document specification file that describes the structure of the documents for which this envelope is intended. When you have finished configuring the envelope, Click OK to save the new envelope or the changes you have made to an existing envelope.

Messaging Port Wizard

Now that we have organizations and documents, we can begin to think about sending messages between them. For that, we need to start thinking about receive locations and transport protocols. You can create a new messaging port either by right-clicking in the results pane of a port search and selecting an option from the New Port menu or selecting an option from the File | New Port menu off the Messaging Manager's main menu. When you create a new port, you have a choice between creating a port for messages to an application (such as you might have defined when configuring your Home Organization) and creating a port for messages to an organization. The paths are slightly different because an application port, dealing as it is with the Home Organization, can be made to talk to an XLANG schedule, whereas a port to an organization cannot make assumptions about the ultimate endpoint of the message. Messages to outside organizations are sent to URLs because the internal applications of those partners are not exposed to our BizTalk Server installation.

The sequence of dialogs followed by the wizard as described in the next two sections is substantially the same as that which you will encounter when editing an existing port, except that you will only have the option of proceeding on to the channel wizard when you first create a port.

Application Messaging Ports

The first stop in the port wizard is the General Information dialog. This dialog, which is also found when creating ports to organizations, is the place where you assign a name to the new port and provide some descriptive comments for your own reference. The name is important, as it is how you will refer to the port when creating channels. Assume, for the moment, that we want to configure a port for a Human Relations application.

Here is what the General Information dialog looks like:

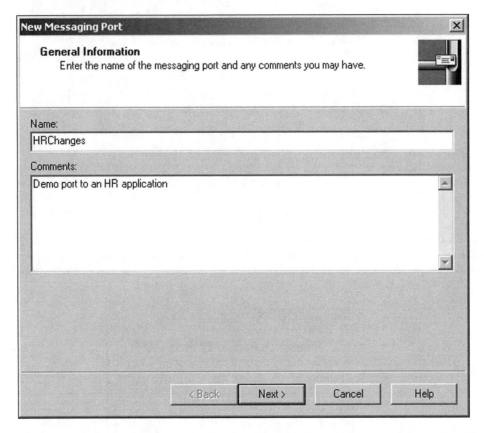

Now you have to specify the destination application. Here is where things can get interesting. If you are developing your business processes with XLANG schedules, you can send MSMQ messages to a running schedule. Otherwise, if you are using an application port to send messages to some legacy application, such as a conventional service or executable image, you may send messages using any supported protocol. Let's assume the sample HR application is an application, not a schedule, named BTSDemoApp. Before we get into details, here's what the Destination Application dialog looks like:

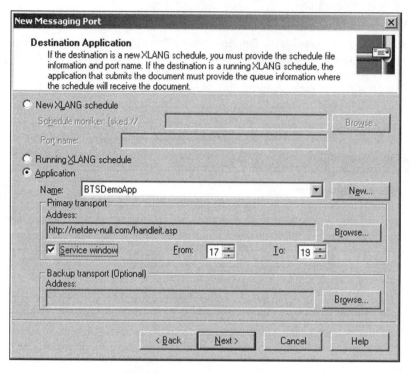

In the illustration above, I've specified a legacy (non-XLANG) schedule, as the destination. That makes the HTTP protocol available to me. The Name listbox drops down to display all the applications currently defined for the Home Organization. Clicking the Browse... button in the Primary transport group opens a dialog to assist you in specifying the primary transport:

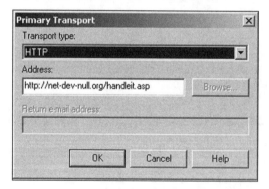

The exact contents of this dialog vary depending on the transport protocol selected. When dealing with an Internet protocol, the protocol portion of the URL is filled in for you, such as http:// for HTTP and mailto: for SMTP. The Browse... button is disabled unless you select Application Integration Component. If you select that option, the Address edit field is renamed Component, and clicking on Browse... brings forth a dialog listing the progIDs of all application integration components (AIC) registered on the local system. Similarly, if you select SMTP for the protocol, the Return e-mail address edit field is enabled, permitting you to enter a return URL for e-mail.

AICs, components used to integrate COM components with BizTalk, are the topic of Chapter 7.

Note in the above example the URL includes the filename of an Active Server Page. This page is the application that would consume messages sent to the port being created. Whatever protocol you select, the run-time messaging engine will use the URL you enter as the destination of the message sent via the port. If you select SMTP, for example, your (or your business partner's) application must either be listening to SMTP, or your e-mail server handling the destination address must have a script that somehow invokes the desired application when a message arrives for the particular e-mail address. BizTalk is finished with the port once it sends a document to the URL you provide using the selected protocol.

> *As of the beta version of Messaging Manager, you cannot enter a URL directly into the* **Address** *field of the* **Destination Application** *dialog. You must click* **Browse...** *and enter the URL in the* **Primary Transport** *dialog.*

You may optionally restrict transmissions to this port to a time window by checking the **Service window** checkbox and entering the opening and closing times of the window. Times may be specified to the nearest hour in the **From** and **To** edit fields, and these times may be modified either through direct entry or by using the spin controls to the right of each field to increment or decrement the time. Messages sent to ports with a service window in effect will be held on BizTalk's Scheduled queue until the window opens, at which time the message will be sent.

Once you have completed specifying the details of the destination application, it is time to talk about the document type this port will accept. This is set through the **Envelope Information** dialog, shown below. Envelopes are specified, you will recall, in terms of the document type they may contain. The drop-down list box lists all envelopes known to Messaging Manager. You may also create a new envelope from this point by clicking the **New...** button and proceeding as discussed under Envelopes, above.

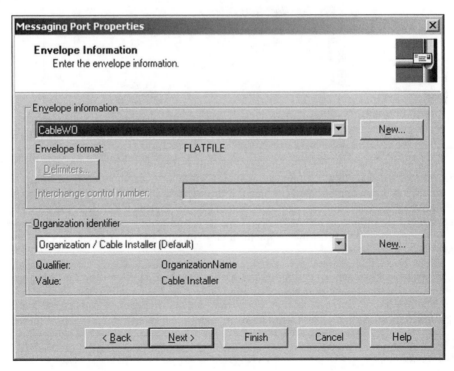

If you are dealing with a custom format, whether XML or some other format, selecting an envelope completes your configuration tasks in this dialog. If you wish to override the default organization identifier or you are dealing with EDI documents, you have a few more tasks to go. EDI envelopes can send more than one document in an envelope. To keep them straight, you need to specify delimiters and identify the interchange with an interchange control number. When you select an envelope, the standard used to create the document the envelope can accept is displayed to the right of the label. Clicking on the Delimiters... button allows you to specify delimiters specific to the needs of the EDI standard (X12 or EDIFACT). EDI also requires an interchange control number, which you specify directly in the Interchange control number edit field. You may also override the organization identifier used for this port through the listbox in the Organization identifier group or by clicking on New... to create a new organization identifier.

The final dialog in the port wizard for application ports allows you to configure security-related information for the port. The settings you specify here will apply to all documents that transit this port.

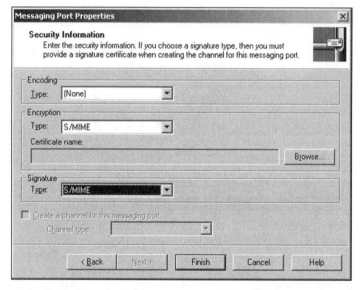

The Encoding type defaults to none, which is perfectly appropriate to text messages. Non-text types may require special encoding to ensure their safe and uncorrupted transmission via Internet protocols. You may change this to MIME, or Custom (when you have extended the system). The latter setting requires that you create a custom encoding component and have it registered on the local system. Next, you may choose to protect the content of documents going through this port by asking BizTalk to encrypt their contents using Secure Multipurpose Internet Mail Extensions (S/MIME). To perform this encryption, BizTalk will require a digital certificate for your partner. You select this by clicking on the Browse... button and hunting for the desired certificate authority and selecting from the list provided. Finally, you may choose to assist the recipient in authenticating your message by specifying the use of an S/MIME digital signature.

Messaging ports work closely with channels, as we have seen, to configure BizTalk messaging. To make your life easier, the messaging port wizard allows you to directly move into the channel wizard by checking the box and selecting a channel type. Your choices are From an Application and From an Organization. For now, though, we'll stop here and examine how to configure a port for an organization.

The details of configuring a channel to go with your port are covered in the Channel Wizard *section later in this chapter.*

Organization Messaging Ports

The basic pattern of configuring a messaging port to an organization tracks the one we just saw fairly closely, so this version of the wizard should seem familiar. We begin as before with the same General Information dialog. After entering a name and, optionally, descriptive text, click Next. At this point the wizard diverges from what we saw when we were configuring an application port. The wizard presents us with the Destination Organization dialog, shown below. While this is analogous to configuring an application destination, the choices are slightly different.

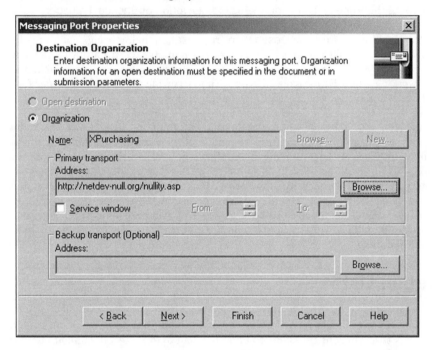

Our first choice is between an open destination and an explicit organization. Open destinations are those which are selected at run time based on information contained in the message. Because the destination is open, the endpoint and transport protocol must be open as well. If you choose this option, all the other controls in the dialog will be disabled   as you can see in the illustration above.

> *Open destinations will be covered in Chapter 10 when we discuss message routing in BizTalk. For now, note that you may not select the open destination option if you wish to send EDI messages through this port. BizTalk cannot construct an X12 or EDIFACT envelope without having a destination organization identifier in advance. Open destination messages must contain the destination information in the body of the messages, and EDI messages do not make provision for this.*

If, however, we are configuring a known, static organization, we must name the organization and proceed to specify the transmission's endpoint. If you have previously configured the organization to which you wish to send messages, you may click Browse... to view a list of organizations known to Messaging Manager. If you overlooked this step, you may recover by clicking the New... button and configuring an organization for use with this port.

You configure the port's endpoint just as you did when we were discussing application ports. Click the Browse... button to see the Primary Transport dialog. That dialog appears and functions exactly as it does when invoked from the application version of the port wizard. Similarly, you may specify a service window for use with this port, configuring the start and end hours for the window.

A final difference displayed by this dialog is the Backup transport group. Messages transmitted outside the home organization are generally less reliable than those transmitted within the organization. You may specify an alternative protocol and endpoint to be used in the event the initial message transmission is unsuccessful. Clicking Browse... in this group invokes a dialog that has the same layout and behavior as the Primary Transport dialog, but a caption of Backup Transport.

Clicking the Next button from the Destination Organization dialog brings you to the Envelope Information dialog. It looks and acts the way it does when invoked from the application port version of the wizard. You select (or create) an envelope, specifying delimiters and an interchange control number if you are working with EDI messages. If you wish to override the default identifier for the destination organization, you may also specify that information at this time.

Clicking the Next button brings you to the Security Information dialog. Once again, this is the same as it is when invoked from the application port version of the wizard. This should not be surprising, as you are specifying the security and authentication information for a message, and this does not depend on the nature of the destination. Security is a function of the class or message, for instance, of its importance; and also of the security of the protocol over which messages will travel, but not of the type of entity receiving the message. You may specify the use of MIME or custom encoding, S/MIME encryption, and digital signing in this dialog. At the end, you may indicate a desire to proceed to the channel wizard immediately upon completion of the port wizard, or invoke the channel wizard later through the File menu.

Distribution Lists

After you've gone to all the trouble of configuring ports, you can very easily leverage that investment to make the rest of your BizTalk-related life easier. If you wish to send the same message to multiple recipients, it is easier to configure a distribution list than to execute a document interchange multiple times.

To create a distribution list, select the File | New Distribution List menu item from Messaging Manager's main menu, or right-click in the search results pane while Messaging Manager is displaying the results of a distribution list search and select the New Distribution List menu item from the context menu. Either mechanism leads to the following dialog:

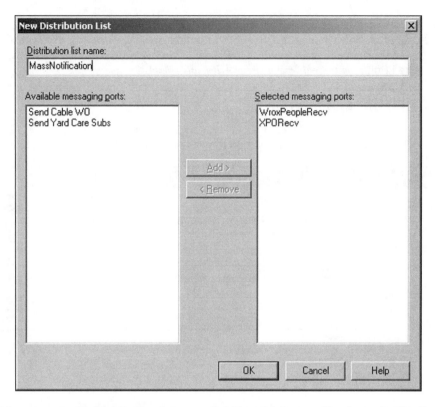

You provide a name in the Distribution list name field by which you will refer to the distribution list elsewhere in Messaging Manager configuration tasks. Messaging Manager, for its part, displays all known ports in the Available ports list. You select or multiselect ports in the list and click Add. Ports belonging to the distribution list are displayed in the Selected messaging ports list and are removed from the available ports list. You can correct any mistakes by selecting ports in the Selected messaging ports list and clicking the Remove button. When you are done, click OK to accept the distribution list configuration.

> *Ports assigned to a distribution list remain available for assignment to other distribution lists or for use individually with channels.*

Channel Wizard

You've reached the final stage of configuring BizTalk for message interchanges. You've specified all the discrete pieces – documents, envelopes, organizations, and ports – and now all that is left is to tie the pieces together with the business agreement that specifies what documents flow between what organizational endpoints over which protocol. That is what channels are all about.

You can create a channel by right-clicking on a port in the search results pane of Messaging Manager when it is displaying port results and selecting the New Channel menu. As an alternative, if a port is selected, you may also select the File New Channel menu from Messaging Manager's main menu. In either case, you have the choice of specifying whether the channel is from an organization or from an application. The two versions of the wizard differ – application and organization – only in the dialog that specifies the source of the document.

The wizard's sequence and behavior is the same when editing existing channels. The dialog caption will change from New Channel *to* Channel Properties, *but otherwise the interface is the same. To edit a channel, select a channel in the results pane of Messaging Manager's main window, then select* File | Edit *from the main menu or right-click and select* Edit *from the context menu.*

Channels from an Application

The first dialog in the channel wizard is the Channel Information dialog. As with messaging ports, this is the dialog where you provide a name and descriptive information. The dialog looks like this:

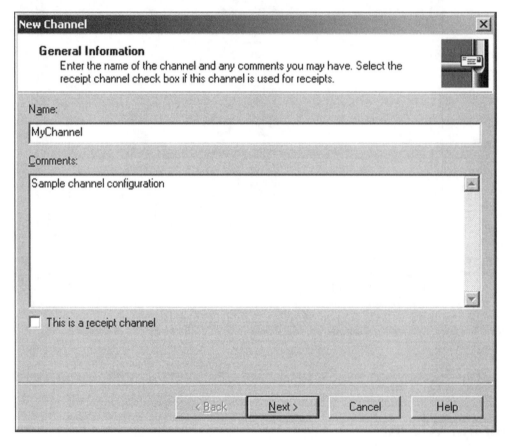

Note the checkbox under the Comments field, however. If you are dealing with EDI messages, BizTalk will let you set up a receipt mechanism without too much trouble. That is what this checkbox does. It is not a general purpose receipt mechanism for custom XML messages.

Receipts are covered in Chapter 10.

Next, you must tell Messaging Manager where the documents processed by this channel originate. Since we are dealing with application channels, the options are XLANG schedules and applications defined for the home organization. The Source Application dialog allows you to specify all the source configuration information:

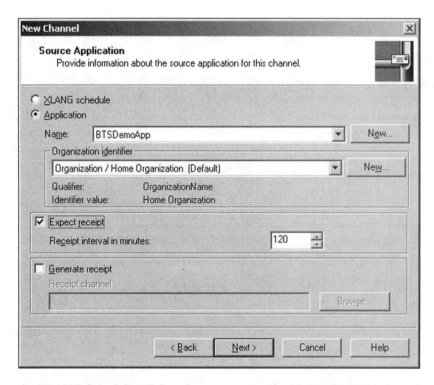

If you select the XLANG Schedule, all the other options are disabled and you are through configuring this dialog. If, however, you are dealing with a home organization application, you have a bit more to specify. First, of course, you must select the application from the drop-down list box or create a new application. Clicking New… invokes the Organization Properties dialog we saw under organization configuration with the Application tab brought to the foreground. The Organization Identifier group allows you to select an existing organization identifier or create a new one. Here again, clicking New… brings up the Organization Properties dialog, this time with the Identifiers tab in the foreground. The application name and the organization identifier are used by the messaging run-time engine to help select the channel to use when a new message is presented to the engine for processing.

The Expect receipt and Generate receipt groups are used with EDI messages as well as messages that use the BizTalk Framework 2.0 standard, known in Messaging Manager as Reliable messaging. Expect receipt, though is used to tell BizTalk how long to expect to wait to hear from the document recipient for an acknowledgement of the message. You use the spin control to configure the expected interval. If no receipt is received within the designated interval, the message is treated as if it had failed to transmit. Generate receipt, by contrast, is used to create an acknowledgement to an outbound message and send that acknowledgement to the originating application. That is, you are sending the message and generating a receipt to acknowledge sending the document, whereas Expect receipt dealt with the case where you sent a message and want to know that it was received.

The Receipt channel refers to the name of another channel that is used to transmit the acknowledging message. Clicking Browse… displays a list of channels that satisfy two conditions. The first is that the channel was designated as a receipt channel by checking the box on the Channel Information dialog. The second is that the destination of the receipt channel is the same as the source of the channel you are currently configuring. When you have completed configuring source application information, click Next to proceed to the Inbound Document dialog.

The Inbound Document dialog, shown below, tells BizTalk about the documents that will be presented to the run-time engine for processing under this channel. This is the specification that describes the document before any mapping or transmission takes place.

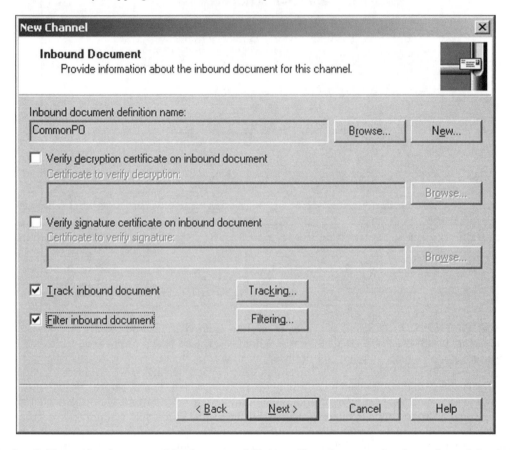

The first field specifies the name of the document definition. If you have previously configured the desired document definition, click on Browse... and select a name from the list provided. If you have a document specification file but have not configured a document definition through Messaging Manager, click New... to access the Document Definition dialog discussed above under *Configuring Document Definitions.*

If the document arrives encrypted, BizTalk's messaging engine will decrypt it prior to processing. Selecting a certificate using the Browse... button allows you to specify the proper certificate so that the decryption may be checked. The certificate must be installed on the certificate store for the BizTalk Server.

Verifying a digital signature is slightly different as it is less restrictive than verifying and performing decryption. Here, it is perfectly acceptable, even desirable, to check a public source for a signature certificate. The public key allows BizTalk to decrypt the digital signature. The signature consists of a checksum that BizTalk may independently compute given the message. If the two match, the document is considered authenticated as only the sender could have encrypted the checksum. Clicking Browse... leads to a dialog containing a list of public certificate authorities, who may be used to obtain the sender's certificate and verify signatures.

When we discussed document definitions, we discussed document tracking fields. You'll recall these were fields in the document's structure that we wished to capture in the DTA (Document Tracking Application) database for future reporting. BizTalk's Document Tracking application accesses this database in response to your query criteria to report on messaging activity in your system. If you wish to augment this information by adding fields to capture from this document when processed by this channel, you may check the Track inbound document checkbox and click Tracking... There you will see the Tracking for Inbound Document dialog, shown below. Note the similarity to the GlobalTracking Properties tab of the Document Definition dialog. The lower portion of the current Tracking dialog looks and behaves just as that tab did. The Global tracking fields list box has been added to depict the selections you made for the document definition. Those choices apply to all instances of the document. The choices you make in this dialog apply only to those instances of the document that are processed under the terms of the channel you are configuring. Note that you cannot remove or change any of the global tracking fields.

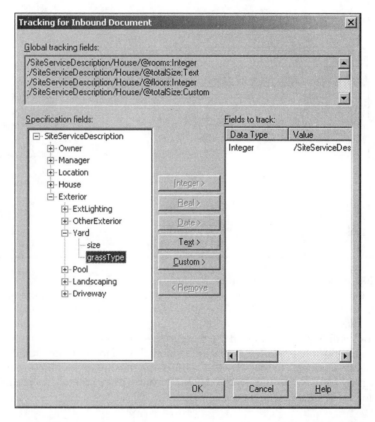

Filtering is the use of fields in a message to augment the channel selection process. You might want to specify special handling for a document based on some properties in the document itself. Normally, BizTalk selects a channel based on the source, destination, and inbound document type, but if you wish to provide special processing, you configure a channel and add one or more filter expressions. These expressions are VBScript expressions involving message fields. When the expression(s) evaluate true, the channel is selected for use. Checking the Filter inbound document checkbox and clicking on the Filtering... button leads to the dialog shown overleaf. In that example, I have established a filter expression based on the lname field of the Owner record in the Site Service Description. Whenever the Owner's last name is Loki, I want to select the channel I am configuring.

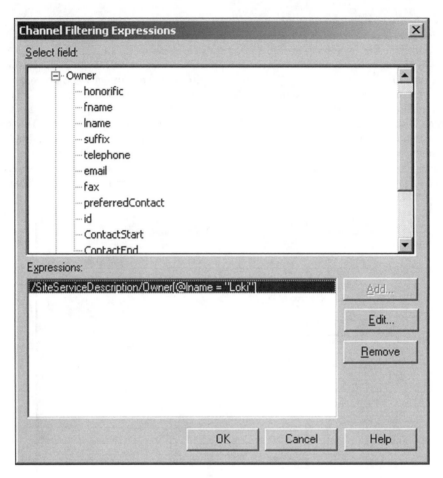

An inbound document is only half the story of a message interchange. There has to be an outbound document as well. The inbound message refers to the document definition of the document as it is presented to the messaging engine. An outbound message refers to the document definition for the message as it leaves BizTalk for its destination. If no mapping of one message on to the other is involved, the two will be the same, but if the two differ, you will need to specify a map for use with this channel. Outbound document configuration for a channel is handled in the Outbound Document dialog. Clicking the Browse... button displays a list of the document definitions currently configured in BizTalk messaging. As you may suspect, the New... button allows you to access the Document Definition dialog to create a new definition.

If the outbound definition you select does not match the inbound definition you selected in the preceding dialog, Messaging Manager automatically checks the Map inbound document to outbound document checkbox. You will need to click the Browse... button to access the WebDAV map repository and select a message map file in this case.

Since you are sending the message, you have the option to have BizTalk digitally sign the document to facilitate message authentication on the receiving end. If you wish to do this, check the Sign outbound document checkbox and click Browse... to select a certificate from your local store. When you are done specifying outbound document information, click Next to proceed to the Document Logging dialog.

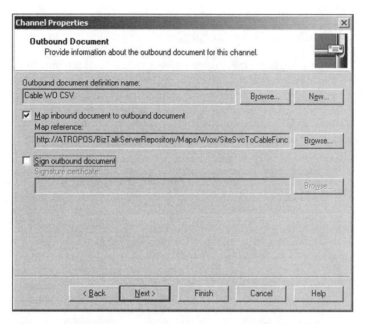

BizTalk can save entire messages in its database for later troubleshooting. You use the Document Logging dialog to configure whether and how this is done. You make separate decisions regarding the inbound and outbound document. In either case, you have the option of saving the message in native format or XML. Recall from the discussion of message maps in Chapter 4 that flatfile documents are converted by parsers into an internal, canonical XML format prior to mapping. This is the XML format referred to in the dialog. Saving in native format, (for instance, in the format in which a document arrived at, or left from the messaging engine) is the default selection. Messaging Manager also defaults to saving the inbound document but not the outbound document.

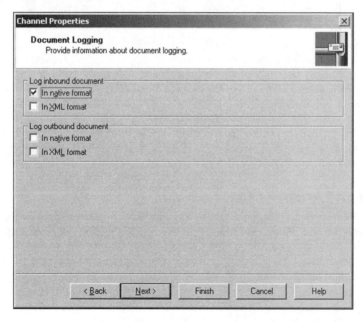

The final stage in channel configuration is the Advanced Configuration dialog. In it, you may use the Group control number field to provide a group control number for EDI interchanges. You may also configure the number of times the messaging engine will attempt to try to send the message and how long it will wait between tries. If the messaging systems exhausts all attempts without successfully sending a message, the message is moved to a queue for failed messages. The Advanced button opens a dialog that permits you to override the envelope and transport protocol selections made in the port configuration for the port used by this channel. That is, messages processed under this channel will use the specified port with a different envelope selection or choice of protocols. When you are done, click Finish to save the channel configuration to the SQL Server database used to store messaging configurations.

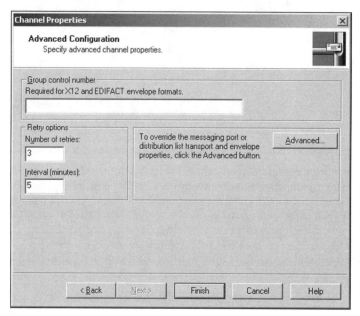

If you elect to override a port that uses the `SendLocalFile` transport, (for instance, you are saving the message to disk), you will have the option of specifying exactly how the document is saved. You may overwrite an existing file, append the document to the end of an existing file (the default), or create a new file. If you append an XML document to the end of an existing file, you will no longer have a well-formed XML document as you now have more than one document element. In consequence, you cannot use Internet Explorer to quickly view the local file. If you choose to create a new file and you expect to have multiple documents on disk in the same location at the same time, use the expression `%tracking_id%` in the filename. This causes BizTalk to save the document under a unique name.

Channels from an Organization

Configuring a channel from an organization is very similar to what you just saw. In fact, the only difference is in the second dialog. As before, you begin with the Channel Information dialog. From there, you reach not the Source Application dialog, but the Source Organization dialog. It is the same as the Source Application dialog except that the first two choices are changed to Open Source (for open routing channels) and Organization (to designate a specific organization for the channel). Clicking Browse... presents you with a list of organizations known to Messaging Manager, while New... allows you to configure a brand new organization. The Organization identifier, Expect receipt, and Generate receipt groups work the way they did for application channels.

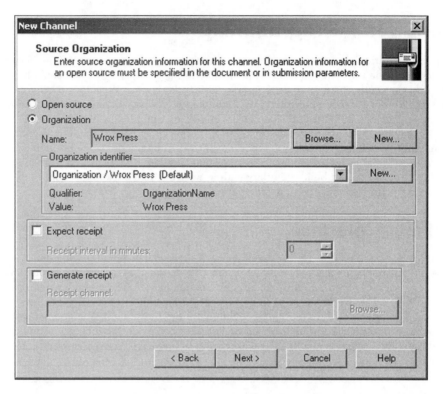

After configuring the source organization, you proceed through the Inbound and Outbound document dialogs, followed by the Document Logging and Advanced Configuration dialogs we discussed under application channels.

While the sequence of events we have just presented for the Channel wizard may seem complicated, it is really quite simple when you abstract it to the steps you must accomplish. Here is the summary:

- ❑ Select an existing port and invoke the channel wizard, specifying whether the source is an application or an organization
- ❑ Configure source parameters, including organization and primary transport information
- ❑ Configure the inbound document, including its specification, tracking, and security
- ❑ Configure the outbound document, including its specification and security; if the outbound document specification is different from the source specification, designate a map file
- ❑ Set logs parameters to use in auditing this channel's activities
- ❑ Set advanced channel parameters and save the channel configuration to the database

This matches well with the concepts we discussed earlier. To deliver a message, you must have a port. A complete interchange, though, starts with an inbound message and continues with an outbound message that goes to the port. To configure a channel, then, we need to describe a port, two documents, and an optional mapping en route. When these are specified, BizTalk has enough information to tie all the details together and drive the messaging service.

Simple BizTalk Programming

With the configuration information we've just covered, you have everything you need to send and receive messages via the common Internet protocols. In many cases, however, you'll find it easier to submit messages via the IInterchange interface BizTalk exposes. We'll take a brief detour, then, to describe this interface. To demonstrate it, we'll build a utility that will let us test channels. When we move into configuring the ports and channels for the Wrox Site Management application, this utility will let us test each channel as we configure them before running the entire schedule. Remember, we have a fully worked-out business process for a hypothetical residential maintenance business, as well as the document specifications to enable it and the maps that translate between the documents. After we discuss IInterchange and build the utility with it, we will come back and set out the messaging configuration to complete our running example.

IInterchange Interface

IInterchange is a streamlined COM interface BizTalk specifies for submitting documents to the run-time messaging engine and checking the queue of suspended messages. An implementation of the interface is provided in the DLLs that accompany BizTalk Server. The type library for this interface is found in cisapi.tlb. By far the most important method of this interface is the Submit() method. It is the method that permits you to submit a document to the run-time messaging engine for asynchronous processing. The remainder of the interface consists of a synchronous version of Submit() and three methods for dealing with messages that fail to process correctly. Here are the details of the IInterchange interface:

Method	Parameters and Meaning
Submit()	Submits the document for asynchronous processing. Messages are copied into a shared queue to await processing by the next available messaging server in the BizTalk server group. Documents are in the queue by the time the method returns. This method returns a string containing a unique handle that may be used to reference the submission in the tracking database.
	OpennessFlag – enumerated type from the BIZTALK_OPENNESS_TYPE enumeration denoting what items, if any, are left to open routing.
	Document – string containing the complete text of the message to send (binary data must be base64 encoded for transmission as text). This parameter is optional; if not passed, FilePath must be provided.
	DocName – string containing the name of the document definition specifying the document instance in Document or FilePath; DocName must not be passed if PassThrough is TRUE.
	SourceQualifier – string indicating the type of organization ID passed in SourceID (for example, Organization Name, DUNS); if this optional parameter is used, SourceID must be passed as well. SourceQualifier cannot be passed if PassThrough is TRUE.
	SourceID – string containing the value of the organization identifier for the originating organization.

Method	Parameters and Meaning
Submit() (continued)	DestQualifier – string indicating the type of organization identifier passed in DestID.
	DestID – string containing the organization identifier of the destination organization.
	ChannelName – string containing the name of the channel to use in processing this message; if passed, BizTalk's normal efforts to determine the channel to use based on source, destination, and document type are bypassed; if PassThrough is TRUE, this parameter must be passed.
	FilePath – string containing the fully qualified path to a file containing the document to submit; paths in URL, UNC, and "drive:" format are accepted. If a remote file server or the shared queue SQL Server is unavailable, Submit() will not timeout for 30 seconds or more. FilePath cannot be used in conjunction with the Document parameter. If PassThrough is TRUE and document mapping is required, FilePath may not be used.
	EnvelopeName – string containing the name of the envelope specification to use with this document. If this optional parameter is passed, the specification must exist and must be valid even if the submitted document is an XML document.
	PassThrough – long value used as a Boolean which, when TRUE, bypasses document decryption, encoding, and signature verification functions. If used, ChannelName must be used and OpennessFlag must be BIZTALK_OPENNESS_TYPE_NOTOPEN. If PassThrough is TRUE and document mapping is required, the document must be XML and the character set must be Unicode.
SubmitSync()	Performs a synchronous document submission. Use of this method will have an adverse effect on the scalability of the BizTalk server group. The interchange is complete by the time the method returns. This method has no return value.
	Parameters are as for Submit() with the following two additions at the end of the parameter list:
	SubmissionHandle – variant containing the unique identifier of the document submission.
	ResponseDocument – variant containing an optional response document. Response documents may be returned from synchronous protocols such as HTTP and AICs.

Table continued on following page

Method	Parameters and Meaning
CheckSuspended Queue()	Checks the shared queue of messages that failed to process (suspended queue) for documents matching the passed criteria. Returns a variant containing a safe array list of document submission handles for interchanges matching the criteria. This may be used in conjunction with GetSuspendedQueueItemDetails to troubleshoot document submissions.
	DocName – string containing the document definition name. If this optional parameter is omitted, all document types are matched.
	SourceName – string containing the name of the source organization; if this optional parameter is omitted, all source organizations match.
	DestName – string containing the name of the destination organization. If this optional parameter is omitted, all destinations match.
GetSuspendedQueue ItemDetails()	Obtains interchange details for a document interchange handle (such as is returned by CheckSuspendedQueue() or Submit()). No return value.
	ItemHandle – string containing an interchange identifier handle.
	SourceName – variant filled by the method with the name of the source organization.
	DestName – variant filled by the method with the name of the destination organization.
	DocName – variant filled by the method with the name of the document definition.
	ReasonCode – variant filled with a value from the CISReasontoQueue enumeration that refers to the reason why the document was moved to the suspended queue.
	ItemData – variant filled by the method with the text of the submitted document.
DeleteFrom SuspendedQueue()	Deletes one or more documents from the suspended queue. No return value.
	DocumentHandleList – a variant containing a list of document interchange handles referring to the documents you wish to delete from the suspended queue.

The first item that needs explanation is the BIZTALK_OPENNESS_TYPE enumeration. While we haven't properly explored open routing yet, know that it is possible to submit messages for processing and have BizTalk determine the proper routing based on values contained within the document itself. For example, I might have a message type I send to a number of recipients using the same protocol for each. The document might contain a field that has the URL or queue name for the recipient. In that case, the port would have an open destination and the value of OpennessFlag would be BIZTALK_OPENNESS_TYPE_DESTINATION. A conventional channel, using a port with an explicit destination URL, would require a flag value of BIZTALK_OPENNESS_TYPE_NOTOPEN.

Open routing is addressed in Chapter 10.

The `OpennessFlag` parameter in `Submit()` and `SubmitSync()` is used to tell BizTalk what, if anything, it needs to determine. The values of the enumeration are as shown in the table below. Note that the enumeration is set up as a bitfield.

You can combine `BIZTALK_OPENNESS_TYPE_SOURCE` and `BIZTALK_OPENNESS_TYPE_DESTINATION` with a logical `AND` operation to instruct BizTalk to dynamically determine both the source and the destination.

Flag name(Value)	Meaning
`BIZTALK_OPENNESS_TYPE_NOTOPEN (1)`	Parameters in the `Submit()` or `SubmitSync()` method explicitly declare all routing information
`BIZTALK_OPENNESS_TYPE_SOURCE (2)`	Source organization is open and must be determined
`BIZTALK_OPENNESS_TYPE_DESTINATION (4)`	Destination organization is open and must be determined

The next thing to consider is the `PassThrough` parameter. This parameter defaults to `FALSE`, and it is relatively uncommon to use the pass-through mechanism, so the parameter is often omitted in calls to `Submit()`. You may wish to bypass the various message support functions in BizTalk when you know your message contains binary information that could be corrupted by encoding, encryption, or digital signing. You might, for example, be passing binary images in your messages. In that case, you set `PassThrough` to `TRUE` and streamline the message processing. Of course, this imposes the restrictions noted in the table on you. This will be most apparent when you need to map a document from one type to another. With encoding disabled, BizTalk cannot convert the message from a non-Unicode character set, so the burden is on the originating application to generate the document in Unicode, which is the character set used internally by BizTalk for XML processing.

Finally, we have to consider the values for the `CISReasontoQueue` enumeration. The value placed in the `ReasonCode` parameter by the `GetSuspendedQueueItemDetails()` method is the only source of error information the interface offers. While sparse, it will help you troubleshoot what has gone wrong with the interchange when the issue is more complicated than a bad organization name. The values are given in the table below:

Code (Value)	Meaning
`noReason (0)`	Not currently supported
`rtdlqParserFailure (1)`	Suspended due to a failure of the parser component
`rtdlqParserDocFailure (2)`	Error trying to parse the document — for example, a well-formedness error in a custom XML document
`rtdlqDocValidation (3)`	Document validation failed

Table continued on following page

Code (Value)	Meaning
rtdlqChannelSelectFailure (4)	BizTalk was unable to select a channel for the interchange
rtdlqInvalidMap (5)	Mapping was required and the specified map was invalid
rtdlqFieldTrackingFailure (6)	Field tracking was specified and BizTalk was unable to comply
rtdlqMappingFailure (7)	Mapping was attempted but was unsuccessful
rtdlqSerializerFailure (8)	Serialization to the desired output format failed
rtdlqEncodingFailure (9)	The channel specified message encoding and the attempt to encode failed
rtdlqSigningFailure (10)	The channel specified a digital signature on the outgoing document and signing failed
rtdlqEncryptionFailure (11)	The channel specified outgoing encryption and encryption failed
rtdlqTransmissionFailure (12)	Document could not be delivered (transport protocol transmission failure)
rtdlqUserMove (13)	System administrator manually moved the document to the suspended queue
rtdlqTimeout (14)	Transmission timeout
rtdlqCustomCompFailure (15)	Failure of a custom component
unkReason (16)	A BizTalk server failed after taking the interchange for processing; upon restart of the server, the interchange was moved to the suspended queue automatically
rtdlqNoChannel (17)	The channel specified for this interchange no longer exists
rtdlqMissingChannel (18)	A channel explicitly named in the Submit() or SubmitSync() method could not be found
rtdlqInvalidChannel (19)	A channel explicitly named in a call to Submit() or SubmitSync() uses an open port
rtdlqOutOfMemory (20)	Insufficient memory is available to complete the interchange
rtdlqBTFRecReqExpired (21)	The document uses the BizTalk Framework and the receiptRequiredBy time has passed
rtdlqBTFExpiresAtExpired (22)	The document uses the BizTalk Framework and the document should no longer be processed because the expiresAt timestamp has been passed
rtdlgCorrelationFailure (23)	A receipt sent as part of the BizTalk Framework failed to correlate (such as a failure to be associated with a sent document)

Channel Tester Utility

Suppose you draw up an orchestration schedule, then go and configure all the message interchanges that make it work. You start the schedule – and the expected results do not occur. Is the fault in the schedule or the messaging configuration? The fact is, any real-world schedule is going to involve a lot of messaging, and that means a lot of configuration. Configuration is still preferable to programming, but it would also be good to test the individual interchange configurations as you go along. That's the idea behind the Channel Tester Utility. This is a small utility we will be building shortly to help check out BizTalk messaging configurations. It lets you load a document and name a channel. It takes that information and submits the document to BizTalk using `IInterchange`. If your configuration is correct, you should get the results you expect from the interchange. Otherwise, you should get some feedback that helps you pin down the problem.

The Interface

The utility is a fairly spartan Visual Basic application consisting of one form. The form is dominated by a scrollable edit field where the document to submit is displayed. This field is enabled for write-access, so you can change a message's contents or enter a message directly. In most cases, though, I expect that you will have a sample document on disk that you wish to open and load. In the illustration below, we've loaded the Site Service Description sample message found in the file `siteservicesample.xml` in the download. The channel name depicted is the channel used to implement the messaging action in the schedule (from Chapter 2) that communicates with the cable installer.

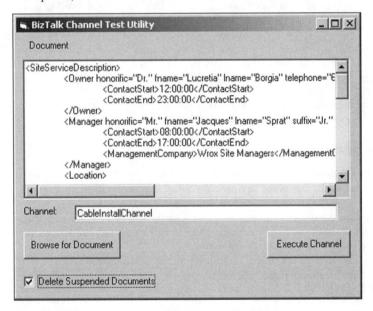

Later on in the chapter, we will be running the channel tester utility on our Wrox Management Services examples. For now, however, it is enough to know that to run the channel tester utility you have to:

❑ Browse for a document you wish to submit via the channel. The one depicted here is the Site Service Description document containing information on Lucretia Borgia's home, which we saw in Chapter 3.

❑ Beneath the Document field is a single line edit field where you enter the name of the channel you wish to test. Enter a channel name.

❑ Click on Execute Channel.

We haven't created a channel to test yet, but we will be doing so later in this chapter.

In terms of channel names for testing, you have to get the name from the Messaging Manager. When we get to the administrative programming interfaces in Chapter 13, we'll interrogate the BizTalk administrative database directly to provide support for this function.

The button labeled **Browse for Document** uses the Common Dialog control (implemented in comdlg32.ocx, typically found in the system32 folder) to open a file dialog, allowing you to browse for your sample document. After obtaining the file and pathname, it uses the File System Object (implemented in scrrun.dll, also in the system32 folder) to open and read the (presumably) text file and write it into the **Document** field.

Clicking **Execute Channel** invokes the IInterchange Submit() method, provided the **Document** field is not empty. If invoked, the method is passed the document and the name of the channel. We then check the suspended queue for documents resulting from this interchange to ensure that no failure resulted from the submission. If there are any such documents and the **Delete Suspended Documents** checkbox is checked, we will delete these documents from the queue.

Setting Up the Project

The utility is a Visual Basic standard executable project. Under **Projects References...**, ensure **Microsoft BizTalk Server Interchange 1.0 Type Library** (in cisapi.tlb, installed in the base BizTalk Server folder in a typical installation) and the **Microsoft Scripting Runtime** (scrrun.dll) are checked. Checking the suspended queue for problems involves another interface, IBizTalkTrackData, which is found in cisdta.dll. You will probably have to browse for this in the base BizTalk Server folder, but once checked it is listed in the project references as **Microsoft BizTalk Server Doc Tracking 1.0 Type Library**. The methods we will use from that interface return ADO recordset objects, so check **Microsoft ActiveX Data Objects Recordset 2.5 Library**, as well.

The form, in addition to the standard controls you see, uses the invisible Common Dialog control. The version I used was 6.0 from the Visual Studio Service Pack 3.

Loading the Document

At start up, the **Document** field is empty. Nothing happens until you click on the **Browse for Document** button. The handler for this is the private subroutine BrowseMsgBtn_Click(). The Common Dialog control was created on the form (found in ChannelTestForm.frm). We're going to need a File System Object for reading the document once we have a pathname, so we'll create that right in the variable declaration. We'll also need a TextStream object, but a method call will create that for us. Here are the declarations and a line of initialization code:

```
Private Sub BrowseMsgBtn_Click()
    Dim objFileSys As New FileSystemObject
    Dim objTextStream As TextStream

    FileDlg.FileName = ""
```

Next, we need to call the Common Dialog's ShowOpen() method to display the file dialog. If you cancel out of the dialog without selecting a file, the dialog control's FileName property will be empty. If it is not, we proceed to open it as a read-only text file using the File System Object, objFileSys. The return value from that call is a TextStream object. We call the ReadAll() method of that object to load the entire file into memory. The return from that method is the content of the file, so we assign it directly to the **Document** field's Text property:

```
      FileDlg.ShowOpen
      If FileDlg.FileName <> "" Then
         Set objTextStream = objFileSys.OpenTextFile(FileDlg.FileName, _
                                                      ForReading)
         MessageText.Text = objTextStream.ReadAll
      End If
   End Sub
```

Submitting the Document

That's all very necessary, but we are here to learn about BizTalk programming. The button handler for the **Execute Channel** button is `ExecuteChannel_Click`. Among the declarations for that subroutine is one for a new `Interchange` object, which is the one that implements the `IInterchange` interface. After the declarations, we check the two input fields to ensure neither is empty, then call `Submit()`:

```
   Private Sub ExecuteChannel_Click()
      Dim objInterChange As New Interchange
      Dim strHandle As String
      Dim rsTracker As New BTSDocTracking
      Dim rsInterchanges As Recordset
      Dim rDocList As Variant

      If MessageText.Text <> "" And ChannelText.Text <> "" Then
         strHandle = objInterChange.Submit(BIZTALK_OPENNESS_TYPE_NOTOPEN, _
                                MessageText.Text, , , , , , ChannelText.Text)
```

Note that the first parameter passed to the method indicates that the channel is not open. The document is passed as a string taken directly from the `Text` property of the `MessageText` edit control. The source, destination, and document name parameters are left empty. Instead, we pass in the name of the channel we want to test, again taken directly from the field where the user entered it: `ChannelText.Text`.

Now we want to check for any problems with the submission. We'll check the suspended queue that is shared by all servers in the BizTalk server group for any messages that are associated with this interchange submission.

The code presented below will not catch all possible errors because `Submit()` is an asynchronous call. Transport protocol timeout errors, in particular, will occur well after we hit this section of the code. As written, though, this code will catch the most common errors, which are those stemming from misconfiguration of BizTalk messaging or problems in the submitted documents. You will usually be testing configuration locally during development, leaving transport problems until you have a well-tested configuration and wish to debug a particular partner. If you wish to catch more errors, you might try calling the Win32 `Sleep()` function to pause execution before hitting the error checking code, or change the submission so that it uses `SubmitSync()`.

The return value from `Submit()` is a string representation of a GUID. If you check some sample values against the suspended queue results in the MMC snap-in, you will quickly find that the GUIDs do not match. This is because BizTalk permits submission of multiple documents in a single interchange, while each document appears individually in the queues. The methods in `IInterchange` that check the suspended queue take either the names of documents, sources, and destinations, or they require the GUID of a particular document in the queue. We cannot use the former method since we are submitting documents using the channel name. Getting individual document GUIDs requires recourse to a document tracking interface, `IBizTalkTrackData`.

Document tracking is covered in depth in Chapter 12.

The object that exposes this interface was declared as a new instance of the `BTSDocTracking` type in the variable `rsTracker`. The `GetInterchanges()` method returns a recordset containing rows with data about interchanges. It takes as its parameter the interchange GUID we got as the return value of `Submit()`. Since our application is submitting a single interchange, we expect to find one row in the recordset. One of the columns in the recordset is `nError`, which will be non-zero if the interchange itself experienced a problem.

```
        'Check for errors
        Set rsInterchanges = rsTracker.GetInterchanges(strHandle)

        rsInterchanges.MoveFirst
        If rsInterchanges("nError").Value <> 0 Then
           MsgBox "Error on interchange: " & rsInterchanges.Fields("nError")
        End If

        CheckForErrors strHandle

    End If
End Sub
```

You may have noticed that I'm calling a routine named `CheckForErrors()` outside the `if` statement that checks the interchange error code. That's because an interchange can be submitted successfully, but documents within the interchange can fail, leaving documents in the suspended queue. Each interchange will involve inbound documents (which we submit to BizTalk), and outbound documents, which are what BizTalk sends on to the destination. If mapping is involved, the two documents will be different. To make sure I'm catching legitimate errors, I always call my error checking routine.

Checking for Errors

The subroutine `CheckForErrors()` has to do two things: get all inbound and outbound documents associated with the interchange that ended up in the suspended queue, and get details regarding each document. Inbound document information is returned as a recordset from the `GetInDocDetails()` method of `IBizTalkTrackData`, while outbound document information is similarly returned by the `GetOutDocDetails()` method. Both methods take the interchange submission GUID as their sole parameter.

Processing each recordset involves iterating through the recordset and retrieving the document GUID, then calling the `GetSuspendedQueueItemDetails()` method of `IInterchange`. Since the processing is similar, I've moved it into a routine of its own that is called by `CheckForErrors()`. Here is the top-level error checking code that grabs the recordsets:

```
Private Sub CheckForErrors(sSubHandle As String)
    Dim rsIn As Recordset
    Dim rsOut As Recordset
    Dim rsTracker As New BTSDocTracking

    Set rsIn = rsTracker.GetInDocDetails(sSubHandle)
    Set rsOut = rsTracker.GetOutDocDetails(sSubHandle)

    If Not (rsIn.BOF And rsIn.EOF) Then
        CheckDocs rsIn, "Inbound"
    End If

    If Not (rsOut.BOF And rsOut.EOF) Then
        CheckDocs rsOut, "Outbound"
    End If
End Sub
```

The low-level code, `CheckDocs()`, takes the recordset and a string denoting the direction of the documents represented in the recordset. The only thing we need from the recordset is the GUID of each document, which is found in the `uidTrackingGUID` column:

```
Private Sub CheckDocs(rs As Recordset, sDir As String)
    Dim i As Integer
    Dim j As Integer
    Dim objIntC As New Interchange
    Dim sDocHandle As String
    Dim vSource As Variant
    Dim vDest As Variant
    Dim DocName As Variant
    Dim vReason As Variant
    Dim vDocData As Variant

    rs.MoveFirst
    While Not rs.EOF
        sDocHandle = rs("uidTrackingGUID").Value
```

With the GUID in hand, we can call `GetSuspendedQueueItemDetails`:

```
objIntC.GetSuspendedQueueItemDetails sDocHandle, vSource, vDest, _
                                     vDocName, vReason, vDocData
```

We pass in the document GUID in `sDocHandle` along with some empty variants that serve as buffers for the data this method returns. The `vReason` variable takes on the value drawn from the `CISReasontoQueue` enumeration. Referring to our earlier table, you can see we are interested in any non-zero value. If we have error information, we format a string that will consist of the error code and the body of the document. Rather than present the user with the raw enumerated value, I have a function `GetFailureString()` that is just one big `Select Case` statement on the `CISReasontoQueue` enumeration:

```
    If vReason <> 0 Then
        sMsg = sDir & " document error: " & GetFailureString(vReason)
        sMsg = sMsg & vbCrLf & "----------" & vbCrLf & vDocData
        MsgBox sMsg
    . . .
Private Function GetFailureString(vReasonCode As Variant) As String
    Select Case vReasonCode

        Case 0
            GetFailureString = "Not supported"
        Case 1
            GetFailureString = "Parser component failure"
        Case 2
            GetFailureString = "Unable to parse the document"
        Case 3
            GetFailureString = "Invalid document"
        Case 4
            GetFailureString = "BizTalk is unable to select a channel"
        Case 5
            GetFailureString = "Document mapping attempted with an _
                               invalid map"
```

```
            Case 6
                GetFailureString = "Unable to comply with the field tracking _
                                    requirements of the channel"
            Case 7
                GetFailureString = "Document mapping was unsuccessful"
            Case 8
                GetFailureString = "Document serialization failed"
            Case 9
                GetFailureString = "Document MIME encoding failed"
            Case 10
                GetFailureString = "Digital signing of the document failed"
            Case 11
                GetFailureString = "Document encryption failed"
            Case 12
                GetFailureString = "Failure to send on the specified transport _
                                    protocol"
            Case 13
                GetFailureString = "Administrator placed this document in the _
                                    suspended queue"
            Case 14
                GetFailureString = "Transmission timeout"
            Case 15
                GetFailureString = "Failure of a custom component (AIC)"
            Case 16
                GetFailureString = "Failure of a BizTalk messaging server while _
                                    the document was in process; you may manually_
                                    attempt to resend by moving the document to _
                                    the work queue"
            Case 17
                GetFailureString = "Specified channel has been deleted"
            Case 18
                GetFailureString = "Named channel not found"
            Case 19
                GetFailureString = "Named channel uses an open port"
            Case 20
                GetFailureString = "Out of memory"
            Case 21
                GetFailureString = "BizTalk Framework receipt required by time _
                                    has passed"
            Case 22
                GetFailureString = "BizTalk Framework timestamp for message _
                                    expiration has passed"
            Case Else
                GetFailureString = "Reason code is out of bounds"
        End Select
    End Function
```

Recall that the user interface had a checkbox signalling the user's desire to clean up the suspended queue by deleting any documents in the queue related to this interchange. We accomplish this by calling the `DeleteFromSuspendedQueue()` method of the interchange object, passing it the GUID of the document:

```
            If DelSuspended.Value = 1 Then
                objIntC.DeleteFromSuspendedQueue sDocHandle
            End If
        End If
        rs.MoveNext
    Wend
End Sub
```

That's all there is to the utility. It is a stand-alone application that may be run on your messaging server to test channel configurations as you build them. You may run it from the Visual Basic development environment or build it as an executable program. When you are specifying multiple configurations needed by a schedule, as we will be doing shortly for the site survey sample application, it is convenient to be able to test each channel as you finish with it, rather than waiting to complete them all and try to debug the entire schedule as a whole. If a channel has a problem in the utility, it is easier to pinpoint it and fix it. If you have a problem with a schedule and all of its required channels worked in the utility, then you know the problem is with the schedule.

Configuring the Wrox Site Management Application

It is time at last to configure the messaging implementations for the orchestration schedule we developed back in Chapter 2. We'll build up the organizations – home, Cable Installer, and Yard Care – then the three documents, envelopes for the flatfile documents, then ports, and finally channels for the messages coming out of the schedule. After we get our first channel built, we'll use the channel tester utility to make sure it works.

After we get the configurations worked out, it will be time to develop a rudimentary client application for the field agents who go out and originate the Site Service Description documents. So, we will:

❏ Configure this application that will send the MSMQ messages for which the schedule waits.

❏ Look at the basics of loading a schedule, although we'll address that topic in its proper detail in the next chapter. The sample application assumes that the schedule is running at all times, so we'll consider how to start it.

❏ And when we're finished, you'll be able to generate a Site Service Description from the client we'll construct, submit it, and watch the Cable Installation and Yard Care messages get sent by the schedule.

Organizations

We'll assume the default Home Organization created by the generic BizTalk Server installation is the Wrox Site Managers organization. After all, it is the one hosting the server group. Make sure that it has the default organization identifier whose qualifier is Organization Name and whose value is Home Organization. This is all the configuration you will need for this organization.

Next, create an organization named Cable Installer with a default organization identifier with the qualifier Organization Name and the value Cable Installer. Finally, create another organization named Yard Care Vendor whose default identifier is similarly qualified, bearing the value Yard Care Vendor. This completes the organization configuration you will need for the example.

Documents and Envelopes

In Chapter 3, we developed three message specifications, the Site Service Description, the Cable Installation document, and the Yard Care document. Now that the organizations have been defined, we need to tell Messaging Manager about these documents.

In Messaging Manager, create a new document definition. On the General tab, provide the name Site Service Description. Click Browse… and select the SiteServiceDescription.xml message specification file you developed in Chapter 3. Repeat this for the other two document types as indicated in the table below:

Document Definition	Specification File
Cable WO CSV	cablewo.xml
Yard Mnx Subscription	yardmnxsubscription.xml

The Site Service Description message does not require an envelope because it is XML in format and so can be read directly by the messaging engine. The other two documents, however, are flatfile format messages, so they require that we define an envelope for each. This is accomplished with Messaging Manager as discussed earlier, providing a name for the envelope and pointing to the document specification file.

Envelope Name	Specification File
CableWO	cablewo.xml
YardCarePosEnv	yardmnxsubscription.xml

The is nothing special about the document and envelope names. You could name them anything you wish. If you want to closely follow the configurations that follow, however, you should to use these names.

Messaging Ports

If you refer back to the business process diagram we developed for this application in Chapter 2, you will be forgiven for thinking that we need to configure three ports:

- ❏ one from the site managers in the field via MSMQ
- ❏ one to the cable installer
- ❏ and finally one to the yard care vendor

That would be a good guess, but alas, you'd be wrong. The port from the site managers uses an MSMQ implementation, not a BizTalk messaging implementation. It is therefore wholly outside the BizTalk messaging engine, so neither a port nor a channel is required. XLANG Scheduler is kind enough to monitor the specified message queue for us and make the proper MSMQ calls to retrieve the message and bring it into the data flow in our schedule. Apparently, the XLANG Scheduler side of the team recognized that many developers would need to monitor message queues for arriving messages, so they built the same sort of functionality into the scheduling engine as exists in MSMQ receive functions (a topic we take up in Chapter 9). It uses MSMQ API calls to wait for an arriving message, at which time it triggers activity in the schedule.

Of course, this also means that BizTalk functions like tracking and mapping are unavailable to us, but the good news for us, right now in this chapter, is that our port and channel configuration tasks just diminished by one third.

You'll also be introduced to the concept of receive functions in Chapter 9. These are BizTalk components that monitor the two protocols for which you cannot easily construct listeners: files and MSMQ messages. Here again, though, these are functions of BizTalk messaging. Since our orchestration schedule uses an MSMQ implementation, we do not have to configure an MSMQ receive function.

We certainly don't want to write applications for our vendors, at least not for the purpose of demonstrating our side of BizTalk messaging. For that reason, we'll use the local file transport protocol for both messaging operations. The mapped document will be written to a location we specify whenever we send a message to our partners. Begin by creating a new port to an organization, configuring it as indicated in the following table. Any items in the port wizard that aren't specified in the table should be left on their default setting:

Port Wizard Item	Setting Value
Name	`Send Cable WO`
Organization Name	`Cable Installer`
Transport type	`File`
Address	`file://c:\temp\cablewo_%tracking_id%.txt`
Envelope Information	`CableWO`
Organization Identifier	`Organization / Cable Installer(Default)`

We've given it an arbitrary name, then selected the previously configured organization, envelope, and organization identifier. The one curiosity is the transport address. In my case, I've elected to write it to the `temp` directory on my local C: drive with a filename beginning with `cablewo_` and ending in the extension `.txt`. The name `%tracking_id%` causes BizTalk to add the tracking GUID to the filename, which results in a unique filename. This allows me to submit lots of cable work orders while keeping each document separate and distinct.

The symbol was certainly useful in allowing us to generate a unique filename. BizTalk messaging supports five such symbols that you may use in filenames:

Symbol	Result	Results in Unique Name
`%datetime%`	Date and time of the messages, expressed in milliseconds from a system-level baseline in GMT	No
`%document_name%`	Name of the document as defined in BizTalk Server	No
`%server%`	Machine name of the computer in the BizTalk cluster that processed the message	No
`%tracking_id%`	GUID	Yes
`%uid%`	Milliseconds from the start of the BizTalk Server host	No

Here's the port configuration for sending documents to the yard care vendor:

Port Wizard Item	Setting Value
Name	`Send Yard Care Subs`
Organization Name	`Yard Care Vendor`
Transport type	`File`
Address	`file://c:\temp\yardcaresub_%tracking_id%.txt`
Envelope Information	`YardCarePosEnv`
Organization Identifier	`Organization / Yard Care Vendor(Default)`

Channels

If you've been following along, you are moments away from being able to transmit a document through BizTalk's messaging engine. We have two channels to configure, and then we can bring the channel tester utility into play.

Begin by selecting the **Send Cable WO** port in the port search results. Right-click on the item and select the **New Channel From an Application** menu item from the context menu. Configure the channel wizard as indicated in this table, again leaving the fields not mentioned in the table set to their defaults:

Channel Wizard Item	Setting Value
Name	`CableInstallChannel`
Source Application	**XLANG Schedule selected**
Inbound document definition name	`Site Service Description`
Outbound document definition name	`Cable WO CSV`
Map inbound document to outbound document	Checked
Map reference	`siteservicetocablefunctoid.xml`

By now you should be gaining an appreciation for the slogan "configuration, not programming". All the configuration work you've done to date comes together here. The channel wizard configuration was largely a matter of selecting things you've already configured. Now we're really dangerous. We have everything we need to start sending messages through BizTalk. Before you rush off to try out the channel tester, here's the other channel configuration you need to implement the messaging for the orchestration schedule from Chapter 2, the channel to the yard care vendor:

Channel Wizard Item	Setting Value
Name	YardMnxSubChannel
Source Application	XLANG Schedule selected
Inbound document definition name	Site Service Description
Outbound document definition name	Yard Mnx Subscription
Map inbound document to outbound document	Checked
Map reference	Siteservicetoyardmnxsub.xml

Testing the Channels

You've waited long enough. Let's make something happen. Open the channel tester utility, which you may have built yourself or downloaded from our site. Click on Browse for Document and select `siteservicesample.xml`.

> *All sample code, including the sample file, is available for download from http://www.wrox.com/. Remember to register compiled code on your machine before use, using the Registry utility or by right-clicking on the component downloaded and selecting Merge from the menu.*

Unless you have absolute confidence in your configuration, leave Delete Suspended Documents unchecked. That way, if you have a problem, you can go into the suspended queue to try to diagnose the cause of the problem. Even if you downloaded the code and the sample, there is always the chance of an error in the configuration. Since we used the local file protocol, the utility will catch the sorts of errors that could occur. Nevertheless, it is nice to be able to go into the BizTalk Server Administration tool (an MMC snap-in) and check and recheck the error messages and the resultant document if there is a problem.

> *We cover the use of the BizTalk Server Administration for troubleshooting in Chapter 9.*

However, I have every confidence in your configuration. So, having browsed successfully for `siteservicesample.xml`:

❑   Enter CableInstallChannel in the edit field labelled Channel

❑   Then, click the Execute Channel button

Since this is the first time you've used the messaging engine since starting your computer, it will take several seconds. If all goes well, you will see nothing. Browse the directory you specified in the port wizard. You should see a file with a name like `cablewo_{56EA95CA-7330-4E1F-81B7-C26805171623}.txt`. The GUID portion of the filename will be different for you, of course – this is a globally *unique* identifier, after all.

You can open the file in Notepad or any text editor and confirm that the Site Service Description document has been transformed into the appropriate cable installation document in CSV format. For the sample message included with the download, the result looks like this:

```
C,Jacques,Sprat,610-555-1212,08:00:00
L,123 Chestnut Ave,Division 6,Philadelphia,PA,19100,First house on left
I,4,4,PREMIUM,12:00:00
```

Now replace the channel name with **YardMnxSubChannel**. Execute the channel again. This time you will see a file with a name like `yardcaresub_{14E60512-321E-47EF-B44E-06AF48EFC179}.txt`. Open that in a text editor and you will see the hybrid positional and delimited format we specified in Chapter 3. Here's a sample of the results:

```
OJacques    Sprat      610-555-121208:00:0017:00:00
A123 Chestnut AvDivision 6      Philadelphia    PA19100
Y10000 rye      4eval
```

You will quickly find that executing these two channels becomes boring. Just for fun, let's introduce some errors. Check the box to delete suspended messages. Now delete the end angle bracket from the Owner element's closing tag and submit the message again with either channel. This time you'll get a parser error. Now delete the entire Owner element. According to the document specification, this is a required record. Submit the document, and you'll get a validation error. You can experiment with other errors and check that the utility detects them.

Wrox Site Management Client

Now that you are satisfied that the individual channels are properly configured, you'll want to execute the schedule from Chapter 2.

Recall the business problem. A field representative of the Wrox Site Service Managers company assesses the features of a residential property using a client application on a portable device, such as a laptop. The client submits the data as a Site Service Description using MSMQ. The schedule receives the message and conditionally generates the messages needed to implement the owner's wishes regarding cable television installation and yard care.

User Interface

The client, for our demonstration purposes, consists of a rudimentary wizard-driven application in Visual Basic. I've implemented five forms, one each for the required Owner, Manager, and Location records, as well as one each for the optional Television and Yard records. Each form except the last has a **Next** button to take you to the next form in the application and so enter information from the form into the Site Service Description document. Every form except the first has a **Back** button to let you retrace your steps. Clicking **Cancel** terminates the application without sending any messages, while clicking **Finish** on the last form completes the document, and sends it via MSMQ. Clicking **Clear** on the Owner form resets the document and all the forms.

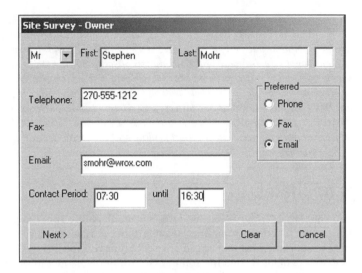

There's very little code other than user interface operations. The Finish button handler has to do some MSMQ messaging. No part of the application is BizTalk-aware. Once the application sends the document to the designated queue, it is up to XLANG Scheduler to receive the message and coordinate BizTalk messaging. Note that the schedule must already be running. We'll cover two ways to do that in later sections.

Only those forms required for the messaging in our schedule are implemented. Thus, you will see only Owner, Manager, Television *and* Yard *service forms.*

Generating XML

Since the end result of the application is an XML document, you might expect to find considerable amounts of XML Document Object Model (DOM) code in this application. In fact, not only is there no DOM code, but the project does not even have a reference to the MSXML component. How are we generating the Site Service Description?

I've wrapped the XML DOM code in a COM component. This component, implemented in SiteMgr.dll and built in the Visual Basic project SiteMgr.vbp (which is all in the sample code), encapsulates all the DOM logic needed to build a Site Service Description document. This is a reasonable approach from both a management and architectural standpoint. There are many developers who are accustomed to using business components to build applications. They are used to getting and setting properties and calling methods. Far fewer programmers know the DOM object model. BizTalk itself, as we have seen, tries to isolate users from the syntax of XML, using records and fields in lieu of elements and attributes. In a production setting, you can have a small team devoted to building business components that serialize themselves as XML documents, and have the bulk of your staff working with BizTalk or Visual Basic at a higher development level.

The component included with the download is substantially derived from one generated by the now-defunct BizTalk Jumpstart VB Addin. Since then, an updated version has been created. The new version is included with the BizTalk Server SDK.

I have manually modified the code generated by the old add-in to eliminate the dependency on the BizTalk Framework envelope format. The source code is neither a definitive DOM sample nor necessarily a complete implementation of the Site Service Description. Instead, it serves two purposes. First, you should become aware of the advantages of encapsulating DOM source code in business components. Secondly, it is a quick and productive way to provide a non-trivial message example while allowing you to focus on BizTalk programming rather than XML. If you wish to dive deeper into DOM programming with the Microsoft COM-based XML parser, read IE 5 Dynamic HTML Programmer's Reference *(Wrox Press, 1999, ISBN 1-861001-74-6) or visit the MSDN XML Developer's Center at http://msdn.microsoft.com/xml/default.asp. The component has only been tested with the sample client.*

Project Dependencies

The client is implemented as a Visual Basic standard executable, built from the project SiteSurveyClient.vbp. There are a number of important references and component dependencies that need to be set. The user interface makes use of spin button controls for the cable connections, TV set-top boxes, and yard size fields. I used the spinner control implemented in the Microsoft Forms 2.0 Library (fm20.dll, usually installed in the system32 folder). The project also uses masked edit fields to control the input of the contact start and end times. This is important as those items are typed as times in the document specification and so an ill-formed time string will cause the message to be suspended. I'm using the Microsoft Masked Edit Control 6.0 from Visual Studio Service Pack 3. This is implemented in msmask32.ocx, also found in the system32 folder.

You will need to add two references to the usual project default references set by Visual Basic. After you build and register the SiteMgr component, browse for it and set a reference. We will use SiteManager.SiteDescription as the entry point for all our XML generation. Next, since we will ultimately be sending the finished XML document via MSMQ, we need a reference to the Microsoft Message Queue 2.0 Object Library (mqoa.dll in the system32 folder).

Form Processing

The forms are very simple, consisting largely of user interface elements. In the Form_Load() procedure, we obtain a reference to the appropriate object representing some major record of the document. These variables – Owner, Manager, Location, Television, and Yard – are declared in the module Globals.bas. In addition to obtaining the reference, the form initialization procedure includes an user interface preparation required by the controls on the particular form. For example, here is the code to get the document reference, set up the combo box, and set a radio button default in the Manager form:

```
Private Sub Form_Load()
    Set Manager = SiteDoc.Manager
    Manager.id = "s" & Trim(Str(Int(10000 * Rnd(Time()))))
    Combo1.AddItem "(None)"
    Combo1.AddItem "Mr"
    Combo1.AddItem "Ms"
    Combo1.AddItem "Dr"
    Combo1.ListIndex = 0
    PhoneOption.Value = True
End Sub
```

The call to `Manager.id` sets an ID for the Manager based on a random number. Although not as good as a GUID, it is sufficient for demonstration purposes.

Each form in the wizard uses the methods of the component to set or reset the various parts of the document. Just as an example, here is the **Next** button handler from the **Owner** form:

```
Private Sub NextBtn_Click()
    If CheckOwnerBeforeNext() Then
        SetOwnerProps
        OwnerForm.Hide
        ManagerForm.Show
    Else
        MsgBox ("First, Last, Telephone, and Contact Period required")
    End If
End Sub
```

The function `CheckOwnerBeforeNext()` checks the form fields to ensure we have the minimal required information: for example, first and last names, phone number, and start and end contact times. `SetOwnerProps()` is a bit more interesting. It interacts with the COM component to set information in the Site Service Description document:

```
Private Sub SetOwnerProps()
    Owner.FName = FName.Text
    Owner.LName = LName.Text
    If Combo1.ListIndex > 0 Then
        Owner.honorific = Combo1.List(Combo1.ListIndex)
    End If
    If SuffixText.Text <> "" Then
        Owner.suffix = SuffixText.Text
    End If

    Owner.Telephone = TelephoneText.Text
    If FaxText.Text <> "" Then
        Owner.fax = FaxText.Text
    End If
    If EmailText.Text <> "" Then
        Owner.email = EmailText.Text
    End If

    If (PhoneOption.Value = True) Then
        Owner.preferredContact = "phone"
    End If
    If (FaxOption.Value = True) Then
        Owner.preferredContact = "fax"
    End If
    If (EmailOption.Value = True) Then
        Owner.preferredContact = "email"
    End If

    With Owner
        .ContactStart = TimeStartText.Text
        .ContactEnd = TimeEndText.Text
    End With

End Sub
```

Note that we only have to check the optional fields. `CheckOwnerBeforeNext()` verified the rest of the fields, so there is no need to recheck them.

When the user clicks Finish, the component's XML property is called to obtain the text of the XML document. It is this property's value that is submitted as the body of the MSMQ message destined for the XLANG schedule.

Submitting Messages

The interesting code in the client occurs in the Finish button handler. We configure an MSMQ message and set its body equal to the text of our XML message. Next, we submit the message to a transactional message queue. Note that there is no use of the `IInterchange` interface or any other BizTalk-aware code. We could replace BizTalk with some other middleware product or a custom application without breaking the client. All the BizTalk logic will be concentrated on the server in the XLANG schedule. As a result, the client machines do not need to have any BizTalk components installed.

```
Private Sub SendMSMQ()
    Dim msmqQueueInfo As New msmqQueueInfo
    Dim msmqTxDisp As New MSMQTransactionDispenser
    Dim msmqTx As MSMQTransaction
    Dim msmqMsg As New MSMQMessage
    Dim msmqQueue As New msmqQueue

    msmqQueueInfo.FormatName = "DIRECT=OS:.\private$\RecvSiteSvcDesc"
    Set msmqQueue = msmqQueueInfo.Open(MQ_SEND_ACCESS, MQ_DENY_NONE)
```

This batch of code declares the MSMQ objects we will need and opens a queue. I'm using a private queue on the local machine for simplicity. In a production environment, you would of course have an MSMQ primary enterprise controller and you would be addressing a public queue on a remote machine. I'm opening the queue for send-only access (`MQ_SEND_ACCESS`) without locking anyone out of the queue (`MQ_DENY_NONE`). While I'm the sole user of this particular application, we're prototyping a system intended to be used by dozens or hundreds of concurrent field agents, so we want to keep the impact on shared resources small.

Now is a good time to open a messaging queue in MSMQ.

> *I recommend that you go into the Computer Management application on your Administrative Tools menu (normally found under Control Panel), then expand the Services and Applications node to expose Message Queuing. From there, select either Private Queues or Public Queues, and use the New Private Queue or New Public Queue menu item off the context menu. The option to mark the queue as transactional is found in the dialog box that results from selecting one of these menu items.*

Name the new queue `private$\RecvSiteSvcDesc` and set its value to `transactional`.

If the queue was opened successfully, I set the body of the message to the XML markup generated by the `SiteMgr` component through its XML property, then send the message. Note that my queue is transactional. It is very important to mark the queue as transactional when you create the queue. XLANG Scheduler expects transactional queues, which is not surprising given that it is intended for robust, mission-critical applications. It would not do to have one BizTalk Server in the group consume a message immediately prior to failing. With transactions, XLANG can recover from such problems.

```
    msmqQueueInfo.Refresh
If msmqQueue.IsOpen Then
    msmqMsg.Body = SiteDoc.XML
    msmqMsg.Label = "SiteServiceDescription"
    Set msmqTx = msmqTxDisp.BeginTransaction
    msmqMsg.Send msmqQueue, msmqTx
    msmqTx.Commit
```

The transaction dispenser object gives us a transaction object, `msmqTx`, which is passed along with the queue object, `msmqQueue`, by the message object in its `Send` call. Having sent the message to the queue, I call `Commit` on the transaction object to commit the transaction and make the message visible to XLANG Scheduler, which is (unbeknown to the client application) waiting for the arrival of a message in the queue. If the queue could not be opened, I present an error message:

```
Else
    'improve error handling in production
    MsgBox "Unable to open messaging queue"
End If
End Sub
```

Watching the Schedule Execute

You can work your way through the Site Survey client application, click Finish, and wait forever for something to happen. The culprit? The schedule is not running. Nothing in the client launches or relaunches the schedule. This is as it should be. You wouldn't want clients controlling the server, particularly clients who are intermittently connected. Managing the schedule is a server-side responsibility.

In Chapter 2 we briefly covered the process of loading a schedule into the XLANG Scheduler using a moniker. Basically, any client that instantiates the moniker via COM will suffice. The following line of Javascript executing on the server will do the trick:

```
objSked = GetObject("sked:///c:\\mypath\\initialorders.skx");
```

This code could be executed anywhere. You might run a script on start-up of the host, or have a service that implements a pool of schedules. This is a moot point for our sample for, as you will see in a just a moment, we can also use the moniker within a tool included with the BizTalk SDK.

In this line of code, mypath stands in for the actual pathname to the compiled schedule file, and the file is found on my `C:` drive. If you've transmitted a message from the client (you can check using the Computer Management application under the Administrative Tools menu on most systems) before you load the schedule, you'll note XLANG Scheduler checks the queue when it reaches the step where it blocks awaiting an incoming message. A check of the queue before and after running the schedule shows that a message was queued and subsequently consumed. The waiting message is plucked from the queue and processed. To verify this, though, you have to look in the folder you configured for the channels and see that files were created by the schedule.

If you didn't modify the default yard size, you will not have a yard maintenance subscription file because of the business rule implemented in the script component.

Now, in a production application, you may have more going on. Data may go into databases, messages may go to remote partners, but one of the secrets of server-side, back-end development is that it is visually boring. There is nothing to see. If you want to have a little fun before we leave this chapter (and learn a bit about what's going on in the schedule), you can launch the XLANG Event Monitor (XLANMon.exe, installed in the XLANG Tools folder of the BizTalk SDK). It looks like this:

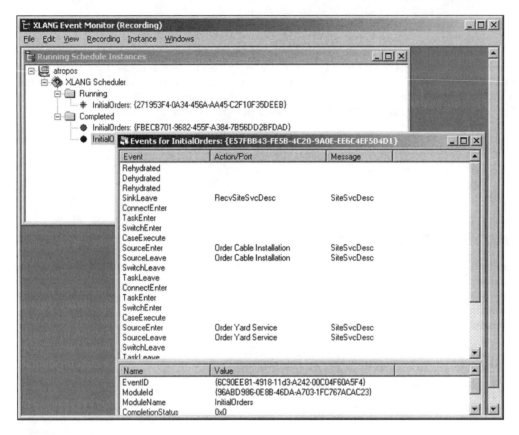

Use the Instance Run... menu item on the main menu to open a dialog that asks for a moniker. Enter the file path only – the Monitor will supply the sked:/// prefix as indicated in the dialog. Once you click OK, a new instance of the schedule should appear under the Running node to indicate a running schedule. If you double-click on the schedule instance the Events for InitialOrders window depicted above will appear. Now compose and send a message using the client utility. Once a message arrives in the queue, events begin to fire in earnest. If you read through the event list, you'll be able to follow the flow through the business process diagram. Try sending messages without cable service or with a yard size smaller than the minimum required to trigger a yard order. You'll see the conditional processing that sends BizTalk messages only when required by our business rules.

At the end, the Relaunch Schedule action occurs. You'll see the schedule you were following (check the GUID) is now under the Completed node of the Running Schedule Instances window and a new schedule has taken its place as the running schedule. When you are finished, you'll want to remove the last running schedule. Select it, then select Instance Terminate on the context menu. The incomplete schedule moves to the Completed node.

Summary

The main lesson I hope you take away from this chapter is that BizTalk messaging is a more a matter of configuration than programming. You learned the basic concepts of BizTalk messaging – organizations, documents, envelopes, ports, and channels. You learned how to use the wizards in the Messaging Manager to configure these entities. You can send messages to outside partners or internal applications without writing a line of code. In some cases, you can receive messages without programming. In other cases, notably HTTP, you'll need to write a little bit of code to receive the message. You'll see an example of this in a later chapter.

Once you begin writing code, you need the IInterchange COM interface. This interface provides a streamlined interface for the purpose of getting documents into the BizTalk messaging engine. It provides no way to take messages out of the engine, however. You must always use the standard protocols supported by BizTalk to receive messages. IInterchange exists largely as a way to access BizTalk messaging from within code. We used it in the channel tester utility, although we needed to resort to other interfaces to check the status of the BizTalk queues.

Finally, we tied together all the strands that we've been developing since Chapter 2. With the details of messaging configured, we were finally able to run the Wrox Site Managers initial orders schedule. We prototyped the client application for the field agents. That application used MSMQ exclusively, demonstrating that BizTalk can be used to integrate legacy applications. Although the client is newly written, it does not have any BizTalk-specific code in it. The server-side details of this application are entirely opaque to the client.

We've tied up a lot of related topics and actually delivered some documents through BizTalk, yet we are not yet halfway through this book. There is much more to BizTalk than basic schedules and fundamental messaging. There are a host of interfaces that perform the programmatic equivalent of the manual tasks we've performed in the last few chapters. It might be better to change our slogan to "configuration, and programming if you want to". There is also the matter of custom components integration. We've also been using BizTalk in a single server configuration while making passing reference to production applications. In a later chapter, we'll give some thought to deployment architectures that taking scaling and reliability into account.

Right now, though, it's time to return to XLANG schedules. There is much that we haven't seen. We need to dive into the details of transactions, both short and long. We've run one schedule at a time, but we can run multiple instances. This provides benefits, but also incurs problems of state management. These are the topics of the next chapter.

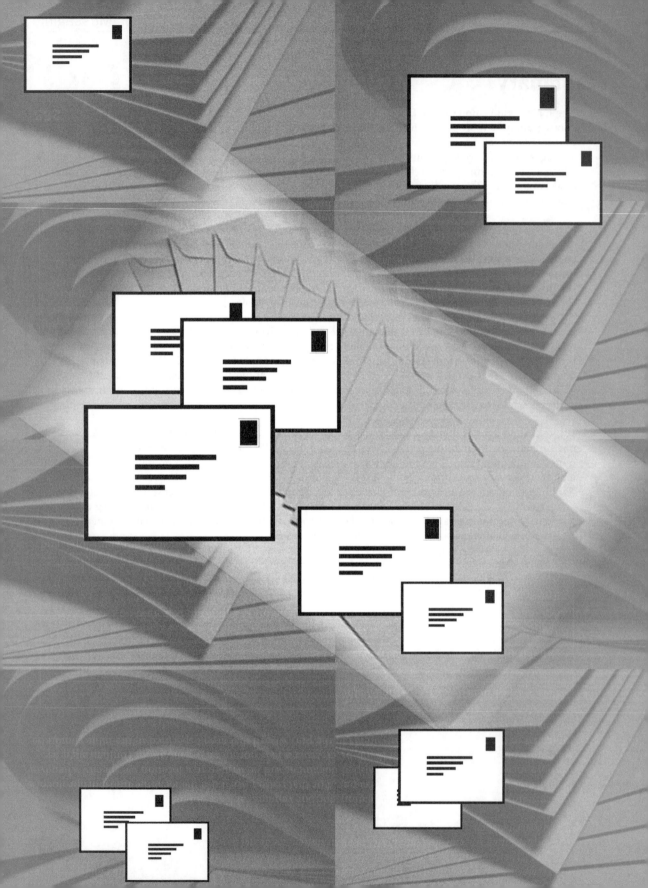

6

Advanced Orchestration

Orchestration is a powerful and flexible way to develop distributed systems through specification rather than programming. In Chapter 2 we saw how a business process diagram makes the workflow in a business process easily visible and accessible to both programmers and managers. By the end of the last chapter, you saw our sample schedule in action. The arrival of a business document joined with an orchestration schedule did the work of custom integration code in an application.

Our sample was fairly simple and lacked features desirable in real-world production systems. For instance, we barely mentioned transactions, and paid little or no attention to scalability. Also, if the receiving server group has dozens of instances of the same schedule executing concurrently, we made no mention of how messages in a long-running business process can be matched with the correct instance of a schedule. This chapter addresses those omissions. Now that you have a basic understanding of orchestration and messaging, we are ready to tackle more advanced topics.

In particular, you will learn the following from this chapter:

- ❑   How to load a schedule in response to channel activation
- ❑   How to load schedules from program code
- ❑   How to communicate between schedules
- ❑   How to help XLANG Scheduler manage schedules for optimum resource utilization, shuttling them between memory and the database through the dehydration and rehydration processes
- ❑   Types of transactions, and what causes them to fail
- ❑   The procedures for recovering from failed transactions in orchestration schedules
- ❑   The clash between concurrency and transactions
- ❑   What techniques XLANG provides for dynamic port binding based on message content

Before we start I will provide some guidance on the proper balance of application code versus system behavior described in XLANG schedules. Orchestration is a powerful capability of BizTalk Server, but you need to fully understand the topics in this chapter to make the most of it. Distributed systems may be similar to client-server applications, but their very nature introduces some challenges in error recovery and message routing. It is these challenges that we will address with orchestration's advanced features.

Architecture: Schedules vs. Applications

Things can get a bit muddled when working with schedules. Orchestration Designer allows you to do quite a bit of work without programming; if you are integrating some manual activities, you might be tempted to go straight to orchestration schedules, avoiding the task of writing applications for the manual processes.

However, this would be a mistake. Schedules are event-driven examples of declarative programming. They are strong on what should happen, but weak on controlling exactly when something happens. XLANG Scheduler will guarantee that a particular action takes place on schedule (forgive the pun!) in response to an event. However, you do not have the line-by-line control that you have in the procedural programming practiced in application development. An application gives you detailed control over what happens; over how the application executes. You also have access to proprietary APIs, including statically linked and non-COM+ dynamically linked libraries.

The point is that *orchestration is intended to coordinate applications, not replace them.* It is a new tool in the programmer's toolkit, one that is well fitted to the high-level view needed in building systems. You might be able to make orchestration work in the low- to mid-level view of application programming, but you will be working against the tool. If you find things growing increasingly difficult to accomplish in a particular schedule, step back a moment and see if you are using the right tool. Perhaps the task you are trying to accomplish should be in a free-standing application that orchestration coordinates, or maybe the task is small, but calls for procedural programming. In that case, a COM component called from the schedule is an ideal choice. Schedules do not replace applications, they complement them.

Loading Schedules

I mentioned in Chapter 2 that it is possible to load an orchestration schedule from a COM file moniker. Indeed, that is how the XLANG Scheduler Monitor loads its schedules. Actually, you have more options for loading a schedule than our discussion suggested, and I did not even touch on an alternative method. One way is to instruct the messaging engine to load a schedule for you when a message arrives, which lets you bypass the entire issue of monikers for simple cases. You can also turn to COM as your method for loading; if you do this you will find that you have a higher degree of control over loading than the discussion in Chapter 2 suggests. Indeed, there are two COM interfaces available to help you work with schedules and their component parts. We'll go into a formal discussion of how to load schedules, focusing on the following:

❑ Loading schedules when a message arrives

❑ The formal syntax of monikers

❑ Programmatic loading using the `IWFWorkflowInstance` and `IWFProxy` interfaces

Loading Schedule on Message Arrival

You may specify a schedule to use when you are configuring a port. The arrival of a message at that port will cause the messaging run-time engine to work with XLANG Scheduler, loading a new schedule or passing the arriving message to a running schedule instance based on your configuration.

The Port Binding Wizard for binding a port to an application accomplishes this on the Destination Application property page. This page is shown below:

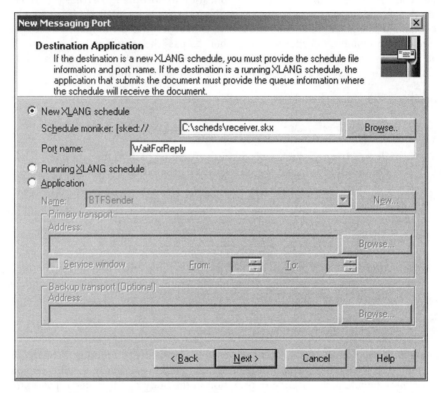

If you check New XLANG Schedule, you must provide a schedule moniker, complete with the port in the schedule that matches this messaging port. On the other hand, if you check Running XLANG Schedule, the document must specify the name of an MSMQ queue that is monitored by the schedule. The latter form is the approach we took in Chapter 2.

Moniker Syntax

Monikers are string names that uniquely identify objects to the COM+ run-time system. A moniker is used to tell the XLANG Scheduler what schedule file to load and on what machine.

In Chapter 2, the discussion at the end of the chapter (regarding how to launch a schedule) disclosed the basics of the XLANG schedule moniker syntax. To unravel the structure of a moniker, it is necessary to understand how the XLANG Scheduler runs. The Scheduler is a COM+ application containing the WkFlow.SysMgr component implemented in skedsmgr.dll, installed with BizTalk Server. Schedules that were running at the time of a system shutdown of the server hosting the XLANG Scheduler are automatically reloaded when the system comes back up courtesy of the Wfsvcmgr.exe service.

The latter point is important to developers. When you are debugging and testing schedules, don't assume that shutting down XLANG Scheduler or rebooting the server will clear everything out. Any schedules that were running at the time you shut down the server or the scheduler will be helpfully restarted by the workflow manager service. They will then run to completion or idle indefinitely, consuming system resources. If you need to clear a schedule outside the normal workflow, use the XLANG Event Monitor (XLANGMon.exe under the XLANG folder of the BizTalk SDK) and explicitly stop the schedule.

Of course, you can create your own COM+ application to host the `WkFlow.SysMgr` component (and hence the core functions we casually refer to as the XLANG Scheduler). This is why COM+ needs to know the name of the machine hosting the XLANG Scheduler, and the name of the application hosting the scheduler's component, in order to know where to pass the moniker. You can use the Component Services management application in Microsoft Windows 2000, which you can find in Start | Programs | Administrative Tools | Component Services, to create such an application.

The form for addressing a schedule via a moniker is this:

```
sked://[host_server]![xlang_host_app]/filepath_to_skx
```

The portion labeled *filepath_to_skx* is the fully qualified path to the compiled schedule file. The XLANG Scheduler uses this to locate the file describing the schedule you want to load.

Two parts of this moniker are optional. If you are using the installed XLANG Scheduler application, you may omit the name of the host application for a moniker that, for example, could look like this:

```
sked://mymachine/c:\schedules\myschedule.skx
```

If you are launching the schedule from the BizTalk Server machine itself and accepting the default COM+ application, you may even omit the machine name, in which case the example above becomes (note the *three* forward slashes this time):

```
sked:///c:\schedules\myschedule.skx
```

There is another way to name a schedule, which is used to address a running schedule instance. This form will fail if the schedule is not running. Its syntax, moreover, is very specific, so you will likely only use it when the schedule records some information in the body of a message it passes to a partner from which it expects a reply. We'll see an example of that later. The form looks like this:

```
sked://[host_server]![xlang_host_app]/{instance_guid}
```

Here again, *host_server* and *xlang_host_app* are optional strings as described above. In this form, however, the path and filename of the schedule are replaced by a GUID that uniquely denotes a running schedule instance. Here is an example:

```
sked://mymachine!XLANG Scheduler/{770C13A4-AB4C-4470-821F-D1FAE5235AE0}
```

Since GUIDs are unique, there is no need to name the schedule, and since the schedule is running (or serialized awaiting message arrival, as discussed under the topic of hydration, below), there is no need to locate the file describing the schedule. The ability to locate a particular instance of a schedule becomes important when you have multiple instances of the same schedule file loaded at the same time and messages coming into the schedule must arrive at a particular instance. We'll develop a sample a little later in this chapter that demonstrates exactly that point, using this form of the schedule moniker.

Schedule monikers have one additional capability: the ability to denote a particular port within a schedule. This feature is useful because it lets any COM-enabled application send messages to a particular step in a running schedule. This will also be demonstrated a little later in the chapter, when we use this capability to send messages to a particular port in a running schedule from another running schedule. In addition to letting schedules communicate, the technique is a very powerful mechanism for integrating schedules with the rest of the Windows platform. The syntax form looks like this:

```
sked://[server]![xlang_host]/<filepath_to_skx | {instance_guid}>/portname
```

In other words, we've just appended the string name of the port (displayed in the port shape on the business process diagram of a schedule), and a forward slash, to the moniker naming the schedule that includes the port. Here is an example of a moniker that locates a port in a particular instance of a running schedule. Note that the line break and whitespace are added for clarity on the page; you would need to remove them if you were launching a real schedule with this moniker:

```
sked://mymachine!XLANG Scheduler/{770C13A4-AB4C-4470-821F-D1FAE5235AE0}
    /WaitForReply
```

In this case, XLANG Scheduler on the server `mymachine` is running the instance of a schedule identified by the GUID. The GUID is obtained from the running schedule itself using a technique you will see demonstrated later. The schedule has a port named `WaitForReply` that we want to address. You should note, however, that a moniker naming a specific port can only be used to address a port bound to COM or script component implementations.

Programmatic Loading

Like the rest of BizTalk Server, schedules and monikers have COM interfaces that let you work with them programmatically. Using these interfaces, you can write applications or scripts that let you check the status of a schedule, obtain information about a schedule or port, and call COM or script component ports. The interfaces in question are:

❑　`IWFWorkflowInstance` for schedules

❑　`IWFProxy` for ports

Both interfaces are implemented in `skedcore.dll`, which is installed with BizTalk Server. That DLL is identified in Visual Basic as **XLANG Scheduler Runtime Type Library**.

Schedules: IWFWorkflowInstance

When you call `GetObject` with a schedule moniker (without a port name at the end), the COM+ runtime passes you a reference to an `IWFWorkflowInstance` interface. This is what lets you launch a new schedule instance, as we saw in Chapter 2. This interface has a number of read-only properties that provide identifying information about the launched schedule, as well as some that allow you to navigate to the ports of the schedule. There is no way, however, to enumerate the ports of the schedule. If the schedule is launched and running, you will be able to navigate to known ports. If the schedule terminates before you make a call to the port, the navigation calls will fail. Let's take a look at these properties.

Property	Meaning
CompletionStatus	Returns a long, denoting the completion status of the schedule. A value of zero denotes successful completion.
FullPortName	Given the short name of a port (for example, WaitForReply), this property returns the full name of the port in terms of the underlying transport protocol. A COM port returns a moniker of the type discussed in this chapter, while an MSMQ binding returns a queue name (for example, mymachine\$private\myqueue). BizTalk messaging bindings identify the channel to be used.
FullyQualifiedName	Returns a full COM moniker for this schedule.
InstanceId	Returns the GUID of the schedule instance.
IsCompleted	Returns a Boolean, indicating whether the schedule has finished running. If false, the schedule is still executing.
ModuleId	Returns the GUID of the XLANG module associated with the current schedule instance. In general, a module will correspond to a single schedule (see the explanatory note below this table).
ModuleName	Returns the name of the XLANG module associated with the current schedule instance.
ParentInstanceID	Returns the GUID of the schedule is the parent of this schedule instance.
Port	Returns an IWFProxy reference to a port, given the short name of the port.

Note that the FullPortName returns the name of the port in terms of the transport protocol. The Port property, by contrast, returns a COM interface reference that enables you to work with a port. The type of this interface is IWFProxy.

The schedules you have seen in Chapter 2, and will see in this chapter, are composed of a single XLANG module. However, the XLANG XML vocabulary also permits a schedule to contain multiple modules. Each module has a name, which is the name you see in the business process diagram and is returned by the ModuleName property. It is also associated with a GUID, which is contained in the ModuleId property.

The IWFWorkflowInstance interface also has a single method:

Method	Usage
WaitForCompletion()	No parameters. When called, this method blocks and does not return until the schedule represented by the IWFWorkflowInstance reference completes execution. The return value is the HRESULT returned by the schedule; in other words, success or an error value.

You might use this method if a moniker is required to launch a schedule that must complete before you can take further action. You could then use the CompletionStatus property to determine whether the schedule completed without error.

Ports: IWFProxy

You can get a reference to an IWFProxy interface instance by calling GetObject() with a port moniker, or by calling the Port property of the IWFWorkflowInstance interface with the name of a port in the schedule. The IWFProxy interface has two properties:

Property	Meaning
FullyQualifiedName	The fully qualified name of the port represented by this object
WorkflowInstance	Returns a reference to the IWFWorkflowInstance object representing the current schedule instance

If you got to the port interface through the parent schedule's Port method, the FullyQualified name gives you the fully qualified moniker that refers to the port. If you bound to the port through a moniker, you can get an interface reference for the parent schedule through the WorkflowInstance property.

There is one other way to use this interface. When the port is bound to a COM implementation, you may call any method or property that is bound to the port. In Visual Basic, for example, if the port DoStuff is bound to a method named Execute(), you could use the following lines to call the bound component's method:

```
Dim Schedule As IWFWorkflowInstance
Dim Port As IWFProxy

Set Schedule = GetObject("sked:///c:\SomeSchedule.skx")
Set Port = Schedule.Port("DoStuff")
Port.Execute()
```

This technique permits you to selectively call any method bound to a port to obtain the benefit of the component.

Instance Dispatching Example

Consider a business process that sends a message to another process, or an outside partner. Suppose the schedule for that business required a reply to the message before processing could continue. For example, we might have a chemical engineering process notifying a quality control application that a batch of material has been completed, or a manufacturing process advising a customer that their order has been completed.

Now suppose that this is a production environment. There are many identical processes going on in the business, so multiple instances of the schedule are running concurrently. It is important that the reply to any given message be returned to the instance that sent the original message.

In the last chapter, when we looked at the MSMQ Binding Wizard, we saw one possible solution. A Receive action can be configured such that each instance creates a new queue. The GUID identifying the queue is appended to the prefix you supply in the Wizard. Similarly, you can set up a dynamic port binding, with the queue name being specified in a message field. Using either technique, you can establish instance-specific messaging provided you are using MSMQ as your transport protocol and you are willing to maintain multiple queues.

We will explore this option in more detail in Chapter 10 when we take up routing.

Take another case where we are using HTTP as our receive mechanism, where the endpoint for receiving messages is a single ASP page. The script code can use `IInterchange` to submit the message to BizTalk's Messaging Services, but that doesn't solve the instance routing problem. Fortunately, we can use the moniker technique to set up a schedule that dispatches messages to the appropriate instance of the schedule we want to address.

In our example, we'll have two schedules on our side. The first is a schedule I'll call the Manufacturing Process schedule. This schedule is found in `Process.skv` and `Process.skx`. It sends a message with instance-specific information in it, then blocks at a `Receive` action awaiting a reply to the message. We will also assume that there are many instances of this schedule running at any given time.

> *The code for this example is found in the `InstanceDispatch` subdirectory of the code download for this chapter.*

The other schedule is the Dispatch schedule, found (unsurprisingly) in `Dispatch.skv` and `Dispatch.skx`. There is only one instance of this schedule running. Its only function is to route an incoming message to the appropriate instance of the Manufacturing Process schedule, and launch a replacement instance of itself. Kept simple, this schedule need not be a communications bottleneck. The Manufacturing Process schedule will presumably be taking many actions, so the mean time to complete this schedule should dominate processing, not the Dispatch schedule. The Dispatch schedule will use monikers to connect to a port in the Manufacturing Process schedule that is bound to COM, and use this connection to forward the message.

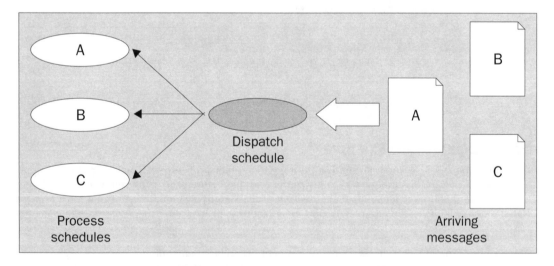

For the purposes of demonstration, we really don't want to build the partner side of the interchange. To simplify things, therefore, we'll implement the following steps:

1. The Manufacturing Process schedule will send its outbound message to an MSMQ queue monitored by the Dispatch schedule. This static queue will receive messages from all instances of the Manufacturing Process schedule.

2. The Dispatch schedule will process the outbound message as if it were the inbound reply message, and route it to the appropriate instance of the Manufacturing Process schedule.

3. The Manufacturing Process schedule will then examine the instance information to ensure it is the one it sent.

The instance GUID of the Manufacturing process schedule, and the instance GUID embedded in the message, will be presented to you in a message box so you can satisfy yourself that the Dispatch schedule is handling the instance-specific routing correctly. If the GUIDs match, you'll know the Dispatch schedule is connecting to the proper Manufacturing Process schedule instance.

Manufacturing Process Schedule

The business process diagram below depicts the operation of the Manufacturing Process schedule:

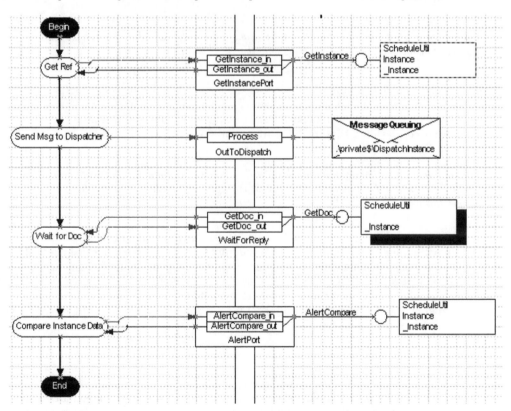

Let's now review this schedule.

1. The first action shape to place is connected to a COM component that will tell us the moniker of the running schedule. We will describe this component once we have looked at the schedule.

This moniker is passed along, through the data flow, to an action that sends a message via MSMQ to the queue we use to communicate with the Dispatch schedule. Now we have to send a message off to the Dispatch schedule's queue. Our message can be very simple since it is really only a holder for the schedule's moniker. Here is a sample message (with whitespace added for clarity):

```
<Process Session=
        "sked://mymachine!XLANG Scheduler/{770C13A4-AB4C-4470-821F-
                D1FAE5235AE0}/GetInstancePort" />
```

2. Go ahead and use BizTalk Editor to create a message specification for this, as we will use it later. Create an XML-based specification with a root-level record named `Process`. Add a required field named `Session` that is an attribute typed as a string.

The shell for this message is always the same, so we can store it in a string constant (named `MsgBlank`:

```
<Process Session="" />
```

You may recall from Chapter 2 that the Data view of a schedule has a shape for constant values that may be added for use in the schedule's data flow.

3. The second action in the schedule, `Send Msg to Dispatcher`, sends the message named `Process` to a private queue. I've created a single private, transactional queue `DispatchInstance` for this purpose. The MSMQ binding for this action's port is similar to what you saw in Chapter 2. Be sure to add `Session` as one of the **Message** fields in the XML Communication Wizard.

Remember that we are taking a shortcut here for the purpose of keeping the demonstration simple. The real-world equivalent would send the message to our partner, or an application, through this port.

4. The next action, `Wait for Doc`, is tricky. It uses a COM messaging implementation, but you will notice from the diagram that the implementation shape has a shadow. This indicates that **No instantiation** was selected in the **Static or Dynamic Communication** property page of the COM Binding wizard. For the first two cases (**Static** and **Dynamic**), a component instance is created. In the **No instantiation** case, however, no component is created and no method is ever called. It is used solely to create a port that someone can connect to using monikers.

This is a little strange at first glance, as we are used to COM being something we call. Usually, anything you get back is the result of action taken in the course of a method invocation. This kind of port binding uses COM for message reception; something else will call the port and pass us a message. The schedule does not call a component. Instead, an outside entity may call into the schedule, using the methods bound to the port. It is therefore tailor-made for communicating with our Dispatch schedule from the outside world.

5. When you connect `Wait for Doc` to the port, remember that you do not want to make a method call, so check the **Wait for a synchronous method call** option.

6. Finally, we have to take some instance-specific action. In our case, that action will be to call a COM component, passing it the schedule's instance GUID as well as the message received at the preceding step.

The component will extract the GUID embedded within the message and put both GUIDs into a message box so that you can verify that the schedules are cooperating properly.

The data flow is the key to the proper operation of the Manufacturing Process schedule. The instance-specific moniker for the schedule comes from the Port References table, which lists the ports in the schedule.

7. You need to pass the port reference moniker into the COM method via a string parameter of the `GetInstance` call. The method (which we'll discuss below), hands the schedule instance moniker back out as the return value of the call.

This is counterintuitive. The problem is that the easiest way to get the instance information from a schedule is through a port. Consequently, we define a port which will be bound to a COM component. The method bound to the port takes the instance information from the port as a parameter. This can be passed in by establishing a link on the Data view, as we shall see shortly. Since we want the port reference in its entirety, we simply pass the in parameter back as the result of the method call. The round-trip exists to allow us to create a port in Orchestration Designer and read its port reference.

8. If you look at the Data flow diagram below, you can see that you need to connect the constant `MsgBlank` to the `Document` property of this message, while the value of the `Session` field comes from the value returned by the `GetInstance` call:

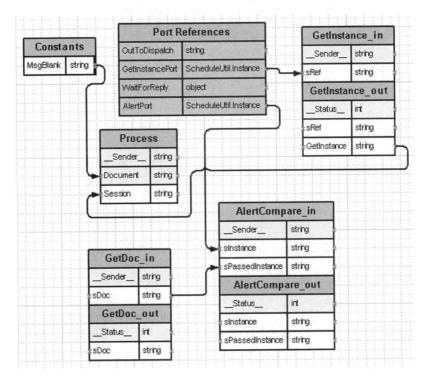

The next action shape, `Wait for Doc`, is the `Receive` action that waits on the placeholder COM port `GetDoc`. The sole parameter of that method is `sDoc`.

9. It is this parameter that XLANG Scheduler will stuff with the value passed to the port by the Dispatch schedule, therefore you need to connect them on the **Data** flow diagram. Consequently, it is the start of the data we need for the rest of the schedule.

The value of `sDoc` is one of the values we want to display in a message box   the passed-in schedule instance moniker. We also want to show the user the value of the moniker for the currently-running schedule so we can ensure they match. The process of showing these values to the user is implemented in a COM method called `AlertCompare()`. This method takes two parameters:

❑ `sInstance`: this is the current schedule's moniker, and is passed in as a reference to the current port. This is exactly the same method we used in `GetInstance`.

❑ `sPassedInstance`: this is the moniker passed in by the Dispatch schedule. The value of `sPassedInstance` comes from `GetDoc`'s `sDoc` parameter, as described above.

The two monikers will differ in the name of the port, but they will have the same GUID if they came from the same instance of the schedule. When the user clicks **OK** on the message box, the `Compare Instance Data` action completes, and the schedule terminates. If the application for another business process wishes to run a new instance of this schedule, it will need to launch a new instance using a moniker.

10. In order to do all this processing, you need to connect `sDoc` to `sPassedInstance`, and the `AlertPort` reference to `sInstance`.

Now it is time to design the Dispatch schedule which will handle the `Process` message sent by our Manufacturing schedule. You can draw your own, based on the instructions in the next section, then compare it with the reference copy, `Dispatch.skv`, in the code download.

Dispatch Schedule

The Dispatch schedule is a bit shorter, but what it does is just as complex as what we saw above. The schedule is shown below:

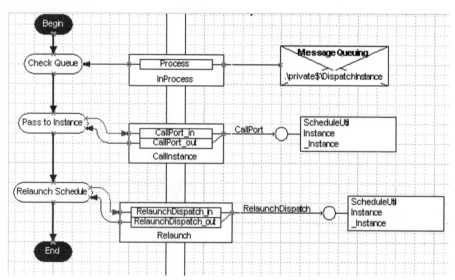

Let's consider each step.

1. The first step is to wait for a `Process` message to arrive in
`.\private$\DispatchInstance`.

Once the schedule has a `Process` message, all it has to do is send that message right back to the sending schedule's `GetDoc()` COM port. To do that, it needs to know the moniker for the port.

2. The `Pass to Instance` action is placed to re-route the `Process` message back to the original schedule. The port used to call the `GetDoc` port is implemented, as you might expect, as a COM port bound to the `CallPort` method of the utility component.

3. When the `Relaunch Schedule` action is taken, the schedule makes a call to the `RelaunchDispatch` method of the utility component. Set that up as shown in the diagram.

As we saw with the Manufacturing Process schedule, the tricky bit is handled in the data flow for the schedule. This is shown below:

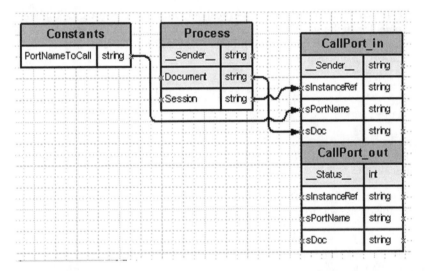

We know implicitly that we want to call a port named `WaitForReply`. This is taken directly from the Manufacturing Process schedule's business process diagram, and stored in the Dispatch schedule as the `PortNameToCall` constant string. The value of that string is passed to the `sPortName` parameter of the `CallPort()` method. The document we want to pass in the `sDoc` parameter is contained in the `Document` property of the `Process` message. This is the text of the message that has just arrived.

We have the port name we wish to call, but the final piece we need is the schedule moniker, which was contained in the `Session` field of the `Process` message. This is why we needed to create a message specification for the `Process` message. When you bind the `CallInstance` port to the `CallPort` method, you can designate a message specification. When you do so, the `Session` field becomes available to you on the property table of the `Process` message, in the **Data** tab for the schedule.

Now the component will receive all the information it needs to connect to the proper schedule instance's COM receive port.

That method uses a known moniker to launch a new instance of the Dispatch schedule, thereby ensuring the system always has that schedule running to await the arrival of a new Process message from the Manufacturing Process schedule, Process.skv, which we created earlier.

Schedule Instance Utility Component

So far, we've made a bunch of COM calls, but their implementation has been left up in the air. All the COM calls we've seen in the two schedules are bundled together in the same component. This component is implemented as a Visual Basic ActiveX DLL. The project is found in ScheduleUtil.vbp, while the code is found in the class module Instance.cls (both of which can be downloaded from the Wrox web site). When you do the port bindings, you are looking for a component with the progID ScheduleUtil.Instance.

The first method we called from the Manufacturing Process schedule was GetInstance(). It took a moniker as a parameter and handed back a moniker, so the body of the method is very simple:

```
Public Function GetInstance(sRef As String) As String
  GetInstance = TrimRef(sRef)
End Function
```

Ideally, we'd just hand back the moniker we received, but it has a port name at the end of it. Since we really want to deal with the schedule's instance moniker throughout this sample, we should trim that name (including the last slash character) off before we hand it back. This is done in GetInstance() using the TrimRef() function:

```
Private Function TrimRef(sRef As String) As String
  TrimRef = Left(sRef, InStrRev(sRef, "/") - 1)
End Function
```

The material we want to trim away is the last part of the string, from the last slash character on. Specifying the character before the location of the last slash gives us the moniker for the instance of the schedule we seek.

The action is then passed to the Dispatch schedule. The first thing it did after retrieving a new Process message from the queue was to call the CallPort() method of our component:

```
Public Sub CallPort(sInstanceRef As String, sPortName As String, _
          sDoc As String)
  Dim port As Variant
  Dim sMoniker As String

  sMoniker = sInstanceRef & "/" & sPortName
  Set port = GetObject(sMoniker)
  port.GetDoc (sDoc)
  Set port = Nothing
End Sub
```

The sInstanceRef parameter must be a schedule moniker without any port name at the end. We build up the moniker we need by taking that passed-in moniker and appending a slash and the name of the port we wish to call, which is passed in through the sPortName parameter. From there, the process is the same as when you wish to launch a new instance of the schedule. The call to GetObject() passes the moniker over to XLANG Scheduler. Since it sees an instance GUID and a port name, it does not launch a new instance of the schedule. Instead, it locates the running schedule and connects us to the port we desire.

The reference XLANG Scheduler gives us is stored in the `port` variable. This is a variant containing an `IDispatch` reference. Since this is a reference to the component port, we can call the `GetDoc()` method directly. Remember, this is a port for which there is no component instantiation, meaning that the component is not called. Instead, the value in `sDoc` is passed to the data flow of the schedule to which we just connected. The method then sets `port` to `Nothing` to ensure COM cleans up references for us.

> *To allow the COM Binding wizard to work properly, we need to have a `GetDoc()` method implemented on the component. This method is never called and is just an empty shell.*

The Dispatch schedule then relaunches itself through the `RelaunchDispatch` method of the component. This is similar to the script component implementation you saw in Chapter 2:

```
Public Sub RelaunchDispatch()
  Dim objSked As IWFWorkflowInstance

  Set objSked = GetObject("sked:///c:\my_local_path\Dispatch.skx")
End Sub
```

Since Visual Basic is a strongly typed language, we can type the variable for the reference returned from the `GetObject()` call as `IWFWorkflowInstance`.

> *Be sure to update the line of code including `GetObject()` to reflect the drive and local folder in which you store the Dispatch schedule file on your local system. Then rebuild the DLL to make this work correctly on your installation. Obviously, in production code you would want to build in some mechanism to allow you to configure the path through a database.*

When the Manufacturing Process schedule got hold of the document through the call to the `GetDoc()` method port, it called the `AlertCompare()` method on our component, to present the information regarding schedule instances to the user:

```
Public Sub AlertCompare(sInstance As String, sPassedInstance As String)
  Dim sRef As String

  sRef = GetSession(sPassedInstance)
  MsgBox "This instance: " & TrimRef(sInstance) & vbCrLf & "Origin: " & sRef
End Sub
```

The `sPassedInstance` parameter is not actually a moniker. If you recall the data flow from the schedule, you'll recall that we connected that parameter to the text of the document passed to `GetDoc()`. We need to strip out the value of the `Session` attribute, and trim off the port name, before we show it to the user. The `GetSession()` function uses the MSXML parser to do this:

```
Private Function GetSession(sDoc As String) As String
  Dim doc As New DOMDocument

  doc.async = False
  doc.loadXML (sDoc)

  If doc.parseError.reason <> "" Then
   GetSessions = "{1}/doc"
  Else
   GetSession = _
     doc.documentElement.selectSingleNode("/Process/@Session").nodeValue
  End If
End Function
```

By setting the `async` property to `False`, we ensure the parser fully loads and parses the document before returning to this function. If the document fails to load in the `loadXML()` method, the string held in the `reason` property of the `parseError` object in the parser will contain some text. In that case, we pass back a hard-coded string with an obviously bad moniker.

If, however, the document is well-formed XML, we use the `selectSingleNode()` method to retrieve the `Session` attribute from the `Process` element. That element will be the `document` element of the document, so we start with the `documentElement` property of the parser and pass it an XPath expression that locates the attribute we want. The string value containing the moniker we want is contained in the `nodeValue` property of the node passed back from the `selectSingleNode` method.

> *XPath is, among other things, a sort of query language for XML. The expression in the call above might be translated into English as "Start at the root of the document, then find the `Process` element, then find the `Session` attribute attached to that element". There is a tutorial on XPath in Appendix B. The W3C XPath Recommendation may be found at www.w3.org/TR/xpath.html.*

With all these pieces in place, you are ready to test the interaction of the two schedules. Satisfy yourself that we really are doing instance-specific binding by launching the schedules in different order. Launch multiple copies of either schedule and watch what happens. In every case, the GUIDs shown to you in the message box will match, indicating that the Dispatch process correctly routed the `Process` message back to the instance of the Manufacturing Process schedule that sent the message in the first place.

Now that we have a thorough understanding of how schedules can be loaded, we can tackle the issue of hydration.

Hydration of Schedules

It would not be unusual to have hundreds of concurrently executing orchestration schedules in a production setting. However, we've noted elsewhere that the time span of distributed applications (like those orchestration integrates) is likely to be considerably longer than that of local applications. The asynchronous nature of most schedules simply compounds this problem. All those HTTP transmissions spanning seconds, and waiting for messages to arrive from other applications and partners, makes for a considerable amount of idle time per schedule. This can potentially lead to a scalability problem, with any system resources allocated by the schedule (memory, components, and so on) being consumed by idle schedules.

Obviously, a product that aims to automate business processes in a high-volume setting needs an answer to this problem. As such, XLANG Scheduler uses a process called **hydration**. Schedules which are not immediately needed in memory write their current state to storage, then are removed from memory in a process called **dehydration**. XLANG Scheduler keeps track of these schedules and retrieves them as needed. The process of restoring a schedule to its in-memory, running state is called **rehydration**. The goal is to have resident in memory only those schedules that are actively engaged in processing.

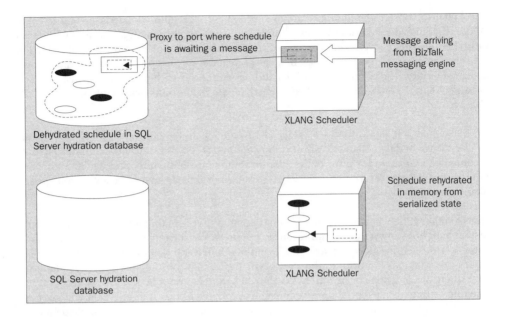

Proxy to port where schedule is awaiting a message

Message arriving from BizTalk messaging engine

XLANG Scheduler

Dehydrated schedule in SQL Server hydration database

Schedule rehydrated in memory from serialized state

SQL Server hydration database

XLANG Scheduler

How It Works

That sounds simple enough, but implementing it is another matter. A bit of reflection on the problem exposes the following thorny issues:

❑ What does XLANG Scheduler do about the state of a schedule?

❑ What can be done about COM components in schedules?

❑ How can schedules be prioritized for dehydration?

Let's consider these one at a time.

Persisting Schedule State

Even the simplest schedule has state. If nothing else, the structure of the schedule and the orchestration shape that is currently executing is state information. For example, a schedule is dehydrated while it is blocked awaiting a message at port X. When the message arrives and the schedule is rehydrated, XLANG Scheduler had better know that port X is on one thread following a fork, another thread exists that is blocked at port Y, and two messages have been received at prior actions in the schedule. The state of the schedule after rehydration must be equivalent to the state prior to dehydration if the schedule is to operate correctly.

Obviously, the persistent state of the schedule must be written to disk. One option is to write the state to an ordinary disk file, perhaps in the form of an XML document. That is the technique used by Orchestration Designer when it is exporting a schedule. Unfortunately, BizTalk Server may be persisting hundreds of schedules, each with more state than its XLANG document. The state contained in the XLANG document is the minimum amount of information needed: every message sent or received during the life of the schedule instance, and every decision made, affects the state of the schedule in some way. Schedules, moreover, are a complex web of dependencies: schedules have actions and ports, ports have implementations and messages, and messages have fields.

It is far better to consign the durable state of a schedule to a relational database. This is exactly what XLANG Scheduler does. A running schedule instance is written to a SQL Server database set up when you installed BizTalk Server. This is no mere serialization of an object into a BLOB field. The current database schema (as of December 2000 in a release candidate version) has 30 tables, and few of them make use of binary fields. The relationships and dependencies within a schedule instance are visible to SQL Server. This, in turn, allows XLANG Scheduler to make sophisticated choices about retrieval and persistence.

When a schedule is idle, awaiting a message, XLANG Scheduler calls on a COM+ application that helps it write a schedule's state to disk. It is not required to do this; it follows an internal and undocumented algorithm for prioritizing what to remove from memory and when. Serializing a schedule to a database and retrieving it imposes substantial performance costs, so you wouldn't want to invoke it unnecessarily.

There is another time when a schedule is persisted, and that is before a transaction boundary. This is consistent with how any transactional resource operates. We introduced the concept of transactions in Chapter 1. Transactions exist so that in the event of a failed transaction we can roll back the state of a system to the state existing prior to the start of the transaction. While, as we shall see later in this chapter, there are activities from which XLANG Scheduler cannot automatically recover, it is worthwhile getting a snapshot of the system state before each transaction. When you get to the section on transactions, you will find several demonstration schedules. If you watch them execute in a tool such as the XLANG Event Monitor, you will see the SchedulePersist event fired as you cross transaction boundaries. This does not mean the entire schedule is dehydrated, however, merely that the persistence application was called to take a snapshot. This snapshot is necessary to reverse the transaction in the event of failure. This is an explicit trade-off between integrity and performance.

Persistence and COM Components

Each port has an implementation, and some of these may involve messaging with COM components. Although it is a good idea to avoid persistent state in a COM component designed for use in a high-volume processing environment, so that component instances may be freely reused without troubling over state, XLANG Scheduler must make allowances for components that do hold state from one message to another. For this, you will need to give XLANG Scheduler a hint.

When you are specifying a COM port implementation, the COM Component Binding Wizard presents the **Advanced Properties** page. On that page is a group marked **State management support**; this group contains a drop-down listbox. The listbox contains three values from which to select to describe the state-management needs of your component:

❑ **Holds no state** – XLANG Scheduler may safely flush the component from memory during dehydration and replace it with a fresh component instance upon rehydration because the component does not maintain persistent state between calls

❑ **Holds state, but doesn't support persistence** – the component does hold state between calls, but does not support the IPersist interface and therefore cannot serialize itself to disk

❑ **Holds state, and does support persistence** – the component holds state between calls and supports the IPersist interface

The last two cases are the important ones when talking about hydration. If components don't keep state, it really doesn't matter what happens to them. Whether XLANG Scheduler keeps them around or destroys them doesn't matter to the schedule's execution, though it will matter to overall performance.

If a component holds state it is up to XLANG Scheduler to somehow maintain that state. A component must support `IPersist` to participate in database serialization. `IPersist` is the interface that lets you assign an object to another object for transport. For example, you can set the `Body` property of an MSMQ message equal to an instance of the MSXML parser. Of course, what is really happening is that MSMQ asks the parser to serialize itself onto a stream provided by the message object. It doesn't matter to you, though, as COM and the component managing the serialization look after the interface negotiations for you.

It is this process that occurs during dehydration. XLANG Scheduler doesn't need to understand the internal persistence scheme of the component. So long as it understands its own information and the component was eligible to be used as a port implementation in the first place, the Scheduler is happy just keeping an opaque stream of data in the database.

When dehydration occurs, XLANG Scheduler offers a stream to a component that supports `IPersist` and directs the component to serialize its state onto the stream. The stream is actually kept in the hydration database. When it is time to rehydrate the schedule, XLANG Scheduler creates a new instance of the component, then hands it a stream with the serialized data on it. The new component instance uses this data to configure itself so that its state matches the state of the component instance that performed the original serialization.

The second of the three options in the list is where the problem lies. If you use a component that holds state but does not support `IPersist`, XLANG Scheduler cannot persist the component's state. It is forced to keep the component instance around, idle, until it is needed by the rehydrated schedule. The resources consumed depend mostly on the amount of state information the component must keep. Still, it is one more thing that must remain in memory in addition to a stub for the schedule. If the component holds scarce system resources such as database connections or transaction locks, scalability will be diminished dramatically.

There is one further concern with components that hold state but cannot be persisted. If a server fails while running a schedule, the schedule will be automatically restored when the server is restarted. This includes rehydrating any state information held in the hydration database. If the schedule is keeping a component that holds state alive at the time the server dies and the component never serialized any information (which is the case if the component does not support `IPersist`), then the full and correct state of the schedule cannot be restored. Components that hold state but cannot participate in hydration and persistence, then, are a reliability problem and should be avoided if at all possible. New components designed for use with BizTalk should either be stateless or support persistence.

Message Latency and Hydration

The hydration algorithm is not documented in BizTalk Server 2000 as of this writing (December 2000). This is probably a good thing. Programmers are always tempted to "wargame" optimization algorithms, trying to outmaneuver the algorithm, and the result is not always good for overall system performance. If one schedule type could, through misuse of resources, conspire to keep itself in memory while idle, it would certainly exhibit excellent performance, but it might starve more deserving schedules of resources. We can also expect the hydration algorithm to be optimized in future versions. BizTalk Server is in its first version, so you would not expect the XLANG team to have determined the final word in hydration efficiency. If you try to beat the Scheduler at its own game, the rules may change in some future version.

The one thing that you can do that is both legitimate, and helpful to performance, is to provide an accurate estimate of the amount of time you expect a schedule to wait at a particular Receive action. The XML Communication Wizard asks for this information on the very first property page. Right under the Receive radio button is a note followed by an edit field. Enter the number of seconds you expect the schedule to have to wait for a message to arrive. If you enter 0, XLANG Scheduler will not dehydrate the schedule when it is blocked at that port.

> *There is a branch of mathematics called **queuing theory** that is used throughout computing (and other fields) to describe the behavior of queued systems. The message latency described above is known there as mean service time. It is one of the key factors that determine how long an item stays in a queue and what sort of queue capacity is required to ensure no data is lost. The better your estimate of the mean message latency for a particular port, then, the more effective the hydration process will be and the higher your system throughput for the BizTalk Server group will be.*

Configuring the Database for Long Transactions

In some early pre-releases of BizTalk Server 2000, the installation procedure did not automatically configure the SQL Server database for schedule hydration. The current release candidate (December 2000) does perform this task. However, there is a slight possibility that you might delete the hydration database, and a somewhat greater chance that you might delete the ODBC DSN or configure it incorrectly. Should that happen, refer to the following steps to configure the database for this hydration.

You will need to use the SQL Server Enterprise Manager application to create a new database. The name of this database does not matter but the location of the physical database files and the configuration of the database will impact on the performance of the XLANG Scheduler in high-volume installations. This information is not, however, specific to hydration, but rather is a function of database activity.

> *Some guidelines on optimizing the SQL Server databases for the overall performance of the BizTalk Server Group are given in Chapter 9. The details of configuring SQL Server databases are given in Professional SQL Server 2000 Programming (2000, Wrox Press, ISBN 1-861004-48-6).*

You must also create an ODBC DSN before XLANG Scheduler can get to the database to persist a schedule's state information. To do this, go into the Component Services application (found in the Start | Programs | Administrative Tools menu on Microsoft Windows 2000) and select the COM+ application that is serving as the host for the Scheduler component. In the default case, this will be XLANG Scheduler. Invoke the Properties dialog and click on the XLANG tab.

> *The XLANG tab is a new addition to the Properties dialog of COM+ applications. It is used to designate an application as a host for XLANG schedule instances, configure the persistence database for schedules, and control running schedules. The tab has two buttons for the latter function. One is used to perform a controlled shutdown of all running schedules, and is used to bring down a server for maintenance or software upgrades. The other button reverses the process, restarting schedules that were dehydrated to the persistence database.*

Click on the Create DSN... button on that page: the ODBC DSN Wizard appears. The default choice on the XLANG tab is to create a File DSN. The Wizard also gives you the option of System or User DSNs. File DSNs do not allow connection pooling and should be avoided in high-volume settings. On the other hand, file DSNs are easily shared across machines. The Wizard guides you through the process of specifying the database to use (the one you created in the preceding step), and most of the defaults are acceptable.

One configuration detail that is important is the name of the DSN. This name must match the name of the COM+ application hosting the scheduler component. For the default installation, then, you would name the DSN XLANG Scheduler. If you wish to change your choices later, you may click the button labeled Configure DSN... and locate the DSN you wish to configure from the File, User, and System property pages.

> *You cannot switch the type of a DSN. You must delete the existing DSN and create a new one. If you wish to do this for your hydration database, to modify the performance of the BizTalk Server installation, make sure you shut down all running schedules before proceeding. You can do this with the Controlled shutdown group on the XLANG tab, then restart them later from the Restart dehydrated XLANG applications group. You may also shutdown and restart schedules from the Event Monitor application XLANGMon.exe.*

After you configure the DSN, the database requires one more step before it can be used. Although you have created a database, there are no tables. The XLANG property page has a button named Initialize Tables... If you click this, you will receive a warning regarding the status of running schedules. If you proceed, all running schedules are shut down. The tables required by the hydration database schema are then created. If you click this button after you have run some schedules, any existing data will be destroyed. If you have running schedules that were dehydrated at the time of this action, their state will be destroyed and the schedules cannot be restarted where they left off. You should always use the XLANG Event Monitor to check for running schedules before taking this action. Use this button only for new installations or after all running schedules have run to completion.

Saving schedules to the database through dehydration is a scalability strategy, as we have seen. There is an additional use: taking snapshots of the schedule before a transaction. We touched on transactions briefly in Chapters 1 and 2, saying that we needed the robust semantics to which we have become accustomed in the relational database world for schedules and their distributed resources. We will now look into the topic of transactions in greater detail.

Transactions and Error Recovery

Transactions are an important part of programming. Any application that must keep two or more entities synchronized – the classic example is a pair of bank accounts undergoing a transfer of funds – needs transactions. Relational databases have long supported transactions. The advent of COM and the Distributed Transaction Coordinator (DTC) in Microsoft Windows brought transactions to resources other than databases. Activities involving message queues, databases, and any COM component supporting the proper interfaces can be manipulated under the formal and reversible behavior of transactions.

BizTalk Orchestration, as we saw in Chapter 2, supports short-lived, DTC-based transactions, and it also understands the transactional behavior built into COM+. Schedules, by their nature, introduce the new idea of long-running transactions. These can span periods longer than it is practical to hold resources under transactional control   for example, while a business partner manufactures goods in response to your purchase order message. The common Internet communications BizTalk messaging supports, moreover, are not transactional. In order to support robust, mission-critical business processes with orchestration, Orchestration Designer must offer mechanisms for long-lived transactions that will be honored by XLANG Scheduler.

This section will teach you about orchestration transactions and by the end of it we will have dealt with:

- Enlisting a schedule in an existing COM+ transaction
- The traditional transactional types (which you may be familiar with already)
- Recovering from a failed transaction
- Long-running transactions
- Nested transactions
- Timed transactions

Nested transactions present an interesting dilemma, particularly when the outer transaction is long-lived in nature. What can you do about an inner transaction that has already successfully committed? There is a mechanism to handle that, and we'll discuss it, too.

Enlisting in COM+ Transactions

We are accustomed to viewing orchestration schedules as the top level of execution. We assume that they are responsible for defining all the transactions we will need within our distributed systems. Since schedules are launched by COM monikers and the COM+ run-time system provides transactional semantics, an orchestration schedule may execute wholly within the bounds of a COM+ transaction started outside the schedule. If you wish the schedule to participate in COM+ transactions, you must configure the entire schedule by setting the Transaction model property for the Begin shape. Doing so, however, incurs limitations we will consider in a moment.

On the Begin shape's Properties dialog, select the Treat the schedule as a COM+ component option from the Transaction model property. This enables the Transaction activation property, which specifies how the schedule will participate in COM+ transactions. You have four options from which to choose:

- Not supported – the default, this setting indicates the schedule will not participate in COM+ transactions
- Supported – the XLANG schedule will participate in a COM+ transaction if one exists
- Required – the XLANG schedule requires a COM+ transaction and will not execute if one does not exist
- Requires New – The schedule requires a new COM+ transaction within which to execute

You do not need to create a new transaction in your COM+ application before calling a schedule with the Requires New setting for its Transaction activation property. In fact, doing so is counterproductive. The XLANG Scheduler automatically creates a new COM+ transaction through the DTC, when it launches a transaction possessing this value for the activation property. If you create one just for executing this schedule, it will be viewed as an existing transaction. XLANG Scheduler will still create a new transaction distinct from the one you created.

Participating in COM+ transactions places some strict limitations on what you can do within a schedule. To begin with, you may not use transactions within the bounds of the schedule. If you use the Fork shape to make use of multi-threading, you must place all calls to COM+ components on one branch of execution. This applies only to COM+ components; older COM-style components do not have this limitation. Calls to transactional resources (for example transacted MSMQ queues) must also be restricted to one thread, and that thread must not be the one with the COM+ components.

Microsoft also suggests that you limit the use of the Fork shape whenever you enlist a schedule in a COM+ transaction. There are some undocumented limitations on COM+ component calls such that all calls to COM+ (not, explicitly, COM components) should be restricted to a single branch of the fork. Similarly, transactional changes should be restricted to a single flow of the fork. While the reason for this is not given, we may presume performance will degrade if these restrictions are not observed.

Short-Lived Transactions

Most of the time, you will not be calling a schedule from a COM+ transaction. Provided you have configured the schedule to support transactions, the most familiar form of transaction will be available to you. This is the short-lived, DTC-based transaction. If you are familiar with database transactions or have worked with the DTC before, you will have a fair idea of what is going on. A short-lived transaction in a schedule works through the DTC to implement its behavior and does not introduce any new features of its own with regard to rolling back transactions. Any DTC transactional resource within the transaction will be rolled back when such a transaction fails.

Any action involving a non-transactional resource (BizTalk messaging via HTTP for instance) will remain in the state it was in at the time the failure occurred. The mechanism which short-lived transactions provide for dealing with this problem gives you the option of creating a new schedule module within the overall schedule that may be invoked whenever the transaction fails. You can then design a sequence of actions to take to correct the state. This might involve sending a message to your partner, indicating that an error occurred in the business process. Provided you include sufficient information to identify the original message sent under the failed transaction, your partner can take appropriate corrective action, such as canceling an order.

Short-lived transactions are especially valuable when you are performing application integration within your own organization. You have tighter control under those circumstances, often with full access to all the resources involved. Message transmission times are generally shorter, too. Under these conditions, short-lived transactions with full recourse to the DTC provide your schedules with the greatest degree of protection. All the formal semantics of transactions, including isolation level, are available for restoring the state of transactional components.

Failure of Short-Lived Transactions

There are three ways a short-lived, DTC-style transaction can fail. First, you can include an `Abort` shape in some branch of your code. When encountered, the schedule will force a failure and move control to any `On Failure Tx` page. You might want to do this if you send a message to a partner and then wait to receive a message in reply. If the reply indicates a catastrophic error condition on the partner's side – a complete failure to process the request – it might be simpler for you to simply invoke the transaction abort module instead of trying to accommodate it in the main module of your schedule.

Paired messages implementing request-response semantics require session management. You can run multiple concurrent schedules on either side of the interchange, so you must ensure the reply is sent to the same instance of the schedule that sent the request. This issue is taken up later in this chapter.

If you've implemented COM messaging, you've seen the second way a short-lived transaction can fail. The Advanced Port Properties page of the COM Component Binding Wizard has an Error handling section. If you check the box inside this section, the transaction will fail if the method call you are implementing returns a failure message. In COM terms, that means an `HRESULT` with a value other than `S_OK`. In Visual Basic, this means calling `Err.Raise` with some non-zero value.

The final way a short-lived transaction can fail is through a failed commit on a transactional resource within the transaction. For example, if one of the actions in the transaction involves sending a message to a transactional queue via an MSMQ messaging implementation, any failure of the message delivery will abort the transaction on the schedule. You can try this yourself. Within a short-lived transaction, create a message queuing implementation, then go to the Computer Management application and deny write access on the queue to all users. No one, including XLANG Scheduler, will be able to send a message to this queue. Now run the schedule, and you will see the transaction fail.

Transaction Failure Recovery

Schedules react to a failed transaction in two ways. First, any actions that are transactional (for example, message queuing implementations on transacted queues that we discussed a moment ago) are rolled back by the DTC. This is automatic, provided you thought ahead, providing transactional components and configuring them to participate in transactions. Remember, the Advanced Port Properties page of the COM and Script Component Binding Wizards allow you to configure such ports so that they ignore transactions.

Next, we must deal with non-transactional resources. Not every action involves transactional resources, yet orchestration must give us a way to deal with failure in a controlled way, even when we are dealing with non-transactional resources. To cope with this, orchestration gives us the On Fail Transaction page. This is a business process diagram, complete with messaging ports and all the other shapes available on the main business process diagram, which is executed when the transaction fails. The idea is to give you a place to take all the actions required to compensate for the failed transaction. You must provide the logic yourself, just as you do in the main diagram, and you must determine the current state of the system mid-way through the failed transaction. Nevertheless, you have an opportunity to address all the distributed resources of the system and restore its state following the failure of a transaction.

Short Transaction Example

Let's try this out with a demonstration schedule. We'll pass a copy of the Site Service Description message encountered in previous chapters into the schedule as an MSMQ message, then send it back out to another queue. The action shape that sends the message out will be enclosed in a transaction. We'll force the transaction to fail by calling a method on a COM component. Start by creating two new private transactional message queues named TxDemo and TxDemoOutput.

Loading the Queue

We need a way to get a document into the queue. You could modify the sample client from the last chapter, but configuring a Site Service Document is fairly tedious, even for the partial implementation provided. However, for our demonstration we don't care about the contents of the message, so we can get by with a script that opens a file and sends the content to a known queue. This is typical MSMQ object-model coding, minus the sort of error handling we need in a production application. This is just a bit of test harness code to drive the experiment. Here is the source of the script, stuff.js:

```
var mqInfo, mqQueue, mqMessage, ofsFSO, mqTxDisp, mqTx;

mqInfo = new ActiveXObject("MSMQ.MSMQQueueInfo");
ofsFSO = new ActiveXObject("Scripting.FileSystemObject");
mqTxDisp = new ActiveXObject("MSMQ.MSMQTransactionDispenser");
if (mqInfo != null)
{
    mqInfo.FormatName = "DIRECT=OS:.\\private$\\TxDemo";
    mqQueue = mqInfo.Open(2, 0);
    mqQueue.Refresh;
```

```
    if (mqQueue != null && mqQueue.IsOpen == true)
    {
       mqMessage = new ActiveXObject("MSMQ.MSMQMessage");
       if (mqMessage != null)
       {
          mqMessage.Body =
                    ofsFSO.OpenTextFile("c:\\mypath\\siteservicesample.xml",
                                        1).ReadAll();
          mqMessage.Label = "SiteServiceDescription";
          mqTx = mqTxDisp.BeginTransaction();
          mqMessage.Send(mqQueue, mqTx);
          mqTx.Commit();
          mqMessage = null;
          ofsFSO = null;
       }
       mqQueue = null;
    }
    // add error handling here for failure to open a queue
       mqInfo = null;
}
```

Note: Be sure to replace `mypath` in the call to `OpenTextFile` with the path to the sample file on your machine.

Before this script will work, you need to create the private queue `TxDemo` in the same manner as the previous example.

This is typical MSMQ object-model coding and is similar to what you saw in the Finish button handler code from the client application in the last chapter. As always, you can download sample code from www.wrox.com.

Business Process Diagram

Construct the business process diagram you see below, following the guidelines overleaf:

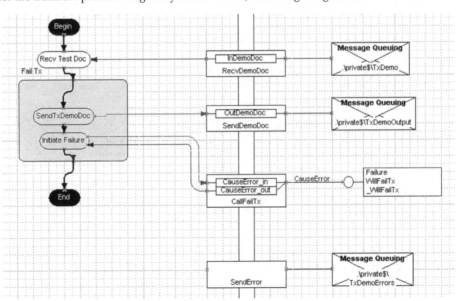

1. The Recv Test Doc action is connected to an incoming MSMQ port named RecvDemoDoc, that connects to the static queue, TxDemo, that you just created. The queue should be private and require transactions.

2. Create the SendTxDemoDoc and Initiate Failure action shapes, then drop a transaction shape on them.

3. Name the transaction Fail Tx. Ensure the transaction type is Short-lived, DTC-style and accept the defaults. The transaction shape will show up on the business process diagram as a black-bordered shape with a filled gray interior through which the included shapes are visible.

Now you need to wire the shapes into the flow through the schedule:

4. Connect the Recv Test Doc action to the top connection point on the transaction shape, then connect that same connection point to the first action within the transaction.

5. Connect SendTxDemoDoc to Initiate Failure, then connect the latter action to the bottom connection point of the transaction.

6. Finally, add an End shape and connect the transaction to it.

7. Now implement an MSMQ port named SendDemoDoc that sends a message to the TxDemoOutput queue. The port must send XML messages to the queue of type SiteServiceDescription. You should point to the message specification we created in Chapter 3.

If you eliminated the Initiate Failure shape and ran the schedule at this point, you would see the incoming message leave TxDemo and arrive at TxDemoOutput. Both queues are transactional, but nothing has prevented Fail Tx from committing.

Causing Failure

We need to do something unusual. We need to think how to deliberately cause a transaction to fail. Normally, programmers spend their time avoiding this outcome, and put time into recovering from failures, but they rarely dream up ways to cause failure. Since we saw that a COM error causes short-lived transactions to fail, the simplest thing for us to do is create a COM component whose sole method does nothing more than raise an error.

To that end, I've created Failure.vbp, a Visual Basic ActiveX DLL project with one class module, WillFailTx.cls (again, these can be downloaded from the Wrox web site). This gives us a COM component with the progid Failure.WillFailTx, which should be sufficient warning to anyone who encounters it in the registry unawares. The class module contains one method implementation:

```
Public Sub CauseError()
    Err.Raise &H8004D002   'XACT_E_COMMITFAILED
End Sub
```

Any failure code would do, but I'm raising the error code you get from the ITransaction interface when a transaction-commit operation fails for an unknown reason. Build the DLL, and we'll proceed to hook it into our schedule.

1. Create a COM messaging implementation that calls our component's `CauseError` method through a port named `CallFailTx`. Make sure the checkbox **Abort the Transaction if the method calls return a failure message** is checked.

2. Turn to the **Data** view and connect the `Document` field of `InDemoDoc` to the `Document` field of `OutDemoDoc`.

Now run the schedule through the XLANG Event Monitor. The inbound document is removed from the `TxDemo` queue, but no corresponding message appears in `TxDemoOutput`. You might decide to move the `Receive` action inside the transaction, which would at least leave the inbound document in the receive queue. Since both queues are transactional, the DTC can restore the state of the queues when the transaction fails. No matter what we do, though, we are left with a silent failure. The schedule should take some positive action when the transaction fails.

The On Fail TX Page

Now we need to provide the diagram for handling the failure of the transaction. This is shown below.

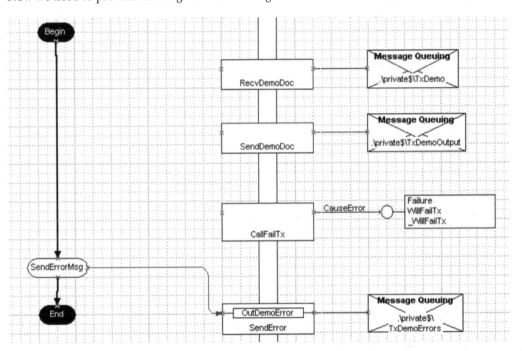

We're going to send an error message to an MSMQ queue. To configure the `On Fail Tx` page:

1. Open the **Transaction Properties** dialog for the `Fail Tx` transaction shape.

2. Check **Short-lived, DTC style** in the **Type** group. In the **On failure** group, click **Add Code** and check the **Enabled** box, then click **OK**. Leave other settings on their defaults.

   Orchestration Designer creates a new tabbed page labeled On **Failure of Fail Tx**. This is initially populated with a `Begin` shape, and the message ports you created on the business process diagram.

293

3. Create an action shape named `SendErrorMsg`, and connect it to the `Begin` shape.

4. Drop an `End` shape on the page and connect it to the action shape.

5. Now create an MSMQ messaging implementation for the `SendErrorMsg` action. Its port should connect to the `TxDemoErrors` queue.

6. The action shape connects to the port by sending an asynchronous message to the queue.

Your `On Failure of Fail Tx` page thus consists of a `Begin` shape connected to the outgoing action shape, which is connected to an `End` shape. The `Action` shape connects to a port bound to MSMQ.

> *Orchestration Designer will not let you connect two ports to the same queue, so we require a new one for the error messages. This is also better and clearer from a design standpoint. Go ahead and create this queue through the Computer Management application.*

We need an error message to send. Ideally we'd write some code to obtain status information, but we would also need session information, which we will discuss shortly. For our immediate purposes, a hardcoded XML message will suffice.

7. On the **Data** page, add a constant called `ErrorMsg`, then give it the value `<ErrorMsg cause="failedTx"/>`.

8. Connect the constant to the `Document` field of the `OutDemoError` message.

Now when the schedule executes, the transaction fails, triggering the execution of the `On Failure of Fail Tx` schedule module. XLANG Scheduler uses the constant `ErrorMsg` as the text of the message it sends to the `TxDemoErrors` queue.

You will see that is exactly what happens. As before, the inbound document is consumed and the `TxDemoOutputs` queue remains empty. With the `On Failure` schedule, however, we now see an `ErrorMsg` document in the `TxDemoErrors` queue. In a real system, whatever application consumed messages from the `TxDemoOutputs` queue would also check the `TxDemoErrors` queue. Error messages would embody status and session information, allowing the application to respond appropriately.

> *You might wonder why we go to this trouble instead of moving the initial* **Receive** *action into the transaction. It is not enough to prevent a failed transaction. We must also notify the consumer of messages – our application – and also the message originator. The application should be made aware that there is a pending problem, and the originator must be notified so that he may take corrective action.*

Long-Running Transactions

Long-running transactions are used in several cases in orchestration schedules:

❑ You can explicitly indicate that a transaction is a long-running transaction. You may choose to do this because the included actions are not transactional, or to indicate that you expect this to be a long process. However, you should note that you do not have to specify this type of transaction to enable dehydration. When nested transactions are involved, the outermost transaction cannot be a short-lived, DTC-based transaction. It must be long-running.

Whether you select a long-lived type or a timed type, a recovery mechanism called **compensation** (which we discuss fully in the *Nested Transactions* section below) becomes available.

Why Long-Running Transactions Fail

Long-running transactions fail in for the same reasons as short-lived transactions:

❑ An explicit `Abort` shape

❑ A COM component returning an error code (when the schedule is configured for this)

❑ The failure of an operation involving a transactional resource

The important difference between long and short transactions is in recovery. The DTC is unavailable to long-running transactions, because it would not be efficient to allow long-lived schedules to tie up transactional resources for long periods of time. Therefore you must specify how to roll back a long-running transaction.

Recovery from Long-Running Transactions

You can recover from long-running transaction failure using an `On Failure Tx` page, just as you did with short-lived transactions. This schedule will be invoked when the transaction fails. Everything in a basic long-running transaction at first seems to be the same as in a short-running transaction, but the difference is in what does not happen automatically.

In our short-lived transaction example, failure of the COM messaging action caused the transaction to fail. That, in turn, caused the preceding transacted message queuing action to be rolled back by the DTC. The action taken on the `On Fail Tx` page was over and above this DTC-based recovery. In a long-running transaction however, the same sequence of events would not roll back the queued message, because the DTC is not involved in long-running transactions. Let's verify that with a brief example.

A Test of Long-Running Transactions

Take the schedule we created in the short-lived example and save a copy as `LongTx.skv`.

1. Open the transaction property page and change the transaction type to long-running.

2. Compile it under the same name with the `.skx` extension.

3. Run `stuff.js` to make sure there is a message in the inbound queue. Now run the schedule.

In the short-lived example, the message in `TxDemo` was consumed, an `ErrorMsg` type document was sent to `TxDemoErrors`, and the message to `TxDemoOutput` was rolled back, leaving that queue unchanged.

Now compare that with the status of your queues after running `LongTx.skx`. The inbound message is still consumed and the error message is sent, as expected, but the `TxDemoOutput` queue has a `SiteServiceDescription` document in it. Changing the transaction type took the DTC out of the processing, so the MSMQ messaging action was not rolled back even though the queue involved with the port is transactional.

Nested Transactions

Transactions become much more interesting when you nest them. Orchestration Designer will permit you to place a transaction around another transaction, but you may not nest transactions any more deeply than this. Nested transactions are useful when the success of a logical transaction is affected by the success or failure of subsequent actions. Rather than attempt to expand the transaction and hold resources longer than necessary, keep the original transaction and throw another transaction around it. The resources held by the inner transaction may be released when the transaction completes, but the resources held by the outer transaction will still be coordinated as a transaction. As we are about to see, compensating action may be taken at the level of the inner transaction in response to a failure of the outer well after the inner transaction has completed its work.

The Dilemma of a Failure in Nested Transactions

Nested transactions present a problem in terms of recovering from an aborted transaction. What do you do about inner committed transactions when an outer transaction fails? You'd like to have something that allows you to "un-commit" the committed transaction. That is very difficult in practice, and when you remember that many BizTalk actions are inherently non-transactional in nature – how do you call back an HTTP POST? – you begin to think this might not be a practical approach.

Fortunately, the On Failure pages suggest an approach. What if you could design a schedule for each transaction that would be invoked in the event of a failed transaction up the line? The process is called compensation.

Recovery Revisited: Compensating Nested Transactions

A **Compensation** module is associated with a transaction, but invoked only in response to the failure of an enclosing transaction. A nested transaction, then, can have two modules associated with it – one for recovering from its own failure, and one for responding to a failure in the enclosing transaction. We can say that the new module compensates for the actions the transaction took. While it is not as rigorous in its actions as a short-lived transaction with the DTC at its disposal, it is just as good as the On Failure Tx page.

In fact, the two pages will be similar. The same mechanisms you devise to restore the state of the system in an On Failure Tx page will work in a compensation page. The only difference in a compensation page is that you know every action in the inner transaction completed successfully – after all, the transaction must have committed, or the outer transaction would not have continued.

It is important to understand the sequence of events in recovering nested transactions. Here is the order of processing in such a situation:

1. Inner transaction commits

2. The outer transaction fails, but *not* because of some action that is inside the inner transaction

3. The compensation page (if it exists) for any enclosed transaction is called

4. The On Failure Tx page for the outer transaction is called

5. Processing in the schedule resumes with the first shape outside the outer transaction

There are a few things to consider here. The first is that On Failure Tx pages and compensation pages may themselves have transactions. These may in turn have recovery pages of their own. All the schedules associated with a page complete before control passes back up the call chain. Therefore, if a transaction in a compensation page fails, the On Failure page for it will be called before XLANG Scheduler calls the On Failure Tx page of the outer transaction.

The other point to remember is that failed transactions do not abort the schedule containing them. This actually applies to any transaction, nested or not. If you want the flow of activity outside a transaction to depend on whether the transaction committed or not, you must test for this condition. So long as you have sent or received at least one message in an On Failure or compensation page, you may readily determine this with a rule in a decision shape. Each message, you may recall, has system defined properties. One of these is __Exists__. Hence to test for a message in a recovery page named IFailed, you would add a decision shape outside the transaction with the rule IFailed.__Exists__. If this evaluates true, you know the transaction in question failed because the recovery page was executed, creating the message in question.

Compensation Example

The best way to understand compensation is through an example. Let's contrive a schedule to model a request from the Home Organization to an organization I'll call Transacted Partner. The sample files are in the NestedTx folder of the code download.

Transacted Partner receives requests from me and takes some action. Such a request consists of an XML-based message called DemoRequest, like this:

```
<DemoRequest requestID="3293" requestType="Buy">
  <Narrative>Please do this</Narrative>
</DemoRequest>
```

The value of the requestID attribute uniquely identifies this request. The value of requestType tells Transacted Partner what to do. The Narrative element provides human-readable back-up instructions. This is, of course, a simplistic specification, but one that is sufficient for our purposes here.

1. Go ahead and create a specification for this message using BizTalk Editor.

The Transacted Partner organization understands that the Home Organization's processes may fail. So the two organizations agree that in such an event, the Home Organization will send Transacted Partner an advisory message containing the requestID and requestType values for the original DemoRequest message, and optionally, a code denoting what step in Home Organization's processes the failure occurred. The latter value is of interest to Transacted Partner only because they may have further communications with the Home Organization. In other words, the step code should not be meaningful to Transacted Partner, but should serve as a token they can pass back (with the requestID value) to the Home Organization as a means of helping the latter keep track of the state of its process. An advisory message for the request shown above might look like this:

```
<DemoRequestFailAdvisory requestID="3293" requestType="Buy"
                         failstep="secondthought"/>
```

Our schedule will be fairly basic.

2. We will be using BizTalk messaging enclosed in a transaction to send a request to the Transacted Partner organization.

3. We'll assume that the schedule then needs to call a COM component to do further evaluation of some sort. Perhaps they are considering their internal manufacturing schedule, or responding to an updated sales forecast.

4. If that process fails, we want to send an advisory to Transacted Partner calling the original request off.

Transacted Partner will then take whatever action they need to reverse any effects of the original request. The business process diagram for the Home Organization looks like this:

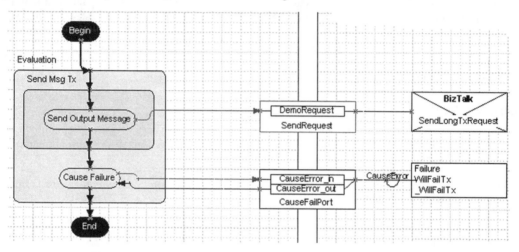

We are reusing our `Failure.WillFailTx` component to force the outer transaction to abort.

5. The compensation page for the Send Msg Tx transaction uses BizTalk messaging to send the `DemoRequestFailAdvisory` message to the Transacted Partner organization.

We're using the local file transport, but the actual protocol is immaterial. The point is that the compensation page will be called after the Send Msg Tx transaction has committed successfully, but after a failure of the Evaluation transaction. The compensation page is intended to undo whatever action resulted at the Transacted Partner organization in response to the DemoRequest message.

6. The On Failure of Send Msg Tx page – which should only be called for a failure of the Send Output of Message action – sends the following message to the local, private queue LongTxErrors:

```
<ErrorMsg cause="sendBTS"/>
```

No error message needs to be sent to our partner because if Send Msg Tx fails, no message was sent to Transacted Partners in the first place. Very little can cause this transaction to fail. Basically, it would come down to a COM error in one of the components implementing the protocol you select to send the message via BizTalk.

7. The On Failure of Evaluation page contains a message queuing implementation that sends the following message to another private queue on the local machine, LongTxEval:

```
<ErrorMsg cause="TxFailed"/>
```

Now, according to theory, if this page is called, the compensation page for the enclosed transaction has already been called. There is no reason to send a message to Transacted Partners from this page because one will have already been sent. The queued message sent here is intended solely to notify the Home Organization's IT staff that something failed.

There is one final bit of configuration to do in this schedule, and it is a bit tricky. We still have to specify the data flow, shown below, but we're going to do something a little unusual.

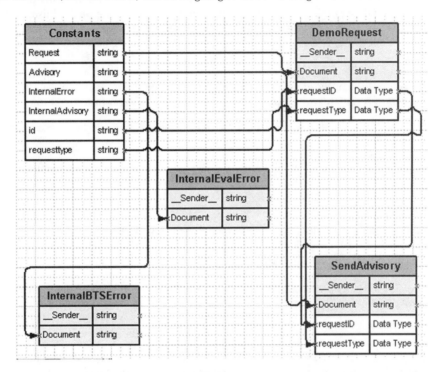

In normal practice, you would use a call to a COM component to generate the various error messages on the On Failure Send Msg Tx and compensation pages. Since this schedule is rigged and we know exactly where it will fail, we don't want to clutter up the schedule and write additional code. Therefore we're going to use constants to compose the messages we need.

8. Define a constant named Request that has as its value the text of a canned DemoRequest message.

9. To fill in the empty requestID and requestType fields of the SendAdvisory message, we first need to assign the constant values id and requesttype to the requestID and requestType properties of the DemoRequest message.

To make Orchestration Designer expose these properties for DemoRequest, you must tell the Binding Wizard that you are sending XML, and you must select those two fields explicitly.

10. The Request constant value is assigned directly to the DemoRequest message's Document property, which is the connection that gives the schedule something to send at the Send Output Message action.

11. The same holds true for the Document properties of the InternalEvalError and InternalBTSError messages. These are the documents rooted with the ErrorMsg element that were shown above.

The tricky part comes with the SendAdvisory message. This message is sent in response to the failed DemoRequest message. Now, since that message's requestId and requestType fields were filled from constants, we could do the same here, but I want to show you that data really does flow through the schedule. Even though DemoRequest is sent from the main module on the business process diagram and the SendAdvisory message is on the compensation page, XLANG Scheduler will have both messages available to it at run-time, and so Orchestration Designer makes them available to you at design time.

12. Therefore, assign the field values from the failed DemoRequest message to the corresponding field values in the SendAdvisory message, thereby connecting them.

13. As with the DemoRequest message, the main body of the SendAdvisory message comes from a constant string.

At run time, XLANG Scheduler will fill in the Document property from the constant, then assign specific values to the requestID and requestType properties from the output of the DemoRequest message.

Running the Example

If you set this schedule in motion, you should see what theory predicts:

1. BizTalk messaging is called to send the DemoRequest message

2. The call to the COM component fails as expected, forcing the compensation page to be invoked

3. The SendAdvisory message is sent via BizTalk messaging

4. The On Failure of Evaluation page is called, at which time MSMQ messaging is invoked to send the InternalEvalError message to our local queue

The On Failure of Send Msg Tx page is never called and so the InternalBTSError message is never sent.

Timed Transactions

There is one final type of transaction to talk about: the timed transaction. Select this to provide a timeout interval for a long transaction. Once selected, the isolation level option cannot be set as you are acting outside the DTC. In the edit field labeled Timeout (seconds), enter the maximum time you wish to allow for the transaction. If you choose this option, the transaction shape will be colored blue on the business process diagram.

A timed transaction is used when you have a series of related actions that are expected to take a comparatively long period to execute, but for which you can set an upper bound on the time they take to complete. You might, for example, be dealing with a partner subject to network delays or whose server is frequently overwhelmed. In such cases, you know that you will receive a message within a certain period or not at all. You will not receive an error message; rather, some Receive action will block indefinitely.

The timeout option becomes more valuable when messaging is combined with lengthy COM calls, or when a series of unreliable calls must be made within a transaction. If the actions are confined to messaging alone, you could always set a time limit on the message reception. However, with multiple calls or involved processing within COM calls, you may not be able to accurately and reliably assess where the delay is coming from. In such cases, a timed transaction is a good solution.

Short-lived, DTC-style transactions may also make use of timeouts. This is not the same as specifying a timed transaction. Select the Short-lived, DTC-style radio button as you normally would. In the Transaction options group, enter a timeout interval just as you did for timed transactions. Now you have the benefits of timeouts and DTC-based isolation.

> *Be careful not to abuse timed transactions. Specify some positive failure measure – an error result from a COM method, a negative reply message from another application – whenever possible. Transactions that are waiting for some action that will never complete block the thread on which they execute. Unnecessary timed transactions and timed transactions with overly generous timeout periods consume system resources unnecessarily.*

We have now finished dealing with the different forms of transactions, so we will move on to deal with *concurrency*. There is a major conflict between transactions and forked flows, and a subtle, hard-to-find performance issue to consider.

Concurrency

The fork and join shapes in business process diagrams offer programmers an easy way to introduce the benefits of concurrent programming into their schedules without a lot of complexity. There are many obvious and not-so-obvious benefits to this. If you need several pieces of information, for example, place the various Send and Receive actions on different flows so that they operate in parallel. If the join shape's Type property is set to AND, XLANG Scheduler will ensure all the flows complete before it proceeds to the first shape following the join.

Do not hesitate to take advantage of concurrent flows in schedules. The implementation in Orchestration Designer is easy to use, yet the ultimate execution implementation in XLANG Scheduler is very powerful. Still, there are a few pitfalls to avoid, and performance issues to watch, when using concurrency.

Concurrency and Transaction Boundaries

Transactions impose a fundamental restriction that conflicts with the fork shape. Every transaction, of whatever type, must have exactly one entry point and exactly one exit   so flows out of a fork shape cannot cross transaction boundaries. Either the transaction lives on one of the flows of a fork, or all the flows of a fork begin and end (via the join shape) within the boundaries of the transaction. This is consistent with the conception of a transaction as an atomic unit of work. If some execution paths lead to one type of exit from a transaction and some lead to another, the internal behavior of the transaction is exposed to outside entities. You can no longer say that the state of the system is inside the transaction or outside it; rather, you have to say that it is inside it on *this* path leading to *that* state.

This problem is easy to recognize because Orchestration Designer will not export a schedule that violates this restriction. Still, if you are well into a schedule implementation when you discover this, it may be difficult to correct the problem. The usual guidelines for transactions and concurrent programming in other programming venues hold in orchestration, as well:

❏ Keep transaction boundaries as small as possible. Transactions are expensive resources, so we try to keep them focused on the smallest possible set of actions that still allow a schedule to complete its tasks correctly.

❏ Minimize the use of concurrent flows. Too many programmers fork a new flow, glibly assuming that there will be a performance gain. This is not always the case. Before introducing a fork shape, think through the task at hand. Ask yourself what overlap you expect to leverage with parallel flows. Make a strong case for the advantage of concurrency before resorting to a fork.

With transactions kept small and concurrency limited, you will not only have fewer conflicts in your schedules, but resolving conflicts, when they occur, will be easier.

Scalability Issues

Fork and join shapes in orchestration schedules permit up to 64 flows. This is more than enough to get you into trouble. First, a schedule with more than a few flows is likely to grow extremely complex. You have the ever-present problem of verifying the correctness of the schedule.

You also have a subtle problem of performance. Any flow that is active will prevent the schedule from being dehydrated. Each flow with one or more `Receive` actions on it has an expected latency set for it. You must ensure that these are balanced between flows, and are accurate. A flow with a receive latency significantly longer than the others will dominate the rest, forcing their resources to be held, inactive, until the long-waiting flow completes or times out, at which time the schedule may be dehydrated. You must profile the performance of any schedule in order to get optimum performance from the overall system, but the problem is much more complicated when you have many flows operating in parallel. It is not unusual for one's estimate of latency to be incorrect, throwing off the overall balance of the concurrent flows.

`Receive` actions are not the only possible pitfall in schedules with many concurrent flows. Distributed systems are almost always slower than their local counterparts due to the overhead of remote communications. HTTP, in particular, can take longer to complete a request than a programmer may be accustomed to allowing for a single operation. Remember that HTTP is a synchronous protocol, and you are not only working across application boundaries, but across the Internet to reach a possibly overloaded server. It is one thing to wait a second or two longer when you are Web surfing, but quite another to wait that long when you are making hundreds of calls on behalf of mission-critical applications.

You must consider the performance of your partner's systems, network congestion, and the time of day when planning a schedule. A single slow outbound call can also delay the execution of the overall schedule when it is part of a concurrent flow whose unifying join shape has its `Type` property set to `AND`.

You also might consider breaking one complex schedule into several schedules that operate independently. If the transactional semantics of your application permit this, you can achieve parallel performance through the concurrent execution of multiple schedules.

We've now covered persistence, transactions, and concurrency, but there is one advanced technique remaining: *dynamic port binding*. This is an approach that will introduce a great deal of flexibility into messaging implementations, and allow us to reduce the number of ports we need in certain situations.

Dynamic Port Binding

In every schedule we've drawn so far, we've been careful to completely specify the protocol-specific binding for each port. Failure to do so would have prevented Orchestration Designer from exporting a schedule in XLANG form. Without a specific idea of where we want the port to go, how could XLANG Scheduler invoke Messaging Services properly? That two-party implementation – XLANG Scheduler invoking the BizTalk Messaging Services – is what enables BizTalk to offer the ability to perform **dynamic port binding**.

Dynamic port binding is the ability to use the same port with different endpoints based on the contents of the document being sent through the port. As far as XLANG Scheduler is concerned, each port is merely data – a configuration to pass along to Messaging Services. Messaging Services, in turn, is not concerned with the overall schedule, nor it is interested in what went before and what will go on after this interchange. So long as an appropriate configuration is passed to it, one that specifies valid ports and protocols, it will attempt to perform the interchange. Messaging Services does not care whether XLANG Scheduler put the configuration together when it exported the schedule or whether it put it together immediately before calling for an interchange.

Orchestration permits us to specify a particular port implementation as dynamic. This means that it will leave the protocol-specific endpoint open until the time XLANG Scheduler reaches the point of trying to send a message through the port. At that time, some field within the message must provide an appropriate endpoint. For MSMQ, that is a queue pathname. For BizTalk messaging, it means the name of a valid channel. For COM, the endpoint is a moniker. At design time, then, we have to go to the data page and indicate which field will provide the needed information.

Why Dynamic Binding?

Besides being a nice trick to show off to your programmer friends, dynamic binding allows us to simplify our schedules. In the demonstration schedules you have seen throughout this book, every action is associated with precisely one recipient. In the real world, an organization is likely to have multiple partners or vendors for a given function. If we did not have dynamic binding, we would be forced to write different branches of the code, each containing nearly identical ports. With dynamic binding, we can reuse the same port in the same thread of execution to perform the same function so long as all the partners are using the same protocol. Only when our partners have different receive protocols, for example one on MSMQ and another on BizTalk messaging, will we have to duplicate ports.

Even then, the issue is not so bad as it seems. BizTalk messaging embraces MSMQ as one of its supported protocols, so we could accommodate both with one dynamic port implemented with BizTalk messaging. BizTalk abstracts the protocol to some degree, so we would not have access to the more intricate features of MSMQ, but the vast majority of messages can be handled this way.

MSMQ and BizTalk Messaging: A Dynamic Binding Example

Let's look at dynamic messaging through an example. There is no hypothetical business case here. We are going to have a client application, written in Visual Basic, that handles a simple message type. That message is just big enough to accommodate comments and the endpoint to which we want a port dynamically bound. Here is a sample of the message:

```
<Notification>
  <DestinationQueue>.\private$\myqueue</DestinationQueue>
  <Comments>This is a test</Comments>
</Notification>
```

The DestinationQueue element's value is the queue to which the message should be delivered. To continue our warning system analogy, an application would know the destination queue assigned to receive warnings. Presumably some application, perhaps one that invoked a pager system, monitors the queue. The textual contents of the Comments element is a descriptive message intended for the recipient, or a log file entry.

The idea is that some notification is coming in, and the schedule must deliver it to the appropriate entity using information provided in the message. You might use this as a sort of central post office or warning system, taking in messages – say, system advisories – and sending them to the appropriate technician.

The reality of our client application is simpler, although somewhat less exciting. Instead of a running application in need of monitoring, we have a Visual Basic form that allows us to enter a destination queue and a descriptive message. Depending on which button you click, you get to test dynamic messaging using either MSMQ or BizTalk messaging. Before we get into the details of the schedule, here is a look at the user interface:

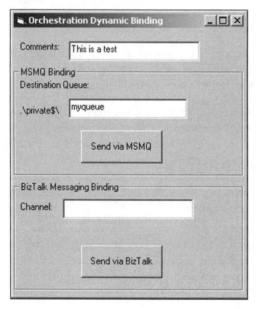

This won't win any awards for style, but it is sufficient for our purposes. We are just trying to get a message into the schedule while allowing the user to specify the MSMQ queue or BizTalk messaging channel of her choice. The comments give you a place to insert a unique message to help you sort out message instances, while the destination queue or channel allows you to send a message to any existing queue or BizTalk messaging channel. That way, you can satisfy yourself that dynamic binding is, in fact, taking place.

Dynamic Binding with MSMQ

When you click on the button labeled Send via MSMQ, the two items of data entered by the user are stuffed into a Notification message, the message is then sent to a local, private queue DynaBind_in, and the schedule DynamicSendMSMQ.skx is loaded. This project has a global variable, doc, that contains an instance of the MSXML parser. The project uses MSMQ, MSXML, and the BizTalk Scheduler run-time object libraries, so be sure to set references to Microsoft Message Queue 2.0 Object Library, Microsoft XML, v2.6 (or later), and XLANG Scheduler Runtime Library (skedcore.dll).

Here's the first half of the button-handler code:

```
Private Sub SendMSMQ_Click()
  Dim objSked As IWFWorkflowInstance

  If DestQueue.Text = "" Then
   MsgBox "You must supply a queue"
  Else
   Call SetMsgValues(doc, ".\private$\" & DestQueue.Text, Comments.Text)
```

We check the edit field to make sure the user has entered a queue name. If so, we call the subroutine SetMsgValues() to set up the Notification message. That document was loaded into a parser instance, without field entries, when the form loaded. SetMsgValues uses XML DOM methods to insert the passed values into the document's fields. Note that we are assisting the user and adding the prefix for a private queue on the local machine.

I've used private queues throughout this book to make the MSMQ samples accessible to readers with workgroup MSMQ configurations. If you are using public queues on an enterprise configuration and you wish to address machines other than the one executing this code, be sure to modify the queue pathname parameter.

In the second half of the button-handler code, we submit the message to the queue DynaBind_in. This is done in the function SendMsgToQueue(). This function takes the text of the message to send, in this case the xml property of the global MSXML document instance, and sends it to the queue. The code is virtually identical to what we have used before for submitting messages to transacted queues. If the queue submission works (SendMsgToQueue returns true), we use the IWFWorkflowInstance interface to load the schedule DynamicSendMSMQ.skx. Be sure to modify the pathname to reflect your configuration. Here's the rest of the code:

```
    If SendMsgToQueue(doc.xml) Then
      ' Launch the schedule
      On Error Resume Next
      Set objSked = GetObject("sked:///c:\temp\DynamicSendMSMQ.skx")
    Else
      MsgBox "Unable to submit message"
    End If
  End If
End Sub
```

The schedule takes matters from there. It looks like this:

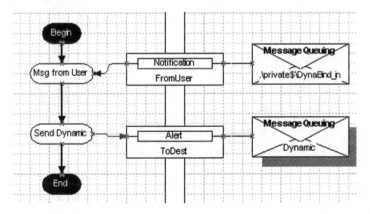

1. The message submitted by the client is plucked from the queue, then sent via the dynamic port `ToDest`.

2. That port is attached to the `Send Dynamic` action, which wants to send a new message, `Alert`:

```
<Alert>
    <To>.\private$\myqueue</To>
    <From>mymachine\private$\DynaBind_in</From>
    <Comments>This is a test</Comments>
</Alert>
```

The `To` field echoes the destination queue, while `From` carries the name of the input port's queue implementation. The `Comments` text entered by the user is passed along unmodified.

3. When you implement the `ToDest` port using MSMQ, the Message Queuing Binding Wizard offers you the choice of a static queue or a dynamic queue (this occurs on the Static or Dynamic Queue Information page). Select Dynamic queue, then click Next.

4. On the Advanced Port Properties page, make sure that the Transactions are required with this queue checkbox is checked if you plan to send messages to transacted queues.

5. When you connect the `Send Dynamic` action shape to the port, configure the XML Communication Wizard for sending a message asynchronously.

6. On the Message Specification Information page, point to the document specification file and add all the fields to the Message fields list. Do the same for the incoming `Notification` message. This will prepare the Data page for a later step.

BizTalk document specification files for these messages are included with the code download for this chapter in the files `alert_spec.xml` *and* `notification_spec.xml`.

The key to making this schedule work is the Data flow, which is shown below:

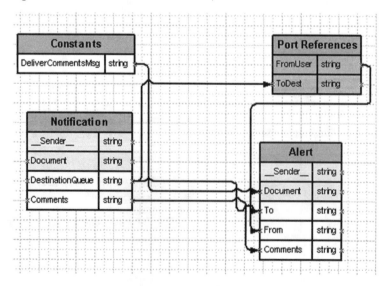

Looking at the screenshot we see that:

7. The `Alert` message body is held in a string constant, `DeliverCommentsMsg`. Connect this to the `Alert` message's `Document` property. Recall that this is a technique we've used before when we wanted to inject a new message into the system.

8. `Alert`'s `To`, `From`, and `Comments` properties are filled by connections to the `DestinationQueue` (`To`) and `Comments` (`Comments`) properties of the inbound `Notification` message, and the `FromUser` port reference (`From`).

This explains how `Alert` gets filled with data, but not how XLANG Scheduler gets told what the desired endpoint is. Now pay special attention to the link to the port reference of our dynamically bound port:

9. Connect the value of the `Notification` message's `DestinationQueue` property, which, as you'll recall, is stuffed with the queue pathname the user entered, to the input of the `ToDest` port reference. This simple connection is what XLANG Scheduler uses to assign the port's endpoint when it invokes MSMQ.

Two final points must be made about dynamic binding:

❑ First, the data flow is absolutely essential. When you choose dynamic binding in the Message Queuing Binding Wizard, you are warned to create a link on the **Data** page between the message field and the port reference. Without it, the dynamic binding cannot occur.

❑ Second, the link is generic, but the data value passed is protocol-specific. In this case, we pass along a valid MSMQ queue pathname because the port implementation uses MSMQ as the underlying communications protocol.

We will find the pattern of specifying dynamic binding does not change with other protocols. What will change is the syntax of the data passed to the port reference. The significance of this will become apparent next, when we implement the BizTalk Messaging case.

Dynamic Binding with BizTalk Messaging

Since the point of the dynamic binding feature is reuse, and since XLANG schedules are data-driven, you may have hoped that implementing the BizTalk messaging version of this project would be very similar to the MSMQ version. It is indeed. The only difference in the button-handler code is in the text of the error messages, the text we pass in for the second parameter of `SetMsgValues` (naming the endpoint), and the name of the XLANG schedule to load:

```
Private Sub SendBTS_Click()
  Dim objSked As IWFWorkflowInstance

  If DestChannel.Text = "" Then
    MsgBox "You must name a BizTalk Messaging channel."
  Else
    Call SetMsgValues(doc, DestChannel.Text, Comments.Text)
    If SendMsgToQueue(doc.xml) Then
      On Error Resume Next
      Set objSked = GetObject("sked:///c:\temp\DynamicSendBTS.skx")
    Else
      MsgBox "Unable to submit message"
    End If
  End If
End Sub
```

Everything in the schedule is identical to the MSMQ schedule, except that the `ToDest` port's implementation uses BizTalk messaging. The data flow is the same. So long as the `Alert` message's `To` field names an endpoint specific to the BizTalk protocol – a channel name – dynamic port binding will work.

There is one final thing to consider with BizTalk dynamic binding. Not only does it permit us a wide range of flexibility in addressing messages – each channel can use a different port – but it also broadens the range of protocols we can use. Unlike COM and MSMQ, BizTalk messaging embraces a number of basic protocols. This is especially valuable when communicating with external partners via the Internet. Some of your partners might use HTTP, while others will want their messages delivered via SMTP. All, of course, will use different URLs. If the applications generating the messages can sort between partners, or a COM component called from the schedule can perform this task for you, dynamic binding will allow you to satisfy all your transmission requirements, in respect of a particular message and step in the process, with a single dynamically bound port.

Summary

Orchestration is one of the most powerful tools BizTalk Server offers you for building distributed systems. Chapter 2 introduced you to the basics of building and using schedules, but it did not expose you to the full range of features offered by XLANG and orchestration. The mission-critical requirements BizTalk Server aims to serve need rich features for transactions and concurrency, as well as a strategy for making efficient use of system resources in long-running schedules. The ability to address partners, applications, and even other schedules in a flexible and dynamic way is a great aid in the automation of important business processes. This chapter showed you the tools orchestration offers for addressing these issues as well as the challenges in using them properly.

Orchestration starts its transactional journey by embracing the DTC and COM+ transactions. You saw that XLANG Scheduler does not offer any new transactional capabilities of its own, but fully participates in the distributed transaction facilities offered by the DTC. By using transaction-aware resources and designing short transactions in schedules, you can have the same transactional behavior in orchestration that you previously enjoyed in the world of COM+ programming.

However, the nature of distributed systems and Internet communications leads to situations that need transactional behavior, but:

❑ They involve resources that are not inherently transactional, or

❑ They involve activities over such a span of time that it is impractical to hold resources in a traditional transaction

For these situations, orchestration offers long and timed transactions, as well as the ability to specify schedules that execute upon the failure of a transaction. We explored the nature of long transactions and when to use them. We also explored how transactions interact when they are nested. Perhaps most importantly, we saw how **On Failure** and **compensation** pages work together to allow you to specify recovery from the failure of transactions when the automatic, DTC-based rollback capabilities do not fully address your needs.

In addition to the severe limitations imposed on concurrency in schedules enlisting in COM+ transactions, we saw the main conflict between **concurrency** and transactions. Transaction boundaries cannot span flows, and forks within transactions must be unified by a join shape within the transaction. A transaction can have one entry and one exit. This is not a problem in demonstration schedules, but can become a problem in complex schedules that you might encounter out in the real world. We offered two strategies:

❑   Keep transactions small, and limit concurrency, to minimize the potential for conflict.

❑   Decompose large schedules into smaller ones that execute independently.

We also cautioned against using concurrency without thinking through how it will affect the performance of your system.

We looked at **hydration** and its role in ensuring that long-running schedules do not tie up scarce resources when they are idle and awaiting input. You saw how XLANG Scheduler uses SQL Server to store the state of an idle schedule and when schedules are serialized.

One of the trickiest topics in programming is making dynamic changes in the flow of control. We explored two forms of dynamic programming in orchestration:

❑   First, we saw how **COM monikers** allow you to address any port in any schedule, including specific instances of a schedule. Using this, we were able to send messages between schedules, gaining access to a COM port for the purpose of passing in information.

❑   Second, under **dynamic port binding**, we saw how a task can be implemented with message passing just once in a schedule, even though the same task may be performed many times with many different recipients. Data in the body of an outgoing message was used to dynamically change the endpoint of the desired messaging action.

As you can see, orchestration is a rich topic with many facets. Between the two chapters, we have covered all the functional areas involved. I hope that these chapters have conveyed at least a hint of the complexity of the topic.

Orchestration involves some conceptual changes for traditional programmers. You must become accustomed to both asynchronous messaging and data-driven behavior. Certainly, programmers accustomed to procedural flows will find the links on the Data page novel, and database programmers will find messaging and COM monikers unusual. As you sort out the different features, learning their strengths and weaknesses, you will find that orchestration provides the same "configuration, not programming" benefits for systems that the Messaging Manager brought to inter-process communications.

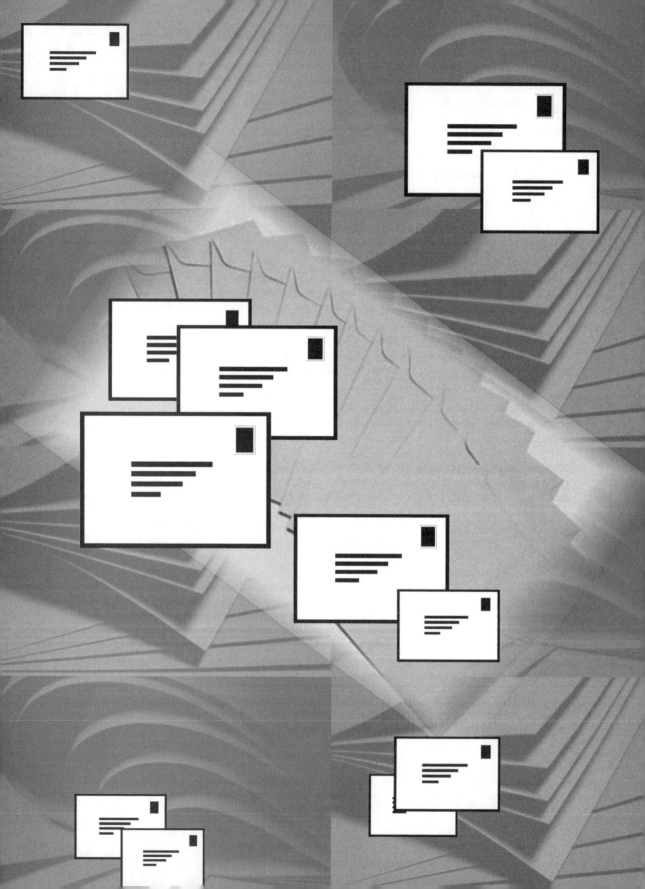

Interfacing Messaging with Applications

7

BizTalk Server provides the plumbing for Enterprise Application Integration (EAI) inside organizational boundaries. It also provides the infrastructure for integration between businesses across the Internet for Business-to-Business e-commerce (B2B).

Although B2B and EAI are useful labels to describe what at first appear to be two separate integration problems, these integration areas commonly overlap. Indeed, in a typical B2B scenario there are usually at least two ancillary EAI transactions. For example, when a product catalog is send out to a B2B trading partner at least two other processes are involved: the first retrieves the catalog data from an internal system before transmission and the second takes the incoming catalog message and delivers it into the trading partner's internal system. Both of these ancillary transactions are EAI, or application-to-application exchanges. The internal systems involved in such exchanges are often labelled Line of Business (LOB) applications and are typically the enterprise stores for order, customer, employee, and accounting information.

When integrating BizTalk with LOB applications you have two choices:

- ❑ Direct integration from BizTalk into the LOB application
- ❑ Indirect integration by creating messages in BizTalk and importing them into the LOB application

The code that integrates BizTalk server to a LOB application is called an adapter, connector, or Application Integration Component (AIC). Although BizTalk Server does not ship with any specific AICs in the box, other than an example SAP connector, Microsoft is working with many LOB application vendors to create pre-packaged AICs for BizTalk Server that may be easily deployed by developers and system integrators. Types of vendors that Microsoft is working with include ERP vendors (examples of ERP systems are: JD Edwards, SAP, PeopleSoft), CRM vendors (examples of CRM systems are: Siebel and Onyx) and market-place vendors (examples of market-place systems are Ariba, Commerce One, VerticalNet, and Clarus). Visit http://www.microsoft.com/biztalk for an up-to-date list of available AICs.

Although application vendors will provide the most commonly requested AICs, system integrators and developers (such as yourself) will encounter a range of custom-built, and legacy applications. In these cases you may have the need to build a BizTalk AIC.

AICs provide BizTalk with the ability to talk directly to existing applications, such as PeopleSoft and SAP. AICs leverage your existing investment in COM, and BizTalk Server provides you with three different AIC interfaces: `IBTSAppIntegration`, `IPipelineComponent` and BizTalk Scriptor components.

In this chapter we will:

- ❑ Briefly examine generic challenges experienced in application integration.
- ❑ Learn how to move a document from the BizTalk Messaging infrastructure into line of business applications by developing and deploying Application Integration Components (AICs).
- ❑ Examine how to build each of the AIC components provided by BizTalk Server.
- ❑ Demonstrate the differences between the `IBTSAppIntegration` and `IPipelineComponent` interface by solving an integration problem for a small bolt vendor, Bob's Bolts. Bob's Bolts wishes to trade electronically with Ken's Cars but also wants to retain its legacy Microsoft Access 2000 ordering application. We will interface BizTalk Server with this legacy application using an AIC.

Application Integration with BizTalk Server

Application Integration involves sending messages to pass state into and out of an application. Messages may originate from:

- ❑ Other applications where details of the internal workings of the source application are not known. Fortunately, only an understanding of the message contents itself is necessary for integration.
- ❑ BizTalk Server Orchestration, which sends out messages as part of an overall business process.

Message to Application Integration

Application Integration involves a number of fundamental steps:

- ❑ Understanding input/output formats from the application
- ❑ Identifying a physical interface to input instance data
- ❑ Sending instance data marked up to the input specification through the input interface
- ❑ Identifying a physical interface to output instance data
- ❑ Retrieving instance data marked up to the output specification through the output interface

Let's apply this methodology to integration with Microsoft Access 2000. Microsoft Access provides a number of interfaces to its internal .mdb file format, including ADO record sets, and flatfile outputs. Flatfile outputs are best suited for batched historical data, while ADO record sets are best suited for real-time query. The physical interface to Microsoft Access for ADO is the ADO Provider for Jet 4.0 that ships with the MDAC layer. Data must be formatted inside ADO Command queries before it is sent to the ADO Provider for Jet so that it matches the input specification for Microsoft Access. Microsoft Access provides a symmetrical interface for ADO; that is, data may be both sent to and retrieved from a Microsoft Access database using an ADO Provider for Jet.

Application Integration into BizTalk Server requires that you understand where AICs are deployed inside BizTalk. From an architectural perspective AICs are the end-points of BizTalk Messaging. Once a document has been submitted into BizTalk Messaging, using the Interchange interface's Submit() or Submitsync() methods or a receive function, the document passes through a channel and is delivered to a messaging port. AIC components are deployed at messaging ports and so the document that the AIC receives is the post-mapped (if mapping has been selected for the channel), and serialized form. The code implemented inside the AIC may then massage the document data so that it is suitable for delivery to the LOB application and finally deliver the data either directly to the legacy application or to an intermediate queue. The legacy application receives the document, performs the appropriate actions and may return a response code back to BizTalk Messaging that indicates success or failure. The response code is logged into the tracking database, and is returned to the Submitsync() caller so that the programmer can take the appropriate action on failure.

The overall process is shown below:

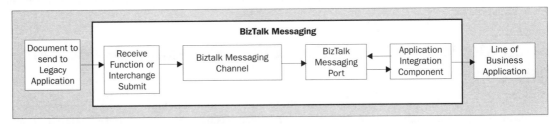

AICs are COM components and may be created in any language that supports COM interface implementation such as Visual Basic and Visual C++.

Business Process to Application Integration

It is common that integration to a specific application is only part of an overall business process. In particular, an EAI scenario may involve a single business process that is responsible for updating content into numerous enterprise stores. For example, a process responsible for updating a user's password into a number of systems would simply interface to each of these systems, wait for them to complete, and then continue to the next system as depicted overleaf:

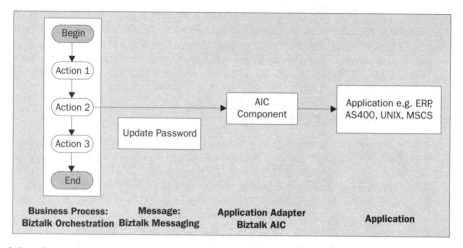

This model is also applicable in very simple B2B scenarios where one trading partner sends an order that is routed directly into the trading partner's legacy application but no return message is required. In these cases, the business process should be modeled in BizTalk Orchestration and the application integration should be performed by sending messages through BizTalk Messaging to the target application.

In the following section we will introduce the Bob's Bolts scenario that we will use to demonstrate how to create AICs.

Scenario: Bob's Bolts – Delivering Messages Directly into Microsoft Access

While Microsoft Access does not necessarily fit into the traditional definition of an enterprise line of business application, numerous small and medium-sized businesses run their entire operation from Access. Further, because of its ubiquitous nature as a member of the Microsoft Office suite it is a useful tool to demonstrate interfacing to BizTalk Messaging with AICs that is accessible to most developers. In our example, we will use none of the XML features built into Microsoft Access 2000. Indeed Microsoft Access 2000 was released before the strong emergence of XML and so it is limited to reading ADO 2.5 or higher record sets persisted in XML format only.

> Note: Whereas native support for reading and writing XML support does not exist in Access 2000 and much of the Office 2000 suite, the next version of Office has extensive XML support that makes interfacing to BizTalk significantly more straightforward. You should be able to use the next version of Office, currently in beta, with this example but the solution presented is not the quickest way to interface the next version of Office with BizTalk.

The same methodology used to build an AIC component for Microsoft Access could be equally well applied to building, for example, an AIC to interface to SAP.

> Out of the box BizTalk Server provides a number of important components to assist with the integration of BizTalk Server and SAP. The SDK\Messaging Samples\SendSAP directory contains an example Pipeline AIC that demonstrates how to send SAP IDOC packets from BizTalk to SAP R/3 systems. These are supplied as unsupported samples only.

The context for this scenario is as follows: Bob's Bolts currently receives purchase orders from Ken's Cars by phone and by fax. Bob's Bolts is a small company and has no automated mechanism to transfer orders into his internal systems. Instead, Bob re-keys all his orders into a trusty Microsoft Access application. On the other hand Ken's Cars is a large business with many suppliers and it is extremely costly for Ken to maintain his current system that also involves re-keying orders. Ken is streamlining his business and has informed all of his suppliers, including Bob, that they must accept electronic orders or lose the business. Bob has investigated the cost of an ERP system to replace Microsoft Access and determined that the expense of this solution is not justified for the low volume of transactions he currently receives from Ken. Bob would like to leverage his existing investment in Microsoft Access *and* receive orders electronically. Biztalk, with the assistance of a custom AIC, will provide Bob with this ability.

Open up Bob's Access database, `BobsAccessDB.mdb`, in Microsoft Access 2000. The table structure for Bob's database is based on a substantially simplified version of the famed `Northwind` example database that ships with Microsoft Access. Bob's database has four tables. The first table contains his customers: currently only Ken's Cars. Each customer has a five letter unique identifier, so Ken's Cars is represented as KENCA. Orders and order detail lines are saved into two tables. Finally, Bob enters information about the bolts he wishes to sell in the Products table. The figure below depicts the relationships between the four tables in the database: Products, Order Details, Orders, and Customers.

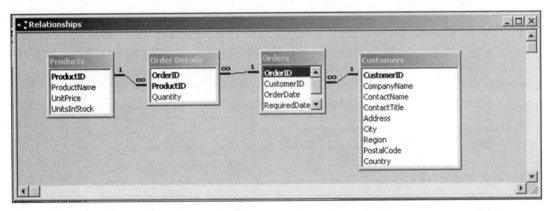

Bob is a businessman (and isn't very technically minded) so, rather than directly editing data in tables, he uses a trusty, if not a little quirky, Access form (shown below). Like many businesses today Bob has a compelling reason to start trading over the Internet, and also has a legacy application that does not support XML.

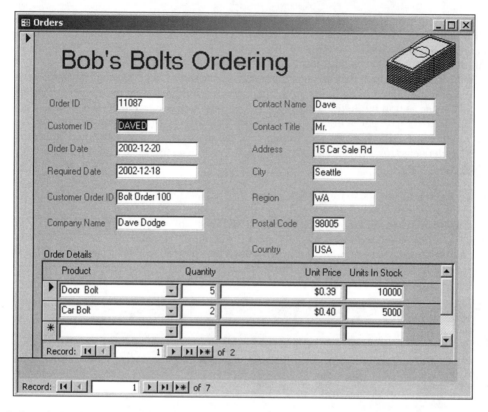

Once Bob and Ken have agreed that they wish to trade electronically, the next step is for them to determine the format and the content of the messages that they will exchange.

Choosing Schemas

To keep this example simple, Bob and Ken have agreed to use XML and a purchase order schema, `BobandKensPOschema.xml`, that maps very nicely to Bob's existing Access database. Although it is not often possible to use the same schema for both businesses, standardization has the benefit of eliminating XSLT mapping steps in message transfer and the associated CPU processing cycles.

The purchase order schema has a header section containing attributes that correlate to the fields in the **Orders** table. Similarly the `Items` section of the purchase order schema has the same fields as the **Order Details** table. An example purchase order instance marked up to the purchase order schema, showing the purchase of five units of item 78 (a door bolt), and two units of item 79 (a car bolt) is presented below. We will use this example later as `testpo.xml`:

```
<PurchaseOrder>
<Header CustomerOrderID="Bolt Order 100"
 CustomerID="KENCA"
 OrderDate="12/12/02"
 RequiredDate="12/20/02"/>
<Item ProductID="78" Quantity="5"/>
<Item ProductID="79" Quantity="2"/>
</PurchaseOrder>
```

Selecting Transport Protocol

Ken and Bob have agreed what information to exchange; next they must determine the transport protocol over which to trade information. They decide that Ken will send the purchase order documents to a folder on Bob's web server via FTP. In this initial phase Ken does not require Bob to send back acknowledgements, or shipping documents – although this may be implemented in the future.

There are a number of cases where using FTP to transport documents might be appropriate, especially for large documents. BizTalk Server 2000 **does not** support FTP as a transport protocol out of the box. However, as incoming FTP results in the delivery of a file to the file system and an FTP server is built into Windows 2000, you can set-up the Windows 2000 FTP server to receive the file to an appropriate directory and then transfer it into BizTalk Server with a simple file receive function.

Should you wish to perform outgoing FTP there are several options. One is to write your own AIC that calls an FTP component. The `wininet.dll` controls that provide client-side FTP functionality are not recommended for server-side processing as they are neither high-performing or thread-safe. Therefore they are currently not recommended in high reliability deployments. However, a number of third-party vendors sell server-safe FTP component implementations. The problem with creating an FTP AIC is that FTP is a connection-based protocol and the AIC will remain in operation until the FTP transfer has been completed. For large files this may have a performance impact on the BizTalk Messaging server. A second approach is to deliver the document you wish to FTP to the file system in a BizTalk Messaging port. Next use one of the third-party FTP executables that will transfer all files delivered in a given directory to an FTP address. Using this approach has the added advantage of loosely coupling the FTP transfer from the BizTalk Messaging system.

Because Bob has no requirement to send back an order confirmation to Ken's Cars we can just use a file receive function in BizTalk Messaging to simulate an incoming FTP transfer of a purchase order.

Bob's Bolts e-Commerce System

We will not implement the business process orchestration at Ken's Cars because we are demonstrating AICs, and neither will we implement the FTP send component that deposits the files on Bob's web server. However, we will completely implement Bob's side of this B2B exchange that takes the incoming files and integrates it into his Microsoft Access 2000 application.

On Bob's web server a receive function is triggered when Ken's FTP module drops a file in the directory.

> *To learn more about receive functions, and configuring BizTalk Messaging channels and ports review the material in Chapter 5.*

The receive function picks up the incoming purchase order from the file system and delivers it to a messaging channel. The channel in turn delivers the document to a messaging port that contains an AIC. The AIC takes the information from the XML document and sends it directly into the Microsoft Access 2000 application. The architecture of Bob's Bolts' e-commerce system, and the names of the various channels, messaging ports, and components we will use are shown below:

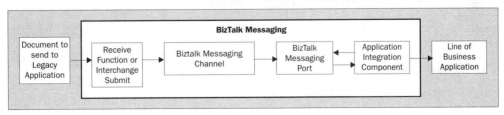

Later in this section we will deploy the AIC component into the BizTalk Messaging Port, but first we need to understand how to implement the appropriate interface to build an AIC. AICs are COM components that implement one of three specific interfaces:

❑ IBTSAppIntegration – Compiled components, designed for simplicity

❑ IPipelineComponent – Compiled components, designed for power because they are both configurable and provide access to interchange meta-data

❑ BizTalk Scriptor components – Interpreted components, designed for debugging and very simple integration scenarios

We will implement Bob's Bolts using the simpler IBTSAppIntegration interface first, and then in the next section we will implement the more powerful IPipelineComponent interface to eliminate some of the concerns that we will raise with the simpler interface. Later in this chapter we will build a BizTalk Scriptor component that could be used as a debugging aid. Although the components in this book are all written in Visual Basic and VBScript, the first two interfaces are available to Visual C++ coders and C++ examples ship with the BizTalk Server itself.

Using IBTSAppIntegration AICs

The IBTSAppIntegration interface is an extremely simple COM interface that exposes a single public method ProcessMessage(). ProcessMessage() takes as its sole input parameter the message that was delivered to the BizTalk Messaging port, and gives you the ability to return a response document. The type library for this interface is stored in btscomplib.tlb. The table below summarises the interface:

Method	Parameters and Meaning
ProcessMessage()	This method processes a document and optionally returns a response. It is called at run time when the server sends a document to a messaging port containing an AIC.
	bstrDocument is a string containing the document contents that have been delivered to the port for processing by the LOB application.
	pbstrResponseDocument is a pointer to the string in VC, or in VB a string, containing the response document to return to BizTalk Messaging.

First we will build an IBTSAppIntegration AIC for Bob's bolts and then we will deploy it into BizTalk Messaging.

Building the IBTSAppIntegration AIC

The Bob's Bolts AIC performs two jobs:

❑ It reads in the purchase order instance from the incoming message by accesses the data inside the XML document.

❑ It inserts the data into the Access 2000 application using ADO.

Reading XML Data

The two common methods for accessing data in XML documents are the XML Document Object Model (DOM), and the Simple API for XML (SAX). Microsoft provides implementations of these technologies in the MSXML SDK.

Both SAX and DOM implementations are contained in `MSXML3.dll`. MSXML 3.0 was released in November 2000 and Microsoft BizTalk Server 2000 is the first Microsoft product to ship with support for this technology. Microsoft SQL Server 2000, which is required for installation of BizTalk, uses the older MSXML 2.6. Fortunately you can install MSXML 3.0 on a machine with Microsoft SQL Server 2000.

The following example requires the MSXML 3.0 DLL as SAX2 was introduced in this release, and its interface is different from the original SAX interface exposed in MSXML 2.6. The MSXML 3.0 DLL ships with Microsoft BizTalk Server so you will have it on your system after the BizTalk Server installation. There is an excellent help file and examples available as part of the MSXML3 SDK, which is available from http://msdn.microsoft.com/xml.

XML DOM and SAX2 are described in detail in the MSXML SDK help files, however it is useful to compare these two implementations to understand why we choose to use the SAX interface for Bob's Bolts.

The XML DOM approach is to load the XML document and retrieve all the nodes into an in-memory tree data structure. Once in memory the data in the tree can be manipulated by calling the methods of the `MSXML.DOMDocument30` interface.

On the other hand, SAX defines an event-based interface; the SAX methods are called as the document is parsed without the document being loaded into memory. SAX is implemented as a number of cooperating interfaces that handle various portions of the document. In particular the context handler interface (`contextHandler`) receives notification of the logical content of a document and gives you the ability to add custom code as a result. The `errorHandler` interface provides a mechanism for writing code that manages errors. SAX 2.0 was introduced in MSXML3. SAX 2.0 adds a number of handlers to the original specification to manage DTDs, declarations and lexical elements.

SAX can parse files of any size, because documents are not first loaded into memory, and it is both fast and simple to use. SAX is also the most useful when you want to build your own data structure representation of the XML contents.

However, because it is event-driven, SAX provides no random access to the document, and it is read-only, in the sense that it doesn't allow you to create changes to the document it is reading. This makes it unsuitable for validation of the document, as well as Extensible Stylesheet Language Transformations (XSLT) that are used for mapping document contents, document creation, and complex searching. The XML DOM is better suited in these cases, at the expense of loading the entire document in memory. Hence, SAX and the XML DOM are complementary, not competitive technologies and the developer should assess which technology is most appropriate for the task at hand.

Bob's Bolts AIC requires read-only access to the purchase order instance and it then transforms the XML data into ADO record inserts. These factors make a SAX2 implementation ideal for our scenario.

Developing Bob's Bolts IBTSAppIntegration AIC

The Bob's Bolts `IBTSAppIntegration` AIC VB project in the download is called `WroxAccessBTSAIC.vbp`. This project contains all the code that is required to accept the incoming purchase order from BizTalk Messaging and deliver it into the Microsoft Access application.

Open the project in Visual Basic. The project references include Microsoft ActiveX Data Objects 2.5 Library for ADO, Microsoft XML v3.0 for SAX, and the Microsoft BizTalk Server Application Interface Components 1.0 Type Library that provides the `IBTSAppIntegration` interface.

The VB Project | References dialog box for the project is shown below:

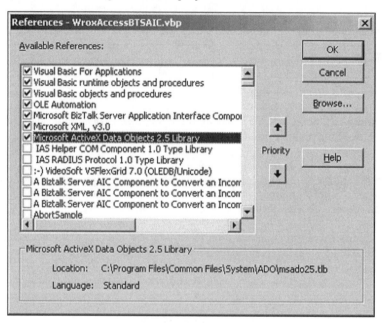

The project contains three source class files:

- ❏ `AICBTSAppIntegration.cls` – which implements the `IBTSAppIntegration` interface and instantiates the SAX parser
- ❏ `ContentHandlerImpl.cls` – which provides an implementation for the SAX content handler code
- ❏ `ErrorHandlerImpl.cls` – which provides an implementation for the SAX error handler code

> **The following example is designed to perform a useful task, taking a purchase order and delivering it into Microsoft Access 2000. It is important not to lose yourself in the details of the SAX2 implementation as you first read over the code that follows. The actual code required to satisfy BizTalk Server's application integration requirements is no more than 3 lines. The remaining code is required to satisfy the legacy application's requirements. This is fairly typical of any BizTalk Server integration project.**

First let's examine the `AICBTSAppIntegration.cls` file.

AICBTSAppIntegration.cls

This class implements the `IBTSAppIntegration` interface. It contains the `ProcessMessage()` method that BizTalk Messaging calls to execute the AIC. The code also calls methods, stored in the other class files, to parse the incoming message and deliver it into Microsoft Access. As you can see from the following listing, the code required to write an `IBTSAppIntegration` AIC is minimal.

The `ProcessMessage()` method function call carries the incoming purchase order data, `bstrDocument`, as a string to the method.

```
Implements IBTSAppIntegration
' This component implements the IBTSAppIntegration interface

Private Function IBTSAppIntegration_ProcessMessage(ByVal bstrDocument As String) _
                                                                As String
```

The `SAXXMLReader30` object is instantiated along with the `contentHandler` and `errorHandler` objects that provide the SAX handlers for reading the document and responding to errors:

```
Dim reader As SAXXMLReader30
Dim contentHandler As ContentHandlerImpl
Dim errorHandler As ErrorHandlerImpl
Dim poFileName As String

Set reader = New SAXXMLReader30              ' This one will do the work
                                             ' These ones will receive
Set contentHandler = New ContentHandlerImpl  ' parsing events
Set errorHandler = New ErrorHandlerImpl      ' and errors
```

The SAX reader `contentHandler` property is assigned to the new `contentHandler` object, and the SAX reader `errorHandler` property is assigned to the new `errorHandler` object:

```
Set reader.contentHandler = contentHandler   ' And they should
Set reader.errorHandler = errorHandler       ' work together
```

The actual work of parsing the document and inserting records into the Microsoft Access database is completed by the `reader.parse()` method that accepts the incoming purchase order document, `bstrDocument`, as its only parameter. Finally all the objects are released:

```
reader.parse bstrDocument                    ' Parse it

Set contentHandler = Nothing
Set errorHandler = Nothing
Set reader = Nothing
End Function
```

The parsing code that is run when `reader.parse()` is called is contained inside the `ContentHandler` routine, which we will examine next.

ContentHandlerImpl.cls

The listing for the `ContentHandler` looks more complex than the previous fragment, but remember that we have already implemented the `IBTSAppIntegration` interface required to use this code inside a BizTalk Messaging port and the code presented here is used to parse the XML document and load it into Microsoft Access. In a SAX implementation the `contentHandler` class, as its name suggests, handles the content, or data, inside our purchase order. In our example this is where most of the work is performed. The SAX interface provides a whole bunch of methods corresponding to events that are generated as the document is parsed. For our purposes we will only write code inside three of these methods:

❑ `startDocument()` – which receives notification when the document is first loaded into the parser.

❑ `startElement()` – which hat receives notification as the parser moves to the start of every new XML element in the document.

❑ `endDocument()` – which receives notification when the document processing is completed.

Note: Even though we only write code inside three of the methods, you must declare all of the methods for the interface for Visual Basic to compile the code sample. To learn more about interfaces review the Visual Basic documentation.

This class file implements the `IVBSAXContentHandler` class. First we declare an `ADODB.Connection` that we will use in the code that follows to transfer data from the incoming purchase order to Bob's Access database. We also declare an `OrderID` variable that is used to overcome a SAX limitation that the document state is not saved during processing.

```
Option Explicit

'The next line is important - it says what is implemented
Implements IVBSAXContentHandler
Private AccessCon As ADODB.Connection
Private OrderID As Double
```

The `startDocument()` method initializes the ADO database connection to the database. A `Connection` object is instantiated, the `ConnectionTimeOut` and `ConnectionString` values are set, the `Connection` is opened, and a transaction is started. Notice that the `ConnectionString` is hard-coded into this component. We could have placed this value in a Universal Data Link (UDL) file, or added some code to read the value from the registry and indeed this would have been much better style. However, I wanted to emphasize that the `IBTSAppIntegration` interface provides no extensible mechanism to pass parameters to the implementation code, because in the `IPipelineComponent` example that follows we will fix this design flaw.

```
Private Sub IVBSAXContentHandler_startDocument()
        Set AccessCon = CreateObject("ADODB.Connection")
        AccessCon.ConnectionTimeout = 30
        AccessCon.ConnectionString = "Provider=Microsoft.Jet.OLEDB.4.0;Data _
        Source=C:\software\BobsBoltsAccessApp\BobsAccessDB.mdb; _
        Persist Security Info=False"
        AccessCon.Open
        AccessCon.BeginTrans
End Sub
```

Note: If you did not install the code sample in the folder c:\software then change the AccessCon.ConnectionString to reflect the location of BobsAccessDB.mdb.

The startElement() method parses each of the elements in the purchase order. The structure of the code in this method is an if... else block that handles the two important elements in the XML document, the Header and Item fields. When the parser reaches the element name Header the values of each of its attributes (CustomerID, OrderDate, RequiredDate, and CustomerOrderID) are determined using sucessive oAttributes.getValueFromName(strNamespaceURI, AttributeName) calls and these are inserted into the database on the same connection that we created in the startDocument() method.

```
Private Sub IVBSAXContentHandler_startElement(strNamespaceURI As String, _
                        strLocalName As String, strQName As String, _
                        ByVal oAttributes As MSXML2.IVBSAXAttributes)
' Called for each element when starting to parse
' oAttributes contains all the attribute nodes
' The target document contains 3 elements: The PurchaseOrder, Header, and Item

    On Error GoTo IVBSAXContentHandler_startElement_Err
    Dim strCommandText As String
    Dim RS As ADODB.Recordset

    If strLocalName = "Header" Then
        ' We are using dynamic SQL for clarify of this example in practice
        ' put this code in an Access Query stored in the DB. This will insert
        ' a record into the Orders table with the Data from the XML file
    strCommandText = "INSERT INTO Orders (CustomerID, OrderDate, _
    RequiredDate, CustomerOrderID) VALUES (" & "'" & _
    oAttributes.getValueFromName(strNamespaceURI, "CustomerID") & "'," & "'" &_
    oAttributes.getValueFromName(strNamespaceURI, "OrderDate") & "'," & "'" & _
    oAttributes.getValueFromName(strNamespaceURI, "RequiredDate") & "'," & "'" &_
    oAttributes.getValueFromName(strNamespaceURI, "CustomerOrderID") & "');"
```

Now we have created a record in the Order table. The schema for the Order table in the Bob's Bolts Access database includes an auto-number field primary key, OrderID, and we need to find out its value because it is also a foreign key in the Order Details table where we will store the Item records shortly. Microsoft Access provides a way to do this by sending the SQL query "SELECT @@IDENTITY" to the database. Effectively this code re-queries the database to find out what auto-number was used in the previous record insert. We take this value of the auto-number and save it in the private variable OrderID. We need to save this value in memory because SAX reads in a serial manner from the start to the end of the document without saving the document in memory or providing a means to search backwards. We will need to use the OrderID value to save the Item details.

```
    AccessCon.Execute strCommandText
    strCommandText = "Select @@IDENTITY"
    Set RS = AccessCon.Execute(strCommandText)
    OrderID = RS.Fields(0)
    Set RS = Nothing
```

When the parser reaches the Item element the code adds a new record to the Order Details table with the values of the ProductID and Quantity attributes and the OrderID variable that we saved in the previous step.

```
    ElseIf strLocalName = "Item" Then
        ' We are using dynamic sql for clarify of this example in practice put
        ' this code in an Access Query stored in the DB
    strCommandText = "INSERT INTO [Order Details] (OrderID, _
            ProductID, Quantity) VALUES ("& OrderID & "," & "'" & _
```

```
        oAttributes.getValueFromName(strNamespaceURI, "ProductID") & "'," & "'" & _
        oAttributes.getValueFromName(strNamespaceURI, "Quantity") & "');"
    AccessCon.Execute strCommandText
  End If
  Exit Sub
```

The `On Error` code rolls back the transaction so that inserts on the `Order` and `Order Details` records are either both completed or neither is completed.

```
IVBSAXContentHandler_startElement_Err:
    AccessCon.RollbackTrans
End Sub
```

The `endDocument()` method contains code to commit the transaction and clears the database connection:

```
Private Sub IVBSAXContentHandler_endDocument()
    AccessCon.CommitTrans
    AccessCon.Close
    Set AccessCon = Nothing
End Sub
```

The `Implements` keyword in VB requires the entire API of the `IVBSAXContentHandler` interface to be declared, but in this case no code is added to following methods:

```
Private Sub IVBSAXContentHandler_endPrefixMapping(strPrefix As String)
End Sub

Private Sub IVBSAXContentHandler_ignorableWhitespace(strChars As String)
End Sub

Private Sub IVBSAXContentHandler_processingInstruction(target As String, _
                                                  data As String)
End Sub

Private Sub IVBSAXContentHandler_skippedEntity(strName As String)
End Sub

Private Sub IVBSAXContentHandler_startPrefixMapping(strPrefix As String, _
                                                  strURI As String)
End Sub
```

> We deliberately keep the code simple and clear in this example by using embedded SQL and monolithic components. When you are writing your own components you should follow the proper n-tier design guidelines of separating the database code into stored procedures, or Access queries in this case, and providing a data access component to retrieve this information to the business logic component layer. If you follow these guidelines you will create a significantly higher performing, more scalable solution as stored procedure code can be pre-parsed, compiled, and stored in the database whereas dynamic SQL must be passed across the network, parsed, and compiled each time it is sent to the database.

Finally, let's examine the error handler class of the SAX interface.

ErrorHandlerImpl.cls

The `ErrorHandler` file implements the SAX error handler interface. For Bob's Bolts it is sufficient to add code to the `fatalError()` method that is called when parsing is forced to abort only. The code inside this method bubbles up error messages to the calling class. The other methods are declared to satisfy the `IVBSAXErrorHandler` interface requirements, but no code is added to them.

```
Option Explicit
Implements IVBSAXErrorHandler

Private Sub IVBSAXErrorHandler_fatalError(ByVal oLocator _
As MSXML2.IVBSAXLocator, strError As String, ByVal nErrorCode As Long)
    Err.Raise vbObjectError+100, "IVBSAXErrorHandler_fatalError:" & strError
End Sub

Private Sub IVBSAXErrorHandler_warning(ByVal oLocator As MSXML2.IVBSAXLocator, _
                        strError As String, ByVal nErrorCode As Long)
End Sub

Private Sub IVBSAXErrorHandler_error(ByVal oLocator As MSXML2.IVBSAXLocator, _
                        strError As String, ByVal nErrorCode As Long)
End Sub
```

Compile the `IBTSAppIntegration` component to make the DLL `WroxAccessBTSAIC.dll`. In the next section we will deploy this component into BizTalk Messaging.

Deploying the IBTSAppIntegration AIC

Deploying the `IBTSAppIntegration` component involves two steps:

❑ Registering the `IBTSAppIntegration` AIC

❑ Adding the `IBTSAppIntegration` AIC to BizTalk Messaging

Registering the IBTSAppIntegration AIC

The `IBTSAppIntegration` project output is the ActiveX library, `WroxAccessBTSAIC.dll`. Compiling the source to a DLL, however, is not quite enough to make the `IBTSAppIntegration` component useful to the BizTalk Messaging sub-system. To explain why this is the case, you need to understand the history of BizTalk Messaging.

The underlying infrastructure for BizTalk Messaging is the Microsoft Commerce Server pipeline technology that was first used in Microsoft Site Server, Commerce Server 3.0. Commerce Server pipelines are used to insulate business logic from ASP pages, so you can think of them as the precursors to BizTalk Orchestration. The Commerce Server product line includes a Pipeline Editor that lets the user add components to a linear, staged pipeline. Developers can mark their components as being available only at a specific stage in a pipeline such as the shipping stage, or in a specific pipeline, such as only being available for the purchase pipeline. There is a GUID category ID value associated with each pipeline, and each stage in a pipeline. As you will see in the `IPipelineComponent` discussion in the next section, BizTalk Server is compatible with existing Commerce Server components, and because of this you need to satisfy some requirements to ensure backwards compatibility.

Although the user is insulated from this through the user-interface, BizTalk Messaging is a pipeline. Components that implement the `IBTSAppIntegration` interface are installed into the pipeline and must be associated with two category IDs in the registry to specify their position in the pipeline and the specific pipeline they are to be used with. Presently, only a single position and a single pipeline are available for developers to install AICs into BizTalk Messaging. As a result the first category ID below marks the component for use in the BizTalk Server Messaging pipeline while the second specifies the position of the component in the pipeline. Both of these values are constant across all `IBTSAppIntegration` components.

There are two ways in which you can register `IBTSAppIntegration` components.

Using regsvr32.exe

When you register the component using `regsvr32`, an unconfigured COM+ application is created. Find the GUID CLSID in the registry, and then add the two GUID category ids from the example below to the implemented key. The process of registration is similar to the one carried out on the functoid in Chapter 4, with the `.reg` file being merged with the existing registry. The exported registry script below shows the two GUID values that are required for an AIC that has a GUID of {F0B9E7E4-748A-480F-B3CD-DF7384840800}. Note that this is the GUID of an example component; by definition a GUID is a unique number and so your component will have a different GUID value.

> *You should back-up your registry before editing key values. The registry is the Windows 2000 database repository for computer configuration information and should you change the wrong information inside the registry you may leave the system in an inconsistent state.*

```
REGEDIT4
[HKEY_CLASSES_ROOT\CLSID\{F0B9E7E4-748A-480F-B3CD-DF7384840800}\Implemented
Categories\{5C6C30E7-C66D-40E3-889D-08C5C3099E52}]
[HKEY_CLASSES_ROOT\CLSID\{F0B9E7E4-748A-480F-B3CD-DF7384840800}\Implemented
Categories\{BD193E1D-D7DC-4B7C-B9D2-92AE0344C836}]
```

Using COM+

Now for the good news – if instead of registering your component as non-configured COM+ component using `regsvr32`, you open up Component Services and add the component to a package inside COM+, that is create a configured component, then the BizTalk Messaging user interface will automatically find it and there is no need to add registry values.

If you wish to debug your component inside COM+ you should set the `TransactionMode` property for the component in VB to `NoTransactions` rather than the default `NotanMTSObject`. You can then use the VB debugger in the IDE to set breakpoints in your components that are triggered on the delivery of documents through the messaging channels to a port containing the AIC. Having the VB debugger available makes it significantly easier to find issues inside AICs. What's more, once you have fixed these errors simply run the component inside the VB environment and the built in VB Component Services Add-in automatically reflects code updates to your component in COM+.

> *To learn more about COM+ and creating VB components that take advantage of COM+ refer to MSDN documentation or* Professional Windows DNA *(Wrox Press, 2000, ISBN 1-861004-45-1).*

Installation into COM+ has the added advantage of enabling you to set a specific security context for the AIC by using the Component Services console. Non-configured AICs will always run in the same account as BizTalk Messaging, which is LocalSystem my default. Furthermore, nonconfigured COM+ applications will run in process with BizTalk Messaging, meaning that if they are badly behaved they have the potential to take down the BizTalk Messaging services, whereas COM+ server packages will run out of process and not have this issue.

Adding the IBTSAppIntegration AIC to BizTalk Messaging

In the previous sections we built the AIC that will consume an XML purchase order and insert the contents into a Microsoft Access database. Next, we either registered and added two category ids to it, or installed it into COM+. The final step required before we can use this AIC is to add it to a BizTalk Messaging port.

So that you can see a complete running example we will build the complete BizTalk Messaging infrastructure including:

❑   Organizations
❑   A document definition
❑   A channel
❑   A receive function
❑   A messaging port
❑   Configuring the messaging port to use the AIC

Note: All the configuration except the last step is not specific to deploying AICs but is required to set-up any BizTalk Messaging process.

Chapters 5 and 8 provide detailed information on how to set up receive functions, channels, and ports for BizTalk Messaging and in a later chapter you will learn how to use the object model that sits behind BizTalk Messaging to generate scripts that assist in the deployment of messaging sites.

Follow the following instructions to setup BizTalk Messaging:

Organizations

In the Messaging Manager, create two new organizations for our trading partners as shown below:

Organisation Name
Bob's Bolts
Ken's Cars

Document Definition

Our trading partners are exchanging a single document, the purchase order. First open BobandKensPOschema.xml (from the download) in the BizTalk Editor tool and store it to the WebDAV root directory. Next, create the document definition in the Messaging Manager as shown below:

Document Name	Specification File from WebDAV
BobandKensPO	BobandKensPOschema.xml

Message Port

Begin by creating a new message port to an application using the Messaging Manager, and configure it as indicated in the following table. Any items in the Message Port Wizard that aren't specified in the table should be left on their default settings:

Message Port Wizard Item	Setting Value
Port To	`Application`
Name	`Bob's Bolts Access 2000`
Application Name	`Press New and create BobsAccessDB`

Now we are ready to add the AIC to the messaging port.

1. Press the Browse button next to the Primary Transport textbox. The primary transport dialog box is displayed.

2. Scroll through the options in the Transport type drop-down and select Application Integration Component as shown below:

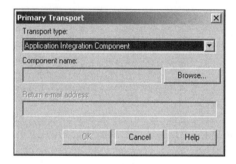

Next we need to specify which Application Integration Component will be attached to this port.

3. Press the Browse button once more and the list of all of the AICs installed on your system will be displayed:

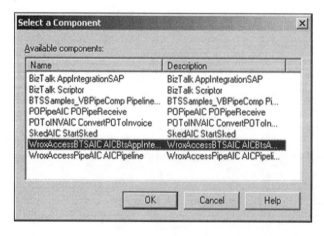

4. Select the `WroxAccessBTSAIC.AICBtsAppIntegration` component and press OK.

If the `WroxAccessBTSAIC.AICBtsAppIntegration` component does not appear in this list then it is most likely that you have not registered the component in COM+ or you have not added the two catalog IDs to the component's CLSID in the registry.

Sometimes for reasons that aren't initially obvious, all of the entries in this dialog box may disappear. This is usually because one or more of the AICs is in an inconsistent state, such as when a newer version exists on the file system and binary compatibility has been broken. If this happens remove your AICs from COM+ and re-add them, and the interfaces will be re-registered; or search for the category IDs in the registry and ensure they point to valid components.

Notice that the `WroxAccessPipeAIC.AICPipeline` component is also displayed in the above list of components (it won't be there on your system yet). This Pipeline component will be the topic for the next section of this chapter.

The completed messaging port dialog box should look exactly like the one below:

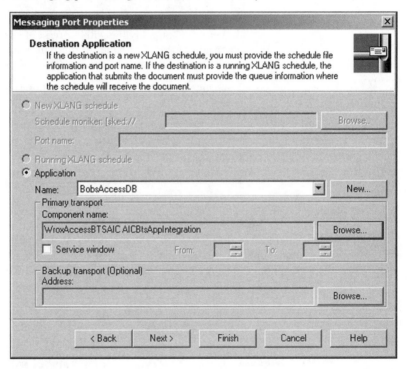

Channels

Now that we have defined the BizTalk Messaging destination, the message port, we need to define the channel to send it to that destination. Create a new channel with the parameters defined below:

Channel Wizard Item	Setting Value
Name	Ken's Cars to Bob's Bolts Access 2000
Source Organisation	Ken's Cars
Inbound document definition name	BobandKensPO
Outbound document definition name	BobandKensPO

Receive Function

Finally we need to define the receive function that waits for Ken to deliver a purchase order by FTP and transfers this purchase order to the channel. Open up the BizTalk Server Administrator and create a new file receive function with the following values:

Receive Function	Setting Value
Name (General Tab)	`Pick up PO from Kens Cars`
Polling location (Services Tab)	This is the directory where you are going to drop the purchase order files. Firstly create a directory on the file system called `c:\Software\BobsPOReceive`, and then fill in this value as: `C:\Software\BobsPOReceive`
Files to poll for (Services Tab)	`Testpo*.xml`. The * is a wild card and tells BizTalk Server to pick-up any file with a prefix of `testpo` and an extension of `xml`. Examples of these files might be: `testpo.xml`, `testpo1.xml`, `testpo100.xml`. You can also use the ? wild card that describes any single character.
Channel Name (Advanced Tab)	`Ken's Cars to Bob's Bolts Access 2000`

Congratulations, you have completed the setup for Bob's Bolts example.

Running the Example

Before we run the example let's review the big picture one more time. We have created a directory on the file system called `C:\Software\BobsPOReceive` where purchase orders will be placed. A BizTalk Messaging receive function, called `Pick Up PO from Kens Cars` processes the purchase orders and delivers them to the BizTalk channel called `Ken's Cars to Bob's Bolts Access 2000`. The channel sends the document to the messaging port, called `Bob's Bolts Access 2000`, which calls an AIC to insert records into Bob's master Access database, `bob.mdb`.

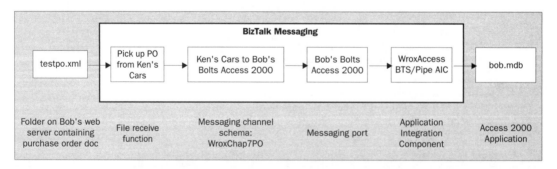

To run the example take the test purchase order instance file, which is supplied as `testpo.xml`, and drop it into the `c:\Software\BobsPOReceive` directory. If everything is set up right then the data stored inside `testpo.xml` will be added to the Microsoft Access database application.

Open up the Access database form called `Orders` and verify that there are new entries in the `Order` and `Order Detail` tables. Each time you drop `testpo.xml` into C:\Software\BobsPOReceive a new entry with a unique `OrderID` is created in the database, and so a new record will be added to the form.

When you are testing the example to examine how it works you will no doubt run the process several times by submitting the test purchase order file. It may be useful to create several copies of this file and change the quantity and price fields in each so that you can distinguish the results of a particular run from the next one.

IBTSAppIntegration summary

`IBTSAppIntegration` components, while extremely easy to implement do have limitations:

❑ You have probably wondered how to pass parameters into an AIC. With an `IBTSAppIntegration` based component it is possible to include these parameters in a header portion of the document itself or in the registry, but not as parameters to the `ProcessMessage()` method.

❑ The second limitation of the `IBTSAppIntegration` interface is that the only information it receives from BizTalk Messaging is the document contents. You might need to find out tracking information about the exchange, or what source and destination organizations were involved in the interchange inside your AIC. Neither of these items is available to an `IBTSAppIntegration` component.

`IPipeline` components provide solutions to both of these issues at the expense of a slightly more complex programming and setup.

Using IPipelineComponent AICs

Before we discuss the semantics of `IPipeline` components, back to our history lesson. Microsoft's early efforts in the B2B arena were pioneered with Site Server 3.0 Commerce Edition and the Commerce Interchange Pipeline in 1997. BizTalk Messaging is backwardly compatible to existing Site Server components through the use of an identical interface: `IPipelineComponent`.

Whereas `IBTSAppIntegration` receives a single parameter, the document itself, the `IPipelineComponent` interface is configurable with the assistance of a second interface called `IPipelineComponentAdmin`.

The `IPipelineComponentAdmin` methods, `GetConfigData()` and `SetConfigData()`, give you the ability to set user-defined properties in the pipeline component.

The interface for the `IPipelineComponentAdmin` is:

Method	Parameters and Meaning
GetConfigData()	This method is used to retrieve fields from the `IPipeline` `CDictionary` object.
SetConfigData()	This method is used to add or update custom fields in the `IPipeline` `CDictionary` object, pDispOrder.

The `IPipelineComponent`'s `Execute()` method receives a **dictionary object** that contains both a pre-defined set of name:value pairs and user-defined properties. The type library for the `IPipeline` components, `pipecomplib.tlb`, is located in \Program Files\Common Files\Microsoft Shared\Enterprise Servers\Commerce, and it is shared between Microsoft BizTalk Server 2000 and Microsoft Commerce Server 2000. Indeed the correct project references to include in every VB project using this interface are: Microsoft Commerce 2000 Core Components Type Library and Microsoft Commerce 2000 Default Pipeline Components Type Library.

The interface for the `IPipelineComponent` is:

Method	Parameters and Meaning
Execute()	This method processes a dictionary object and returns a response document, if available. This method is called at run time, immediately after the `IPipelineConfig` interface's `SetConfigData()` method, when the server has sent a document to the component.
	pDispOrder is the dictionary object containing the document, and interchange and tracking details
	pDispContext is a required parameter for this interface that is not utilised by BizTalk. It is still part of the method signature to provide compatibility between Commerce Server, where this object is used, and BizTalk Server pipeline components.
	lFlags is a reserved parameter.
EnableDesign()	This method is called when the component is in design mode, such as when dictionary properties are being set at design time.

Whereas the `IBTSAppIntegration` interface's `ProcessMessage()` method receives the sole parameter of the document data, pipeline components receive a dictionary object, `pDispOrder`, which contains the document data, in a field called `working_data`, and many additional fields such as the source and destination organization involved in the exchange. The names and descriptions of these fields as well as an example of the data they may contain are detailed in the table below:

Dictionary Name	Description	Example

working_data	Contents of the submitted document	`<PurchaseOrder>`
		  `<Header CustomerOrderID=`
		    `"Bolt Order 100"`
		    `CustomerID="KENCA"`
		    `OrderDate="12/12/02"`
		
		  `RequiredDate="12/20/02">`
		  `</Header>`
		  `<Item ProductID="78"`
		    `Quantity="5">`
		  `</Item>`
		  `<Item ProductID="79"`
		    `Quantity="2">`
		  `</Item>`
		`</PurchaseOrder>`

Dictionary Name	Description	Example
Doc_type	Root Node Name of incoming doc	PurchaseOrder
Out_doc_doc_type	Root Node Name of outgoing doc	PurchaseOrder (no transforms completed)
Src_ID_Type	The type of identifier used for the source organization	OrganizationName
Src_ID_Value	The value of the source organization identifier	Ken's Cars
nbr_bytes	Number of bytes in the message	476
Tracking_ID	ID for tracking, stored in dta_outdoc_details.uidTrackingDetails	{303CC95D-26E9-4ACD-A545-5F5A2F04E700}
in_doc_key	In Document Key, stored in dta_indoc_details.NinDocKey in InterchangeBTA	213
Document_Name	The name of the inbound document definition	WroxChap7PO
in_doc_tracking_id	Tracking ID for in bound document, stored in dta_indoc_details .uidTrackingGUID	{B8BD8382-39F8-4427-B060-D4F541568F77}
Syntax	Document standard property	"Custom XML"
Dest_ID_Type	The type of identifier used for the destination organization	OrganizationName
Dest_ID_Value	The value of the destination organization identifier	Home Organization
submission_id	Submission ID, stored in dta_interchange_details .UidSubmissionGUID	{9A1C8E4C-A029-43C2-BF00-7C3CA5D4F87D}
in_interchange_key	Interchange key, stored in dta_interchange_details .nInterchangeKey	424
Responsefield	Used to return a text-based response to the caller.	Acknowledged/Failed

As you will see later in Chapter 12, many of the values can be tracked in the tracking database.

Some of the values, such as the Tracking_ID *are not persisted to the Tracking database unless specific options, in this case tracking the outbound document, are selected in the channel setup of the Messaging Manager. You will learn how to set up the channel to tracking outbound exchanges in Chapter 12.*

All of the dictionary values are input parameters except for Responsefield. This field is most useful when used in conjunction with an IInterchange.SubmitSync() call where the caller submits a document to BizTalk Messaging, and waits synchronously for a response. The Responsefield can be interrogated to determine if the result was successful. The code fragment below demonstrates such a synchronous call from a document stored in strDocument to a BizTalk Messaging channel called "My Channel". The last parameter to the SubmitSync() call, strResponseData contains the Responsefield value.

```
Dim objectInterchange, strDocument, strSubmitHandle, strResponseData

Set objInterchange = CreateObject("BizTalk.Interchange")
objInterchange.SubmitSync BIZTALK_OPENNESS_TYPE_NOTOPEN, strDocument, , , , , _
,"MyChannel", , , , strSubmitHandle, strResponseData

If strResponseData <> "Completed" Then
     'An error has occurred stop processing
Else
     'Continue processing
End If
```

Let's get back to the main event. It's time to apply our new found knowledge of the IPipeline interface and the IPipelineAdmin helper interfaces, and apply them to the Bob's Bolts scenario to solve several design issues with the IBTSAppIntegration component.

Building the IPipelineComponent AIC

One design problem with Bob's IBTSAppIntegration example is that the database connection string is hard coded into the component. We could have placed this information in a registry key or a UDL file, but it would be easier for system administrators if there was a more direct interface built into messaging to set properties such as the ConnString. We will use an IPipelineComponent to expose the database connection string through the BizTalk Messaging Manager interface. First let's take the Bob's Bolts IBTSAppIntegration code and convert it into an IPipelineComponent.

Developing the Bob's Bolts IPipelineComponent AIC

The Pipeline component project is called WroxAccessPipeAIC.vbp in the download. Open up the project in VB. The structure of the WroxAccessPipeAIC project is similar to the WroxAccessBTSAIC project. It consists of 3 class files:

❑   AICPipeline.cls – which implements the IPipelineComponent and IPipelineComponentAdmin interfaces and instantiates the SAX parser.

❑   ContentHandlerImpl.cls – which provides the SAX content handler code.

❑   ErrorHandlerImpl.cls – which provides the SAX error handler code. The code for the errorHandler() method is identical to that in the previous project and so it is not further described below.

AICPipeline.cls

The main Pipeline AIC class file implements both the IPipelineComponent interface and its helper interface IPipelineAdmin.

The code in the Execute() method is very similar to the IBTSAppIntegration example except for two important differences.

First, before calling the SAX2 reader the contentHandler.ConnString property is set to the value of strConn. This enables the value of strConn to be passed from the AICPipeline class to the ContentHandlerImpl class:

```
Implements IPipelineComponent
Implements IPipelineComponentAdmin
' This component implements the IPipelineComponent and IPipelineComponent
interfaces
Dim strConn As String

Private Function IPipelineComponent_Execute(ByVal pdispOrder As Object, _
                ByVal pdispContext As Object, ByVal lFlags As Long) As Long
    Dim reader As SAXXMLReader30
    Dim contentHandler As ContentHandlerImpl
    Dim errorHandler As ErrorHandlerImpl
    Dim poFileName As String

    Set reader = New SAXXMLReader30            ' This one will do the work
                                               ' These ones will receive
    Set contentHandler = New ContentHandlerImpl   ' parsing events
    contentHandler.ConnString = strConn
```

Second, the directory object pDispOrder("working_data") is passed to the parse method of the SAX2 reader rather than bstrDocument in the previous example because this is the directory name:value pair that contains the document data.

```
    Set errorHandler = New ErrorHandlerImpl    ' and errors
    Set reader.contentHandler = contentHandler ' And they should
    Set reader.errorHandler = errorHandler     ' work together

    reader.parse pDispOrder("working_data")            ' Parse it

End Function
```

The two IPipelineAdmin functions are straightforward. The GetConfigData() method creates a dictionary object, and sets the value a new item in the dictionary called ConnString to the internal strConn variable:

```
Private Sub IPipelineComponentAdmin_SetConfigData(ByVal pDict As Object)
    strConn = CStr(pDict("ConnString"))
End Sub
```

The SetConfigData method performs the reverse role to GetConfigData. It sets the strConn variable to the value of the dictionary connection string:

```
Private Function IPipelineComponentAdmin_GetConfigData() As Object
    Dim objectConfig As New CDictionary
    objectConfig.Value("ConnString") = strConn
    Set IPipelineComponentAdmin_GetConfigData = objectConfig
End Function
```

You must add the `EnableDesign()` method because it is part of the `PipelineComponent` interface and whenever you implement an interface you must declare each of the methods. The `EnableDesign()` method is used by BizTalk server to tell the component it is running in design mode, but you should not add any code to this method. Setting properties on the component in design mode will be covered shortly, but first here is the code for our Pipeline component:

```
Private Sub IPipelineComponent_EnableDesign(ByVal fEnable As Long)
End Sub
```

Now we will examine the `IPipelineComponent` version of the Content handler class that performs the parsing.

ContentHandlerImpl.cls

The `contentHandler` implementation code is almost identical to that which we used for the `IBTSAppIntegration` component except that the connection string is no longer hard-coded into the class. Instead a new property has been added to the form that enables the user to set a variable called `strConn`. The `ADODB.ConnectionString` call in the `startDocument` method refers to this variable.

```
Private strConn As String

Public Property Get ConnString() As String
   ConnString = strConn
End Property

Public Property Let ConnString(strnewConn As String)
   strConn = strnewConn
End Property

Private Sub IVBSAXContentHandler_startDocument()
      Set AccessCon = CreateObject("ADODB.Connection")
      AccessCon.ConnectionTimeout = 30
      AccessCon.ConnectionString = strConn
      AccessCon.Open
      AccessCon.BeginTrans
End Sub
```

The SAX error handler interface, `ErrorHandlerImpl.cls`, is identical for both the `IPipeline` and the `IBTSAppIntegration` components.

Writing the Property Sheets for the WroxAccessPipeAIC

Now that we have built the Pipeline component, we need to build the front-end to the component's `SetConfigData()` and `GetConfigData()` methods so that the `ConnString` value can be edited at design time in the BizTalk Messaging Manager.

Site Server 3.0, Commerce Edition exposed a third interface, `IPipelineComponentUI`, to give developers the ability to build front-end ActiveX components. BizTalk Server 2000 simplifies the user interface coding by using ASP pages instead of ActiveX components. The developer creates two ASP pages with special filenames and places them into the \Program Files\Microsoft BizTalk Server\MessagingManager\pipeline directory where the BizTalk Messaging Manager automatically recognizes them.

The two ASP files must conform to the following naming structure:

❑ *Projectname_classname*.asp – Where Projectname is the filename of the VB project, and classname is name of the pipeline class file. This combination is also called the Prog ID for the component. This file displays the user interface for the Pipeline component.

❑ *Projectname_classname*_post.asp – This file is named as per the previous file except it has the word post added to it. The file accepts form posts from the user interface ASP file and stores them into the commerce dictionary.

So, for the Bob's Bolts example IPipelineComponent AIC we need to write two ASP property pages to set the value of the ConnString dictionary object. Both ASP pages include the standard header and footer code that is the basis for all pipeline property pages.

The user-interface page, called wroxaccesspipeaic_aicpipeline.asp is displayed below:

```
<%@ LANGUAGE = VBScript %>
<!--#INCLUDE FILE="pe_edit_header.asp" -->
<%
call InputText("ConnString")
%>
<!--#INCLUDE FILE="pe_edit_footer.asp" -->
```

As you can see, there are very few lines in this ASP page. Most of the work is completed in the include files and I wrote a single line to call the InputText() method with ConnString parameter as its sole parameter. When this page is executed it renders a text box with the label ConnString as shown below:

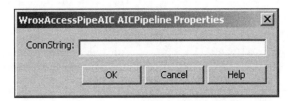

The include files are also located in the pipeline directory. Let's examine what these two include files do, not only because this information is useful to understand when you write ASP page interfaces to pipeline components, but also because it isn't documented in the BizTalk Server help file. If you don't want to create complicated interfaces to Pipeline components you might want to skip over the details of how this actually works and concentrate on the two tables below that provide you with a list of pre-built functions you can use to display and capture design-time information.

The pe_edit_header.asp include file performs several actions. Firstly, it includes a set of HTML edit control functions from pe_global_edit.asp.

```
<!--#INCLUDE FILE="pe_global_edit.asp" -->
```

pe_global_edit.asp itself includes a number of other ASP files such as pe_config_util.asp, pe_dlg_util.asp and strings.asp to support the various HTML controls it exposes, which are documented overleaf:

HTML based edit control descriptor	Purpose
InputTextArea(field)	Displays the field in a textbox.
InputTextAccel(field, accel)	Displays the field in a textbox and creates an accelerator key to access it.
InputText(field)	Displays the field in a textbox.
InputPasswordAccel(field, accel)	Displays the field in a textbox with the password mask and creates an accelerator key to access it.
InputPassword(field)	Displays the field in a textbox with the password mask.
DisplayReadonlyText(field)	Displays the field as read-only.
InputSelection(field, list, accel)	Displays a drop-down box with the field as the label, the list as the items in the drop-down box, and creates an accelerator key to access it.
InputArrayAccel(field, arr, accel)	This is equivalent to InputSelection.
InputArray(field, arr)	This is equivalent to InputSelection except you can't specify an accelerator key.
InputSimpleListAccel(field, listname, accel)	Displays a drop-down combo box with field as the label, from a dictionary object called listname and creates an accelerator key to access it.
InputSimpleList(field, listname)	Displays a drop-down combo box with field as the label, from a dictionary object called listname.
InputOption(name, value)	Adds an option with a specified name and value to a drop-down combo box.
InputRadioAccel(name, value, custom_title, table_entry, accel)	Displays a radio button with a different display name, custom_title, with optional descriptive text included in the table_entry variable and creates an accelerator key to access it.
InputRadio(name, value, custom_title, table_entry)	Displays a radio button with a different display name, custom_title, with optional descriptive text included in the table_entry variable.
InputCheckboxAccel(name, accel)	Displays the name label next to a checkbox and creates an accelerator key to access it.
InputCheckbox(name)	Displays the field label next to a checkbox.
InputNumberAccel(field, accel)	Displays the numeric field in a textbox and creates an accelerator key to access it.
InputNumber(field)	Displays the numeric field in a textbox.
InputFloatAccel(field, accel)	Displays a floating point field in a textbox and creates an accelerator key to access it.
InputFloat(field)	Displays the floating point field in a textbox.

Secondly, it calls the `sGetPostScriptName` function from `pe_config_util.asp` and takes the name of the current ASP file, appends `_post` and returns the value in `postURL`.

```
<%
postURL = sGetPostScriptName()
%>
```

Thirdly, it creates a form to host the HTML controls and sets up the form to post to the page defined in `postURL`. In our example the first ASP page is called `wroxaccesspipeaic_aicpipeline.asp` and it posts to a second page called `wroxaccesspipeaic_aicpipeline_post.asp`, which we will examine shortly.

```
<FORM METHOD="POST" ACTION="<% = postURL%>" id=propform name=propform
style='margin:0px;padding:0px'>
```

Finally, `pe_edit_header.asp` defines a number of hidden fields that are posted to the `wroxaccesspipeaic_aic_pipeline_post.asp`. These are all used to store the `IPipelineComponent` values into BizTalk Server.

```
<INPUT type="hidden" id=compname name=compname value="<% = g_sCompName%>">
<INPUT type="hidden" id=pipedbid name=pipedbid value="<% = g_lPipeDbid%>">
<INPUT type="hidden" id=agrdbid name=agrdbid value="<% = g_lAgrDbid%>">
<INPUT type="hidden" id=configtype name=configtype value="<% = g_nConfigType%>">
<INPUT type="hidden" id=compprogid name=compprogid value="<% = g_sCompProgId%>">
<INPUT type="hidden" id=comppage name=comppage value="<% = g_sCompPage%>">
<INPUT type="hidden" id=configdata name=configdata value="">
<INPUT type="hidden" id=posted name=posted value="1">
```

The footer include file, `pe_edit_footer.asp`, contains code to render either an **OK** button, or the combination of **OK**, **Cancel**, and **Help** buttons at the bottom of the dialog box. It also closes the `<FORM>` and `<HTML>` tags.

Now we will examine the second ASP page, `wroxaccesspipeaic_aicpipeline_post.asp`, which receives the `ConnString` variable from the first ASP page. Once again this page is very simple as much of the work is already done for us by the two include files. The only line that we have written calls the `GetInputText()` method and passes it the `ConnString` field name, and the minimum and maximum field size.

```
<%@ LANGUAGE = VBScript %>
<!--#INCLUDE FILE="pe_global_edit.asp" -->
<%
call GetInputText("ConnString", 0, bufsize_medium)
%>
<!--#INCLUDE FILE="pe_post_footer.asp" -->
```

As well as defining the user-interface HTML controls, `pe_global_edit.asp` defines a set of `GetInput` functions that receive data posted from the Input functions used in the first ASP page. These functions are described overleaf:

Function descriptor	Purpose
`GetInputPassword(field, min, max)`	Processes the result of a password field with specified minimum and maximum length.
`GetInputText(field, min, max)`	Processes the result of a textbox field with specified minimum and maximum length.
`GetSelection(field, min, max)`	Processes the result of a drop-down combo box with specified minimum and maximum length.
`GetInputNumber(field, min, max)`	Processes the result of a text box containing a number with specified minimum and maximum length.
`GetInputFloat(field, min, max)`	Processes the result of a text box containing a floating point number with specified minimum and maximum length.
`GetCheckBox(field)`	Processes the result of a checkbox field with specified minimum and maximum length.

All of these functions work in a similar manner, so we will only examine how the `GetInputText()` method works. The first step is to retrieve the form variable from the previous page. `GetInputText()` uses the `Commerce.Page` object, which is part of the underlying BizTalk infrastructure. This object provides you with an easy way to handle form posts and query strings and validate them for size all in one call. The `GetInputText()` method then passes the result into the `ProcessInput()` method that performs preprocessing and eventually saves the new value in a dictionary object:

```
Set mscsPage = Server.CreateObject("Commerce.Page")


Sub GetInputText(field, min, max)
   if min=0 then
      inp = mscsPage.RequestString(field, "", min, max)
   else
      inp = mscsPage.RequestString(field, null, min, max)
   end if
   call ProcessInput(inp, field, min, max, "text")
End Sub
```

There were a lot of details in the previous section which will assist you in writing complex user interfaces to `IPipelineComponents` should you wish to do so.

If this is not the case, in summary, the steps required are:

1. Create an ASP page named after the component's Prog ID with the "." replaced with a "_". Add one line of code to the ASP per design-time parameter.

2. Create an ASP page with "_post" appended to the base name above. Add one line of code per design-time parameter.

3. Deploy the ASP pages into the \Program Files\Microsoft BizTalk Server\MessagingManager\Pipeline directory.

Now that we have created the raw materials, the component DLL and two ASP pages, we need to deploy them.

Deploying the IPipelineComponent AIC

Deploying the `IPipelineComponent` involves two steps:

❑ Registering the component

❑ Adding the component to a BizTalk Messaging port

Registering the IPipelineComponent AIC

Pipeline components are installed into BizTalk Messaging in an identical manner to `IBTSAppIntegration` components. To remind you: install the `IPipelineComponent` into a COM+ package or register it and add two category IDs to the CLSID. Next you need to add the component to BizTalk Messaging.

Adding the IPipelineComponentAIC to BizTalk Messaging

We will use the same BizTalk Messaging infrastructure that we set up for Bob's Bolts in the `IBTSAppIntegration` example to demonstrate the Pipeline component. However, we want to swap out the `IBTSAppIntegration` component for the `IPipelineComponent`.

Open up the BizTalk Messaging Manager and edit the messaging port named **Bob's Bolts Access 2000**. Change the **Primary Transport** from the `IBTSAppIntegration` component to the `WroxAccessPipeAIC.AICPipe` AIC as shown below:

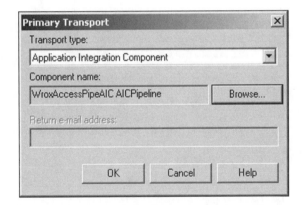

Whereas this completed our set-up for the `IBTSAppIntegration`, we have not completed the set-up for `IPipeline` component because we need to set the design-time `ConnString` property. Copy the two ASP files `wroxaccesspipeaic_aicpipeline.asp` and `wroxaccesspipeaic_aicpipeline_post.asp` into the \Program Files\Microsoft BizTalk Server\Messaging Manager\Pipeline directory if you have not already done so.

Configuring the IPipelineComponent AIC

No doubt when you installed the pipeline AIC into the messaging port you expected to find a way to trigger the two ASP pages to set the `ConnString` property. No matter, how hard you look for it (I looked long and hard the first time I went to set up a pipeline component), you will not find this configuration on the messaging port. It is in fact attached to the messaging channel. Pipeline AICs are still executed on receipt of a message into a BizTalk Messaging port.

So, why do you set up the pipeline AIC properties on the channel? Recall that you can set up many channels to deliver a message from many sources to a single port/destination. By setting the pipeline AIC properties at the channel level you are able to create a unique set of properties for each set of documents that flow through a channel to the port containing the AIC, rather than setting a single set of parameters for all documents delivered to a messaging port.

Now we know that we need to edit the channel, so where do we set the new value?

The user-interface is not especially clear, but the design-time pipeline AIC properties are set through the Advanced Configuration page of the Channel Properties dialog for each channel that is connected to a port containing the pipeline AIC.

1. Open up the Channel Properties for the Ken's Cars to Bob's Bolts Access 2000 channel.

2. Navigate to the final property page by pressing the Next button on each of five property pages.

The dialog box appears as shown below:

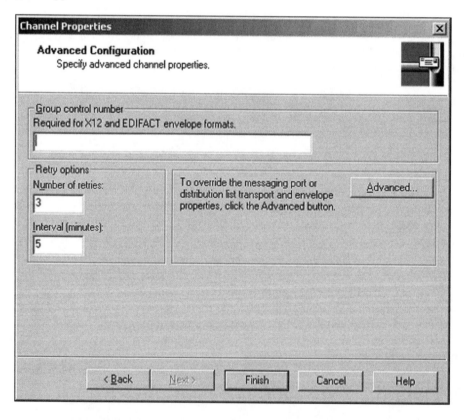

3. Press the Advanced button and a dialog box appears that shows the name of the AIC and a Properties button:

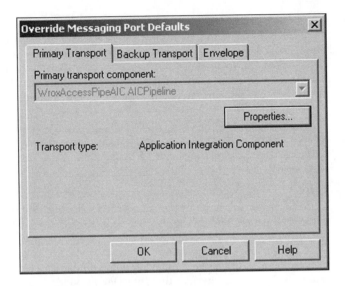

1. When you press the Properties button you execute the property ASP page `WroxAccessPipeAIC_AICPipeline.asp` that you placed in the Messaging Manager\Pipeline directory.

For Bob's Bolts this page displays a simple textbox with the label `ConnString`:

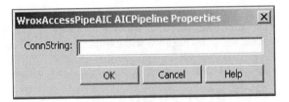

2. Enter the `ConnString` value which may be: `Provider=Microsoft.Jet.OLEDB.4.0;Data Source=c:\software\BobsBoltsAccessApp\BobsAccessDB.mdb;Persist Security Info=False` in the textbox and press OK to save the information by executing the `WroxAccessPipeAIC_AICPipeline_post.asp` ASP page.

Note: If you did not install the software in the c:\software directory then you should change the Data Source to point to the actual directory containing the Microsoft Access database.

If you were not prompted with the dialog box above and instead you received an error message box containing the text: the property page is not available then the ASP files are either missing or incorrectly named.

Scripting errors inside ASP pages, such as missing <%, missing brackets on method calls, and so on are harder to track down because the BizTalk Messaging user interface doesn't return error codes directly to the user – instead you receive error boxes with not particularly useful descriptions such as: "*localhost* [where localhost is the name of the web server] was not found".

However, the property pages are just ASP pages running in the Messaging Manager virtual directory of your default web site so the best places to look for error messages are the web logs for the site. The error description below shows the results of one of my early attempts to create Bob's Access AIC where I did not typecast the `ConnString` to a string value using `CStr(pDict("ConnString"))` in the `SetConfigData()` method. As a result the `HTMLEncode()` method in the ASP page returned a type mismatch because the HTML page was trying to apply string logic to a numeric field.

```
2000-10-25 21:03:24 172.28.101.185 mydomain\myusername 172.28.101.185 80 GET
/MessagingManager/pipeline/WroxAccessPipeAIC_AICPipelineComponent.asp
|155|800a000d|Type_mismatch:_'HTMLEncode' 500 0 3296
Mozilla/4.0+(compatible;+MSIE+5.5;+Windows+NT+5.0)
MSCSProfile=745D84CBF04D14A48AA6FF9C89D722C0F6C3451F1FA0251D531B6B3B2F69456DFDFE90
D5ADFE7B6101847157D4646496AEA8223E2482B87AFA380CB89D6E85A4C8B496C7D37A5F19542211C5
8CE3D1B27634A12BB0D75513ADA3B0C9D0C948CEA42F5A7BDC6FE66AE0883F0BFDB2203AA4D1CF765E
65D09C361D551CF83354E3A6700D4F09DB9B32;+ASPSESSIONIDGQQGQLPQ=JJEBCADDIGEJBILLLKCPM
IBA -
```

If you want to use a higher-level interface for debugging then you can set up the property pages in Visual Interdev and use the debugging interface that InterDev provides.

You can debug VB code inside Pipeline components at run time in a similar manner to the `IBTSAppIntegration` component that was described earlier. You can also debug the `IPipelineComponentAdmin` code at design time as you enter values into the ASP pages. To do this, first set breakpoints in the `SetConfigData()` and `GetConfigData()` methods of your AIC before pressing the properties button in BizTalk Messaging; then you can step through each of the method calls and troubleshoot where appropriate.

This section completes our Bob's Bolts scenario, although we will use the Bob's Bolts messaging port and channel setup in the next section where we will explain how to use simple BizTalk Scriptor AICs.

Using BizTalk Scriptor AICs

BizTalk Scriptor AICs provide the developer with a simple interface to the underlying functionality of `IPipelineComponent`, but through interpreted VBScript or JScript. Site Server, Commerce Edition developers will recognize the Scriptor interface. BizTalk Scriptor AICs are most useful for creating very simple functions or scripts to be used as debugging aids. BizTalk Scriptor components are interpreted and do not provide the best performance in an enterprise environment; furthermore all data types in the scripting engine are represented as variants and this causes issues when you need to data-type to transfer information entered by the user through to a database application.

We will create a small BizTalk Scriptor AIC that provides debugging information by logging the document contents and meta-data into a text file. First we need to replace the `IPipelineComponent` at the Bob's Bolts Access 2000 messaging port with the BizTalk Scriptor. To do this, open up the primary transport dialog box for this messaging port and choose the BizTalk Scriptor as shown opposite above:

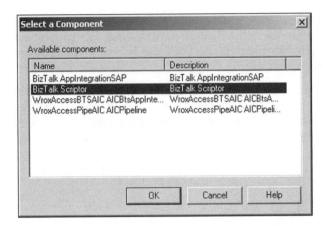

1. Open the Channel Properties wizard for Ken's Cars to Bob's Bolts Access 2000, navigate to the last property page and press the Advanced button to reveal the Override Messaging Port Defaults page.

2. Select the Properties button, just as you did when you set design-time properties for the IPipeline component in the previous section.

The dialog box below appears:

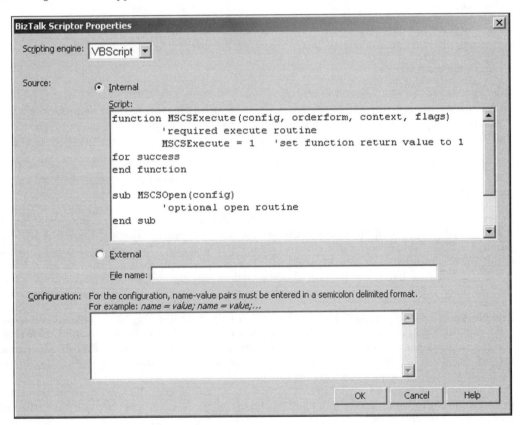

The BizTalk Scriptor component provides you with the user interface to enter script or access an external script file. At the top of this dialog box you choose whether you want to write your BizTalk Scriptor component in VBScript or JScript. Script code is either stored internally with the pipeline, or externally on the file system.

By now it will be no surprise to you that the BizTalk Scriptor dialog box is actually the ASP page `BizTalk_Scriptor_1.asp` located in the **\Program Files\Microsoft BizTalk Server\MessagingManager\Pipeline** directory and that it includes the standard header file `pe_edit_header.asp`, and the standard footer file `pe_edit_footer.asp`.

3. Select VBScript as the language, external source for the script, and enter the file path to `ExampleScriptorAIC.wsf`, which is supplied with the source code for this book.

4. Type: `machinename=BobsMachine` in the configuration box.

What do you achieve by completing this step? `IPipeline` AICs provide you with two methods, `GetConfigData()` and `SetConfigData()` to set and retrieve user-defined properties, however, BizTalk Scriptors have a more simplistic interface. You simply enter the name: value pairs in the configuration textbox and they are appended to the configuration dictionary.

That completes the setup for our external BizTalk Scriptor component. Let's examine how the BizTalk Scriptor works, and the contents of the code inside `ExampleScriptorAIC.wsf`.

The BizTalk Scriptor component interface is a simplified version of the `IPipeline` interface with three public methods:

❑ Function MSCSExecute(config, orderform, context, flags)
❑ Function MSCSOpen(config)
❑ Sub MSCSClose()

You can think of the `MSCSOpen()` and `MSCSClose()` methods as constructors and destructors. If you wish to have some code run before `MSCSExecute()` then you may write the code inside the `MSCSOpen()` method. Conversely, if you wish to have some code run after `MSCSExecute()` then you may write the code inside the `MSCSOpen()` method.

The `MSCSExecute()` method is the only required method for a BizTalk Scriptor component. Its `orderform` parameter is equivalent to the `IPipeline` component's `pDispOrder` dictionary object parameter and holds the same name:value pairs, such as `working_data`.

Whereas user-defined `IPipeline` parameters were added to the `pDispOrder` dictionary through the use of two ASP pages, scripting components take a different approach. The `MSCSExecute()` config parameter is a dictionary object that contains all of the configuration information as name:value pairs. Configuration information is entered into the BizTalk Scriptor component interface directly. The MTS `context` dictionary parameter is required in the method signature but its contents are not available to BizTalk Scriptor components, and `flag` parameters are currently reserved inside BizTalk Server 2000.

The file `exampleScriptorAIC.wsf` (where `wsf` is a windows scripting file), available in the source code with this book, contains a simple VBScript BizTalk Scriptor component. This BizTalk Scriptor component has been designed to assist you with debugging – it writes all of the BizTalk Messaging meta-data out to a log file. Open up `exampleScriptorAIC.wsf` in Notepad. The first few lines of the `MSCSExecute()` method creates a log file called `"c:\software\ExampleScriptorAIC\output.txt"` and opens it for writing, overwriting any previous file of the same name. If you have moved the sample code to a different directory then of course change this filename.

```
Function MSCSExecute(config, orderform, context, flags)
    On Error Resume Next
    Dim FileSys, File, strTmp, stm, strD
    strTmp = "c:\software\ExampleScriptorAIC\output.txt"
    Set FileSys = CreateObject("Scripting.FileSystemObject")
    Set File = FileSys.OpenTextFile(strTmp, 2, True)
```

If the file open operation is successful then the Responsefield, which is the sole output parameter of the orderform dictionary, is set to "Scriptor successfully saved text file" and the next few lines retrieve and format the working_data, which is of course the document data that was sent out of BizTalk Messaging, from the orderform object and append it to a string called a:

```
if Err.Number = 0 then
    orderform.ResponseField = "Scriptor successfully saved text file"
    dim a, b
    a ="working_data:"
        for i=1 to Len(orderform.working_data)
        a = a & Chr(AscB(Mid(orderform.working_data,i,1)))
            b = CInt(AscW(Mid(orderform.working_data,i,1))/256)
            if b > 0 then a = a & Chr(b)
        next
```

The remaining pre-defined orderform dictionary name:value pairs are each appended to the string a:

```
a = a & vbNewLine & "Doc_Type:" & orderform.Doc_Type
a = a & vbNewLine & "Out_doc_doc_type:" & orderform.Out_doc_doc_type
a = a & vbNewLine & "Src_ID_Type:" & orderform.Src_ID_Type
a = a & vbNewLine & "Src_ID_Value:" & orderform.Src_ID_Value
a = a & vbNewLine & "nbr_bytes:" & orderform.nbr_bytes
a = a & vbNewLine & "Tracking_ID:" & orderform.Tracking_ID
a = a & vbNewLine & "in_doc_key:" & orderform.in_doc_key
a = a & vbNewLine & "Document_Name:" & orderform.Document_Name
a = a & vbNewLine & "in_doc_tracking_id:" & _
                               orderform.in_doc_tracking_id
a = a & vbNewLine & "Syntax:" & orderform.Syntax
a = a & vbNewLine & "Dest_ID_Type:" & orderform.Dest_ID_Type
a = a & vbNewLine & "Dest_ID_Value:" & orderform.Dest_ID_Value
a = a & vbNewLine & "submission_id:" & orderform.submission_id
a = a & vbNewLine & "in_interchange_key:" & _
                               orderform.in_interchange_key
a = a & vbNewLine & "Responsefield:" & orderform.Responsefield
```

Next a user-defined configuration parameter called machinename is retrieved from the config dictionary and appended to the string:

```
a = a & vbNewLine & "Machinename (Configuration parameter):" & _
                                config.machinename
```

The string a is written into the file which is then closed. The MSCSExecute() function returns a value of 1 indicating that it completed successfully:

```
File.WriteLine a
File.Close
MSCSExecute = 1 'success
```

347

If on the other hand the initial file creation process failed then the `orderform` output `Responsefield` is set to the string message `"Scriptor could not open text file"` and the `MSCSExecute()` function returns the value of 0 indicating that it did not complete successfully:

```
        else
            MSCSExecute = 0
            orderform.ResponseField = "Scriptor could not open text file"
        end if
```

To complete the `MSCSExecute()` function error handling is restored and the dimensioned variables are destroyed:

```
            Err.Clear
            set File = nothing
            set FileSys = nothing
            On Error Goto 0
    End Function
```

For our simple example the `MSCSOpen(config)` and `MSCSClose()` routines contain no additional code:

```
Sub MSCSOpen(config)
      'optional open routine
End Sub

Sub MSCSClose()
      'optional close routine
End Sub
```

It's time to test the BizTalk Scriptor component: drop the test purchase order, `testpo.xml`, into the C:\software\BobsPOReceive directory and the AIC will create the output file as c:\software\ExampleScriptorAIC\output.txt. The contents of this file will look similar to those shown below:

```
working_data:<PurchaseOrder>
      <Header CustomerOrderID="Bolt Order 100" CustomerID="KENCA"
OrderDate="12/12/02" RequiredDate="12/20/02"/>
      <Item ProductID="78" Quantity="5"/>
      <Item ProductID="79" Quantity="2"/>
</PurchaseOrder>
Doc_Type:PurchaseOrder
Out_doc_doc_type:PurchaseOrder
Src_ID_Type:OrganizationName
Src_ID_Value:Ken's Cars
nbr_bytes:436
Tracking_ID:{B79217EA-5BB4-4968-A6A9-6AD1655C0375}
in_doc_key:189
Document_Name:BobandKensPO
in_doc_tracking_id:{31E434D5-AFB5-4645-9C1C-CC5022FAC144}
Syntax:Custom XML
Dest_ID_Type:OrganizationName
Dest_ID_Value:Home Organization
submission_id:{05D09015-070C-4544-97A2-3D1278EE8DB2}
in_interchange_key:371
Machinename (Configuration parameter):osmium2
Responsefield:Scriptor successfully saved text file
```

This completes our discussion of how to write and use Scriptor components. Any treatment of Scriptor components would not be complete without explaining their limitations and when not to use them.

Disadvantages of Scriptor Components

A major disadvantage of BizTalk Scriptor components is that they can be very challenging to debug. There is no way to step through these components on a line-by-line basis, and writing to a log file is the preferred method of debugging. When an error occurs inside a scriptor component the error is recorded in the Application Log and often using the Event Viewer is your best run-time analysis tool.

A second disadvantage of BizTalk Scriptor components is that all of the variables are declared as variants. The lack of data typing can often cause issues, such as type mismatches, when you are transferring variables captured in scripts to more strongly typed database access components.

If your components have any level of complexity then I would recommend migrating them from the BizTalk Scriptor to Visual Basic and the `IBTSAppIntegration` or the `IPipeline` component interface depending on their requirements. Most of the code will port nicely with only a few alterations – such as renaming the `orderform` object and the debugging abilities that Visual Basic provides are more than worth the effort involved.

Caveats Using AICs

There are two AIC caveats that are useful to remember before we complete this chapter. The first, which if you have been reading carefully you will have noticed is that the failure codes used in the various components are somewhat inconsistent. To return an error message from:

❑ The `IBTSAppIntegration.ProcessMessage()` method use `Err.Raise` which throws an exception.

❑ The `IPipelineComponent.Execute()` method use 1 for failure (and 0 for success) or `Err.Raise`

❑ The Scriptor `MSCSexecute()` method use 0 for failure (and 1 for success) or `Err.Raise`.

When an AIC error occurs BizTalk Messaging will automatically send the document to the retry queue. `Err.Raise` is the preferred method for signalling an error because `Err.Description` will be sent to the Application Log, which makes it easier to diagnose the source of the error. When the retry count has been exhausted the document will be placed into the suspended queue. You can access the documents in the suspended queue using the BizTalk Server `CheckSuspendedQueue()` method of the `Interchange` interface.

A second caveat is that if you create transactional COM+ AICs and then implement abort code using the COM+ `SetAbort()` method calls you will not get the expected behavior. If you use `SetAbort()` then you will disable all of BizTalk Server's database connections and cause them to roll back. If the call to the AIC was synchronous then the only database access is to the tracking database and this will be rolled back and the caller should catch this. If the call to the AIC was asynchronous then document will be delivered directly to the suspended queue. To avoid this use the AIC return values (which are HRESULTs) to inform BizTalk of a failure inside an AIC.

Summary

This chapter explained how to deliver a document from inside the plumbing of BizTalk Messaging to business processes and line-of-business applications.

You learned that messaging ports containing Application Integration Components provide useful exit points to directly interface to legacy applications. Whereas most of the time you spent on BizTalk Messaging in Chapter 5 revolved around configuring messaging ports and channels this chapter was about writing code to create AICs. BizTalk Messaging Server provides you with three different foundations to help you build these components. Firstly, you learned how to use the simple `IBTSAppIntegration` component that accepts the document data as its only input. We used the example of an integration project with Access 2000 and SAX to explain some of the general principles involved in parsing XML documents and passing the data to legacy systems. Secondly, you learned about the more complex `IPipelineComponent` and `IPipelineComponentAdmin` interfaces that allow you to pass parameters into your AIC, and provide you with access to more information about your Interchange. Finally, you learned how to build simple script components with the BizTalk Scriptor.

Once AICs have been created, third-party vendors may redistribute them with their systems. An example of this is the SAP AIC connector that ships with BizTalk Server 2000 Enterprise Edition in the box. Developers can leverage this functionality by installing the component and setting the appropriate properties, without needing to understand the black magic involved in translating from one application to another. This means that a majority of developers will be more productive creating and integrating businesses and business processes rather than spending time understanding the internal specifics of individual interfaces.

In the next chapter we will drill-down into the messaging sub-system and show you how to interface messages with schedules.

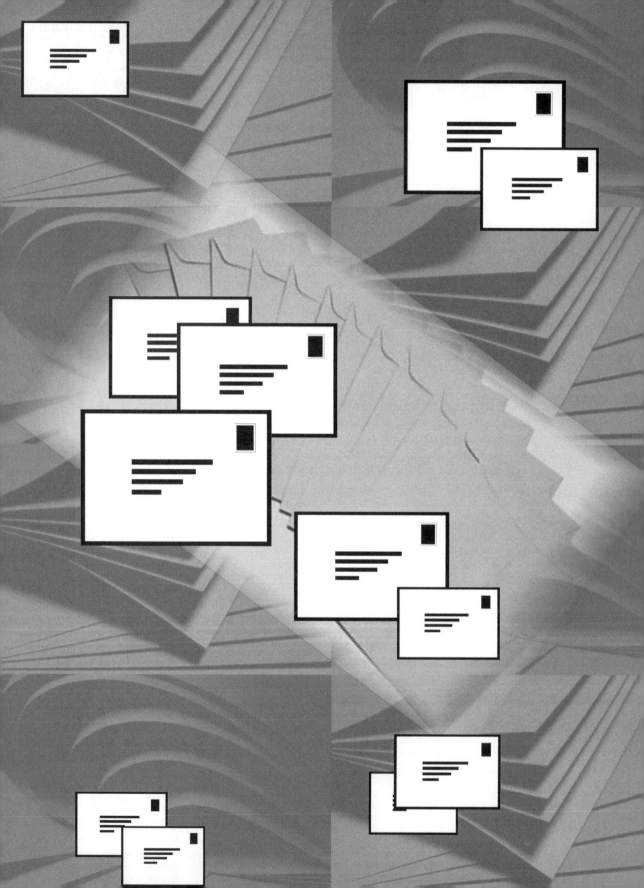

8

Interfacing Messaging with Schedules

In Chapter 7, we used BizTalk Messaging to pass a single message containing a purchase transaction to an application. Obviously there are more steps involved in most business-to-business (B2B) or enterprise application integration (EAI) exchanges than just a single message that is sent to, or received from, an application or organization. These integration problems more commonly involve the outputs of a number of business processes running both within and between organizations.

For example, consider the Bob's Bolts scenario that we introduced in Chapter 7. The following actions could conceivably accompany the purchase transaction:

- ❑ On receipt of a purchase order, Bob may need to send Ken an estimated arrival time of the complete order.

- ❑ On receipt of a purchase order, Bob may also need to manufacture more bolts to fulfill that order or to stock up for future orders.

- ❑ When Bob needs to manufacture bolts he may choose to send out the order when all components of the order are ready, or as each piece is completed.

- ❑ When Ken receives an invoice for his order he also receives the physical goods. This in turn will enable him to continue the process of car manufacturing.

- ❑ Once Ken has completed car manufacturing he sells the cars to his customers.

Each of these steps represents a business process or a portion thereof. A B2B exchange can often be described as the passing of messages from business processes in one organization to a second set of business processes in another organization.

Similarly EAI exchanges commonly involve interacting business processes across applications within an organization.

BizTalk Orchestration provides the ability to represent holistic business processes graphically. The plumbing BizTalk Server uses to send and receive messages to integrate these business processes across application or organization barriers is called BizTalk Messaging. Note that sending an outgoing message from a business process, such as a B2B purchase order, may be just one step in the *middle* of an overall business process rather than the last step. The receipt of a message may **activate** a new business process – such as when a supplier receives a purchase order. On the other hand, it may allow an existing business process that is waiting for a message to proceed, such as when a supplier returns an invoice to the vendor whose overall business process involves sending out a purchase order, waiting to receive an invoice, and then submitting this information into an accounting application.

Too often in the past, developers' toolsets have been biased towards the creation of the individual components of business processes, while not assisting in the creation of a framework for long-running business processes that may span between days and months. Typically this leads to large amounts of unnecessary coding to develop the business process that sits around the individual components. One of the key features of BizTalk Server is that its orchestration environment provides a mechanism to create agile and scalable holistic business processes. When building orchestration diagrams the developer may now think from a business process perspective rather than a piece-by-piece approach. An orchestration schedule may perform an action, such as sending out a purchase order, and then wait for days, weeks, or months before continuing to the next step in the overall business process, which may be the receipt of an invoice. The process of returning a business message to a specific instance of waiting orchestration schedule is labeled **correlation**.

In Chapter 2 you learned how to orchestrate business processes using the BizTalk Orchestration Designer to create XLANG, an XML language based on PI calculus, which was executed by the BizTalk Orchestration COM+ engine. In that chapter you also learned the first piece of the integration puzzle: how to send out a message from a business process defined as an orchestration into the BizTalk Messaging, using BizTalk Messaging binding in the BizTalk Orchestration Designer. In this section we will extend this to show how to integrate messaging with schedules to achieve the following:

❑ Activate a new orchestration based on delivery of a message – to start business processes in response to the receipt of messages

❑ Correlate to an existing orchestration based on delivery of a message – to allow existing business processes to resume in response to messages

❑ Integrate two disparate business processes, created in orchestration, using BizTalk Messaging where either the Internet or an Intranet separates these processes

At the end of this chapter you should understand when to use BizTalk Orchestration and BizTalk Messaging in the solutions that you create, and how to move messages in and out of orchestration

Assumed Knowledge

This section assumes you have a solid understanding of BizTalk Messaging and BizTalk Orchestration. In particular you will need to know how to:

❑ Construct messages using the BizTalk Editor as discussed in Chapter 3

❑ Construct maps using the BizTalk Mapper as discussed in Chapter 4

❑ Construct messaging ports and channels using the BizTalk Messaging Manager as discussed in Chapter 5

❑ Create actions in the BizTalk Orchestration Designer as discussed in Chapter 2

❑ Interface to simple COM or script components using the BizTalk Orchestration Designer as discussed in Chapter 2

❑ Use the XML Communication Wizard in the BizTalk Orchestration Designer to expose message fields on the Data Page as discussed in Chapters 2 and 6

❑ Control flow on the Data page in Orchestration Designer to and from both messages and COM/script components as discussed in Chapters 2 and 6

If you are unsure how to perform any of these tasks, you should review earlier chapters of this book before reading this chapter.

Activating a New Orchestration from Messaging

The receipt of a business message often requires the execution of a new business process:

❑ The receipt of a purchase order initiates a supplier-side business process that culminates in fulfillment of the order to the customer.

❑ The receipt of a faulty merchandise message initiates a supplier-side business process that culminates in replacement of the faulty merchandise.

❑ The receipt of a letter of acceptance from a potential employee culminates in the addition of that new employee to the enterprise's internal systems.

BizTalk Server represents business processes in orchestration schedules, while it sends and receives messages with BizTalk Messaging. In this section we will build a simple example to show **orchestration activation** – instantiating an orchestration schedule in response to a message delivered through BizTalk Messaging. The example will consist of the following steps:

1. A message document is received from the file system into BizTalk Messaging.

2. The document is delivered through a channel and to a messaging port.

3. The messaging port instantiates a new orchestration schedule instance, and passes the message it receives from the channel to the orchestration schedule.

4. The orchestration schedule receives the message, extracts a field from within the message, and displays that field in a message box.

Message boxes are used extensively in this section to visually demonstrate the individual steps in orchestration schedules. In a production environment you should never use message boxes because orchestration schedules will stop processing until you press OK to dismiss them. However, they are useful tools to use when you are debugging your business process in a developer environment.

As you can see overleaf, the BizTalk Messaging configuration for orchestration activation is very similar to the one we encountered for Application Integration Components in Chapter 7. For both cases configuration to activate a schedule, or an Application Integration Component is completed at the messaging port.

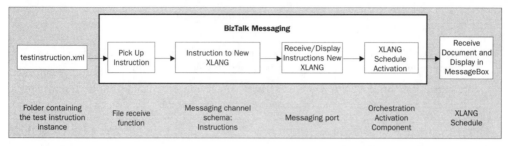

First we will discuss how to create the BizTalk Orchestration schedule so that it can be activated from BizTalk Messaging. Then we will explain how to set up BizTalk Messaging to activate with this schedule.

Creating an Orchestration Schedule for the Example

The Orchestration schedule we will use is shown in the screenshot below:

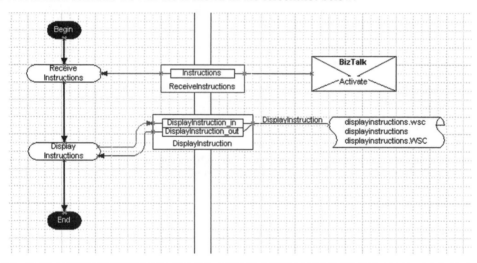

Note: you can download a package containing this schedule (**ReceiveandDisplayInstructions.skv**) and the remaining files used in this section with the software for this book from **www.wrox.com**.

Beware: The text for this chapter assumes that you have downloaded the software and unzipped it into the **c:\software** directory. The **ReceiveandDisplayInstruction.skx** is part of the example located in **c:\software\btmtonewsked**. Although it is much simpler to use the directory structure supplied, you may move the files to other directories or drives. Should you wish to do this you will need to change the following settings:

1. All references to BizTalk Orchestration schedules in the BizTalk Messaging ports should be changed to the new drive and location.

2. All references to the windows scripting components inside the BizTalk Orchestration Designer Script Binding Wizard should be changed to their new drive and location. You may also need to re-run the XML Communication Wizard to re-generate the message specification and finally re-draw the lines on the **Data** page to and from the scripting components as a result.

> 3. All references to the message specifications for any incoming and outgoing messages
> attached to BizTalk or Message Queue implementation shapes should be changed by
> running the XML Communication Wizard on each message and changing the path
> containing the message specification to its new location.
>
> 4. All references to the drive/directory path in the BizTalk Server Administrator
> receive functions should be updated.

The `ReceiveandDisplayInstructions.skv` schedule contains just two actions. The first action is
bound to a BizTalk Messaging implementation shape, and is the key to linking BizTalk Messaging to
BizTalk Orchestration, as you will see shortly. The BizTalk Messaging implementation shape receives
an XML message that conforms to the `Instructions.xml` specification – this specification was
created in the BizTalk Editor. The test message that we will use for the remainder of this section is an
instance marked up to the `Instructions.xml` specification, called `TestInstruction.xml`.
`testinstruction.xml` contains a single element, Instruction, and a single attribute, Continue that
contains a string value as shown below:

```
<Instruction Continue="Everything is fine, Schedule was started
sucessfully"></Instruction>
```

If you examine the XML Communication Wizard **Message Specification Information** page of the
`Instructions` message in the `ReceiveandDisplayInstructions.skv` schedule you will notice
that we have exposed the `Continue` attribute as a message field. Once the `Continue` attribute has
been exposed, it becomes part of the global data space and is available to send to other messages or
components in the BizTalk Orchestration **Data** page.

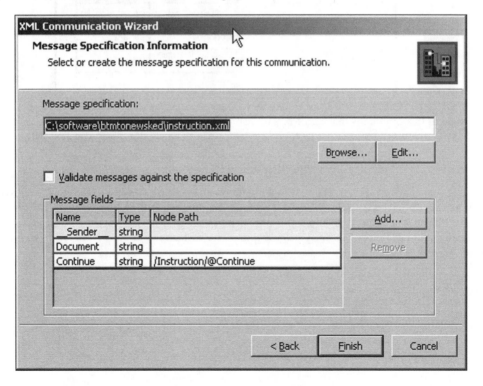

The second action is bound to a simple script component that takes a single input parameter Continue and displays it in a message box. The important code in the script component is shown below:

```
Function DisplayInstruction(Continue)
    MsgBox(Continue)
End Function
```

The easiest way to create Windows Script Component (.wsc) files is to download the Microsoft Windows Script Component Wizard from msdn.microsoft.com/scripting. This wizard takes care of all the GUID and XML formatting issues for you. XML-based COM components are ideal prototyping tools, as you can generate the interface sections for your components rapidly using the wizard, and use these interfaces to complete your orchestration schedules. Some time later, once you have implemented the code that lies underneath the interfaces for each component with Visual Basic or Visual C++, you can then swap out the script components for these production components.

If you examine the Data page of Orchestration Designer, shown below, you will see that the Continue attribute of the Instructions message is bound to the DisplayInstruction_in input parameter of the same name.

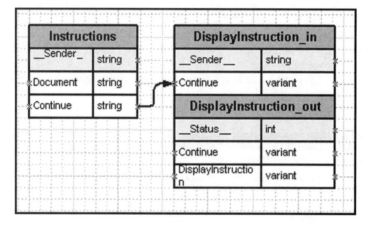

The effect of this binding is that MsgBox will display the text string contained in the Continue attribute on the screen. For our testinstruction.xml message instance, the displayed text will be:

Everything is fine, Schedule was started successfully!

Let's examine the BizTalk Messaging implementation shape more closely. Right-click on the object and examine the properties with the BizTalk Messaging Binding wizard. The name of the port is ReceiveInstructions. Remember this port name, because we will need to enter it in BizTalk Messaging to correlate back to this particular port. The first screen of the wizard is shown opposite above:

The second page of the wizard shows that this port has been set up as a receive port (remember the point of this scenario is to receive a message from BizTalk Messaging and activate a new orchestration instance).

The final page of the wizard is the **XLANG Schedule Activation Information**, and it shows that we have set the receive port to instantiate a new schedule instance on the arrival of a message. Note that there are two restrictions on receive ports that are used to instantiate schedules: only a single action on the left-hand side of orchestration can be connected to each receive port, and the receive port must not be used within a loop. If you want to use a BizTalk Messaging implementation shape in Orchestration to create a new instance of a schedule on response to a message then you **must** answer Yes in this wizard as shown below:

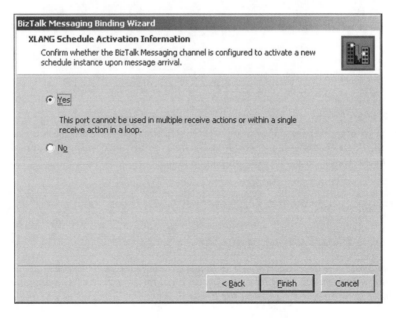

Make the XLANG orchestration schedule from the BizTalk Orchestration designer using the **File-Make XLANG** Menu Item and accept the default name of receiveanddisplayinstructions.

Configuring BizTalk Messaging for the Example

We have now created an orchestration schedule with a BizTalk Messaging receive port that will instantiate the schedule on receipt of an incoming message and display a field from that message in a message box. In this section we will configure BizTalk Messaging to call this schedule. Let's go through the (hopefully familiar) process of configuring message documents, ports, channels, and receive functions to set up the BizTalk Messaging infrastructure.

Configuring Message Documents

First copy the Instruction.xml schema into your WebDAV repository by opening the file from c:\software\btmtonewsked in the BizTalk Editor and storing it into the root WebDAV folder. Next open up the BizTalk Messaging Manager and set up the following document definition:

Document Name	Specification File from WebDAV
Instructions	Instruction.xml

The **New Document Definition Wizard** is shown below:

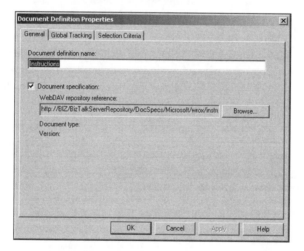

Configuring Message Ports

Begin as usual by creating a new message port to an application, name it Receive/Display Instructions New XLANG, and press **Next**. There are only two settings that are specific to XLANG activation. On the **Destination Application** page, choose **New XLANG schedule**. Enter the path to the schedule:

```
C:\software\btmtonewsked\receiveanddisplayinstructions.skx
```

Then enter the exact name of the orchestration port bound to the BizTalk Messaging implementation shape. In our case this is called: ReceiveInstructions.

> *Note: You must type in this port name so that it is exactly the same as the name used for the port in the orchestration schedule or the process will fail and a XLANG Scheduler WFBinding error will be recorded in the Event Viewer.*

> **Beware!** BizTalk Orchestration uses *ports*, while BizTalk Messaging uses *message ports*. Ports in Orchestration are an abstract functionality such the MSMQ, COM, Scripting, and BizTalk Messaging implementation shapes, while message ports are the destination points for the delivery of messages from channels. Indeed you can think of message channels and ports as somewhat analogous to shipping channels and shipping ports. The port that you specify in the **Destination Application** dialog box of the BizTalk Messaging Port Wizard is the orchestration port defined in the schedule. This overloading of the term port can be confusing at first, but once you understand that a messaging port is not an orchestration port but it may call an orchestration port that may be bound to a BizTalk Messaging implementation shape then you'll have no trouble.

The Message Port Wizard set up information is summarised below:

Wizard Item	Setting Value
Port To	`Application`
Name	`Receive/Display Instructions New XLANG`
Schedule moniker: [sked://	`C:\software\btmtonewsked\receiveanddisplay instructions.skx`
Port Name	`ReceiveInstructions`

This means that the completed messaging port dialog box should look like the one below:

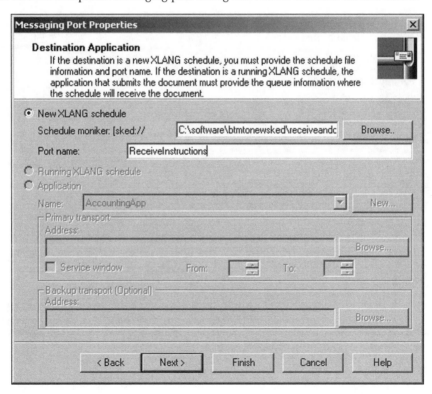

Configuring Channels

Now that we have defined the BizTalk Messaging destination, the message port, we need to define the source organization in the channel. Create a new channel from an application, called `InstructionSource`, to the `Receive/Display Instructions New XLANG` messaging port with the following information:

Channel Wizard Item	Setting Value
Name	`Instruction to New XLANG`
Source Application...New	`InstructionSource`
Inbound document definition name	`Instructions`
Outbound document definition name	`Instructions`

The first page of the New Channel wizard is shown below:

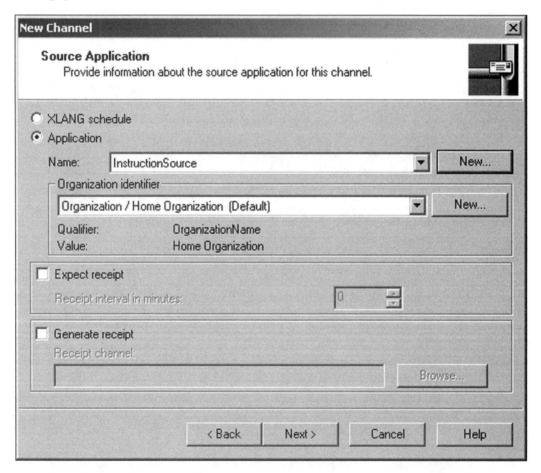

Configuring the Receive Function

Finally we need to define the receive function that waits to receive the message instance, `testinstruction.xml`, into a specific directory, c:\software\btmtonewsked\InstructionReceive, and delivers it to the Channel. Open up the BizTalk Server Administration tool and create a new file receive function with the following values:

Receive Function Item	Setting Value
Name (General Tab)	`Pick up Instruction`
Files to poll for (General Tab)	`testinstruction.xml`
Polling location (General Tab)	`C:\software\btmtonewsked\InstructionReceive`
Channel Name (Advanced Tab)	`Instruction to New XLANG`

Note: the value for the Polling location (the directory where you drop your Instruction file instances) requires that you have created a directory on the file system called C:\software\btmtonewsked\InstructionReceive. If you create the directory after the receive function then it is possible that the receive function has noticed that the directory it is supposed to poll from does not exist and has disabled itself. To re-enable the receive function right click on the name of the receive function, open the Properties *and uncheck* Disable receive function *on the General tab.*

Running the Example

Congratulations, you have now completed the setup for both BizTalk Messaging and Orchestration. To run this example, drop the `testinstruction.xml` message into the c:\software\btmtonewsked\InstructionReceive directory. The message will be picked up by the receive function, delivered to the BizTalk Messaging channel through to the BizTalk Messaging port, and finally to the BizTalk Orchestration schedule, which will display a message box (shown below) on your screen as its second action.

Note the first time you run the example BizTalk Orchestration reads the XLANG Orchestration schedule from disk and compiles it to its own internal representation. This compilation has a small performance hit. The second and subsequent times you run the example you will notice it is significantly faster because it does not need to re-compile the XLANG Orchestration schedule.

Underneath the covers

So how does BizTalk Messaging pass the message to BizTalk Orchestration? One of the fundamental requirements for good application integration architecture is loosely coupling the systems so that dependencies between disparate applications are reduced. The goal is to isolate one application from another in case the second application is down for a period of time. For example if your back-end order processing is down, then this must not stop your web server from collecting new orders from customers. An excellent mechanism to provide this level of insulation is to use message queues between the applications.

In our example case, the web front-end may continue to collect orders and deposit them in a message queue, completely unaware of a system fault in a back-end application. BizTalk Messaging and BizTalk Orchestration are integrated together using a message queuing application. To examine how this works, find the XLANGMon.exe (XLANG Event Monitor) tool located in the \Program files\Microsoft BizTalk Server\SDK\XLang Tools folder. By default the XLANG Event Monitor captures only a sub-set of the COM+ events generated by Orchestration that are most useful to developers. To view all of the events, choose the View-Events Filter menu item and check the COM and MSMQ binding checkboxes.

Now leave XLANG Event Monitor running, and drop the testinstructions.xml message into the c:\software\btmtonewsked\InstructionReceive directory. Once the message is picked up by the receive function, and delivered through the channel to the messaging port, the XLANG schedule is started. When the XLANG schedule is started the XLANG Event Monitor tool will show a new running schedule and the ReceiveAndDisplayInstructions.skx message box will be displayed. When you press the OK button on the message box, the schedule completes and it moves from the Running folder to the Completed folder. It should now be displayed with a black icon in the XLANG Event Monitor tool.

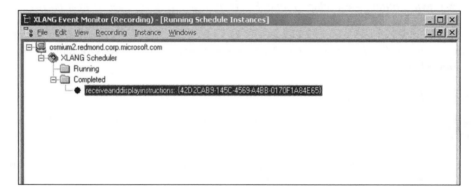

If you double-click on the name of the completed schedule in the XLANG Event Monitor, tool then you can explore the schedule actions inside the schedule on a step-by-step basis. Double click on the black icon to examine all of the steps involved in starting, running and completing the schedule. The results are shown below:

XLANG Event Monitor shows three columns. The first column is the events, such as ScheduleStart and ScheduleEnd. The second column has the actions involved, these are the same names as you used in the BizTalk Orchestration designer when you created the schedule. The third column is the message that was involved. Clearly, XLANG Event Monitor is a very useful tool for debugging events. You will also see XLANG errors in this tool.

Notice that the BizTalk Messaging implementation shape bound to the Receive Instructions action in orchestration is implemented as a message queue (MSMQReceive). If you select the MSMQReceive then you will see on the ChannelID line that the message queue is a private message queue, with the name of the BizTalk Orchestration port and a GUID value. In the screenshot above the value is: .\private$\ReceiveInstructions{6F347663-1E40-43C9-99CD-CC8E906E72} .

If you open Computer Management in the Control Settings panel in your Windows Start menu, and view the message queues on your system while the example is running, then you will see a temporary private queue with the same channel name and a different GUID. The message queue is called a **per-instance message queue** because a unique message queue is created for each transfer from BizTalk Messaging to BizTalk Orchestration. The queue has a label of XLANG Scheduler. When the orchestration is completed, the per-instance message queue is removed.

The maximum size of a message that may be placed in a message queue is 4 Mb. Message queues store messages in UNICODE format and the maximum sized message that can be transferred into BizTalk Orchestration from BizTalk Messaging is a 2 Mb ANSI XML message. If you have larger messages that you wish to send into BizTalk Orchestration then you will need to provide a facility to chunk these messages into small pieces before submitting them to BizTalk Orchestration. Each Windows 2000 server can currently accommodate up to 2.6 Gb of messages at any one time. Like SQL, message queuing is disk intensive – so to optimize message queuing performance place message queues on high-performance disks.

Correlating to an Existing Orchestration

In the previous section you learned how to pass a message from the file system, through BizTalk Messaging, to a new instance of a BizTalk Orchestration XLANG schedule and thus display the message in a message box. However, most B2B business processes involve at least two messages per organiZation:

1. An outgoing message containing a request

2. An incoming message containing receipt information

Similar concepts apply when two different business processes interact on the same machine, or on different machines within an organization. These business processes could be implemented by two short-lived orchestration schedules that each perform a small number of actions and then exit. However, in reality, it is not always the case that complete business processes run for a short time period.

For example when a business sends out a purchase order to a supplier it may take days or weeks to receive back the invoice. BizTalk Server enables you to think in a business process holistic sense, and the above example is a single business process so it should be represented as such in a single orchestration schedule. BizTalk Server gives you the power to create long-running business processes inside the orchestration environment. These business processes might involve sending out a message, and then waiting for a considerable length of time to receive an incoming message before performing further functioning. Clearly this may result in many thousands of business processes running on a machine simultaneously as each starts and then waits to receive further information to continue processing.

To achieve scalability, BizTalk Orchestration utilizes an XLANG Persistence database and automatically dehydrates the BizTalk Orchestration schedules into this database on any sync actions, such as waiting to receive a message from BizTalk Messaging, or at the start of a transaction. The schedule will remain on the system, surviving reboots and the passage of time, until a message is received that causes it to rehydrate from the XLANG Persistence database and complete processing. Dehydration and rehydration are provided for you automatically by the BizTalk Server infrastructure; you do not need to control this manually. You can programmatically determine whether a particular instance is in memory using the `IWFGroupAdmin.InstanceIsResident` property.

Since we may have several instances of a schedule running on a machine at the same time, we must also make sure that messages are passed back to the schedule's instances from which they originated. To achieve this, each orchestration schedule instance has its own GUID identifier, making it uniquely addressable. **Correlation** is the process of returning a message to a specific instance of a running schedule.

In this section, to illustrate correlation, we are going walk through an example that will showcase the following aspects of integrating BizTalk Messaging with BizTalk Orchestration:

❑ Receiving a message into BizTalk Messaging, and transferring this message to a new BizTalk Orchestration instance (this is the example demonstrated in the previous section)

❑ Sending a message from this BizTalk Orchestration instance through BizTalk Messaging, to a second business process that may or may not be represented as a BizTalk Orchestration and could be running on either a different machine within the enterprise or on a trading partner's machine across the Internet

❑ Correlating a message back from the second business process to the **original** business process

The BizTalk Server implementation of this scenario is different depending on the message transport. You will learn how to perform the steps above for the following cases:

❑ Two BizTalk Servers interacting over HTTP

❑ Two BizTalk Servers interacting over a non-HTTP transport, such as file, SMTP, or MSMQ

❑ A BizTalk Server and any external business process interacting over HTTP

In order to compare and contrast each of these cases, we will use the same scenario throughout the following sections and implement it differently where required. Our example will use the following two business processes: an **Instruction** business process will receive an Instruction message and send this to an **Acknowledgement** process, which (you've guessed it) then sends back an Acknowledgement message to the Instruction process.

In a business scenario, the Instruction might be a message such as:

❑ A purchase order

❑ A request for quote

❑ A new employee setup form

The Acknowledgement could be a message such as:

❑ An invoice

❑ A quote

❑ An acknowledgement of an employee being set up in internal systems

These are the seven steps BizTalk goes through to accomplish our example. A more detailed, technical, step-through showing the two interacting business processes is:

1. An Instruction message file is created and dropped into a file share.

2. A new schedule instance of the Instruction business process receives this Instruction file.

3. The Instruction BizTalk Orchestration schedule displays a message indicating that a schedule has been activated, and sends the message out to BizTalk Messaging to deliver it to the Acknowledgement business process (which is either running on an internal application or at an external trading partner).

4. The Instruction message is transferred with BizTalk Messaging to the Acknowledgement business process.

5. The Acknowledgement process receives the message and displays it in a message box on start-up of the schedule. It then creates an Acknowledgement message, which it sends into BizTalk Messaging.

6. BizTalk Messaging transfers the Acknowledgement message between organization or application boundaries.

7. The Instruction business process receives the message back to the same instance that sent out a message to the Acknowledgement process, and it displays the message contents.

The message boxes are simply used as a visual indicator for each step in the process. The complete process with numbering that matches the bullet points above is shown below:

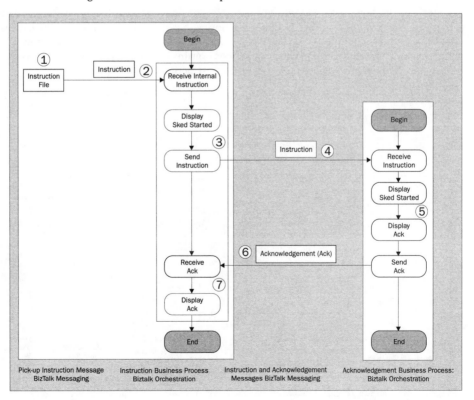

You should be familiar with a number of the individual steps in the scenario already. In particular, the first two steps: retrieving a file, and then delivering it to a new schedule instance were explained in the previous section. For this reason, the instructions below provide only the necessary information to configure BizTalk. If you need additional help then please review the earlier example in this chapter and then the earlier chapters in this book (in particular Chapters 2, 5, and 6). We will start with the HTTP correlation example with two business processes running on two BizTalk servers separated by the internet.

HTTP-Based Correlation Between Two BizTalk Servers

The manner in which you perform schedule correlation is different for schedules exchanging messages over HTTP transports or non-HTTP transports, although there are many common elements. The BizTalk Messaging binding implementation shape in Orchestration has built-in support for HTTP, so this is the example we will examine first.

Let's discuss a generic case of HTTP-based correlation before we move on to build a specific example. Consider two business processes: the Instruction business process and the Acknowledgement process. The bulleted points that follow below will step you though the processes of:

❑ Sending the Instruction message out from the Instruction business process

❑ Receiving the message at the Acknowledgement business process, and returning an Acknowledgement message

❑ Receiving the Acknowledgement message on the Instruction business process side, and correlating this back to the existing Instruction business process

In this generic example we assume that the Instruction business process has been started. The diagram below illustrates the overall process. At this point notice that there are two business processes created as BizTalk Orchestration schedules, and that BizTalk Messaging is used to send messages from the Instruction business process to the Acknowledgement business process and also to receive messages from the Acknowledgement business process to the Instruction business process.

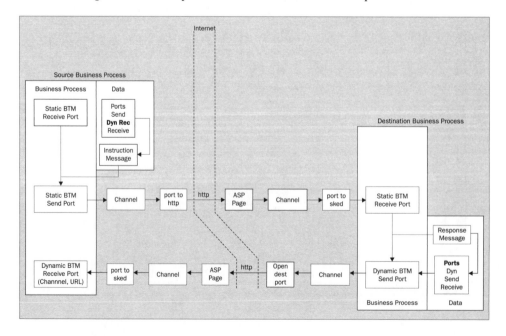

Sending the Message out from the Instruction Business Process:

To configure sending the message out of the Instruction business process, we need to do the following:

❑ Create a static BizTalk Messaging binding port in the Instruction BizTalk Orchestration schedule, to send the Instruction message.

❑ Create a BizTalk Messaging implementation shape in the Instruction BizTalk Orchestration schedule to accept return messages. In the properties of the implementation shape specify the BizTalk Messaging channel to receive return information and `ReceiveResponse.asp`, an ASP page that both receives the Acknowledgement message upon its return and submits it to BizTalk Messaging.

❑ Save the return BizTalk Messaging orchestration port information into the physical Instruction message using theorchestration **Data** page.

❑ Create a messaging port to the Acknowledgement system using HTTP, and an accompanying channel.

Receiving the Message at the Acknowledgement Business Process and Returning an Acknowledgement Message

Now we consider the actions required to configure the receipt of the message by the Acknowledgement business process:

❑ Create a dynamic BizTalk Messaging implementation shape in the BizTalk Orchestration schedule, to return the message.

❑ Flow the return BizTalk Orchestration port information from the physical message to the dynamic BizTalk Messaging Orchestration port using orchestration data flow.

❑ Create an open destination messaging port.

❑ Create a BizTalk Messaging channel to the open destination messaging port, specifying the inbound and outbound document types as the schema for the document to return to the original schema. This channel/port combination works with the dynamic BizTalk Messaging Orchestration port to Instruction to deliver the message from the Acknowledgement business process to the Instruction side of the exchange.

Receiving the Response Message and Correlating This Back to the Existing Instruction Business Process:

Finally, these actions are required to configure the receipt of the response message and its correlation in the Instruction business process:

❑ Physically add `ReceiveResponse.asp`, an ASP page that both receives the message and submits it to BizTalk Messaging and to the web environment on the Instruction system.

❑ Create a BizTalk Messaging port to the running XLANG schedule. This will deliver the message to the schedule BizTalk Messaging binding port.

❑ Create a BizTalk Messaging channel to the port to the Instruction system.

Let's expand on these generic steps and build the complete scenario.

Pick-up Internal Instruction and deliver to new Instruction Business Process

All of the source files for this example are located in the c:\software\skedtoskedhttp directory. The two steps take the internal Instruction, testinstruction2.xml, from the file system and deliver it through BizTalk Messaging to the Instruction Orchestration schedule C:\software\skedtoskedhttp\Instruction.skx.

Configuring a Message Document

Open Instruction2.xml from the c:\software\skedtoskedhttp directory in the BizTalk Editor and save it into root directory of the WebDAV repository. This file is the message specification for our test instance Instruction file, testinstruction2.xml. Open up Messaging Manager and set up the following document definition:

Document Name	Specification File from WebDAV
Instructions2	Instructions.xml

Configuring a Messaging Port

Now set up a messaging port to an application as summarized below:

Message Port Wizard Item	Setting Value
Port To	Application
Name	Receive Internal Instructions2 New XLANG
Schedule moniker: [sked://]	C:\software\skedtoskedhttp\Instruction.skx
Port Name	ReceiveInternalInstruction

Configuring a Channel

Create a new BizTalk Messaging channel from an application with the following information:

Channel Wizard Item	Setting Value
Name	Internal Instruction2 to New XLANG
Source Application...New	InternalInstructionSource
Inbound document definition name	Instructions2
Outbound document definition name	Instructions2

Configuring a Receive Function

Open up the BizTalk Server Administration tool and create a new file receive function to pick up the testinstruction2.xml with the following values:

Receive Function Item	Setting Value
Name (General Tab)	`Pick up Instruction2`
Files to poll for (General Tab)	`Testinstruction2.xml`
Polling location (General Tab)	`C:\software\skedtoskedhttp\InstructionReceive2`
Channel Name (Advanced Tab)	`Internal Instruction2 to New XLANG`

Note*: the value for the Polling location (the directory where you drop your Instruction files) requires that you have created a directory on the file system called C:\software\skedtoskedhttp\InstructionReceive2 first*.

We have now defined the infrastructure to receive a message into the Instruction schedule, `Instruction.skx`. Now let's examine the `Instruction.skv` file in the BizTalk Orchestration Designer.

Receiving Internal Instructions into BizTalk Orchestration, Sending Instructions and Receiving Acknowledgements

Load the schedule source file `Instruction.skv` into the Orchestration Designer. A screenshot is shown below:

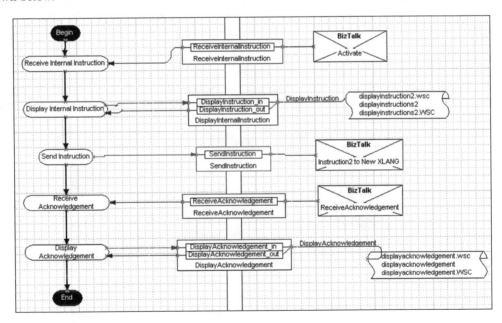

Let's consider each action in turn in the schedule:

BizTalk Messaging delivers the `testinstruction2.xml` to the XLANG schedule through the Orchestration BizTalk Messaging receive port called `ReceiveInternalInstruction`, which is tied to the action `Receive Internal Instruction`. In the BizTalk Messaging Binding Wizard for `Receive Internal Instruction`, the value of **XLANG Schedule Activation** is set to YES. This means that each time a message is received to this port a new instance of the schedule is started, and the text **Activate** is added to the BizTalk Messaging implementation shape.

The second action calls a simple windows script component that displays a message box containing the name of the schedule, the number of the schedule (where Instruction is the first schedule, and Acknowledgement is the second schedule), and the contents of the Continue attribute passed in from testinstruction2.xml message.

Once the message box is displayed, the document is then sent out to BizTalk Messaging with a BizTalk Messaging implementation shape in the Send Instruction action. In the BizTalk Messaging binding wizard the BizTalk Messaging channel "Instruction2 to http" is used to send the message. We will define this BizTalk Messaging channel shortly. The BizTalk Messaging Binding Wizard is shown here:

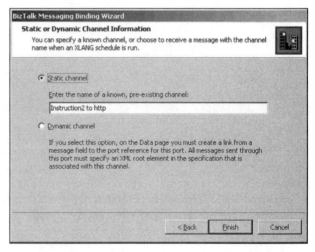

After sending out the Instruction to the second XLANG schedule, this orchestration schedule waits to receive an Acknowledgement. At this point the schedule is dehydrated into the XLANG persistence database. In the BizTalk Messaging wizard for the Receive Acknowledgement action, the value of **XLANG Schedule Activation** is set to **NO**. This is because we wish to correlate the message received in this port back to the original instance of the schedule, not start a new instance of a schedule. In the BizTalk Messaging Wizard **Channel Information** dialog, the BizTalk Messaging channel that interfaces with the schedule is ReceiveAcknowledgement. We will define this channel in BizTalk Messaging later in this section. The URL to receive on is http://localhost/ReceiveResponse.asp. This setup is shown below:

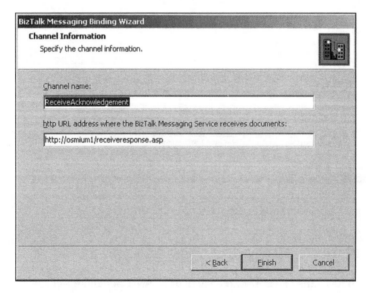

`Receiveresponse.asp` ships with Microsoft BizTalk Server 2000. Copy the `ReceiveResponse.asp` file from the `\Program Files\Microsoft BizTalk Server\SDK\Messaging Samples\ReceiveScripts` directory in the root directory of your default web site.

When the Acknowledgement message is received it is displayed in a message box in the action `Display Acknowledgement`.

Now turn to the **Data** page for this Instruction schedule, which shows the message flow. This is shown below:

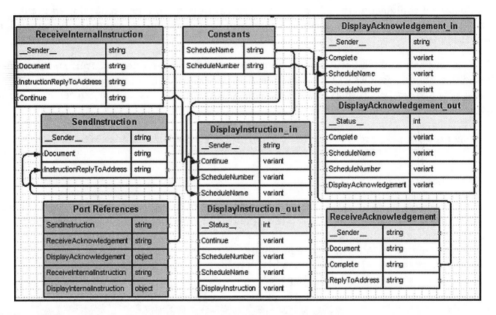

This diagram is quite complex so let's look at the main building blocks first.

There are three messages:

❑   The `ReceiveInternalInstruction` message, which contains the incoming internal Instruction

❑   The `SendInstruction` message, which contains the message to send out to the Acknowledgement process

❑   The `ReceiveAcknowledgement` message which contains the message returned from the Acknowledgement process

There are also two windows script components:

❑   `DisplayInstruction`, which displays the Instruction message to be sent to the Acknowledgement process

❑   `DisplayAcknowledgement`, which displays the Acknowledgment message returned from the Acknowledgement process

We have defined two constants:

- ❑ ScheduleName with a value of instruction.skv
- ❑ ScheduleNumber with a value of 1

These constants are used so that we can call the same windows script component on both the Instruction and the Acknowledgement side and display the name of the schedule, and its order (for example, "The instruction schedule is the first schedule") in a message box.

The document contained in the ReceiveInternalInstruction message is flowed to the SendInstruction message, so that the contents of the document are sent to the Acknowledgement business process.

The two constants and the Continue attribute from the ReceiveInternalInstruction message are flowed to a simple windows COM script, DisplayInstruction, as input parameters. DisplayInstruction displays these parameters in a message box, as you can see from the script shown below:

```
function DisplayInstruction(Continue, ScheduleNumber, ScheduleName)
    MsgBox("Schedule Started: " & ScheduleNumber & " (" & ScheduleName & "): " _
        & Continue)
end function
```

We need to save a piece of state from the schedule in the outgoing message to the Acknowledgement business process so that we can later return to the original instance of the Instruction schedule. In the outgoing message specification, instruction2.xml, we have created a field called InstructionReplyToAddress. The incoming Instruction message instance, testinstruction2.xml contained this **blank** field. It is important that this field is initially blank, because we will set it through the Data page.

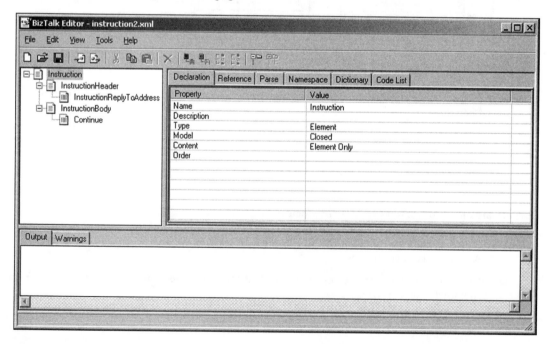

Flow the `ReceiveAcknowledgement` port string to the `InstructionReplyToAddress` field of the `SendInstruction` message. So what is stored in the `ReceiveAcknowledgement` port string? The string looks similar to this:

http://localhost/receiveresponse.asp?channel=receiveacknowledgement&qpath=machinename.mydomain.com\private$\receiveacknowledgement{72aae5ca-4138-92f1-3b651e5ed787}

As you can see this string contains the return URL and channel that you earlier specified in the BizTalk Messaging Wizard for the `ReceiveAcknowledgement` Orchestration port, as well as a per-instance message queue. When a message is returned to this per-instance message queue it will correlate to the schedule. When the Acknowledgement organization wishes to return back to this specific instance of the orchestration schedule it needs to use this information, as we shall see later.

Finally, once the Acknowledgement message is received from the Acknowledgement business process, the Windows scripting object `DisplayAcknowledgement` displays it in a message box. This object is very similar to the `DisplayInstruction` object: it accepts three parameters, the constants `ScheduleName` and `ScheduleNumber`, and the `Complete` attribute from the **Acknowledgement** document.

Sending Instructions through BizTalk Messaging to a New BizTalk Orchestration via HTTP

The `Send Instruction` action of the XLANG schedule delivers the outgoing `Instruction` message to the BizTalk Messaging channel `Instruction2 to http`. This channel in turn delivers the message to a messaging port that sends the message over the Internet, using HTTP to the Acknowledgement business process.

At the Acknowledgement side of the exchange, the ASP page `receiveinstruction.asp` receives the message, and delivers it via BizTalk Messaging to a new schedule. The most important line in this ASP page is the call to the `Submit()` method of the `Interchange` interface, with the name of the channel to deliver the message to, and the `openness` parameter of 1 (not open):

```
Call Interchange.Submit(1,PostedDocument,,,,,,"Instruction2 to New XLANG")
```

Copy `receiveinstruction.asp` to your web root directory for the Acknowledgement business process. If you are creating this example on a single machine just copy it to your web root directory. Let's now cover the BizTalk Messaging setup for this step. Firstly, we need to set up the HTTP messaging port to send the Instruction message from the Instruction organization to the Acknowledgement organization.

Configuring a Message Port to HTTP

Create a new message port to a new organization with the following values:

Message Port Wizard Item	Setting Value
Port To	`Organization`
Name	`http to acknowledgement`
Organisation...New	`Acknowledgement Org`
Primary Transport	`http://localhost/receiveinstruction.asp`

> **Note:** If you are setting up this scenario across two machines then replace `localhost` with the name of the target machine.

Configuring a Channel to HTTP Port

Create a new channel from an application with the following information:

Channel Wizard Item	Setting Value
Name	`Instruction2 to http`
Source	`XLANG Schedule`
Inbound document definition name	`Instructions2`
Outbound document definition name	`Instructions2`

Now we will configure the messaging port and channel on the Acknowledgement business process side that receives the Instruction message from `receiveinstruction.asp` and delivers it to the Acknowledgement BizTalk Orchestration schedule.

Configuring a Message Port to Acknowledgement XLANG

Create a new message port to a new application with the following values:

Message Port Wizard Item	Setting Value
Port To	`Application`
Name	`Receive Instructions2 to Acknowledgement.skx New XLANG`
New XLANG Schedule	`C:\software\skedtoskedhttp\acknowledgement.skx`
Port Name	`ReceiveInstructions2`

Configuring a Channel from the ASP Page to Acknowledgement XLANG Messaging Port

Create a new channel from an application with the following information:

Channel Wizard Item	Setting Value
Name	`Instruction2 to New XLANG`
Source	`XLANG Schedule`
Inbound document definition name	`Instructions2`
Outbound document definition name	`Instructions2`

We have now configured BizTalk Messaging to deliver the Instruction to the Acknowledgement XLANG schedule. In the next sub-section we will examine the contents of this schedule.

Receiving Instructions and Sending Acknowledgments in BizTalk Orchestration

Take a look at the source of the XLANG schedule for the Acknowledgement business process, stored in `acknowledgment.skv`:

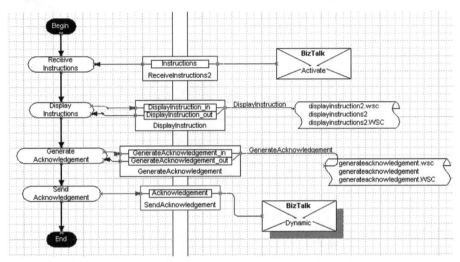

The schedule receives the `instructions2` message through the BizTalk Messaging port from the `Instruction2 to New XLANG` channel. In the same way as we did for the BizTalk Messaging implementation shape that activated the Instruction business process, **XLANG Schedule Activation** is set to `YES` for this BizTalk Messaging binding, because a new instance of the schedule is created on receipt of every message.

Once the message is received into the `displayinstruction2.wsc` component (identical to the one used in `instruction.skx`), it is called to display the message contents. The windows scripting component `generateacknowledgement` creates an Acknowledgement message by loading the XML instance `testacknowledgement.xml` from the file system and returning it to the schedule. Once the XML has been loaded, the function displays a message box as shown:

The message box contains a string representation of the Acknowledgement message. The code for `generateacknowledgement` is shown below:

```
Function GenerateAcknowledgement()
    Dim XMLDoc
    Set XMLDoc = CreateObject("Msxml2.DOMDocument")
    XMLDoc.load("c:\software\skedtoskedhttp\testacknowledgement.xml")
    GenerateAcknowledgement = XMLDoc.xml
    MsgBox("Acknowledgement generated :" & CStr(XMLDoc.xml))
    Set XMLDoc = Nothing
End Function
```

Finally the Acknowledgement message is sent out from the schedule through a **dynamic** BizTalk Messaging Orchestration port. The use of a dynamic port (shown below) is vital for correlation back to the same instance of the Instruction schedule.

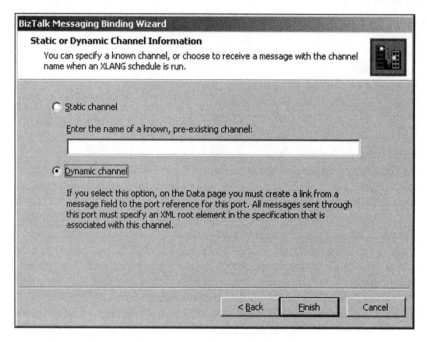

Notice we do not specify a target channel in the BizTalk Messaging Wizard. We will set this information on the Data page. Open up the Data page for the Acknowledgement schedule:

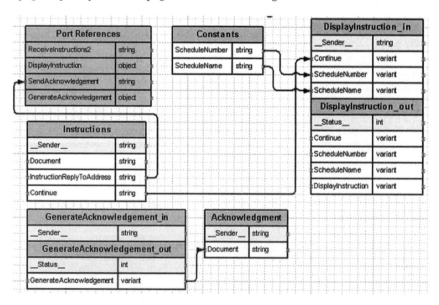

Once again this diagram is quite complex so let's look at the main building blocks first.

There are two messages:

- ❏ The `Instructions` message received from the Instruction business process
- ❏ The `Acknowledgement` message that contains the message returned from the Acknowledgement process

There are also two Windows script components:

- ❏ `DisplayInstruction`, which displays the Instruction message to be sent to the Acknowledgement process; this is the same component as used on the Instruction business process side
- ❏ `GenerateAcknowledgement` that displays the acknowledgment message returned from the Acknowledgement process

We have defined two constants:

- ❏ `ScheduleName` with a value of `acknowledgement.skv`
- ❏ `ScheduleNumber` with a value of 2 (because this is the second schedule)

The most important data flow is from the `InstructionReplyToAddress` of the incoming message to the dynamic port `SendAcknowledgement`. This transfers the HTTP URL stored in the Instruction message to the Dynamic port so that BizTalk knows which particular instance of the Instruction business process to return the message on:

http://localhost/receiveresponse.asp?channel=receiveacknowledgement&qpath=machinenam
e.mydomain.com\private$\receiveacknowledgement{72aae5ca-4138-92f1-3b651e5ed787}

Remember that the GUID will be different for each transfer.

The parameters for the `DisplayInstructions` Windows script component are the two constants `ScheduleName` and `ScheduleNumber`, as well as the `Continue` attribute of the incoming Instruction message.

Finally the Acknowledgement document is flowed from the output of the `generateacknowledgement` script to the outgoing `Acknowledgement` message.

Returning the Acknowledgement message to the Original Instance of the Instruction Schedule (Acknowledgement Side)

Dynamic messaging port bindings in schedules work in conjunction with open destination messaging ports in BizTalk Messaging – the dynamic port submits to a channel that delivers the document to an open port. The open destination messaging port then executes the HTTP URL (generated above, and also stored in the return message in the section directly above), to call the ASP page on the Instruction system. This ASP page then receives the document.

> **Every time you create a dynamic orchestration port you must create a channel for the outgoing document specification to an open destination messaging port to complete the setup.**

Let's now go through the BizTalk Messaging setup for the document, open destination messaging port ,and channel on the Acknowledgement organization that delivers the `Acknowledgement` message back to the Instruction organization.

Configuring the Acknowledgement Document

Open `Acknowledgement.xml` from the `c:\software\skedtoskedhttp` directory in the BizTalk Editor and save it into root directory of the WebDAV repository. This file is the message specification for our test instance Instruction file created by the Windows scripting component `GenerateAcknowledgement.wsc`. Open up Messaging Manager and set up the following document definition:

Document Name	Specification File from WebDAV
Acknowledgement	`Acknowledgement.xml`

Configuring the Open Destination Message Port

Create a new message port to a new organization with the following values:

Message Port Wizard Item	Setting Value
Port To	`Organization`
Name	`Receive Acknowledgement and Send Out Open Destination`
Destination Organisation	`Open Destination`

> Note: The primary transport does not need to be set up in this open destination port because the dynamic BizTalk Messaging send port in Orchestration passes this information to the open destination messaging port.

Configuring the Channel to the Open Destination Message Port

Create a new channel from an application with the following information:

Channel Wizard Item	Setting Value
Name	`Send from Acknowledgement XLANG Open Destination`
Source	`XLANG Schedule`
Inbound document definition name	`Acknowledgement`
Outbound document definition name	`Acknowledgement`

It is important that for each document specification there is only a single channel/open destination port combination. If there is more than one channel/open destination port combination, then BizTalk will get confused and you will receive an XLANG Scheduler WFBinding error message in the Event Log.

We have now configured the Acknowledgment process to send the Acknowledgement message, via HTTP, to the Instruction side of the exchange. Now we will address how the Instruction process receives the HTTP post and directs the message back into the existing BizTalk orchestration.

Returning the Acknowledgement Message to the Original Instance of the Instruction Schedule (Instruction Side)

Next, the ASP page `receiveresponse.asp` is called with the URL containing query string values for the channel and for the queue path (qpath below). The URL is shown below:

http://localhost/receiveresponse.asp?channel=receiveacknowledgement&qpath=machinename.mydomain.com\private$\receiveacknowledgement{72aae5ca-5807-4138-92f1-3b651e5ed787}

The ASP page parses the incoming document, queue path, and channel from the query string. It takes the `queuepath` query string that contains the return queue in the MSMQ pathname syntax and translates it to an MSMQ format name syntax by pre-pending `queue://Direct=OS:`. Then it calls `Submit` to deliver the document as `PostedDocument` to the specific queue and channel name, which is in this case `receiveacknowledgement` as you can see from the query string above, into BizTalk Messaging:

```
' Parse the query string
queuepath = Request.QueryString("qpath")
queuepath = "queue://Direct=OS:" & queuepath
channelname = Request.QueryString("channel")
' Code to retrieve posted document omitted for clarity
' Please refer to receiveresponse.asp for more information
Set interchange = CreateObject( "BizTalk.Interchange" )
' Submit the document back into BizTalk Messaging at the Instruction side
Call Interchange.Submit(4,PostedDocument,,,,,queuepath,channelname)
```

You should have already copied `receiveresponse.asp` from `\Program Files\Microsoft BizTalk Server\SDK\Messaging Samples\ReceiveScripts` to your web root directory in a previous step.

Here's how to set up BizTalk Messaging for the `receiveacknowledgement` channel and its destination port back to the **original running instance** of the Instruction XLANG schedule.

Configuring the Message Port to Correlate Back to Instruction XLANG

Create a new message port to a new application with the following values:

Message Port Wizard Item	Setting Value
Port To	Application
Name	Receive Acknowledgment into existing XLANG
Running XLANG Schedule	Running XLANG Schedule

> Note: you do not need to specify anything other than `Running XLANG Schedule` for this messaging port, as the `Interchange.Submit` call contains the per-instance queue to return to. This correlates the message back to the ReceiveAcknowledgement Orchestration port.

Configuring the Channel from the ASP Page to Instruction XLANG

Create a new channel from an organization with the following information:

Channel Wizard Item	Setting Value
Name	`ReceiveAcknowledgement`
Source	`AcknowledgementOrg`
Inbound document definition name	`Acknowledgement`
Outbound document definition name	`Acknowledgement`

> It is vital that is a channel from an organization not an application, especially if you run this example on a single machine. If you create a channel from an application then you will have two channels to open destination ports that both fit the Acknowledgement specification (**ReceiveAcknowledgement** and **Receive Acknowledgement into existing XLANG**). BizTalk Messaging must only find one such channel.
>
> The error you will receive is:
>
> **The Message Queuing message could not be sent.**
> **Instance ID: {05A6CD4C-E42D-49C7-8DB5-66ED63BB820E}**
> **Port name: SendAcknowledgement**
> **Queue path:**
> **http://machinename/receiveresponse.asp?channel=receiveacknowledgement**
> **&qpath=machinename.domainname\private$\receiveacknowledgement{1f60d7**
> **08-b86b-4641-afab-866aa77fd769}**
> **Message type: Acknowledgement**
> **Message name: Acknowledgement**
> **Correlation ID: {11CC1423-46BA-4B08-BB73-41277C0D79C0}-0000006f**
> **MSMQ object error description: A valid open destination channel could not be found. The document definition is Acknowledgement. You might need to create a channel for this document definition.**
>
> Note: When you see this error, if you are certain that you have created a valid open destination channel for a document definition, check to ensure you have not created two of them by mistake.

Well done! You have now completed the setup so that the Acknowledgment message will be *correlated* with the original XLANG schedule. The XLANG schedule displays the Acknowledgement and completes processing.

Running the example

When you run this example by copying the Instruction message `testinstruction2.xml` to `c:\software\skedtoskedhttp\instructionreceive2`, the flow of message boxes displayed on the screen is:

Event	Message Box contents displayed
On receipt of the Instruction into `Instruction.skx`:	Schedule Started: 1 (Instruction.skx) Everything is fine, message was delivered to schedule successfully.
On receipt of the Instruction into `Acknowledgement.skx`:	Schedule Started: 2 (Acknowledgement.skx) Everything is fine, message was delivered to schedule successfully.
On creation of the Acknowledgement message in `Acknowledgement.skx`:	Acknowledgement generated
On receipt of the Acknowledgement into `Instruction.skx`:	Correlated back to Schedule: 1 (Instruction.skx): Everything is fine, Acknowledgement was returned to initial schedule successfully.

In the diagram below, the data flow for this whole HTTP-based correlation process, between schedules running on BizTalk Servers, is shown. The table below the diagram defines the functionality of Steps A to O.

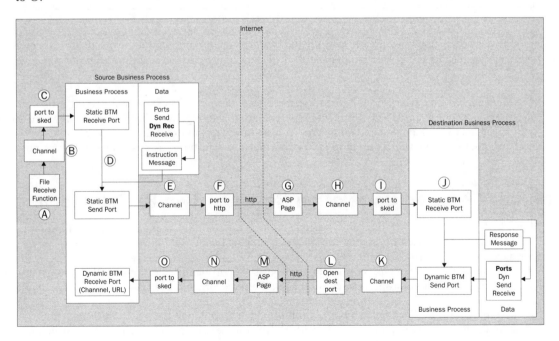

Step	Function	Name
A	Receive Function	`Pick up Instruction2`
B	Channel	`Internal Instruction2 to New XLANG`
C	Port	`Receive Internal Instructions2 New XLANG`
D	Schedule	`Instruction.skx`
E	Channel	`Instruction2 to http`
F	Port	`http to acknowledgement`
G	ASP Page	`ReceiveInstruction.asp`
H	Channel	`Instruction2 to New XLANG`
I	Port	`Receive Instructions2 to Acknowledgement.skx New XLANG`
J	Schedule	`Acknowledgement.skx`
K	Channel	`Send from Acknowledgement XLANG Open Destination`
L	Port	`Receive Acknowledgement and Send Out Open Destination`
M	ASP Page	`ReceiveResponse.asp`
N	Channel	`ReceiveAcknowledgement`
O	Port	`Receive Acknowledgment into existing XLANG`

HTTPS transmissions can be performed in a similar manner to that outlined above, except you need to modify the Instruction schedule file. Modify the **ReceiveAcknowledgement** port so that the receive URL has an HTTPS prefix, and change the BizTalk Messaging ports so that they send out using HTTPS.

Now that we have covered HTTP-based transport correlation, in the next section we will explain the necessary steps for a non-HTTP transport implementation, and highlight the differences between these non-HTTP and HTTP implementations. We will also introduce an example, re-implementing the scenario above, except we will use non-HTTP transports to transfer messages between the two business processes.

Non-HTTP-based Correlation Between Two BizTalk Servers

If we wish to use non-HTTP transports, we encounter a problem: the dynamic orchestration port and the Orchestration BizTalk Messaging receive ports support the HTTP transport only. For example, you need to enter the return URL in the Orchestration BizTalk Messaging receive port. Fortunately, this does not mean that we can't use non-HTTP transports for correlation, it just means that you need to do some more work to use transports such as MSMQ, file transport, and SMTP.

As we did in the HTTP example above, we will provide an outline of the overall process before examining the specific setup involved. As with HTTP, the steps below assume that the Instruction business process has been started; and as you can see the three basic steps, sending out an Instruction, creating an Acknowledgement, and returning that Acknowledgement are identical to those used for HTTP (although the details are different).

The complete process for non-HTTP based correlation between the Instruction organization and the Acknowledgement organization is illustrated below:

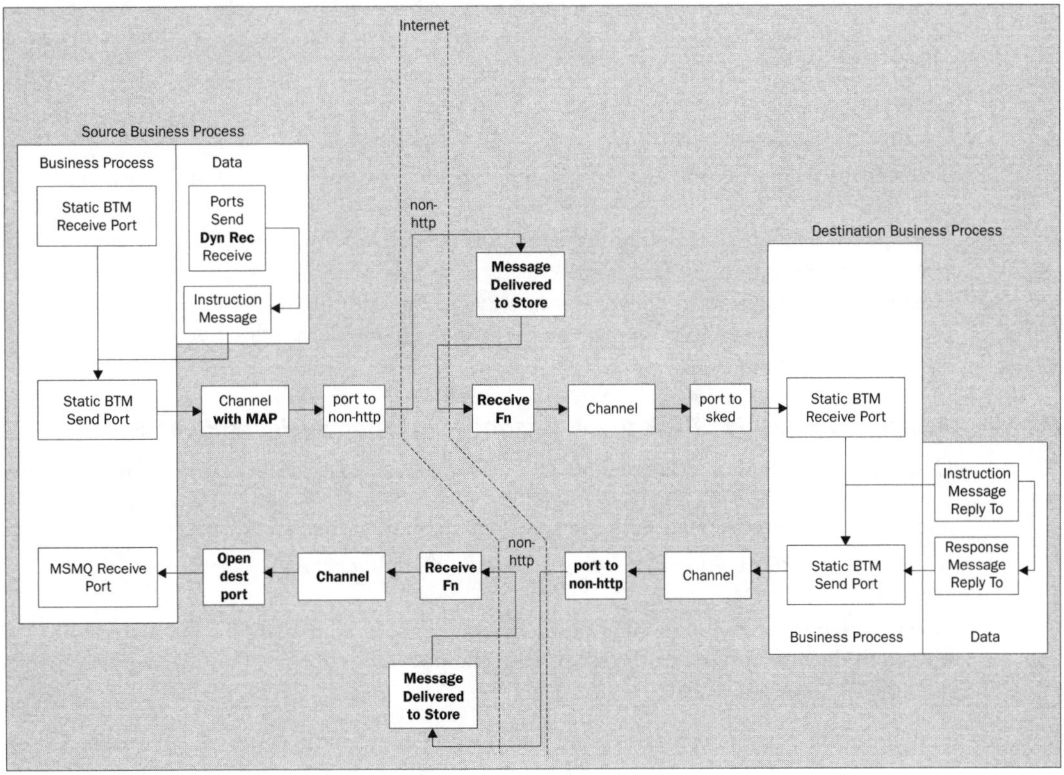

Below are the actions we will be performing to implement these steps. It all may look complex, but there is no need for alarm – we will be stepping through all of these actions with a practical example.

Sending the Message Out from the Instruction Business Process:

❑ Create a static BizTalk Messaging port binding in the Source schedule to send out messages.

❑ Create a MSMQ binding to accept return messages into the Source schedule.

❑ Save the return BizTalk Messaging binding information (specified above) into the physical message using orchestration data flow.

❑ Create a map in the BizTalk Mapper tool to convert the message queue format name to a path name, so that it can be used to correlate back to the schedule.

❑ Create a messaging port that delivers using a non-HTTP transport such as SMTP, file transport, or MSMQ.

❑ Deploy the map created to convert the message queue format to a path name in the outgoing messaging channel in the port created just above. Note: This is a new step for non-HTTP transports.

Receiving the Message at the Acknowledgement Business Process and Returning an Acknowledgement:

- ❑ Create a receive function (or use a receive script) at the Acknowledgement organization, to receive the message from the message store, whether it is a file system, mail box or message queue, and deliver it into BizTalk Messaging.
- ❑ Create a port to start the new schedule.
- ❑ Create a channel to the port.
- ❑ Transfer the incoming BizTalk Messaging return information to a field in the response message.
- ❑ Create a BizTalk Messaging binding static port in the Destination schedule, to send back the response message.
- ❑ Create a messaging port to deliver the message using a non-HTTP transport to a physical store on the Source organization (for example, a message queue, file, or mailbox).
- ❑ Create a channel to this port.

Receiving the Acknowledgement Back to the Existing Instruction Business Process:

- ❑ Create a receive function (or use a receive script) at the Destination organization, to receive the message from the message store (whether it is a file system, mailbox, or message queue) and deliver it open destination to the specified channel in BizTalk Messaging.
- ❑ Create an open destination messaging port that will deliver the message back to the Source schedule.
- ❑ Create a channel to the open destination messaging port, specifying the inbound and outbound document types as the schema for the document to return to the original schema (in our case Acknowledgement).

At this point, let's compare and contrast HTTP and non-HTTP scenarios now we have looked at both:

- ❑ The receive port in the original XLANG schedule is not a BizTalk Messaging shape; rather it is a per-instance MSMQ shape.
- ❑ The correlation embedded in the message for HTTP was always an HTTP URL. Regardless of the actual transport used, SMTP, MSMQ, File, etc. the correlation information embedded in the message for the non-HTTP scenario is the per-instance MSMQ.
- ❑ Unlike HTTP transports Non-HTTP transports require the use of a channel map to translate the MSMQ path name to a format name.
- ❑ Whereas in the HTTP scenario the two ASP pages accepted messages and delivered them to BizTalk Messaging in a single step, for the non-HTTP scenario the outgoing message may be first delivered to a message store, such as Exchange, Message Queue, or a file, before being received into BizTalk Messaging.
- ❑ For the HTTP scenario, a dynamic orchestration port binding is used to return the message back to the source organization. For the non-HTTP scenario a static BizTalk Message port binding is used to transfer the message back to the Instruction system. Whereas in the HTTP scenario the Acknowledgement message did not need to contain correlation information, for the non-HTTP scenario the reply-to-address is also embedded in the Acknowledgement message.
- ❑ For the HTTP scenario the open destination messaging port was on the Acknowledgement side of the exchange. For the non-HTTP scenario the open destination messaging port is executed on the Acknowledgement system and it delivers the message directly to the per-instance queue.

Although many of the steps involved in the non-HTTP and HTTP cases are similar, for the sake of clarity we will present the entire non-HTTP flow in its completeness. We will also use the same step numbering as before, but highlight the key differences between HTTP and non-HTTP flow as we build out the scenario.

Where the channels and ports in BizTalk Messaging have similar functionality in both scenarios, the non-HTTP case uses the postfix `non-http` tagged onto the name used for the HTTP case. Note that in this non-HTTP scenario we assume that both the Instruction and Acknowledgement business processes have access to a shared file system – in other words the non-HTTP transport used in the following example is the *file* transport. The same methodology can however be applied to SMTP and MSMQ transports and potentially other user-defined transports (for example, FTP) implemented through an Application Integration Component.

Pick-up Internal Instruction with BizTalk Messaging and Deliver to the Instruction Business Process

Except for the filenames and directory paths, configurations are identical for the non-HTTP and HTTP cases. First we set up BizTalk Messaging to receive the internal Instruction file, `testinstruction2.xml`, and deliver it to the XLANG schedule `C:\software\skedtoskednonhttp\Instructionnonhttp.skx`.

Configuring Documents

If you haven't already completed this step for the HTTP case, open `Instructions2.xml` (the message specification for the `testinstruction2.xml` instance) into your WebDAV repository using the BizTalk Editor. Next open up Messaging Manager and set up the following document definition:

Document Name	Specification File from WebDAV
Instructions2	`Instruction2.xml`

Configuring the Message Port

Set up a message port to an application as summarized below:

Message Port Wizard Item	Setting Value
Port To	`Application`
Name	`Receive Internal Instructions2 New XLANG non-http`
New XLANG schedule Schedule moniker: [sked://]	`C:\software\skedtoskednonhttp\Instructionnonhttp.skx`
Port Name	`ReceiveInternalInstruction`

Configuring a Channel

Create a new channel from an application with the following information:

Channel Wizard Item	Setting Value
Name	`Internal Instruction2 to New XLANG non-http`
Source Application...New (if it doesn't already exist)	`InternalInstructionSource`
Inbound document definition name	`Instructions2`
Outbound document definition name	`Instructions2`

Configuring a Receive Function

Open up the BizTalk Server Administration tool, and create a new file receive function, with the following values:

Receive Function Item	Setting Value
Name (General Tab)	`Pick up Instruction2 non-http`
Polling location (General Tab)	`C:\software\skedtoskednonhttp\InstructionReceive2`
Files to poll for (General Tab)	`Testinstruction2.xml`
Channel Name (Advanced Tab)	`Internal Instruction2 to New XLANG non-http`

Note: *the value for the Polling location (the directory where you drop your Instruction files) requires that you have created a directory on the file system called C:\software\skedtoskednonhttp\instructionreceive2 .*

We have now defined the infrastructure to receive the message into the Instruction schedule `instruction.skx`. As we did before with HTTP, let's now examine the contents of the Instruction schedule file.

Receiving Internal Instructions into BizTalk Orchestration, Sending Internal Instructions and Receiving Acknowledgements

Load the schedule source file `instructionnonhttp.skv` into the Orchestration Designer. It should look like this:

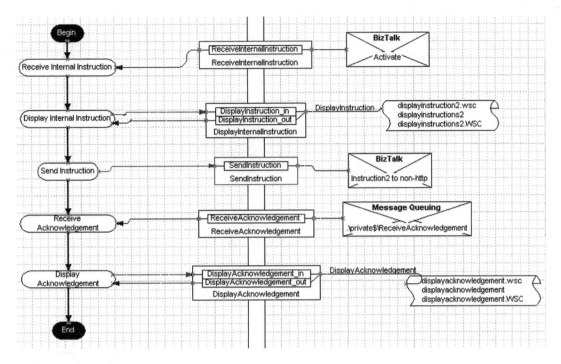

Let's consider each action in turn.

BizTalk Messaging delivers the `testinstruction2.xml` to the XLANG schedule through the BizTalk messaging binding receive port called `ReceiveInternalInstruction`. This port is tied to the action `Receive Internal Instruction`. In the BizTalk Messaging binding wizard for `Receive Internal Instruction` the value of **XLANG Schedule Activation** is set to YES. This means that each time a message is received to this port, a new instance of the schedule is started.

The second action calls a simple Windows script component that displays a message box containing the name of the schedule, the number of the schedule instance, and the contents of the `Continue` attribute passed in from `testinstruction2.xml`.

The document is then sent out to BizTalk Messaging with a BizTalk Messaging binding shape. In the BizTalk Messaging binding wizard for the `Send Instruction` action, the BizTalk Messaging channel `Instruction2 to non-http` is used to send the message.

After sending out the Instruction to the Acknowledgement XLANG schedule, this process then waits to receive an Acknowledgement message, and then displays it. Notice that the receive binding is an MSMQ, because the BizTalk Messaging receive binding object can only be used with HTTP.

The **Data** page for this schedule, shown overleaf, describes the message flow:

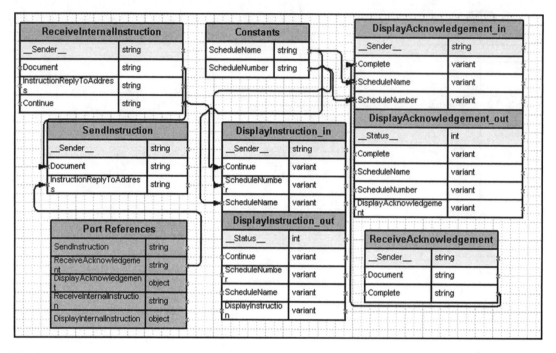

The document contained in the ReceiveInternalInstruction message is flowed to the SendInstruction message, so that the contents of the document will be sent to the Acknowledgment process.

Note that we have defined two constants: ScheduleName (with a value of instructionnonhttp.skv) and ScheduleNumber (with a value of 1). These two constants, and the Continue attribute from the ReceiveInternalInstruction message, are flowed to the simple COM script Displayinstruction as input parameters. Displayinstruction displays this information in a message box, as you can see from the script below:

```
function DisplayInstruction(Continue, ScheduleNumber, ScheduleName)
    MsgBox("Schedule Started: " & ScheduleNumber & " (" & ScheduleName & "): " _
          & Continue)
end function
```

The most important data flow is from the ReceiveAcknowledgement port reference to the InstructionReplytoAddress field of the SendInstruction message. As for the HTTP case this step is vital for correlation. We need to save the return schedule information into the outgoing message, so that we can use it later in the second schedule to return back to this same instance of the Instruction schedule. The string saved in the ReceiveAcknowledgement port reference looks similar to this:

machinename.mydomain.com\private$\receiveacknowledgement{72aae5ca-5807-4138-92f1-3b651e5ed787}

As you can see, this string contains the MSMQ pathname for the per-instance message queue (where the return message must be delivered to correlate back to the schedule), as opposed to the HTTP URL contained in the message for the HTTP case.

Once the Acknowledgement is received, the COM scripting object `DisplayAcknowledgement` then displays it in a message box. This object is very similar to the `DisplayInstruction` object; it accepts three parameters – the constants `ScheduleName` and `ScheduleNumber`, and the `Complete` attribute from the Acknowledgement document.

Sending Instructions through BizTalk Messaging to a New BizTalk Orchestration via non-HTTP

The `Send Instruction` action of the XLANG schedule delivers the outgoing Instruction message to the BizTalk Messaging channel `Instruction2 to non-http`. This channel in turn delivers the message to a port that sends the message to the file system for the Acknowledgement business to import. Whereas in the HTTP case, the channel just delivered the message to the messaging port to HTTP, in the case of the non-HTTP transport, the channel here does more than just deliver the message to the port – it also applies a map.

Recall that the `ReceiveResponse.asp` page in the HTTP case took the MSMQ pathname to the MSMQ format name by pre-pending `queue://Direct=OS:`. For the non-HTTP example we no longer have this ASP to complete the work. Fortunately, we can apply a map to do the same work.

The map, called `mapPathNametoFormatName.xml` (supplied in the `c:\software\skedtoskednonhttp` directory), takes the `instruction2.xml` schema as both its input and output document specification, and uses the Concatenate functoid from the String palette to pre-pend `queue://Direct=OS:` to the value of `InstructionReplytoAddress`. The screenshot below shows BizTalk Mapper with this map loaded:

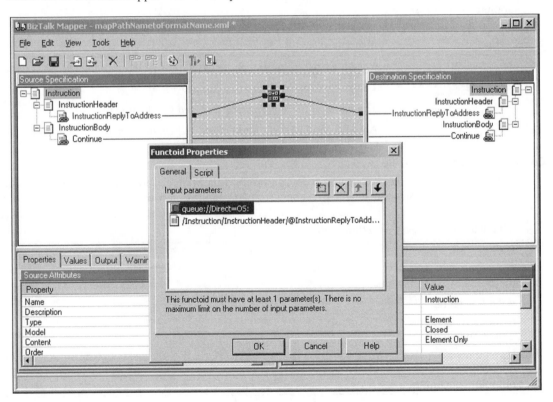

Once the Instruction message has been sent to the file system, a receive function picks up the message for the Acknowledgement process. The receive function delivers it through a channel to a messaging port that activates the Acknowledgement business process. Remember that for the HTTP case, it was an ASP page, rather than a receive function, that performed this role.

The BizTalk Messaging setup for the ports, channels ,and receive functions involved in this non-HTTP-based correlation process are detailed below.

If you are setting up the scenario on two machines, you will need to create the `Instructions2` document definition, otherwise it will be already set up in a previous configuration step.

Configuring Message Port to File

Create a new message port to a new organization with the following values:

Wizard Item	Setting Value
Name	`Non-http to acknowledgment`
Organization...New	`Acknowledgement Org`
Primary Transport	`file://c:\software\skedtoskednonhttp\instruction2acknowl` `edgementreceive\testinstruction2%tracking_ID%.xml`

Note that `%tracking_ID%` is used as part of the filename to ensure that each message is delivered as a unique file. If a filename without the `%tracking_ID%` is used then BizTalk Server will append each message to this single file. Other symbols that may be used as part of the file name (but do not guarantee uniqueness) are:

Value	Meaning
`%datetime%`	The date time in milliseconds (based on GMT) when the file was created
`%document_name%`	The name of the document being processed
`%server%`	The name of the server that processed the document
`%uid%`	A millisecond counter that is restarted when the server is rebooted

Configuring a Channel to File

First open `mapPathNametoFormatName.xml` in the BizTalk Mapper and then store it into the root WebDAV directory. Next, create a new channel from an application with the following information:

Channel Wizard Item	Setting Value
Name	`Instruction2 to non-http`
Source	`XLANG Schedule`
Inbound document definition name	`Instructions2`
Outbound document definition name	`Instructions2`
Map inbound document to outbound document	`http://localhost/BizTalkServerRepository/Maps/mapPathNam` `etoFormatName.xml`

Now we will set up the BizTalk Messaging on the Acknowledgement side of the exchange that receives the file output and sends it to the Acknowledgement XLANG schedule.

Configuring a Message Port to Acknowledgement XLANG

Create a new message port to a new application with the following values:

Wizard Item	Setting Value
Port To	`Application`
Name	`Receive Instructions2 to Acknowledgement.skx New XLANG non-http`
New XLANG Schedule	`C:\software\skedtoskednonhttp\acknowledgementnonhttp.skx`
Port Name	`ReceiveInstructions2`

Configure a Channel to Acknowledgement XLANG

Create a new channel from an application with the following information:

Channel Wizard Item	Setting Value
Name	`Instruction2 to New XLANG non-http`
Source	`XLANG Schedule`
Inbound document definition name	`Instructions2`
Outbound document definition name	`Instructions2`

Configure the Receive Function

Open up the BizTalk Server Administration tool, and create a new file receive function with the following values:

Receive Function Item	Setting Value
Name (General Tab)	`Pick Up at Acknowledgement non-http`
Polling location (General Tab)	`C:\software\skedtoskednonhttp\instruction2acknowledgementreceive`
Files to poll for (General Tab)	`*.xml`
Channel Name (General Tab)	`Instruction2 to New XLANG non-http`

> **Note**: *the value for the Polling location requires that you have created a directory on the file system called C:\software\skedtoskednonhttp\instruction2acknowledgementreceive.*

BizTalk Messaging is now configured to deliver the Instruction message to the Acknowledgement XLANG schedule.

393

Receiving Instructions and Sending Acknowledgments in BizTalk Orchestration

The XLANG Acknowledgement schedule `acknowledgmentnonhttp.skx` is shown below:

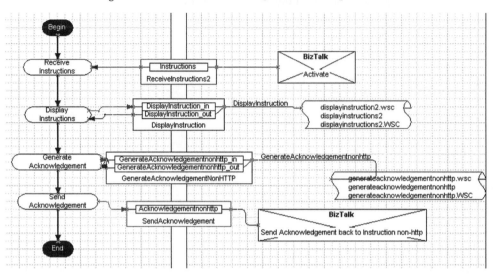

As you can see, the schedule receives the `instructions2` message through the BizTalk Messaging binding to the BizTalk Messaging `Instruction2 to New XLANG` channel. In the same way as for `instructionnonhttp.skx`, **XLANG Schedule Activation** is set to YES for this BizTalk Messaging binding, because a new instance of the schedule is created on receipt of every message. Once the message is received into the `displayinstruction2.wsc` component, which is identical to the one used in `instructionnonhttp.skx`, the component is called to display the message contents.

For the HTTP example in the preceding section, the `generateacknowledgement` COM object simply created the return message, and the `InstructionReplyToAddress` field was tied to an outgoing dynamic BizTalk message binding that then routed the reply back to the Instruction business process. However, *dynamic BizTalk message bindings only provide support for HTTP*. For non-HTTP transports we need to embed the `InstructionReplyToAddress` inside the return message, and send it back to the Instruction business process because the correlation address is a private per-instance message queue on the Instruction machine.

The scripting COM object `generateacknowledgementnonhttp` creates an Acknowledgement message by loading the XML instance `testacknowledgement.xml` from the file system, appending a new element called `InstructionReplyToAddress` with the value of the `InstructionReplytoAddress` parameter and returning it to the schedule. The important code from `generateacknowledgementnonhttp` is shown below:

```
function GenerateAcknowledgementnonhttp(InstructionReplyToAddress)
    Dim XMLDoc, Newelement
    Set XMLDoc = CreateObject("Msxml2.DOMDocument")
    XMLDoc.load("c:\software\skedtoskednonhttp\testacknowledgement.xml")
    Set newelement = XMLDoc.createElement("InstructionReplyToAddress")
    newelement.Text = InstructionReplyToAddress
    XmlDoc.documentElement.appendChild(Newelement)
    GenerateAcknowledgementnonhttp = CStr(XMLDoc.xml)
    MsgBox("Acknowledgement generated :" & CStr(XMLDoc.xml))
    Set XMLDoc = Nothing
end function
```

Once the XML has been loaded, the function displays a message box.
Finally the Acknowledgement message is sent out of the schedule through a static BizTalk Messaging binding send port called `Sendacknowledgement`.

If you turn to the **Data** page, shown below, you should note the flow of the `InstructionReplyToAddress` from the incoming message, `Instructions`, to the `generateacknowledgement` COM object, and then out of the COM object as part of the `acknowledgementnonhttp` response message.

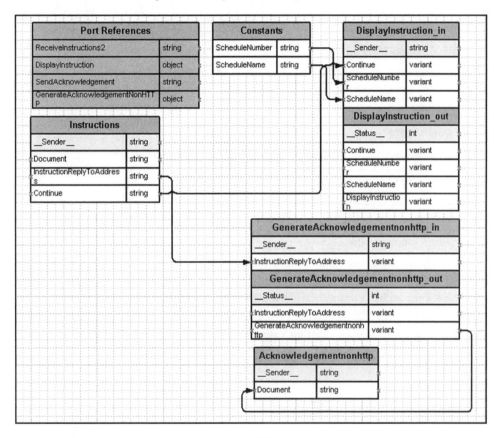

The parameters for the `DisplayInstructions` COM script are the two constants `ScheduleName` (with the value of `Acknowledgementnonhttp.skx`) and `ScheduleNumber` (value of 2), as well as the `Continue` attribute of the incoming Instruction message.

Finally, the generated Acknowledgement document is flowed from the output of the `generateacknowledgementnonhttp` script to the outgoing message.

Returning the Acknowledgement Message to the Original Instance of the Instruction Schedule (Acknowledgment Side)

The static BizTalk messaging binding `SendAcknowledgement` calls the BizTalk messaging channel `Send acknowledgment back to instruction non-http`. This channel then delivers the document to the file system, for the Instruction business process to retrieve.

Let's now review the BizTalk Messaging port and channel set up.

Configuring a Message Port to File

Create a new message port to a new organisation with the following values:

Message Port Wizard Item	Setting Value
Port To	Application
Name	Acknowledgement to non-http
Destination Organisation..New	InstructionOrg
Primary transport	file://c:\software\skedtoskednonhttp\acknowledgement2instructionreceive\acknowledgement%Tracking_id%.xml

Configuring Documents

Open Acknowledgementnonhttp.xml (the message specification for the testacknowledgement.xml instance) into your WebDAV repository using the BizTalk Editor. Next open up Messaging Manager and set up the following document definition:

Document Name	Specification File from WebDAV
Acknowledgementnonhttp	Acknowledgementnonhttp.xml

Configuring a Channel to File

Create a new channel from an application using the following information:

Channel Wizard Item	Setting Value
Name	Send Acknowledgement back to Instruction non-http
Source	XLANG Schedule
Inbound document definition name	Acknowledgementnonhttp
Outbound document definition name	Acknowledgementnonhttp

Note that the document definition Acknowledgementnonhttp is different from the acknowledgmenthttp schema used for the HTTP case for two reasons. First it contains the field InstructionReplyToAddress, and second the document contains routing information.

Open acknowledgmentnonhttp.xml in the BizTalk Editor. You should see the following window contents:

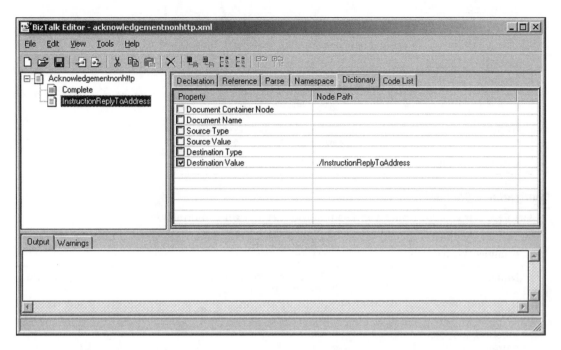

Select `InstructionReplyToAddress` – you will see that this field is used to specify the destination value. When the document is delivered to the open destination channel, this destination value is used to determine where the document should be delivered. This process is called self-routing and is discussed in detail in another chapter of this book. Note that we did not need to complete this step for the HTTP transport, because it was automatically taken care of by the Dynamic Orchestration BizTalk messaging binding and open destination messaging port combination.

The Acknowledgment process is now set up to send the Acknowledgement message to a file system that is accessible to the Instruction schedule.

Returning the Acknowledgement Message to the Original Instance of the Instruction Schedule (Instruction Side)

A receive function picks up the incoming Acknowledgement message file, and delivers it to BizTalk Messaging. BizTalk Messaging then uses a channel to an open destination port to deliver the message back to the original schedule instance. The reason that we could not use an open destination port on the Acknowledgement side of this exchange is because the open destination port drops the message on a private message queue, which is not available on a remote machine.

Here's how to configure BizTalk Messaging for the `receiveacknowledgement` channel and its destination port:

Configuring a Message Port to Correlate Back to Instruction XLANG

Create a new message port to a new organisation with the following values:

Message Port Wizard Item	Setting Value
Port To	`Organization`
Name	`Receive Acknowledgement and Send Out Open Destination non-http`
Destination Organization	`Open Destination`

Configuring a Channel from File to Instruction XLANG

Create a new channel from an application with the following information:

Channel Wizard Item	Setting Value
Name	`Receive Acknowledgement into existing XLANG non-http`
Source	`XLANG Schedule`
Inbound document definition name	`Acknowledgementnonhttp`
Outbound document definition name	`Acknowledgementnonhttp`

Configuring a Receive Function

Open up the BizTalk Server Administration and create a new file receive function with the following values:

Receive Function Item	Setting Value
Name (General Tab)	`Pick Up Return Instruction non-http`
Polling location (General Tab)	`c:\software\skedtoskednonhttp\acknowledgement2instructionreceive`
Files to poll for (General Tab)	`*.xml`
Openness	`Open Destination`
Channel Name (Advanced Tab)	`Receive Acknowledgement into existing XLANG non-http`

> **Note**: *the value for the Polling location (the directory where you drop your Instruction files) requires that you have created a directory on the file system called* c:\software\skedtoskednonhttp\acknowledgement2instructionreceive.

Now the acknowledgment message is all set up to correlate back to the original XLANG schedule. To complete the process, the XLANG schedule displays the Acknowledgement in a message box.

Running the Example

You can run this example by copying `testinstruction2.xml` (the Instruction message) to `c:\software\skedtoskednonhttp\instructionreceive2`. The flow of message boxes displayed on the screen is:

Event	Message Box contents displayed
On receipt of the Instruction into `Instruction.skx`	Schedule Started: 1 (Instruction.skx) Everything is fine, message was delivered to schedule successfully.
On receipt of the Instruction into `Acknowledgement.skx`	Schedule Started: 2 (Acknowledgement.skx) Everything is fine, message was delivered to schedule successfully.
On creation of the Acknowledgement message in `Acknowledgement.skx`	Acknowledgement generated: <Acknowledgementnonhttp Complete = "Everything is fine, Acknowledgement was returned from initial Schedule successfully"><InstructionReplyToAddress> queue://Direct=OS: machinename.mydomain.com\private$\receiveacknowledgement{ 72aae5ca-5807-4138-92f1-3b651e5ed787} </InstructionReplyToAddress><Acknowledgementnonhttp>
On receipt of the Acknowledgement into `Instruction.skx`	Correlated back to Schedule: 1 (Instruction.skx): Everything is fine, Acknowledgement was returned to initial schedule successfully.

As with the HTTP case, we now describe the full correlation process in diagram and table form:

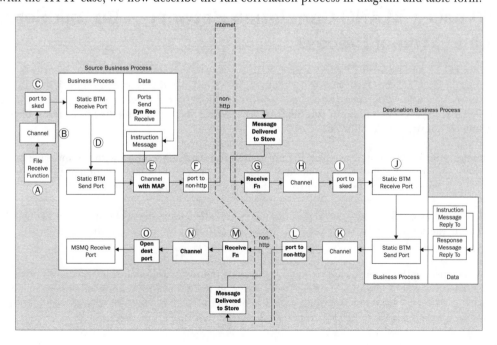

Step	Function	Name
A	Receive Function	`Pick up Instruction2 non-http`
B	Channel	`Internal Instruction2 to New XLANG non-http`
C	Port	`Receive Internal Instructions2 New XLANG non-http`
D	Schedule	`Instructionnonhttp.skx`
E	Channel	`Instruction2 to non-http`
F	Port	`Non-http to acknowledgement`
G	Receive function	`Pick Up at Acknowledgement non-http`
H	Channel	`Instruction2 to New XLANG non-http`
I	Port	`Receive Instructions2 to Acknowledgement.skx New XLANG`
J	Schedule	`Acknowledgementnonhttp.skx`
K	Channel	`Acknowledgment to non-http`
L	Port	`Send Acknowledgement back to Instruction non-http`
M	Receive function	`Pick Up Return Instruction non-http`
N	Channel	`Receive Acknowledgement into existing XLANG non-http`
O	Port	`Receive Acknowledgement and Send Out Open Destination non-http`

HTTP-based XLANG Correlation Between a BizTalk Server and an External Process

For the HTTP and non-HTTP cases above, both the source and destination business processes were running BizTalk Server Orchestration schedules. However, schedule correlation back to a BizTalk Server orchestration **does not require** a second BizTalk Server. Indeed one of the key design goals of BizTalk Server 2000 was to allow it to inter-operate with other environments not running BizTalk Server (or indeed not running Windows).

The reason for this is simple: we pass the correlation information around with the message as it moves from the source to the destination schedule. As long as we retain the information at the destination, and return it to the source, then we can correlate back to the original schedule.

In this section we will discuss correlation that uses an external process *not* running on BizTalk Server. Following the same pattern as for previous cases, we will start by looking at the generic case, and then move on to consider an example.

First, let's review the generic case. Note that the steps below assume that the Instruction business process has been started and is running BizTalk Server 2000, but the Acknowledgement business process is defined in another technology on another platform. The three basic steps are identical to those used for non-HTTP/HTTP correlations between two BizTalk Servers.

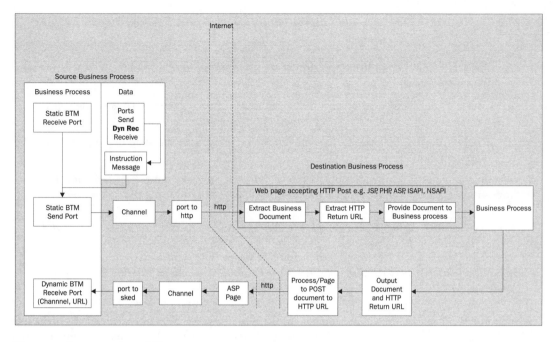

The overall process is as follows:

Sending the Message Out from the Instruction Business Process:

❑ Create a static BizTalk Messaging binding port in the Instruction schedule, to send the Instruction message.

❑ Create a BizTalk Messaging binding port in the Instruction schedule to accept return messages. In the binding, specify the BizTalk Messaging channel to receive return information. Specify a **modified version** of the original `ReceiveResponse.asp`, an ASP page that both receives the message and submits it to BizTalk Messaging.

❑ Save the return BizTalk Messaging orchestration port information, specified in the previous step, into the physical message using orchestration data flow.

❑ Create a messaging port to the Acknowledgement system using HTTP, then a messaging channel.

Receiving the Message at the Acknowledgement Business Process and Return the Acknowledgement:

❑ Create a dynamic web-based receive mechanism that can accept HTTP posts, for example the ASP page `ReceiveInstruction.asp` we will discuss shortly. The target page will receive the channel name and the queue path as query string variables, and the document, called the entity body, in a form variable. Any web-based receive mechanism could be potentially used: ASP, ISAPI, Java Server Pages (JSP) and Servlets, PHP, Apache server plug-ins, and NSAPI (meaning that this could run on a non-Windows platform). For the example overleaf we will use an ASP page.

Receiving the Response Message and Correlating this Back to the Existing Source Business Process:

❑ Physically add the **modified version** of ReceiveResponse.asp to the web environment on the source system.

❑ Create a BizTalk Messaging port to the running XLANG schedule. This will deliver the message to the schedule BizTalk Messaging binding port.

❑ Create a BizTalk Messaging channel with the same name as specified in the first step to the messaging port.

We will now implement our Instruction/Acknowledgement process example scenario, for the case of a trading partner running ASP pages on a Windows 2000 box, but **not** using BizTalk server.

If you are running this scenario on a single box, then of course it will have BizTalk Server installed on it. However, the destination business process will not use any of the functionality provided by BizTalk. If you are in a LAN based environment then you can set up this scenario across two machines. Further, you could extend this scenario to run with other web page serving technologies on other platforms.

To simplify this scenario, we will not implement the business process on the Acknowledgement side. We will simply receive the document in an ASP page, and then return the Acknowledgement from the same ASP page.

All of the steps on the Instruction business process are identical to those in the previous HTTP scenario with two BizTalk servers, and we can create the entire scenario from the HTTP scenario by simply replacing the ReceiveInstruction.asp and the ReceiveResponse.asp files in the web root with the new copies from c:\software\skedtoskedhttpnonbiztalk. Whereas in the HTTP scenario with two BizTalk servers this ASP page accepts the Instruction and submits it back to BizTalk Messaging on the Acknowledgement side, in this scenario the ASP page accepts the Instruction message, parses out the return URL, loads the Acknowledgement response, and sends the Acknowledgement back to the source process.

We have added logging to the ReceiveInstruction.asp file. Of course you would remove the logging before using this ASP page in production, but it makes it easier to understand the flow of data. By default the log text file is called ReceiveInstruction.txt and is placed in the c:\software\skedtoskedhttpnonbiztalk directory. Modify this file path is you have installed this sample in another directory. The code to load the Instruction message into the variable PostedDocument is the same as that used for ReceiveInstruction.asp:

```
PostedDocument = PostedDocument & Stream.ReadText
Stream.Close
Set Stream = Nothing
' This section is NEW
' Save the posted document to the log file
' Edit the directory path below if appropriate

set fso = server.CreateObject("Scripting.FileSystemObject")
set myFile = fso.CreateTextFile("C:\software\skedtoskedhttpnonbiztalk\ _
& ReceiveInstruction.txt")
myFile.WriteLine("The document contents received are:" & PostedDocument)
```

The `PostedDocument` document in our case is the contents of the `testinstruction2.xml` message. The `InstructionReplyToAddress` attribute in the `InstructionHeader` contains the URL to return to the Instruction schedule. The ASP page loads the `PostedDocument` into an XML DOM, extracts the `InstructionReplyToAddress` value, and writes this to a log file:

```
dim xmlDoc
set xmlDoc = Server.CreateObject("MSXML2.DOMDocument")
xmlDoc.LoadXML PostedDocument
'Get the InstructionReplyToAddress from the XML Document
dim InstructionReplyToAddress

InstructionReplyToAddress = xmlDoc.documentElement.childNodes.Item(0).
Attributes(0).nodeValue
myFile.WriteLine("InstructionReplyToAddress is:" & InstructionReplyToAddress)
```

At this point we have the information we need to correlate back to the source schedule, and we could start some business process, returning a resulting document. For our scenario this section is blank.

```
' INSERT BUSINESS PROCESS HERE
```

To simulate the creation of a response document from a business process we load the `testacknowledgement.xml` message just as we did for the previous HTTP example. We then log the Acknowledgement message:

```
xmlDoc.load("c:\software\skedtoskedhttp\testacknowledgement.xml")
Acknowledgement = CStr(xmlDoc.xml)
myFile.WriteLine("Acknowledgement generated:" & Acknowledgement)
set xmlDoc = Nothing
myFile.close
set myFile = Nothing
set fso = Nothing
```

Finally we need to send the Acknowledgement message back to the source schedule. MSXML3 provides us with a high-performance HTTP control for this purpose. We open the URL in the `InstructionReplyToAddress` field, and then submit the `Acknowledgement` document.

```
'Send the Acknowledgement to the ASP page URL in the document using POST
set objXMLHTTP = Server.CreateObject("MSXML2.XMLHTTP")
objXMLHTTP.Open "POST", InstructionReplyToAddress, false
objXMLHTTP.send Acknowledgement
Response.Status = "202 Accepted"
Response.End
```

The document is delivered to the modified `ReceiveResponse.asp` on the Instruction side of the exchange. This page has been modified for two reasons. Firstly, it logs information into `C:\software\skedtoskedhttpnonbiztalk\receiveresponse.txt` for debugging purposes as shown below:

```
set fso = server.CreateObject("Scripting.FileSystemObject")
set myFile =
fso.CreateTextFile("C:\software\skedtoskedhttpnonbiztalk\receiveresponse.txt")
myFile.writeline("total bytes accepted:" & Request.TotalBytes)
L_HTTPReqFailed_Text = "400 Request failed"
queuepath = Request.QueryString("qpath")
queuepath = "queue://Direct=OS:" & queuepath
channelname = Request.QueryString("channel")

myFile.writeline("channelname:" & channelname)
myFile.writeline("Extracted queuepath:" & queuepath)
myFile.writeline("contenttype:" & ContentType)
```

Secondly this page ensures that the ContentType is set to text/xml rather than the default of text/HTML.

```
ContentType = "text/xml"
```

Then, ResponseResponse.asp submits the message through BizTalk Messaging, and back to the original instruction.skx instance through the existing BizTalk Messaging channel ReceiveAcknowledgement.

Finally, this instance displays the Acknowledgement in a message box, shown below, and the Orchestration schedule completes processing.

Although we won't examine non-HTTP correlation between a BizTalk Server and a non-BizTalk Server, we can alter the non-HTTP-based BizTalk Server to BizTalk Server process in a similar way to the HTTP-based.

Other Approaches to Correlation

All of the schedule correlation examples we have seen require a reference to the schedule instance to be sent in an outgoing message, and then used to return to the original schedule. We simplified the examples above by passing the correlation data in the message throughout the entire process.

However, there are many cases where you are unable to send the correlation data as part of the message. For example, if you are sending an IDOC out from BizTalk into SAP then there is no space on the IDOC specification to include the correlation information.

In these cases where it is not possible to transfer the correlation address to a target system, you can create an AIC component that saves the correlation data along with a unique piece of business information that will be sent to and returned from the target. For example the IDOC sent into SAP may be for a unique purchase order and the document that is returned from SAP also contain this unique number. The AIC should save the unique business information and correlation data pairs into a local data store, such as a SQL Server database, before transporting the message to its destination.

When the target system returns a response, a second component can then retrieve the correlation information based on the unique piece of business information and then submit the message back into BizTalk messaging.

The overall process for this scenario is shown opposite:

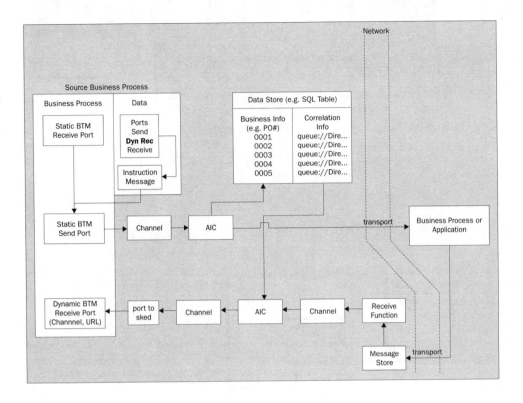

Summary

Whereas the focus of Chapter 7 was integrating BizTalk Messaging with line-of-business applications in a point-to-point manner, the focus of this chapter was integrating BizTalk Messaging with holistic business processes defined in Orchestration schedules.

BizTalk Messaging provides the mechanism to **activate** new business processes on the receipt of documents, which we demonstrated early in this chapter with aid of an example. In reality, a source business process often sends an output message to another process, waits for a message response, and then uses the response to trigger the reactivation of the source process. The process of returning the message response to the source process is called **correlation**.

Correlation in BizTalk Server is performed by storing unique identifying information about a schedule instance into an outgoing message. BizTalk Messaging provides the mechanism to send documents between business processes. You learned how to perform schedule correlation for two schedules interacting over either HTTP or non-HTTP transports. Then we modified the HTTP correlation example so that it could be used in a mixed environment, involving a single BizTalk server and a business process implemented by another application (which may also be on another platform, such as UNIX). Finally, we discussed how to save correlation information in a local data store, and then use a unique piece of business information to retrieve this correlation data on receipt of an incoming message.

As you can see, even the simplest business processes require a good deal of configuration. The management and administration of these configurations will be tackled in the next chapter.

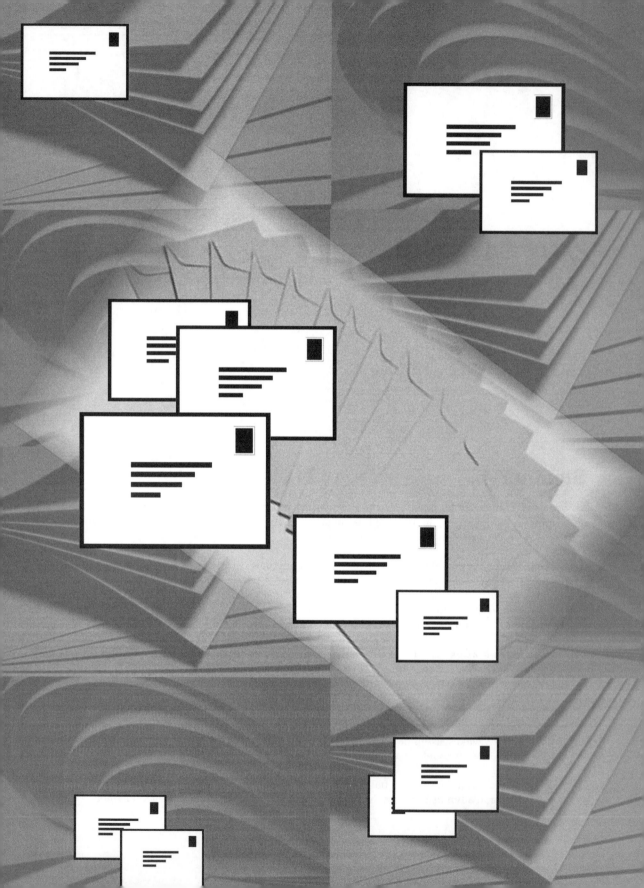

9

Administration

Any server product must include some tool for managing and administering the server, especially if the product allows clusters of servers cooperating on the same task, as in the Enterprise edition of BizTalk Server. For all our work with BizTalk Server, we've yet to come to grips with BizTalk Server administration. We've taken the presence of a server largely for granted. We've used Messaging Manager extensively, but that isn't the same thing as server administration.

Therefore, in this chapter we are going to learn about **BizTalk Server administration**. We'll begin by learning the difference between administration and management in BizTalk Server, then review the basic entities that exist in a BizTalk Server installation. You learned some of this in Chapter 1, but now we'll go into more detail and pay attention to what must be done to administer these entities. Next, we'll introduce a new topic, **receive functions**, that are set-up through the BizTalk administrative tool but extend the reach of the messaging system. We'll see an example of receive functions as we modify the InitialOrders.skx schedule from Chapter 2 to use another source of messages.

The heart of the chapter, though, is devoted to an examination of the **BizTalk Server Administration snap-in** for the Windows MMC. We'll have a look at adding servers and server groups through the snap-in, as well as how to configure them. We'll introduce you to the common tasks of BizTalk Server Administration and how to perform them using the administration snap-in. The snap-in also permits you to modify the performance-related configuration of the system, as well as providing a view of the shared messaging queues. We'll build on that view to learn how to use the snap-in to troubleshoot problems encountered with the messaging system and XLANG Scheduler.

When you have finished this chapter, you will be able to do the following:

❑ Understand the major functional entities of a BizTalk Server installation

❑ Create and configure file and MSMQ receive functions

❑ Understand how to use receive functions with the BizTalk messaging system

❑ Create, configure, and delete groups and servers

❑ Diagnose messaging problems in a running BizTalk Server group

❑ Respond to messaging problems through manual intervention

❑ Secure BizTalk through server configuration and the use of roles

❑ Identify performance factors in BizTalk Server groups and design high-performance physical configurations

Administration may not be a flashy topic, but it is essential. When you are facing an interchange (a single transmission, regardless of how many documents or attachments are included) that should work but does not deliver the expected results, you'll be glad you know your way around the administrative tool. Finally, when it is time to put your brilliant prototypes into high-volume production, being able to design a high-performance installation will make you very popular.

Administration versus Management

If it isn't administration, what is it we've been doing with Orchestration Designer and Messaging Manager all this time? Answer: we've been managing the system. In a product where the job gets done through "configuration, not programming", management might as well be programming. We've specified the logical configuration of systems and applications. We replaced programming with declarative specifications, but we were still concerned with a logical, abstract flow of processing.

However, none of this configuration had any effect on the server itself. We just assumed that the BizTalk Server group would be there, running quietly and efficiently in the background. As any good database administrator will tell you, however, there is a lot of administration that needs to get done if applications are going to run – and run well – on a given server installation. You must configure the software and data storage to ensure that every server in the group has access to the data and services it needs. You must secure the group, ensuring access is granted only to authorized users, and then only with the proper permissions.

BizTalk Server 2000 isn't really a single server application. Instead, like most modern server products – and certainly most Web-related server products – BizTalk Server is a collection of cooperating servers and tools. It comprises the following services:

❑ BizTalk Messaging Services and the XLANG Scheduler.

❑ Internet Information Server on which WebDAV depends for HTTP support.

❑ You may use HTTP and SMTP components in your channels, which brings in IIS again and may bring in Exchange or some other SMTP server.

❑ The servers in a group are tied together by the Messaging Management database, which brings in at least one SQL Server.

Administration is all about properly connecting the pieces at a minimum, and ideally configuring all the pieces for optimum performance.

BizTalk is aimed at mission-critical, high-volume systems. The big win in deploying business-to-business software is in stripping out friction and overhead from essential, and therefore high-volume, activities. Even when you are using BizTalk for internal application integration, you are going to use it for critical line-of-business applications. The overhead of designing messaging solutions is warranted only when you have a variety of applications cooperating on the same task, or when the task to be coordinated is an extremely high value activity. Reliability and performance, then, are of the utmost importance in a BizTalk Server installation.

This is where administration comes in. While developing a BizTalk solution, you need to be able to troubleshoot problems. The BizTalk Server Administration interface lets you do that by giving you a window into the state of the servers and the shared queues upon which the product is based. When you deploy your solution, you need to move from a development platform – typically a group composed of a single server – to a production environment. A production server group will have more than one BizTalk server, and reliability measures like clusters will be in effect on the SQL Server side. When a solution is in operation, you will need to monitor performance to ensure you are getting the best use out of your hardware resources. When the time comes to expand your installation, you will need to know what to upgrade and then you will have to manage the upgrade process. All this is administration, not management. While it is not as interesting, perhaps, to programmers, administration is vitally important to a successful BizTalk solution.

BizTalk Groups, Servers, and Shared Data

BizTalk Server is a new product, and if you are just starting out and running the examples, you're probably working with a single server that hosts all the BizTalk and SQL Server software. You probably think of BizTalk as a single machine, even if you are using the Enterprise edition, with a view to eventually implementing BizTalk on several machines.

Any BizTalk installation, however, consists of a **server group**. This is a cluster of individual servers, each configured with the BizTalk Server software, that share a common body of data. This is what allows BizTalk to scale to high volumes and ensure high availability of the messaging servers. The data, which controls the flow of messages as well as the overall configuration of the group, resides in four SQL Server databases. The group cooperates to process orchestration schedules and messages. Although you may address individual machines through schedule monikers, as we saw in Chapter 6, applications and organizations outside the BizTalk group will normally view the group as a single logical machine.

Take a look at the schematic of a production BizTalk server group overleaf. We'll refer to it in the sections that follow. At the end of the chapter, we'll come back to it again, and make suggestions to enhance performance.

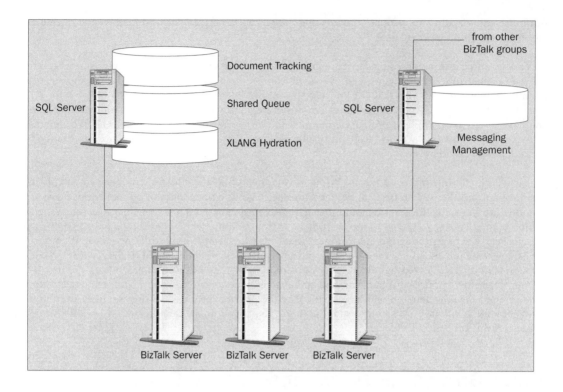

BizTalk Servers

Let's start with the three servers at the bottom of the diagram. A single BizTalk **Server** consists of a computer with the BizTalk Server software installed. At run time, it hosts Messaging Services and (probably) an instance of XLANG Scheduler. Each BizTalk Server includes this software, as well as any AICs or custom components that might be used in BizTalk messaging ports, channels, and schedules. Each Server shares the processing of the overall traffic coming and going with the other machines, much in the way an HTTP server in a round-robin web farm shares the load on a busy web site. The analogy cannot be taken too far, however. In a web farm, incoming traffic is load-balanced across Servers by routing an incoming request to the next available server in the farm. In a typical BizTalk installation, the Servers share queues of incoming and outgoing messages.

BizTalk Servers also rely on the Internet Information Service (IIS), because WebDAV access to the repository relies on HTTP services. For the record, Messaging Manager and message tracking functions are also implemented as web-based services.

> *There is one area in which individual BizTalk Servers can differ: receive functions. We will discuss these in a moment. Such functions are defined individually for each Server. The software needed to operate receive functions, however, is common to each Server. A receive function specified for a particular server in a group, then, is really a specialized configuration of common software.*

BizTalk Server Groups

A BizTalk **Server group** is a collection of Servers with a common messaging configuration. They share the queue of messages to process, giving each Server an identical view of the work. Logically, since all Servers in the group share the message processing, they must also share the document tracking database. All XLANG hydration data is stored in a shared database for access by the Servers in the group. The configuration of the group is maintained in a shared database, as well.

There is no central server coordinating the activities of the group. Instead, each server shares the load. This occurs through a shared queue of messages implemented in the SQL Server database. Each server, then, protects the integrity of message processing in the group by grabbing a message for processing within the bounds of a database transaction. This arrangement keeps individual servers in the group from attempting to grab the same message for processing. If a server needs to see a global view of the group, it refers to the shared queue database. All the tools for managing and administering BizTalk Server are built with knowledge of the shared data schema, and the registry on each Server contains keys that identify the databases and their hosts. In consequence, you may administer any BizTalk Server from any other BizTalk Server.

The three BizTalk Server machines in the diagram opposite belong to the same BizTalk group. They are unified by the Shared Queue and Tracking databases. The configuration of the group is stored in the Messaging Management database. Each Server may perform the same functions as either of the other two Servers, including administration. Each Server operates independently on a unit of work (a message). It is the shared databases that make these individual Servers a group, not some centralized software.

Each installation of BizTalk has at least one Server and at least one group. As you can see from the diagram, each group may have more than one Server, but Servers can only belong to exactly one group. You can add additional groups, say, for scalability. Adding additional Servers increases throughput; adding additional groups not only adds Servers, but it allows you to segregate your configurations functionally and distribute the enterprise load between groups of related Servers.

To illustrate this point, think back to the Messaging Manager. You are able to view all the configurations, such as channels, known to the Server. While you can refine your search and there is no explicit limit to the number of channels permitted in the database, there is the potential for the results of the search to be so numerous as to overwhelm you. As you add configurations to your Server, you may find it increasingly difficult to keep track of what channel belongs to what application. Therefore, although you can scale your installation without adding a new group, doing so permits you to organize your enterprise, as well as fine-tune security and performance for the specific needs of individual groups and departments.

Each configuration has each own unique pattern of usage and traffic load. In consequence, the load related to each configuration can be in conflict with the demands of other configurations. It is therefore beneficial to organize your messaging and orchestration information by business function, or some other unifying factor, as your use of BizTalk expands – to be better able to keep track of each function.

For example, you might split internal systems from external partners, putting each in its own group, or segregate by such business functions as purchasing and scheduling. Not only does this make it easy for you to understand what Messaging Manager shows you, but you can better understand your bandwidth and hardware requirements. If you have assigned a BizTalk Server group to a business function that is forecasting expansion, you know that you will need to add Servers to the group. Conversely, if the load on the Servers in another function-specific group spikes, you will understand that activity in the related business function also spiked. Although you can determine this information even if you do not organize by Server group, it is more difficult.

While each group maintains its own view of the workload, all group configuration information is maintained in a single database – in the diagram above, this is shown as the Messaging Management database. Note that while the three Servers in the group depicted are the only machines connecting to the Server hosting the Shared Queue and Tracking databases, there is an additional connection to the Messaging Management database marked from other BizTalk groups. Each Server hosting BizTalk throughout an enterprise will connect to the same Messaging Management database.

> *There is no restriction in the software that enforces different groups to use the same Messaging Management database. If two groups do not share the database, however, you will not be able to administer one group from a server belonging to the other group. The two groups will be isolated. The load on the Messaging Management database is comparatively light, so there is no practical benefit to be gained from hosting multiple Messaging Management databases and isolating groups.*

BizTalk Databases

The shared databases are clearly of great importance to the operation of BizTalk Server 2000. They are what enable servers to cooperate, and therefore they are also what enable BizTalk Server 2000 to scale. There are four databases needed. You may name them anything you wish during installation, but I've shown the default database names below:

- ❑ **Shared Queue** – InterchangeSQ
- ❑ **Tracking** – InterchangeDTA
- ❑ **Messaging Management** – InterchangeBTM
- ❑ **XLANG Hydration** – XLANG

Since the databases are shared, it makes sense to provide certain functions as stored procedures on the database. If you examine any of the databases using the SQL Server Enterprise Manager, you will find a host of stored procedures. These tend to be basic building blocks, such as getting the next message on a MSMQ queue, or locating a particular interchange, and by having these building blocks available, the tools and Servers that interact with the shared databases are able to call the appropriate stored procedure. SQL Server maintains the transactional integrity of the database, giving each Server the sense that it is the only entity working with the shared information.

> *There is no need to investigate the stored procedures. Indeed, they are subject to change with the database schemas. Studying them is an exercise in studying the source code of an application. They are mentioned here to provide you with a sense of BizTalk Server's architecture.*

As noted before, each Server group maintains its own Shared Queue, Tracking, and XLANG Hydration databases. Each enterprise installation usually maintains a single Messaging Management database.

The *Tracking* database maintains the record of all document interchanges that passed through the BizTalk Server group. Any document processed by a Server belonging to the group, whether being sent or received, is recorded in this database. The data maintained depends on the selection criteria you established in the document definition (set in the Global Tracking Tab of the Document Definition Properties dialog in Messaging Manager) or channel tracking configuration (specified in the Inbound Document page of the Channel Properties wizard in Messaging Manager).

We've seen what purpose the *XLANG Hydration* database serves. It is largely opaque to administrators and programmers and functions as a private store for the XLANG Scheduler. Because SQL Server maintains integrity in the face of system failures, the XLANG Schedule Restart service (`wfsvcmgr.exe`) is able to reliably determine what schedules were executing at the time and restart them when the system is recovered. The *Messaging Management* database also has stored procedures that enable the BizTalk Server Administration MMC snap-in to implement an administrator's desires regarding the addition, deletion, and movement between groups of Servers.

The one database that we have skipped over so far is the *Shared Queue* database. As the name suggests, it implements some queues that BizTalk Messaging Services uses to process document interchanges. Here the stored procedures and transactions provided by SQL Server are critically important. Without them, it would be impossible to have more than one Server. A particular Server must be able to obtain a message from a queue in an atomic transaction if the Servers are not to interfere with one another. An understanding of the queues implemented by this database will therefore be useful to you when you try to troubleshoot failed interchanges. With this in mind, let's take a closer look at queues.

Queues

It is easy to see why BizTalk would need a queue of messages. Arriving and departing documents are queued, and the Servers in the group de-queue each message in turn for processing. In this way, the queue acts as a buffer to ensure no data gets lost when the traffic presented to the group exceeds the capacity of the group's Servers to process messages.

If you recall that channels can be scheduled, you might have imagined that there is another queue, reserved for scheduled messages. That way, Servers would not waste their time repeatedly de-queuing and re-queuing messages that cannot be sent at present. Actually, BizTalk supports *four* queues in the Shared Queue database. It is not until you realize that document interchanges can fail that the need for the additional queues becomes apparent. The queues implemented by this database are:

- **Work**
- **Scheduled**
- **Retry**
- **Suspended**

We'll now consider each of these in turn.

Work Queue

This is the queue for documents awaiting processing. Documents arrive in this queue as a result of an `Submit()` or `SubmitSync()` method call on the `IInterchange` interface, which we discussed in Chapter 5. The queue exists to support immediate processing, so it will be rare for you to see messages in this queue when you open the BizTalk Server Administration snap-in while the BizTalk Server is running. In fact, you will only see messages in this queue when the load exceeds the group's capacity to process traffic and the queue is acting as a buffer. This queue is not the primary buffer for Messaging Services, however. Every effort is made to process arriving documents promptly, but should you see messages there, you may manually move them to the Suspended queue, if you wish to prevent them from being processed for some reason.

Scheduled Queue

Documents that have passed through the Work queue, and are on their way to their destination, go into the Scheduled queue. If you see messages in this queue, it will generally be because the port involved in the interchange has a service window associated with it and the document must wait for transmission. Messages involved in interchanges without a service window may also end up in the Scheduled queue, however. The table that implements the Scheduled queue permits null values in the columns defining service windows. This queue is the primary buffer for the Server group. Again, administrators may manually move documents from the Scheduled queue to the Suspended queue.

Retry Queue

Interchanges may fail for any number of reasons. If a message fails because the interchange is improperly or incompletely specified, the document will be immediately transferred to the Suspended queue. If, however, the configuration is good but the interchange fails due to problems with the communications protocol, for example, no response from an HTTP server, documents may end up in the Retry queue, and the BizTalk messaging system will then try the interchange again. By default, BizTalk will retry the transmission three times, at five minute intervals. Remember, though, that in the Channel Wizard for BizTalk messaging there is a Retry options group on the Advanced Configuration page. There are controls within that group that permit you to change the number of retry attempts and the interval between them.

Suspended Queue

We are all human, and therefore subject to error, so we all get to know the Suspended queue rather better than we would like, especially while we are learning our way around BizTalk messaging. An error in the processing of an interchange will cause the document to be placed in this queue. If a transmission failure persists through all retry attempts, the document in question will end up in the Suspended queue. The Suspended queue is where documents go to die when things go wrong.

There are a number of things you can do with documents in the Suspended queue. Your initial inclination might be to delete the message, and while that is the ultimate destination for documents in this queue, there is still a wealth of information that may be gleaned from suspended documents. As a result the Suspended queue is the best place to look for information when troubleshooting a failed interchange.

Documents in the Suspended queue are said to exist in a **state**, which reflects where the failure occurred in the BizTalk messaging process. The BizTalk Server Administration tool will let you view the contents of either the document or the entire interchange, depending on the state of Messaging Services when the failure occurred. These states and what you may view are listed in the table below. Regardless of the state, Biztalk Server Administration lets you view the error information returned by Messaging Services.

State	Meaning	Viewable Contents
Initial	First step in processing an interchange	Interchange
Parsing	Parsing the document	Interchange
Document Validation	Validating a document against its specification	Document

State	Meaning	Viewable Contents
Channel Selection	Selecting a messaging channel for processing a document	Document
Mapping	Mapping a document to the desired output format	Document
Serializing	Serializing the document from the internal XML form native to BizTalk Server to the output format	Document
Field Tracking	Recording specified fields in the BizTalk DTA database	Document
Encoding	MIME encoding of contents	Interchange
Signing	Digital signing of an interchange for authentication	Interchange
Encrypting	Message encryption	Interchange
Custom Component	Custom parser/serializer/correlator invoked	Interchange
Transmitting	Transmission via communications protocol	Interchange
Correlating	Relating a receipt message with its associated outbound document	Document

Having reviewed the services in BizTalk Server which require administration, let's now move on to look at the tool we will use to do so: BizTalk Server Administration.

BizTalk Server Administration User Interface

Every administrative task you will perform manually is accomplished through a snap-in to the Windows MMC. The resulting tool is referred to as BizTalk Server Administration, and its user interface is shown below:

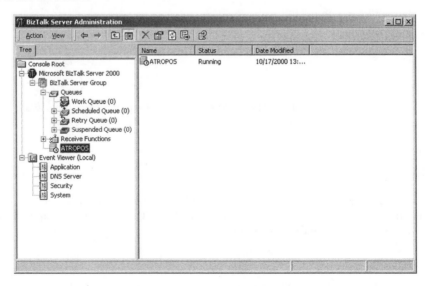

It shares the overall theme common to MMC snap-ins. You can see a two-pane window that has menus named Action and View. The left-hand pane contains a tree view of the entities under administration. The right-hand view displays information about the entity selected in the tree view.

The Console Root has only two child entries: Microsoft BizTalk Server 2000 and the Event Viewer. The latter is the same system event log that you see when you start the Event Viewer application from the Administrative Tools menu in Windows. The Application Log is a good source of information for troubleshooting interchanges, and we'll come back to that when we take up troubleshooting.

The BizTalk node has as many nodes as there are BizTalk server groups in the Messaging Management database. In general, this should be the number of groups installed at your location. Each group has nodes for the shared Queues, each Server belonging to the group (my server in the screenshot above is called ATROPOS), and a node for Receive Functions.

Displaying Shared Queue Properties

Each queue entry has a number behind it, displaying the total number of messages in the queue. These numbers are not dynamically updated, and to get a current view of the number of messages in each queue, you should right-click on the queue you are interested in and select the Refresh command when it becomes available.

On a lightly loaded system, you would expect to see no messages in the Work and Scheduled queues, but you might see messages in the Retry queue, and you will find messages in the Suspended queue if there is a problem. You will see messages in the Scheduled queue if traffic rises to the point where a backlog develops, or if you have established a service window on a port through which you try to send a message.

Selecting a queue causes the messages in the queue to be listed in the right-hand pane. The context menu for queues allows you to refresh the snapshot of the queue, which updates the total. The columns available for display in the right-pane vary according to, and reflect the purpose of, the selected queue. All queues offer the basic properties Timestamp, Source, and Destination for display.

Work Queue

To this basic list, the Work queue adds the following properties:

- ❑ Document/Interchange
- ❑ Processing Server
- ❑ State

Scheduled Queue

Once an interchange moves on to the Scheduled queue, additional information is available. Beyond the three basic properties, the Scheduled queue offers these for display:

- ❑ Processing Server
- ❑ Service Window

The Service Window property is added to reflect the likelihood of interchanges subject to service windows and the fact that service has actually been scheduled. Curiously, the Document/Interchange property is not available for the Scheduled queue.

Retry Queue

If the interchange moves to the Retry queue, the following properties are available in addition to the three basic properties:

❑ Last Retry

❑ Retry Interval

❑ Remaining Retries

❑ Processing Server

❑ Service Window

This reflects the additional information related to retrying a transmission.

Suspended Queue

If the interchange encounters a problem and moves to the Suspended queue, you may view the following properties in addition to the basic properties of Timestamp, Source, and Destination:

❑ State

❑ Error Description

❑ Document/Interchange

❑ Interchange ID

By default, all available properties are displayed as columns in the Properties pane.

Displaying Receive Function Properties

If you select a Receive Function in the left-hand pane, properties of that function are displayed. Receive functions are an important capability of BizTalk Server that we have not discussed yet. We'll discuss these functions next, but for now know that the properties available for display are:

❑ Name

❑ Protocol Type

❑ Processing Server

❑ Date Modified

The context menu for receive functions allows you to delete or refresh an entry, as well as display its properties. Properties are exposed in a dialog we'll discuss in the next section. If a receive function is disabled, a red X is shown over its icon in the left-hand pane.

Displaying Server Properties

Selecting a Server in the left-hand pane causes its properties to be displayed in the right-hand pane. The available properties are Name, Status, and Date Modified. If the Server is running, its icon in the left-hand pane has a right-facing green triangle. If it is stopped, a red diamond is displayed over the icon. The context menu gives you more choices than any other context menu we have seen so far.

❑ You may start or stop the BizTalk Messaging Service on that Server

❑   You may delete a Server, which removes it from its Server group

❑   You can refresh the view of the server

❑   There is an additional menu item, **All Tasks**, that expands to its own menu with the single item **Free Interchanges**; this task lets you free an interchange from a stopped Server and move it to another Server

Receive Functions

In Chapter 2, we saw that messages could go directly into an orchestration schedule by arriving at an MSMQ queue monitored by XLANG Scheduler. Chapter 6 showed how messages could arrive in schedules via COM ports, called using the No instantiation option of the COM binding wizard. In Chapter 5, documents moved into BizTalk Messaging Services via the IInterchange interface.

An HTTP endpoint might consist of an ASP that retrieves the message from the Request object and submits it to messaging via IInterchange. A message arriving via SMTP can be similarly processed using an Exchange script. There are two protocols, however, that are very important yet leave us no convenient way to submit incoming messages to Messaging Services. These are the *local file protocol*, for documents dropped into local folders, and *MSMQ*. Neither the file system, nor the MSMQ software, gives us ready access to a scripting engine.

Receive functions are components in BizTalk that may be configured to poll a queue or file folder. When a specified document arrives, the receive function uses IInterchange to submit the document to Messaging Services, then deletes it from the monitored location. BizTalk Server supports receive functions specifically for the file system and message queuing. The general flow of processing for a receive function is depicted in the schematic below:

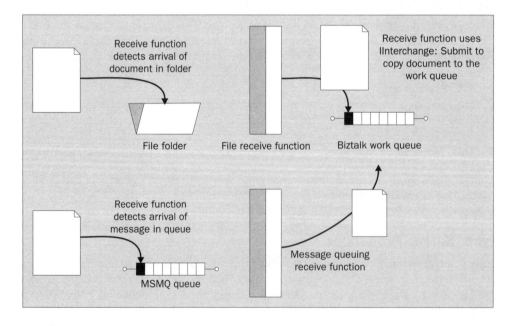

Let's take the case of a **file receive function** first. The file receive function uses an operating system event to poll the designated file folder, looking for files that match the filename specifications entered into the Server Administrator (we will be looking at how these are entered later on in this chapter). When one arrives, it copies the file and passes it to Messaging Services via IInterchange. If the call to Submit() worked, the file is deleted from the folder, and the message is in the BizTalk work queue awaiting processing. If it fails, the file is left in the folder and an error is written to the event log. In both cases, the receive function is an add-on to the system. So far as the sending application is concerned, the process ended with the delivery of the message to the folder or queue. The receive function used features of the operating system to detect message arrival, then used IInterchange to bring the message into BizTalk.

The process for an MSMQ receive function is nearly identical to the one for file receive functions, except the administrator specifies a particular queue to poll instead of a folder. When a message arrives, the message queuing receive function de-queues the message from the queue and submits it to BizTalk. If it works, the message is put in the BizTalk work queue and the MSMQ transaction is committed. If the call to Submit() fails, the transaction is rolled back, leaving the document visible in the monitored queue.

In both file receive functions and MSMQ receive functions, the functions in question are quite resilient, and data that fails to be picked up by them is not lost – the incoming data will simply remain in the folder or queue it was to be collected from.

Configuring Receive Functions

There are a few quirks of receive functions that explain why we are talking about them in a chapter on BizTalk Server Administration, rather than back in the chapter on messaging (Chapter 5).

- ❑ First, the BizTalk Server Administration tool is where these receive functions are configured, for reasons of processing efficiency (see below), as opposed to being configured in the Messaging Manager.

- ❑ Second, receive functions are assigned to a specific Server within the group. All BizTalk Servers have the software to support receive functions, but they are expensive resources that are dedicated to very specific locations. In consequence, if you want more than one Server to monitor the same folder (on a mapped drive, perhaps) or queue, you will have to create an appropriate receive function for each Server and repeat the configuration.

Adding a Receive Function

You add a receive function by right-clicking on the Receive Functions node and selecting the New submenu. Later in this chapter we will experiment with adding such a function for our Wrox Site Managers example. When the submenu appears, choose the type of receive function you wish (either file or message queuing). The dialog that appears in response to your selection differs little between the two choices. The type is reflected in the dialog caption, of course, but there is an additional difference we'll get to in a minute. The screen shotshown overleaf shows the dialog for a new file receive function:

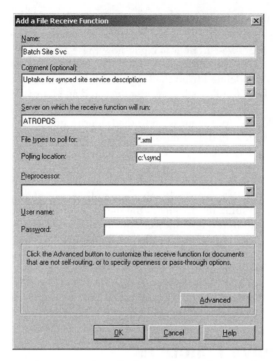

The first thing to do is provide a name by which to refer to the new function. You may also provide comments.

Be as specific as possible in your comments. Since receive functions are machine-specific, you may end up with several receive functions similarly configured. If there is a difference, or you have put a unique receive function on a Server for a particular reason, you will want to record that information.

Next, you need to specify which Server will host the receive function. The drop-down list box contains entries for all the Servers in the Server group.

Now we come to the other difference between the two types of functions I alluded to a moment ago. In the case of a file receive function, you are allowed to specify a filename mask. The function, when operating, will poll the designated folder searching for files that match the filename mask. If I wanted to poll for the Site Service Description documents we have developed in previous chapters, I could specify s*.xml to sort out such documents from other XML messages.

Although personally I prefer to create new folders to act as a receive location for each file receive function, you may wish to have a common folder or you may have little control over the location. A common example would be a folder used for files pushed to the site via FTP. You may have a common folder for all files pushed by your partners, or your network administrator might have created a folder for each partner as a security measure designed to isolate one partner from another and from the rest of the network. In either case, the single folder will contain many different types of documents. While it is true that FTP has been removed from the final release of BizTalk as a port option for sending, this should not affect their receipt through receive functions. It is unknown whether FTP will ever be restored as a port option – however, it may well reappear in subsequent service pack releases. In any case the ability to support FTP sending directly is largely unnecessary so long as file receive functions are available.

Message queuing receive functions do not make this distinction based on filenames or types – there is no capability, say, to differentiate documents based on message labels. What both types of receive functions require, however, is for you to specify a polling location. For file receive functions, this is the file system folder where documents will be deposited as files.

Message queuing receive functions, on the other hand, require a named queue as the polling location, but there is an important restriction placed on the information you provide for this item. The implementation of message queuing receive functions works with the low level MSMQ API. The functions in that API work with format names rather than queue path names. The syntax to use is:

```
DIRECT=OS:<server_name>\<queue_name>
```

So, to create a message queuing receive function on the private queue Incoming on my Server (atropos), I would enter the following into the polling location box:

```
DIRECT=OS:atropos\private$\Incoming
```

Next, you have the option of selecting a preprocessor component. These are custom COM components that may be invoked prior to parsing if your documents require special processing or clean-up prior to formal parsing. An example of this would be for messages compressed for transport. A pre-processor could be used to decompress the file prior to the start of parsing.

The next two items in the dialog box are a **Username** and **Password**. For file receive functions, this is optional. You would provide this information if the polling location was secured with restrictive access permissions. In that case, you would need to provide the user name and password of an account with read and delete privileges for the folder. On the other hand, message queuing receive functions require the user name and password of an account with access to the MSMQ service and the particular queue in question.

The last remaining control (other than the ubiquitous **OK**, **Cancel**, and **Help** buttons) on the dialog is the ominous **Advanced** button. The advanced options are used to tell a receive function what to do with a document once it has it. If the documents for which the receive function is configured are self-routing, you are don't need to concern yourself with this, and may safely click **OK**. But, since we won't cover self-routing and open messages until Chapter 10, we will be using the **Advanced** button for now.

Advanced Configuration of Receive Functions

In a nutshell (and a fairly small one, at that), **open routing** means that fields within the message determine some or all of the routing. All the configurations we have made so far for messaging ports and channels (as distinct from XLANG schedules) have made all the decisions for Messaging Services.

> *It would be more elegant to say they are "closed", but for some reason BizTalk Server does not use that term. There is "openness" in various degrees, or "not open", but no "closed" routing.*

Messaging Services routes a message based on the type of message, its source, and its destination. Since channels encapsulate all this information, specifying a channel by name is shorthand for specifying the full routing information. You may leave the source, destination, or both, open as your need for flexibility dictates.

What this means for receive functions is that the **Advanced Options** dialog first asks you to specify the degree of openness: **Not open**, **Open Destination**, or **Open Source**. For the kinds of routing we've been doing, the choice is **Not open**:

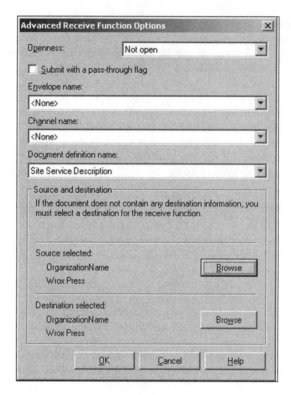

Next, you need to specify whether the document should be processed as a **pass-through submission**. A pass-through, as the term suggests, bypasses the parsing, decoding, decryption, and signing functions of Messaging Services. All that happens is that the message is passed directly to the channel for transmission. You use a pass-through to transmit binary data or non-Unicode text through BizTalk (taking advantage of Messaging Service's ability to shift a message from the protocol that brought it to BizTalk to another protocol for the outbound transmission).

The next three list boxes exist to let you specify the routing of a non-open interchange as rapidly as possible. All three display only configurations that exist in the Messaging Management database, so you cannot misconfigure a receive function by making a typing mistake. You must specify an envelope for non-XML document types, as always. Next, you can specify a channel and document definition to complete the routing.

If the message is not self-routing, you may select an organization by clicking on the appropriate Browse button. This information will be passed in the call to IInterchange. If you did not select a channel by name in the Channel name drop-down list, you must specify the source and destination information so that Messaging Services can select a channel at runtime.

Note that the Browse buttons are disabled when a channel is selected.

A Browse button is provided because you must provide both the organization qualifier and organization identifier value when you specify the source or destination. Clicking Browse brings up the Select Source or Select Destination dialog, shown opposite above. When finished selecting the source or destination, click OK to go back to the main dialog.

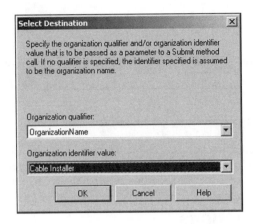

Editing or Disabling Receive Functions

You may wish to alter the configuration of a receive function, or disable the receive function. A receive function that has been disabled remains in the database, but is not actively loaded and polling. The only things you cannot do to an existing receive function is change its underlying protocol (file or message queuing) or change the name of the receive function itself.

You can reconfigure properties by double-clicking on a receive function in the Properties pane, or by right mouse-clicking and selecting the Properties menu item from the context menu. The property dialog that is presented has three tabs as depicted in the screenshot below:

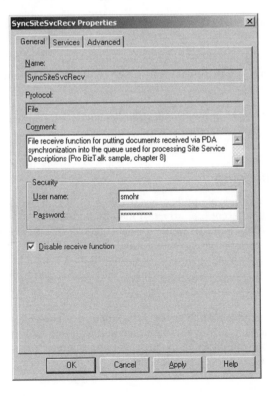

As you can see, the tabs are General, Services, and Advanced. These duplicate the functions on the Add New Receive Function dialog, but some items have been moved. The layout of the tabs is as follows:

❑ General – name and protocol (read-only), comment, security, disable receive function

❑ Services – host server, polling location, and preprocessor. For file receive functions, file type is added

❑ Advanced – routing information, unchanged from the new function dialog

Checking the Disable receive function checkbox and clicking OK or Apply retains the receive function configuration but stops it from executing on the host server. The icon for the receive function in both panes will have a red X on it. Unchecking the box restores the receive function to operation.

Using Receive Functions

When would you want to use receive functions? At first sight, they would seem redundant in the case of message queuing as we have seen that a XLANG schedule can monitor a queue without any help. For files, certainly, applications depositing files on local drive could use IInterchange to submit documents directly. The easy answer, of course, is that you will use file receive functions whenever you have no control over the application saving the files. FTP, as noted above, is one such case. Legacy applications are another prime example. Of course, you will need to use receive functions when you are using BizTalk messaging but not XLANG schedules.

In the case of MSMQ messaging, the question is a little more difficult, as we saw that no modification was needed to get a message into a schedule. There are two cases that illustrate some uses for receive functions.

❑ The first concerns applications for which orchestration is not required: file conversion processing.

❑ The other illustrates a situation in which we either have a legacy application that cannot make use of the queuing API, or situations in which remote access to message queuing is impossible or undesirable.

We'll talk about the first in passing, as it replicates the features of a number of products on the market whose capabilities are limited to file format conversion. We'll develop the latter as a practical sample of file receive functions.

File Conversion Processing

Let's suppose you have a number of applications that export files in one file format, and other applications that require a different file format. It may be undesirable to add format conversion code to either set of applications; if the number of file formats increases, you have a many-to-many situation in which you need an exponential number of file format mappings. We saw this problem in Chapter 4 when we discussed the motivation for BizTalk Mapping. Rather than add format conversion code to the applications, we'd like to place BizTalk messaging in the middle, performing the file conversion in the course of an interchange.

This is what a number of products, such as Mercator, focus on. They let you specify a mapping and file locations. Files arriving in a location are transformed and dropped into the other location in the new format, and for many organizations, such file processing is enough. You should be able to see that this is easily replicated using BizTalk Server, which is designed to map differing file formats on to messages.

Designing an orchestration schedule for this task would be simple. A receive action would take the document in, and a send action would transmit the document via BizTalk messaging. The channel involved would specify the desired mapping. The hard part, though, is how to get the documents, which are being saved directly to disk by a legacy application you cannot change, into the schedule. You would have to resort to a component that polls for files – exactly what a file receive function does.

A file receive function can solve this problem and eliminate the need for a schedule. The file receive function can specify the desired channel directly, causing BizTalk messaging to be utilized in response to the appearance of a file. The desired output file is created without recourse to a schedule. The XLANG Scheduler is strictly overhead for this sort of application.

Wrox Site Managers: An Alternative Path for Site Service Description

Now we are going to configure our own file receive function, for the Wrox Site Management example we have been building up through the chapters so far.

Recall for a moment the basic business proposition we set out in Chapter 2. Field agents using client software on laptops or PDAs generate Site Service Description documents, which are queued for submission to the InitialOrders.skx schedule. We assumed that each client device would have wireless communications with the home office. At worst, we assumed reliable MSMQ messaging at the client, so that if the client was disconnected from the home office, messages would be queued locally and sent once communications are restored.

Both wireless communications and MSMQ are available for PocketPCs, and both are certainly available for laptops. But wireless is expensive for PDAs, so having to fit MSMQ, wireless software, and the client on some devices might be a bit of a stretch. It is all too easy to envision the management of Wrox Site Managers coming back to you – the programmer of the system – shortly after rollout asking for a "small enhancement". They'd like some way of processing documents that have been stored on the PocketPCs and then synchronized with a machine at the home office upon the field agent's return. No changes should be made to the server-side software.

Happily, file receive functions make this possible. You can configure a file receive function that polls the synchronization folder on the home office machine. The function will look for Site Service Descriptions, and submit them to BizTalk messaging using a channel. BizTalk messaging, of course, supports MSMQ messaging, so we make the target of that messaging the RecvSiteSvc queue that is the entry point of the InitialOrders schedule. The schedule is designed to be resident in memory, executing, at all times.

In theory, then, the existing system should work without modification. The orchestration schedule has no idea how a message got into the queue and, indeed, couldn't care less. Whether the client called the messaging API or BizTalk did, the message arrived and it is time to get to work. The general scheme of processing is shown overleaf – all you need to do is configure a file receive function, a BizTalk port, and a BizTalk channel. Configuration, not programming, is our goal here. We should be able to get it done before lunch. Let's try it!

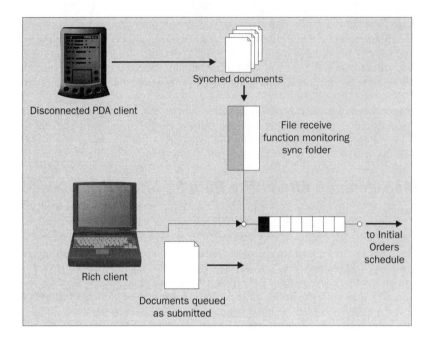

Port Configuration for Receiving Documents

When all is said and done, the file receive function we are going to set up will turn to BizTalk Messaging Services to dispose of the documents it plucks from the target folder. Since nothing can be done without the proper configurations, we should start with BizTalk. Now, we have existing organizations and document definitions from Chapter 5, but we are going to need a new port and channel to do what we want. Remember, the schedule we devised in Chapter 2 monitored the queue without Messaging Services' help, and documents arrived in that queue via MSMQ API calls, not through BizTalk messaging.

There are a lot of different ways we can organize the port and its associated channel. What makes sense is to treat this as an example of application-to-application integration within the Home Organization. Wrox Site Managers is the Home Organization here (we could certainly rename it if we so desired). The new port and channel are taking files that are synced from PDAs, and putting them in a queue that feeds another application. Although there are no actual applications performing these functions, they are logical functions that may be treated as applications. It will help us keep things straight.

Here's what to do:

1. First of all, open up the Biztalk Messaging Manager application.

2. In the left-hand pane, click on **Organizations** and click **Search** now.

3. Double-click on the **Home Organization** (or whatever you have renamed the Home Organization). This should bring up its **Properties** dialog:

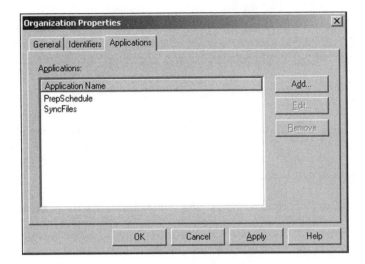

4. In the Applications tab of the Home Organization's Properties dialog, add two new applications, SyncFiles and PrepSchedule.

5. Click OK to dismiss the Properties dialog.

Now we are ready to define a messaging port that sends documents to the logical PrepSchedule application.

6. Create a new messaging port to an application and call it LoadSchedQueue.

7. Select the Application radio button on the Destination Application page, and locate and select the PrepSchedule application from the list:

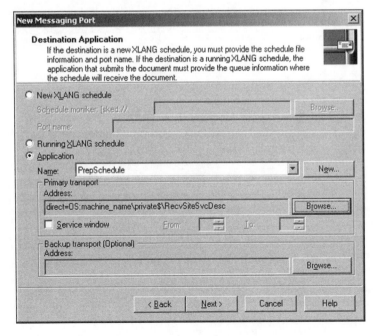

8. Under Primary transport, if you have selected Message Queuing and provide the address `direct=OS:machine_name\private$\RecvSiteSvcDesc`. Be sure to replace machine_name with the actual machine name of the computer hosting the target queue.

You will not require an envelope since the Site Service Description message is based on XML, which is the default parser anyway.

9. Accept the defaults on the Envelope Information and Security Information pages.

10. Before clicking Finish, however, check Create a channel for this messaging port and select the From an Application option.

11. Click Finish to complete the port configuration and begin configuring a channel.

Creating a Channel to Get the Message into the Queue

Now we're going to create the channel for our receive function.

12. Give the channel the name SyncFilesToQueue. It is useful to provide comments stating that this channel is to be used by a file receive function. As you create more channels, you will find that you quickly forget which channel goes with which system or application, so lots of descriptive comments become important.

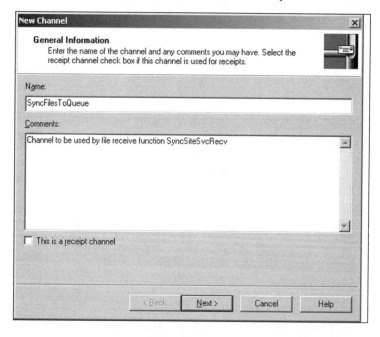

13. Select Site Service Description as both the inbound and outbound document definition name.

14. You may accept the defaults on the remaining pages unless you are interesting in tracking the passage of these files. On the last page, click Finish to save the channel configuration.

Now we'll configure the file receive function.

File Receive Function Configuration

Begin by opening the BizTalk Server Administration tool, and expanding the Server group node for the group on which you are running the Site Managers system.

15. Right mouse-click on Receive Functions and select the New File Receive Function menu item from the context menu.

16. In the Add a File Receive Function dialog, enter `SyncSiteSvcRecv` for the name of the receive function, and also enter some comments describing what the receive function is intended to do for us.

17. Select the Server on which you want the file receive function to execute.

In my case, the choice is easy for two reasons: I only have one BizTalk Server, and I've implemented the `RecvSiteSvcDesc` queue as a private queue. My file receive function needs to execute on that machine. In the hypothetical case of Wrox Site Managers, we'd want to put the receive function on the machine to which the PDAs synchronize their files.

We have no preprocessing tasks – the input is guaranteed to be well-formed and valid because it is built by a component that uses the XML processor – so we'll skip over that control. Assume that the client software is saving the documents with filenames of the form `siteservicecXXX.xml`, where the XXX stands in for a sequential serial number. The client starts at `000` and rolls over after `999`, so field agents have the incentive to visit the home office and synchronize their PocketPCs on a timely basis.

18. With this convention, we should specify the File types to poll for entry as `siteservice*.xml` (this will also catch the sample document we will be using in this example - `siteservicesample.xml`, residing in the code for Chapter 3).

19. In the Polling location field, enter the synchronization folder using a conventional drive designation or UNC pathname.

20. If the folder has special security restrictions on it, enter the user ID and password of the account to use to access the folder for read-write access.

The account under which Messaging Services executes must have rights to the polling location folder.

21. Click the Advanced button.

22. In the Advanced Receive Function Options dialog, make sure the Openness property reads Not open, as our message is not self-routing.

There are a number of different ways to specify routing, but we will take the easiest, specifying a BizTalk messaging channel by name.

23. Select the channel you just configured in Messaging Manager, `SyncFilesToQueue`.

24. Click OK to close the Advanced Properties dialog, then click OK on the main dialog to save the receive function configuration.

Using the Receive Function with the InitialOrders Schedule

It's time to see if our theory accords with reality. We should be able to drop a Site Service Description document into the folder monitored by the file receive function, and have it processed by the orchestration schedule. We assumed that the schedule would always be running so that it could process documents as they came in from the field via MSMQ, so be sure to start the schedule using a script or, for test purposes, the XLANG Event Monitor.

> *Remember that the schedule has two business rules that determine whether or not the cable installation and yard service subscription messages get sent. Be sure that the sample document you drop into the folder has information that will send at least one message. The sample available for download, `siteservicesample.xml`, will trigger both outbound messages.*

Now drop a copy of a Site Service Description document into the folder monitored by the file receive function. It may take several seconds for you to see anything depending on where you are in the receive function's polling interval and how fast Windows Explorer refreshes its view of the folder, but after several seconds, the file will disappear from the monitored folder. Depending on the content of your sample message, the output cable installation and yard service messages will appear in the file folder you designated.

If you launched the initial schedule instance using the XLANG Event Monitor, you can check it at this point. A new instance should be holding at the MSMQ receive action. The completed instance will show events for receiving the message that the file receive function dropped into the queue, and for sending the output messages. The events you see should be identical to those you saw in Chapter 5.

Common Administrative Tasks

Receive functions were something of a detour from the main purpose of the BizTalk Server Administration snap-in. They were a programming solution, allowing you to solve problems in your applications and systems. At the start of this chapter, though, we said the focus was going to be on administration, not management. Rather than build new solutions, the aim of administration is to operate and administer the solutions and Servers you have.

This is what we shall focus on in the next section of this chapter. A BizTalk system administrator faces common tasks on a daily basis. These tasks are accomplished through BizTalk Server Administration. We're going to go through each task and show you how to get the job done. We will focus on the following:

- ❏ **Remote Administration**
- ❏ **Server Group Administration**
- ❏ **Server Administration**
- ❏ **Securing BizTalk Server groups**

Some of these tasks may seem mundane. Remember, though, that without a properly running BizTalk Server group, even the cleverest BizTalk-enabled system is useless. While the tasks described here are seldom so dramatic in their impact, knowing how to administer BizTalk efficiently and effectively will aid you in debugging and deploying BizTalk solutions. If your installation is running smoothly, you have more time to devote to the interesting business of designing and developing new solutions.

Rights and Remote Administration

BizTalk Server Administration needs to connect to the individual Servers in the various BizTalk Server groups in order to configure them. In addition, it needs to work through the Messaging Management database in SQL Server to effect changes in the composition of the groups and the existence of the groups themselves. For its own purposes, BizTalk creates a user group, named **BizTalk Server Administrators** by default, when you install the software. When you establish database connections during installation, you are prompted for a user ID and password for an account that has administrative privileges on the host SQL Server. You are able to update the database connection information, as we shall see in a moment, from within BizTalk Server Administration.

> *BizTalk Server also creates a group for access to document tracking. This group is named* **BizTalk Server Report Users** *by default.*

Since BizTalk Server Administration is a snap-in to the Windows MMC, a user who is a member of the BizTalk Server Administrators group is able to perform administrative tasks remotely. You must start the MMC with access to the common console file BTSmmc.msc. This document is installed in the root of the BizTalk Server folder subtree, **Program Files\Microsoft BizTalk Server**, by default when the product is installed.

Setting Enterprise Properties

The Messaging Management database sets the configuration for the entire installation. To establish it as the BizTalk configuration database for all groups under administration, you must select the node labelled **Microsoft BizTalk Server 2000**. This is the parent of all the Server group nodes. Right-click on it and select the **Properties** menu item from the context menu, or select it and choose the **Action | Properties** menu item on the main menu, to expose the **Properties** dialog for the entire BizTalk Server 2000 installation:

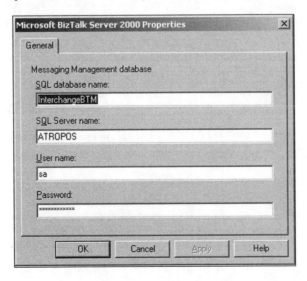

BizTalk Server Administration has to read this information on startup. Note that you must use an existing SQL Server account. It can get all the subordinate information, for example, the names of Server groups by reading this database, but it has to have a starting point that locates this database. All the information on this page is recorded in the local Server's registry.

Setting Group Properties

If you right-click on any server group name in BizTalk Server Administration's left-hand pane and select the Properties menu item from the context menu, or select the server group and click Action | Properties on the MMC main menu, you will gain access to the BizTalk Server Group Properties dialog box. This dialog, shown below, permits you to set all the important properties of the Server group:

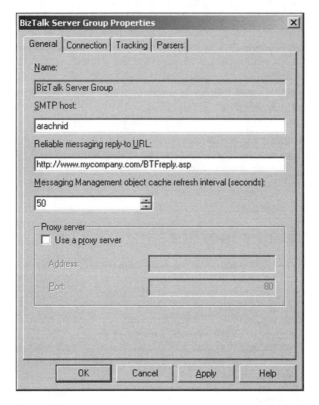

The dialog consists of four pages:

- ❑ General – properties governing access to Internet protocol servers and access to the Internet
- ❑ Connection – identity and access to the Shared Queue and Document Tracking databases
- ❑ Tracking – general policies governing document logging
- ❑ Parsers – identity and order of access to parser components

This dialog allows you to perform administrative tasks that govern the Server group as a whole. Let's examine each of these pages in turn.

General Properties

The name of the Server group is presented as a read-only property. You cannot change the name from this dialog. In fact, you cannot change it anywhere; all you can do is delete it and create a new one.

The next entry is the name of the SMTP server handling SMTP relaying (the protocol used for sending e-mail to mail systems such as Exchange). Configurations throughout BizTalk Messaging Services are able to abstract the identity of the SMTP Server. They simply say, in effect, "pass this message off to the SMTP Server for transmission to the following address". Somewhere, of course, Messaging Services, through the SMTP send component, must be able to look up the name of the server. This is recorded in the Messaging Management database, but you enter it – and edit it – here.

The Reliable messaging reply-to URL field refers to an HTTP script that processes replies to documents sent according to the BizTalk Framework. This Framework is referred to via the euphemism "reliable messaging" throughout BizTalk Server. Under the Framework, every message receives a reply (more on this in the next chapter). You may set this up as an ASP that processes message replies. If you are not using the Framework, you may leave this entry blank.

> *We'll present an extended sample that uses the BizTalk Framework 2.0 in the next chapter, as an example of open routing.*

Information entered into the Messaging Management database is cached by Messaging Services. The faster the refresh interval, the sooner changes take effect. A fast refresh interval decreases performance by frequently interrupting Messaging Services for database queries, so you should estimate how often you expect to make configuration changes and set this value accordingly. Finally, sites using a proxy server may configure this information on this page.

Database Connections

Messaging Management was just one of the shared databases. It was also the only one shared by all server groups. Now that we are dealing with the properties of a single Server group, we can finish configuring the location, identity, and access account for the shared databases. The Connection page contains groups for the Tracking and Shared Queue databases. Each elicits the database name, the machine name of the hosting SQL Server, and the user name and password of the account through which to access the database.

Note that each of the three databases is configured separately. Each may be on a different machine, accessed through a different account. This will be an important tool for optimizing performance when we take up that topic toward the end of this chapter.

Tracking

This page is fairly sparse. As we have seen, the details of tracking are configured through the Messaging Manager (the tool, not the database). The properties configured through this page are global settings across all Servers and channels. This page first asks you to indicate whether to enable document tracking. By default, this is turned on. Under that heading, you have three more properties to specify by clicking the checkboxes:

❑   Log incoming interchange – on by default

❑   Log outgoing interchange – on by default

❑   Log the original MIME-encoded message – off by default

Parsers

In Chapters 3 and 4, we discussed the general sequence of processing for a message: a parser looks at the document, mapping may occur, and a serializer writes the document to the desired output format. Along the way, decisions are made: channels are selected according to the type of the document, and routing may be accomplished depending on the value of designated fields. We noted that there are different parser components to handle XML, EDI formats, and flatfiles. In Chapter 10, you see how to create your own specialized parser components to handle other types of files, even binary formats. How does BizTalk Messaging Services know which component is to handle each incoming message?

The answer is that it tries each component in turn. We want the service to select the proper parser component as quickly as possible. To address this need, BizTalk Server Administration lets you change the order in which parsers are tried. If you have a Server group devoted to UN/EDIFACT EDI processing, for example, it makes sense to put this parser at the top of the list of components to be tried. The parser page displays the parsers registered with the system under the component category BizTalk Server Parsing Components. The components are displayed in the order in which Messaging Services will apply them to an unknown message type. You may select a particular component and raise or lower its standing in the order of parsing attempts by clicking the up or down arrow controls on the page. The default order of parsing attempts is:

- ❑ XML
- ❑ UN/EDIFACT
- ❑ ANSI X12
- ❑ Flatfiles

It is also possible to develop your own serializers/parsers for a particular format.

Adding a Server Group

You were prompted to create a Server group when you installed BizTalk Server. That's a good thing, too, or we'd have had nothing to configure through the last few sections. Hopefully, though, your company's use of BizTalk Server will grow and your responsibilities as a BizTalk administrator with it. When that happy day occurs – *before* you ask for a raise, please – you will need to add a new Server group to your BizTalk installation.

To perform this task, select the Microsoft BizTalk Server 2000 node in the left-hand pane and right mouse-click on it, selecting the New Group menu item from the context menu. If you prefer to use the main menu, the equivalent menu item is Action | New Group. You will be presented with the New Group dialog box. This dialog box is very similar to the Connection page on the Server Group Properties dialog. The first entry is the only difference. It asks for the name of the new group.

> *BizTalk Server Administration uses Windows Management Instrumentation, the standard underlying the Windows MMC in general, for its implementation. Names are therefore subject to the WMI naming restrictions. If you create a name using non-alphanumeric characters, the name may be rejected. More information is available from* msdn.microsoft.com/library/default.asp. *Look in the Platform SDK, under* Windows Management Instrumentation | WMI Overview | Terms and Concepts | Object Paths; *this contains a general description. The formal specification is provided in the* Reference *section under the heading* Backus-Naur Formal Syntax.

From there on, the dialog is the same as the Connection page. You are asked to provide the name, server machine name, and account information for the Tracking and Shared Queue databases for the new group. Remember, these will be entirely different from any other group. Only the Messaging Management database is held in common.

If, for some reason, the databases do not exist or are damaged, you may reinstall them using SQL Server's Enterprise Manager and Query Analyzer tools. *Enterprise Manager* lets you add and delete databases. *Query Analyzer* lets you load SQL scripts and execute them on existing databases. Once you have created the Tracking and Shared Queue databases, go to the setup folder under the BizTalk installation (or on the installation CD) and locate the following script files: BTS_Core_Schema.sql, BTS_Tracking_Schema.sql, and SQL_Reporting.sql. Loading and executing each of these script files in turn will configure the shared databases for use. Be careful to set the proper database in the Query Analyzer before running the script. Alternatively, if you prefer a graphical interface or need to redirect the group to an existing database, you may use the database setup application, BTSsetupDB.exe, found in the setup (BTSsetupDB.exe) folder.

Adding a Server to a BizTalk Server Group

Once you add a Server group, you will need to add Servers to that group to perform processing. In fact, long before you need a second group, you will need to add Servers to your original group. The initial software installation adds the Server on which the software is being installed automatically. After that, you need to add Servers to an existing group manually.

This is one of the easiest tasks you can perform in BizTalk Server Administration. Select the node representing the Server group to which you wish to add a Server. Right mouse-click and select the New Server menu item from the context menu, or select the Action | New Server main menu item. You are given the Add a BizTalk Server dialog. This dialog asks for only one piece of information: the name of the Server to be added to the group.

> *When you are installing BizTalk Server 2000 to additional machines, you have the option of performing a silent install. In this case, you specify, among other items, the group name from the command line. The syntax of the command line for installation is covered in Appendix A. If the name you supply exists in the Messaging Management database as the name of an existing BizTalk Server group, the machine on which the software is being installed is added to the group and adopts the specified Tracking and Shared Queue databases assigned to the group.*

Deleting and Moving Servers

If you wish to remove a Server from a group, select the Server's node in the left-hand pane, right mouse-click, and select Delete from the context menu, or select the Action | Delete main menu item. This procedure also lets you move servers from one group to another. Deleting a Server from a group does not remove the BizTalk Server 2000 software. You can immediately add the Server to another group.

> *While the BizTalk Server software is installed in this case, you may not have any application components or custom BizTalk components such as functoids, parsers, and serializers installed that are required by the new group. Similarly, when you delete a Server, you will reconfigure any receive functions set to execute on that Server. When you are moving Servers between groups in a production setting, always review the status and configuration of your components.*

There is an additional consideration to take into account when moving Servers. If you are moving Servers between Messaging Management databases, or simply deleting Servers from use by BizTalk Server, be careful not to remove all Servers from a Messaging Management database you intend to continue to use. If you have deleted the last Server from the database, and there are no Servers in any of the groups under the Messaging Management database, you will need to run the BizTalk Server Database Setup Wizard to restore the Messaging Management database to active use. The wizard is found in the setup folder. When you run the wizard, it is not necessary to create a new Messaging Management database. Instead, use the option to select an existing database found on the Configure a BizTalk Messaging Management database page.

Starting and Stopping Servers

You may start and stop BizTalk Messaging Services on any Server in a group. Note this is restricted to Messaging Services, and has no effect on XLANG Scheduler, which is controlled through the Component Services administrative console. You will want to start and stop Messaging Services when taking a Server out of service for maintenance or hardware upgrades. A controlled stop permits you to redistribute interchanges that were in process on the Server at the time the service was stopped.

To stop a running service, select the node representing the Server in question and right mouse-click. Select the Stop menu item on the context menu. The same action may be taken from the main menu with the Action | Stop menu item. The Server icon will change so that a red circle is displayed over the icon, and the Status column for the Server in the right hand Properties pane will show Stopped. You may restart stopped Messaging Services by using the Start menu item on the context menu or Action | Start from the main menu. The red circle icon is replaced with one displaying a green right-facing arrow, and the Status column shows Running.

In addition to facilitating maintenance, starting and stopping BizTalk Messaging Services forces a refresh of the messaging cache. If you do not want to wait for a configuration update to take effect, as you might when working on a development Server, this is a simple way to force the information to flow through to Messaging Services immediately.

Freeing Interchanges

If you stop a running BizTalk Server in a production environment, you run the risk that interchanges assigned to Messaging Services will be stranded. Remember that an interchange is a single transmission that may include more than one message. Once you stop the Server, however, you may make the interchanges available for reassignment by freeing the interchanges. Select the stopped Server's node in the left-hand Tree pane and right mouse-click, selecting the All Tasks Free Interchanges menu item. From the main menu the menu item is Action | All Tasks Free Interchanges.

> **Attempting to free interchanges on a running server results in an error message.**

When this command is initiated, a stored procedure is executed on the Shared Queue database. Among other things, it marks the interchange as not having a Server assigned. Messaging Services reassigns the freed interchange to the next available Server.

Setting Server Properties

Although BizTalk Server groups are intended to consist of multiple Servers with interchangeable configurations, it is still possible to make some performance-related property settings for individual Servers. Before making changes to a Server's properties, you must stop Messaging Services as described above. Making changes to a Server's properties is accomplished through the Server Properties dialog box. You open this dialog through the context menu's Properties menu item, or by selecting Action | Properties from the main menu. It is shown below:

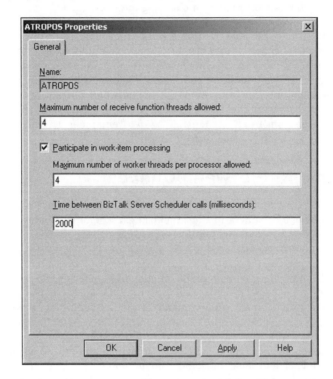

The machine Name displayed is, as you might expect, read-only. Changing this property would have too many effects outside of BizTalk for it to be safe to permit changing the machine name casually for any one application.

You may set the maximum number of threads devoted to receive functions. Note this does not mean that this number of threads is automatically created; rather, it is an upper limit. Ordinarily, an increased number of threads results in an increase in performance. This is because both file and MSMQ operations involve I/O operations that are slow compared to operations in memory, so threads executing instructions (for example, threads processing messages for the messaging service), can continue to operate while a receive function thread is blocked waiting for an I/O operation to complete. This boosts CPU utilization. However, there is a cost involved in switching the processor between threads – a process called context switching. If processing is not dominated by I/O, context switching can actually diminish performance. If you need to adjust the default setting, you should carefully measure your actual performance using the Performance Monitor application, and experiment with different settings for this value. In general, though, you may begin by slightly increasing the maximum number of threads for a machine running many receive functions.

The checkbox labeled Participate in work-item processing might seem surprising to you. It means exactly what you might think. When checked, this Server will participate in processing documents submitted to Messaging Services. Unchecked, this property prevents the Server from drawing messages from the work queue for processing. You will virtually always want to leave this box checked. You might, however, have many schedules that do not use BizTalk messaging implementations, or you might need a lot of receive functions. In the latter case, you may wish to devote one or more Servers exclusively to hosting receive functions. In such cases, you could devote one or more Servers to these functions and take them out of normal BizTalk message processing. This would increase their performance by eliminating the distraction of checking the work queue.

If, however, the Server is to participate in normal work processing, you will want to review the next two settings. Like the Receive function thread property, the Maximum worker threads per processor property is a performance-related setting. Increasing this number can increase performance in I/O-bound operations, but you should measure your actual performance carefully before changing this setting by a significant amount. The last property, Time between BizTalk Server Scheduler calls, refers to the interval at which the Server checks the shared queues, not XLANG Scheduler. It takes a count of milliseconds on the range from 1 to 2^{32}-1 (4,294,967,295). Remember that this involves a database query, so it is pointless to specify a value that is too small.

Moving Documents Between Queues

At times, usually during development, you will realize that a message needs to be terminated during processing. You may have a document in a channel using a scheduled window and you might wish to try an alternative channel. Any document in the Work, Scheduled, or Retry queues may be moved to the Suspended queue to terminate processing.

In the Tree pane, select the queue containing the document in question, then select the message in question in the Properties pane. Right mouse-click on the message and select the All Tasks Move to Suspended Queue menu item on the context menu, or select Action | All Tasks Move to Suspended Queue from the main menu. This takes the document out of the normal flow of processing.

If you are intent on terminating the interchange, you may then go to the Suspended queue, select the document, right mouse-click and select the Delete menu item on the context menu. Not only does the Action | Delete main menu item perform the same function, but the stylized X icon on the taskbar of the main window will delete the message as well.

Now, you may have a document in the Suspended queue that can be rescued. Connectivity to the outside world may be re-established, or you may have changed an incorrect configuration. In that case, you can try the submission again. Select the document in the suspended queue, then right mouse-click and select the All Tasks Resubmit menu item on the context menu, or select the message and click on the Action | All Tasks Resubmit menu item on the main menu. This causes the document to be resubmitted to Messaging Services.

Exporting Administrative Information

The BizTalk Server Administration snap-in supports a feature that may be convenient in the event that you have a lot of information displayed in the Properties pane – you can export the contents of the Properties pane to a text file at any time:

1. Select an item in the Tree pane, then select Action | Export List... from the main menu.

2. You are presented with a Save As file dialog. Choose a folder and filename and click OK.

The lines below are a sample exported from the Suspended queue. Note the column headings. Columns are tab-delimited. In the sample, I have broken the entry onto several lines for clarity:

```
Timestamp              State          Error Description  Source
10/24/2000 21:36:33    Serializing    User Move          DestOrg

Destination    Document/Interchange    Interchange ID
                                       {4BB01B52-96D9-4EC0-A9D8-8DF7A9BD4BEB}
```

Tracking Errors through the Administrative Interface

A complete BizTalk messaging service interchange is a long series of interdependent steps, any one of which can fail for good reason. It can be challenging, therefore, for a BizTalk novice to diagnose a failed submission. Fortunately, the BizTalk Server Administration snap-in provides valuable information, which, when taken with an understanding of the sequence of events in a BizTalk interchange, can help you solve problems. If you submit a document to Messaging Services and do not get the desired outcome – a schedule triggered by a channel, a message written to disk or queue – your first stop should be BizTalk Server Administration.

Checking Group and Server Status

Generally, in development your problems will stem from a bad configuration or incorrect document. In production, though, if a working channel suddenly fails, you should make a quick check of the Server group and individual Servers to ensure they are functioning properly.

Your first stop is to check the status of the group as a whole. Select the Microsoft BizTalk Server 2000 node in the Tree pane and then look at the Status column in the Properties pane. Each group's state will be listed. Groups can be in one of the following states:

❑ **Connected** – the normal operating state, this indicates that the group is able to connect to the shared queue and tracking databases

❑ **Tracking connection failed** – the group cannot connect to the tracking database, leading to faults regarding in-transit tracking and message interchange reporting

❑ **Shared queue connection failed** – the group is unable to connect to the shared queue database and is therefore unable to process messages

❑ **Tracking and shared queue connections failed** – the group has no database connections to shared information and is therefore unable to perform messaging service functions

Any of the last three states is critical. When encountered, be sure to check the properties in the Connection page of the Server group properties. If the hosts are correctly listed and you have network connectivity to them, check the account information against the user information in SQL Server.

Next, you will want to check the status of the individual Servers in the group. Select the group in question in the Tree pane. The Properties pane displays icons for the queues and receive functions, followed by the Servers assigned to the group. The Status column will display one of the following states:

❑ Running – the Server's messaging server is active and you have administrative privileges on the machine

❑ Access denied – you lack administrative privileges for the machine

❑ Error – BizTalk Server 2000 has been removed from the machine

❑ Stopped – BizTalk Messaging Services has been stopped

❑ Unknown – the Server is unavailable for an unknown reason

The problem states can usually be solved by ensuring you have administrative rights to the Servers, that BizTalk Server is installed on the Servers and the messaging system is running, and that you have network connectivity with the Servers.

Viewing Error Information for Suspended Documents

If the preceding steps show a healthy network environment and properly connected groups and Servers, you must look at the results of the specific BizTalk interchange. The State and Error Description columns of a document's properties are a prime clue to what went wrong. The state of the failed document or interchange reflects where in the chain of processing the error occurred, and that will help focus your search by pointing you to the proper tools.

Back in the section on shared queues at the start of this chapter, we listed the various states of documents in the Suspended queue and what kind of information was available for viewing. Here is a table of the same states, paired with comments regarding what you should check. This includes the data in the documents as well as the tools you should use.

Document State	What to check...
Initial	the parameters of the submission
Parsing	document syntax, for example, well-formedness in XML documents
Document Validation	the inbound document against the specification in BizTalk Editor
Channel Selection	routing parameters and document type against channel configurations in Messaging Manager
Mapping	the mapping process in BizTalk Mapper, including functoid processing
Serializing	the outbound document against the message specification in BizTalk Mapper
Field Tracking	the document's fields against tracking criteria in Messaging Manager; also check the DTA database for errors
Encoding	data submitted against the specified MIME type
Signing	certificate information in Messaging Manager and the Windows certificate store

Document State	What to check...
Encrypting	certificate information in Messaging Manager and the Windows certificate store
Custom Component	custom parsers and serializers against inbound and outbound documents, respectively
Transmitting	port configurations to ensure proper URLs; check connectivity and access to servers for SMTP, MSMQ
Correlating	messages against the custom parser and correlator components

For problems with parsing, validation, mapping, serializing, and channel selection, view the contents of the document or interchange. This is an area where knowledge of XML is helpful. Even if you are going from one flatfile format to another, the tools in the middle stages are XML-based. Validation is particularly easy to check. You can copy and paste the document contents from the Document content window. The content is displayed in an edit control, so you can select the content and use *Ctrl+Insert* to copy the text to the clipboard. Paste this into a text editor and save it to a file, then use BizTalk Editor to validate this document instance against the inbound message specification.

Mapping is a bit harder. BizTalk Mapper lets you test the map, but it only shows you the mapping to the internal, XML-based form. If you suspect trouble spots, you can enter the values from the submitted document into the values fields in Mapper for those fields and see what happens. Are the values picked up properly? Is there a type conflict, particularly when functoids (discussed in Chapter 4) are being used?

Serializing may be the hardest of all. The results of the mapping are the input for the serialization, but you cannot easily test the serializer. Still, you can look at what the Mapper displays and compare that by hand with the message specification for the outbound document specification. Problems in this state usually arise when the mapping creates intermediate content which, when serialized, does not validate against the outbound document specification.

In all cases, view the error description for the suspended message. The text displayed is often truncated, so the data displayed in the Suspended Queue Entry Error Description dialog box will often be of some help.

Information Available in the Event Logs

It is almost always worth looking a bit further down in the Server Administration snap-in. The last major node is the local event viewer. This offers access to the Server's event logs. If you run the administration console on the Server handling the interchange, you can look at the Application log to see what Messaging Services and its components had to say about the failure. The data written by the components is particularly revealing as they generally write detailed failure information. While this can be cryptic, it may also shed new light on the error descriptions in the Suspended queue. The standard BizTalk parsers, serializers, and transport components write particularly descriptive information.

If you need access to the logged information, you might wish to go into the system Event Viewer and save the log so that it is not inadvertently removed.

Securing BizTalk

So far we've made only passing reference to special security measures. We've mentioned the use of certificates, encryption, and digital signing in conjunction with Messaging Manager, but we haven't talked about the administration of security in BizTalk Server. This is due in some degree to the fact that, like many Windows applications and services, BizTalk Server 2000 builds on the security measures native to Windows. There are some aspects of BizTalk administration, however, that will require us to take another look at security.

Using Windows, SQL Server, and BizTalk security measures, you can control who has access to key services and who can submit documents for processing. Combined with security measures for the services hosting your Internet protocol endpoints, you can fully secure BizTalk Server for reliable communications with your partner over the public Internet.

User Roles

The first step in securing BizTalk is to secure access to Messaging Services. This is done through the **Component Services** application, which is found on the Administrative Tools menu in most Windows installations. `IInterchange` is the gateway to BizTalk Messaging Services, and it is implemented in a COM+ component that is installed in the **BizTalk Server Interchange Application** COM+ application. You can find this application by connecting to the computer hosting BizTalk Server, expanding its node, then expanding the COM+ Applications node.

> **We will assume throughout this discussion that you have administrative access to all the Servers in the Server group you wish to administer. Note also that when we are talking about securing a particular component or COM+ application, you will have to perform this configuration task on every Server in the group, as each machine runs its own copy of the software. Each Server must be identically configured in order to create a secure configuration.**

Securing IInterchange with Roles

Within the Interchange Application, you have three nodes: components, BizTalk.Interchange.1, and Roles, which is empty following installation of the software. The component listed is the one implementing the `IInterchange` interface. We are going to add roles, then assign specific users to those roles. The roles thus created will control access to the `Submit()` and `SubmitSync()` methods of the interchange component.

First, we have to enable security for the COM+ application. To do so, select the BizTalk Server Interchange Application node, then right-click and select Properties, or select Action | Properties from the main menu.

1. In the Properties dialog that appears, click on the Advanced tab

2. Uncheck the Disable changes check box and click OK. Click Yes in the warning dialog that appears.

This step tells Component Services to allow configuration changes to the COM+ application. BizTalk Server disables changes by default when it installs. You must click OK and close the dialog for the change to take effect.

3. Reopen the Properties dialog and click on the Security tab.

4. Check the box labeled Enforce access checks for this application to turn on security checking.

This is not enough by itself, however. We need to be able to check the identity of the users of each component instance. In its default setting, COM+ will only control this at the process level, making it impossible to control individual submissions.

Check the radio button for checking access at the process and component level. Your property page should look like this:

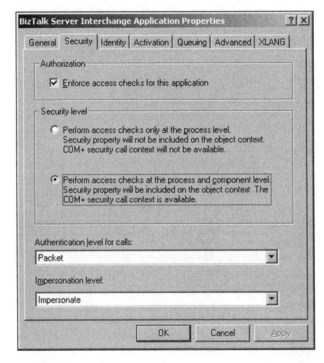

With the settings shown above, the COM+ runtimes will force authentication of each packet being sent as part of a method call, and security will be enforced by having the COM+ runtime impersonate the requesting user. This is exactly what we want.

Now move to the Roles node.

5. Right-click on the node and select New Role, or select the node and select the Action | New Role main menu item.

6. Enter a name for the role, such as *InterchangeSubmitter* and click OK.

7. The role appears as a new node under Roles.

8. Expand this new node, and select the Users node.

9. Right-click, and select New User.

10. From the Select Users or Groups dialog (shown below), add the users you want to have rights to the list, then click OK:

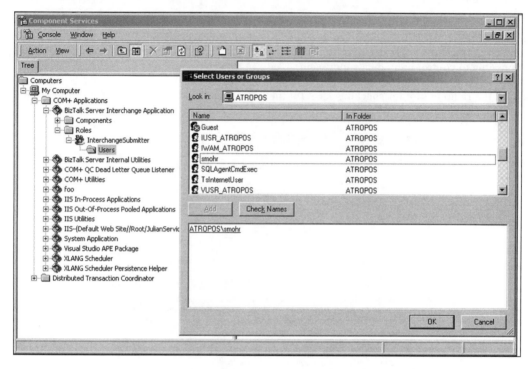

The users you selected appear under the Users node of the new role.

11. Now select BizTalk.Interchange.1 under the Components node and expand it.

12. Expand Interfaces and Methods, and select Submit.

13. Right-click and select the Properties menu item.

14. On the dialog that appears, select the Security tab.

15. In the Roles explicitly selected for selected item(s) list, check the box for the role you created.

16. Click OK.

Repeat the process for SubmitSync(). The users you assigned to the role will now be the only ones able to use IInterchange to submit messages to BizTalk Messaging Services.

If you have difficulty viewing the interfaces on the component, and you have come directly to this step from creating the role, turn security off for the COM+ application, then re-enable it.

Securing Remote Users

That's fine for the server, but what about users on remote clients? After all, it will be a rare server, indeed, that invokes IInterchange remotely. Messages will come into the server via a protocol such as HTTP, SOAP, or SMTP, where a script or component will call IInterchange locally. The work you just did securing IInterchange will work so long as you are on an intranet and you have not changed the default settings. During installation, BizTalk Server configures IIS for Basic and Integrated Windows authentication for its own applications, such as Messaging Manager itself. If you configure your own applications this way, the ASP that serves as an HTTP receive point will impersonate that user when it calls IInterchange.

You may not be able to use this method to secure your external partners. You may not be in a position to create a user account for external users, or they may not be willing to use basic authentication, which passes passwords across the network in clear text. In such cases, you should use server administration methods to severely restrict the sites that can reach your endpoints. For example, in IIS, you can restrict access to a domain name, for instance, mypartner.com, a single IP address, or a range of IP addresses. If you use this method, be sure to use certificates and whatever secure methods the protocol provides, for example, secure HTTP (HTTPS). For more information on securing access to your site, see *Alex Homer's Professional ASP Web Techniques* (Wrox Press, ISBN 1-861003-21-8).

Securing Orchestration

The other major piece of BizTalk Server is, of course, orchestration. Since XLANG Scheduler is a COM+ application, you would, rightfully, assume that you can perform the tasks described above to create roles for the application. You can, but it won't be necessary. If you open XLANG Scheduler in the **Component Services** application, you will find that access check enforcement was turned on during installation of the software. If you expand the **Roles** node, you will find four roles:

- ❑ **XLANG Schedule Creator** – needed to launch new instances of a schedule

- ❑ **XLANG Scheduler User** – required by users who will interact with a running schedule, for instance – calling a COM port to send a message into the schedule

- ❑ **XLANG Scheduler Administrator** – role for users who administer XLANG Scheduler

- ❑ **XLANG Scheduler Application** – role used by XLANG Scheduler itself when it launches a COM+ application from a schedule

If you look at the **User** nodes for each role, you will find that the installation process added the **Everyone** group identity to each role except **XLANG Scheduler Administrator**, which picked up the local **Administrators** group identity. Since access checks are enabled and roles have been created, though, it is very easy to secure orchestration. Decide who needs what level of access and assign them to the appropriate role.

The last two roles in the above list require a bit of elaboration. XLANG Scheduler Administrator applies to users performing the following tasks:

- ❑ Designating whether a COM+ application may host the XLANG Scheduler component

- ❑ Controlling persistence, including setting the type of DSN to be used by XLANG Scheduler

- ❑ Shutting down all schedule instances

- ❑ Starting, stopping, or terminating a running schedule instance

If you launch or interact with a COM+ application from an XLANG schedule, the XLANG Scheduler will use the XLANG Scheduler Application role. Any identity required by the other application must be added to the XLANG Scheduler Application role in XLANG Scheduler or you will not be able to work with the other COM+ application.

Designing for Scalability

If you are just learning about BizTalk Server 2000, it is likely that you are working with a typical development environment. You have a Server group consisting of one Server, and SQL Server is installed on the machine as well. All the interlocking parts of a BizTalk environment – Messaging Services, XLANG Scheduler, SQL Server, IIS, and your own custom components – are installed and executing on the same computer. That's a great development environment, but you won't be deploying BizTalk in production that way.

BizTalk is intended to be an Enterprise-class Server (although it is also sold in a single-server, non-clustered version), handling large volumes of mission-critical message traffic. A large part of administering BizTalk Server, then, is designing and deploying it for scalability. As we write this (December 2000), BizTalk has not reached general release; it is consequently hard to make any scalability suggestions based on experience. There are some sound suggestions that can be made, however, based on the design of the product and experience with database applications.

Designing a scalable BizTalk Server installation divides roughly into two parts: deploying the SQL Server databases, and deploying services and components.

Deploying the Databases

It would be easy to forget the role of SQL Server in a BizTalk Server installation. It is intended to be part of the infrastructure, hidden away behind the main product and its COM APIs. BizTalk Server, though, is tied together by its shared databases. Deploying SQL Server correctly offers potentially large gains in performance.

The first, and easiest, choice you might make is to move SQL Server off the BizTalk Server hosts (which we'll refer to hereafter as BTS machines) and onto a server of its own. This will not disturb the configuration of the group. The databases are intended to be shared, so if SQL Server is deployed on a BTS machine, it is local to that Server but remote to the rest of the Servers in the BizTalk Server group. Moving SQL Server to its own machine takes the database load off all the BTS machines and allows you to concentrate your hardware resources on the database server.

This is especially important when you factor reliability into the system. The data in SQL Server is, by definition, persistent. It requires a failover cluster (Microsoft Cluster Services) to avoid becoming a single point of failure. The BTS machines, by contrast, do not hold state. Failure of one BTS machine would only affect interchanges in process by that server; even those messages need not be lost. If the processing server fails, the BizTalk administrator may manually free the interchanges assigned to that server, at which time BizTalk will reassign them to the remaining Servers in the group. You need not implement a BTS machine as a failover cluster. Your BizTalk network, then, might look like this:

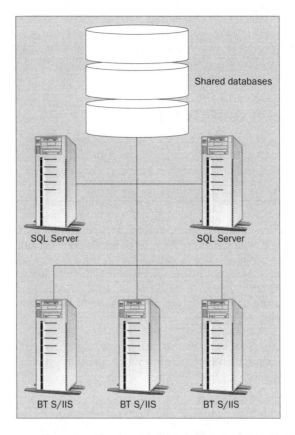

We can go further, however, if we consider how the database interacts with BizTalk Messaging Services. The Messaging Management and Shared Queue databases are accessed frequently by all Servers, as an interchange moves through the various states. These will be heavily utilized databases, and their use is somewhat interwoven.

The DTA database will also be heavily used – it is used at well-known points during an interchange, but the degree to which it is used is harder to predict. You will also have requests for service that are unrelated to interchanges and Messaging Services. Users and administrators querying the database will impose load on the DTA database in patterns completely unrelated to the operation of Messaging Services. Remember, you have the option of controlling how much data is logged, as well as whether the complete inbound and outbound messages are logged.

It is useful to move the DTA database to its own server, as it is largely decoupled from the other two databases, but the degree of improvement you will see depends on your own choices regarding what information is logged and how tracking data is utilized.

The end result of moving SQL Server off the BTS machines in the Server group is that we are able to overlap database requests and the other tasks in interchange processing. The BizTalk Servers will settle into a pattern of CPU and memory intensive processing. A large number of relatively inexpensive BTS machines can be associated with a small number of expensive database servers. While the one interchange in a BTS machine is waiting for data, other interchanges that are not waiting may complete. On the database server, a large number of requests result in a similar pattern. In that case, queries blocked for I/O are overlapped with queries that are fetching data from memory or are bound by the processor.

Finally, predicting the behavior of the Orchestration Hydration database is more difficult. For one thing, schedules and their hydration requirements can vary widely. In general, their utilization will be governed by how long they wait for inbound messages (some BizTalk transactions can wait hours or even days to complete), and how many transactions are used. You should experiment with your own schedules before deciding how to host the hydration database.

Deploying Services and Components

Once you've carefully considered your database options, profiled usage, and settled on a deployment scheme, you are left with the BTS machines themselves. What can we do to scale the Messaging and Orchestration Services?

A BTS machine hosts a variety of services. You have BizTalk Messaging Services, XLANG Scheduler, IIS, and any custom components or COM+ applications that may be used by Messaging Services or orchestration. There is little reason to try to split these across machines. Orchestration and Messaging Services will almost always interact closely. Receive channels may activate schedules, and schedules may use BizTalk messaging. While you may call across machines to use schedules – we saw how this might happen in Chapter 6 – you want to keep the two services together to maximize the possibility of local COM invocations. Similarly, you want local access to IIS. Local use of Messaging Manager requires use of IIS, and, more importantly, you need IIS and ASP – or some other HTTP server with application capabilities – for HTTP receive endpoints.

If you cannot specialize your Servers, is there anything you can do to improve scaling on the application side of your BizTalk Server installation? There are four approaches you might consider:

❑ Separately deploy receive and send services

❑ Replace HTTP with SMTP, or place messages on a local queue, to handle surges in demand

❑ Isolate ASP applications from BizTalk receive functions

❑ COM+ load balancing with App Center

Separately Deploy Send and Receive Services

Earlier in the chapter, we saw that you need to explicitly deploy file or message queuing receive functions to specific machines. The same holds true in practice for HTTP receive functions. Since these are usually ASP pages, they have a specific URL – in short, they reside on a specific machine. It is only after they submit the inbound message to Messaging Services that all the machines in the BizTalk Server group process the traffic as a cluster.

This gives you the opportunity to specialize some BTS machines as receive servers, leaving others free to process a greater share of the messaging service traffic. This is useful when you have an inbalance in the amount of inbound and outbound traffic, or when the time to process one or the other is substantially greater. For example, if an ASP receives a message that triggers an elaborate schedule that takes a substantial amount of time to process, you can concentrate all the message reception on one machine knowing that the remainder of the machines will take up the slack running the schedule.

You can use the Windows Load Balancing Service, or a hardware load balancing device, to create a web server farm of BizTalk Servers running HTTP receive functions. Windows Load Balancing Service routes incoming requests transparently to a series of HTTP servers in a round-robin fashion. So far as BizTalk Server is concerned, all the Servers are part of the same group. A subset of the Servers may be running ASP pages under IIS that act as receive functions. The machines share a common URL, with the load balancing solution sharing out traffic equally. Thus, you can cluster receive functions, while the remainder of the BTS machines in the server group handle the schedules and outbound BizTalk messaging. The HTTP receive servers will still participate in this activity through BizTalk's normal shared processing, but the disproportionate loading of receive functions will displace the other BizTalk activity, leaving it for the rest of the BizTalk servers. This setup is illustrated below:

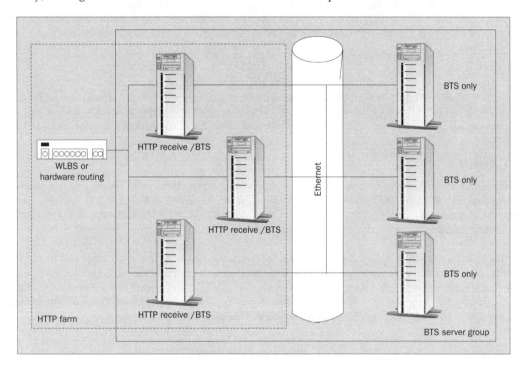

Surges in Demand

HTTP is popular for communicating with external partners. Firewalls are easily configured to pass HTTP traffic, stateless HTTP applications are easily clustered with web farms (as depicted in the last section), and secure HTTP (HTTPS) protects documents transmitted over the Internet. There is a problem with scaling HTTP, however. It is a synchronous protocol. A request, even an HTTP POST operation, expects a response. Many message schemas take advantage of this when they expect a reply message. Under average loads or below, this is no problem. When traffic temporarily surges above the capacity of the HTTP server farm, requests are lost. This is what happens when you click on a link to a very busy site and get no reply.

The traditional way to handle this problem is through queuing. Queues with adequate buffer capacity allow messages to accumulate in the queue during surges. When traffic levels drop, the application drains the queue. You can take advantage of this in BizTalk if your business process does not demand an immediate response. You can replace HTTP with SMTP, or use the Submit() method of the IInterchange interface (which asynchronously queues documents in the shared queue). Or you can use MSMQ message queuing from your HTTP receive function to introduce queuing behavior in the receive portion of your deployment. If you are using Submit() from an ASP, you can send a perfunctory reply indicating the success of the Submit() function as the response to the HTTP request. You should only use SubmitSync() when the reply must be meaningful in business terms. In such cases, you have no choice but to wait for the interchange to be processed.

Isolate ASP Applications from BizTalk Receive Functions

BizTalk Server is an application-integration product. Many new internal applications are constructed as ASP applications on intranets. Be sure to observe the distinction between HTTP receive functions and ASP applications. Even though the BTS machine hosting the receive function is running IIS and ASP, you do not want to put the load of a high volume application on a BizTalk machine. These machines should be limited to BizTalk messaging and schedules – functions only they can perform. If you are communicating with an ASP application, host the application on an IIS server that is not part of the BizTalk Server group.

> *The next release of Microsoft's XML parser, MSXML 3.0, available at msdn.microsoft.com/xml/general/xmlparser.asp includes an HTTP POST interface which is safe for use in ASP pages for server-to-server HTTP communications. This component is expected to be included in release form with the commercial release of BizTalk Server 2000.*

App Center

Orchestration schedules will frequently call COM+ components. In normal usage, you will install these components locally on the BizTalk Servers. If the components prove to be handling a substantial amount of the overall processing of the system, you may wish to consider clustering COM+ components using App Center.

In this case, calls to the COM+ component are transparently load-balanced across a number of COM+ servers. App Center helps with the administration and management of the component server cluster, offering a single console for management of the cluster. It also helps ensure all servers in the cluster receive the same component configuration when deploying a new application. The BizTalk Servers are reserved for Orchestration and Messaging Services. This setup is shown below:

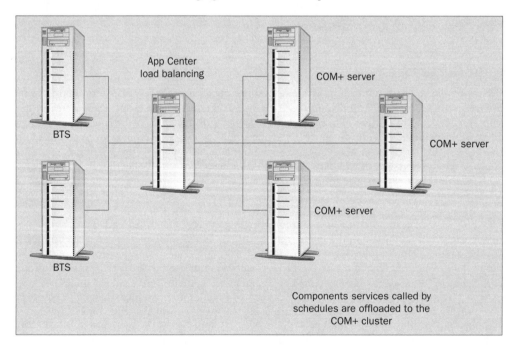

App Center is an enterprise-class server product similar in complexity to BizTalk Server. For additional information on the product, as well as using it to effectively manage component deployment, please refer to Professional Application Center 2000 *(Wrox Press, 2001, ISBN 1-861004-47-8).*

Summary

This chapter built on your knowledge of the concepts and entities used by BizTalk Server, by introducing you to receive functions for files and message queuing. You saw that such functions round out the ability of BizTalk Messaging Services to receive traffic on the protocols it supports. Additionally, file receive functions give you a way to handle FTP interchanges even though that protocol is not directly supported by BizTalk Server. Receive functions also give you a way to accommodate less capable clients without rewriting the schedules and messaging of your systems.

Perhaps most importantly, we examined what it means to administer BizTalk Server 2000. Prior to this chapter, you were managing messaging, a design-time task. Administration moved you into the realm of operating a production BizTalk environment, and we covered the common tasks of administration and how they are accomplished through the BizTalk Server Administration tool. You learned how to configure server groups and individual servers, and in the process, you learned what information is shared by the group and what is specific to each server. We showed you how multiple server groups may easily coexist and be administered in a single BizTalk installation.

As a direct result of learning to configure server groups, we learned a bit more about the shared queues BizTalk Messaging Services uses and how messages move between them. This became important when we took up the topic of troubleshooting. BizTalk Server Administration provides a window directly into the queues, and the information they contain helps you in diagnosing failed messaging interchanges and suggests where to look and what tools to use to fix the problem. You also learned what an administrator can do to retry failed interchanges, terminate running interchanges, and free interchanges stranded by a server failure or maintenance so that they may be processed by other servers in the group.

You learned how to secure BizTalk Messaging Services and XLANG Scheduler using the native security measures provided by Windows. We secured BizTalk at a fundamental level by assigning COM+ roles to the methods of the IInterchange interface. No matter what protocol is used to receive messages, inbound traffic is entered into Messaging Services via this interface. Complementing this, we looked at what you could do to secure access to your system when dealing with external partners, and although you no longer had the advantage of native Windows security, you could use digital certificates and IIS administration to control access to the receive endpoints.

Finally, we got a brief glimpse of deploying BizTalk Server with performance in mind. As with many PC-based enterprise systems, the short answer to scalability is "more servers with shared state". How many machines and how services are assigned to them makes all the difference to the performance of the overall BizTalk system. While the story of BizTalk performance is still being written by the BizTalk development team at Microsoft and their early-adopter partners, some strategies are already apparent; database techniques, in particular, are well known from the world of web site hosting.

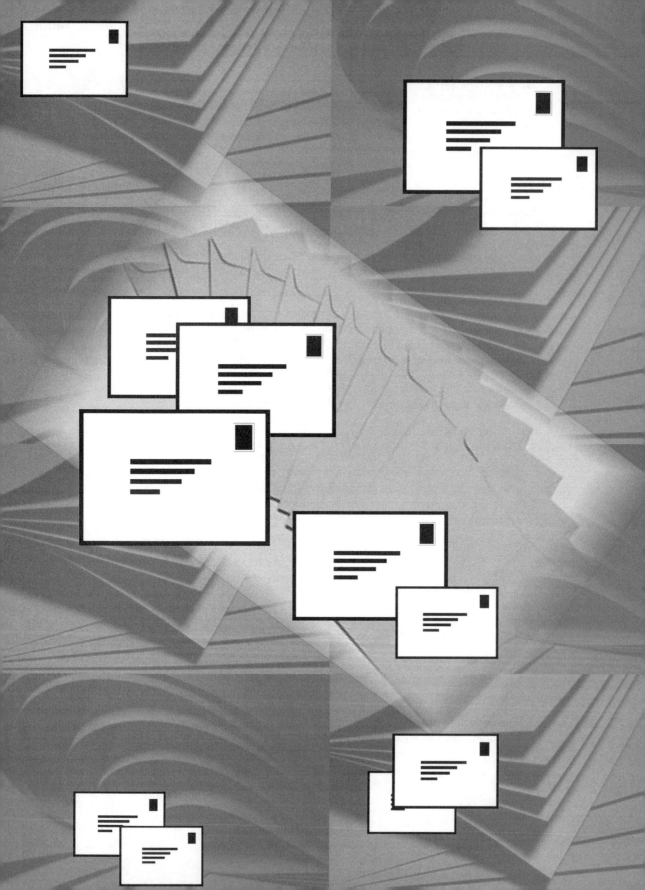

10

Routing and Acknowledging Receipts

Whenever we've configured the BizTalk messaging service for message exchange, we've been careful to specify the source and destination of the document. This is what you'd expect by analogy with the real world you send a letter by writing an address on the envelope. If you expect a reply, you need to supply your return address too. When you place a telephone call, you enter the number of the other party. When they return your call, they have to have your telephone number to place the call.

BizTalk showed us a few tantalizing hints that suggest there might be an alternative to explicitly providing routing information in port configurations. In Chapter 5, we looked at distribution lists, whereby one message can be sent to a long list of recipients. In Chapter 6, we found that orchestration lets us dynamically bind to ports based on the content of the message being sent.

This is what we really want. You will frequently encounter situations when you want to execute the same process with the same document, but with only one out of a number of partners. While using a distribution list allows us to send messages to the whole list, it won't let us select a single entry from the list. For example, say you have a purchasing application that you want to connect to your supplier's supply chain applications. Your application generates a specific purchase order. Based on what is being bought, the application knows who the desired supplier is. We need to perform the same function – transmitting the purchase order but to just one out of many partners. We don't want to have to configure a channel for each vendor. Wouldn't it be easier if the application could insert the identity of the recipient into the message, and then let BizTalk select the appropriate port based on that information?

This is one function of **routing** in the messaging service. Routing is the process by which BizTalk selects a port and a channel in order to determine the target destination. In the cases we have seen so far in this book, BizTalk used submission routing, providing all routing information in the configurations or the API calls to IInterchange. The correct selection of channel and port depended on information submitted to Services during the call to the Submit() method of the IInterchange interface.

In this chapter we will also look at acknowledging that you have received a message in the form of a receipt. This enables the concept of reliability, whereby you can be sure that the intended party has received the message that you sent them. BizTalk Server provides ways in which you can request a receipt if you are sending a message, generate a receipt if you receive a message, and how to correlate a receipt with the record of the original document, and thus confirming that it has been sent (and saving the server from trying to resend the message again).

While BizTalk Server can deal with most of the formats you are likely to be working with out of the box, if you need to work with a custom format, you will need to write a custom parser and serializer, to generate the intermediate form of XML that BizTalk Server uses internally. We will look at custom parsers and serializers in this chapter as well. Also, if we are working with custom formats, you may need to deal with receipts in custom formats, so you will also need to write a custom correlator to match the receipt with its original message.

This chapter broadens the routing picture. During its course:

❑ We'll review how BizTalk goes about routing and what information it needs.

❑ We'll introduce **self-routing**, the process by which documents contain the information BizTalk needs to route them to their destination.

❑ We'll cover open ports, where the final destination is left open to the routing process.

❑ We'll see how we can request and generate receipts for messages we send and receive.

❑ We'll look at how we can deal with formats that BizTalk server does not provide native support for, by using custom parsers, serializers, and correlators.

❑ Finally, by way of illustrating these concepts, we'll develop a self-routing example using HTTP.

To make things interesting, we'll use **reliable** messaging, BizTalk Server's implementation of the BizTalk Framework. Reliable messaging uses an envelope that is consistent with the BizTalk Framework. When reliable messaging is specified, the messaging service follows the rules provided in the Framework for reliable delivery and acknowledgement of messages.

Basic Routing Requirements

All the various bits of configuration that you do in Messaging Manager gives the BizTalk messaging service the information it needs to process a given interchange. In Chapter 5, you learned that the channel is the top-level concept that ties all the other configurations together for the purposes of a message interchange. Clearly, then, when the messaging service is presented with an interchange for processing, its first and most important task after parsing the document is to select a channel from the Messaging Management database. Routing is how BizTalk Server implements this task.

The BizTalk messaging service requires three bits of information to select a channel:

❑ the source organization

❑ the destination organization

❑ the document definition

If more than one channel matches the combination, all of the matching channels are executed with the submitted interchange document, resulting in multiple transmissions. If none match, the submitted interchange is moved to the `Suspended` queue. BizTalk permits different routing techniques depending on how these items are identified and what entity provides them to BizTalk Server. You may furnish routing information in the document itself, in the configuration, in the `Submit` call, or in some combination of these.

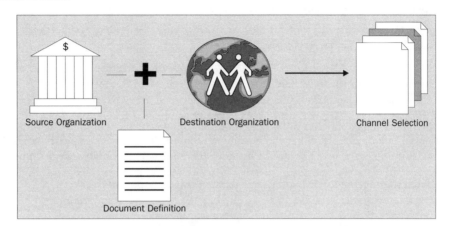

There are four kinds of routing in the BizTalk messaging service. Together, they provide a great degree of freedom in determining how your messages will be processed. Understanding them will help you determine the proper form of routing for your application integration needs. The four methods are:

❑ **Call-based routing** – Here the source and destination are supplied as parameters of the `IInterchange` methods `Submit()` or `SubmitSync()`.

❑ **Channel specification** – In this case the name of the channel is supplied as a parameter of `Submit()` or `SubmitSync()`.

❑ **Self-routing** – Self-routing means that the document to be processed contains the information within known fields in the body of the document.

❑ **Non-self-routing receive function** – Here the items are specified as properties of a custom receive function.

Channel specification is the method employed by the Channel Tester utility in Chapter 5. We employed non-self-routing in the receive functions of Chapter 8. We'll cover all four methods in this chapter, but self-routing will get extensive treatment. In fact, we'll demonstrate self-routing twice: once in a custom message specification, and once in an extensive sample employing the BizTalk Framework.

Call-based Routing

Take a look at the Visual Basic method signatures for `IInterchange` methods `Submit()` and `SubmitSync()`:

```
strHandle Submit(lOpenness, Document, DocName, SourceQualifier, SourceID, _
    DestQualifier, DestID, ChannelName, FilePath, EnvelopeName, PassThrough)

SubmitSync(lOpenness, Document, DocName, SourceQualifier, SourceID, _
    DestQualifier, DestID, ChannelName, FilePath, EnvelopeName, PassThrough, _
    SubmissionHandle, ResponseDocument)
```

The first parameter of each method, lOpenness, is an enumerated flag that indicates whether the associated port can be "open". We'll cover the specification of open ports a little later on, but you can get some idea about openness from the choice of values for this parameter (the numeric value of the defined constant follows in parentheses):

❑   BIZTALK_OPENNESS_TYPE_NOTOPEN (1) – the configuration of the port must be fully specified in terms of source and destination

❑   BIZTALK_OPENNESS_TYPE_SOURCE (2) – the port's source may be left open for resolution based on some field in the message itself

❑   BIZTALK_OPENNESS_TYPE_DESTINATION (4) – the port's destination may be left open for resolution based on some field in the message itself

The lOpenness parameter is important to routing and is the only one which is not optional. Although each of the remaining parameters of both methods are optional, some combination of these parameters must be present. For example, either the document to be processed must be passed in string form through Document, or FilePath must designate a file on disk that contains the document.

For call-based routing, the following message parameters are important:

❑   DocName

❑   SourceID

❑   DestID

❑   SourceQualifer

❑   DestQualifier

DocName is a string containing the document definition name, as defined in the Messaging Manager database. The document definition, in turn, points to a document specification file. DocName, then, is all that is needed to specify one of the three critical routing items, the document definition.

The source and destination organization items are a little more complex. The organization identifiers are passed in SourceID or DestID respectively. However, BizTalk gives you many ways to identify an organization. The default method, and the one we have used throughout this book, is the Organization Name. This is where the SourceQualifier and DestQualifier parameters come in; they are strings that denote the type of the identifier passed in SourceID or DestID. If SourceQualifier or DestQualifier is passed, SourceID or DestID must be passed as well.

If you are using the default of organization name, you should pass the string literal OrganizationName for the qualifier. For the other organization identifier types, however, you need to pass the string form of the integer index BizTalk uses to identify the various types of qualifiers. This index is found in the Organization Properties dialog of Messaging Manager, on the Identifier page in the Qualifier column. For example, if you are identifying an organization by its telephone number, you would pass the string 12 as its qualifier. The somewhat lengthy list of standard identifiers is provided in the dialog box. The qualifier value for each is provided by Messaging Manager when you select a standard identifier and may be viewed but not changed in the dialog:

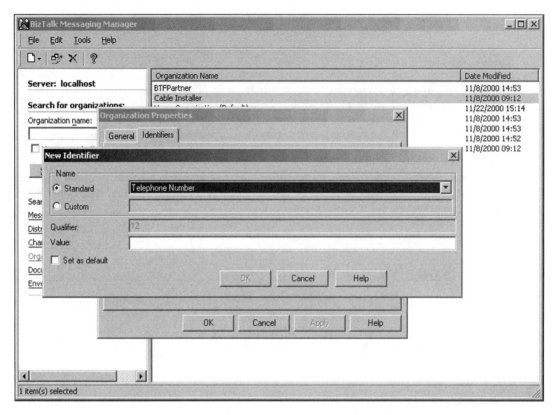

For an organization name, the value of the ID is the name of the organization itself; for example **Home Organization**. Note that you may specify the source, the destination, or both, depending on the value of lOpenness. If the port you need is using an open port source, lOpenness should be BIZTALK_OPENNESS_TYPE_SOURCE, and all four source and destination-related parameters should be passed.

Let's have an example of call to the Submit() method. Say we wanted to execute the Wrox Site Managers to Cable Installer interchange from our InitialOrders schedule as a separate BizTalk messaging interchange. Outside the schedule, the call to Submit() would look like this:

```
strHandle = objInterChange.Submit(BIZTALK_OPENNESS_TYPE_NOTOPEN, _
    MessageText.Text, "Site Service Description", "OrganizationName", _
    "Home Organization", "OrganizationName", "Cable Installer")
```

As we would expect, the value of lOpenness must be BIZTALK_OPENNESS_TYPE_NOTOPEN, because the port we configured explicitly specifies a destination, and the channel that goes with it explicitly names a source organization.

We used the organization names Home Organization and Cable Installer, so SourceID and DestID have those values, and the qualifiers are both OrganizationName. Providing a name for the organization was simpler than creating a value for one of the other standard identifier types. The document name as defined in Messaging Manager is Site Service Description, and the text of the message was contained in an edit control named MessageText.

What kind of situations suit call-based routing with this level of detail? Well, if you have an application in which you develop the source and destination, it is easier to specify this than to remember the channel names in your system. The organizations, after all, are part of your business environment, so if you use representative names (or telephone numbers, or some other identifier), this information will be easy to obtain. If you wish to send a notification to a business contact that your assignment has changed, you might decide to use the contact's telephone number as his organization identifier. This is the sort of information that derives from the business situation and maps directly into BizTalk routing requirements. Channel names are a BizTalk abstraction, so asking a user to pick one, or trying to develop the information from some other business-related approach could be difficult. For example, if we extended the Wrox Site Managers example from earlier in this book, we might well have several cable installers, each covering a different region. A staff member at the company would certainly know that they had a business relationship with, say, the ComCoxCast Cable company, but not know that someone had developed a channel for the relationship named SoudervilleTownshipSvcChannel. The channel name is arbitrary, but the organization name (and other items, like telephone number) are artifacts of the business relationship.

Channel Specification

The fastest way to pick exactly the channel you desire is to pass the name of the channel in the submission. Channels, remember, encapsulate all of the information needed for a message exchange, so passing the name of an existing channel forces the messaging service to bypass any routing information in the document itself. This is the same approach we used in the Channel Tester utility; here is the relevant line from that application:

```
strHandle = objInterChange.Submit(BIZTALK_OPENNESS_TYPE_NOTOPEN, _
            MessageText.Text, , , , , , ChannelText.Text)
```

Once again, we pass the mandatory 1Openness parameter. The next parameter is the text of the interchange document as before. The parameters dealing with document type, source, and destination are omitted. The final parameter passed is the name of the channel as provided by the user.

Note that the document definition is missing from this call. Since all of the messages used with our Channel Tester utility are XML-based, the messaging service can determine this information for itself by looking at the document element. If we wanted to pass a flatfile format document, we would have to include the EnvelopeName parameter as well. This would allow the messaging service to determine the document definition, as well as permitting it to parse and serialize the message itself.

Envelopes and flatfile format messages were covered in Chapter 5.

The use of channel specification routing in a real-world application will be less common. It might be useful, however, if you can bundle a group of processing parameters together, and then associate them with some concept from the business problem you are trying to solve. For example, you might maintain your business contract information in a database and select a vendor on the basis of that information. Since the practical business details must include agreement on document specifications and destination URL and protocol, it would also be convenient to configure a channel for each agreement and store the name of the channel with the rest of the agreement information. This would have the advantage of streamlining routing, and also slightly increasing throughput by allowing the messaging service to go straight to the information it requires.

Self-Routing

Sometimes it is convenient to hide all the port and agreement information from the applications that participate in a BizTalk Server integration project. That's where self-routing documents come in. Self-routing documents contain some or all of the information the messaging service requires for routing, within the message itself. The messaging service parses the document, extracts the routing information, then uses it to select the appropriate channel.

Of course, this means that the messaging service must somehow be told where to find the routing information in the document. That's where the Dictionary information in a document specification comes into play. The Dictionary tab in BizTalk Editor generates XPath expressions that locate fields or records that you choose. If the interchange submission provides routing parameters, the messaging service turns to the message specification. If it finds Dictionary information, it extracts the field values specified for routing, then performs channel selection using this information.

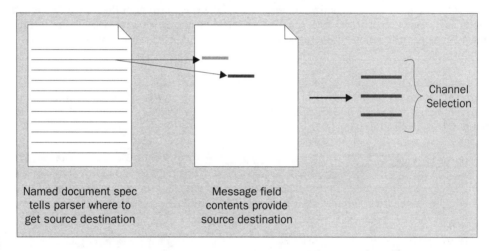

Named document spec
tells parser where to
get source destination

Message field
contents provide
source destination

Channel
Selection

Self-routing, then, is most useful when you or your partner have control over message formats or you adopt a standard format. In any case, the controlling entity must have anticipated the desire for self-routing and designated fields in the message for this purpose. It offers the greatest flexibility, but you must be able to control the message specification. Some envelope formats are built for exactly this purpose. We have used the postal envelope analogy throughout this book, but only used it to describe the contents of the message within. An envelope that provides routing information completes the postal analogy. The BizTalk Framework, which we'll examine a bit later is substantially dedicated to providing an envelope that includes routing information.

The envelope format schema for BizTalk Framework is discussed in Appendix C.

Self-Routing Document Specifications

The document specification for a self-routing document is of the utmost importance. Without it, the routing information you provide within the message would be lost to the messaging service. After you create and specify the fields and records that make up your document, you need to specify the routing information for documents of this type.

Start BizTalk Editor and open a message specification. When you click on the Dictionary tab of the BizTalk Editor, you will see six items of information:

❑ Document Container Node – record whose child element(s) constitute the message itself

❑ Document Name – field or record whose value names the type of the message

❑ Source Type – the qualifier for the source organization identifier

❑ Source Value – the source organization identifier

❑ Destination Type – the qualifier for the destination organization identifier

❑ Destination Value – the destination organization identifier

If you check a box, the field/record selected in the tree view becomes the source of information for the item you checked. For example, in the following screenshot, the content of the To record has been selected for the destination organization identifier. If the specification of the selected tree node precludes its use in a particular role, the item associated with that role is disabled. For instance, only element-type records can act as the document container node because attributes cannot contain elements.

Once an item is checked, BizTalk Editor generates the XPath expression that locates that node in the document. When an interchange is processed, the messaging service passes this expression to the document parser to get the node instance in question, then retrieves the value of the node in order to obtain one of the routing items.

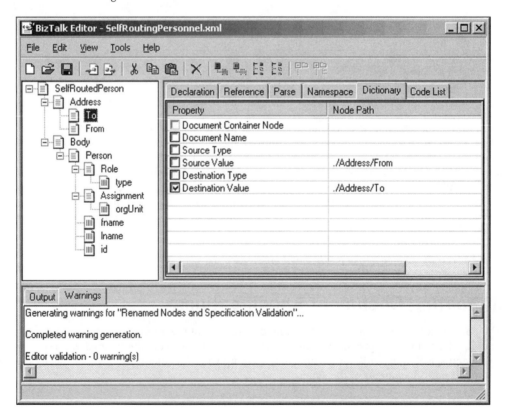

An Example of Self-Routing

We'll illustrate self-routing documents with a brief example. Suppose you needed to forward personnel information, including a person's name and organizational assignment, to a business partner or remote office. If we also include fields for routing information, we can route the document by inserting the name of the partner or remote office in the appropriate record or field. When you submit the document to the messaging service, it will extract the information, then select the proper port and channel to use. Changing the routing information in document instances causes the document to go to a different destination.

Creating The Document

Let's create a highly simplified version of such a document. A more complex and practical sample will be presented later when we build the sample application. Using XML as the document standard, we can create a document specification that matches the following :

```
<SelfRoutedPerson>
  <Address>
   <To>Regional Managers</To>
   <From>Wrox Site Managers</From>
  </Address>
  <Body>
   <Person fname="Esther" lname="Morris" id="gov000x">
     <Role type="Governor"/>
     <Assignment orgUnit="Wyoming"/>
   </Person>
  </Body>
</SelfRoutedPerson>
```

The `Address` record contains the routing information in its child records `To` and `From`. The body of the document, which contains the personnel information we want to send to the receiving business application, is contained within the `Body` element. Here's a brief summary of the specification:

Records	Properties
SelfRoutedPerson	Closed model, element only content, XML standard
Address	Closed model, element only content, minimum occurrences=1, maximum occurences=1
To	Closed model, text only content, minimum occurrences=1, maximum occurrences=1
From	Closed model, text only content, minimum occurrences=1, maximum occurrences=1
Body	Closed model, element only content, minimum occurrences=1, maximum occurrences=1
Person	Closed model, element only content, minimum occurrences=1, maximum occurrences=1
Role	Closed model, empty content, minimum occurrences = 0, maximum occurrences = *

Table continued on following page

Records	Properties
Assignment	Closed model, empty content, minimum occurrences = 0, maximum occurrences = 1
Fields	**Properties**
type	Attribute type, required = Yes
orgUnit	Attribute type, required = Yes
fname	Attribute type, required = No
lname	Attribute type, required = Yes
id	Attribute type, required = No

> *The specification for this document is included with the software download for this chapter in the file* SelfRoutingPersonnel.xml.

Having decided on the structure of the document specification, these are the stages involved in creating a document definition:

1. Turn to the Dictionary tab

2. Select the To record and check the Destination Value item

3. Select the From node in the tree view and check the Source Value item in the Dictionary tab

4. Save the document specification as SelfRoutingPersonnel.xml in the WebDAV repository.

5. In Messaging Manager create a document definition named Self Routing Person that uses this specification

Creating Ports and Channels

The next step is to create ports and channels:

1. Create two or more ports, one for each organization to which you wish to route documents.

The sample under discussion has two ports, each of which uses the file protocol to deliver appropriately named documents to disk.

2. Create two channels, one to go with each port.

These channels associate your message originator with the destination port. The names you provide for the ports and channels are entirely up to you, but you must remember the channel names for use in the next step.

Submitting Documents

We could modify the Channel Tester from Chapter 5 to submit these documents. All we have to do is change one line.

1. Replace the line that makes the call to the `Submit` method of `IInterchange` with the following line of code:

```
strHandle = objInterChange.Submit(BIZTALK_OPENNESS_TYPE_NOTOPEN, _
                    MessageText.Text)
```

This calls the same method, but now the submission parameters do not include any routing information. Our ports are not open, so `lOpenness` takes the value `BIZTALK_OPENNESS_TYPE_NOTOPEN`. The only other parameter passed is the document body itself. This forces the messaging service look to the document itself for routing information. When the parser discovers a document that begins with the `SelfRoutingPerson` record, it is able to find the document definition. This gives it a link to the document specification file in the repository, which in turn tells it where to look for the routing information.

If you modify the Channel Tester from Chapter 5, you either need to remember to enter some text in the channel edit field or comment out the check for this information.

Testing

If you modify the Channel Tester (or use the modified version included with the download), you can open a sample document (or enter one directly), modify the `To` and `From` records, and submit the interchange. The messaging service will send the document to the appropriate location based on the routing information provided in the document.

A sample document conforming to this specification is found in the file `SelfRoutingSample.xml`.

Using Open Ports

You can configure a port so that you set up parameters such as encoding and signing, but leave the destination open. This allows you to send the same class of documents using the same processing to different locations using possibly different protocols. Such a port configuration is called an **open port**.

The advantage of using open ports is that you can create a single port for a particular messaging policy rather than a host of ports that are identically configured except for the destination and protocol. You can create such a port by checking the **Open Destination** radio button on the **Destination Organization** page of the port creation wizard. When you do this, most of the options for configuring the port are disabled. The choices that are left to you are: envelope information; encoding; signature.

Now, how does the messaging service resolve the destination when a document is presented to it for processing? The destination and protocol must be supplied through submission parameters (call-based routing) or within the submitted document (self-routing). We've looked at both, yet there doesn't seem to be a place for a URL. `Submit()` has parameters for the destination, but they pertain to the destination identifier. Similarly, the **Dictionary** page of BizTalk Editor lets you designate the same information within the document, but it too lacks anything labelled "URL" or "protocol".

In fact, the destination identifier does double duty in this case. When the first parameter has the value `BIZTALK_OPENNESS_TYPE_DESTINATION`, the destination ID is used as the URL, complete with protocol identifier, to the destination. The following line would send the submitted document from the Wrox Site Managers organization to the URL http://www.mybiz.com/partners/recv.asp:

```
strHandle = objInterChange.Submit(BIZTALK_OPENNESS_TYPE_DESTINATION, _
        MessageText.Text, , , "Wrox Site Managers", , " _
        http://www.mybiz.com/partners/recv.asp ")
```

The interchange will work as long as you have a channel that involves Wrox Site Managers and the supplied document type. That channel must be associated with an open port. We could get the same effect with a self-routing document provided we identified a field or record as the Destination Value, and filled this field with the URL required. In that case, the messaging service would be picking the URL out of the document instead of the name of the destination organization.

You should note that open ports are a one-to-one association, like the conventional ports we have seen previously. They differ from a distribution list in that a single copy of the submitted interchange goes to a single destination. They are also unlike distribution lists in that the destination may be dynamic. While distribution lists may send multiple transmissions, the locations are static. Open ports allow you to send an interchange to any location to which you have a URL and connectivity.

> **Note that you cannot have encryption with an open port as a known certificate is required to perform encryption. Since the organization is never identified as such – the URL merely locates a resource – a certificate cannot be located.**

There is one more enumerated value for the `1Openness` parameter, and that is `BIZTALK_OPENNESS_TYPE_SOURCE`. We can have an open source configured through the channel. To configure an open source when you are configuring a channel from an organization, check the **Open source** radio button on the **Source Organization** page of the channel wizard. This will disable the controls for specifying the organization identifier, of course, as well as the **Expect receipt** and **Generate receipt** boxes. When you save this channel, you may submit an interchange as you did with the open destination, except that you will use `BIZTALK_OPENNESS_TYPE_SOURCE` for the first parameter, and you must be sure to provide the source organization identifier in its usual place.

Open sources offer the flexibility of sending the same document type, with an optional mapping, to the same destination from multiple sources. Note, however, that you may not combine open source channels with open destination ports.

Non-Self-Routing Receive Functions

There is one more way to route documents. Anything coming through a receive function (file or MSMQ) can have routing parameters specified for it. This method is used instead of self-routing documents. You can use these so-called **non-self-routing receive functions** when you are dealing with non-XML or legacy XML document formats that do not have routing built into the specification, but which are going to known endpoints. This is also useful when you expect to receive batches of messages. For example, you might have a partner that uses FTP to send you a batch of messages once a day. You would devote a file folder to that organization and configure a file receive function that monitored the folder. Since you know the organization, you can provide the proper routing information in the receive function's configuration.

You may configure receive functions for routing through the **Advanced** page of the receive function property dialog. There are several ways to go about this. First, you must specify the openness property of the receive function. Your choices and their meanings are the same as for the first parameter of the IInterchange method Submit(). Next, you have the option of specifying a channel by name. This is the approach we used in Chapter 7 when we devised a file receive function. If you do this, you can stop. Your routing information is fully configured. In fact, the rest of your routing options will be disabled.

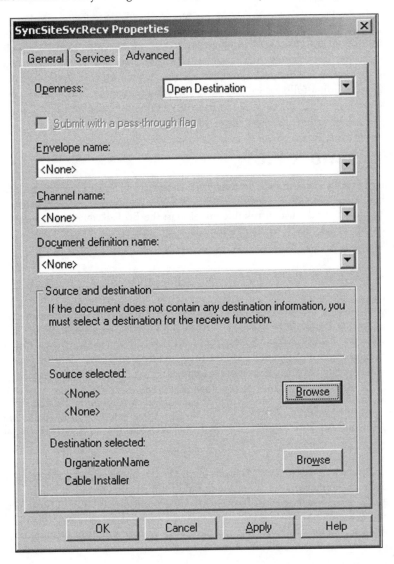

Now, depending on the openness property, you may wish to specify a source or destination. In both cases, clicking the **Browse** button gives you a dialog that allows you to select the organization qualifier and organization identifier. In contrast to what you can submit in conjunction with open ports, though, your choices are limited to the organizations you have already configured in the Messaging Manager database. The screenshot above shows a receive function configured for an open destination.

Routing and the BizTalk Framework

In terms of the routing capabilities of BizTalk Server 2000, we are finished. There is one important implementation of self-routing built into the messaging service that deserves explanation however, before we dive into another routing sample. That is the **BizTalk Framework**.

On the face of it, the Framework's document envelope specification is just another implementation of a self-routing document. If it stopped there, the native BizTalk Framework implementation in BizTalk Server would be useful simply for the productivity enhancement of having the envelope generation and routing done for you. The Framework, however, also adds a layer of reliability in that it incorporates – indeed insists on receipts. We'll see how this works as we work through the specification in this section. In the section that follows, we'll build a BizTalk Framework sample application that peels back the encapsulation offered by BizTalk Server to give you an appreciation of what is going on inside the Framework implementation offered by the product.

BizTalk Framework 2.0

BizTalk Framework is in draft for the second version of the message envelope specification as we write this (November 2000). BizTalk Server recognizes BizTalk Framework 1.0 messages, but fully supports version 2.0. When you make use of reliable envelopes, the BizTalk messaging service generates BizTalk Framework 2.0 envelopes and receipts. In typical usage, this is transparent to you. The messaging service implements the basic semantics prescribed by the Framework for message exchange over HTTP.

> *The Framework itself provides for the use of protocols other than HTTP.*

Still, the form of BizTalk Framework envelopes changed dramatically between the two versions. The Simple Object Access Protocol (SOAP) was introduced with wide enthusiasm well after BizTalk Framework version 1.0 was published. SOAP moved almost immediately to version 1.1 and picked up support from major vendors, such as IBM and Iona, in addition to Microsoft. At the same time, Microsoft was in the late stages of formulating their .NET architecture. That architecture relies heavily on so-called **Web Services**, and SOAP is an important enabling technology for such services. Many of the challenges faced by BizTalk Framework 1.0 had already been encountered and solved in SOAP. Therefore it became useful to use SOAP envelopes as fully as possible in BizTalk, so that there would be commonality between BizTalk Framework and other Web services embraced by Microsoft's .NET initiative.

We'll restrict ourselves in this chapter to a discussion of the basic message routing and receipt delivery functions of BizTalk Framework 2.0 as implemented by BizTalk Server 2000. There are important, optional elements provided in the full Framework specification that have important implications for state management and XLANG schedules, but they are beyond the scope of this chapter. In addition, these features are not automatic parts of the Framework implementation provided by BizTalk Server. A full reference to the current BizTalk Framework 2.0 draft specification is provided in Appendix C.

BizTalk Business Document Structure

The Framework's first major contribution to routing and delivery is the specification of a BizTalk document structure. A BizTalk document is an envelope such as we have become accustomed to in the rest of BizTalk messaging. The general structure of a simple BizTalk document is shown in the simplified illustration below.

The BizTalk envelope's document element, `Envelope`, has two main children:

❑   Header

❑   Body

Your document is embedded as an immediate child of the `Body`.

The `Header`, in turn, consists of three major sections:

❑   Endpoints – denotes the source and recipient organizations

❑   Properties – provides such important properties of the document as its time of transmission and its unique identity

❑   Services – allows the source organization to specify requests regarding reliable delivery

The BizTalk Framework document structure is built on XML and relies heavily on the **namespaces** feature of that standard. Namespaces allow you to associate collections of related terms and structures by assigning a URI (Uniform Resource Identifier) to them.

A URI is a string of characters which identifies some resource. A prefix is assigned to the URI, and element and attribute names are then qualified by the prefix corresponding to the namespace from which the names are drawn. This allows chunks of useful syntax to be developed without fear of name collision. Each chunk is a separate namespace. Thus, the `Envelope` element bears the prefix `SOAP-ENV` (i.e., `SOAP-ENV:Envelope`), which tells us that this usage of `Envelope` comes from the SOAP envelope namespace. This namespace is declared with the following attribute in XML: `xmlns:SOAP-ENV="http://schemas.xmlsoap.org/soap/envelope/"`

A BizTalk envelope is composed of names drawn from several namespaces under the BizTalk Framework banner. There are six namespaces, of which four relate to major areas of the business document. They are identified here by the prefixes used for them in BizTalk Server envelopes:

❑   `SOAP-ENV` – denotes the main parts of the envelope (Envelope, Header, Body)

❑   `eps` – endpoints

❑   `prop` – properties

❑   `services` (note no prefix) – used to request receipt services

❑   `biz` – endpoint address types

❑   `xsi` – a W3C namespace used in conjunction with XML schemas

> In this book we've tried to stay away from the specifics of XML, especially
> namespaces and name scope, in this book as the product encapsulates all its supported
> formats, including XML, in the fields and records model. However, you can obtain
> further information on XML namespaces from Professional XML (Wrox Press, 2000,
> ISBN 1-861003-11-0) or the W3C Namespaces Recommendation at
> **http://www.w3.org/TR/REC-xml-names/.**

The following sample envelope will illustrate how this basic structure is fleshed out in practice:

```xml
<?xml version="1.0"?>
<SOAP-ENV:Envelope xmlns:SOAP-ENV="http://schemas.xmlsoap.org/soap/envelope/"
         xmlns:xsi="http://www.w3.org/1999/XMLSchema-instance">
  <SOAP-ENV:Header>
   <eps:endpoints SOAP-ENV:mustUnderstand="1"
      xmlns:eps="http://schemas.biztalk.org/btf-2-0/endpoints"
      xmlns:biz="http://schemas.biztalk.org/btf-2-0/address/types">
     <eps:to>
      <eps:address xsi:type="biz:OrganizationName">
        BTFPartner
      </eps:address>
     </eps:to>
     <eps:from>
      <eps:address xsi:type="biz:OrganizationName">
        Wrox Site Managers
      </eps:address>
     </eps:from>
   </eps:endpoints>
   <prop:properties SOAP-ENV:mustUnderstand="1"
      xmlns:prop="http://schemas.biztalk.org/btf-2-0/properties">
     <prop:identity>
      uuid:8FFBA256-34AC-4A61-BC5D-29FB49F28962
     </prop:identity>
     <prop:sentAt>2000-10-28T01:12:41+00:00</prop:sentAt>
     <prop:expiresAt>2000-10-28T01:22:41+00:00</prop:expiresAt>
     <prop:topic>root:SiteServiceDescription</prop:topic>
   </prop:properties>
   <services xmlns="http://schemas.biztalk.org/btf-2-0/services">
     <deliveryReceiptRequest>
      <sendTo>
        <address xsi:type="biz:httpURL">
         http://atropos/BTFPartner/BTFReceipts.asp
        </address>
      </sendTo>
      <sendBy>2000-10-28T01:22:41+00:00</sendBy>
     </deliveryReceiptRequest>
   </services>
  </SOAP-ENV:Header>
  <SOAP-ENV:Body>
   . . . // your document(s) goes here
  </SOAP-ENV:Body>
</SOAP-ENV:Envelope>
```

Let's have a look at the pieces of this message:

- ❑   The `endpoints` section provides a home for routing information that encompasses the source and destination organizations.

- ❑   The `properties` section provides a series of document interchange properties. Some of these identify the interchange and its subject. Others are time related and help implement the reliable messaging behavior mandated by the BizTalk Framework. This is complemented by the `services` section that follows it.

- ❑   The `services` section is where the parameters of the receipt function are found.

These sections complete the `Header` of the envelope. The payload of the interchange, consisting of one or more business documents, is held in the `Body` of the envelope.

We will discuss the `endpoints`, `properties`, and `services` elements in more detail in a little while. They are important to this chapter as they are the basis for routing and receipts. Before we do that, however, we will examine the structure of the receipt messages BizTalk Server sends to the source organization when it receives a BizTalk document.

BizTalk Receipt Document Structure

BizTalk Framework documents are *always* acknowledged by a receipt. The BizTalk document that was received specifies how long the recipient has to reply and the reply-to URL for the receipt, which must be sent. If the originator does not receive a receipt, the original message will be retried. If a receipt and a retransmission overlap, i.e., a second copy of the same message is received by the recipient, it is the responsibility of the recipient to examine the message and determine that the second copy is in fact a copy and not act on it.

The number of transmission attempts and the interval between attempts is configurable through Messaging Manager, but the messaging service must keep trying to deliver the message until it has proof (a receipt) that the message was received. This is why BizTalk Framework envelopes are termed **reliable envelopes** in BizTalk Server.

The overall structure and namespaces in a receipt are very similar to that of a BizTalk document. The outer envelope contains `Header` and `Body` sections. But, unlike the original message, the `Body` of the receipt is an empty element   there is no payload to a BizTalk receipt. All of the information that must be conveyed to the original server is part of the envelope header.

This makes sense. A receipt is part of the infrastructure of the BizTalk Framework messaging scheme. A BizTalk document's payload is part of the business process itself. A receipt, being part of the infrastructure, should not inject any information into the business process. At the level of the business process, the receipt is important only to the extent that it adds a measure of reliability to the protocol, HTTP, which isn't designed to be inherently reliable.

The namespaces used in receipt messages are the same as those used in the BizTalk Framework document, with one addition. The receipt has a new section, `deliveryReceipt`, which adds a namespace whose prefix is `rcpt`.

The `Header` section bears the familiar child elements `endpoints` and `properties` that we found in the business document. The `deliveryReceipt` element replaces the `service` element, though. This element contains other elements that allow the recipient (the source of the original message) to identify the message to which this receipt applies and find out when the message was received.

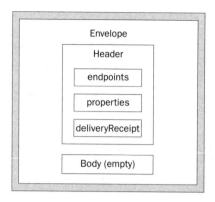

Here is a sample BizTalk receipt. Skim over it for now; we will elaborate on the meaning of the individual sections in a moment.

```
<SOAP-ENV:Envelope xmlns:SOAP-ENV="http://schemas.xmlsoap.org/soap/envelope/"
        xmlns:xsi="http://www.w3.org/1999/XMLSchema-instance">
 <SOAP-ENV:Header>
  <eps:endpoints SOAP-ENV:mustUnderstand="1"
        xmlns:eps="http://schemas.biztalk.org/btf-2-0/endpoints"
        xmlns:biz="http://schemas.biztalk.org/btf-2-0/address/types">
   <eps:to>
    <eps:address xsi:type="biz:httpURL">
     http://atropos/BTFPartner/BTFReceipts.asp
    </eps:address>
   </eps:to>
   <eps:from>
    <eps:address xsi:type="biz:OrganizationName">
     BTFPartner
    </eps:address>
   </eps:from>
  </eps:endpoints>
  <prop:properties SOAP-ENV:mustUnderstand="1"
       xmlns:prop="http://schemas.biztalk.org/btf-2-0/properties">
   <prop:identity>
    uuid:F4F3633F-8717-4871-8DD4-0E30C2365EC1
   </prop:identity>
   <prop:sentAt>2000-11-01T15:14:24+00:00</prop:sentAt>
   <prop:expiresAt>2000-11-01T16:14:24+00:00</prop:expiresAt>
   <prop:topic>
    http://schemas.biztalk.org/btf-2-0/message-type/receipt
   </prop:topic>
  </prop:properties>
  <rcpt:deliveryReceipt
     xmlns:rcpt="http://schemas.biztalk.org/btf-2-0/receipts"
     SOAP-ENV:mustUnderstand="1">
   <rcpt:receivedAt>2000-11-01T15:14:24+00:00</rcpt:receivedAt>
   <prop:identity
       xmlns:prop="http://schemas.biztalk.org/btf-2-0/properties">
    uuid:D47765BA-1845-41F8-8FE4-DF0A21EADE02
   </prop:identity>
  </rcpt:deliveryReceipt>
 </SOAP-ENV:Header>
 <SOAP-ENV:Body/>
</SOAP-ENV:Envelope>
```

Routing in the Framework

The messaging service needs to get three things from the document if it is to be completely self-routing and able to select the proper channel:

❑ Document Type

❑ Document Source

❑ Document Destination

Now, if the messaging service is creating the BizTalk envelope, these items are known by the time the envelope is created. The recipient, however, may not know the document type or source. In fact, the only way to know the exact destination and document type is to create specific receive URLs for specific document types and applications. While this will sometimes be the case, the Framework should not rely on this. Organizations with a limited amount of messaging traffic may well establish a single receive location for example an ASP page that accepts all their incoming traffic. They would then be relying on The messaging service to sort messages out for them, and that in turn will require that the envelope contains the necessary information explicitly.

> *Remember that the Framework does not require any particular implementation software. Microsoft explicitly states that the Framework does not require BizTalk Server. The sample BizTalk Framework application that follows this discussion will create its own envelopes outside the messaging service, then use BizTalk Server on the recipient's end to route the message.*

The Framework, as we have already noted, goes beyond the simple routing requirements of BizTalk Server to add a basic mechanism for reliable delivery to HTTP. We'll discuss this mechanism, then see where the BizTalk envelope carries the required information.

Delivery

To deliver the message we need to know:

❑ Who sent the message

❑ Who it is intended for

❑ What sort of message it is

At first sight this may appear simple, but we shall see that there is more to it than meets the eye when we attempt to implement it. In BizTalk Server alone, we have seen that there are many ways to identify an organization. That is why there is a qualifier for organization identifiers as well as the identifier itself. The first two items, with qualifiers, are carried by the envelope in the endpoints element. The remaining item, the message type, is found among the document properties recorded in the properties element. Let's now take a closer look at these elements.

The endpoints Element

BizTalk Framework uses the endpoints element, for which a namespace is declared, to contain the source and destination identifiers. The namespace is given the prefix eps in the BizTalk Server implementation of the Framework. The element's child elements also belong to this namespace.

The `endpoints` element begins by declaring two namespaces: its own, and a related one used to define address types:

```
<eps:endpoints SOAP-ENV:mustUnderstand="1"
     xmlns:eps="http://schemas.biztalk.org/btf-2-0/endpoints"
     xmlns:biz="http://schemas.biztalk.org/btf-2-0/address/types">
```

There is an attribute, drawn from the SOAP envelopes namespace, called `mustUnderstand`. The namespace declaration was found on the `document` element in the listing above, and it established the `SOAP-ENV` prefix that you see on the `mustUnderstand` attribute. This is a boolean that indicates whether or not the message recipient must understand the element to which it is attached in order to process the message. If the value is "true" (`1`, as above), then the receiving software must stop processing the message if it does not have knowledge of this element. This is important. Note that this does not mean a recipient may or may not understand the BizTalk Framework. It means that it may or may not understand this attribute in order to properly process this message. It tells us that `endpoints` is essential to this message's processing when the value is `1`.

As you can see, BizTalk is borrowing liberally from SOAP. SOAP intentionally provides an open model to facilitate such borrowing and to enable all sorts of uses of SOAP. For our purposes, software that cannot understand the `endpoints` element – which comes from BizTalk, not SOAP – cannot possibly comply with the processing required by the BizTalk Framework.

The immediate children of the `endpoints` element are `to` and `from`, denoting destination and source, respectively. Each is composed of an `address` element whose textual content is the endpoint's identifier. There are many sorts of identifiers, as we have seen, so the contents of the element must be typed. For this, BizTalk borrows the type attribute from the W3C schema namespace. In this case, the value of the attribute is taken from the BizTalk types namespace: `biz:OrganizationName`, as you can see:

```
<eps:to>
 <eps:address xsi:type="biz:OrganizationName">
   BTFPartner
 </eps:address>
</eps:to>
<eps:from>
 <eps:address xsi:type="biz:OrganizationName">
   Wrox Site Managers
 </eps:address>
</eps:from>
</eps:endpoints>
```

In this way, the `endpoints` element is able to convey two of the three items needed for routing in a manner consist with SOAP envelopes.

The properties Element

The `properties` element carries the third item, the document type, within it, as well as a number of other properties related to the interchange. We'll get back to those properties when we discuss the reliability mechanism. Since document type and reliability are fundamental parts of the BizTalk Framework, `properties` carries the `mustUnderstand` attribute with a value of 1:

```
<prop:properties SOAP-ENV:mustUnderstand="1"
   xmlns:prop="http://schemas.biztalk.org/btf-2-0/properties">
```

Moving into the element, we find it is a flat collection of properties tied to the interchange. The one in which we are presently interested is `topic`. This element, defined in the Framework, is purposefully vague. It is intended to carry a URI that denotes the overall purpose of the document being transmitted. In this case, BizTalk Server uses the root element of the business document to give the purpose. This is reasonable, in that each business document type should correspond to a specific business purpose. In addition, by naming the `root` element, it allows the receiving messaging service to locate the proper document definition.

```
<prop:identity>
    uuid:8FFBA256-34AC-4A61-BC5D-29FB49F28962
</prop:identity>
<prop:sentAt>2000-10-28T01:12:41+00:00</prop:sentAt>
<prop:expiresAt>2000-10-28T01:22:41+00:00</prop:expiresAt>
    <prop:topic>root:SiteServiceDescription</prop:topic>
</prop:properties>
```

Here we can see that `SiteServiceDescription` is the root element.

Reliable Delivery Behavior

The `endpoints` and `properties` elements give the BizTalk messaging service enough information to carry out its routing tasks. Using these elements alone, a BizTalk Framework envelope is just another example of a self-routing document. Another of BizTalk Framework's design goals, however, is to add a layer of reliability necessary for e-commerce to the inherently unreliable nature of HTTP and other internet protocols. **Reliability** in this context is considered to mean:

❑ A message is delivered to its destination

❑ The sender receives positive acknowledgement of its delivery

❑ The destination is able to deliver the document to the business layer exactly once

These requirements necessitate a messaging scheme that uses both *retransmission* and *document identity*.

Reliable Messaging

An originating server that is compliant with the BizTalk Framework 2.0 sends a message and waits for a receipt. If a receipt is not received for the message, it is free to repeat the transmission. The recipient, in return, is obliged to respond to the transmission with a receipt message that is clearly associated with the original message. When the receipt is received, the originating server must stop retransmitting.

That's the outline of reliable messaging according to the BizTalk Framework, but there are obviously more implementation details. For example, variable latency in the network and in servers should be expected. In fact, it is possible for a receipt to arrive at the originating server after a retransmission despite being sent before the retransmission. Clearly, then, all messages exchanged under BizTalk must include a timestamp.

It is unreasonable to make the sending server wait indefinitely for a receipt, but it is equally unreasonable to expect a synchronous response to a message in the form of an immediate receipt. A scalable server will probably reserve the option to send the receipt at a later time. Messages that request receipts, then, should specify a time by which they expect to receive a receipt.

These time specifications actually makes things easier for both parties. The originator may convey its retransmission interval by the difference between the expected receipt time and the transmission time. The receiving server, in turn, may calibrate its delay, balancing the demands of scalability against the expected receipt time.

Now, given the potential for many retransmissions and network latency, there is a finite chance that a given document instance will be delivered to the destination more than once. For the same reason, there is a possibility that a receipt may be delivered to the source more than once. In each case, it is important that the source be able to correlate a receipt with the document to which it replies.

Within the layer of the BizTalk Framework, the source needs to be sure that it cancels retransmissions when a receipt is received, and performs this only once for the proper message. This means that the receipt must bear the original message's identity, and also have an identity of its own, so that the source may recognize duplicate receipts. More importantly, the destination needs to deliver the document to the business layer, (the application) exactly once; because it is assumed that some action will be taken in response to a business document, sending the same document to the application more than once would have unanticipated, negative consequences. Forcing all applications using BizTalk Framework-compliant servers to perform their own checks for duplicated messages would diminish the value of using the Framework. The BizTalk Framework-compliant software – in our case BizTalk Server – then, performs a valuable service by ensuring that a particular message is delivered only once, regardless of how many copies may be received.

There is one further requirement that is less a function of the BizTalk reliability mechanism and more an assumption of the business process. Many messages are time sensitive. If not received and acted upon within a particular window, the message should be discarded, as the business conditions or requests it conveys may no longer be in effect. Situations like this include a time limited bid in a supply chain application, or a notification of some event in a manufacturing process.

The result is that the reliability mechanism in BizTalk Framework requires the following items in a BizTalk document:

- ❏ Message identity
- ❏ The time sent
- ❏ The time a receipt is expected
- ❏ The time the message expires

A BizTalk receipt message, in turn, requires the following items under the Framework mechanism:

- ❏ Its identity
- ❏ The identity of the original document
- ❏ Time the receipt was sent

Additionally, the receipt should contain the time the original message was received and the time the receipt expires, although these are not strictly required to implement the reliability mechanism just described. Let's return to the envelope for the BizTalk document and see where BizTalk puts these items.

Another Look At The properties Element

The properties element carries, as we previously noted, properties relating to the document it encapsulates. Returning to that element, we can now understand the other properties that were transmitted as children of the properties element:

```
<prop:properties SOAP-ENV:mustUnderstand="1"
    xmlns:prop="http://schemas.biztalk.org/btf-2-0/properties">
  <prop:identity>
    uuid:F4F3633F-8717-4871-8DD4-0E30C2365EC1
  </prop:identity>
  <prop:sentAt>2000-11-01T15:14:24+00:00</prop:sentAt>
  <prop:expiresAt>2000-11-01T16:14:24+00:00</prop:expiresAt>
  <prop:topic>
    http://schemas.biztalk.org/btf-2-0/message-type/receipt
  </prop:topic>
</prop:properties>
```

The first is the `identity` element. This is a URI that uniquely identifies the message. In the case shown, the prefix `uuid:` is used to indicate that this identifier is a GUID (sometimes known as a Universally Unique ID, rather than Globally Unique, hence `uuid`). The transmission time of the document is kept in the `sentAt` element, while the expiry time of the message follows in the `expiresAt` element. Both have values expressed as ISO-compliant date-time strings. The `topic` element is a URN that identifies the topic of the message to the receiving server. In this case, the URN identifies the BizTalk Framework itself and denotes this message as being a BizTalk Framework receipt message.

The services Element

That only leaves the receipt deadline unaccounted for. The BizTalk document requests a receipt as a service of the messaging system, so the `services` element, shown below, includes the `deliveryReceiptRequest` element. The deadline is found in the `sendBy` element, again in the form of an ISO-compliant date-time string.

```
<services xmlns="http://schemas.biztalk.org/btf-2-0/services">
  <deliveryReceiptRequest>
    <sendTo>
      <address xsi:type="biz:httpURL">
        http://atropos/BTFPartner/BTFReceipts.asp
      </address>
    </sendTo>
    <sendBy>2000-10-28T01:22:41+00:00</sendBy>
  </deliveryReceiptRequest>
</services>
```

There is an additional item of information in the request for a receipt. The `sendTo` element, with its child `address` element, tells the recipient where to send the receipt. This allows the sender to establish a single point to receive all receipts, or as many endpoints as it desires to segregate its business process. The only promise made to the recipient is that if a receipt is sent to that endpoint, the responsibilities of the recipient under the reliability mechanism will be satisfied. Note the `xsi:type` attribute on the `address` element. In contrast to the `xsi:type` attributes on the `address` elements in the `endpoints` element, this one has the value `biz:httpURL`, signifying an HTTP URL rather than an organization identifier.

Receipts

Now let's see how the destination server fulfils its responsibilities regarding reliability in BizTalk Framework. It needs to pass its identity, the identity of the original message, and the time the original message was received. After looking at this in the framework, we will then go on to look at the general concepts surrounding receipts and how they are implemented in BizTalk Server.

The endpoints Element

The receipt message carries an `endpoints` element that is the inverse of the one in the original message. The `to` element now points to the source of the original message, while the `from` element refers to the destination server sending the receipt:

```
<eps:endpoints SOAP-ENV:mustUnderstand="1"
      xmlns:eps="http://schemas.biztalk.org/btf-2-0/endpoints"
      xmlns:biz="http://schemas.biztalk.org/btf-2-0/address/types">
  <eps:to>
   <eps:address xsi:type="biz:httpURL">
     http://atropos/BTFPartner/BTFReceipts.asp
   </eps:address>
  </eps:to>
  <eps:from>
   <eps:address xsi:type="biz:OrganizationName">
     BTFPartner
   </eps:address>
  </eps:from>
</eps:endpoints>
```

Note also that the `to` element points to the URL passed in the `sendTo` element of the original message's `deliveryReceiptRequest` element, not the original organization identifier.

The properties Element

The `properties` element of a receipt carries the same sort of information as it does in a BizTalk document. Two points should be observed, however. First, the `identity` property passed here is the identity of the receipt, not that of the original document. Second, the `topic` element reflects that this is a receipt.

```
<prop:properties SOAP-ENV:mustUnderstand="1"
    xmlns:prop="http://schemas.biztalk.org/btf-2-0/properties">
  <prop:identity>
   uuid:F4F3633F-8717-4871-8DD4-0E30C2365EC1
  </prop:identity>
  <prop:sentAt>2000-11-01T15:14:24+00:00</prop:sentAt>
  <prop:expiresAt>2000-11-01T16:14:24+00:00</prop:expiresAt>
  <prop:topic>
   http://schemas.biztalk.org/btf-2-0/message-type/receipt
  </prop:topic>
</prop:properties>
```

The `sentAt` and `expiresAt` elements refer to the receipt, as well.

The deliveryReceipt Element

If you refer back to the receipt schematic, you'll recall that there is no services section. Why? Because the receipt is providing the service, a receipt, requested in that section. In consequence, the services section is replaced with the `deliveryReceipt` element:

```
<rcpt:deliveryReceipt
   xmlns:rcpt="http://schemas.biztalk.org/btf-2-0/receipts"
   SOAP-ENV:mustUnderstand="1">
  <rcpt:receivedAt>2000-11-01T15:14:24+00:00</rcpt:receivedAt>
  <prop:identity
     xmlns:prop="http://schemas.biztalk.org/btf-2-0/properties">
     uuid:D47765BA-1845-41F8-8FE4-DF0A21EADE02
  </prop:identity>
</rcpt:deliveryReceipt>
```

The `receivedAt` element conveys the time the original message was received. The `identity` element reflects the identity passed in the original message, thereby allowing the original source to correlate the receipt with the original message. With this information, the receipt has checked off all its responsibilities under the BizTalk Framework's reliability mechanism.

Having seen how the Framework provides a mechanism for ensuring reliability of messages, we will now have a closer look at the concepts surrounding receipts and how BizTalk Server implements the process of acknowledging a document it receives.

Acknowledging Receipt

If we are exchanging documents with trading partners, we need a way of processing receipts that our partners return, as well as a way of generating them ourselves.

Throughout our earlier discussions we have referred to the structured message data as documents. This is invariably the correct view to take – we are modeling business processes, where the data often takes the form of a business document. We haven't yet considered in any detail the idea of **receipts**, the idea that in many cases, the messaging system and the receiving application should pass an acknowledgement back to the sender, so that the sender knows that the interchange has been successful. To implement this, on one hand we may wish to employ a series of handshakes, so that any breaks in the workflow are detected early, and remedial action can be taken within that same workflow. On the other hand, we may also wish to have a receipt from the receiving organization confirming that an important document has actually been received into their systems (and if we do not get a receipt we need to resend); this latter receipt is a document too in the business process sense.

Clearly, in the workflow sense, the receipt of a document often drives another process we need to look at. That process in turn may produce a document that drives another process, and so on. Even in the simplest "buyer orders goods, supplier delivers goods, supplier invoices buyer" scenario, some acknowledgement of the delivery of the goods should precede the buyer's receipt of the invoice! This state of affairs is often enforced in the workflow: the invoice isn't sent by the supplier until the delivery advice note has been received by them from the buyer. Of course, the supplier could add a workflow rule instead, that says "wait seven days from dispatch before invoicing"; this approach avoids the need to have yet another 'piece of paper'. But, this banks on the fact that fulfilment gets the goods to the customers within seven days for the majority of the time.

However, we are striving (in a utopian sense) towards totally-integrated business processes, with the highest achievable level of automation. If the buyer receives the goods, and that fact is recorded electronically in a computer system, then the buyer can use this information to ensure they do not receive any invoices for undelivered goods, by offering up an electronic delivery advice that then drives the invoicing process.

In this section we will see:

- ❑ How we can configure receiving Servers to generate a receipt and return it to the sender
- ❑ How we can configure the sending Servers to handle a receipt when it is returned
- ❑ What information can be obtained from tracking the receipt and its status in the database
- ❑ An example of generating and receiving a receipt

Configuring BizTalk Servers to Handle Receipts

Considering the different message formats that BizTalk can deal with, it is hardly surprising that there is more than one way to handle the processing of receipts. In fact there are two, and the one you choose depends on the type of message you are dealing with:

❑ **Reliable messaging** when using a reliable message with the XML parser, which processes receipts automatically

❑ **Configuration of channel properties in Messaging Manager** when using an X12, EDIFACT, or custom parser that requires receipts

When dealing with receipts, both parties in an exchange need to be able to work with the receipts. The *recipient* of a message has to be able to generate a receipt, while the *sender* of the original message has to be able to accept the receipt, and then correlate this with the message that was sent. This means that both the destination and source systems must be configured (if they are BizTalk Servers, or written in custom code if not,) to deal with the sending and receiving of receipts.

Processing Receipts Using Reliable Messaging

If you are using XML, you can automatically process receipts by using reliable messaging. Reliable messaging is far easier to configure than implementing receipt processing for EDI documents. In this section we will see how we can configure Messaging Services to send and receive receipts using reliable messaging envelopes, which are compliant with BizTalk Framework 2.0.

In Messaging Manager, you can configure a messaging port to use a reliable envelope format for a message if you require a receipt. Envelopes that use reliable messaging must include a `reply-to` URL address in the header, which is used by the destination as the address to return the receipt to.

Configuring the Source System for Reliable Messaging Receipts

When we want to use messages which require receipts, using reliable messaging, we have to perform the following steps:

❑ Set the property of the `reply-to` URL on the server that sends the message and requires a receipt

❑ Create an envelope that uses the reliable envelope format

❑ Create a messaging port for transporting the message to the destination

❑ Create a channel to process the sent message

Let's start by setting the reliable messaging `reply-to` URL address property, so that the server receiving the document knows where to send the receipt. We do this in the BizTalk Server Administration tool:

1. Expand Microsoft BizTalk Server 2000 and click the Server group that you want to configure

2. On the Action menu click Properties

3. In the BizTalk Server Group Properties dialog box, shown below, find the Reliable messaging reply-to URL box, and type the URL that this Server group uses to receive reliable messaging receipts

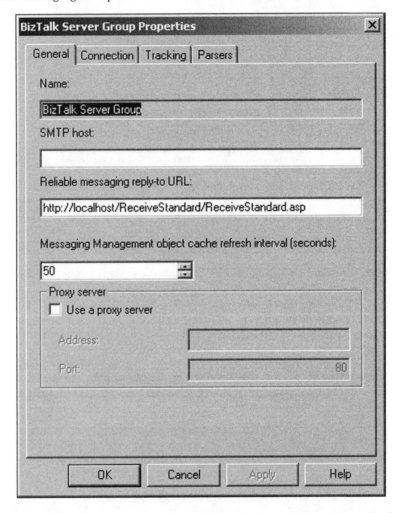

When you create the outgoing message, which uses a reliable messaging envelope, the Server will automatically insert the URL that the receipts have to be sent to in the header of the message. It also places the original message into the retry queue. The Server then uses the retry options specified for the channel to determine how often, and for how many times, it should try to send the message, until it has got a receipt back.

If you would like to see what a reliable messaging envelope looks like, have a glance through Appendix C as the subject of Reliable envelopes and their reliance on SOAP is discussed in more depth and an example is included.

Next, we switch from the BizTalk Server Administration tool to Messaging Manager, as we have to create an envelope that uses the reliable envelope format:

4. In the New Envelope dialog box, find the Envelope format list, and select RELIABLE:

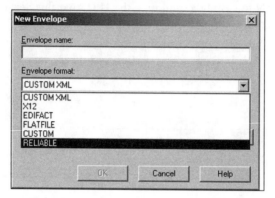

As you can see from the way **RELIABLE** is highlighted, if you choose the custom XML format, like we did in the above screenshot, and do not select a specification, the envelope format defaults to reliable format anyway.

5. Give the Envelope a name; in our case we have called it Regional.

After that, we must create a messaging port for transporting the message to the destination application. Use the New Messaging Port Wizard to do this.

6. On the Envelope Information page, in the Envelope information area, select the envelope you created previously, because ours was called Regional it appears in the drop down box:

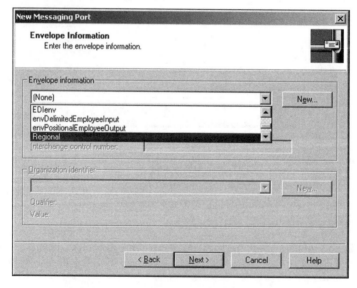

Finally, we must create a channel to process the original interchange, using the channel wizard.

7. On the Source Application or Source Organization pages (whichever you are dealing with), *do not* set any receipt properties.

8. On the Advanced Configuration page, in the Retry Options group, you can specify the Number of retries and the Interval:

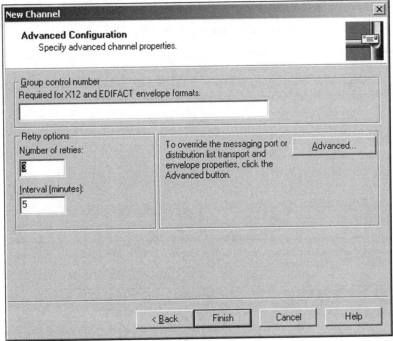

Your Server will now be configured to send a reliable message that requires a receipt, and it will know:

❑ How long to wait for a receipt before trying to resend the message

❑ How many attempts it should make to send the message

Configuring the Destination System for Reliable Messaging Receipts

When a destination Server receives an interchange in a reliable message format, it uses a special document definition, channel, and messaging port to process and transport a receipt to the sender. To do this it uses special system objects that you cannot view in Messaging Manager, and you cannot create instances of the objects using their system names.

The destination Server uses the `reply-to` URL address included in the header of the message it receives, as the address to send the receipt to. When you have to send a receipt from a reliable message, you do not need to do anything to configure Messaging Services to send the receipt, unless the source system specifies an SMTP address in the reply-to URL address. We'll see how to send a receipt back to an SMTP address next.

Configuring a Server to Send a Receipt for a Reliable Message via SMTP

If you have to send a receipt via SMTP, you need to configure your Server to include a `From` address in the header of the receipt. When you install BizTalk Server, an organization identifier is created for the Home Organization, which is named Reliable Messaging Acknowledgement SMTP From Address, and cannot be removed. If you are sending a receipt via SMTP, the Server inserts the value that you specify for this organization identifier into the interchange header as the `From` address.

To configure Messaging Services to send a receipt back to the sender of the original reliable message, using SMTP, you must perform the following steps:

❑ Configure the Reliable Messaging Acknowledgement SMTP From Address

❑ Create a messaging port for transporting the original message to its intended destination.

❑ Create a channel to process the original message

To configure the Reliable Messaging Acknowledgement SMTP From Address organization identifier of the Home Organization in BizTalk Messaging Manager:

1. Open the Home Organization by checking the Home Organization checkbox and then clicking on Organizations in the search pane

2. In the Organization Properties dialog, click the Identifiers tab

3. In the Organization identifiers list, click Reliable Messaging Acknowledgement SMTP From Address, and click Edit

4. In the Identifier Properties dialog box, locate the Value box and type in a value for the identifier

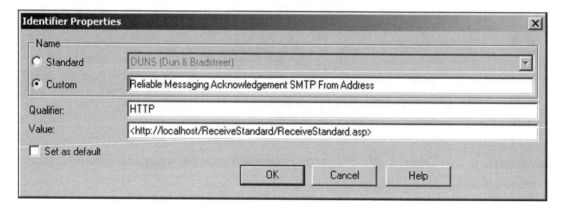

Only modify the identifier value – do not modify the identifier name or qualifier.

Next we have to create a messaging port for transporting the original message to its intended destination. We covered this in Chapter 5. Luckily, this does not require any other special configuration.

Finally, we have to create a channel to process the original message – again no special configuration is required for this. We covered this in Chapter 5 too.

If you have configured document tracking for this message, the inbound interchange is logged to the DTA, but the receipt is not.

Configuring Channel Properties to Process Receipts

When using the X12 or EDIFACT parser, or a custom parser that requires receipts, things become a little more complicated. BizTalk Messaging Services allow you to configure channel properties to control the processing of necessary receipts.

In the following illustration, you can see what is involved in the processing of a receipt. again we have to configure both source and destination systems – both of which are configured using channel properties.

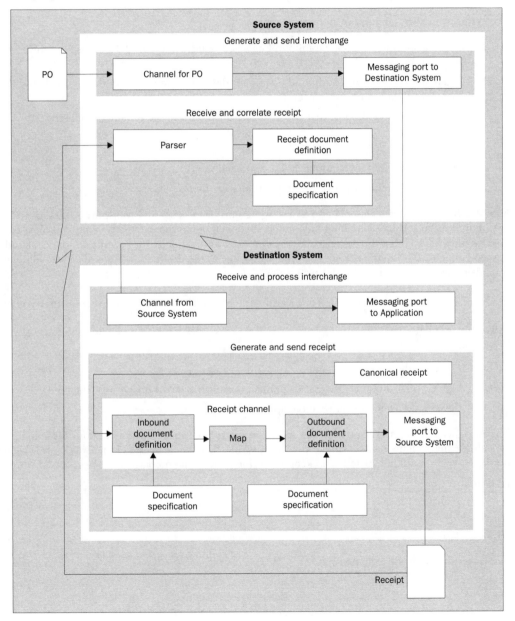

> Remember that correlating the receipt with the message that was sent is important. If you have built or bought a custom parser, you will need to buy/write a custom correlation component as well.

Configuring the Source to Generate and Receive Receipts

In this section we will see how we can use Messaging Services to send a message to a partner, and how we can use channel properties to process a receipt.

To do this, we have a number of steps to perform:

- ❑ Create a specification for the inbound and outbound document definitions, and the receipt we expect to be returned
- ❑ Create the inbound and outbound document definitions for creating the channel, and the document definition for the receipt
- ❑ Create the messaging port that will send the document to the intended recipient

On the destination machine we need to:

- ❑ Create the channel for sending the receipt back
- ❑ Create a channel to process the original message being received

First you have to create a channel and a messaging port, to process and transport a message to the destination system. While you don't have to create a channel to receive the receipt, you must create a document definition that the Server can use to process, and validate, the receipt. We have already seen how to configure Messaging Services to send a message to the destination system, so we will focus on processing the receipt using channel properties.

1. To start, open up BizTalk Editor and create a specification for the receipt that you expect.

When the destination system processes your sent message that requires a receipt, the parser does the following:

- ❑ It extracts the header elements
- ❑ It generates a canonical receipt (canonical form is discussed further in Chapter 4)
- ❑ It inserts the elements into the receipt

Therefore we have to make sure that the specification on the source system contains these fields, so that we can use these elements to correlate the receipt with the original message that was sent. If we did not do this, it would not know whether to keep on trying to send the message.

In X12 the important elements are:

- ❑ `functional_identifier`
- ❑ `standards_version`

In EDIFACT, the header elements are

- ❑ `functional_identifier`
- ❑ `standards_version_type`
- ❑ `standards_version_value`

Next we have to open up Messaging Manager and create the inbound and outbound document definitions for creating the channel, and the document definition for the receipt. Here you must select the specification that you just created.

On the destination Server:

2. Create a messaging port and a channel for sending the receipt back before you create the channel for processing the original message.

It might seem a bit strange to start by configuring the receipt channel first. However, when you are creating the channel to process the original message that is sent from the source, you need to specify the receipt channel. So you must create a messaging port for transporting the receipt to the source system, and its associated receipt channel to process the receipt, before creating the channel for the original document.

On the source Server:

3. Create the messaging port that will transport the interchange to the destination system.

On the destination Server:

4. Create a channel to process the original message that you are receiving.

When using the channel wizard to do this, on the Source Application or Source Organization page, make sure that you have selected the Expect Receipt check box.

If your business process requires a receipt, you will also want to be able to act if one is not sent, since the receipt may be required for data integrity (such as correct stock levels and accounts), or for some further part of the process to execute.

Because you are expecting a receipt, you will also need to be able to specify an amount of time you can wait for the receipt before you take some action – usually resending the message. You can set the time you want to wait for a receipt before resending the message in the Receipt interval in minutes box.

The receipts are submitted to Messaging Services just as any other document would be. Once the receipt has been submitted, the X12 or EDIFACT parsers can distinguish the receipt from other documents, and direct the server to correlate the receipt with the original document that was sent.

Configuring the Destination to Generate Receipts

Now, let's have a look at how we set the destination server to generate the receipt. Again, we are using channel properties, so this is the method to use for working with messages that use the X12, EDIFACT or a custom parser.

To do this you have to create a channel and messaging port to process the outbound interchange, and transport it to the destination. You don't need to create a channel or a messaging port to process the receipt that the destination system returns. A parser will process the receipt just using the document definition.

Open up BizTalk Editor. Then:

5. Create the specifications for the inbound and outbound document definitions that are used to create the receipt channel.

For the inbound definition of the receipt channel you use the canonical receipt specification, which is in the WebDAV repository. For the outbound document you must do what we have seen already:

6. Create specs for inbound and outbound document definitions that are used to create the channel to process the original message from the source.

Now open the Mapper tool. We need to specify a map which is used to transform the canonical receipt into the correct doc type for the outbound document:

7. Create this map for the receipt channel.

Note that you can use a map provided with BizTalk Server, if it matches the document type required for your business process in the WebDAV repository. If not, you can create your own, using the canonical receipt specification, and a specification that matches the document type of your business process.

Next, switch to Messaging Manager:

8. Create document definitions for the receipt channel, using the receipt specification that you created, and then the channel itself to process the message.

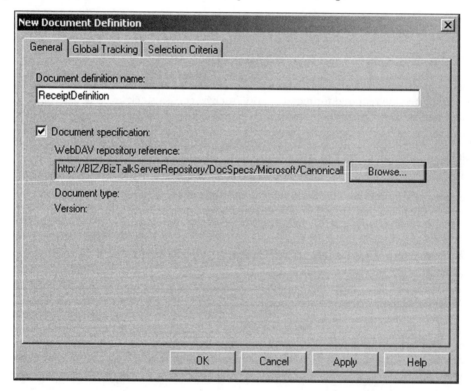

9. You must also create document definitions for the channel to process the original message

10. Now create a messaging port to transport the receipt to the source system

This must create this messaging port before creating those that are used in the original interchange, because when you create them, you must specify the receipt channel.

11. Create a receipt channel from an application for processing the receipt

12. On the channel wizard's General Information page, select the This is a receipt channel check box.

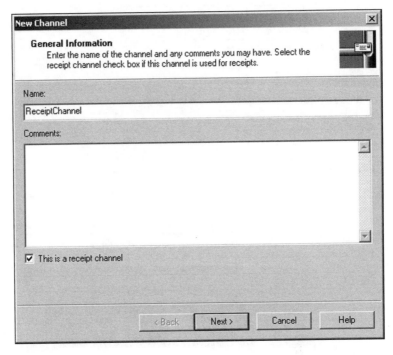

13. On the Source Application page, in the Name list, select an application (you can create an application for the Home Organization that you use to designate receipts that are generated by the parsers).

14. On the Inbound Document page, click Browse, and find the document definition that you created earlier that uses the canonical receipt specification.

15. On the Outbound Document page of the channel wizard, click Browse, and find to the document definition that you created earlier, that uses the specification defining the document type required for your business process.

16. Create a messaging port for transporting the docs contained in the original message to their intended destination – this port does not require special config to process receipts.

17. Create a channel to process the original interchange from your trading partner.

18. In the channel wizard on the Source Organization page select the Generate receipt check box.

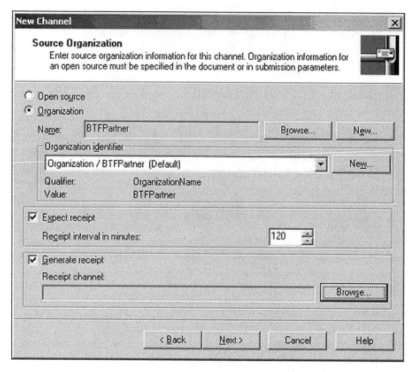

19. In the Generate Receipt area click Browse and select the receipt channel that you created to process the receipt.

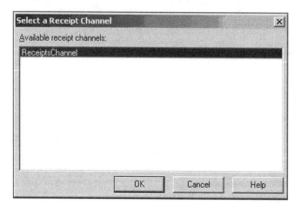

20. On the Advanced Configuration page, in the Retry options area, you can set the number of retries and the time interval for them.

Working with Tracking and Receipts

If you are tracking your documents, the original interchange will be logged in the DTA database. In this database, there is a receipt status field, which will be set to Expect when the message is first sent. This will then change to reflect the status of the receipt.

In the following diagram, you can see how the receipt flow works in the DTA database:

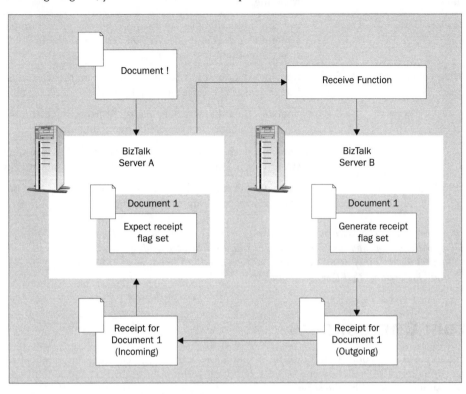

Document 1 is processed by Server A, and the DTA database's Expect receipt flag is set. Then Server B receives the document with a receive function, which sets a Generate receipt flag. Server B then processes the document and generates the receipt, which is sent back.

Document Tracking Application Database

Let's have a look at the document-instance record results. These appear as a row of fields that describe the document information.

The Receipt field provides a link to receipt information.

The following fields are for *outgoing* documents only:

Field	Meaning
Receipt status	Specifies receipt status. Values are: none pending overdue accepted accepted with errors rejected

Table continued on following page

Field	Meaning
Real 1, Real 2	Specifies data that has been captured from the document content as a real number. As you can see, there are two fields that can contain real numbers.
Integer 1, Integer 2	Specifies data that has been captured from the document as an integer value. There are two fields that can contain integers.
Date 1, Date 2	Specifies data that has been captured from the document as a date value. There are two fields that can contain dates.
String 1, String 2	Specifies data that has been captured from the document as a string value. There are two fields that can contain strings.
Custom Search	Indicates additional data that has been captured as a string value. There is a limit on the field of 2 GB.

If you configure fields (such as integers, strings, dates or custom fields) in the document definition as being optional, and you configure them to be tracked, when the fields are not included in the document instance they do not appear in the query results. There is no error or warning generated because you declared that they were optional.

Custom Components

BizTalk exposes some objects and interfaces that allow you to write custom components for extending the functionality of BizTalk Server and for integrating with applications that you are not able to natively with the support offered by the server.

BizTalk ships with capabilities for dealing with the majority of types of file that you are likely to have to deal with in your integration work. However, there are some other, custom formats that you might need to work with. You can use custom components to help you handle this type of file.

❑ Custom parsers help you parse the file into a format that BizTalk will understand

❑ Custom serializers help you to send the data out of BizTalk in a format that is required by the next application

❑ Custom correlators associate a custom receipt with it's corresponding original message

If you think about how BizTalk handles messages, their purpose and role becomes obvious. The parser will take an incoming document and transform it into an XML form that BizTalk can deal with (and perform any extra programming logic that cannot be performed within the file format), while the serializer will take the intermediate XML form once BizTalk has finished with it, and generate a custom format to pass out of the server to the next application. Custom correlators, meanwhile, will match a receipt with an original message that was sent. We will look at the objects and interfaces that BizTalk exposes in the rest of this chapter, before coming to an example of receipt.

Extension of BizTalk Server is done through the Adapter and Integration Model, parts of which we have seen already (in Chapter 9). In all it includes:

❑ Custom Application Integration Components (AICs), which we met in Chapter 7 to allow custom post processing of documents.

❑ Security components for tasks like custom encoding, encryption, digital signatures, or 3rd party plug-ins

❑ Custom parsers and serializers

❑ Custom correlators

Why Build Custom Parsers and Serializers?

While BizTalk Server does support most of the formats you are likely to come across, if you have to integrate with an application that uses a format other than those with native support, you need to write a parser that will handle the incoming document, and a serializer that will generate the correct outbound format.

Custom Parsers

Custom parsers are components that parse the incoming document that is in a custom format not supported by BizTalk Server out of the box. Custom parsers implement the IBizTalkParserComponent interface. BizTalk then uses the object to convert the document that is in a custom format into XML for the server to process and to identify the BizTalkChannel objects that are needed to process the XML documents.

You can also use the parser to implement complex logic that has to be enforced but which is not supported in the document format.

> **Custom parsers can only currently be written in C/C++ because the interface is not automation compliant.**

If you want to write a custom parser, it has to implement the IBizTalkParserComponent interface. When you register the custom parser with BizTalk, the parser advertises itself to the server as being able to deal with a certain format of files through the ProbeInterchangeFormat() method on the IBizTalkParserComponent interface. BizTalk then knows that it can use the parser with that kind of document. When the server passes the parser a document type it was designed for, it then parses the incoming format and generates the intermediate XML that BizTalk can work with.

Let's take a closer look at the IBizTalkParserComponent interface

IBizTalkParserComponent

IBizTalkParserComponent has the following methods:

Method	Description
`ProbeInterchangeFormat()`	Identifies the format of the interchange.
`GetInterchangeDetails()`	Gets information about the organization identifiers of the source and destination `BizTalkOrganization` objects.
`GroupsExist()`	Determines if the interchange contains groups.
`GetGroupDetails()`	Gets details of the group for the Tracking database. This method is called only if there are groups in the interchange.
`GetGroupSize()`	Gets the size of the group after all documents in the group are parsed. This method is called only if there are groups in the interchange.
`GetNextDocument()`	Examines the data in a document and determines when to get the next document if this is not the last document.
`GetNativeDocumentOffsets()`	Identifies offsets from the beginning of the stream for final details about the group in the Tracking database for final logging.

So, that BizTalk can recognize the existence of a parser, and so that it can work with files it was designed to, you have to register the parser on the server. As with Application Integration Comonents, custom parsers must be registered with two category IDs: one for all pipeline components and one for the specific type of pipeline component, in this case `BizTalkParserComponent`.

Custom Serializers

Of course, parsers are great for getting documents into BizTalk server so that it can work with them, but we also need a way of sending out the native format a document arrived in, which is where serializers come in. Custom serializers take the intermediate XML form that BizTalk uses internally and create a document according to the custom format you want. In order to integrate applications with custom formats, we might need to write a custom parser/serializer pair.

> **Custom serializers can only be written in C/C++ because the interface is not automation compliant.**

When you write a custom serializer component, it needs to implement the `IBizTalkSerializerComponent` interface to access the methods of the `BizTalkSerializerComponent` object.

This interface is designed to work on one interchange at a time, to get the information from the component, which simplifies the process of building one (as there is only one instance per thread, and you do not need to be thread safe for multiple threads).

As with the custom parser, it needs to be registered properly with BizTalk server so that it can use it and know which formats it uses using the `BizTalkSerializerComponent` CATID.

IBizTalkSerializerComponent Interface

The methods of the `BizTalkSerializerComponent` object are shown in the following table.

Method	Description
AddDocument()	Adds an XML document for storage by the serializer component.
GetDocInfo()	Gets details of the document.
GetGroupInfo()	Gets details of the group, such as size and offset, for the Tracking database.
GetInterchangeInfo()	Gets information about the interchange created.
Init()	Outputs the document instance to the serializer component and indicates where it should be sent.

Custom Correlator

If you have a custom parser/serializer pair, and have to deal with receipts, you will need to write a custom correlator to correlate the original document with its acknowledgement.

Correlating a receipt with the original message that was sent and triggered the generation of the receipt is very important. If we did not do this, BizTalk would not know that the message had been received, and would keep trying to send the original or give up, depending on how we set the message properties.

When we are using reliable messaging we do not need to worry about correlation, as BizTalk will take care of this for us. If we are working with custom, unsupported formats, however, we have to write our own code to correlate the original message and the receipt.

Custom correlators can only be used in conjunction with a custom parser, and have to implement the `IBizTalkCorrelation` interface. When the custom parser's `GetNextDocument()` method of the `IBizTalkParser` interface is called, the custom correlator's `ProgID` is returned as a parameter.

This will only work for simple correlation of a message with its acknowledgement. If you wanted to be able to perform more complex tasks you would need to design it as part of the workflow with nested loops in orchestration.

> **Custom correlators can only currently be written in C/C++ because the interface is not automation compliant.**

IBizTalkCorrelation

A custom correlator has to implement the `IBizTalkCorrelation` interface, which must make a method called `Correlate()` available. The `Correlate()` method extracts the relevant information from the document, document group, or interchange.

The syntax is as follows:

```
HRESULT Correlate(
    IUnknown* Acknowledge,
    IDictionary* Dict
);
```

The parameters it takes are `Acknowledge` and `Dict`. `Acknowledge` which is a pointer to the `IBizTalkAcknowledge` interface (which we look at next) to invoke and set the receipt flag. `Dict` is a pointer to an `IDictionary` interface that contains the receipt information.

IBizTalkAcknowledge

BizTalk provides an object called `BizTalkAcknowledge` to process receipts that are sent back to the server in response to a message it has sent out.

Method	Description
AckDocument()	Processes receipts received for documents.
AckGroup()	Processes receipts received for document groups.
AckInterchange()	Processes receipts received for document interchanges.

You use these different methods when you have send single documents, groups of documents, and document interchanges.

AckDocument() Method

The `AckDocument()` method processes receipts for documents. It is only used with receipts for individual documents. If the receipt needs to be mapped, you have to create a document definition that points to `CanonicalReceipt.xml`. The syntax is as follows in C++:

```
HRESULT AckDocument(
    BSTR bstrSyntax,
    BSTR bstrTrackingId,
    DTA_ACK_STATUS enumAckStatus
);
```

Alternatively, if you are working in Visual Basic:

```
object.AckDocument(
    bstrSyntax As String,
    bstrTrackingId As String,
    enumAckStatus As DTA_ACK_STATUS
)
```

`bstrSyntax` is a `BSTR` in C++ and a `String` in VB holding the syntax of the document that required the acknowledgement, for example, X12 or EDIFACT.

bstrTrackingId is a BSTR in C++ and a String in VB holding a unique tracking identifier of the document, which is a GUID that can be found in the Tracking_ID field in the dta_outdoc_details table.

enumAckStatus is an Enumeration value of the status of the receipt. Valid values are from the DTA_ACK_STATUS enumeration.

Name	Value	Description
DTA_ACK_NONE	0	No receipt is expected.
DTA_ACK_PENDING	1	The receipt is expected but has not yet arrived.
DTA_ACK_OVERDUE	2	The receipt has timed out.
DTA_ACK_ACCEPTED	3	The receipt has arrived with a status of accepted.
DTA_ACK_PARTIALLY_ACCEPTED	4	The receipt has arrived with a status of accepted with errors.
DTA_ACK_REJECTED	5	The receipt has arrived with a status of rejected.

AckGroup() Method

If you are working with document groups, you need to use the AckGroup() method to process receipts.

The syntax in C++ is as follows:

```
HRESULT AckGroup(
    BSTR bstrSyntax,
    BSTR bstrVersion,
    BSTR bstrRelease,
    BSTR bstrFunctionalGroupId,
    BSTR bstrControlId,
    BSTR bstrSrcAppName,
    BSTR bstrDestAppName,
    DTA_ACK_STATUS enumAckStatus
);
```

Whereas in Visual Basic the syntax is:

```
object.AckGroup(
    bstrSyntax As String,
    bstrVersion As String,
    bstrRelease As String,
    bstrFunctionalGroupId As String,
    bstrControlId As String,
    bstrSrcAppName As String,
    bstrDestAppName As String,
    enumAckStatus As DTA_ACK_STATUS
)
```

bstrSyntax is a BSTR in C++ and a String in VB that holds the syntax of document that was sent from the server and which is being acknowledged, for example, X12 or EDIFACT. You must use the exact strings for the following syntax types: X12, EDIFACT, Custom XML .

The main use for the next four properties is when dealing with EDI documents.

❑   `bstrVersion` is a BSTR in C++ and a `String` in VB, that contains the version of the syntax.

❑   `bstrRelease` is a BSTR in C++ and a String in VB, that contains the release of the version of the syntax.

❑   `bstrFunctionalGroupId` is BSTR in C++ and a String in VB, holding the code for the type of documents in a group.

❑   `bstrControlId` is a BSTR in C++ and a `String` in VB, that contains the unique identifier for the control number, used primarily for EDI.

`bstrSrcAppName` is a BSTR in C++ and a String in VB, which holds the name of the source application.

`bstrDestAppName` is a BSTR in C++ and a String in VB, which holds the name of the destination application.

Finally, the `enumAckStatus` property is an Enumeration value that indicates the receipt status. Valid values are from the `DTA_ACK_STATUS` enumeration, which were listed with the `AckDocument()` method.

AckInterchange() Method

The `AckInterchange()` method processes receipts for document interchanges.

In C++ the syntax is as follows:

```
HRESULT AckInterchange(
    BSTR bstrSyntax,
    BSTR bstrInterchangeId,
    BSTR bstrVersion,
    BSTR bstrControlId,
    BSTR bstrSrcAliasQualifier,
    BSTR bstrSrcAliasId,
    BSTR bstrSrcAppName,
    BSTR bstrDestAliasQualifier,
    BSTR bstrDestAliasId,
    BSTR bstrDestAppName,
    DTA_ACK_STATUS enumAckStatus
);
```

Whereas in Visual Basic it follows this syntax:

```
object.AckInterchange(
    bstrSyntax As String,
    bstrInterchangeId As String,
    bstrVersion As String,
    bstrControlId As String,
    bstrSrcAliasQualifier As String,
    bstrSrcAliasId As String,
    bstrSrcAppName As String,
    bstrDestAliasQualifier As String,
    bstrDestAliasId As String,
    bstrDestAppName As String,
    enumAckStatus As DTA_ACK_STATUS
)
```

`bstrSyntax` is a BSTR in C++ and a `String` in VB that holds the syntax of document that was sent from the server and which is being acknowledged, for example, X12 or EDIFACT. You must use the exact strings for the following syntax types: X12, EDIFACT, Custom XML

`bstrInterchangeId` is a BSTR in C++ and a `String` in VB containing the unique tracking identifier of the interchange, which is a GUID.

Again, the next properties are primarily used with EDI documents:

❑   `bstrVersion` is a BSTR in C++ and a `String` in VB, that contains the version of the syntax.

❑   `bstrControlId` is a BSTR in C++ and a String in VB, which holds the unique identifier for the control number.

`bstrSrcAliasQualifier` is a BSTR in C++ and a `String` in VB that contains the qualifier of the source organization. This indicates how the `bstrSrcAliasID` parameter is to be interpreted. Valid values come from the organization identifier qualifiers that are created when the user creates an alias for an organization. Common qualifiers include the DUNS number, telephone number, and BizTalk. The default qualifier for all new organizations is Organization Name and refers to the name of the organization in the database. If a BizTalk Framework 1.0–compliant document is submitted and a qualifier is not found during parsing, the qualifier defaults to BizTalk.

`bstrSrcAliasId` is a BSTR in C++ and a String in VB, which holds the value of the qualifier of the source organization. For example, if the `bstrSrcAliasQualifier` parameter is `Telephone`, this value is the telephone number.

`bstrSrcAppName` is a BSTR in C++ and a String in VB containing the name of the source application.

`bstrDestAliasId` is a BSTR that contains the value of the qualifier of the source organization. For example, if the `bstrDestAliasQualifier` parameter is `Telephone`, this value is the telephone number.

`bstrDestAppName` is a BSTR that contains the name of the destination application.

`enumAckStatus` is an Enumeration value that indicates the receipt status. Valid values are from the `DTA_ACK_STATUS` enumeration which we saw in the `AckDocument()` method.

A BizTalk Framework Routing and Receipt Example

Having gone to all that trouble to understand the BizTalk Framework and the mechanisms by which we send and acknowledge receipts, we should now take a look at a practical example. The example will demonstrate the following:

❑   Creation of a BizTalk Framework envelope

❑   Delivery of a message in that envelope to a partner via HTTP

❑   Routing of the message at the partner based on the envelope

❑   Generation and transmission of a receipt message to the message originator

For our example we will be using BizTalk Framework. Although BizTalk Framework is one of many such e-commerce initiatives, it is backed by a repository of message schemas for a variety of industries and functions. More importantly from our standpoint, support for the Framework is built into BizTalk Server. If you want to add a layer of application functionality above the core messaging service of BizTalk Server, using BizTalk Framework through its implementation as reliable messaging in BizTalk Server is an easy and effective way to go.

Ideally, if you are setting up a real-world BizTalk Framework interchange between two organizations, the process should be relatively easy.

- ❑ You set up an organization configuration for your partner,

- ❑ You create the message specification for the message you wish to send.

- ❑ You then specify an outgoing channel and port that sends an interchange to your partner.

- ❑ Ensure the port specifies the use of a reliable envelope.

Your partner, meanwhile, configures an organization for you, a message specification for your document, and a port and channel for receiving BizTalk messages. When he receives your interchange, his messaging service generates the receipt for which your messaging service are waiting. Again, the receipt process is transparent to your partner and his applications provided his server implements the BizTalk Framework.

However, in this case we're assuming that you are learning BizTalk Server and probably only have access to a single host computer. This presents a problem. You can create a port and channel for the outgoing side of the interchange, but when you try to create a port and channel for your hypothetical partner's side you will have a conflict. Both channels will specify the same combination of source, destination, and message type. While source and destination are reversed, Messaging Manager sees that you are sending the same type of document between the same organizations and will not accept the channel. We cannot easily perform the entire loop on a single host BizTalk Server computer.

In order to model a BizTalk Framework environment for the purposes of a sample that can be run effectively on one machine, we'll bypass the outgoing BizTalk Server. We're going to develop a client application that creates a BizTalk Framework message, including the envelope, and sends it via HTTP to an ASP that acts as the receive function for your partner. That way, there is only one messaging interchange involving BizTalk Server. You will only need a single port, channel, and document specification for each partner and so there will be no conflict. The client will allow you to insert the organizational identifier for your partner. By monitoring the output of the channels, you will be able to verify that BizTalk Server can perform self-routing functions according to the BizTalk Framework 2.0 specification.

Example Scenario

Since this is an atypical scenario, designed to work around the shortcomings of possessing only a single server, it is important to understand the sequence of events in this sample. We are demonstrating the capabilities of BizTalk Server to perform BizTalk Framework routing, and we want you to be satisfied that the BizTalk Server messaging service is indeed doing the job. As a bonus, you'll get a glimpse of how to implement an HTTP receive function using ASP.

The sequence of events required is shown in the diagram below:

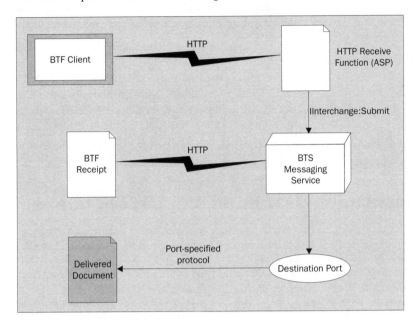

The process can be summarized as:

1. The BTF client application formats a BizTalk Framework message, and transmits it via an HTTP POST operation to a particular URL

2. The URL locates an ASP page that serves as our partners' receive function

3. The message is plucked out of the transmission and submitted to the messaging service via the `IInterchange` interface

4. Seeing a reliable envelope, i.e., a BizTalk Framework envelope, the BizTalk Server messaging service uses its implicit knowledge of the Framework to select an appropriate channel for the interchange.

5. Messaging service uses the associated port to send the document it received from the client to the organization named in the port, via the specified protocol.

6. Messaging service creates a BizTalk Framework receipt message and sends it to the reply URL in the original interchange's envelope

If you think about it, this sequence of events demonstrates the claim Microsoft makes for the BizTalk Framework: we don't need BizTalk Server to use it. It is certainly a useful implementation, but we are performing a BizTalk Framework interchange between a partner who is not using BizTalk Server (the BTF Client) and a partner (who is the destination organization).

The HTTP receive function, and hence the destination organization, has no way of knowing what sort of implementation generated the incoming message. So long as the exchanged document adheres to the Framework's guidelines, the software does not matter. Similarly, the message originator has no way of knowing what software its partners are using and for the same reasons.

As we progress through the sample, you will get a glimpse of a minimal BizTalk Framework implementation without BizTalk Server, and you will see what BizTalk Server does for you when you use the Framework. Therefore, the limitation of using a single server here actually turns out to have a beneficial side effect.

In order to put this example to this test:

❑   We will write `BTFClient.exe` to use as our client application.

❑   We will create a virtual directory and insert the `ReceiveStandard.asp` and `BTFReceipts.asp`, which are our receive functions for the purposes of this example.

❑   We will configure the necessary ports, envelopes, and channels in BizTalk.

❑   We will then test these configurations through the transmission of a sample document.

Client Application User Interface: BTFClient.exe

All the work outside the BizTalk messaging service is performed in the BTF client application, `BTFClient.exe`. This is a Visual Basic application similar in its interface to the Channel Tester utility from Chapter 5. However, the Channel Tester used the messaging service through the `IInterchange` interface, whereas `BTFClient.exe` will use HTTP.

The user interface of `BTFClient.exe` consists of a single form that displays the body of a Site Service Description document. The user may alter the document's contents so long as it does not render the document invalid. The key difference from the Channel Tester is the presence of an edit control labeled **Destination**. Rather than entering the name of a channel to use, the user will enter the organizational identifier of the partner to which the message is to be sent. The user interface is shown in the screenshot below:

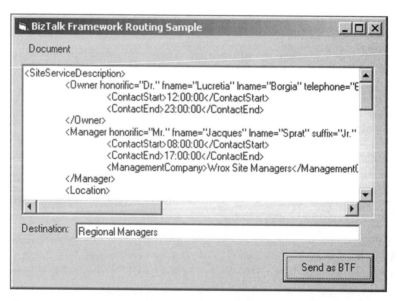

The document that is displayed in the form is actually a window into the body of a BizTalk Framework message. When the user clicks the button labeled **Send as BTF**, the application fixes up the envelope to reflect the time of submission and the desired destination. The result is then transmitted via HTTP to a known HTTP receive endpoint.

Form Load Events

There are three things we need to do when the form loads:

- First and foremost, we need to set up the template for our BizTalk Framework message. Since we don't have the messaging service generating the reliable envelope for us, we'll load a sample file from disk. That way, all we have to do to submit the message is fix up the various fields in the envelope before we send it rather than creating an envelope from scratch.

- At the same time, to allow you to modify the body of the message for easier tracking, we'll grab the body of the message – a complete Site Service Description, and stuff it into the edit field in the client form.

- Finally, we need to set up the destination URL of the recipient. Here's the form load event handler, Form_Load(), found in BTFClientForm.frm:

```
Set objParser = New DOMDocument30
sURL = "http://mymachine/BTFPartner/ReceiveStandard.asp"
```

1. We've set our global variable, objParser, equal to a new instance of the MSXML parser. We've also set our global URL variable to the destination of the document.

Be sure to modify this URL to reflect the location of the ASP acting as your HTTP receive function – we will be configuring the virtual directory later, so don't worry, you can come back to this line once you know the absolute path for the directory. The file ReceiveStandard.asp in the code download for this chapter will act as this ASP for now, and later we will be looking at using BTFReceipts.asp as well.

2. Now, we'll load the sample message, complete with reliable envelope, from a file located in the same directory as the application:

```
objParser.async = False
objParser.Load ("file://" & App.Path & "\BTFSample.xml")
```

3. We've specified synchronous loading to be sure our file is loaded and fully parsed before we do anything with it. App.Path is the location from which the application was started, and the Load() method is MSXML's way of loading a document from a URL. Note we've used the file protocol to indicate that the document should be loaded from disk.

```
If (objParser.parseError = 0) Then
   MessageText.Text = objParser.selectSingleNode( _
        "/SOAP-ENV:Envelope/SOAP-ENV:Body/SiteServiceDescription").xml
Else
   MsgBox "Error: " & objParser.parseError.reason
```

By the time the user sees the form, we have a parsed template resident in memory and a destination URL set. The body of the template is displayed in the edit control, but it is not tied in any way to the body of the template in memory.

Setting the Endpoints

When the user clicks on the **Send as BTF** button, we can now assume the body of the message is up to date. Unfortunately, the rest of the template is in bad shape. The version on disk was generated in October 2000, with a particular identity and destination. The time of the message, its expiry time, and the desired time of a receipt are also not current. We need to start fixing things up before we send the message on its way.

> ❑   The first thing to fix is the destination. The originator remains fixed; it will be coming from the Home Organization. The recipient, however, will vary depending on what the user entered in the form. It is this destination that the BizTalk messaging service will use to route the message when it is submitted by the receive function.

Be sure to edit the template document if you have renamed your Home Organization. You will also have to edit the URL in the template document (BTFSample.xml included in the code for this chapter). We will return to editing the URL after we create our virtual directory.

Since the template document is parsed and resident in an instance of the Microsoft XML parser, we can use an XPath expression to locate the node containing the name of the destination. The method of the parser object to use is called `selectSingleNode()`. It returns an instance of a DOM node, which we must declare ahead of time. The first few lines of the button handler, `SendBTF_Click()`, look like this:

```
Dim node As IXMLDOMNode, body As IXMLDOMNode
Dim objBody As New DOMDocument30
Dim sExpires As String

Set node = objParser.selectSingleNode( _
    "/SOAP-ENV:Envelope/SOAP-ENV:Header/eps:endpoints/eps:to/eps:address")
node.childNodes(0).nodeValue = DestinationName.Text
```

The destination is inside the `SOAP-ENV:Header` element, in the `eps:address` element, which is a grandchild of the `eps:endpoints` element. The way XPath works is to specify a path that the parser must traverse to reach the desired node. In our case, it is easy to specify:

- ❑ Start at the document's root (denoted by the `/` character)
- ❑ Traverse to its `SOAP-ENV:Header` child
- ❑ Go to its `eps:endpoints` child
- ❑ Then to that element's `eps:to` child element
- ❑ Finally to that element's `eps:address` element

The method `selectSingleNode()` returns the first node that matches this path. We may safely use it because we know there will be only one such element in the entire document.

The element is qualified by an attribute, `xsi:type`, describing what type of organization identifier is expressed in the text value of the element. The sample has the value `biz:OrganizationName` for this attribute. We can leave that alone, so all we have to do is set the value of the element's text to the value the user entered in the destination edit field.

Doing this requires knowing about a small oddity in the DOM. The text of an element is actually a child node of the element. That explains the left-hand side of the above assignment: node is the `eps:address` element, so `node.childNodes(0)` is the first child of the `eps:address` element. This element only has one child, which we know to be the value we wish to set.

Setting Properties

We can proceed in the same vein as before to set a few more elements in the header. Most of them are found in the header's `prop:properties` element. These are:

❑ the `prop:sentAt element`   the timestamp of the document

❑ the `prop:expiresAt` element   tells the recipient when the message expires (and therefore the message should be ignored if it is received at a later time)

❑ the `sendBy` element (under the `deliveryReceiptRequest` element in `services`)   the desired deadline for receiving a receipt

❑ the `prop:identity` element   a unique identifier for the message.

Let's take a look a the first three time-related elements first.

Setting Time Elements

We're certainly going to use XPath and `selectSingleNode()` to retrieve the nodes to change in the template, but we need to have a value to which to set them. BizTalk uses Coordinated Universal Time, known as UTC (after the French translation). You may know this under another name, Greenwich Mean Time (GMT).

> *Strictly speaking, UTC and GMT are not the same thing, but they are within a second or so of each other and the difference is strictly technical.*

Times in XML are expressed as ISO standard strings, in the form `yyyy-mm-ddThh:mm:ss`. An expression of the form `hh:mm` is appended with a plus or minus sign to indicate the time zone in which the time was taken by telling the receiver what the adjustment should be. For example the following represents a time taken in France at 19:20 GMT:

```
19:20+01:00
```

We'll continue BizTalk's method of using UTC, so we'll have to get the local clock time from the system, adjust for the time zone (and possibly the daylight time adjustment in some countries during the summer months), and format the result in ISO format. It is useful to be consistent, settling either on local time or UTC, so as to avoid errors. Since BizTalk always displays UTC, we've adopted the same approach.

The sentAt Element

❑ Visual Basic gives us the `Now()` function to retrieve the current, local clock time, but the result is a variant. Here are the lines to set the `sentAt` element in `SendBTF_Click`:

```
Set node = objParser.selectSingleNode( _
      "SOAP-ENV:Envelope/SOAP-ENV:Header/prop:properties/prop:sentAt")
vDTG = Now()
node.childNodes(0).nodeValue = FormatISODTG(vDTG)
```

The first line is the XPath selection that should look familiar to you from the last section. The second line grabs the local clock time and saves it to a variable for future reference. In the third line, we set the value of the sentAt node's text to be a formatted value. We've stuffed the code to format a variant in ISO form in the function FormatISODTG().

Let's sidetrack for a moment to discuss FormatISODTG() in more detail. This function uses a system API call, GetTimeZoneInformation(), to retrieve the time zone and daylight time adjustments. That call and its associated data structure are declared in the form's general declarations as follows:

```
Private Const TIME_ZONE_ID_STANDARD = 1
Private Const TIME_ZONE_ID_DAYLIGHT = 2

Private Type SYSTEMTIME
  wYear As Integer
  wMonth As Integer
  wDayOfWeek As Integer
  wDay As Integer
  wHour As Integer
  wMinute As Integer
  wSecond As Integer
  wMilliseconds As Integer
End Type

Private Type TIME_ZONE_INFORMATION
  Bias As Long
  StandardName(0 To 63) As Byte ' used to accommodate Unicode strings
  StandardDate As SYSTEMTIME
  StandardBias As Long
  DaylightName(0 To 63) As Byte ' used to accommodate Unicode strings
  DaylightDate As SYSTEMTIME
  DaylightBias As Long
End Type

Private Declare Function GetTimeZoneInformation Lib "kernel32" _
(lpTimeZoneInformation As TIME_ZONE_INFORMATION) As Long
```

The first two declarations support the return type of GetTimeZoneInformation() and tell us whether standard or daylight time is in effect. The SYSTEMTIME structure is only of interest to us since it is used as a type within the TIME_ZONE_INFORMATION structure. The latter structure is passed into the function and filled out upon return. The Bias member of TIME_ZONE_INFORMATION is the number of minutes to be added to UTC to arrive at the current time. Time zones to the east of Greenwich have positive values for Bias, while zones to the west are negative. DaylightBias, which functions like Bias, is the additional adjustment to compensate for daylight time.

All this is just preparation for FormatISODTG(). This function, listed below, accepts a local date and time in variant form and returns an ISO time string expressed as UTC (in other words the string ends with +00:00). We start with some declarations, then we get the time zone information, then calculate the adjustment to apply:

```
Private Function FormatISODTG(vDate As Variant)
  Dim strDTG As String
  Dim lRetVal As Long
  Dim lBias As Long
  Dim lDaylight As Long
  Dim lZone As Long
  Dim vDateAdjusted As Variant
  Dim tz As TIME_ZONE_INFORMATION
```

```
lRetVal = GetTimeZoneInformation(tz)

If lRetVal = TIME_ZONE_ID_STANDARD Then
 lDaylight = 0
Else
 lDaylight = tz.DaylightBias
End If
lBias = tz.Bias + lDaylight
```

Following the API call, we determine whether we need to compensate for daylight time or not, based on the return value of the call to `GetTimeZoneInformation()`. When we are done, the variable `lBias` holds the total number of minutes to add to the local time in order to arrive at UTC.

Now we need to get that count of minutes into variant form to add to the time value passed in. The Visual Basic function `TimeValue` will do the trick for us, but we need to give it a formatted string. For simplicity, we've assumed that all time zones are some integral multiple of hours offset from UTC.

There are a few isolated time zones with half hour adjustments. If you live in one, you will need to modify the next line of code.

```
lZone = lBias / 60
vDateAdjusted = vDate + TimeValue(lZone & ":00:00")
```

The variable `lZone` now contains the number of hours by which we need to adjust. We prepend that to a string denoting zero minutes and seconds, then pass the result to `TimeValue`. The result of that function, a variant expressing the adjustment to apply to local time, is added to the value passed into our function. Now we have to take the result, `vDateAdjusted`, and format it using the Visual Basic function `Format()`:

```
strDTG = Format(vDateAdjusted, "YYYY-MM-DDTHH:MM:SS+00:00")

FormatISODTG = strDTG

End Function
```

`Format()` accepts a variant time value and a formatting string. We give it the adjusted time and a template for an ISO format time string, then assign the result as the return value of the function.

The expiresAt Element

Let's head back to the button handler routine which uses `FormatISODTG()` now. You might be forgiven at this point for forgetting where we were in the routine. We had just located the `sentAt` element and were setting it to the current time expressed as UTC:

```
Set node = objParser.selectSingleNode( _
    "SOAP-ENV:Envelope/SOAP-ENV:Header/prop:properties/prop:sentAt")
vDTG = Now()
node.childNodes(0).nodeValue = FormatISODTG(vDTG)
```

❑   Now we need to set the expiry time of the message in the `prop:expiresAt` element. A message received after its expiry time is to be disregarded by the recipient. We need to choose a window for our message. There is no rule for this in the BizTalk Framework, but you should choose a time frame consistent with the expected latency of the transmission protocol, any time windows on your partner's ports, and your business process.

SMTP, for example, might have a latency measured in minutes. An example of a business factor might be a time sensitive price proposal or order request. After a certain amount of time, the offer might not be valid (price proposal) or you might not need the item you were ordering (order request). We'll arbitrarily use a value of one hour from the time the message was sent. We add one hour to the `sentAt` time, then set a string variable to the results of `FormatISODTG`. We'll discuss why we do that in a moment:

```
vDTG = vDTG + TimeValue("01:00") ' require reply in one hour
sExpires = FormatISODTG(vDTG)
Set node = objParser.selectSingleNode( _
     "SOAP-ENV:Envelope/SOAP-ENV:Header/prop:properties/prop:expiresAt")
node.childNodes(0).nodeValue = sExpires
```

We calculate the time, find the right node using `selectSingleNode()`, then set the node's textual value to the calculated time in ISO string format.

The sendBy Element

❑ At this point, we have one more time-related element to set in our template: `sendBy`. This element, found in `deliveryReceiptRequest` under `services` in the `header` element, is the time by which we expect a reply from the recipient, acknowledging receipt. If we have not gotten a reply by that time, we will resend the message. One hour seems like a more than adequate time for an HTTP round-trip, so we'll reuse the time string from `expiresAt`:

```
Set node = objParser.selectSingleNode( _
  "SOAP-ENV:Envelope/SOAP-ENV:Header/services/deliveryReceiptRequest/sendBy")
node.childNodes(0).nodeValue = sExpires
```

Setting the Unique Message Identifier

❑ We also need to set an element, `prop:identity` in the `prop:properties` element, to uniquely identify the message. We cannot retain the value in the template if we need to keep message instances straight. BizTalk Framework allows a variety of identifiers, but a globally unique ID (GUID) satisfies the criteria and can be generated using a system API call.

This one is harder to implement. GUIDs are 128 bit entities, with some rules regarding how it is broken up. We'd like to see something like this:

8FFBA256-34AC-4A61-BC5D-29FB49F28962

In other words a block of eight characters, followed by three blocks of four, finished off by a block of twelve characters. We'll write a function, `GetGUID`, to generate one for us. The values are hexadecimal in nature. Here's how we declare the API call and a structure that is going to let us get into the return result for formatting:

```
Private Type GUID
  Data1 As Long
  Data2 As Integer
  Data3 As Integer
  Data4(7) As Byte
End Type
```

The GUID type is simple for the first three blocks. A Long is a four byte data type, which may fill the entire first block when expressed as a hexadecimal string. An Integer is a two byte data type, which nicely fits the next two blocks. There are no integral types, though, which will expand as hexadecimal strings that are 16 characters in length. Instead, we can declare an array of 8 single byte values and do the expansion on a byte by byte basis.

The function CoCreateGuid takes this structure and fills it using a combination of the system time and the machine's network identity to generate a GUID. The return value is an HRESULT. So long as it has the value 0, the function worked. Here is how we use this function to set the value of the prop:identity element:

```
Private Declare Function CoCreateGuid Lib "OLE32.DLL" (pGuid As GUID) As Long

Set node = objParser.selectSingleNode( _
    "SOAP-ENV:Envelope/SOAP-ENV:Header/prop:properties/prop:identity")
node.childNodes(0).nodeValue = "uuid:" & GetGUID()
```

As before, we use XPath to retrieve the node, then set the textual content to the desired value. The convention in BizTalk Framework is to preface the GUID with the prefix uuid:, so we've added that as well. Let's take a look at the function GetGUID() to see why we couldn't simply call the API function directly.

> *The code which follows is slightly adapted from code posted to a Microsoft KnowledgeBase article at http://support.microsoft.com/support/kb/articles/Q176/7/90.asp.*

Here's how it starts:

```
Private Function GetGUID() As String
  Dim udtGUID As GUID
  If (CoCreateGuid(udtGUID) = 0) Then
```

We declare a variable of the user type GUID we previously declared, then pass it to the API function CoCreateGuid(). If the result indicates success, we'll format the value that came back in the structure. The value that comes back is not formatted for hexadecimal. If we displayed it directly, we'd have a long decimal number. We need the hexadecimal form nicely formatted to a string. Here's how we go about it for the first three blocks:

```
GetGUID = _
    String(8 - Len(Hex$(udtGUID.Data1)), "0") & Hex$(udtGUID.Data1) & "-" & _
    String(4 - Len(Hex$(udtGUID.Data2)), "0") & Hex$(udtGUID.Data2) & "-" & _
    String(4 - Len(Hex$(udtGUID.Data3)), "0") & Hex$(udtGUID.Data3) & "-" & _
```

The first three blocks have to be eight, four, and four characters in length respectively. If they fall short, we need to pad them with leading zeroes, hence the call to Visual Basic's String() function. After each block, we append a hyphen to separate the blocks.

The remaining block needs zero padding on each byte if the value is less than sixteen (hex 10). We'll take the first two bytes, Data4(0) and Data4(1), to make up the last block of four characters, then string the remaining values together. We use the IIf statement to prepend a 0 if the value of the byte is less than 16 (hexadecimal 10):

```
IIf((udtGUID.Data4(0) < &H10), "0", "") & Hex$(udtGUID.Data4(0)) & _
IIf((udtGUID.Data4(1) < &H10), "0", "") & Hex$(udtGUID.Data4(1)) & "-" & _
IIf((udtGUID.Data4(2) < &H10), "0", "") & Hex$(udtGUID.Data4(2)) & _
IIf((udtGUID.Data4(3) < &H10), "0", "") & Hex$(udtGUID.Data4(3)) & _
IIf((udtGUID.Data4(4) < &H10), "0", "") & Hex$(udtGUID.Data4(4)) & _
IIf((udtGUID.Data4(5) < &H10), "0", "") & Hex$(udtGUID.Data4(5)) & _
IIf((udtGUID.Data4(6) < &H10), "0", "") & Hex$(udtGUID.Data4(6)) & _
IIf((udtGUID.Data4(7) < &H10), "0", "") & Hex$(udtGUID.Data4(7)))
```

Replacing the Body of the Message

The point of displaying the body of the template message is to allow you, the user, to modify the values. This will help convince you that routing is actually taking place. The message we are going to send, however, is the message that is resident in the XML parser object.

1. To fix things up, then we need to find and replace the SOAP-ENV:Body element's child element: the document element of the message you are sending. In other words, the document inside the BizTalk wrapper.

Clearly, we can use our trusty friend selectSingleNode() to locate the node in question, but our method of setting the textual content fails completely when it comes to replacing an entire subtree. For that, though, we can use the node interface's replaceChild() method. Let's start by locating the node to replace and getting the new message body into a DOM tree:

```
Set node = objParser.selectSingleNode( _
          "/SOAP-ENV:Envelope/SOAP-ENV:Body/SiteServiceDescription")
objBody.async = False
objBody.loadXML (MessageText.Text)
```

The last two lines here initialize a fresh instance of the XML parser component, and load the XML in the edit control into the parser. The loadXML method takes a string of markup rather than the URL of a document. Now, if the markup passed parsing, we perform the replacement:

```
If (objBody.parseError = 0) Then
   Set body = objParser.selectSingleNode("/SOAP-ENV:Envelope/SOAP-ENV:Body")
   body.replaceChild objBody.documentElement, node
```

The method we are using is called replaceChild(), so we have to find the parent of the node we wish to replace. The line calling selectSingleNode() with the XPath expression locating the SOAP-ENV:Body element does just that. Next we call replaceChild(), passing it the document element of the new message – SiteServiceDescription – and the node we previously located and wish to replace.

2. At this point, the document is totally fixed up and ready to send. We'll do that in a subroutine called SendDoc. That routine takes a string representing the text of the message and a URL to which to send it. The other clause of the If statement passes a warning to the user if the edited message body failed parsing:

```
SendDoc objParser.xml, sURL
Else
   MsgBox "You may have corrupted the body text: " & _
                      objParser.parseError.reason
End If
```

Posting the Document via HTTP

Our subroutine `SendDoc` takes advantage of an interface on the MSXML parser that allows us to do HTTP operations. This interface, `XMLHTTP30`, is intended for client-side use. The latest version of the parser includes a new interface that is safe for use within an ASP. While the interface is part of the XML parser component, the document you send need not be XML, although in our case it will be.

The `XMLHTTP30` interface consists of a method, `open()`, that prepares the component by telling it which method will be performed and to which URL. Next, you set the HTTP headers using the `setRequestHeader()` method to indicate what type of content is being passed, then you call the `send()` method to execute the HTTP operation. Here is the subroutine in its entirety:

```
Private Sub SendDoc(sDoc As String, sURL)
  Dim objHTTP As New XMLHTTP30

  Call objHTTP.open("POST", sURL)
  Call objHTTP.setRequestHeader("Content-Type", "text/xml")
  objHTTP.send (sDoc)

End Sub
```

We are performing a `POST` as required by BizTalk. This operation also does not have the length limitations of a `GET`, somewhere around 2K bytes for the request. The value we've passed in the parameter `sURL` was declared in the General declarations section, named in the form load handler routine, and names the receive function of our message recipient:

```
sURL = "http://mymachine/BTFPartner/ReceiveStandard.asp"
```

We will be coming back to modify this URL to reflect your host server and virtual directory.

The message we are sending is XML and there are no MIME attachments, so we can set the `Content-Type` header to the value `text/xml`. Finally, we call `send()`, and launch the message is on its way.

The HTTP Receive Function

Since we are simulating an outside partner, we haven't called the `Submit` method of the `IInterchange` interface to pass the document to the messaging service. That means we have an HTTP receive function to grab the document passed to it, and then we use the `Submit` method to bring BizTalk Server to bear on the interchange.

An ASP works nicely as a receive function. It has the ability to call COM interfaces, specifically `IInterchange`, and it has built-in objects that help us deal with HTTP `POST` operations. What happens after the receive function passes the document to the messaging service illustrates how BizTalk Server deals with the BizTalk Framework 2.0 on a native basis.

ReceiveStandard.asp

The SDK that ships with BizTalk Server has just such an ASP included. It is called `ReceiveStandard.asp` and is found in the **MessagingSamples/ReceiveScripts** folder under the SDK. This page is sufficient for our purposes and a good starting point for building a fully functional receive function for HTTP.

1. ReceiveStandard.asp deals with getting the document into Unicode for submission to Submit, and it checks the Content-Type header. It does not deal with multi-part messages and it does not handle MIME attachements. Our example doesn't require that support, so we can use the page as it is. Let's examine a few key lines to see what is happening:

The code that follows in this section is taken from Microsoft's ReceiveStandard.asp *sample and is copyright property of the Microsoft Corporation.*

```
ContentType = Request.ServerVariables( "CONTENT_TYPE" )
. . .
if ( ContentType = "" or Request.TotalBytes = 0) then
  Response.Status = "406 Not Acceptable"
```

After some preliminary lines, the receive function checks to see if the Content-Type header is present. This is required in order to detect multi-part MIME messages. The page doesn't do much with them besides announcing the type of the message. The page also checks to make sure something is passed. If nothing was passed, it rejects the transmission by returning a 406 error.

```
EntityBody = Request.BinaryRead (Request.TotalBytes )
Set Stream = Server.CreateObject("AdoDB.Stream")
Stream.Type = 1 'adTypeBinary
stream.Open
Stream.Write EntityBody
Stream.Position = 0
Stream.Type = 2 'adTypeText
Stream.Charset = CharSet
PostedDocument = PostedDocument & Stream.ReadText
Stream.Close
Set Stream = Nothing
```

2. Here, the page goes through the request and converts it to Unicode before submitting it to the messaging service. This readies it for parsing by the XML parser. The page does the conversion by reading the Request stream as binary data (Request.BinaryRead), writing it into an ADO stream object, then letting the ADO stream object convert it to text. The result is written into a string variable.

```
SubmissionHandle = interchange.submit( 1, PostedDocument )
Set interchange = Nothing

Response.Status = "202 Accepted"
Response.End
```

Finally we reach the messaging service with the posted document. The document copied from the Request object and converted to Unicode is submitted via Submit(). Note this is an asynchronous submission with no routing parameters. The first parameter indicates whether the port associated with the channel for this submission can be open. The receive function passes the constant value BIZTALK_OPENNESS_TYPE_NOTOPEN. The document passed in the second parameter will be self-routing, but the port it passes through must have a specific destination associated with it.

Finally, having sent the document to the messaging server, the ASP returns the "202 Accepted" response. Note that it is not passing back a business document generated by processing the transmitted document. The submission may not be processed as yet. Furthermore, this is not the receipt document. That will be sent directly from the messaging service when it processes the message.

Virtual Directory

❑ Now is a good time to create the virtual directory. We have the client-side code and the HTTP receive function. We're about ready to try things out. Complete the following steps to define a virtual directory from which to serve the ASP.

❑ If you have an Administrative tools entry on your Start menu, you can open the Internet Services Manager. Otherwise, open the Control Panel, open the Administrative Tools folder in it, and double click on the Internet Services Manager.

❑ Open the node for the host server, then right click on the default web site node.

❑ Select New Virtual Directory from the context menu. The Virtual Directory Creation Wizard opens.

❑ Enter an alias for the virtual directory on the Virtual Directory Alias page. This is the portion of the URL the follows http:// and precedes the name of the ASP.

❑ On the next page, enter the path of the directory containing the downloaded ASPs.

❑ On the Access Permissions page, ensure Read and Run scripts are checked. Click Next, then Finish on the page that follows.

The ASPs should now be ready to be served in response to HTTP requests. They do not need to be edited.

When BizTalk Receives The Submission

The messaging service gets the submission and must turn to the document itself for routing information, since neither routing parameters nor a channel name were passed in. The first thing that happens is that the messaging service attempts to apply the parser components to the message. The XML parser works, and the messaging service recognizes the reliable envelope by its structure. This alone tells the messaging service where to look for the source and destination. The remaining item, the document type, is readily determined by looking at the child of the SOAP-ENV:Body element. The service looks there because the BizTalk Framework envelope schema is built into it. For any other envelope, the service would have to access the envelope's message specification and check the information entered in the Editor's Dictionary tab. These three pieces of information are enough for the messaging service to locate the matching channel, assuming one exists, and its associated port.

The messaging service will always send a receipt when it detects an inbound reliable message. This also means it ignores the channel properties regarding whether you want to send a receipt and if so, what receipt channel to use. Instead, the messaging service looks at the value of the sendTo element's address child. This is a URL, so it provides both the messaging protocol to use and the protocol endpoint. In the case of the sample, we've specified the URL:

```
http://mymachine/BTFPartner/ReceiveStandard.asp
```

Besides the usual caveat about changing the hostname and virtual directory to reflect your configuration, we need to point out one other fact. This address is not related to the Reliable messaging reply-to URL property configured for the server group in the BizTalk Administration snapin. That value is used when the messaging service is sending a reliable message. Its value is inserted into the address child of the sendTo element in the envelope. We will return to the reply-to URL property shortly.

❑ The receipt is automatically generated by the messaging service based on the information in the submitted BizTalk Framework envelope. The messaging service is finished with the submission once the receipt is sent.

Viewing the Receipt

BizTalk treats reliable messages differently than other message types that request receipts. Since the BizTalk Framework is well-known to BizTalk Server, it incorporates the entire receipt cycle. With any other type of messages needing receipt, you would have to specify receipt channels for both sending and receiving receipts; however, BizTalk Server will ignore that information when you are using reliable envelopes, as we saw in the last section.

When receiving an interchange in a reliable envelope, the messaging service automatically creates a BizTalk Framework receipt message and sends it to the URL specified in the sendTo element, because this is what is called for by the Framework. When sending an interchange using reliable messaging, the service automatically expects a receipt within the window defined by the sentAt time and the receipt sendBy time. The sent interchange goes from the Scheduled queue to the Retry queue, with the retransmission parameters you set in the interchange's channel. If a receipt for this message is not received within the window, the interchange is moved to the suspended queue, and an error message is written to the application log.

Of course, something has to handle the incoming receipt. BizTalk Server has a hidden, predefined channel, port, and document definition for this purpose. They are named Reliable Message Acknowledgement Channel, Reliable Message Acknowledgement Port, and Reliable Message Acknowledgement, respectively. While you cannot view these in Messaging Manager, you also cannot create channels, ports, and document definitions with these names.

The result of all this is that if you use ReceiveStandard.asp as your HTTP receive function for accepting receipts, the interchange will work, but you will not see the receipt message: the messaging service consumes it.

> *If this seems harsh, go to Chapter 10 and consider what you need to do to process receipts in messaging schemas other than BizTalk Framework. A substantial amount of custom component development is involved.*

BTFReceipts.asp

If you are curious, you need to modify your receive function ASP. We've done that in BTFReceipts.asp. The line in ReceiveStandard.asp that calls Submit() is replaced with the following lines:

```
Set objFS = CreateObject("Scripting.FileSystemObject")
Set objStream = objFS.OpenTextFile("C:\temp\outputfile.txt", 8, True)
objStream.WriteLine "----------------- Received at " & Now() & " ------------"
objStream.WriteLine PostedDocument
objStream.WriteLine "----------------- End Received at " & Now() & " --------"
objStream.Close
Set objStream = Nothing
Set objFS = Nothing
```

Rather than send the receipt through the messaging service, we open a known text file using the scripting File System Object. It is opened set for appending rather than overwriting. We write a header line, followed by the posted document, followed by a closing line. This lets you inspect the receipt returned by the messaging service in response to the interchange submitted in ReceiveStandard.asp when the client application sent it the outgoing message.

Testing the Sample and BizTalk Framework Routing

There is no need to point to a specification for the envelope as BizTalk implicitly understands the BizTalk Framework 2.0 envelope format. When you send an interchange, you do not need to create the BizTalk envelope, as the messaging service takes care of that for you, inserting your message into the SOAP-ENV:Body element. The messaging service moves the interchange to the Retry queue, where it remains until a receipt is received from your partner. The receipt behavior is entirely hidden from you. You have gained a minimal level of reliability for the price of some configuration.

After all that work, BizTalk Server had better perform self-routing on messages that use reliable envelopes! To test this, you need to set up several ports and channels to simulate your business partners. In the real world, the client would be transmitting to different URLs. Then again, in the real world, with multiple servers and partners, we wouldn't be using the HTTP client application. We'd be submitting our outgoing interchanges to the messaging service and routing would occur on our side.

In the sample, the receive function submits the interchange it receives to the messaging service, and routing occurs there. You may think of this as routing between applications on the partner side if you wish. What we will demonstrate is that messages arrive in different places depending on what you enter for the destination in the edit field of the client application.

Preparation

Before we go on to configure BizTalk, let's check that everything so far is in order. By now,

- ❑ We have looked at BTFClient.exe, our client application
- ❑ We have glanced through the ASP pages we will be using as our receive functions
- ❑ We have created a virtual directory containing the ASP receive functions
- ❑ We have touched upon the sample document containing the BizTalk Framework message we intend to send

❑ Now is an excellent time to make sure that the URL we will be using for the receive function is consistent in the various elements of our example.

- ❑ Look at the client application. Make sure the URL specified in General Declarations is the one leading to the ReceiveStandard.asp in your virtual directory.
- ❑ Now open up the sample document, BTFSample.xml, included with the code for this chapter. Make sure the URL in the code also reflects the address of ReceiveStandard.asp.
- ❑ Open up the BizTalk Server Administrator tool. Right click on the server group, and select Properties. On the General tab, enter the URL for ReceiveStandard.asp.

Now we are ready to configure the ports and channels for this system in BizTalk.

Configuring the Ports

- ❑ You may configure any number of ports and channels to represent partners, but we'll consider just two here. We'll assume you have two partners who need to receive Site Service Description messages, BTFPartner and Regional Managers. The protocol for moving the document to them doesn't really matter, so for simplicity we've opted for the local file protocol. That way, you get immediate feedback. So long as the documents are dropped to the same folder but with different names, you need only watch the folder in Windows Explorer to see the results of the BizTalk Framework routing. Send a message to BTFPartner and an appropriately named file arrives seconds later. Send one to Regional Managers, and a file named for them appears.

Let's discuss the port to Regional Managers. In a stunning burst of originality, we've named it Regional Managers BTF Port.

Because of the way we submit the documents in the receive function, we have to specify a particular organization for the port. It cannot be an open destination port.

❑ In the Messaging Manager, select New Port To An Organization

❑ Name it Regional Managers.

❑ While we're in the Destination Organization page, we select the File protocol and provide the URL file://c:\temp\regional_btf_%tracking_id%.xml.

This will result in a series of XML files in our c:\temp directory whose name begins regional_btf_ and ends with a GUID.

❑ On the next page, Envelope Information, select None for the envelope.

This is important if you are using ReceiveStandard.asp to handle receipt messages. Since a Framework document is submitted to the messaging service, it will generate a receipt message. If you use the reliable envelope on the message, it will expect to receive a receipt in return. However, since ReceiveStandard.asp is sending the message to a file location, no receipt is returned and the outgoing message ends up in the Retry queue.

If you use no envelope, no receipt is expected. The document that ends up on disk will not have the BizTalk Framework envelope, however. Once you are satisfied with the receipt process, try changing your receipt endpoint to BTFReceipts.asp and use a reliable envelope with this port.

❑ Select the defaults for the Security Information page, but check the box for creating a channel.

❑ Specify From an organization and click Finish.

Configuring the Channel

The New Channel wizard should now appear.

❑ Enter BTF to Regional Managers Channel for the name and click Next.

❑ Our template bears Wrox Site Managers as the originator, so select that organization as the source of the interchange.

❑ Leave the receipt-related check boxes on the Source Organization page unchecked.

Remember, this is reliable messaging, so the messaging service has default behaviors built in and will ignore anything you specify here anyway.

❑ Select Site Service Description as both the inbound and outbound document definition.

❑ We also recommend changing the Retry Options defaults to one attempt and a one-minute interval.

That way, if you make a mistake configuring the channel and the interchange ends up on the Retry queue, it will fail quickly and move to the suspended queue without making a lot of retransmission attempts. A one-minute window is more than adequate time for the receipt to arrive on a single machine handling both sides of the interchange.

❑ From here on, accept the defaults, clicking Finish to save the channel.

Completing the Test

Repeat the port and channel configurations for at least one other organization. This will give you several partners with which to test the routing capabilities of BizTalk Framework in conjunction with the messaging service.

❑ Now start the sample client, `BTFClient.exe`. Make any modifications you desire to the Site Service Description displayed in the edit control.

❑ Enter an organization name, **Regional Managers** say, in the Destination edit field, and then click the **Send as BTF** button.

❑ Check the folder specified in the port configuration for the partner organization – in our case, this is `C:/temp`. A file with the appropriate name should appear within seconds.

Now change the **Destination organization** in the client. Make other changes to the document if you wish. Send the document and check the destination folder. A new file bearing the name of the new partner appears. If you made changes to the content of the document, you can open the file and see the changes. BizTalk Server messaging service is routing the interchanges you submit based entirely upon the content of the reliable envelope and its implicit knowledge of the BizTalk Framework.

BTFReceipts.asp as Receive Function

Now, try reconfiguring the example again. This time, the URL it should be pointed at is BTFReceipts.xml.

❑ Change the URL in BTFClient.exe and re-compile the executable.

❑ Change the URL in the sample document BTFSample.xml.

❑ Go back into BizTalk Server Administration and alter the reply-to URL to the new address.

Everything happens as before, with one notable exception – open up the messaging ports and instead of specifying **None** for the envelope, create a new envelope, this time of type RELIABLE.

Now, run the example again.

This time, your sample document will appear in `C:/temp/`, but under the name `output.txt`. `BTFReceipts.asp` has taken the sample document, and held it in the queue while it awaits the receipt requested by the reliable messaging envelope. This is handled by the ASP receive function, and the `output.txt` file is written to the destination.

Summary

When you began this chapter, you were accustomed to completely specifying all the routing information for an interchange through Messaging Manager. This was not a very flexible way of sending messages. By discussing the topic of routing, we have expanded the horizons of routing to encompass the full range of routing and delivery capabilities in BizTalk Server.

You learned that there are four types of routing in the messaging service:

❑ Call-based

❑ Channel specification

❑ Self-routing documents

❑ Non-self-routing receive functions

We also visited the topic of open ports, observing how you could use a single port configuration to uniformly serve multiple destinations. Complementing that is the idea of open sources in channel configurations. With that, you can establish uniform processing to a single destination from multiple sources determined dynamically at the time of message exchange.

With these options, you are free to create innovative applications that meet the requirements of your business situation. If you have access to `IInterchange`, say in new applications programmed with an awareness of BizTalk Server, you can have complete control of routing through call-based or channel specification routing. Legacy applications and formats may be served with non-self-routing receive functions. All sorts of applications, legacy or otherwise, that use formats that can be updated may make use of self-routing documents for the greatest degree of freedom in message routing.

We also looked at how we can request that an acknowledgement is generated once a message has arrived at its destination, and how we can configure BizTalk server to generate receipts for messages. This is vital in order to ensure reliability in message delivery.

The other topic we briefly looked at was how to deal with formats that BizTalk server does not provide native support for in the form of custom parsers, serializers, and correlators. In the cases when we have to deal with formats that BizTalk Server is not programmed to work with, we will need to consider writing components.

With the core routing capabilities covered, we moved into the BizTalk Framework as an example of a self-routing envelope format that also adds a measure of reliability to otherwise unreliable Internet messaging. We covered BizTalk Server's implementation of BizTalk Framework 2.0 in terms of routing and reliability. A complete reference to this specification is found in Appendix C. We saw that the Framework, introduced to you in Chapter 1, easily accommodates self-routing through its `endpoints` element. We discussed its basic reliability mechanism and the requirements that imposes. Following that, we looked at BizTalk business documents and receipts, locating where the information needed to satisfy the reliability requirements is carried in those envelopes.

Completing the treatment of BizTalk Framework, we developed a basic example of BizTalk Framework routing under the BizTalk Server implementation. By chance, the restrictions of running the entire example on a single server in a kind of loop-back role allowed us to explore the envelope format more closely. We were forced to find ways to handle time and GUID issues through the Win32 API and insert the results in an XML document. The restrictions imposed also allowed us to demonstrate that BizTalk Server can interoperate with other BizTalk Framework implementations. Indeed, one side of our exchange bypassed BizTalk Server entirely. While it was scarcely robust and would definitely not be an implementation you would consider for a production environment, we proved that simple XML and HTTP tools were enough to get us started with BizTalk Framework.

Routing in BizTalk Server messaging service is a powerful and flexible tool. It complements the flexibility of orchestration that we saw in Chapter 6, but in a similar way it can be confusing at first glance. Flexibility and dynamic methods of routing require thought and careful consideration to fully understand. Even more consideration is needed to select the right method for your application integration architecture. Yet with experience in applying BizTalk Server and XML message formats, you are free to implement systems that are capable of sophisticated and dynamic behavior. You will be able to move from limited, static systems to ones that are as flexible as the business process they are intended to model. After all, that is the point of doing application and partner integration using a middleware tool such as Microsoft BizTalk Server.

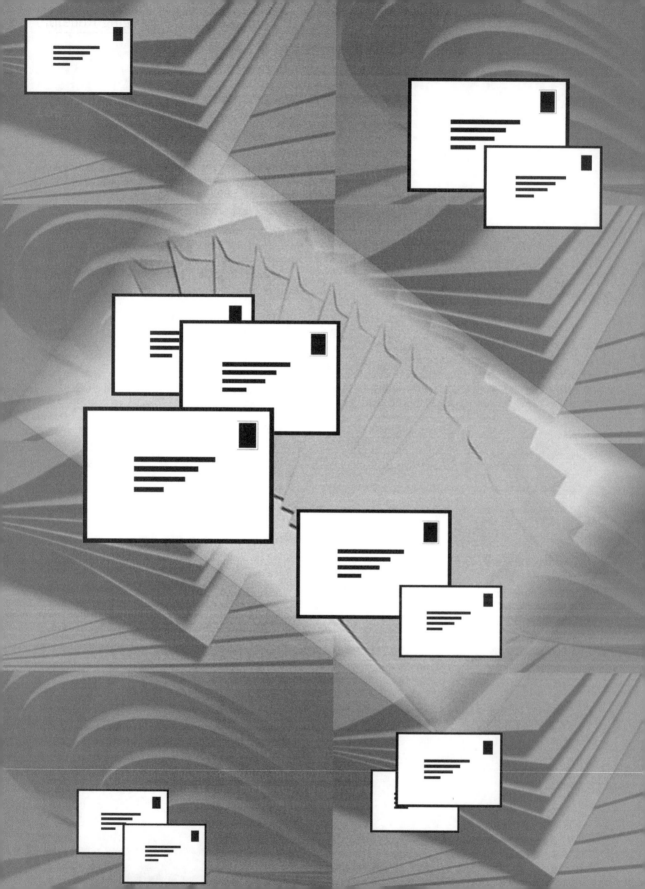

11

Tracking

Tracking document exchanges is an important aspect of message transfer between business processes both within and across organizations. Tracking data can help a business to resolve customer enquiries "My goods have not arrived yet; when did you send them?" and even disputes such as "You haven't sent my goods, have you?" In application-to-application transfers tracking data can provide you with performance and usage trends that may be used to determine which machines require additional capacity. Unfortunately applications occasionally malfunction, and tracking data can also provide an audit trail for programmers to help diagnose application issues as well as message format issues, and understand which messages need to be fixed and re-processed. Indeed, businesses are often required to retain records of all electronic transactions for a given length of time for legal or taxation reasons.

Too often developers design and build core systems for information transfer, and then add tracking capabilities at the end of the development cycle, almost as an after-thought. Unsurprisingly, this often leads to unsatisfactory results where large portions of the message transfer go untracked. Of course, the tracking capabilities are all hand coded, and so each time the core message transfer engine is modified the tracking code may also need to be revised.

One of the key benefits of BizTalk Server is that you get document tracking right out of the box. Even if you initially develop your solution with little knowledge of the document tracking capabilities that BizTalk provides, by simply setting the appropriate configuration information you can automatically take advantage of BizTalk's tracking capabilities.

There are two main considerations for tracking in BizTalk Server:

- ❑   Recording interchange message data and meta-data
- ❑   Displaying the tracking data

You can configure BizTalk Messaging channels and document specifications to determine how much interchange and document-specific data is tracked at each stage in the messaging process. The tracking data is saved in a SQL Server database called the **Document Tracking and Activity** database (DTA), which contains 23 tables and several stored procedures that load data into the system. The DTA also includes a number of stored procedures that support the BizTalk Tracking user interface, which is itself an ASP driven, web-based query tool used to examine interchange data. Of course there are occasions when you may wish to write your own custom programs or reports to access the tracking information in a different format not through a web page.

In the following sections you will learn:

❏ How to capture tracking information at run time

❏ How to display tracking information through the tracking user interface

❏ How the tracking interface works so that you can modify it

❏ How to access the tracking data in your own programs or reports

Capturing Tracking Information

Before we can analyze tracking data we need to configure the BizTalk environment to retain the tracking data that we require. You recall that you should create business processes in BizTalk Orchestration and send/receive messages from these business processes through BizTalk Messaging. You will not be surprised that BizTalk Messaging has industrial strength tracking built in. If on the other hand you need to track BizTalk Orchestration steps then Microsoft provides a sample that you will need to extend for your own purpose. This sample, called `workflowaudit`, is briefly discussed at the end of this chapter.

It is important that you understand how messages flow both in to and out of BizTalk Messaging before we examine the various tracking configuration settings.

Configuring BizTalk Messaging Tracking

In this section we will configure BizTalk Messaging to save tracking information at run time. However, before we do this it is important that you understand how BizTalk represents documents internally. Further, we are going to examine tracking by using an enterprise application integration scenario at Ken's Cars. First we will explain this scenario, and setup the generic BizTalk Messaging pieces to run the scenario. Then we will configure the scenario to save tracking information.

Understanding How BizTalk Converts Messages

BizTalk Server is an XML-based engine to its core. This means that any incoming non-XML document is first converted into an intermediate XML representation. For each potential incoming format, a parser and an envelope (that describes an instance of the format), assist in this conversion. Out of the box BizTalk Server supports XML, EDIFACT, X12, and flatfiles. The envelope is specified as an XDR schema created in the BizTalk Editor with the Standard property set to the appropriate format as shown above opposite for the XDR schema we will use as our example for this section:

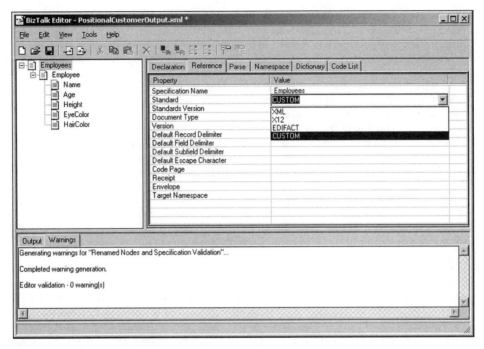

Parsers for XML, EDIFACT, X12, and flatfiles also ship in the box. You can view the list of currently installed parsers by right-clicking the BizTalk Server group in the BizTalk Server Administrator tool and viewing the BizTalk Server Group Properties.

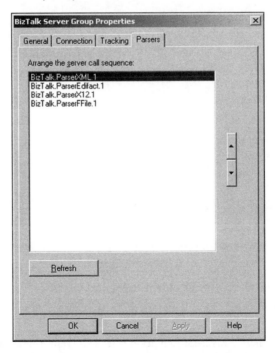

Should you ever have the need to write a custom parser to support some custom format then you may do so in Visual C++. Custom parsers and serializers are the subject of Chapter 11.

By translating any incoming format into XML before further processing, BizTalk is able to use the power of XML to transform any input file to any output file. For example, Extensible Stylesheet Language Transformations (XSLT) created in the BizTalk Mapper may be applied. Once transformations have been completed, a second XDR schema envelope and a serializer are used to create the output file format.

The business scenario that we will address in this chapter is unfortunately all too commonplace in many businesses today. Ken's Cars uses an accounting system that runs on an AS400 box. Ken also owns a human resource management (HRM) system that is hosted on an UNIX box. The accounting system pays his staff, while the HRM system tracks the hours worked. The manufacturers of these two systems do not provide a mechanism for them to exchange messages, so in the end Ken is left in the dubious position of updating his employee information manually on both systems.

Ken wishes to update employee information in a single system and have it automatically update into the second system. He learns that while neither of these legacy systems supports XML, the UNIX HR system can output messages as delimited flatfiles while the AS400 accounting system can input messages as positional flatfiles. He will use BizTalk to perform this conversion and examine the various ways that BizTalk can track this message exchange.

The diagram below illustrates the BizTalk processing cycle for the conversion of the delimited flatfile document to the positional flatfile. You should note that, in this example, XML is neither the incoming nor outgoing file format. However, the incoming delimited flatfile document is converted to XML, mapped to a second XML format and then output as a positional flatfile. One key advantage of this method of document conversion is that, if a document can be represented in the XML unified format then the combination of a parser/serializer and an XDR envelope will enable the conversion of any document format to any other document format supported by BizTalk Server.

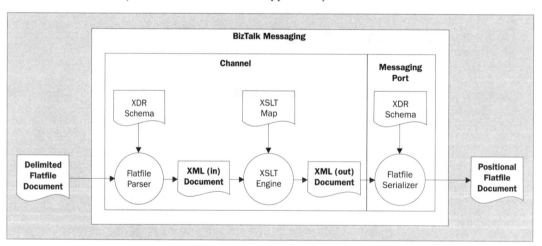

The key from a tracking perspective is that the document passes through four separate states as it moves through BizTalk Server:

- ❑ Initial native document (the delimited flatfile document)
- ❑ First intermediate XML representation (the XML representation of the flatfile that is passed to the XSLT Engine)
- ❑ Second intermediate XML representation (the XML representation of the positional file that emerges from the XSLT Engine)
- ❑ Final native document (the positional flatfile)

The conversion steps from the incoming native format to the intermediate XML format, and from the intermediate XML to the outgoing native format are called **translation.** The XSLT mapping step is called **transformation**, and was discussed in detail in Chapter 4. BizTalk Tracking gives you the ability to track **all four** possible document states during an interchange.

Configuring the HR to Accounting System Transfer in BizTalk Messaging

If you are not familiar with document definitions, messaging channels and ports, and receive functions then please read the earlier chapters in this book before continuing. The instructions below provide you with the essential information to setup this scenario only.

Configuring the Document Definition

Open up each of `DelimitedEmployeeInput.xml` and `PositionalEmployeeOutput.xml` in the BizTalk Editor and save these to the root directory of your WebDAV repository. Open up the BizTalk Messaging Manager and setup the following document definitions:

Document Name	Specification File from WebDAV
DelimitedEmployeeInput	`DelimitedEmployeeInput.xml`
PositionalEmployeeOutput	`PositionalEmployeeOutput.xml`

Now that we have configured the document definitions, we need to deploy the XDR schemas that are used with the parser to create the intermediate XDR representations of the flatfiles.

Configuring the Envelopes

In this case, the envelopes are the same as the document definitions as an envelope contains a single document. Open up the BizTalk Messaging Manager and setup the following envelopes:

Envelope Wizard Item	Setting Value
Envelope **Name**	`envDelimitedEmployeeInput`
Envelope **Format**	`FLATFILE`
Envelope **Specification**	`DelimitedEmployeeInput.xml`
Envelope **Name**	`envPositionalEmployeeOutput`
Envelope **Format**	`FLATFILE`
Envelope **Specification**	`PositionalEmployeeOutput.xml`

Next we need to configure a BizTalk Messaging port and channel combination to accept the incoming delimited file and output a positional file.

523

Configuring a Messaging Port

Set up a messaging port to an application as summarized below:

Message Port Wizard Item	Setting Value
Port To	`Application`
Name	`Deliver HR accounting positional msg`
Application..New	`AccountingApp`
Primary transport Address:	`file://c:software\delimitedtopositionaltrack\`
	`accountingout\output%Tracking_id%.txt`
Envelope Information	`envPositionalEmployeeOutput`

For an explanation of the `%Track_id%` variable refer to the discussion in Chapter 8.

Configuring a Channel

Create a new BizTalk Messaging channel from an application with the following information:

Channel Wizard Item	Setting Value
Name	`Take HR delimited msg and transform to accounting positional msg`
Source Application...New	`HRApp`
Inbound document definition name	`DelimitedEmployeeInput`
Outbound document definition name	`PositionalEmployeeOutput`
Map inbound to outbound document	`DelimitedEmployeeInputtoPositionalEmployeeOutput.xml`

Finally you need to configure a receive function to take the delimited file output from the HR system into BizTalk Messaging.

Configuring a Receive Function

Open up the BizTalk Server Administration tool and create a new file receive function to pickup the test instance file `input.txt` and deliver it to BizTalk Messaging:

Receive Function Item	Setting Value
Name (General Tab)	`Delimited Input from HRApp`
Polling location (General Tab)	`c:\software\delimitedtopositionaltrack\receivehrapp`
Files to poll for (General Tab)	`*.txt`
Envelope Name	`envDelimitedEmployeeInput`
Channel Name (Advanced Tab)	`Take HR delimited msg and transform to accounting positional msg`

Note: the value for the Polling location (the directory where you drop your instruction files) requires that you have created a directory on the file system called c:\software\delimitedtopositionaltrack\hrreceive first. Of course you may choose to use any directory rather than this one.

We have now created the BizTalk Messaging infrastructure to pickup the delimited file output from the HR system and deliver the positional file to the accounting system. As yet we have not configured tracking at all, but before we do you should run the example to check that you have completed the set up successfully.

Running the Example to Transfer the Delimited Message from the HR App to the Accounting App

Open up `input.txt` from `c:\software\delimitedtopositionaltrack` directory supplied with the book's software download in `Notepad`. The input file includes two employee records (including name, age, height, eye colour, and hair colour) delimited with CR and LF with each item in the record delimited with a comma:

```
Lisa Patel,28,6.20,Blue,Brown
James Johnson,45,5.10,Brown,Dark Brown
```

Drop a copy of this file into the `c:\software\delimitedtopositionaltrack\receivehrapp` directory. The receive function will pickup the file and deliver to through the BizTalk Messaging channel/port combination to the output file: `output{GUID}.txt` (where `{GUID}` is a GUID value) in `c:\software\delimitedtopositionaltrack\accountingout`. Open up the output file in Notepad to check that it is in the positional format that is required for the accounting application:

```
Lisa Patel      28  6.20  Blue   Brown
James Johnson   45  5.10  Brown  Dark Brown
```

Now we have a foundation to work on, let's add tracking capabilities to this scenario.

Tracking the Message Transfer

By now you should also be well aware that BizTalk Messaging is a code-light environment that provides configurable access trading partner relationships. Configuring tracking inside BizTalk Messaging is no exception to this code-light approach. BizTalk Tracking provides you with access to two types of information:

❑ The meta-data involved in document translations, such as:

    ❑ The document source and destination

    ❑ The document name

    ❑ The document type

❑ Business specification information contained in document **fields**, such as the `Total` field for each purchase order sent out, or in our scenario the name of each employee. This enables you to perform business analytical functions, such as reporting the total value of purchases over a specific time period, or examining your employee turnover.

As with any tracking technology the programmer should spend some time evaluating how much tracking data needs to be recorded to satisfy business requirements. Increasing the amount of tracking information results in increased disk writes to the tracking database and as such there is an impact on performance. Of course more disk writes to the tracking database also results in a larger disk footprint for the tracking database. While on the subject of performance, for optimal throughput you should install the tracking database on a separate disk from the work-items database, and it is even better to off-load the work to a separate machine.

Tracking options may be set for any of the following BizTalk Messaging entities:

❑ Server Groups

❑ Channels

❑ Document Definitions

We will now examine each of these in turn by changing the settings for our transfer between the HR application and the accounting application.

Server Group Tracking Options

Server Group tracking settings give you the ability to make changes to tracking across all of the servers in a group. Open the BizTalk Administrator console, right-click on the BizTalk server group and select the Tracking tab to examine the tracking options as shown below:

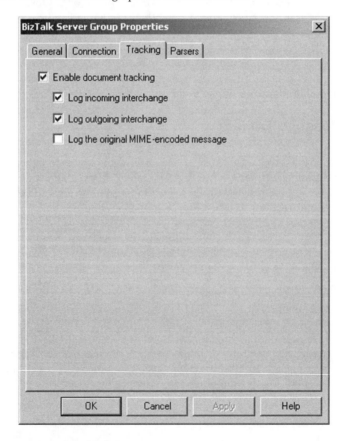

There are four tracking options as shown above. These options have a global effect across the server group and you should review the information below carefully before changing any of them. Let's examine them individually.

When the Enable document tracking option is not selected all document interchange tracking is turned off for the server group. Removing all document tracking removes your ability to view any of the four documents involved in the HR application to accounting application exchange. Indeed, you will receive a system warning if you try to disable this option. When Enable document tracking is not ticked you can not set any of the other options in this dialog box.

> *You may need to turn off document tracking when you are working with large files. This is because the recommended maximum document size for an interchange, a single file containing a collection of documents, is 20 Mb with logging turned on. The 20 Mb figure is the UNICODE XML representation of the native format. If you are submitting an ANSI EDI format then the practical maximum is 7-10 Mb because the intermediate UNICODE XML representation of this format will be close to 20 Mb. Should you wish to work with larger interchanges then you must disable the document-tracking option or expect significantly reduced (unacceptable) performance.*

The Log incoming/outgoing interchange options tell BizTalk Server to keep a copy of the input and output documents in their native formats. Non-repudiation and commerce law concerns often require you to log messages in this manner. As we will see, when this option is ticked not only the document itself but also information about the interchange such as the source and destination organisations, and the transport used will be recorded.

The Log the original MIME-encoded message option tells BizTalk Server that S/MIME-encoded documents should be stored in the Tracking database in their original format, before decoding of the S/MIME sections is completed. This setting is not turned on by default during the installation of BizTalk server but if you are receiving MIME documents and you need to store them in their original format then turn this option on.

Note that if you choose not to log incoming and outgoing interchanges or original MIME-encoded messages you can still track document-specific information, rather than the interchange meta-data.

For our HR application to accounting application scenario we will accept the default options of Enable Document Tracking, Log incoming interchange, and Log outgoing interchange. Now let's examine the document definition tracking options:

Document Definition Tracking Options

You can also set tracking information for individual document definitions stored in WebDAV. This enables you to store specific information inside the business messages that you transfer, so that you can later query or aggregate the data. These settings are applied to **all** instances of a document definition used inside BizTalk Messaging.

Open up the Messaging Manager and then the document definition, DelimitedEmployeeInput, that is the message specification for the document that is received from the HR application. Select the Global Tracking tab. A graphical representation of the message specification fields is displayed in the left-hand pane of the dialog box. The Document Definition Properties dialog box is shown overleaf:

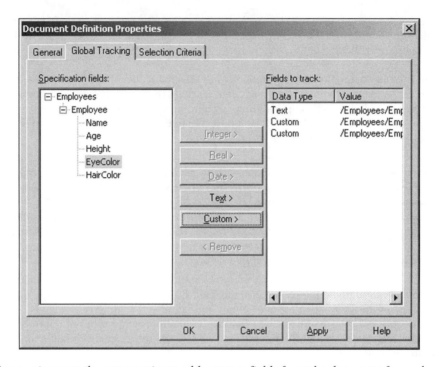

BizTalk Server gives you the opportunity to add any two fields from the document for each of the data types: integer, real, date, and text. These fields will be saved in SQL Server database columns of the same data type inside the tracking database so that they can be queried with simple SQL select statements. To track the Name field in the document definition select the field and press the **Text** button to add the XPath query for the Name field to the right-hand pane.

In addition, you can add an unlimited number of custom fields from inside the document definition to be tracked. The difference between custom fields and data-typed fields is that the custom document fields are all stored inside a single XML message in the tracking database rather than in separate columns. A direct result of this storage mechanism is that you will need to parse these XML messages to obtain access to the custom tracking data. To track the Age and the EyeColor fields as custom fields, select each one and press the **Custom** button to add them to the right-hand pane.

The tracking user interface, which will be explained in the next section, provides easy access to both the data-typed and the custom tracking fields.

> **It is important that you assign data types to the fields in your own schema if you wish to use BizTalk Tracking. If you receive the error message box "Object or data matching name, range, or selection criteria was not found within the scope of this operation" then check your schema to ensure that the schema contains at least one field with a data type. Only fields with data-types assigned can be tracked because they are stored into strongly typed SQL Server columns.**

Please also note that any fields selected in both the source and destination specifications in a single document interchange will be ignored in the source specification.

Document Definition Tracking Caveats

The BizTalk Editor currently supports setting data types for fields/attributes but not records/elements. If you need to track elements then you must assign data types to those elements. To explain this clearly let's work through an example: below is a simple XML document containing one element, MyElement, and a single child attribute, MyAttribute.

```
<MyElement MyAttribute="MyAttribute_1">MyElement_1</MyElement>
```

Import this schema into the BizTalk Editor and assign a string data type to MyAttribute as shown:

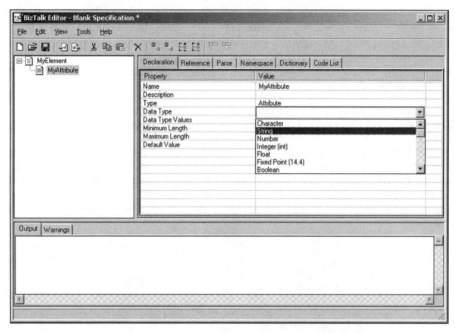

Now save the XDR schema and open it into Notepad. You will see, as shown below, that the BizTalk Editor has been assigned a data type d:type="string" to MyAttribute so it is available to BizTalk Tracking.

```
<?xml version="1.0"?>
<!-- Generated by using BizTalk Editor on Sat, Dec 02 2000 12:38:28 PM -->
<!-- Microsoft Corporation (c) 2000 (http://www.microsoft.com) -->
<Schema name="MyElement" b:BizTalkServerEditorTool_Version="1.0"
                    b:root_reference="MyElement" b:standard="XML"
                    xmlns="urn:schemas-microsoft-com:xml-data"
                    xmlns:b="urn:schemas-microsoft-com:BizTalkServer"
                    xmlns:d="urn:schemas-microsoft-com:datatypes">

    <b:SelectionFields/>

    <ElementType name="MyElement" content="textOnly" model="closed">
        <b:RecordInfo/>
        <AttributeType name="MyAttribute" d:type="string">
            <b:FieldInfo/></AttributeType>
        <attribute type="MyAttribute" required="no"/>
    </ElementType>
</Schema>
```

On the other hand, you can see that the element, `MyElement`, has no data type, and there is no interface to set this inside the BizTalk Editor, so it is not available for tracking.

Fortunately, there is a work-around – you can manually edit the resulting document specification in `Notepad`, or any XML editor, to add data-typing information to the element, and then BizTalk tracking will allow you to select the element node for tracking. Alter the definition of the element to add data typing information, as shown below, and then the element is available for tracking.

```
<ElementType name="MyElement" content="textOnly" model="closed" d:type="string">
```

In this sub-section you learned how to set up tracking for all documents that fit a specific document definition. Often you will want to track fields inside document definitions for certain messaging channels, but not for other messaging channels. If this is the case then you should set up these fields in channel tracking, rather than inside document definition tracking.

Channel Tracking Options

Channel tracking options let us further refine document tracking for a specific set of interchanges. The interface is very similar to the Document Definition Properties dialog box.

Open up the Messaging Manager and the `Take HR delimited msg and transform to accounting positional msg` channel. Tracking is set from the Tracking button on the third page of the Channel Wizard. As you can see below, the XPath for the global tracking fields that we set in the document definition are displayed at the top of the dialog box because they are tracked for all instances of the document definition. Let's add one further field the Employee Height as a Real.

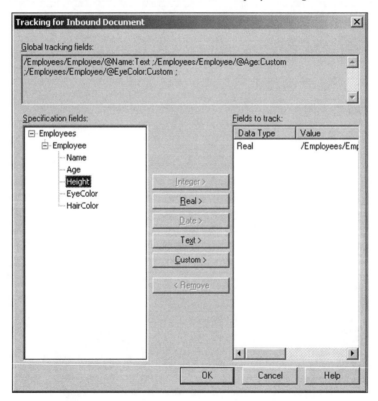

The final channel specification setting determines which of the four documents in the channel, the inbound native and XML documents, and the outbound native and XML documents are saved into the tracking database. Navigate to the second last page of the Channel Properties wizard.

If you are not performing any transformations in a particular channel, then just log the inbound documents, as the two sets of documents will be identical. If you are using XML documents the native format will be the same as the XML format so logging both is unnecessary. Set the `Take HR delimited msg and transform to accounting positional msg` channel to log the entire document so that we can later examine how these are saved in the tracking database.

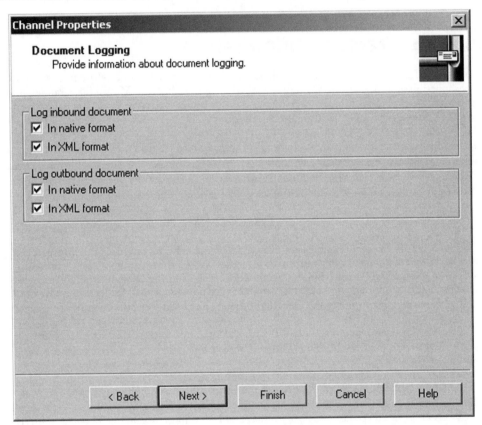

How and Where Document Definition and Channel Tracking Options are Stored

The document definition and channel tracking options are persisted into the BizTalk Messaging database, `InterchangeBTM`, along with all the other BizTalk Messaging configuration information. As you will learn in Chapter 13, BizTalk Server provides complete programmatic access to this database through the BizTalk Object model. The example code snippet below shows how to create the document definition `DelimitedEmployeeInput`, which we built using the wizard in an earlier section in this chapter, with VBScript and how to assign tracking information to it:

```
Set BT = CreateObject("BizTalk.BizTalkConfig")
set doc = BT.CreateDocument
doc.clear
doc.name = "DelimitedEmployeeInput"
doc.reference = "http://" & myServerName &
"/BizTalkServerRepository/DocSpecs/DelimitedEmployeeInput.xml"
```

There may be many tracking fields for each document definition, so these are added to the document definition using a dictionary object:

```
Set doc.TrackFields = CreateObject("Commerce.Dictionary")
doc.TrackFields.s_value1 = "/EmployeeInfo/Employees/@Name"
Doc140003 = doc.create
```

Now that you have setup BizTalk Tracking re-run the transfer of the delimited file from the HR system to the accounting system and we will examine the results in the tracking user interface.

Displaying Tracking Information

Drop a copy of input.txt into the c:\software\delimitedtopositionaltrack\receivehrapp directory. The receive function will pick up the file and deliver through the BizTalk Messaging channel/port combination to the output file: output{GUID}.txt (where {GUID} is a GUID value) in c:\software\delimitedtopositionaltrack\accountingout.

Open the BizTalk Document Tracking application and select Home Organization | HRApp as the source selection and Home Organization | Accounting App as the destination selection. This will restrict the tracking user interface to finding documents involved in the exchange between the HR application and the accounting application. You can also set a date and time range if you wish.

> Note: BizTalk Document Tracking is available to all users belonging to the Windows 2000 BizTalk Server Report Users group. The tracking interface uses the Microsoft Office web components that ship with Microsoft BizTalk Server 2000 and installs two client-side packages: the windows common controls, and the BizTalk Document Tracking Installation control. These controls are downloaded to Internet Explorer the first time you open the application. If you trust your local web site, then to avoid a security message in Internet Explorer when you open each page of the tracking interface, you should add the BizTalkTracking web site to the Trusted site zones on the Security tab of the Internet Options dialog box.

Press the Show Documents button to display the list of all the documents exchange between these two applications. On the author's machine two documents are visible in the document type selection list: the Employees and the CustomerInfo. If you have only set up the exchange between the HR and the accounting application for Employee information as shown at the start of the chapter then you will only see the Employees document.

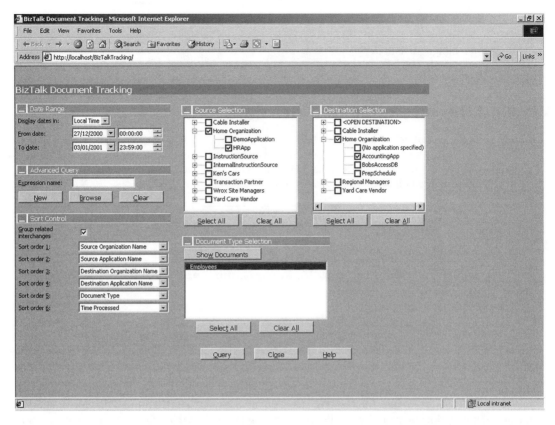

Press the Query button to display the tracking meta-data with incoming and outgoing interchanges grouped together, and the records displayed in the sort order: source organization, source application, destination organization, destination application, document type, and processing time as specified on the BizTalk Document Tracking form.

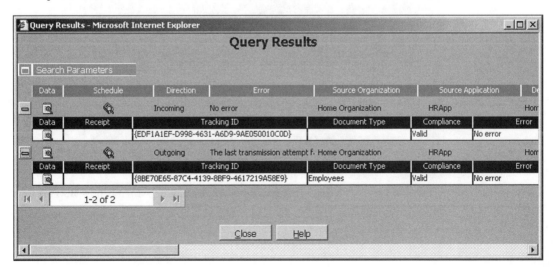

You can use Query Results to view:

❑ Interchange meta-data

❑ Document specific data

Viewing the interchange Meta-data

In our example we turned on logging for both incoming and outgoing interchanges at the server group so both interchanges are displayed. Each interchange contains a single document. The document itself contains two records. If you press the document data icon associated with the **incoming** interchange then you can view the delimited document as shown below:

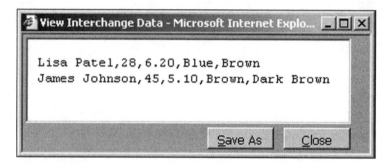

Also recorded against the interchange are the source and destination organizations, the number of documents sent, which in this case is a single document, and the processing date/time. Expand the incoming interchange to view information about the document itself. Next press the document data icon for the incoming document and you will see the dialog box below that once again presents the single document involved in this interchange but also provides you with the option to View native format or to View XML format.

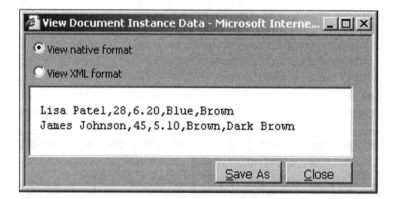

Select View XML format to reveal the first intermediate XML document, which is how BizTalk Server represents the delimited file internally.

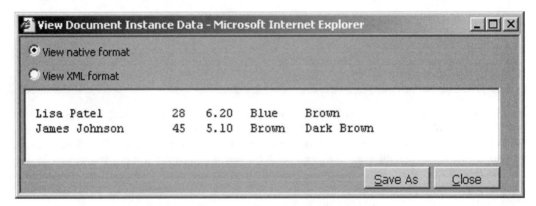

In the outgoing interchange, the intermediate XML document is mapped to a second intermediate XML document, and it is finally serialized as a positional format. If you expand the second interchange you can examine the document instance data to reveal the second intermediate XML document or the outgoing positional file that is shown below:

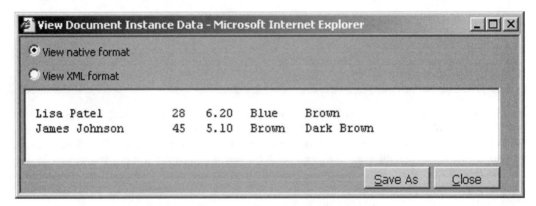

BizTalk Document tracking displays a summary line for each document involved in the interchange. This summary includes the name of the document's specification, and whether the document was successfully processed.

Viewing Document-specific Data

The BizTalk Document Tracking is not limited to examining the meta-data surrounding the document interchange. The results of the document and channel tracking field setup that we completed earlier are also visible.

Recall that we set up tracking for the document definition to record the employee's name as Text. On the channel, we also added tracking for the employee's height as a Real. The data-typed fields are immediately visible on the outgoing document record. The screenshot overleaf shows the details:

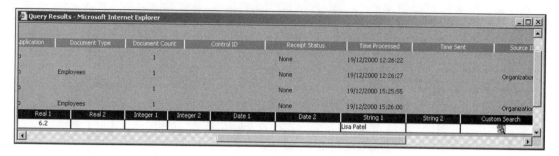

The first record in this document contains the name Lisa Patel that is saved into **String 1**. It also shows a height of 6.2 that is saved into **Real 1**.

On the document definition we also set up two custom fields: Age and EyeColour.
To view the custom fields you need to press the **Custom Search** icon. The Age, (28) and the EyeColor (Blue) values for the first record are displayed below:

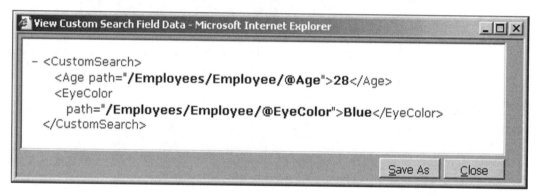

Examining each custom field in each document interchange to determine whether it contained a certain piece of business-specific information would be a painful way to examine the custom data. Fortunately, BizTalk Document Tracking provides a more convenient user interface for this task. Return to the main BizTalk Document Tracking page and press the **New Advanced Query** button. We will create a query that returns all documents where the Age custom field is greater than 27. Select the Age field from the **Source Selection** drop down, select the > operator and enter 27 in the value field. Press **Done** to save the setting. The result is shown opposite above:

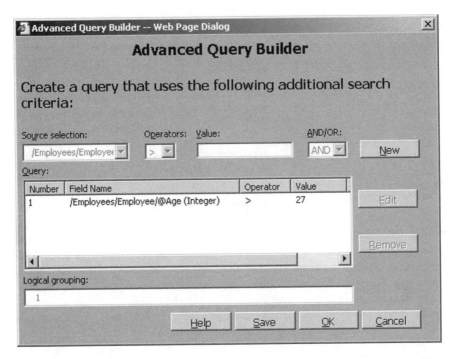

You will then be prompted to save the query with a name so that you can recall it later. To use the query enter its name in the Expression name text box on the main tracking screen or Browse for the name. Then press the query button.

While BizTalk Tracking is a useful tool to examine interchanges and document data for a system administrator, to really understand how to access the business information stored in BizTalk server requires knowledge of the COM interface to tracking and the underlying database structure. We will examine this shortly, but first we will briefly examine the files that compose the BizTalk Document Tracking user interface that we have used in this section, and the stored procedures they call to retrieve tracking information. We will reuse several of these stored procedures in our own tracking user interface.

Inside the Tracking Interface

The BizTalk Document Tracking interface is a 2-tier web application composed of ASP pages in the http://localhost/BizTalkTracking virtual directory and a number of SQL stored procedures prefixed with dta_ui in the DTA database. The tracking user interface files are stored in \Program files\Microsoft Biztalk server\BizTalkTracking and this is also the file set for the virtual IIS root directory http://localhost/BizTalkTracking.

While the tracking interface provides access to most of the tracking data it is not a complete solution. For example the response document that is returned by Application Integration Components is not available in the interface but is stored in the database. If you wish to modify the tracking interface it is useful to understand what functions belong to what ASP pages, and what stored procedures these pages call to retrieve tracking data. The table overleaf lists the ASP pages, describes their function, and also lists the stored procedures that are used:

ASP/HTML Page	Function	Stored Procedure(s) used
BrowseQuery.htm	Display the **Advanced queries** dialog box	dta_ui_get_userqueries
BrowseQuery.asp	Used for testing purposes, redirects to Browsequery.htm	
DTAComponentDownload.htm	Retrieves the CAB files required for use of the tracking interface	
DTAComponentInstall.htm	Installs the CAB files required for use of the tracking interface	
InterchangeWorkflowStatus.asp	View XLANG Schedule Summary	dta_ui_get_interchange_workflow_status
QueryBuilder.asp	Used for testing purposes, redirects to QueryBuilder.htm	
QueryBuilder.htm	Advanced query builder user interface	dta_ui_get_one_userquery dta_ui_get_custom_field_names
RawCustomSearchField.asp	Retrieves the custom search field information	dta_ui_get_document_customsearchfield
RawDocData.asp	Retrieves the native document data	dta_ui_get_document_XMLdata dta_ui_get_document_data
RawInterchangeData.asp	Retrieves the interchange data	dta_ui_get_interchange_data
Results.htm	Return the results for an interchange query	dta_ui_get_interchangeNavigation dta_ui_get_interchange dta_ui_get_document
submit.htm	Startup screen for BizTalkTracking containing the main interface	dta_ui_get_version dta_ui_get_doctypes
ViewCustomSearchField.asp	Displays custom search fields	
ViewDocumentData.asp	Show document data in xml/native	
ViewInterchangeData.asp	Show interchange data	

In the following section we will use some of the BizTalk Tracking stored procedures in conjunction with the COM interface to obtain tracking data. The methodology we use could be applied to writing custom reports for examining BizTalk Server document information.

Programmatic Access to the Tracking Information

There are three approaches to accessing data from the tracking database. You can:

❑ Write your own custom queries with SQL code to extract data

❑ Call an existing stored procedure

❑ Use the COM interface

BizTalk provides the same COM interface with two different names, `BizTalkTrackData` for C++ users and `BTSDocTracking` for VB users. For simplicity we will call it the `BTSDocTracking` interface because this book generally targets the VB programmer. The underlying structure of the tracking database will most likely change as the product undergoes future revisions, and so the code you write today calling stored procedures may not work in the future. In contrast, the COM `BTSDocTracking` interface provides a level of abstraction on top of the stored procedures that should be more resistant to change over product revisions. That is, the underlying code may change, but the code in the COM interface should insulate you, the end user, from this change. Let's examine the `BTSDocTracking` interface in some detail.

BTSDocTracking Interface

`BTSDocTracking` is a simple interface with three main methods each requiring a single parameter, the submission ID, and returning a recordset rich in tracking information. When you perform an `Interchange.Submit()` or `SubmitSync()` to pass messages to BizTalk server the submission ID is returned to the calling application. The type library for the `BTSDocTracking` interface is stored in `CISDTA.dll`. The tables below contain a lot of information, but as it is not presented in this manner inside the BizTalk Server help files, you will find this to be useful reference information.

The first of `BTSDocTracking`'s methods is `GetInterchanges()`. This method returns an ADO recordset that contains a list of interchanges returned from the `IInterchange.Submit()` call, including all the data from the Tracking database.

Input:	`bstrSubmissionID`: A unique identifier for a previous document submission to BizTalk Server.
Output:	`nInterChangeKey`: Foreign key to dta_interchange_details table used to retrieve interchange detail information such as the interchange data contents.
	`nInterChangeDataKey`: Primary key for each unique interchange.
	`nResponseDocDataKey`: Foreign key to dta_document_data used to retrieve the interchange response document.
	`uidSubmissionGUID`: GUID representing the parent submission. One submission may result in many interchanges and documents.

Table continued on following page

Output:	dtProcessedTimeStamp: The time the interchange record was recorded.
(continued)	NvcSyntax: Code for document syntax (XML, X12, EDIFACT, FLATFILE, etc.). For pass-through submission or on certain errors, described later, this field has a value of "UNKNOWN".
	nvcVersion: The particular version of the syntax.
	nvcControlID: Unique control ID used both for EDI and also BizTalk Reliable Messaging.
	nDirection: 0 if the interchange is outbound, 1 if the interchange is inbound. This field is the foreign key to the dta_direction_values table where the textual representation of 0 and 1 is stored.
	dtTimeSent: Timestamp for successful transmission.
	nError: Error code, the description for which is stored in the dta_error_message table.
	nTestMode: Reserved field, not currently used.
	nvcSrcAliasQualifier: The qualifier for the sending organisation, such as OrganisationName.
	nvcSrcAliasID: The identifier value for the source organization, such as Home Organization.
	nvcSrcAppName: The source application name.
	nvcDestAliasQualifier: The qualifier for the destination organization.
	nvcDestAliasID: The identifier value for the destination organization.
	nvcDestAppName: The destination application name.
	nAckStatus: A code representing the receipt status. The textual descriptions for receipt status are stored in dta_ack_status_values.
	nvcSMTPMessageID: The SMTP transport message identifier (for EDIINT). EDIINT is currently not supported in BizTalk Server 2000 and this field is reserved for a future implementation.
	nDocumentsAccepted: The number of documents accepted in this interchange.
	nDocumentsRejected: The number of documents rejected in this interchange.
	nTransportType: A code for the transport type. The textual descriptions of the transport types, such as HTTP, FTP, etc. is stored in dta_transport_type_values.
	nvcTransportAddress: The transport address, for example file://c:\test.xml.
	nvcServerName: The processing server name.
	nNumberOfBytes: The size of the interchange, in bytes. This field represents what is tracked in the related dta_interchange_data record and can be greater than what is actually transmitted because of additional envelope processing and data format conversion during transmission.
	nNumOfTransmitAttempts: The number of transmit attempts required to sent this interchange to the destination.

The second of `BTSDocTracking`'s methods is `GetInDocDetails()`. This method returns an ADO recordset containing a list of the documents that were included in the return from the `IInterchange.Submit()` call.

Input:	bstrSubmissionID: A unique identifier for a previous document submission to BizTalk Server.
Output:	nOutDocKey: Primary key from each out document.
	nInDocKey: Foreign key to dta_indoc_details for each incoming document.
	nGroupKey: Foreign key to the dta_group_details table.
	nInterchangeKey: Foreign key to the dta_interchange_details table that contains the actual interchange document.
	nRoutingKey: Foreign key to dta_routing_details that contains the destination routing information.
	nDocumentDataKey: Foreign key to dta_document_data that contains the actual document.
	nDebugDocDataKey: Foreign key to dta_debugDoc_data that contains the XML form of the received document.
	uidTrackingGUID: Master tracking GUID unique identifier.
	dtProcessedTimeStamp: The time the record was created.
	nvcSyntax: Code for document syntax (XML, X12, EDIFACT, FLATFILE, etc.). For pass-through submission or on certain errors, described below, this field has a value of UNKNOWN.
	nvcVersion: The particular version of the syntax.
	nvcRelease: The release of the particular version.
	nvcDocType: Document type or transaction set identifier.
	nvcControlID: Unique Control ID used for processing EDI functional groups.
	nError: Error code, the description for which is stored in the dta_error_message table.
	nIsValid: Validation code. Values allowed are 0 (invalid), 1 (valid), or 2 (pass-through).
	nAckStaus: Code for the status of the receipt. This is a foreign key to dta_ack_status_values that contains the textual descriptions of the receipt statuses.
	nReceiptFlag: A flag whose value indicates whether the receipt is related to an interchange (1), group (2), indoc (4), or outdoc (8).
	nReceiptKey: A unique number that identifies the receipt information.
	dtReceiptDueBy: Receipt deadline timestamp, computed to be the processing timestamp.
	nRealName1: Foreign key to dta_custom_field_names.
	nRealValue1: Tracking real value capture field 1.
	nRealName2: Foreign key to dta_custom_field_names.
	nRealValue2: Tracking real value capture field 2.

Table continued on following page

Output:	nIntName1: Foreign key to dta_custom_field_names.
(continued)	nIntValue1: Tracking integer capture field 1.
	nIntName2: Foreign key to dta_custom_field_names.
	nIntValue2: Tracking integer capture field 2.
	nDateName1: Foreign key to dta_custom_field_names.
	nDateValue1: Tracking date capture field 1.
	nDateName2: Foreign key to dta_custom_field_names.
	nDateValue2: Tracking date capture field 2.
	nStrName1: Foreign key to dta_custom_field_names.
	nvcStrValue1: Tracking string capture field 1.
	nStrName2: Foreign key to dta_custom_field_names.
	nvcStrValue2: Tracking string capture field 2.
	nvcCustomSearch: Capture of the custom search fields as XML.

BTSDocTracking's final method is GetOutDocDetails(). This method returns an ADO recordset containing a list of the documents that were generated as a result of the IInterchange.Submit() call.

Input:	bstrSubmissionID: A unique identifier for a previous document submission to BizTalk Server.
Output:	nInDocKey: Primary key for each document.
	nGroupKey: Foreign key to dta_group_details.
	nInterchangeKey: Foreign key to dta_interchange_details that contains the actual interchange data.
	nDocumentDataKey: Foreign key to dta_document_data that contains the actual document.
	nDebugDocDataKey: Foreign key to dta_debugDoc_data that contains the XML form of the received document.
	uidTrackingGUID: Master tracking GUID unique identifier.
	dtProcessedTimeStamp: The time the record was created.
	nvcSyntax: Code for document syntax (XML, X12, EDIFACT, FLATFILE, etc.). For pass-through submission or on certain errors, described below, this field has a value of UNKNOWN.
	nvcVersion: The particular version of the syntax.
	nvcRelease: The release of the particular version.
	nvcDocType: Document type or transaction set identifier.
	nvcControlID: Unique Control ID used for processing EDI functional groups.
	nError: Error code, the description for which is stored in the dta_error_message table.
	nIsValid: Validation code. Values allowed are 0 (invalid), 1 (valid), or 2 (pass-through).

Building a VB Tracking User Interface

In the earlier example in this chapter we submitted a delimited file, `input.txt`, from the HR application to BizTalk Messaging with a file receive function. Now we will write a VB application that programmatically submits the document, obtains the submission ID and then demonstrates how to access tracking data through the `BTSDocTracking` interface.

Before we delve into the code for this sample, open up the project file `programmatictrack.vbp` from `c:\software\programmatictrack` or wherever you have placed it on your machine. Edit the source code to update all references from `c:\software\programmatictrack` to your directory, and change the `ConnectionString` if your SQL Server is not your local machine or if you have changed the default username from `sa` and blank password. Then run the application. Initially the form is blank and the only available buttons are the **Submit Document Input.txt** and the **View Latest Interchange** buttons.

The purpose of the **View Latest Interchange** *button will be explained at the end of this sub-section.*

When you press the **Submit Document Input.txt** button Visual Basic loads the delimited file `input.txt` file from **c:\software\programmatictrack** using the envelope `envDelimitedEmployeeInput`, and delivers it to the channel `Take HR delimited msg and transform to accounting positional msg` using the `Submit()` method. The channel then maps the delimited file to a positional file and outputs the result in the **C:\software\delimitedtopositionaltrack\outputpositional**. Whereas the file receive function used earlier in the chapter resulted in a destructive read of the source document, the programmatic submit does not remove the source document and so we can submit the document multiple times from the same location.

Immediately after you submit the document the incoming Interchange grid as well as the incoming document grid is populated with data retrieved from the `BTSDocTracking` call. The `Submit()` method is asynchronous and hence it returns before the outgoing interchange is completed. To retrieve the outgoing interchange and the outgoing document information press the **GetOutDoc Information** button repeatedly. If the interchange is completed the grid will be refreshed with data; if the interchange has not yet completed it will remain blank.

As an exercise you can modify the example to use the synchronous SubmitSync() *method.* SubmitSync() *does not return to the method caller until the outgoing interchange has completed and so using this method you will always see the outgoing interchange.*

The sample also allows you to view the contents of the interchange, as well as the native and XML versions of the incoming and outgoing documents. A screenshot of the sample showing interchange and document information is below:

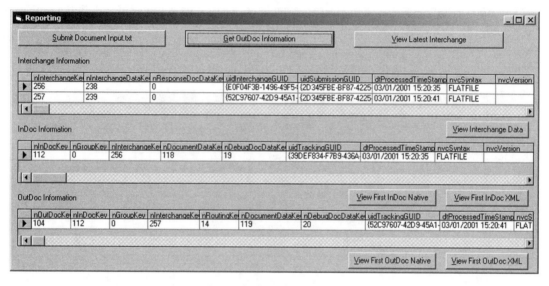

If you only receive one line, then check your BizTalk Messaging setup, the suspended queue, and the Event viewer, and resolve the problem before continuing. This example requires the messaging port/channel setup that you performed at the beginning of the chapter.

The native inbound and outgoing documents are the delimited document, and the positional document. Note that because Windows message boxes use a proportional font, the positional document does not line up properly. Using message boxes makes this sample relatively code-light, but if you need to show these documents in practice you should write a form to display them.

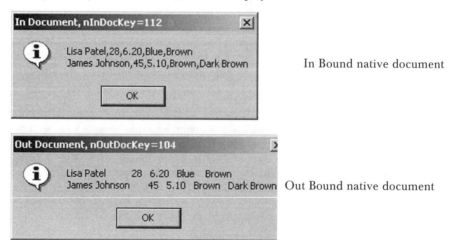

In Bound native document

Out Bound native document

Now we will examine the code behind this sample. Open up the form and view the code. The
BTSDocTracking interface object, dimensioned as mytrackingdata, has three methods that return
results as the ADO resultsets dimensioned as myInDocInterchanges, myInDocDetails, and
myOutDocDetails:

```
Option Explicit

Dim myInDocDetails As ADODB.Recordset
Dim myOutDocDetails As ADODB.Recordset
Dim myInterchanges As ADODB.Recordset
Dim mytrackingdata As New BTSDocTracking
```

The BTSDocTracking interface does not provide us with the complete set of tracking information, in
particular it does not return the interchange, indoc, or outdoc document data directly; instead it
provides a handle to these data items. We need to access the InterchangeDTA directly using stored
procedures to obtain this information. The connection object, myConnection, and a command object,
myCommand, are dimensioned for this purpose. mySubmissionID is dimensioned to save the
submission ID from an Interchange.Submit() call so that it can be queried a second time with the
Get OutDoc Information button:

```
Dim myRS As New ADODB.Recordset
Dim myConnection As New ADODB.Connection
Dim myCommand As New ADODB.Command
Dim mySubmissionID As String
```

The Form_Load() method opens a new connection to the tracking (InterchangeDTA) database. If
your database is not on the local machine then edit the ConnectionString as appropriate.

```
Private Sub Form_Load()
  ' open the SQL database
  myConnection.ConnectionString = "Provider=SQLOLEDB.1;Persist Security
Info=False;User ID=sa;Initial Catalog=InterchangeDTA"
  myConnection.Open
  myCommand.ActiveConnection = myConnection
  myCommand.CommandType = adCmdStoredProc
End Sub
```

When you press the **Submit** button the btnSubmit_Click() method is executed. Initially the source
input.txt file is read from disk into the variable myDocument:

```
Private Sub btnSubmit_Click()

  Dim myInterchange As New Interchange
  Dim myFile As New Scripting.FileSystemObject
  Dim myTextFile As TextStream
  Dim myDocument As String

  Set myTextFile = myFile.OpenTextFile("c:\software\programmatictrack\input.txt")
  myDocument = myTextFile.ReadAll
```

The data grids that display the interchange, and in/out document details are cleared:

```
Set myInDocDetailsGrid.DataSource = Nothing
Set myInterchangesGrid.DataSource = Nothing
Set myOutDocDetailsGrid.DataSource = Nothing
```

myDocument is submitted to BizTalk Messaging, using the myInterchange.Submit(), to the channel Tracking Delimited File Output with the envelope "envDelimitedCustomerInput" and then the interchange object is released:

```
mySubmissionID = myInterchange.Submit(BIZTALK_OPENNESS_TYPE_NOTOPEN, myDocument, , _
    , , , , "Tracking Delimited File Output", , "envDelimitedCustomerInput") _
    Set myInterchange = Nothing
```

The return from the Submit() call is mySubmissionID, which is the key to obtaining tracking information for this particular submission. mySubmissionID is passed as the sole parameter to the GetInDocDetails() (which retrieves the incoming document details) and GetInterchanges() (which retrieves the incoming interchange details) methods of the tracking object, mytrackingdata.

```
Set myInDocDetails = mytrackingdata.GetInDocDetails(mySubmissionID)
Set myInterchanges = mytrackingdata.GetInterchanges(mySubmissionID)
```

Both of these methods return recordsets that are assigned to the data grids for display:

```
Set myInDocDetailsGrid.DataSource = myInDocDetails
Set myInterchangesGrid.DataSource = myInterchanges
```

The last step in the btnSubmit_click() method is to enable many of the buttons on the form so that the user can integrate BizTalk for further information about this exchange. As you can see the grids display a great deal of tracking information.

```
btnGetOutDocDetails.Enabled = True
btnViewInDocXML.Enabled = True
btnViewInDocNative.Enabled = True
btnViewInDocXML.Enabled = True
btnViewInterchange.Enabled = True
End Sub
```

When you press the GetOutDoc Information button to retrieve out document details, the tracking object GetOutDocDetails() is called with the same submission ID:

```
Private Sub btnGetOutDocDetails_Click()
    Set myOutDocDetails = mytrackingdata.GetOutDocDetails(mySubmissionID)
    Set myOutDocDetailsGrid.DataSource = myOutDocDetails
```

If the resulting recordset has records (RecordCount > 0) then the interchange has completed and the outgoing document information is recorded in the data grid, enabling the detail buttons:

```
If myOutDocDetails.RecordCount > 0 Then
    Set myInterchanges = mytrackingdata.GetInterchanges(mySubmissionID)
    Set myInterchangesGrid.DataSource = myInterchanges
    btnViewOutDocNative.Enabled = True
    btnViewOutDocXML.Enabled = True
End If
End Sub
```

One glaring omission from each of the incoming/outgoing and interchange recordsets is the actual document contents. The COM BTSDocTracking interface does not provide you with a direct mechanism to access these.

For its own tracking interface, BizTalk Tracking, Microsoft created several stored procedures to return this information. We will leverage these existing stored procedures and the information inside the tracking records to retrieve the actual document data.

> **We are now directly accessing stored procedures, rather than the COM interface and can not guarantee that these will be identical in future versions of the product.**

For example, dta_ui_get_document_XMLdata, is used to retrieve the XML representation of the data. If the @tnDirection parameter is one, then it refers to an incoming document. If the @tnDirection parameter is zero, then it refers to the outgoing document. The second parameter required by this stored procedure, @nDocumentKey, is set to the tracking record myInDocDetails("nInDocKey") to retrieve information specific to our interchange:

```
Private Sub btnViewInDocXML_Click()
    myCommand.CommandText = "dta_ui_get_document_XMLdata"
    myCommand.Parameters.Refresh
    myCommand.Parameters("@nDocumentKey") = myInDocDetails("nInDocKey")
    myCommand.Parameters("@tnDirection") = 1 'for incoming
    Set myRS = myCommand.Execute
```

After the stored procedure myRS("ntxtDocumentData") contains the actual document, which is displayed in a message box:

```
    MsgBox myRS("ntxtDocumentData"), vbInformation, "In Document XML, nInDocKey=" & _
myInDocDetails("nInDocKey")
End Sub
```

The code for viewing the outbound document is almost identical to the incoming document with two exceptions. The stored procedure parameter @tnDirection is set to zero for outgoing, and the @nDocumentKey is set to the myOutDocDetails("nOutDocKey") value:

```
Private Sub btnViewOutDocXML_Click()
    myCommand.CommandText = "dta_ui_get_document_XMLdata"
    myCommand.Parameters.Refresh
    myCommand.Parameters("@nDocumentKey") = myOutDocDetails("nOutDocKey")
    myCommand.Parameters("@tnDirection") = 0 'for outgoing
    Set myRS = myCommand.Execute
    MsgBox myRS("ntxtDocumentData"), vbInformation, "Out Document XML, nOutDocKey=" _
& myOutDocDetails("nOutDocKey")
End Sub
```

A second stored procedure, dta_ui_get_document_data is used to retrieve native documents from InterchangeDTA. dta_ui_get_document_data receives the same two parameters as dta_ui_get_document_XMLdata and returns the document in myRS.Fields("imgDocumentData"):

```
Private Sub btnViewInDocNative_Click()
    Dim myStream As ADODB.Stream
    Dim MyString As String
```

```
myCommand.CommandText = "dta_ui_get_document_data"
myCommand.Parameters.Refresh
myCommand.Parameters("@nDocumentKey") = myInDocDetails("nInDocKey")
myCommand.Parameters("@tnDirection") = 1 'for incoming
Set myRS = myCommand.Execute
```

Whereas XML documents are suitable for direct display to the screen, the native document is stored in a binary stream. Before we display the document we first write it as binary into an ADODB stream called `myStream`, assign it the character set specified in the return recordset, `myRS.Fields("nvcCharSet")`, and read from the stream as text. The result is text representation that is human-readable. Finally we ensure that the resulting string is Unicode and display the result in a message box:

```
Set myStream = CreateObject("ADODB.Stream")
myStream.Open
myStream.Charset = myRS.Fields("nvcCharSet")
myStream.Position = 0
myStream.Type = adTypeBinary
myStream.Write myRS.Fields("imgDocumentData")
myStream.Position = 0
myStream.Type = adTypeText
MyString = myStream.ReadText
myStream.Close
MyString = ConvertToUnicode(MyString)
MsgBox MyString, vbInformation, "In Document, nInDocKey=" & _
myInDocDetails("nInDocKey")
End Sub

Function ConvertToUnicode(MyString As String) As String
  ConvertToUnicode = Replace(MyString, Chr(0), "")
End Function
```

It will come as no surprise to you that viewing the outgoing native document involves calling the `dta_ui_get_document_data` stored procedure with `@tnDirection` set to zero and `@nDocumentKey` set to `myDocDetails("nOutDocKey")`:

```
Private Sub btnViewOutDocNative_Click()
    Dim myStream As ADODB.Stream
    Dim MyString As String

    myCommand.CommandText = "dta_ui_get_document_data"
    myCommand.Parameters.Refresh
    myCommand.Parameters("@nDocumentKey") = myOutDocDetails("nOutDocKey")
    myCommand.Parameters("@tnDirection") = 0 'for outgoing
    Set myRS = myCommand.Execute

    Set myStream = CreateObject("ADODB.Stream")
    myStream.Open
    myStream.Charset = myRS.Fields("nvcCharSet")
    myStream.Position = 0
    myStream.Type = adTypeBinary
    myStream.Write myRS.Fields("imgDocumentData")
    myStream.Position = 0
    myStream.Type = adTypeText
    MyString = myStream.ReadText
    myStream.Close
    MyString = ConvertToUnicode(MyString)
    MsgBox MyString, vbInformation, "Out Document, nOutDocKey=" & _
myOutDocDetails("nOutDocKey")
End Sub
```

The stored procedure `dta_ui_get_interchange_data` is used to return interchange information. It receives a single input parameter `@nInterchangeKey` which is set to the tracking recordset value `myInterchanges("nInterchangeKey")`:

```
Private Sub btnViewInterchange_Click()
    Dim myStream As ADODB.Stream
    Dim MyString As String
    Dim xmldom As New DOMDocument30

    myCommand.CommandText = "dta_ui_get_interchange_data"
    myCommand.Parameters.Refresh
    myCommand.Parameters("@nInterchangeKey") = myInterchanges("nInterchangeKey")
    Set myRS = myCommand.Execute
```

As the result is stored in binary, it is processed similarly to the native documents before being displayed in a message box:

```
    Set myStream = CreateObject("ADODB.Stream")
    myStream.Open
    myStream.Charset = myRS.Fields("nvcCharSet")
    myStream.Position = 0
    myStream.Type = adTypeBinary
    myStream.Write myRS.Fields("imgInterchangeData")
    myStream.Position = 0
    myStream.Type = adTypeText
    MyString = myStream.ReadText
    MyString = ConvertToUnicode(MyString)
    myStream.Close
    MsgBox MyString, vbInformation, "Inbound Interchange, nInterchangeKey=" & _
myInterchanges("nInterchangeKey")
End Sub
```

If you use a message queue or a file receive function as a mechanism to input documents into BizTalk Server, then you do not get a `submissionID` return handle. However, in this case, or if you wish to retrieve any subset of the aggregate tracking data in the server, you can write simple SQL queries, such as the one below, which returns all the `submissionGUID` values from the InterchangeDTA:

```
select distinct uidSubmissionGUID from dbo.dta_interchange_details
```

You are probably wondering what the function of the **View Latest Interchange** button is in the Visual Basic programmatic tracking example. It is included to demonstrate how to select the `uidSubmissionGUID` directly from the database. Each record in the `dta_interchange_details` table contains a datetime stamp, `dtProcessedTimeStamp`. The Command object, `myCommand` executes dynamic SQL that selects the `dta_interchange_details` record that was most recently submitted based on the `dtProcessedTimeStamp` column:

```
Private Sub btnLatestInterchange_Click()
  myCommand.ActiveConnection = myConnection
  myCommand.CommandType = adCmdText
  myCommand.CommandText = "select top 1 uidSubmissionGUID from
dbo.dta_interchange_details order by dtProcessedTimeStamp desc
  Set myRS = myCommand.Execute
```

The submission GUID is extracted from the recordset and displayed in a message box and the grid data is updated with the `interchange`, `indoc`, and `outdoc` information based on the submission ID. If the submission has completed before this method is completed then two interchange records will be retrieved:

```
    mySubmissionID = myRS("uidSubmissionGUID")
    MsgBox "Submission GUID ID:" & mySubmissionID & " selected.", vbInformation, _
"Last Interchange Submission"

    Set myInDocDetails = mytrackingdata.GetInDocDetails(mySubmissionID)
    Set myInterchanges = mytrackingdata.GetInterchanges(mySubmissionID)
    Set myOutDocDetails = mytrackingdata.GetOutDocDetails(mySubmissionID)
```

Once the data is retrieved, the data grids are refreshed:

```
    Set myInDocDetailsGrid.DataSource = myInDocDetails
    Set myInterchangesGrid.DataSource = myInterchanges
    Set myOutDocDetailsGrid.DataSource = myOutDocDetails
```

Finally the command buttons are enabled:

```
    btnGetOutDocDetails.Enabled = True
    btnViewInDocXML.Enabled = True
    btnViewInDocNative.Enabled = True
    btnViewInDocXML.Enabled = True
    btnViewInterchange.Enabled = True
    btnViewOutDocNative.Enabled = True
    btnViewOutDocXML.Enabled = True
End Sub
```

In this section you learned how to access the tracking database programmatically through VB. This will give you the power to create custom interfaces to the tracking meta-data as well as the custom reports on business-specific information. In the next section we will explore the main tracking database tables and understand what values are written to these as a document passes through BizTalk Messaging.

Understanding Document Tracking at the Database Level

When you run the HR web to accounting example, BizTalk Server executes three stored procedures in succession: `dta_log_debugdoc_data`, `dta_log_inbound_details`, and `dta_log_outbound_details` to insert data into the tracking tables. The options that we have selected for the server group, channel, and document definition determine what information is logged into these tracking tables. The key tracking database tables are:

Table Name	Purpose
dta_interchange_details	Contains one row for every interchange submitted to (incoming) or sent by (outgoing) BizTalk Server. The record contains details of the interchange such as the source and destination organisations and applications, the submission and interchange GUIDs, the file syntax, the date submitted, the number of documents accepted and rejected, the transport address, the number of bytes processed, and the interchange direction. The interchange key uniquely identifies an interchange record.
dta_interchange_data	Contains one row for every interchange submitted to (incoming) or sent by (outgoing) BizTalk Server. The record contains the data from the interchange and the original filename if it is an incoming interchange and the server group log interchange option is selected. The interchange key links this record to the dta_interchange details record.
dta_indoc_details	Contains one row for every document submitted to (incoming) BizTalk Server. The interchange key links this record to the dta_interchange details record.
dta_document_data	Contains one row for every document submitted to (incoming) or sent by (outgoing) BizTalk Server.
dta_debugdoc_data	Contains one row for the incoming and outgoing intermediate XML format if this option is selected on the messaging channel.
dta_outdoc_details	Contains one row for every record sent by (outgoing) BizTalk server. The record contains the outgoing document including the document definition tracking fields for integer, real, date, and text and the custom search fields.
dta_MIME_data	Contains one row for every MIME document submitted to BizTalk Server if the log MIME interchange option is selected.

Tracking may occur at each of the steps involved in document processing inside BizTalk Server:

1. Submission of the incoming document to the server – in our case `input.txt` through a receive function

2. Decoding and decryption – not performed in our example

3. Parsing and validation – parsing to create the intermediate XML document

4. Select channel and checkpoint document – `Take HR delimited msg and transform to accounting positional msg`

5. Perform channel mapping – applying `DelimitedEmployeeInputtoPositionalEmployeeOutput.xml`

6. Select outgoing port – `Deliver HR accounting positional msg`

7. Serialize output

8. Envelope addition – creating `output{GUID}.txt` internally

9. Transmission of the outgoing-document – saving `output{GUID}.txt` to the file system

We will examine what is recorded when the `input.txt` file is submitted through BizTalk server and also what information is recorded when an error occurs. This section is most useful for you if you want to understand what is tracked in the various tracking tables when an error occurs. For a definition of the field names below refer back to the COM interface documentation in the tables above.

Submission of the Incoming-Document to the Server

Normal action within BizTalk:

❑ When `input.txt` message is submitted to BizTalk using the receive function the interchange information is logged into the `dta_interchange_details` table with the `nvcSyntax` field set to the filetype of `FLATFILE` and `nIsValid` set to 1.

Other cases:

❑ If the specified channel does not exist then the `dta_interchange_details` record is logged with `nvcSyntax = UNKNOWN`.

❑ If the document is submitted as pass-through (meaning that the pass-through flag has been set to `yes`) and the channel specified by the caller exists, then the `nvcSyntax` records of the `dta_interchange_details` and `dta_indoc_details` tables are both set to `UNKNOWN`. The `dta_indoc_details` is effectively a dummy record, because as BizTalk server does not process the document it is unable to determine document information. In addition `nIsValid` is set to 2 to signify a pass-through submission.

Decoding and Decryption

Normal action within BizTalk:

❑ The `input.txt` document does not contain any MIME sections and no record is added to the `dta_MIME_data` table.

Other cases:

❑ If the document contains MIME data then it is logged in the SQL Server image field `imgMIMEData` of the `dta_MIME_data` table and keyed with the `SubmissionID` that is an output parameter from the `Submit()` method of the `IInterchange` interface.

Parsing and Validation

Normal action within BizTalk:

❑ `Input.txt` contains an interchange of a single document for the flatfile parser. The flatfile parser records document tracking information to the `dta_indoc_details`. The DTA logs the first document instance of every interchange into the `dta_interchange_details` record, and also the last document instance because the log incoming interchange option is set for the BizTalk server group. The summary interchange fields: `nDocumentsAccepted`, `nDocumentsRejected`, and `nNumberofBytes` are also updated.

Other cases:

❏ If the interchange is not recognized by any installed parser, then the DTA logs a dta_interchange_details record with nvcSyntax set to UNKNOWN.

❏ If the interchange can be recognized by an installed parser but the parser returns a fatal error, such as a failed HRESULT, then the DTA logs both the dta_interchange_details and the dta_indoc_details records with interchange and parsing errors. The nvcSyntax of both records is set to the parser-specific value.

❏ If the document is invalid and failed either validation or parsing, then the DTA logs the dta_indoc_details record with document parsing or validation errors.

Select Channel and Checkpoint Document

Normal action within BizTalk:

❏ Because a single channel is selected, and both native and XML inbound document data is logged, dta_document_data and dta_debugdoc_data records are created.

Other cases:

❏ If no channel is found, then the DTA logs a dt_indoc_details record with a document channel selection error.

❏ If more than one channel is selected only one set of dta_document_data and dta_debugdoc_data records are created for each dta_indoc_details record.

Mapping

Normal action within BizTalk:

❏ Document mapping succeeds and the intermediate XML data representation is created and logged to the dta_debugdoc_data table because outbound XML data is logged for the Tracking Delimited File Output channel.

Other cases:

❏ If a channel matches more than one port, a single instance of the intermediate XML format is added to the dta_debugdoc_data table.

❏ If mapping fails then the dta_outdoc_details record contains a document translation error but the dta_interchange_details record does not contain a error.

Select Outgoing Port

Normal action within BizTalk:

❏ A single outgoing port, Tracking Positional File Output, is matched and the DTA logs a dta_outdoc_details record.

Other cases:

❏ If a channel matches more than one port then multiple dta_outdoc_details records are created.

❏ If a port cannot be found for the document then dta_outdoc_details contains a find port error, but the dta_interchange has no error.

Serialize Output

Normal action within BizTalk:

❑ The flatfile serializer creates the delimited output text file. The Log native outbound data option is selected for the channel, Tracking Delimited File Output, and so a record is written to the dta_outdoc_details. The log outgoing interchange option is selected for the server group and as a result an entry is written to the dta_interchange_details table.

Other cases:

❑ If serialization fails then the DTA logs a dta_outdoc_details record with a document serialization error, but the dta_interchage_details record has no error.

Envelope Addition

Normal action within BizTalk:

❑ The envelope is successfully added to the document and no additional DTA logging is recorded.

Other cases:

❑ If enveloping fails then the DTA logs a dta_interchange_details record for each interchange, encoding, signing, or encrypting error, but the dta_outdoc_details record has no error.

Transmission of the Outgoing-Document from the Server

Normal action within BizTalk:

❑ The document is successfully delivered to the output directory. The DTA logs any response data and logs to the dta_outdoc_details and the dta_interchange details records information from the serializer component.

Other cases:

❑ If transmission fails then the DTA logs a dta_interchange_details record with an interchange transmission error, but the dta_outdoc_details record contains no error.

If you need to study the tracking database workings at its lowest level then submit a document to the database with the SQL Profiler running with the SQL:StmtCompleted event selected. Each line of SQL run against the InterchangeDTA database will be recorded to the SQL Profiler log.

Preprocessors and Document Tracking

Although a preprocessor was not used in this example, these components are useful for altering incoming document data before submitting it into BizTalk Messaging. For example, if you wish to send messages compressed over the Internet, then a preprocessor can decompress these before document processing. As preprocessors are called before submitting the document to BizTalk Messaging, the incoming document is not tracked. If you need to track the document before it is preprocessed then you must manage this logging yourself inside the preprocessor component by loading the document data that enters the parsing component, vDataIn, and logging its contents to the appropriate table. For more information on preprocessor components refer the BizTalk Server help file.

Managing the Tracking Database

For each document submitted to a BizTalk server with logging turned on, information is written to the SQL tables in the `InterchangeDTA` database. You can set a SQL 7 or SQL 2000 database to auto-grow so that the disk space allocated to SQL Server increases when it is appropriate. However, to avoid unnecessary disk allocation the SQL settings of **Truncate log on checkpoint** and **Auto shrink** should be set on both the `InterchangeDTA` and `InterchangeSQ` databases. This action has the side-effect of removing the "Up-to-the minute" recovery mechanism built into SQL Server.

SQL Server automatically triggers checkpoints during the normal use based on the number of entries in the transaction logs. When a checkpoint occurs the transaction logs are truncated and the physical disk space is recovered. Even with these settings in place, over time the size of this database will increase to the point where it requires maintenance to remove older records. The `debugdoc_data` table takes up a large amount of space in the tracking database. This is because the `debugdoc_data` table contains a database row storing the incoming and outgoing interim XML format for each message submitted to BizTalk Server.

Another source of unnecessary database usage, in particular for EDI handling, are the records in the `dta_outdoc_details` table that expected receipts to come back but whose waiting period has subsequently timed out.

Fortunately, BizTalk Server ships with a SQL job script, `DTA_SampleJobs.SQL` in the **SDK\Messaging Samples\SQLServerAgentJobs** directory to assist with these two issues. The SQL script creates two SQLServerAgent jobs. `dtaJob_receipt_monitor_InterchangeDTA` is scheduled to run, by default, every 30 minutes to remove unnecessary receipts. Similarly, the `dtaJob_purge_database_InterchangeDTA` job runs every 30 minutes by default and trims the `debugdoc_data` table to 25,000 records by removing the oldest records. You can modify the time periods between each job and the number of records trimmed by editing the SQL scripts.

Configuring BizTalk Orchestration Tracking

BizTalk Orchestration tracking settings are not integrated into the BizTalk Orchestration process. Indeed, by default there is no tracking information stored for BizTalk Orchestration XLANG schedules. Instead, the tools required to build tracking for XLANG schedules are supplied in the \Program Files\Microsoft BizTalk Server\XLANG Samples\WorkflowAudit and WorkflowAuditClient directories:

❑ The `WorkflowAudit` component listens to COM+ events associated with running XLANG schedules and saves the results into DTA tables: `dta_wf_EventData` and `dta_wf_WorkFlowEvent`.

❑ The `WorkflowAuditClient` sample is a simple VB application that instantiates an instance of the `WorkflowAudit` component. For XLANG schedule monitoring to be active this VB application must be running and with logging enabled.

An interactive VB application is not especially suitable for an enterprise environment, so you will need to re-host the `WorkflowAudit` in an NT service for it to be of most use. Further, the `WorkflowAuditclient` currently collects all Orchestration events and writes them into the SQL Server tables. Logging milestones, rather than all events in an Orchestration schedule to the database may be a more suitable approach because it both reduces the performance impact of database writes for each action, and also increases the usefulness of the collected data.

Summary

Tracking is an essential part of document transfer because it provides non-repudiation, as well as the ability to understand when error conditions occur. The BizTalk Messaging manager gives you the ability to select the extent of the tracking information that you collect. Tracking can be configured on a per server group, per document, and per channel basis. Tracking information is stored in the document, tracking, and activity database called `InterchangeDTA`. The BizTalk Tracking interface is a web site that unlocks the tracking data – providing the user with the ability to query both interchange meta-data and business information.

Programmatic access to tracking information is provided through the combination of a COM interface and stored procedures empowering the programmer to create custom interfaces or views of tracking data to suit the individual requirements of a particular business model.

The stages involved in tracking a document through BizTalk Server were also explained to assist with problem solving and to provide you with a deeper understanding of the tracking process. Finally we examined how to manage growth of the tracking database.

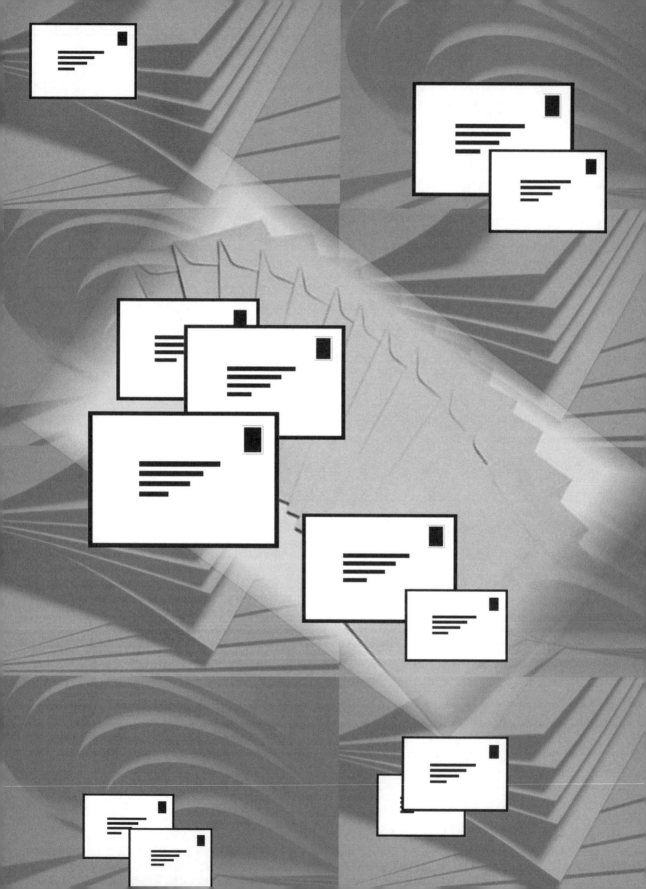

12

Configuration Programming

Microsoft BizTalk Server is deeply dependent on COM. It accesses other services through COM, its major services are COM+ applications, and the services themselves are built from COM+ components. One of the nice things about component software is that components usually expose all the features of the product through COM interfaces, allowing you, the developer, to build your own applications with the same resources the development team had in building the product. You can integrate your own applications as closely as you wish with BizTalk Server, and you can control the configuration and operation of the messaging service through programs.

Like many other products built for Windows, BizTalk Server offers a full object model for controlling its features from code. In Chapter 5 we saw how you use IInterchange to submit documents to the messaging service, and in Chapter 6 we saw how you can use COM to launch an orchestration schedule or call into a running schedule. We've also seen how to use COM interfaces to check on the status of interchanges. Now we're going to go further and see how you can manipulate the various messaging-related entities we described in Chapter 5 – documents, ports, channels, and so forth – to control the configuration of the messaging service through COM.

❏ First we'll present two scenarios in which you might wish to do messaging configuration from code.

❏ After examining the business cases, we'll move straight into a study of the fourteen interfaces that make up the messaging configuration object model.

❏ Finally, we'll try out these interfaces by creating a configuration utility of our own.

You might think that of all the tasks in managing and administering BizTalk Server, administrative programming is one you would always wish to do manually. In fact, there are many situations where administrative programming can be effective. Some sites using BizTalk will want to dynamically create and tear down configurations as their businesses evolve. They might, for example, automate the process by which they accept new trading partners. Upon acceptance, they could use the contents of a message sent through a publicly accessible port to create the items needed to exchange messages specifically with that partner. Most sites, though, will be more cautious. Even the most careful BizTalk administrator, however, can make good use of administrative utilities that extend the capabilities of Messaging Manager. The messaging-configuration object model for BizTalk makes such utilities possible. Administrators can make use of this to aid in deploying a working configuration to a new machine. Scripts may be written for execution under the Windows Scripting Host that configure the new machine to match the old one.

Don't let the number of new interfaces intimidate you. There are a few utility interfaces, but most of the interfaces we'll encounter have a direct correspondence to one of the administrative entities in the BizTalk messaging service. Since you are already familiar with their features and how to configure them, the properties and methods of these interfaces will be readily understood.

Uses for Configuration Programming

The use and benefits of the IInterchange interface are obvious. It is used at runtime to provide access to the messaging service from within programs. The utility of the configuration object model may not be as clear at first glance. It is used at design time to configure the specifications that guide the messaging system. You would expect that this is a job for a BizTalk administrator. There will be occasions, however, when it is useful to be able to create messaging specifications. We'll briefly present two situations where the configuration object model is useful. These are certainly not the only cases where you might use the interfaces we're going to study in this chapter, nor are they an exhaustive solution. They are provided as a catalyst for your own solutions.

Configuration Export

The first situation in which you might want to use the configuration object model is in exporting and importing the configuration of the server group. You do not need this capability within a given server group; point a new server to the Messaging Management database and it has all the configurations it needs. You still need to be sure it has installed any custom COM components required by your systems, but the messaging configuration is otherwise complete. You might use this capability in the following situations:

❑ Having a complete configuration backup is a good measure for emergency recovery. If all your other reliability measures fail, you have only to install BizTalk Server and import the configuration.

❑ More commonly, you are going to have useful configurations in your organization that you would like to share with other server groups. A workgroup might pioneer a particular form of processing. Once proven, the system might be adopted as the organizational standard solution to that particular problem. If the pioneering organization is able to export the messaging configurations specific to that system, rollout of the new standard would be greatly facilitated. Other parts of the organization, running their own BizTalk Server groups, would simply import the configurations exported by the pioneers.

Such an export-import capability is partially implemented by the BTConfigAssistant *sample in the SDK. This utility copies the specifications and maps of your configuration to a specified folder, then generates a script that uses the configuration object model to reproduce the configuration of the BizTalk Server on which it is run.*

An exported configuration would consist of some body of data – perhaps an XML document – a collection of schedules, message specification files, and message maps, and code to read the Messaging Management database and serialize it as data outside the relational database. The import process would involve complementary code to read the data and recreate the configuration in the gaining server group's Messaging Management database. The code needed to export the entire messaging service configuration is relatively straightforward. It need only enumerate everything in the source database.

The export code for a selective export is more interesting. You might start with a desired channel, then trace its dependent relationships downward and outward until all required ports, documents, maps, and organizations were accounted for. Such a process would take you through most if not all of the configuration object model.

This example is an instance in which the configuration object model lets us program a utility application designed to make BizTalk administrators more productive. There is nothing in it that could not be done manually through BizTalk Messaging Manager. Automating the process, however, improves productivity and promotes reliability when you need to transfer a snapshot of some configuration. Once the utility code is fully tested, you can be sure that no details are overlooked in an export. The equivalent manual process always runs the risk of missing a crucial detail.

Dynamic Configuration

Let's take the export-import process a step further and cross firewall boundaries. One of BizTalk Server's main uses is to connect trading partners for business-to-business e-commerce. At runtime, everything is automated. Design time, though, is a problem. There are many efforts to create third-party industry portals to facilitate the connection of two partners. The schema repository on BizTalk.org, the BizTalk Framework site, is one such effort. Still, downloading a document schema or even a BizTalk-style document specification is just the beginning. Partners still have to exchange all sorts of configuration information before they can begin exchanging messages. The configuration object model and the export-import concept we just presented provide an opportunity to streamline the process.

Imagine that two prospective partners have reached agreement on the business details of a partnership. This could happen in a variety of ways. They might work through the intermediary of a third party portal, or one partner might advertise for service. In the latter case, a firm might issue a request for proposals and indicate that all replies had to be sent to a particular URL in a particular format. Just because a prospective trading partner is able to use the protocol mandated by the specified URL doesn't mean they prefer it for ongoing exchanges. Similarly, they might wish to switch to a different data format. That is, they might support X12 EDI for the purposes of setting up the business transaction, but they might internally use different formats. We've moved from a business agreement to the task of seeking agreement on technical details.

At this point, we can use the configuration object model to streamline the process. Having established sufficient trust to do business together, a partner might then be willing to reveal that they are using BizTalk Server for their messaging implementation, and they might also reveal what standard formats, if any, they are using. While it is unlikely that one standard will displace all others in any given industry, it is likely that a handful of data formats will dominate their industry. The other partner could then offer message specification files, maps from their formats to and from the standard formats, and a configuration export along the lines of the last section.

In theory, we could have a configuration document that does not assume the use of BizTalk Server, but that is stretching things a bit. While any messaging passing B2B scheme must deal with certain concepts, for example message formats, endpoints, and protocols, it would be hard in practice to develop an XML configuration vocabulary broad enough to satisfy all potential messaging schemes.

What does all this enable? Well, if the business negotiation can be automated, it becomes possible to automate the entire trading relationship. Consider the following steps:

❑   Organization seeks trading partner

❑   Partner is found through portal

❑   Organizations reach business agreement

❑   Partners reveal use of BizTalk Server

❑   Organizations exchange specifications, maps, and configurations

❑   Organizations import their partner's configurations using the configuration object model

❑   Messaging begins

It is unrealistic to think that a strategic relationship might be forged without human intervention. An auto manufacturer, for example, is unlikely to commit to a relationship worth hundreds of millions of dollars in materials purchasing on the basis of an automated exchange. Human intervention, though, costs money. A firm might be willing to automate the relationship process for low-value trades or for single transactions. The cost savings could outweigh the additional trust gained by human intervention. Without the configuration object model, the data exchanged might as well be paper documents and telephone calls. With the object model, all this information can be reduced to machine-readable XML that is transferred automatically, and the trading relationship can, at least in theory, be established without human intervention.

BizTalk Configuration Object Model

The BizTalk messaging-configuration object model is a series of COM interfaces representing the major entities of the BizTalk messaging service. Its primary use is to give you programmatic access to the configuration data maintained in the Messaging Management database similar to that granted manually through the BizTalk Messaging Manager utility. Each entity in the messaging service, for example ports and channels, has an interface in the object model. In addition, two utility interfaces exist to assist with the task of storing and retrieving various configuration properties.

You might wonder why an elaborate COM object model is required. The messaging service is driven entirely by the configurations stored in the Messaging Management database for the BizTalk server group. As this is a SQL Server database, why not simply use ADO and SQL statements? Simplicity is one answer, certainly, but there is a more important consideration. The integrity of the database, and therefore the functioning of the messaging service, is dependent on constraints and stored procedures defined in the database. The business rules represented by the stored procedures must be enforced if the messaging service is to work properly. Direct access to the underlying database tables could allow a program to bypass these rules with unpredictable results.

The configuration object model, then, acts as the middle tier of a three-tier system that protects the messaging service from improperly programmed applications. The object model was written with the constraints and stored procedures in mind. The methods and properties of the object model hide these details from application code while ensuring that they are called appropriately. If an application makes calls that would violate the integrity of the database, an error message is returned. This is certainly preferable to violating integrity and causing the failure of the messaging service.

The configuration object model should not be used to modify configurations that are in active use. This may result in unpredictable behavior. Even when used as intended, applications that access the object model will have a dramatic impact of the behavior of Messaging Services. This, in turn, will have a dramatic impact on the operation of the systems you build with orchestration schedules and BizTalk messaging. Quite simply, the object model touches the configurations that tell BizTalk Server how to exchange messages and what may be exchanged. The interchange of messages is the heart and soul of BizTalk Server's model of distributed processing. Because of the importance of the configuration object model, applications that make use of it must run under a user account that belongs to the BizTalk Server Administrator security group.

Making Sense of the Configuration Object Model

The configuration object model consists of thirteen principal interfaces and two utility interfaces. The model is actually even simpler than that. A top level interface, IBizTalkConfig, represents the Messaging Manager utility or the Messaging Management database as a whole. You gain access to the object model through that interface. Another interface, IBizTalkBase, exists to define some methods and properties that are common to various other interfaces. Those interfaces are derived from IBizTalkBase. You will never instantiate a component that exposes IBizTalkBase. Instead, you create instances of the components you need. If the interface supported by the component is derived from IBizTalkBase, the methods and properties defined by the base interface are exposed as if they were defined by the derived interface.

Of the remaining eleven interfaces, six define the primary entities you deal with in the messaging service: organizations, documents, envelopes, ports, distribution lists (known as port groups in the object model), and channels. The remaining five interfaces deal with related configuration items on the various pages of the Messaging Manager Wizards. These are:

❑ Endpoints – the source or destination of an interchange

❑ Service windows – time constraints on the use of ports

❑ Transports – the configuration of communications transport protocols

❑ Certificate Information – configuration and use of digital certificates for security

❑ Logging Information – details of what data is tracked in the DTA database and in what form

Entering the Configuration Object Model

The following diagram represents the relationship between the top-level interface and the principal interfaces that correspond to a major entity in the messaging service. All the principal interfaces are derived from the IBizTalkBase interface. The labels associated with the lines name the properties of IBizTalkConfig through which you reach the other objects. The Certificates property, a collection of objects offering the IBizTalkCertificateInfo interface does not represent a major entity. Because of the importance of certificates to the messaging service, however, the designers of IBizTalkConfig decided it is important to have direct access to this lesser configuration interface from the top-level object.

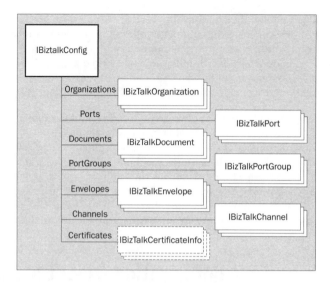

Interfaces and Relationships with Other Objects

A look at the `IBizTalkChannel` interface reveals something interesting. This interface relies on a number of the secondary interfaces for its configuration. Interfaces such as `IBizTalkLoggingInfo` and `IBizTalkEndPoint` are represented through references to specific objects in properties of the interface. Yet, while a channel is undeniably associated with a port, there is no reference to `IBizTalkPort`.

The resolution to this problem is simple. The major entities in the Messaging Management database are identified by unique **handles**. These handles are long values that are keys to certain tables in the database. All relationships between the major entities, then, are modeled by having one object have a property that is the handle to the related object in the database. Thus, the port that is associated with the channel is represented by the long value of the `IBizTalkChannel` interface's `Port` property. All properties that hold an interface reference rather than a handle have relationships with secondary configuration objects. Here is a diagram depicting the live, object-to-object relationships in the `IBizTalkChannel` interface:

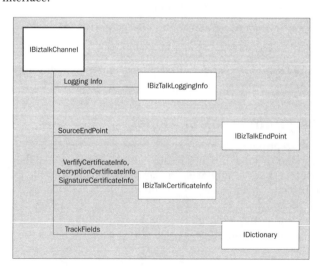

A similar situation holds for the IBizTalkPort interface. Here, though, we see something new. The Channels property, which records information about all the channels that use the port, is a reference to an ADO recordset object. The contents of the recordset are basic data types, not interface references.

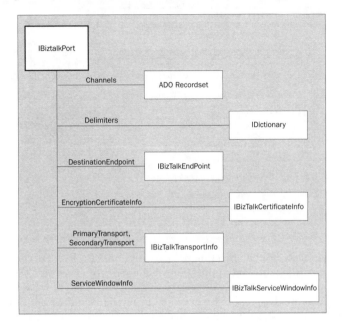

The remaining major interfaces – IBizTalkEnvelope, IBizTalkPortGroup, IBizTalkOrganization, and IBizTalkDocument – have somewhat simpler relationships with live objects.

- ❑   IBizTalkEnvelope has no interface references at all. All its properties are strings.

- ❑   IBizTalkPortGroup uses ADO recordsets to model the relationship between a distribution list, otherwise known as a port group, and the channels that use it, as well as the ports it contains.

- ❑   IBizTalkOrganization uses IDictionary to record all the organization qualifier-indentifier pairs that identify the organization. It uses an ADO recordset to record information about the applications defined for the Home Organization.

- ❑   Finally, IBizTalkDocument uses IDictionary to record information for EDI documents as well as the document fields that are to be tracked in the DTA database.

In each case, a major interface that is somehow related to another major interface, for example a port object and the envelope it uses, models the relationship with a property that holds the value of a handle, or key, to the row in another table that represents the object instance of the other interface.

Implementation of the Configuration Object Model

The messaging configuration object model is implemented in BizTalkObjectModel.dll. This DLL is found in the root directory of the BizTalk Server installation. In Visual Basic, you may select the reference labelled Microsoft BizTalk Server Configuration Objects 1.0 Type Library to get typed access to the object model.

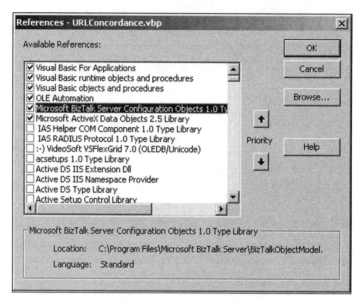

The components that make up the object model must run on a BizTalk Server host machine, so there is little point in writing intranet applications that consist of client-side scripts. You can, however, write such an application using server-side scripts. Similarly, you might write scripts to automate configuration tasks that are designed to be executed using the Windows Scripting Host. All the interfaces that make up the object model are dual COM interfaces, so they may be used from late-bound scripting languages as well as from early-bound languages like C++ or Visual Basic.

The Windows Scripting Host gives you the ability to run scripts from the command line.

If you wish to use the object model interfaces from a scripting language, you must create an instance of `IBizTalkConfig` using one of the following calls:

```
configObj = CreateObject("BizTalk.BizTalkConfig")    ' VBScript
configObj = new ActiveXObject("BizTalk.BizTalkConfig"); // Javascript
```

Once you have an instance of a component supporting `IBizTalkConfig`, you may create the other objects you need through the methods of `IBizTalkConfig`, for example `CreatePort()`, or access existing configuration information using the various properties of the interfaces discussed below.

Maintaining Referential Integrity while Working with Configuration Objects

If you try to delete, say, a port that is in use by one or more channels using the Messaging Manager, you will get an error message and you will not be able to delete that object. That is because the Messaging Manager enforces the referential integrity of the Messaging Management database. If you could delete a configuration object that is needed by another configuration, the messaging service would be unable to function properly. A channel, for example, that needed a port would be unable to process an interchange if it was unable to locate the `port` object. The messaging configuration object model respects the same referential integrity rules. Instead of popping up a message, however, the object model raises errors. In Visual Basic, these errors end up in the global `Err` object. The numeric code associated with the error is found in `Err`'s `Number` property.

The configuration object model raises errors in a number of classes. There are a number of errors stemming from the COM system. Errors directly related to the BizTalk messaging service or the configuration object model may also be raised.

> *There are thirteen COM error codes and over one hundred BizTalk error codes documented in the object model. Please refer to the BizTalk Server documentation for these codes and their meanings. This information is found in the* BizTalk Server 2000 Programming Reference | Using the BizTalk Messaging Configuration Object Model | Object Model Reference section.

Since the object model makes use of other COM interfaces, there are still more errors that may be raised. The major category is OLEDB errors stemming from the use of the ADO recordset object. The use of digital certificates involves the use of the Windows CryptoAPI, which also raises errors when trouble is encountered.

Avoiding errors is always preferable to detecting them and reading the codes. The best way to do this is to follow the same rules and practices that work for you in Messaging Manager. When creating new configuration objects, start at the bottom and work up. Progress from objects with no external dependencies, for example organizations, to the objects that rely on them, for example ports, to objects such as channels that rely on almost all the other objects. Work in the other direction when deleting objects. Delete the channel, then the port, and so forth. Port objects make things a bit easier for you. IBizTalkPort has a Channels property that lists all the channels that rely on the port. Before attempting to delete a port, then, always check that property for dependencies. Although you may have just deleted a channel that depends on the port, you cannot be sure that no one else has reused the port in conjunction with another channel. A quick check will avoid runtime errors.

IBizTalkBase

The IBizTalkBase interface is unique in the messaging configuration object model in that you never instantiate a component built for this interface alone. The interface is a base upon which other interface implementations build. In the reference sections that follow, the derived interfaces will only list properties and methods added to those in IBizTalkBase. The following interfaces inherit the methods and properties of IBizTalkBase:

- ❏ IBizTalkOrganization
- ❏ IBizTalkDocument
- ❏ IBizTalkPort
- ❏ IBizTalkChannel
- ❏ IBizTalkEnvelope
- ❏ IBizTalkPortGroup

> *If you are having trouble remembering what each object represents in BizTalk Messaging Services, refer to the section on* BizTalk Management Concepts *in Chapter 5.*

This does not mean that you query one of these components for the IBizTalkBase interface. Instead, the interfaces listed above inherit from IBizTalkBase. This means that you will never see IBizTalkBase per se; the methods and properties of IBizTalkBase are found by name within the interfaces listed above. Nevertheless, it is instructive to examine this interface to get some sense of what underlies the other interfaces.

Method	Parameters and meaning
Clear()	No parameters, no return value.
	Reinitializes the object in memory. Properties revert to their default values.
Create()	No parameters; returns a long value handle to the newly created database object.
	Creates a new object of the proper type in the Messaging Management database.
Load()	lHandle – a long value denoting an object.
	Loads the object from the Messaging Management database into the object.
LoadByName()	sName – string value of 64 characters or less denoting the name of a database object.
	Calls Clear to initialize the object, then loads the object from the database into memory for manipulation.
Remove()	No parameters, no return value.
	Removes the object associated with this component from the database.
Save()	No parameters, no return value.
	Saves the object in memory into the database.

It is important to understand the linkage between the running component and the object in the database. The messaging service deals exclusively with the Messaging Management database. Consequently, when you deal with a component whose interface is derived from IBizTalkBase, you are dealing with a component that represents a specific entity in the database. Clear() initializes the component in memory. The Create() method is used to create a new entity in the database. Load() or LoadByName() loads the configuration of a specific entity, for example port, from the Messaging Management database into the component so that you may work with it programmatically. The entity is referenced within the database either by name or by a unique, long-valued handle. Once you've made changes, Save() writes those changes back to the database. You may delete an object from the database by loading it with Load() or LoadByName(), then calling Remove().

Property	Meaning
DateModified	Read-only. Returns a string denoting the date and time the object was last modified in the database. The timestamp is of the form yyyy-mm-dd hh:mm:ss and is UTC.
Handle	Read-only. Returns a long value that is the database handle to the object.
Name	Read/write. Gets or sets the name of the object.

This pattern of a configuration object in the database being paired with a running component instance is reflected in the properties of this interface. DateModified reflects the date and time the object represented by the component was created in or last written to the database. Handle gives the database handle for the configuration entity, while Name gives you the friendly name of the configuration.

IBizTalkConfig Interface

This interface represents the Messaging Management database as a whole. Put another way, you need a single point from which to enter the messaging configuration model, and this is it. Its collection properties provide access to the rest of the object model, while its methods allow you to create new objects programmatically. Here are the methods of the `IBizTalkConfig` interface:

Method	Parameters and meaning
CreateChannel()	No parameters, returns an interface to a new IBizTalkChannel object.
	Call this method to create a new channel object with default configuration. You may use the returned interface to configure the new channel. This method does not automatically write a new channel object to the database.
CreateDocument()	No parameters, returns an interface to a new IBizTalkDocument object.
	Like CreateChannel(), this method creates a newly initialized document object in memory.
CreateEnvelope()	No parameters, returns an interface to a new IBizTalkEnvelope object.
	Use this method to create a new envelope object.
CreateOrganization()	No parameters, returns an interface to a new IBizTalkOrganization object.
	The organziation created exists only in memory and has default values for its configuration.
CreatePort()	No parameters, returns an interface to a new IBizTalkPort object.
	Creates a new port object with default configuration.
CreatePortGroup()	No parameters, returns an interface to a new IBizTalkPortGroup object.
	Creates a new port group (also known as a distribution list) in memory with default values. The object must be saved to the database before use.

The methods of this interface are remarkably uniform. They take no parameters and serve only to create a new object of a particular type with default values. You create the object in question, use the methods and properties of its interface to configure it, then call that interface's Save() method to write it to the Messaging Management database. At that time, the configuration is available for use by the messaging service.

We said that `IBizTalkConfig` serves as a single point of entry to the configuration object model. The methods of this interface certainly bore this out in terms of creating new configuration objects. The properties of the interface, which are all collections, perform a similar service for accessing existing configuration objects.

Property	Meaning
Certificates	Read-only; returns an ADO recordset containing all the certificate objects that match the criteria passed into this property. The property takes the following parameters:
	StoreType – an enumerated value from the BIZTALK_STORE_TYPE enumeration; denotes what certificate store to search
	UsageType – an enumerated value from the BIZTALK_USAGE_TYPE enumeration; tells the object to search for objects according to the task for which they are used
	sNameFilter – a string used to filter certificate names; names that begin with the filter value will be matched
	Each certificate in the recordset has four columns:
	Name – string naming the certificate
	Reference – string value naming the certificate reference
	Store – BIZTALK_STORE_TYPE enumeration denoting where the certificate is stored
	Usage – BIZTALK_USAGE_TYPE enumeration denoting how the certificate is to be used
Channels	Read-only; returns an ADO recordset containing all channels.
	Each channel in the recordset contains the following columns, listed in order:
	id – long-value handle to the channel in the database
	name – name of the channel
	datemodified – string representation of the UTC time the channel was created or last modified
Documents	Read-only; returns an ADO recordset containing all documents configured in the Messaging Management database.
	Each document has the following columns, listed in order:
	id – long-value handle to the document in the database
	Name – read-write; name of the document
	DateModified – read-only; string representation of the UTC time the document was created or last modified

Property	Meaning
Envelopes	Read-only; returns an ADO recordset containing all envelopes in the Messaging Management database.
	Each envelope has the following columns, listed in order:
	`id` – long-value handle to the envelope in the database
	`Name` – name of the envelope
	`DateModified` – string representation of the UTC time the envelope was created or last modified
	`Format` – a string denoting the type of envelope. The value of this column must be one of the following strings:
	`x12` – ANSI X12 EDI
	`edifact` – UN/EDIFACT EDI
	`custom xml` (default) – XML
	`custom` – custom format requiring custom parser
	`flatfile` – flatfile other than XML
	`reliable` – BizTalk Framework 2.0
Organizations	Read-only; returns an ADO recordset containing all organizations configured in the Messaging Management database.
	Each organization in the recordset has the following columns, listed in order:
	`id` – long-value handle to the organization in the database
	`Name` – name of the organization
	`DateModified` – string representation of the UTC time the organization was created or last modified
	`defaultflag` – variant (Boolean) indicating whether this organization is the default organization
PortGroups	Read-only; returns an ADO recordset containing all the port groups configured in the messaging service.
	Each port group in the recordset has the following columns, listed in order:
	`Handle` – long-value handle to the port group in the database
	`Name` – name of the port group
	`DateModified` – string representation of the UTC time the port group was created or last modified
Ports	Read-only; returns an ADO recordset containing all the ports known to the messaging service.
	Each port in the recordset has the following columns, listed in order:
	`id` – long-value handle to the port in the database
	`name` – name of the port
	`datemodified` – string representation of the UTC time the port was created or last modified

These collections are interesting in that they work through ADO recordsets. You iterate through them using ADO methods, and they throw ADO/OLEDB errors in addition to the errors the BizTalk configuration object model generates. The information in the recordset is read-only. If you wish to change something, you need to access the object through its handle, make the changes, and save the object. This will become apparent as we go through the interfaces for each object.

We alluded to the BIZTALK_STORE_TYPE enumeration. Here are its enumerations and their values. Note that you may not combine enumerations through a bitwise AND.

Enumeration Constant	Numerical Value	Meaning
BIZTALK_STORE_TYPE_MY	1	Certificate is authorized by the organization
BIZTALK_STORE_TYPE_BIZTALK	2	Certificate is stored in the dedicated BizTalk certificate store

Similarly, here are the BIZTALK_USAGE_TYPE enumerations:

Enumeration Constant	Numerical Value	Meaning
BIZTALK_USAGE_TYPE_ENCRYPTION	1	Encryption certificate
BIZTALK_USAGE_TYPE_SIGNATURE	2	Certificate used for messaging signing
BIZTALK_USAGE_TYPE_BOTH	4	Certificate used for both functions

IBizTalkOrganization Interface

This interface represents organizations in the BizTalk Messaging Management database. For the purposes of this interface, organization identifiers are known as aliases. This interface inherits from IBizTalkBase and exposes all the methods and properties of that interface. In addition to those methods, here are the methods added by the IBizTalkOrganization interface:

Method	Parameters and meaning
CreateAlias()	No return value; this method has the following parameters:
	sName – string bearing the name of the identifier
	vDefault – variant (Boolean) indicating whether this is the default identifier for the organization
	sQualifier – string containing the identifier's qualifier
	sValue – string containing the value of the identifier
	Creates and configures a new organization identifier, or alias, for the organization.

Method	Parameters and meaning
CreateApplication()	No return value; this method has the following parameter:
	sName – string naming the application
	Creates a new application for the organization.
GetDefaultAlias()	This method takes no parameters and returns the long-valued handle that references the default alias in the database.
LoadAlias()	This method has no return value and takes the following parameters:
	lAliasHandle – long-valued database handle of the alias in the database
	vName – variant filled with the name of the alias upon return
	vDefault – variant filled with a Boolean upon return indicating whether this is the default alias
	vQualifier – variant filled upon return with the alias qualifier
	vValue – variant filled upon return with the alias value
	Given an alias handle, this method loads the configuration of the alias from the database.
LoadApplication()	This method has no return value and has the following parameters:
	lAppHandle – long-valued database handle of the application in the database
	vAppName – variant filled upon return with the name of the application
	Loads an application configuration from the database given its handle.
RemoveAlias()	This method has no return value and the following parameter:
	lAliasHandle – long-valued handle of the alias in the database
	Removes the alias configuration (identifier qualifier and value pair) referenced by the handle. This method will generate an error if you attempt to remove the default identifier.
RemoveApplication()	This method has no return value and the following parameter:
	lAppHandle – long-valued handle of the application in the database
	Removes the application denoted by the handle.

Table continued on following page

Method	Parameters and meaning
SaveAlias()	lAliasHandle – handle of the alias to save
	sName – name of the alias
	vDefault – variant containing a boolean flag indicating whether this is the default identifier for the organization
	sQualifier – alias qualifier
	sValue – alias value
	This method has no return value.
	Given the handle of an existing alias, this method saves the configuration passed in.
SaveApplication()	lAppHandle – database handle of the application
	sAppName – name of the application
	This method has no return value.
	Given the handle of an existing application, this method saves the application configuration (name).

You may recall from Chapter 5 that Messaging Manager only permits the creation of applications for the home organization. The object model does not enforce this restriction. If you create an application for an external partner, however, it will not be available for use through the Messaging Manager and its wizards. Note that this precludes the creation of channels and ports involving applications.

A number of methods of this interface require an alias handle. This value may be obtained from the Aliases property, listed below.

In addition to the properties of the IBizTalkBase interface, this interface exposes the following properties:

Property	Meaning
Aliases	Read-only; returns an ADO recordset with the collected aliases (organization identifiers) of the organization.
	Each row of the recordset contains the following columns, listed in order:
	Handle – long-value database handle of the alias
	Name – value passed in the CreateAlias() method
	Default – Boolean flag passed in the CreateAlias() method
	Qualifier – value passed in the CreateAlias() method
	Value – identifier value passed in the CreateAlias() method

Property	Meaning
Applications	Read-only; returns an ADO recordset containing all the applications configured for the organization. Each row of the recordset has the following columns, listed in order: Handle – application handle in the database Name – application name specified in the CreateApplication() method
Comments	Read/write; this property holds the string comments provided for the organization.
IsDefault	Read/write; a variant holding a boolean value that indicates whether this is the default (home) organization.

IBizTalkDocument Interface

The IBizTalkDocument interface represents the configuration of a document in the Messaging Management database. This interface also inherits from IBizTalkBase, exposing all the methods and properties of that interface. The methods and properties listed below are those added by this interface.

Method	Parameters and meaning
LoadByPropertySet()	This method has no return value and the following parameter: PropertySet – an IDictionary interface to an object containing the name-value pairs by which an EDI document is selected. The criteria apply to the functional group header. Loads an EDI document by its property set.

Property	Meaning
Content	Read-only; string denoting the content of the document specification.
NameSpace	Read-only; string containing the namespace URI used to resolve name collisions in the document.
PropertySet	Read/write; this property is an IDictionary interface to an object containing EDI document selection critieria. The criteria apply to the functional group header.
Reference	Read/write; WebDAV URL of the document specification.
TrackFields	Read/write; this property is an IDictionary interface to an object containing the names of the document fields used to track the document in the messaging service.
Type	Read-only; string containing the identity of the standard on which the document is based, for example X12, XML.
Version	Read-only; string containing the version of the document.

The Reference property follows the same rules you must follow in Messaging Manager regarding when the database reflects changes made in BizTalk Editor. The Reference property is checked when the IBizTalkBase-derived Create() and Save() methods are called. If Reference is not empty when Create() is called, Content is set to the contents of the document specification Reference points to, and NameSpace is set to the namespace declaration found in the document specification. If Reference has not been changed since the last Create() or Save() call at the time Save() is called, the values of Content and Namespace will not be updated in the Messaging Management database. Once Reference is set, changes made to the specification so referenced will not be reflected in the database until the specification is renamed and Reference modified to reflect the new name.

Please see IDictionary Interface, below, for the methods and properties used to configure a dictionary object for use with this interface.

IBizTalkPort Interface

This interface, derived from IBizTalkBase, represents a messaging port configuration in the Messaging Management database. The interface has no methods other than those defined by IBizTalkBase. In addition to the base proeprties, IBizTalkPort has the following properties:

Property	Meaning
Channels	Read-only; an ADO recordset containing information on all the channels that use this port. Each channel row has the following columns listed in order:
	Handle – long value denoting the configuration's database identitiy
	Name – string name of the channel
	Channel identifier – a GUID identifying the channel
Comments	Read/write; the text comments describing the port.
ControlNumberValue	Read-write; a string denoting the interchange control number for the port.
Delimiters	Read/write; an IDictionary interface to an object bearing the field, record, and document delimiters for interchanges and documents used with this port. This property is required when the Format property of the envelope used with the port is X12, EDIFACT, or Custom. Standard delimiters are provided for EDI formats.
DestinationEndpoint	Read/write; IBizTalkEndPoint interface describing the destination of the port.
EncodingType	Read/write; an enumerated value from the BIZTALK_ENCODING_TYPE enumeration indicating the type of document encoding used with the port.
Encryption CertificateInfo	Read/write; the value of this property is an IBizTalkCertificateInfo interface to an object describing the certificate used with this port.

Property	Meaning
EncryptionType	Read-write; a value from the BIZTALK_ENCRYPTION_TYPE enumeration denoting the type of document encryption used by the port.
Envelope	Read-write; handle of the envelope object in the database describing the envelope used with the port.
PrimaryTransport	Read-write; an IBizTalkTransportInfo interface describing the primary transport protocol of the port.
SecondaryTransport	Read-write; an IBizTalkTransportInfo interface describing the secondary transport protocol of the port.
ServiceWindowInfo	Read-write; an IBizTalkServiceWindowInfo interface describing the service window in effect for the port.
SignatureType	Read-write; a value from the BIZTALK_SIGNATURE_TYPE enumeration denoting what sort of digital signing will be performed on documents passing through this port.

The EncodingType property uses values from the BIZTALK_ENCODING_TYPE enumeration. The values defined by this enumeration are as listed in the table below:

Enumeration Constant	Value	Meaning
BIZTALK_ENCODING_TYPE_NONE	1	No encoding used
BIZTALK_ENCODING_TYPE_MIME	2	MIME encoding
BIZTALK_ENCODING_TYPE_CUSTOM	3	Custom encoding

The EncryptionType property takes its permissible values from the BIZTALK_ENCRYPTION_TYPE enumeration as listed below:

Enumeration Constant	Value	Meaning
BIZTALK_ENCRYPTION_TYPE_NONE	1	No encryption
BIZTALK_ENCRYPTION_TYPE_CUSTOM	2	Custom encryption
BIZTALK_ENCRYPTION_TYPE_SMIME	4	S/MIME encryption

The SignatureType property uses values from the BIZTALK_SIGNATURE_TYPE enumeration to describe what signing and verification will be used in conjunction with this port. Calling Clear() on the port sets the value to BIZTALK_SIGNATURE_TYPE_NONE. You must save all channels associated with this port with a valid IBizTalkCertificateInfo object prior to setting this property to BIZTALK_SIGNATURE_TYPE_SMIME as certificates are required to perform signing. The values of the BIZTALK_SIGNATURE_TYPE enumeration are:

Enumeration Constant	Value	Meaning
BIZTALK_SIGNATURE_TYPE_NONE	1	No signing
BIZTALK_SIGNATURE_TYPE_CUSTOM	2	Custom digital signing
BIZTALK_SIGNATURE_TYPE_SMIME	4	S/MIME signing

IBizTalkChannel Interface

IBizTalkChannel is an interface derived from IBizTalkBase that is used to describe the channels configured in the Messaging Management database. As such, it is crucial to controlling the behavior of the messaging service. This interface has the following methods in addition to those defined in IBizTalkBase:

Method	Parameters and meaning
GetConfigComponent()	No return value.
	eConfigType – BIZTALK_CONFIGDATA_TYPE value passed in to indicate what configuration is requested
	lPortHandle – long-valued handle denoting the port used with the channel
	sCLSID – string representation of the component's CLSID (filled on return)
	Fills sCLSID with the CLSID of a COM component associated with the channel's port object. This component is used to implement the intentions of the channel with respect to transport, encryption, signing, encoding, and serialization.
GetConfigData()	No return value.
	eConfigType – BIZTALK_CONFIGDATA_TYPE value passed in to indicate what configuration is requested
	lPortHandle – long-valued handle denoting the port used with the channel
	vType – variant filled with the transport type upon method return
	vDictionary – an IDictionary interface to an object describing the primary transport configuration
	Gets the configuration of the channel's port.

Method	Parameters and meaning
SetConfigComponent()	No return value.
	eConfigType – BIZTALK_CONFIGDATA_TYPE value passed in to indicate what configuration is requested
	lPortHandle – long-valued handle denoting the port used with the channel
	sCLSID – string representation of the component's CLSID
	Sets the CLSID of the component associated with the channel's port for the purpose described by eConfigType.
	BIZTALK_CONFIGDATA_TYPE_PRIMARYTRANSPORT and BIZTALK_CONFIGDATA_TYPE_SECONDARYTRANSPORT may not be used as values for the eConfigType parameter in this method.
SetConfigData()	No return type.
	eConfigType – BIZTALK_CONFIGDATA_TYPE value passed in to indicate what configuration is requested
	lPortHandle – long-valued handle denoting the port used with the channel
	vType – variant filled with the transport type upon method return
	vDictionary – an IDictionary interface to an object describing the primary transport configuration
	Sets the port configuration data for this channel.

A number of methods use values from the BIZTALK_CONFIGDATA_TYPE enumeration to indicate what configuration information they are to retrieve or set. The enumeration is described in the following table:

Enumeration Constant	Value	Meaning
BIZTALK_CONFIGDATA_TYPE_PRIMARYTRANSPORT	0	Primary transport protocol
BIZTALK_CONFIGDATA_TYPE_SECONDARYTRANSPORT	1	Secondary transport protocol
BIZTALK_CONFIGDATA_TYPE_ENCRYPTION	2	Encryption certificate
BIZTALK_CONFIGDATA_TYPE_ENCODING	3	Encoding type
BIZTALK_CONFIGDATA_TYPE_SIGNATURE	4	Signature certificate
BIZTALK_CONFIGDATA_TYPE_SERIALIZER	5	Serializer component

In addition to the properties defined by the `IBizTalkBase` interface, `IBizTalkChannel` supports the following properties:

Property	Meaning
Comments	Read/write; a string containing the user-supplied comments regarding the channel.
ControlNumberValue	Read/write; string containing the group control number value for the channel. Required for channels using X12, EDIFACT, or Custom envelopes with their port.
DecryptionCertificateInfo	Read/write; the `IBizTalkCertificateInfo` interface to the object describing the decryption certificate for the channel.
ExpectReceiptTimeout	Read/write; a long value representing the number of minutes to wait for a receipt.
Expression	Read/write; a string containing an XPath expression used to help select the channel.
InputDocument	Read/write; a long value containing the handle of the document definition in the database for the input document. Note: This property cannot be changed after `Create()` or `Save()` is called.
IsReceiptChannel	Read/write; a variant containing a Boolean value. When True, this property indicates that the channel is a receipt channel.
LoggingInfo	Read/write; `IBizTalkLoggingInfo` interface to an object describing the logging configuration for the channel.
MapContent	Read-only string containing the contents of the map file pointed to by the `MapReference` property. This property is set when `Create()` and `Save()` are called.
MapReference	Read/write string containing the WebDAV URL for the map file; required when `InputDocument` and `OutputDocument` are not the same.
OutputDocument	Read/write; long value containing the database handle of the output document definition. This property cannot be changed after `Create()` or `Save()` is called.
Port	Read/write; long value containing the database handle of the channel's port. Either `Port` or `PortGroup` must be set for the channel. This property cannot be changed after `Create()` or `Save()` is called.

Property	Meaning
PortGroup	Read/write; long value containing the database handle of the channel's port group (distribution list). Either Port or PortGroup must be set for the channel.
	This property cannot be changed after Create() or Save() is called.
ReceiptChannel	Read/write; long valued handle of the receipt channel for the channel.
	The following restrictions apply to this property:
	❑ It may be set only if IsReceiptChannel is False.
	❑ The channel referenced by this property must have an IsReceiptChannel property of True.
	❑ The destination endpoint object of the receipt channel must be the same as the source endpoint object of this channel.
RetryCount	Read/write; long value (between 0 and 999, inclusive) denoting the number of times to retry a failed transmission under this channel configuration.
RetryInterval	Read/write; long count of minutes (between 1 and 63,999, inclusive) to wait between retransmission attempts.
SignatureCertificateInfo	Read/write; IBizTalkCertificateInfo interface describing the certificate used for signing documents under this channel.
SourceEndpoint	Read/write; IBizTalkEndPoint interface describing the source of the channel.
TrackFields	Read/write; an IDictionary interface containing a description of the fields used to track documents under this channel configuration.
	A set of predefined fields is defined for this object. When additional user-selected fields are required, they are added to an ISimpleList object. Each entry in the Dictionary or List is an XPath expression locating the tracking field.
VerifySignatureCertificateInfo	Read/write; IBizTalkCertificateInfo interface describing the certificate used to verify document signatures.

The dictionary object (IDictionary interface) used to specify tracking fields is preconfigured with eight standard fields, two each for the integer, real, date, and string types. Additional tracking fields are added by adding them to an ISimpleList interface object. That interface reference is stored in the dictionary as the value of the x_custom_search field. The names of all the fields in the dictionary object and their data types are as noted in the table overleaf:

Field name	Data type
i_value1	Integer
i_value2	Integer
r_value1	Real
r_value2	Real
d_value1	Date
d_value2	Date
s_value1	String
s_value2	String
x_custom_search	ISimpleList containing additional expressions locating fields to track

IBizTalkEndPoint Interface

The IBizTalkEndPoint interface describes the source of a channel and the destination of a port. It describes the properties of one endpoint of the message interchange. This interface has no methods and the following four properties, in adition to those of IBizTalkBase:

Property	Meaning
Alias	Read/write; a long value containing the database handle of the endpoint's alias (organization identifier).
Application	Read/write; long value containing the database handle of the endpoint's application configuration.
Openness	Read/write; a value from the BIZTALK_OPENNESS_TYPE_EX enumeration; this property denotes whether the endpoint is open and if so, in what regard. This property cannot be set on a pre-existing endpoint.
Organization	Read/write; a long value containing the database handle of the organization.

The Openness property takes its values from the BIZTALK_OPENNESS_TYPE_EX enumeration whose values are as follows:

Enumeration Constant	Value	Meaning
BIZTALK_OPENNESS_TYPE_EX_NOTOPEN	1	The endpoint is not open
BIZTALK_OPENNESS_TYPE_EX_SOURCE	2	The endpoint's source organization is open
BIZTALK_OPENNESS_TYPE_EX_DESTINATION	4	The destination is open

Enumeration Constant	Value	Meaning
BIZTALK_OPENNESS_TYPE_EX_FROMWORKFLOW	8	The endpoint receives its document from an XLANG schedule
BIZTALK_OPENNESS_TYPE_EX_TOWORKFLOW	16	The endpoint is sending a document to an XLANG schedule

As you might expect, the endpoint object faces the same restrictions on openness as hold for ports and channels configured through the Messaging Manager. Endpoints represent either the source, which is associated with a channel, or the destination, which is associated with a port, of an interchange configuration. An open port is one in which the destination is not set. An open channel, you may remember, is one in which the source is not set. So if the Openness property of the endpoint is BIZTALK_OPENNESS_TYPE_EX_SOURCE, we have an open channel and the port, which represents the destination of the channel cannot have the SignatureType property set. The document could be coming from various sources and so we cannot specify that it must be signed. The port, similarly, cannot be part of a port group (also known as a distribution list).

If Openness is set to BIZTALK_OPENNESS_TYPE_EX_FROMWORKFLOW on an endpoint associated with a channel, the organization associated with that channel must be the default organization. If the Openness property for a destination endpoint such as a port, is set to BIZTALK_OPENNESS_TYPE_EX_DESTINATION, the PrimaryTransportType for the channel must be set to BIZTALK_TRANSPORT_TYPE_OPENDESTINATION. The transport type is a property of the port, and the Openness property indicates that the port, which is the channel's destination, is open. Consequently, the transport type cannot be fixed. Similarly, open destination endpoints cannot have the EncryptionType property set on the port object. The port object cannot be associated with a port group, either, because port groups (which we knew as distribution lists in Messaging Manager) cannot use open ports.

IBizTalkEnvelope Interface

The IBizTalkEnvelope interface represents an envelope configuration in the Messaging Management database. Although this interface does not add any methods to the IBizTalkBase interface, it exposes all the methods defined by that interface. The following additional properties are defined by IBizTalkEnvelope:

Property	Meaning
Content	Read-only; a string containing the contents of the envelope specification file.
Format	Read/write; a string indicating the standard on which the envelope specification is based.
NameSpace	Read-only; a string containing the namespace declaration of the envelope. The length of the NameSpace string combined with the length of Name cannot total more than 255 characters.
Reference	Read/write; a string containing the WebDAV URL of the envelope specification file. This is a required property for envelopes whose Format property has the value custom.
Version	Read-only; a string containing the version of the envelope configuration.

The value of the Content property is controlled by the status of the Reference property. If Reference has a valid URL at the time Create() is called, Content is updated to reflect the contents of the file pointed to by the value of Reference. The NameSpace property is set to reflect the namespace in the referenced file under the same conditions. Content (and NameSpace) will be updated when Save() is called only if Reference has been changed since Create() or Save() was last called. Once Reference is set and the configuration saved (or created), any changes made to the envelope specification file through BizTalk Editor will not be reflected in the Content property. To cause such changes to be reflected in Content, you must rename the specification file, change Reference to reflect the new filename, and call Save() on the envelope object.

The Format property's value must be one of the following strings:

❑ x12

❑ edifact

❑ custom xml

❑ custom

❑ flatfile

❑ reliable

The custom xml value is the default value for this property and is the value to which a newly created envelope object's Format property is initialized. If you set Format to some other value, the configuration will result in an error when an interchange is attempted using the configuration.

IBizTalkPortGroup Interface

This interface is used to manipulate the configuration of a distribution list. The configuration object model uses the term "port group" to refer to the same entity. This interface is derived from IBizTalkBase and exposes all the properties and methods of that interface.

> *Many of the names that are used in the configuration object model reflect names that were used throughout the product in early pre-releases of BizTalk Server. Thus, a distribution list used to be known as a port group. If some of the names seem obscure, this is probably the reason.*

IBizTalkPortGroup adds the following methods to the IBizTalkBase interface:

Method	Parameters and meaning
AddPort()	No return value.
	lPortHandle – a long value containing a database handle to an existing port
	Adds the referenced port in the Messaging Management database to the port group.
RemovePort()	No return value.
	lPortHandle – database handle of a port in the port group
	Removes the port refernce by lPortHandle from the port group.

A port group object must contain at least one port object before the configuration may be used. The Openness property of the endpoint object representing a port must have the value BIZTALK_OPENNESS_TYPE_NOTOPEN, which means the port may not be open. Port groups may not contain the same port object more than once. The following additional properties are defined by IBizTalkPortGroup:

Property	Meaning
Channels	Read-only; an ADO recordset containing all channels using this port group. Each channel in the recordset has the following columns:
	Handle – long value containing the database handle of the channel
	Name – string name of the channel
Ports	Read-only; an ADO recordset containing all ports in the port group. Each port in the recordset has the following columns:
	Handle – a long value containing the handle of the port in the Messaging Management database
	Name – a string naming the port

Calls to the Channels and Ports properties may result in OLEDB errors being thrown as those properties utilize ADO recordsets.

IBizTalkServiceWindowInfo Interface

This interface describes a service window specified for a port. A service window, you will recall, is the interval during which messages may be sent to the port. This interface has no methods but defines the following properties:

Property	Meaning
FromTime	Read/write; a string representing the earliest time that the port may be used for interchange transmissions.
IsEnabled	Read/write; a variant containing a Boolean which, when True, indicates the service window is in effect for the port with which it is associated.
ToTime	Read/write; a string representing the latest time the port may be used for interchange transmissions.

Interchanges submitted outside an enabled service window for a port remain in the Scheduled queue until the service window opens.

IBizTalkTransportInfo Interface

This interface is used to configure the primary and secondary transport protocols for a port object. When you create a new port object, default objects supporting IBizTalkTransportInfo are automatically created. The following properites are defined in this interface:

Property	Meaning
Address	Read/write; string containing the protocol/appropriate URL of the endpoint with which this object is associated.
Parameter	Read/write; string containing the reply-to URL for SMTP transports.
Type	Read/write; value from the BIZTALK_TRANSPORT_TYPE enumeration denoting the transport protocol in use. An error will result if the URL value of Address is inappropriate for the protocol selected by this property when an interchange is attempted using this configuration. Errors are drawn from the range of error enumeration values named BTS_E_TRANSPORT_SYNTAXxxx, where xxx names the transport.

The Type property denotes the transport protocol that will be used. Its value guides the messaging service in selecting the proper transport COM component for use with an interchange. Here are the values of the BIZTALK_TRANSPORT_TYPE enumeration:

Enumeration Constant	Value	Meaning
BIZTALK_TRANSPORT_TYPE_NONE	1	This object does not select a transport
BIZTALK_TRANSPORT_TYPE_HTTP	4	HTTP is selected
BIZTALK_TRANSPORT_TYPE_SMTP	8	SMTP is selected
BIZTALK_TRANSPORT_TYPE_APPINTEGRATION	32	The message will be transported via COM to an AIC
BIZTALK_TRANSPORT_TYPE_MSMQ	128	MSMQ is the selected transport protocol
BIZTALK_TRANSPORT_TYPE_FILE	256	A file will be written using the local file system
BIZTALK_TRANSPORT_TYPE_HTTPS	1024	Secure HTTPS is selected as the transport protocol
BIZTALK_TRANSPORT_TYPE_OPENDESTINATION	2048	The messaging port is open
BIZTALK_TRANSPORT_TYPE_LOOPBACK	4096	Documents submitted using SubmitSync and this configuration will be processed and returned as the reply document
BIZTALK_TRANSPORT_TYPE_ORCHESTRATIONACTIVATION	8192	The interchange will be submitted to an orchestration schedule

It is essential that the value of the Address property agree with the protocol indicated in Type. The following prefixes are used in the value of Address for the different protocols supported by BizTalk Server (N/A denotes Not Applicable):

Protocol	Prefix	Comments
AIC	N/A	URL consists of a CLSID delimited with braces and hyphens, for example {12345678-1234-1234-1234-1234567890AB}
Local file	`file://`	
HTTP	`http://`	
HTTPS	`https://`	
Loopback	N/A	
MSMQ	N/A	Requires DIRECT MSMQ transport routing
None	N/A	
Open destination	N/A	
Orchestration activation	N/A	Full pathname to the `skx` file; the `file://` prefix must not be used
SMTP	`mailto:`	

When HTTP or HTTPS is the selected transport protocol, the default configuration is to use a proxy server. You may override this default by using the `SetConfigData()` method of `IBizTalkChannel` and setting the `UseProxy` field of the `IDictionary` parameter to `false`.

> *Be sure to change this if you are not using a proxy server.*

As you may recall from Chapter 5's discussion of ports, we used the `%tracking_id%` macro in conjunction with the local file protocol to cause the messaging service to create a unique filename for transported documents. A number of other macro symbols are defined for use with this protocol:

Macro symbol	Meaning
`%datetime%`	UTC timestamp of file creation, expressed in milliseconds
`%document_name%`	Name of the document definition processed
`%server%`	Machine name of the server that processed the interchange
`%tracking_id%`	Generates a GUID for each file created
`%uid%`	Count of milliseconds since the server was last booted

Note that only `%tracking_id%` guarantees a unique filename. You may, of course, combine multiple macros to form a descriptive filename, for example `%document_name%_%tracking_id%.xml` would yield a unique filename reflecting the document definition of the processed interchange.

IBizTalkCertificateInfo Interface

Digital certificates are used by ports and channels to implement signing and encryption of documents. The `IBizTalkCertificateInfo` interface is used to programmatically configure certificate information. An object supporting this interface is automatically created when you create a port or channel object, where it is referenced in the various `xxxCertificateInfo` properties.

The following additional properties are defined by IBizTalkCertificate:

Property	Meaning
Name	Read-only string containing the certificate name.
Reference	Read/write string referring to the certificate. Note: Setting this value can result in the generation of errors defined by the CryptoAPI interfaces.
Store	Read/write; a value from the BIZTALK_STORE_TYPE enumeration indicating where the certificate is stored (see IBizTalkConfig for the values of this enumeration).
Usage	Read-only; a value from the BIZTALK_USAGE_TYPE enumeration indicating how the certificate is used by the messaging service (see IBizTalkConfig for the values defined by this enumeration).

Certificates used for signing and decryption must be stored in the certificate store denoted by BIZTALK_STORE_TYPE_MY. Certificates used for signature verification and encryption must be stored in the store denoted by BIZTALK_STORE_TYPE_BIZTALK.

IBizTalkLoggingInfo Interface

You may recall that the **Document Logging** page of the Channel Wizard asks you to specify whether inbound and outbound documents are logged and in what format. This interface captures the same information. An object supporting this interface is automatically created when a channel object is created using the CreateChannel() method of the IBizTalkConfig interface. This interface has the following four properties:

Property	Meaning
LogNativeInputDocument	Read/write; a variant containing a Boolean, which, when True, tells the messaging service to log inbound documents in their native format.
LogNativeOutputDocument	Read/write; a variant containing a Boolean, which, when True, tells the messaging service to log outbound documents in their native format.
LogXMLInputDocument	Read/write; a variant containing a Boolean, which, when True, tells the messaging service to log inbound documents in XML format.
LogXMLOutputDocument	Read/write; a variant containing a Boolean, which, when True, tells the messaging service to log outbound documents in XML format.

You can access this interface through the LoggingInfo property of IBizTalkChannel.

IDictionary Interface

This interface does not directly represent any messaging service entity. Instead, it is a utility interface that permits the aggregation of an arbitrary collection of name-value pairs and as such should be familiar to anyone with database experience. The interface is implemented by a number of DLLs including `mscscore.dll`, which is usually located in a folder under the Program Files\Common Files folder. This interface is useful to a variety of BizTalk-related COM interfaces because it can be used for the ad hoc storage of named properties. Every item stored by this interface is typed as a variant for maximum flexibility in the data that may be aggregated by this interface. Different interfaces used in the configuration object model specify named values to reflect their configuration needs. This interface supports the following methods:

Method	Parameters and meaning
GetMultiple()	No return value.
	lNumItemsToRetrieve – a long count of the number of items to retrieve from the collection
	rsNames – an array of names for which values are to be retrieved
	rvValues – an array of variants which is filled upon return from the method with the values associated with the passed-in names
	This method allows the programmatic retrieval of multiple values given their names.
	Note: This method will fail in VBScript because some types required by this method are not supported in that language.
PutMultiple()	No return value.
	lCountOfPairs – long valued count of the number of items in the following array parameters
	rsNames – array of strings naming the new items
	rvValues – array of variants containing the values to be added
	This method is used to create or set name-value pairs in the dictionary.
	Note: This method fails in VBScript because some data types required by this method are not supported by that language.

These methods reflect the loose structure of the dictionary. The interface itself does not specify any named values. When created, the dictionary is empty. `PutMultiple()` adds name-value pairs to the object or changes existing values. A named value may be an instance of the `IDictionary` interface. To retrieve the value of one or more name-value pairs, fill an array with the names for which you want values and call `GetMultiple()`.

`IDictionary` supports the following properties:

Property	Meaning
Count	Read-only; a long value indicating the number of name-value pairs stored in the dictionary object
NewEnum	Read-only; this property returns an IUnknown interface pointer, which may be successfully queried for an IEnumVariant interface pointer, permitting the enumeration of the pairs in the collection
	This interface allows you to iterate through the collection using the Next method, which returns an object representing the name-value pair. The value of the pair is exposed by the Value property of that object.

Table continued on following page

Property	Meaning
Prefix	Read/write; a string containing a prefix filter.
	Values for names beginning with the prefix are not saved to the Messaging Management database when the contents of the dictionary are saved.
	Note: This property has a default value of _. Names beginning with this character will not be saved unless the value of the property is changed.
Value	Read/write; this property takes a string parameter denoting the name of the property desired and sets or retrieves the corresponding value.
	This is the default property of the interface, so the following lines are equivalent:
	❏ `Dictionary.Value(name)`
	❏ `Dictionary(name)`

In Visual Basic, you can access the contents of the dictionary in two ways. If the names of the pairs are known in advance, `GetMultiple()` and `PutMultiple()` are the most efficient way to get at the values of the pairs. As an alternative, you may access pairs individually using the `Value` property. Applications written in C++ may iterate through the collection and determine names and values using the `NewEnum` property, but names must be known for access in Visual Basic.

ISimpleList Interface

`IsimpleList`, which like `IDictionary` is implemented in `mscscore.dll`, is similar to `IDictionary` in that it allows the ad hoc creation, modification, and deletion of variant values in a collection. Unlike that interface, `ISimpleList` offers an ordered collection indexed through integer indices. This interface is used by the `TrackFields` property of the `IBizTalkChannel` interface to add custom fields to the tracking criteria for a channel.

The `ISimpleList` interface exposes the following two methods:

Method	Parameters and meaning
Add()	No return value.
	vValue – variant value to add to the collection
	This method is used to add new values to the list object.
Delete()	No return value.
	lIndex – long value containing the zero-based index of the item to remove from the collection
	This method removes the value stored at the indexed location, modifying the `Count` property and the indices of existing items in the process.

Unlike `IDictionary`, values are accessed by their ordinal index and they have no name. Care must be exercised to ensure that the proper index is passed to retrieve a particular value. Indices are altered by calls to `Delete()`. The total number of items stored in the list is increased by calls to `Add()`. That method appends a new item to the end of the list. You should always use indices immediately and not hold them across calls to Add and Delete.

ISimpleList supports the following properties:

Property	Meaning
Count	Read-only; long value indicating the total number of items in the list.
	Count will be one more than the maximum valid index.
Item	Returns a variant containing the value of the item stored at the passed in index.
	lIndex – zero-based index of the item to add or change
	Adds or changes an item. If lIndex refers to an existing item in the collection, the item is changed.

URL Concordance Example

A busy BizTalk Server installation can easily end up with a large number of ports. If those ports involve external partners, it is entirely possible that the URLs used to submit documents to your partners can change over time. Web sites are restructured and applications can be changed. The configurations in your Messaging Management database can be intact, yet interchanges can begin to fail. It is prudent, then, to periodically check the URLs on which you rely.

We'll build a URL concordance checker to demonstrate the use of the configuration object model in building administrative utilities. This application will let a BizTalk administrator enumerate all the URLs used by the channels in use by a given BizTalk server group. This application will show you how to navigate the object model in Visual Basic and illustrate a key concept in the object model.

All code in this example can be downloaded from the Wrox web site (http://www.wrox.com).

User Interface

Our application is a Visual Basic application consisting of a single form. The form is dominated by an instance of the MSFlexGrid control. This control, which offers a simple grid interface, ships with Visual Basic and is implemented in msflxgrd.ocx, typically found in the system32 directory. The grid will support three named columns:

❑ Channel, in which the name of the BizTalk channel is displayed.

❑ URL, where the protocol-specific URL of the channel's destination is displayed.

❑ Service Window, in which the service window (if one is defined and enabled) of the destination port is displayed.

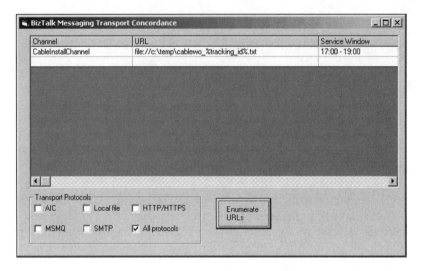

There are a series of checkboxes underneath the grid, one for each protocol (other than loopback) supported by the BizTalk messaging service, and one for all protocols. When the user clicks the button labelled **Enumerate URLs**, the application will enumerate all channels in the server group configuration and list all URLs that use the selected protocol. Note that ports that do not participate in any channels will be missed. Our intent is to enumerate all actively used URLs. Any port that is not associated with a channel cannot be used by the messaging service, so enumerating the channels to get at the ports ensures we only see active ports.

Setting Up the Project

In addition to software components installed by BizTalk Server, you will need ADO 2.5 or later and the Microsoft FlexGrid control. The latter component is implemented in msflxgrd.ocx, which is installed to the system32 folder by a number of development tools. Start by creating a standard EXE project in Visual Basic named URLConcordance. Name the form URLForm. Using the Project | Components... menu item, select the Microsoft FlexGrid Control 6.0. Using Project | References..., set the following references:

❑ Microsoft BizTalk Server Configuration Objects 1.0 Type Library
(BizTalkObjectModel.dll) – BizTalk messaging configuration object model

❑ Microsoft ActiveX Data Objects 2.5 Library (msado15.dll) – ADO recordset support

The component setting gives us access to the MSFlexGrid control for the user interface. The BizTalk configuration object model is obviously necessary, while ADO recordset support is needed because one of the properties we shall use is an ADO recordset.

In the General declarations area of the form, add the following line:

```
Dim BTSConfig As New BizTalkConfig
```

This gives us a global instance of the component that implements the IBizTalkConfig interface. As you should recall, that interface is the entry point for the entire configuration object model. Any other objects we require from the object model will be created as we need them.

Enumerating Channels

The first thing we want to do when the user clicks on the button is enumerate the channels. The `IBizTalkConfig` interface has a property, `Channels`, that will do that for us. Recall that the value of the property is an ADO recordset object. Here is how the button handler starts:

```
Private Sub EnumBtn_Click()
  Dim rsChannels As ADODB.Recordset
  Dim i As Integer, sChannelName As String, sWindow As String
  Dim channel As BizTalkChannel
  Dim port As BizTalkPort
  Dim pTransport As BizTalkTransportInfo

  ResetGrid

  Set channel = BTSConfig.CreateChannel
  Set port = BTSConfig.CreatePort
  Set rsChannels = BTSConfig.Channels
  For i = 1 To rsChannels.RecordCount
    . . .
    rsChannels.MoveNext
  Next i
End Sub
```

`ResetGrid()` is a subroutine that uses the methods of the grid control to set up the column headers and clear out any existing rows. We retrieve the value of the `Channels` property, then we iterate through the recordset and perform some action for each channel found. What, though, are those lines where `CreateChannel()` and `CreatePort()` are called?

The contents of the recordset are simple data types, not interface references. We have information about the channels, not references to the channels themselves in the recordset. We have to use the methods of the `BTSConfig` object to create empty channel and port objects. The next few lines are key to understanding how to navigate the object model:

```
For i = 1 To rsChannels.RecordCount
  channel.Load rsChannels.Fields("id").Value
  sChannelName = channel.Name
```

The `id` column of the recordset is a database handle. The `Load()` method of `IBizTalkBase` (and hence of all interfaces, like `IBizTalkChannel`, derived from it) loads the object's data from the database given the handle. This is the pattern we'll use throughout the object model:

❑ get the handle from a collection property of the top-level object

❑ create an empty object

❑ then load the persistent state of the object desired from the database

In the code fragment above, we can get the name of the channel, which is destined for the first column of the grid control, from a property of the newly loaded channel object.

We have the channel, but we really want the URL of the channel's destination. In fact, there are two possible URLs: one each for the primary and secondary transports. That information requires that we have the configuration of the port associated with the channel. Continuing with the pattern we just saw, we load the `port` object:

```
port.Load channel.port
```

Accessing Port Information

The port has a bit of information that we're going to need, the service window. The user interface displays this so that a user can determine when a port may be used. Before we delve into the transports, then, let's get that information:

```
sWindow = GetWindow(port.ServiceWindowInfo)
```

GetWindow() is a function that takes an IBizTalkServiceWindowInfo interface reference and returns a string composed of the start and end times of the service window. If no window is defined, or a defined window is not enabled, we want an empty string.

```
Private Function GetWindow(pSW As BizTalkServiceWindowInfo) As String
  Dim sWin As String
  sWin = ""
  If pSW.IsEnabled Then
    sWin = pSW.FromTime & ":00 - " & pSW.ToTime & ":00"
  End If
  GetWindow = sWin
End Function
```

The IBizTalkServiceWindowInfo interface's IsEnabled property lets us skip any window that is not enabled. The FromTime and ToTime properties are strings, but you have to remember that they only list the hour. To make a string that is obviously a time, then, we have to add the :00 fragments ourselves.

Transport Information

The GetWindow() function gave us the data we're going to put into the third column of the grid. The most important piece of information, the URL, requires a visit to the primary and secondary transport configurations:

```
If Not IsNull(port.PrimaryTransport) Then
  Set pTransport = port.PrimaryTransport
  If CheckCriteria(pTransport) Then
    WriteEndPt sChannelName, pTransport.Address, sWindow
  End If
End If

If Not IsNull(port.SecondaryTransport) Then
  Set pTransport = port.SecondaryTransport
  If CheckCriteria(pTransport) Then
    WriteEndPt sChannelName, pTransport.Address, sWindow
  End If
End If
```

The two blocks follow the same pattern. If a transport exists, we pass it to the CheckCriteria() function. That function checks the type of the transport and returns true if the checkbox for that protocol or the **All protocols** checkbox is checked. If the transport type matches the user's filter criteria, we pass the channel name, URL (found in the Address property of the IBizTalkTransportInfo interface), and the string we got from GetWindow() to WriteEndPt(), a subroutine that uses the methods of the grid control to push the data into a new row in the control. Here's the body of CheckCriteria():

```
Private Function CheckCriteria(pTrans As BizTalkTransportInfo) As Boolean
  Dim bRet As Boolean
  ' All or nothing
  If pTrans.Type = BIZTALK_TRANSPORT_TYPE_NONE Then
   CheckCriteria = False
   Exit Function
  End If

  If AllCheck.Value = 1 Then
   CheckCriteria = True
   Exit Function
  End If

  bRet = False
  Select Case (pTrans.Type)
   Case BIZTALK_TRANSPORT_TYPE_HTTP
     If HTTPCheck.Value = 1 Then bRet = True
   Case BIZTALK_TRANSPORT_TYPE_HTTPS
     If HTTPCheck.Value = 1 Then bRet = True
   Case BIZTALK_TRANSPORT_TYPE_SMTP
     If SMTPCheck.Value = 1 Then bRet = True
   Case BIZTALK_TRANSPORT_TYPE_APPINTEGRATION
     If AICCheck.Value = 1 Then bRet = True
   Case BIZTALK_TRANSPORT_TYPE_MSMQ
     If MSMQCheck.Value = True Then bRet = True
   Case BIZTALK_TRANSPORT_TYPE_FILE
     If FileCheck.Value = 1 Then bRet = True
  End Select
  CheckCriteria = bRet
End Function
```

The Type property is a value from the BIZTALK_TRANSPORT_TYPE enumeration. If the value is BIZTALK_TRANSPORT_TYPE_NONE, there is nothing to display so we return false. If the All protocols checkbox is checked, we always want to list the URL, so we return true. For the rest, we have to compare the value of Type to the status of the related checkbox.

In case you are interested in how to use the FlexGrid control, here is the body of WriteEndPt():

```
Private Sub WriteEndPt(sName As String, sURL As String, sWindow As String)
   Dim sRow As String
   ' The grid control uses the tab character as a column delimiter
   sRow = sName & vbTab & sURL & vbTab & sWindow
   ResultsGrid.AddItem sRow, 1

End Sub
```

Given our parameters for display, the routine composes a string consisting of the parameters delimited by a tab character. The control uses that character to indicate a new column. The AddItem() method inserts a new row. Its first parameter is the string we just built, and its second is the index where we want to see the row appear. The control numbers rows beginning with 1.

> *Additional usage of the control is demonstrated in Form_Load and ResetGrid routines in the code download for this project.*

Summary

The BizTalk messaging configuration object model is quite extensive, comprising fifteen interfaces. The relationships aren't hard to understand, though. One interface, `IBizTalkBase`, is a common base used to derive the interfaces for the major entities of the messaging service. `IBizTalkConfig` is a contrived interface designed to act as the entry point for the entire object model. That interface has a series of properties that query the Messaging Management database and return an ADO recordset representing that portion of the database.

Each major configuration entity is identified in the database by a handle or key, which is a long interger value. This handle lets you retrieve a specific configuration through the `Load()` method of the `IBizTalkBase` interface. An object created through one of the methods of the `IBizTalkConfig` interface is empty and initialized to default values. It is the `Load()` method that queries the Messaging Management database for the specific configuration requested.

The remaining interfaces of the object model represent collections of related data, usually corresponding to controls on a page of one of the configuration wizards in Messaging Manager. Properties whose values are references to these interfaces are live, which means the property returns a COM interface initialized to the values of the configuration. Examples of these interfaces are `IBizTalkServiceWindowInfo`, in the `IBizTalkPort::ServiceWindowInfo` property, and `IBizTalkTransportInfo`, in the `PrimaryTransport` and `SecondaryTransport` properties of the `IBizTalkPort` interface. We are able to navigate the entire object model with two techniques. Accessing the major entities involves iterating through a recordset and loading the objects from their database handles, while the minor objects are pre-loaded into interface instances found in the properties of the major objects.

The configuration object model is a useful tool for building utilities for working with the messaging service. We can use it as a window into the Messaging Management database, as with our sample, or a way to export and import server group configurations. Using the object model for dynamic configuration of the messaging service requires care. The configuration object model is best used to configure new messaging objects or modify existing objects when the messaging service is not running. If used with a running server group, great care must be taken not to interfere with configurations that are in use. The port and port group interfaces, for example, have properties that enable us to look back up the object model to the channels that uses those objects. This is a help in avoiding conflicts. If care is taken though, the object model offers the possibility of automating the technical side of establishing a B2B trading relationship. We sketched out the outlines of such an application.

The configuration object model is an example of one of the benefits of component software. Building BizTalk Server from COM components yields the dividend of a series of COM-based object models for accessing and manipulating the major subsystems of the product. `IInterchange` gave us access to the runtime side of the messaging service. The configuration object model completes our picture of the messaging service with access to the design-time side. BizTalk's Messaging Management implements this side of the service, so we could get by with SQL and ADO. The object model, however, observes the constraints and rules needed to preserve the relational integrity of the database. It is also easier to navigate the object model than it is to navigate the Messaging Management database with SQL queries.

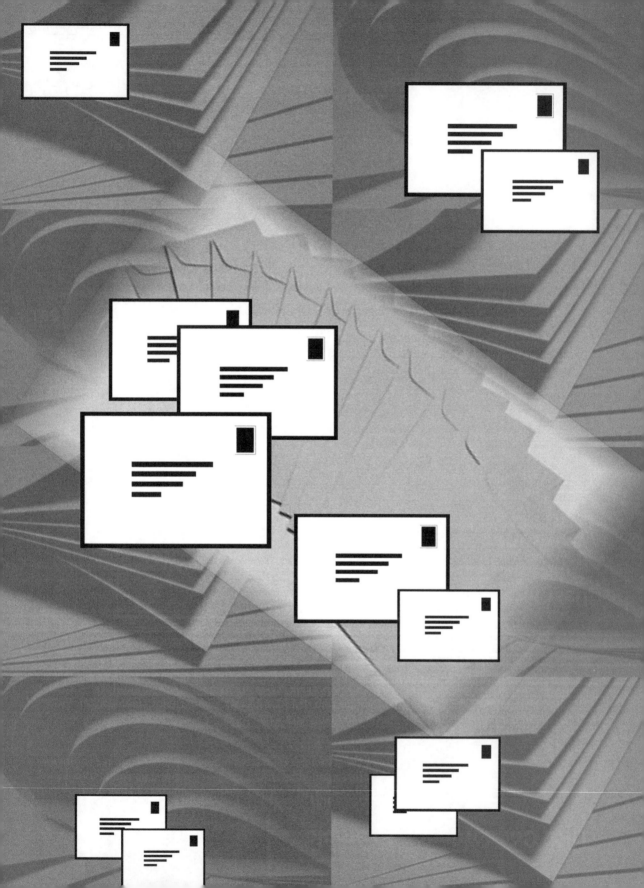

Setup and Installation

This appendix summarizes the setup and installation process for Microsoft BizTalk Server 2000. We examine the hardware and software prerequisites, particularly in terms of the other software products on which BizTalk Server relies. Installation is covered in terms of manual installations as well as command line installations such as you might use to deploy the product to all the servers in a BizTalk server group.

Options, sequences of events, and screenshots are based on a late pre-release version of Microsoft BizTalk Server 2000. Minor changes to screenshots and names may occur. For the latest settings, please refer to the BizTalk Server documentation.

System Requirements

Microsoft has established a minimum recommended hardware configuration for BizTalk Server 2000. Since the product is intended for use in enterprise-scale integration settings, the minimum configuration is unlikely to be seen in a typical environment. Consequently, some suggestions are made regarding how to make use of additional servers deployed in a BizTalk installation.

Regardless of the host hardware configuration, Microsoft BizTalk Server 2000 relies on several other software products. In most cases, the required configuration is quite specific in terms of version and patches.

Minimum Recommended Hardware Configuration

The following is the minimum suggested hardware required to install and run the complete BizTalk Server product:

❑ Pentium 300 Mhz class processor.

❑ 128 megabytes of RAM.

❑ A 6-gigabyte hard disk.

This configuration is sufficient to install and run the development tools and the runtime services, but is not sufficient to handle high volumes of messaging traffic. A single server meeting these minimum hardware requirements will also fail to meet commonly accepted standards for reliability. This configuration should be taken as the minimum configuration needed for evaluation or as a stand-alone development machine. It may be sufficient in a production environment if multiple machines with this configuration are deployed in a BizTalk server group.

Hardware Recommendations for Performance

BizTalk Server is designed to scale through the use of clusters of cooperating BizTalk servers. A typical production configuration will include multiple servers with BizTalk Server installed. Beyond the use of BizTalk Server itself, BizTalk is highly reliant on SQL Server for data services. The shared databases are one area in which multiple servers may profitably be used to increase message through-put. The suggested growth path is as follows:

❑ Single server – BizTalk Server and SQL Server collocated on a single machine.

❑ Two servers – one machine is dedicated to BizTalk Server, with SQL Server moved to the second machine.

❑ Three servers – one BizTalk Server computer, one SQL Server machine hosting the shared queue and messaging management databases, and one SQL Server computer hosting the document tracking database.

❑ Four or more servers – two computers configured with SQL Server as in the three machine case, with the remaining servers running BizTalk Server.

BizTalk Server is designed to let multiple machines share the messaging load equally without special configuration or additional clustering software.

Disk configuration is not especially critical for the computers hosting BizTalk Server. Persistent data resides exclusively in SQL Server, so RAID arrays should be reserved for those servers.

Software Dependencies

Microsoft BizTalk Server 2000 requires three other commercial products for a complete installation and runtime processing. In addition, production deployments may make use of custom COM components which must be installed on all BizTalk servers. The list of software dependencies is as follows:

❑ Windows 2000 Server, Advanced Server, or Professional Service Pack 1 – Messaging Manager and Document Tracking are Web applications and require Internet Information Server. Additionally HTTP receive functions require IIS, as does WebDAV access to the document repository. Certificate storage requires ActiveDirectory, and SMTP transmission requires access to an SMTP server. Runtime services may run on Windows 2000 Professional provided some functions are hosted on a separate computer running one of the Server versions of the operating system. All Windows versions must have NTFS as the file system to run BizTalk Server.

❑ SQL Server 7.0, Service Pack 2 or SQL Server 2000 – BizTalk Server maintains all configuration, schedule, and messaging state in four SQL Server databases. Runtime services require that SQL Server be available.

❑ Visio 2000 SR-1A – Orchestration Designer is implemented as a VBA application within Visio 2000. You may run exported schedules without Visio, but you will not be able to design or export schedules without it.

❑ Any custom COM components used by message mapping or orchestration schedules.

Pre-release documentation calls for Service Pack 1 to Windows 2000. Late pre-release versions (November 2000) require bug fixes past the service pack. The authors anticipate that a second service pack will be available and required by the time BizTalk Server 2000 is released.

Note that the Windows installation must include Internet Explorer 5.0 or later. Messaging Manager and Document Tracking are browser-hosted applications that make extensive use of COM controls and dynamic HTML. It is possible to install the development tools separately from the runtime services. In that case, Windows 2000 Professional may be used as the operating system, and SQL Server is not required.

The release version of BizTalk Server 2000 supports installation of the runtime services to a machine running Windows 2000 Professional. In practice, the dependencies on IIS and, to a lesser extent, ActiveDirectory, make this a challenging option. We recommend that this be considered only for a standalone developer's machine, and then only with great care.

Manual Installation and Setup

The manual installation process for BizTalk Server 2000 utilizes the Windows Installer and is completely wizard-driven. While the entire process is fairly simple and the wizards guide you through the process, you do have to make a few choices along the way. There are several types of installations from which to choose, and you must configure administrative access. Additionally, you have some choices to make with regard to the four SQL Server databases.

Installation Types

There are three types of manual installations possible with the included `setup.exe` executable:

❑ Complete – all tools and services required to run and administer the BizTalk messaging service and XLANG Scheduler

❑ Tools – Orchestration Designer, Editor, Mapper, Document Tracking, and BizTalk Server 2000 documentation

❑ Custom – user-selected choice from all BizTalk tools and services

You should be logged into the machine on which you are installing BizTalk through an account with administrator-level access. Some of the choices involve configuring a new user group or installing the software with different degrees of visibility. All three types of installations start the same way. You are first presented with a screen that lists the licensing terms and asks you to accept or reject them. Provided you accept, you are taken to a screen that asks for the name of the licensed user and the product ID key from the CD case. On this screen, you have the choice of installing the software so that it appears on the starup menu for all users or just the currently logged in user. The next page gives you the chance to select an installation folder for the program and its related files.

The next screen, shown below, is where you must make your first critical choice. You are given the chance to select which type of installation you wish to pursue.

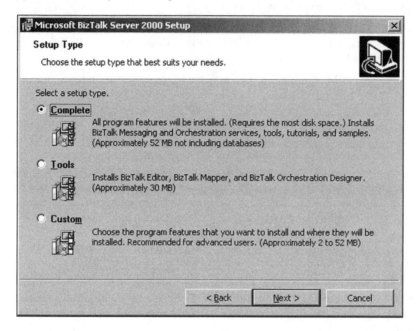

If you choose **Complete**, you are taken immediately to the page for configuring administrative access. If you choose **Custom**, you go through the following page which gives you the chance to select which options to install:

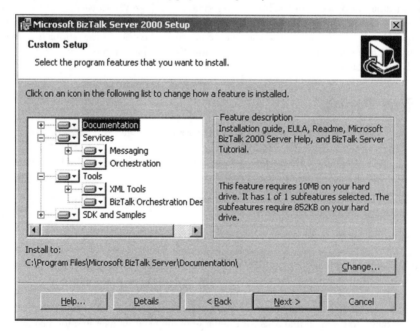

The default is to install all options that would be installed in the Complete installation.

If you select the Tools installation type, you will not have access to runtime services or the IInterchange interface. You may export the COM+ BizTalk Server Interchange Application to install the IInterchange interface component to other machines.

Your next task is to configure a user group for administrative access to BizTalk Server. You should make note of the name you give to this group for future reference. The name you choose should follow the normal rules for user group names. The value you enter is added to the registry under `HKEY_LOCAL_MACHINE\SOFTWARE\Microsoft\BizTalk Server\1.0\NTGroups`. If you change the name later, you must change the value of this key. The default group name is BizTalk Server Administrators.

On the next page you have the option to install BizTalk so that it operates under either the local system account or a specific user account. Normally, you will select the former so that BizTalk can operate whenever the machine is running regardless of whether an interactive user is logggged in. However, you may choose to run BizTalk under a particular user account if you want to restrict access or control when it runs, e.g., on a developer's machine when the developer is logged in. That page also has a checkbox, normally selected, for starting BizTalk's runtime services when setup completes.

After completing that page, you are given a page that reviews your installation options and informs you that setup is ready to install BizTalk. If you click Next, all the components, executables, and related software for BizTalk Server are installed and registry keys are set up.

Immediately upon completion of the software installation process, the database configuration wizard starts with a welcome page. After clicking through the welcome page, you are taken to the page for configuring the Messaging Management database. This page follows a pattern that is repeated on all the other database configuration pages. You are given a choice between creating a new database or connecting to an existing one.

At the bottom of the page are SQL Server connection options: server name, user account name, password, and database name. If you elect to create a new database and give it the name of an existing database, any existing data is wiped out. The user account you supply must have administrative access to the database (in the case of an existing database) or will be granted such access (for a new database).

After completing this page, you are taken to a page for configuring a BizTalk server group. You may create a new group, which defaults to the name BizTalk Server Group, or select from any existing groups that are known to the server on which you are installing the product.

Following configuration of the group, you repeat the database selection process for the Tracking database and Shared Queue database. The defaults BizTalk offers for the database names are:

- InterchangeBTM – messaging management
- InterchangeDTA – tracking
- InterchangeSQ – shared queue

After you have completed your selections, you are given a page which reviews the options you have selected. If you wish to change anything, click Back to go back to the appropriate page in the wizard. Otherwise, clicking Next takes you to the completion page. Clicking Finish here causes the databases to be created or configured. When this process completes, you are presented with the welcome page to the BizTalk Server Orchestration Persistence database wizard.

This wizard, while distinct from the preceding one, is almost identical in terms of the user interface. You again have the choice to create a new persistence database, which defaults to the name XLANG, or select an existing one. If you create a new database, any schedules in process on that machine will be lost. After making your selecction, you reach the installation page. Click Finish, and the hydration database will be created or configured, ending the manual installation process.

Installing to a Server Group: Silent Installation

If you are installing the software to all the machines in a server group, you will probably not want to manually install each in turn. This section describes the command line syntax Windows Installer will accept for BizTalk Server. The following is the command line structure:

```
msiexec /I filepath\Microsoft BizTalk Server.msi /qb [/Lv* logfile_path]
  [INSTALLLEVEL=<200 | 100>] ALLUSERS=1 PIDKEY="key" DSNCONFIG="filepath"
```

The executable msiexec is the Windows installer. Everything following the /I switch is the command line for installation. The most critical piece of information is the path to the installation file, Microsoft BizTalk Server.msi. The /qb switch presents a minimal user interface consisting of a progress bar. The /Lv* switch generates an installation log for which you may supply a name and path. It defaults to install.log in the directory from which the software is installed. If you do not supply the INSTALLLEVEL option, it will default to 100, which is the Tools installation. If you wish to install runtime services, include this option with the value 200. Other options permit you to control what gets installed. The ALLUSERS option takes the value of 1 to insure all users can see the software and its registry keys. PIDKEY is the product key from the CD case. The 25 character key should be entered without hyphens. The DSNCONFIG option supplies database connection information for all four databases. We shall discuss its structure later.

There are additional command line options available to you as listed in this table:

Option	Default value	Meaning
USERNAME	Logged on user (installer-provided property)	Name of the installing user; corresponds to the User information page of the manual installation
COMPANYNAME	Logged on company (installer-provided property)	Name of the installing user's compnay; corresponds to the user information page of the manual installation
PIDKEY	""	Product key without hyphens
INSTALLLEVEL	100	100 = Tools, 200 = server installation
INSTALLDIR	"{Program Files}\Microsoft BizTalk Server" (installer-provided property)	Installation folder root for the software

Option	Default value	Meaning
BTS_GROUP_NAME (complete installation only)	"BTSAdmin"	Name of the user group for BTS administration
BTS_GROUP_DESCRIPTION (complete installation only)	"Members can fully administer Microsoft BizTalk Server"	Description for the group named in BTS_GROUP_NAME
BTS_USERNAME (Complete installation only)	""	Name of the user under which BTS starts; may be qualified by a domain name
BTS_PASSWORD	""	Logon password for the account named in BTS_USERNAME
BTS_SERVER (Complete and Tools installations)	"localhost"	Name of the BizTalk Server
BTS_SDK_SERVER (Complete and tools installations)	"localhost"	Name of the server to access for DCOM (IInterchange)
DSNCONFIG	""	Qualified filename to the database initialization file (all databases)
BTSSETUPDB.INI	""	In lieu of DSNCONFIG, you may provide the qualified name of an initialization file to be used for the messaging service database configuration
XLANGSETUPDB.INI	""	In lieu of DSNCONFIG, you may provide the qualified name of an initialization file to be used for the XLANG database configuration

The initialization file(s) for database configuration are simple .ini text files. There are five sections:

❑   InterchangeBTM – messaging management database configuration

❑   Group – BizTalk server group naming

❑   InterchangeDTA – tracking database configuration

❑   InterchangeSQ – shared queue database configuration

❑   Orchestration – schedule hydration database configuration

Each section has four possible keys, with the exception of the Group section. All sections and keys are optional. If omitted, the default values shown below are used. The four database section keys are:

❑ Server – machine name; defaults to localhost

❑ Username – logon user account, defaults to sa

❑ Password – logon user account password, defaults to empty string

❑ Database – database name; defaults to the name of the section

For example, the section to configure the messaging management database on the SQL Server MyData under the user account lockbox with the password volusia and the database name MessagingMgt would look like:

```
[InterchangeBTM]
Server=MyData
Username=lockbox
Password=volusia
Database=MessagingMgt
```

The Group section is used to configure the BizTalk server group. It has one key, GroupName, which defaults to BizTalkGroup. If the group already exists, the keys for the tracking and shared queue dfatabases are ignored in favor of the values found in the messaging management database.

Windows Installer has its own set of command line switches. The /qb, /I, and /Lv* switches shown above are specific configurations of installer command line switches. For a complete list of command line switches and their options, refer to Windows Installer documentation.

Note that if your schedules and maps require custom components, you must separately install these for the machines in the server group to process interchanges and scedhules correctly.

Security Settings for Document Tracking

The Document Tracking application that is installed with BizTalk Server is a Web-based application. It uses ActiveX components and accesses data outside the Web application. For most Internet settings, Internet Explorer will generate a warning. If you wish to avoid these warnings, select the Tools | Internet Options menu item in Internet Explorer. Select the Security tab of the properties dialog. On that tabbed page, click Trusted Sites in the Web Zone area, then click the Sites… button below that area. Type the server URL, beginning with https:// for the IIS machine hosting the BizTalk tracking function, then click Add to add this machine to your list of trusted sites.

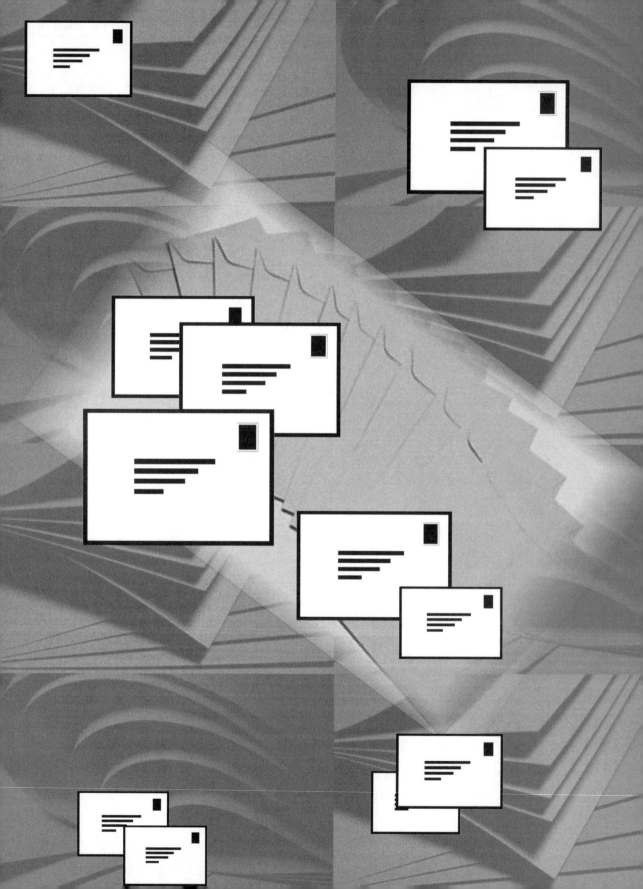

B

XSLT and XPath

This appendix is designed to give you enough information about XSLT, the XML transformation language, to enable you to write useful stylesheets; and about XPath, the query language used by XSLT stylesheets to access XML data.

We haven't got room here for a complete description of these languages or a detailed guide showing how to take advantage of them: for that see the Wrox Press book *XSLT Programmer's Reference*, written by Michael Kay (ISBN 1-861003-12-9). The aim is, instead, to cover enough to give a useful working knowledge.

In this appendix, we'll go through the following:

❑ We'll start with an overview of the XSLT language: what it's for, and how it works

❑ Then we'll take a detailed look at the XPath query language, which is used in XSLT stylesheets to access data in the source document

❑ Having done that, we'll look at the role of template rules and match patterns in an XSLT stylesheet, and review all the instructions you can use within a template

❑ Finally, we'll look at the top-level elements you can use in a stylesheet to define processing options

That's a lot of technical detail, so at the end we'll relax with some soccer; using XSLT to display soccer scores from an XML file.

What is XSLT?

XSLT is a high-level language for defining XML transformations. In general, a transformation takes one XML document as input, and produces another XML (or indeed, HTML, WML, plain text, etc.) document as output.

In this sense it's a bit like SQL, which transforms source tables into result tables, and it uses similar declarative queries to express the processing required. The obvious difference is that the data (both the input and the output) is arranged as a hierarchy or tree, rather than as tables.

XML transformations have many possible roles in the architecture of a system. For example:

❑ The most familiar application of XSLT is to format information for display. Here, the transformation is from "pure data" (whatever that means) to data with formatting information: usually the target will be HTML or XHTML, though it might be other formats such as SVG, PDF, or Microsoft's RTF. Of course these aren't all XML-based formats, but that doesn't matter, because as we'll see they can be modeled as XML trees, and that's all is needed.

❑ XSLT is also very useful when managing data interchange between different computer systems. This might be as part of an e-commerce exchange with customers or suppliers, or simply application integration within the enterprise. The increasing use of XML doesn't mean that data conversion will be outdated. What it does mean is that in future, data conversions will often be translating one XML message format into another XML message format.

❑ XSLT can perform some of the roles traditionally carried out by report writers and 4GLs. As well as pure formatting, this can include tasks such as information selection, aggregation, and exception highlighting. For example, if your web-shopping site generates a transaction log in XML format, it is quite possible to use XSLT to produce a report highlighting which areas of the site were most profitable and which category of customers visited that area.

A program written in XSLT is referred to as a stylesheet. This reflects the original role of the language as a way of defining rules for presenting XML on screen. XSLT grew out of a bigger project called XSL (eXtensible Stylesheet Language), which aimed to provide this support, not only for on-screen display but for every kind of output device including high-quality print publication. XSLT was separated out into a sub-project of its own, because it was recognized that transformation of the input was an essential part of the rendering process, and that the language for transformation was usable in many other contexts. The other part of XSL, which handles the formatting specifications, is currently still under development.

XSLT transformations can be carried out on the server or on the client. They can be done just before the user sees the data, or early on while it is being authored. They can be applied to tiny XML files a few bytes long, or to large datasets. There are no rights and wrongs here: like SQL, the XSLT language is a versatile tool that can be applied in many different ways.

XSLT processors are available from a number of vendors, and in this appendix, we'll stick to describing the language, as defined by W3C, rather than any specific product. There are open source products available (Saxon and Xalan are popular choices), as well as closed source free products from Microsoft and Oracle, and some development tools available commercially. Many of these are written in Java, so they will run on any platform, but processors are also available written in C++ and Python. Here are some pointers to the web sites:

❑ Microsoft (MSXML3): http://msdn.microsoft.com/xml
❑ Oracle (Oracle XML parser): http://technet.oracle.com/
❑ Saxon: http://users.iclway.co.uk/mhkay/saxon/
❑ Xalan: http://xml.apache.org/xalan/overview.html

A good place to look for information about XSLT, including pointers to other products available, is http://www.xslinfo.com/.

One word of warning: when Microsoft shipped Internet Explorer 5, back in 1998, they included a processor that handled a language based on an early draft of XSLT, with many omissions and Microsoft extensions. Microsoft refers to this language as XSL, but it is a distant cousin of XSLT as eventually standardized by W3C. The language is now dated, and Microsoft themselves have a conformant XSLT processor, but millions of copies have shipped and are still being shipped with every copy of IE5 and IE5.5, so it won't go away in a hurry. This chapter is about XSLT, not about Microsoft's 1998 XSL dialect: don't get confused between the two.

Many readers will probably find it simplest to start with the Microsoft XSLTprocessor (MSXML3). At the time of writing, this is available for download from the MSDN web site, but it is expected to become part of Internet Explorer 6 in due course. In the meantime, do read the installation instructions very carefully, because it is easy to find yourself trying to run XSLT stylesheets through the old 1998 XSL processor, and wondering why nothing happens. Note that MSXML3 also includes a conversion utility for old stylesheets: it's only 90% of the job, but that's still easier than doing it all yourself.

The Transformation Process

We described XSLT as a way of transforming one XML document into another, but that's a simplification. The diagram below illustrates what is really going on:

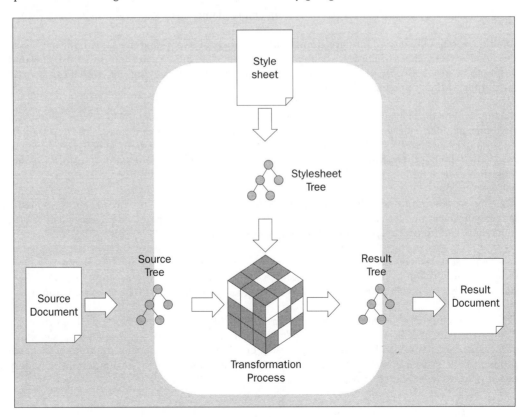

There are three separate stages of processing here:

❑ An XML Parser takes the source XML document and turns it into a tree representation

❑ The XSLT Processor, following the rules expressed in a stylesheet, transforms this tree into another tree

❑ A Serializer takes the result tree and turns it into a XML document.

Very often these three bits of software will be bundled together into a single product, so the joins may not be obvious, but it's useful to understand these three stages because it affects what a transformation can and can't do.

On the input side, this means the stylesheet isn't in control of the XML parsing process, and it can't do processing based on distinctions that are present in the source document but not in the tree produced by the parser. For example, you can't write logic in the stylesheet that depends on whether an attribute in the XML was written in single quotes or double quotes. Perhaps less obviously, and on occasions more frustratingly:

❑ You can't tell what order the attributes in a start tag were written in.

❑ You can't discover if the source document contained entities or character references: these will all have been expanded by the time the XSLT processor sees them. Whether the user originally wrote © or © makes no difference; by the time the XSLT processor sees it, the distinction has disappeared.

❑ You can't tell whether the user wrote an empty element as <a></a> or as <a/>.

In all these cases the distinctions are simply different ways of expressing the same information, so you shouldn't need to know which way the input was written. The only frustration is that if you want the output to be physically the same as the input, there is no way of achieving this, which can be irritating if the output XML is to be further edited.

Equally, on the output side, you can't control these details. You can't tell the serializer to write the attributes in a particular order, or to use © in preference to ©, or to generate empty elements as <a></a> rather than <a/>. These constructs are supposed to be equivalent, so you aren't supposed to care. XSLT is about transforming the information held in documents, not about transforming their lexical representation.

Actually, on the output side, the designers of the language were a little pragmatic, and provided a few language features that let you give hints to the serializer. However, they made it very clear that these are hints only, and no processor is obliged to take notice of them.

The fact that stylesheets are reading and writing trees has another important consequence: you read and write elements as a unit, rather than processing each tag separately. There is simply no way of writing a start tag without a matching end tag, because writing an element node to the tree is an atomic operation.

The tree structure used by XSLT is very similar to the DOM model but it has some important differences, which we'll see later. Many products do in fact use a DOM representation, because this allows standard parsers and serializers to be used, but there are inefficiencies in this approach, so other products have chosen to represent the XSLT tree structure more directly. It's important to understand this structure so we'll describe it in detail later.

XSLT as a Programming Language

You can teach a simple subset of XSLT to HTML authors with no programming knowledge, by pretending that it's just a way of writing the HTML you want to generate with some simple extra tags to insert variable data from an input file. But XSLT is actually much more powerful than this, and as this book is written for programming professionals, it makes more sense to treat XSLT as a programming language and to compare and contrast it with other languages you may have used in the past. In this section, we'll draw out a few of its more striking features.

XML Syntax

Firstly, an XSLT stylesheet is an XML document. Instead of the braces and semicolons of most programming languages, it uses the angle brackets and tags of XML. Therefore, you can write things like this:

```
<xsl:if test="title='Introduction'">
    <b>SUMMARY</b>
</xsl:if>
```

In a conventional language, you might write something like this:

```
if (title='Introduction')
{
    write('<b>Introduction</b>');
}
```

There are a number of reasons for this. One is that you can write the output XML that you want to generate as part of the stylesheet, as with the SUMMARY in the example above. In fact, some stylesheets consist mainly of fixed output text with a few XSLT instructions mixed in. Another reason is that you can easily write stylesheets that transform other stylesheets, which sounds like a strange thing to do but can actually be extremely useful. Pragmatically, it also means that stylesheets are very consistent with XML in things such as handling of character encodings, name syntax, whitespace, and the like.

The downside is that it's verbose. Typing out hundreds of angle brackets is no-one's idea of fun. Some people like to use specialized editors to make the job easier; but when it comes down to it, typing effort has very little to do with the true ease of use of a language.

Rule-based

There's a strong tradition in text processing languages, like Perl and awk, of expressing the processing you want to do as a set of rules: when the input matches a particular pattern, the rule defines the processing to be performed. XSLT follows this tradition, but extends it to the processing of a hierarchy rather than a sequential text file.

In XSLT the rules are called template rules, and are written in the form of <xsl:template> elements in the stylesheet. Each rule has a match pattern that defines what kind of nodes in the tree it applies to, and a template body that defines what to do when the rule is fired. The template body can consist of a mixture of result nodes to be copied directly to the output tree, and XSLT instructions that can do things such as reading data from the current position in the source tree, or writing calculated results to the output tree. So a simple template rule might say:

```
<xsl:template match="price">
    <b>$<xsl:value-of select="format-number(., '#0.00')" /></b>
</xsl:template>
```

The pattern here is "price", which matches any <price> element; the action is to output the value of the <price> element, formatted as a number with two decimal digits, preceded by a $ sign and enclosed in a <b> element.

One particularly important XSLT instruction is <xsl:apply-templates>, which tells the processor where to go next; whereas in a text processing language, each line can be processed in sequence, with a hierarchy it is possible to process nodes in any order. Normally, however, the template rule for an element will contain an <xsl:apply-templates> instruction to process its children. When it does this, each of the children will be processed by finding the template rule in the stylesheet that matches that node.

Here is an example of a collection of template rules that process <item> elements within <record> elements. The rule for <record> elements outputs a <tr> element, and within it outputs the results of finding and applying the appropriate rule for each of its child elements. There are two template rules for <item> elements depending on whether the element has any text content or not. If it has, it outputs a <td> element containing the string value of the element; otherwise, it outputs a <td> element containing a non-breaking space character (which is familiar to HTML authors as the value of the   entity reference, but is written here as a numeric Unicode character reference).

```
<xsl:template match="record">
   <tr><xsl:apply-templates /></tr>
</xsl:template>

<xsl:template match="item[.!='']">
   <td><xsl:value-of select="." /></td>
</xsl:template>

<xsl:template match="item[.='']">
   <td> </td>
</xsl:template>
```

XPath Queries

When you write an XSLT stylesheet you are actually using two different languages. You use XSLT itself to describe the logic of the transformation process, and within it, you use embedded XPath expressions or queries to fetch the data you need from the source document. It's comparable to using Visual Basic with SQL.

Although its role is similar, the syntax of XPath is not at all like SQL. This is because it's designed to process hierarchic data (trees) rather than tables. A lot of the syntax in SQL is there to handle relationships or joins between different tables. In a hierarchic XML document or tree, most of the relationships are implicit in the hierarchy, so the syntax of XPath has been designed to make it easy to reference data by its position in the hierarchy. In fact, the most obvious resemblance is to the way filenames are written to access files in a hierarchic filestore.

It's easiest to show this by some example XPath expressions:

Expression	Meaning
/invoice/billing-address/postcode	Starting at the root of the document, get the invoice element, then within that the billing-address element, then within that the postcode element.

Expression	Meaning
`../@title`	Starting at the current node, get the title attribute of this node's parent element.
`/book/chapter[3]/section[2]/para[1]`	Get the first `<para>` element, that is a child of the second `<section>` element, that is a child of the third `<chapter>` element, which is itself, a child of the root of the tree.

Functional Programming

Most programming languages are sequential in nature: the program carries out a sequence of instructions, modified by testing conditions and looping. They can create variables to hold values, and later in their execution, they can access the variables to retrieve results that were calculated earlier.

At one level XSLT looks quite similar. It has constructs like `<xsl:if>` to test conditions and `<xsl:for-each>` to do looping, and you can write a sequence of instructions, and the stylesheet then looks very much like a conventional sequential program. However, below the surface, it's not like that at all. XSLT is carefully designed so that the instructions can be executed in any order. The innocuous `<xsl:for-each>` instruction, for example, may look like a loop that processes a list of nodes, one at a time, in a particular order, but it's carefully designed so that the processing of each node doesn't depend at all on how the previous node was handled, which means it's actually possible to do them in any order or even in parallel.

To achieve this, the theory underlying XSLT is that of functional programming, more often found in rather academic languages such as Lisp and Scheme. The idea is that each piece of the output is defined as a function of a particular piece of the input. These functions are all independent of each other, so they can be done in any order: in theory at least this means that if only a small piece of the input changes, you can work out how to change the output without executing the whole stylesheet again from scratch. Another benefit of this approach is that it's much easier to stop a stylesheet being stuck in an infinite loop.

What this means in practice is that although a stylesheet may look superficially like a sequential program, it has no working storage. As we'll see, XSLT does have variables, but they aren't like the variables in sequential programming languages, because they are effectively "write-once". You can't update variables, so you can't use them to accumulate a running total and read them later, or count how many times you've been round a loop, because that would only work if things were done in a particular order. For simple stylesheets you probably won't notice the difference, but for more complex transformations you'll find you need to get used to a rather different style of programming. It may be frustrating at first, but it's worth persevering, because once you have learnt to think in functional programming terms, you'll find that it's a very elegant and concise way of expressing solutions to transformation problems.

Data Types

Many of the different properties of different programming languages are determined by their type system. In XSLT, the type system is defined largely by the query language, XPath.

The characteristic data type of XPath is the node-set. Just as SQL queries return a set of table rows, XPath queries like those shown in the previous section return a set of nodes from the input tree. Even if a query returns only a single node, it is always treated as a node-set that just happens to have only one member. A node-set behaves like a mathematical set: there's no intrinsic order to the nodes in the set, and there can't be any duplicates (the same node can't appear more than once).

Many instructions that process node-sets actually handle the nodes in **document order**. This is, essentially, the order in which the nodes appeared in the original XML document. For example, an element appears in document order before its children, and its children appear before the next sibling of their parent element. Document order in some cases isn't fully defined, for example there is no guarantee what the order of the attributes for a particular element will be. The fact that there is a natural ordering to nodes doesn't prevent node-sets being unordered sets, any more than the natural ordering of numbers prevents {1,2,3,5,11} being a pure set.

XPath queries aren't the only data type that node-sets can return; they can also return character strings, numbers, or Boolean values. For example, you can ask for the name of a node (a character string), the number of children it has (a number), or whether it has any attributes (a Boolean):

❑ Character strings in XPath follow the same rules as character strings in XML. They can be of any length (from zero upwards), and the characters they may contain are the Unicode characters that you can use in an XML document.

❑ Numbers in XPath are in general floating point numbers: of course, this includes integers. Integers will usually behave the way you expect, with the possible exception of rounding errors; for example, percentages may not add up to exactly 100. The floating-point arithmetic follows the same rules as Java and JavaScript (specifically, the rules defined in IEEE 754). You don't need to understand these rules in detail, except to know that there is a special value NaN (not a number), which you will get when you try to convert a non-numeric character string (such as "Unknown") to a number. NaN behaves very much like Null in SQL. If you do almost any operation on NaN, the result is NaN. For example, totalling a set of values in which one is the character string "Unknown" will return a total of NaN.

❑ Booleans are just the two values True and False. XPath doesn't have three-valued logic as in SQL – absent values in the source data are represented not by a special Null value, but by an empty node-set. Like SQL Nulls, empty node-sets sometimes give counter-intuitive results. For example, an empty node-set is not equal to itself.

An XSLT stylesheet can declare variables. These variables can hold the result of any XPath query, that is, a node-set, a string, a number, or a Boolean. A variable can also hold a temporary tree constructed by the stylesheet itself: for most purposes, this variable is equivalent to a node-set containing a single node, namely the root of this tree. These trees are referred to as **result tree fragments**.

As we mentioned earlier, XSLT variables are "write-once" variables; they are just names for values. Some people have suggested they should really be called constants, but that wouldn't be accurate, since variables can hold different values on different occasions. For example, within a template rule that is processing a <chapter> element, you might set a variable to hold the number of paragraphs in the chapter. The variable will have a different value for each chapter that you process, but for a given chapter, its value will not change during the course of processing.

Here are some examples of variables of each kind:

Variable declaration	Explanation
`<xsl:variable name="x" select="//item" />`	The value is a node-set containing all the `<item>` elements in the source document.
`<xsl:variable name="y" select="count(@*)" />`	The value is a number containing the number of attributes of the current node. "`@*`" is an XPath expression that selects all the attributes.
`<xsl:variable name="z" select="@type='T'" />`	The value is True if the current node has a type attribute whose value is 'T', False if it does not.

`<xsl:variable name="tree">`
  `<table>`
  `<tr>`
  `<td>`
    `<img src="button1.gif"/>`
  `</td>`
  `<td>`
    `<img src="button2.gif"/>`
  `</td>`
  `</tr>`
  `</table>`
`</xsl:variable>`
	The value is a tree (or result tree fragment) whose root contains the table structure as written.

Although values have different data types, the data types don't have to be declared in variable declarations. XSLT is therefore a dynamically typed language, like JavaScript.

In general, type conversions happen automatically when required, for example if you write `<xsl:value-of select="@name" />` then the node-set returned by the expression @name (it will contain zero or one attribute nodes) is converted automatically to a string. There are some situations where explicit conversions are useful, and these are provided by the XPath functions `boolean()`, `number()`, and `string()`, described later in this chapter.

The XPath Data Model

Understanding the XPath tree model is crucial to stylesheet programming.

The tree structure used in XSLT and XPath is similar in many ways to the DOM, but there are some important differences. For example, in the DOM, every node has a nodeValue property, while in XPath every node has a string-value property. But the nodeValue of an element node in the DOM is null, while in XSLT and XPath, the `string-value` property of an element is the concatenation of all its descendant text nodes.

The properties available for every type of node in an XSLT tree are the same. Each node has a name and a string-value. You can also ask for the node's children, its parent, its attributes, and its namespaces. Where the property is inapplicable (for example comments don't have names) you can still ask for the information, you'll just get an empty result.

There are seven types of node in an XSLT tree:

Node type	Usage
Root	Represents the root of the tree, corresponding to the Document node in the DOM. This is not the same as the "document element" (the outermost element in the tree). In fact, an XSLT tree does not always represent a well-formed document, so the root may contain several element nodes as well as text nodes. In a well-formed document, the outermost element is represented by an element node, which will be a child of the root node.
	The root node's properties are as follows:
	❑ Its name is an empty string
	❑ Its string-value is the concatenation of all the text nodes in the document
	❑ Its parent is always Null
	❑ Its children may be any collection of elements, text nodes, processing instructions, and comments
	❑ It has no namespaces or attributes
Element	Each element node corresponds to an element in the source document: that is, either to a matching start tag and end tag, or to an empty element tag such as `<A/>`.
	An element node's properties are as follows:
	❑ Its name is derived from the tag used in the source document, expanded using the namespace declarations in force for the element
	❑ Its string-value is the concatenation of all the text between the start and end tags
	❑ Its parent is either another element, or if it is the outermost element, it parent is the root node
	❑ Its children may be any collection of elements, text nodes, processing instructions, and comments
	❑ Its attributes are the attributes written in the element's start tag, plus any attributes given default values in the DTD, but excluding any `xmlns` attributes that serve as namespace declarations
	❑ Its namespaces are all the namespace declarations in force for the element, whether they are defined on this element itself or on an outer element

Node type	Usage
Attribute	❑ There will be an attribute node for each attribute explicitly present in an element tag in the source document, or derived from a default value in the DTD. However, the xmlns attributes used as namespace declarations are not represented as attribute nodes in the tree. An attribute will always have a name, and its string-value will be the value given to the attribute in the source XML. An attribute node's properties are as follows: ❑ Its name is derived from the attribute name used in the source document, expanded using the namespace declarations in force for the containing element ❑ Its string-value is the attribute value ❑ Its parent is the containing element (even though the attribute is not considered to be a child of this parent) ❑ An attribute node has no children, attributes, or namespaces
Text	Text nodes are used to represent the textual (PCDATA) content of the document. Adjacent text nodes are always merged, so the tree can never contain two text nodes next to each other. It is possible, however, for two text nodes to be separated only by a comment. The properties of a text node are as follows: ❑ Its name is Null ❑ Its string-value is the text content, after expanding all character references, entity references, and CDATA sections ❑ Its parent is the containing element (or in the case of a result tree fragment, a text node can also be a child of the root node) ❑ A text node has no children, attributes, or namespaces Any entity references, character references, and CDATA sections occurring within the source XML document are expanded by the XML parser, and the XSLT tree contains no trace of them. All that is present on the tree is the string of characters that these constructs represent. Text nodes that consist only of whitespace can be treated specially: the XSLT stylesheet can indicate that such nodes should be removed from the tree. By default, however, whitespace that appears between elements in the source document will be present as text nodes on the tree and may affect operations such as numbering of nodes.

Table Continued on Following Page

Node type	Usage
Processing Instruction	Processing-instruction nodes on the tree represent processing instructions in the XML source document. Processing instructions in XML are written as `<?target data?>`, where the target is a simple name and the data is everything that follows. The properties of a processing-instruction node are: ❑ Its name is the target part of the source instruction ❑ Its string-value is the data part ❑ Its parent is the containing node, always either an element node or the root ❑ It has no children, attributes, or namespaces Note that the XML declaration at the start of a document, for example `<?xml version="1.0"?>`, looks like a processing instruction, but technically it isn't one, so it doesn't appear on the XPath tree.
Comment	Comment nodes on the tree represent comments in the source XML. The properties of a comment node are: ❑ Its name is Null ❑ Its string-value is the text of the comment ❑ Its parent is the containing node, always either an element node or the root ❑ It has no children, attributes, or namespaces
Namespace	Namespace declarations are increasingly used in XML processing, however you will very rarely need to make explicit reference to namespace nodes in the XPath tree, because the namespace URI that applies to a particular element or attribute is automatically incorporated in the name of that node. Namespace nodes are included in the model for completeness: for example, they allow you to find out about namespace declarations that are never referred to in an element or attribute name. An element has one namespace node for every namespace that is in scope for that element, whether it was declared on the element itself or on some containing element. The properties of a namespace node are: ❑ Its name is the namespace prefix ❑ Its string-value is the namespace URI ❑ Its parent is the containing element ❑ It has no children, attributes, or namespaces

Names and Namespaces

Namespaces play an important role in XPath and XSLT processing, so it's worth understanding how they work. Unlike the base XML standards and DOM, where namespaces were bolted on as an afterthought, they are integral to XPath and XSLT.

In the source XML, an element or attribute name is written with two components: the namespace prefix and the local name. Together these constitute the qualified name or QName. For example in the QName `fo:block`, the prefix is `fo` and the local name is `block`. If the name is written without a prefix, the prefix is taken as an empty string.

When a prefix is used, the XML document must contain a namespace declaration for that prefix. The namespace declaration defines a namespace URI corresponding to the prefix. For example, if the document contains an `<fo:block>` element, then either on that element, or on some containing element, it will contain a namespace declaration in the form `xmlns:fo="http://www.w3.org/XSL/"`. The value `"http://www.w3.org/XSL/"` is the namespace URI, and it is intended to uniquely distinguish `<block>` elements defined in one document type or schema from `<block>` elements defined in any other.

The namespace URI is derived by finding the appropriate namespace declaration for any prefix used in the QName. In comparing two names, it is the local name and the namespace URI that must match; the prefix is irrelevant. The combination of local name and namespace URI is known as the expanded name of the node. In the XPath tree model, the name of a node is its expanded name (namespace URI plus local name). Namespace prefixes will usually be retained intact, but the system is allowed to change them if it wants, so long as the namespace URIs are preserved.

Where a qualified name includes no namespace prefix, the XML rules for forming the expanded name are slightly different for element names and for attribute names. For elements, the namespace URI will be the default namespace URI, obtained by looking for a namespace declaration of the form «xmlns="..."». For attributes, the namespace URI will be the empty string. Consider the example shown below:

```
<template match="para" xmlns="http://www.w3.org/1999/XSL/Transform"/>
```

Here the expanded name of the element has local name `"template"` and namespace URI `"http://www.w3.org/1999/XSL/Transform"`. However, the expanded name of the attribute has local name `"match"` and a null namespace URI. The default namespace URI affects the element name, but not the attribute name.

XPath expressions frequently need to select nodes in the source document by name. The name as written in the XPath expression will also be a qualified name, which needs to be turned into an expanded name so that it can be compared with names in the source document. This is done using the namespace declarations in the stylesheet, specifically those that are in scope where the relevant XPath expression is written.

If a name in an XPath expression uses no namespace prefix, the expanded name is formed using the same rule as for attribute names: the namespace URI will be Null.

In the example above, which might be found in an XSLT stylesheet, "para" is the name of an element type that this template rule is designed to match. Because para is written without a namespace prefix, it will only match elements whose expanded name has a local name of "para", and a null namespace URI. The default namespace URI does not affect the name written within the match pattern. If you wanted to match elements with a local name of "para" and a namespace URI of "urn:some-namespace" you would have to assign an explicit prefix to this namespace in the stylesheet, for example:

```
<template match="my:para"
    xmlns="http://www.w3.org/1999/XSL/Transform"
    xmlns:my="urn:some-namespace" />
```

XSLT uses many names to identify things other than XML elements and attributes; for example, it uses names for templates, variables, modes, keys, decimal formats, attribute sets, and system properties. All these names follow the same conventions as XML attribute names. They are written as qualified names; any namespace prefix they use must be declared in a namespace declaration; the equivalence of two names depends on the namespace URI, not the prefix; and if there is no prefix, the namespace URI is Null (the default namespace declaration is not used).

Controlling namespace declarations in the output document can sometimes prove troublesome. In general, a namespace declaration will automatically be added to the output document whenever it is needed, because the output document uses a prefixed element or attribute name. Sometimes it may contain namespace declarations that are surplus to requirements. These don't usually cause a problem, although they might do so if you want the result document to be valid against a DTD. In such cases you can sometimes get rid of them by using the attribute exclude-result-prefixes on the <xsl:stylesheet> element.

In very rare cases, you may want to find out what namespace declarations are present in the source document (even if they aren't used). This is the only situation in which you need to explicitly find the namespace nodes in the tree, which you can do using an XPath query that follows the namespace axis.

XPath Expressions

To write an XSLT stylesheet you'll need to write XPath expressions. At the risk of finding you impatient to see a stylesheet in action, we'll talk about XPath expressions first, and then describe the way they are used by XSLT in a stylesheet. Although XPath was designed primarily for use within an XSLT context, it was separated into its own specification because it was seen as being useful in its own right, and in fact, it's increasingly common to see XPath being used as a freestanding query language independently of XSLT.

In this section, we will summarize the rules for writing XPath expressions. We can't hope to give the full syntax, let alone all the rules for how the expressions are evaluated, because of the limited scope of the book, but we'll try to cover all the common cases and also warn you of some of the pitfalls.

Context

The result of an XPath expression may depend on the context in which it is used. The main aspects of this context are the context node, the context size, and the context position. The context node is the node on the source tree for which the expression is being evaluated. The context position is the position of that node in the list of nodes currently being processed, and the context size is the number of nodes in that list. The context node can be accessed directly using the expression, "." (period), while the context position and context size are accessible using the functions position() and last().

Other aspects of the context of an XPath expression, obtained from the containing XSLT stylesheet, include the values of variables, the definitions of keys and decimal formats, the current node being processed by the stylesheet (usually the same as the context node, but different within an XPath predicate), the Base URI of the stylesheet, and the namespace declarations in force.

Primaries

The basic building blocks of an XPath expression are called primaries. There are five of them, listed in the table below:

Construct	Meaning	Examples
String literal	A string constant, written between single or double quotes (these must be different from the quotes used around the containing XML attribute).	`'London'` `"Paris"`

Number	A numeric constant, written in decimal notation. Although XPath numbers are floating point, you can't use scientific notation.	`12`
		`0.0001`
		`5000000`

Variable Reference	A reference to a variable defined elsewhere in the stylesheet. This is always written with a preceding $ sign.	`$x` `$my:variable-name`

Function call	A call on either a system-supplied function, or an extension function provided by the vendor or the user, together with its arguments if any. Each argument is an XPath expression in its own right.	`position()`
		`contains($x, ';')`
		`ms:extension`
		`('Bill', 'Gates')`

Parenthesized expression	An XPath expression contained in parentheses. Brackets may be used to control operator precedence as in other languages.	`3 * ($x + 1)` `(//item)[1]`

Operators

Many of the operators used in XPath will be familiar, but some are more unusual. The table below lists the operators in order of precedence: those that come first in the table are evaluated before those that come lower down.

Operator	Meaning
A [B]	A filter expression. The first operand (A) must be a node-set. The second operand (B), known as the predicate, is an expression that is evaluated once for each node in the node-set, with that node as the context node. The result of the expression is a node-set containing those nodes from A where the predicate succeeds. If the predicate is a number, it succeeds if it equals the position of the node in the node-set, counting from one. So `$para[1]` selects the first node in the `$para` node-set. If it is not a number, then it succeeds if the value, after converting to a Boolean using the rules of the `boolean()` function, is True. So `$para[@name]` selects all nodes in the `$para` node-set that have a `name` attribute.

Table continued on following page

Operator	Meaning
A / B A // B	A location path. Location paths are discussed in detail below. The first operand, A, defines a starting node or node-set; the second, B, describes a step or navigation route from the starting node to other nodes in the tree.
A | B	A union expression. Both operands must be node-sets. The result contains all nodes that are present in either A or B, with duplicates eliminated.
– A	Unary minus. The value of A is converted if necessary to a number (using the number() function) and the sign is changed.
A * B A div B A mod B	Multiply, divide, and modulus (remainder after division). Both arguments are converted to numbers using the number() function, and the result is a floating-point number. These operators are often useful in formatting tables: for example `<xsl:if test="position() mod 2 = 1">` will be True for the odd-numbered rows in a table, and False for the others.
A + B A – B	Addition and subtraction. Both arguments are converted to numbers using the number() function. Because hyphens can be included in names, there must be a space or other punctuation before a minus sign.
A > B A >= B A < B A <= B	Tests whether one operand is numerically greater or smaller than the other one. When the XPath expression is written in a stylesheet, remember to use XML entities: < for <, > for >. Special rules apply when either or both operands are node-sets: see the section on *Comparing Node-sets* below. If the operands are strings or Booleans, they are converted to numbers using the rules of the number() function. If either operand cannot be converted to a number, the result will always be False.
A = B A != B	Tests whether the two operands are equal or not equal. Special rules apply when either or both operands are node-sets: see the section on *Comparing Node-sets* below. In other cases, if one operand is a Boolean, the other is converted to a Boolean; otherwise if one is a number, the other is converted to a number; otherwise they are compared as strings. Comparison of strings is case-sensitive: 'Paris' is not equal to 'PARIS'.
A and B	Boolean AND. Converts both arguments to Booleans, and returns True if both are True.
A or B	Boolean OR. Converts both arguments to Booleans, and returns True if either is True.

Comparing Node-sets

When you use the comparison operators =, !=, <, >, <=, or >=, then if either or both of the operands is a node-set, the comparison is made with every member of the node-set, and returns True if any of them succeeds. For example, the expression //@secure='yes' will return True if there is an attribute anywhere in the document with the name secure and the value "yes". Similarly, //@secure!='yes' will return True if there is an attribute anywhere in the document with the name secure and a value other than "yes".

If you compare two node-sets, then every possible pair of nodes is compared. For example, `//author=//artist` returns True if there is at least one `<author>` element in the document that has the same string-value as some `<artist>` element in the document. In relational terms, it returns True if the join of the two sets is not empty. (Depending how clever the processor is at optimizing, this could of course be a very expensive query to run on a large document.)

This rule has consequences that may not be intuitive:

❑ Comparing anything with an empty node-set (even another empty node-set) always returns False, regardless of the comparison operators you use. The only exception is when you compare an empty node-set with the Boolean value False: this returns True.

❑ When either A or B is a node-set, testing `A!=B` doesn't give the same result as testing `not(A=B)`. Usually you want the latter.

❑ The expression: `.=/`, doesn't test whether the context node is the root, it tests whether the string-value of the context node is the same as the string-value of the root node. This is likely to be True, for example, if the context node is the outermost element in the document. To compare nodes for identity, use the `generate-id()` function.

Location Paths

Location paths are the cornerstones of the XPath expression language, the construct that gave the language its name.

Because location paths are frequently used, the language provides many shorthand abbreviations for common cases. It's useful to know when you're using a shorthand form, so I'll present the full verbose syntax first, then show the abbreviations.

I'll start with some examples, and then describe the rules.

Example location paths

Some examples are given in the table below:

Location path	Meaning
`para`	Select the `<para>` elements that are children of the context node. Short for `./child::para`.
`@title`	Select the `title` attribute of the current node (if it has one). Short for `./attribute::title`.
`../heading`	Select the `<heading>` elements that are children of the parent of the context node. Short for `./parent::node()/child::heading`.
`//item`	Select all the `<item>` elements in the document. Short for `/descendant-or-self::node()/item`.

Table continued on following page

Location path	Meaning
`section[1]/clause[2]`	Select the second `<clause>` child element of the first `<section>` child element of the context node.
`heading [starts-with(title, 'A')]`	Select all the `<heading>` child elements of the context node that have a `<title>` child element whose string-value starts with the character 'A'.

Syntax rules for location paths

A full location path takes one of the following forms:

Format	Meaning
`/`	Selects the root node.
`/ step`	Selects nodes that can be reached from the root by taking the specified step. Steps are defined in the next section.
	For example, `/comment()` selects any top-level comment nodes, that is, comments that are not contained in any element.
`E / step`	Selects nodes that can be reached from nodes in `E` by taking the specified step. `E` can be any expression that returns a node-set; it can be another location path, for example (but not the root expression `/`), or a variable reference, or a call on a function such as `document()`, `id()`, or `key()`, or a union expression `(A|B)` in parentheses.
	For example, `../@title` selects the `title` attribute of the parent node.
`step`	Selects nodes that can be reached from the context node by taking the specified step. For example, `descendant::figure` selects all `<figure>` elements that are descendants of the context node.

Steps

In these constructs, a step defines a route through the tree representation of the source document. A step has three components:

- ❑ An axis, which defines the relationship of the required nodes to the starting nodes; for example, whether child nodes, following sibling nodes, or ancestor nodes are required. If no axis is specified explicitly, the child axis is assumed.

- ❑ A node test, which defines two things: the type of nodes that are to be selected, for example elements, text nodes, or comments, and the names of the nodes to be selected. It is also possible to select nodes regardless of their type. There are three kinds of name test: a full name test, which selects only nodes with that name; a namespace test, which selects all nodes in a particular namespace, and an any-name test, which selects nodes regardless of their name. The node-test is always present in some form.

- ❑ Zero or more predicates, expressions that further restrict the set of nodes selected by the step. If no predicates are specified, all nodes on the axis that satisfy the node test will be selected.

The full syntax for a step is:

```
axis-name «::» node-test ( «[» predicate «]» )*
```

We'll look separately at the axis-name, the node-test, and the predicates, and then describe the various ways in which the full syntax can be abbreviated.

Axis Names

XPath defines the following axes that you can use to navigate the tree structure.

Axis name	Contents
ancestor	Contains the parent of the starting node, its grandparent, and so on up to the root.
ancestor-or-self	Contains the node itself plus all its ancestors.
attribute	For any node except an element, this axis is empty. For an element, it contains the attributes of the element, including any that were given default values in the DTD. Namespace declarations are not treated as attributes.
child	Contains the children of the starting node. The only nodes that have children are the root and element nodes; in all other cases, this axis is empty. The children of an element include all the nodes directly contained within the element: they don't include attributes or namespaces.
descendant	Contains the children of the starting node, their children, and so on, recursively.
descendant-or-self	Contains the starting node itself, plus all its descendants.
following	Contains all nodes in the document that follow the starting node in document order, other than its own descendants. In source XML terms, this means all nodes that begin after the end tag of the starting element.
following-sibling	Contains all the nodes that are children of the same parent as the starting node, and follow it in document order.
namespace	Contains nodes representing all the namespace declarations that are in scope for an element. Nodes other than elements have no namespace nodes.
parent	Contains the parent of the starting element. This axis is empty if the starting element is the root.
preceding	Contains all nodes in the document that precede the starting node in document order, other than its own ancestors. In source XML terms, this means all nodes that end before the start tag of the starting element.
preceding-sibling	Contains all nodes that are children of the same parent as the starting node, and that precede it in document order.
self	Contains the starting node itself.

Node-tests

The node-test within a step appears after the «::», and is used to select the type of nodes you are interested in, and to place restrictions on their names. It must be one of the following:

QName	A name optionally qualified with a namespace prefix, for example "para" or "fo:block". Selects nodes with this name that are of the principal node type for the axis. For the attribute axis, the principal nodes are attributes; for the namespace axis, they are namespace nodes; and in all other cases, they are elements.
prefix:*	Selects nodes of the principal node type for the axis, which belong to the namespace defined by the given prefix.
*	Selects all nodes of the principal node type for the axis.
node()	Selects all nodes, regardless of their name and type.
text()	Selects all text nodes.
comment()	Selects all comment nodes.
processing-instruction()	Selects all processing instruction nodes.
processing-instruction('name')	Selects all processing instructions with the given name. Note that the name must be in quotes.

Predicates

A step can optionally include a list of predicates, which define further conditions that the nodes must satisfy if they are to be selected. Each predicate is an XPath expression it its own right, written in square brackets. Each predicate acts as a filter on the node-set, the node-set is passed through each filter in turn, and only those nodes that satisfy all the predicates are selected.

For example the predicate [@title='Introduction'] selects a node only if it has a title attribute whose value is Introduction; the predicate [position() != 1] selects a node only if it is not the first node in the node-set passed through from any previous filter.

The predicate is evaluated for each node in turn. The context for evaluating the predicate is different from the context of the containing expression: specifically, the context node is the node being tested, the context size is the number of nodes left over from the previous filtering operation, and the context position is the position of the context node in this list of remaining nodes. So the predicate [position()=last()] will be True only if the node being tested is the last one in the list.

If the axis is a forwards axis, then position() gives the position of each node within the node-set considered in document order; if it is a reverse axis, then the nodes are taken in reverse document order. The only reverse axes are ancestor, ancestor-or-self, preceding, and preceding-sibling.

A predicate can be either numeric or Boolean. If the value is a number N, this is interpreted as a shorthand for the expression position() = N. So following-sibling::*[1] selects the immediately following sibling element (because this is a forwards axis) while preceding-sibling::*[1] selects the immediately preceding sibling element (this is a reverse axis, so [1] means the last element in document order).

The syntax for predicates within a step is extremely similar to the syntax for predicates within a filter expression, and the two can easily be confused. In the following examples, the predicate is part of a step:

```
item[1]
preceding-sibling::*[@type='D'][1]
```

In the following example, the predicate is part of a filter expression:

```
$item[1]
(preceding-sibling::*)[@type='D'][1]
```

The only real difference is that in a filter expression, the nodes are always considered in forwards document order, while in a step, they are taken in axis order. This means that in the second example above, the last sibling having `@type='D'` is taken, whereas in the fourth example, the first sibling with this attribute is used. It only makes a difference if the predicate is numeric, or uses the `position()` function.

Abbreviations

We've already been using some shortcut notations for location paths, but it's time to describe them more formally.

❑ The symbol . (period) is an abbreviation for the step `self::node()`. It refers to the context node itself. You can't follow it with any predicates; if you want to test whether the context node is a `<para>` element, write `<xsl:if test="self::para">`.

❑ The symbol .. is short for the step `parent::node()`. The same considerations apply.

❑ The child axis is the default axis, so you can always omit `child::` from a step. For example, `/section/item` is short for `/child::section/child::item`.

❑ The symbol @ can be used to indicate the attribute axis, it is short for `attribute::`. So `@title` means the same as `attribute::title`.

❑ The operator // is short for `/descendant-or-self::node()/`, and is a useful short-cut when searching for all the descendants of a node. For example `//item` retrieves all the `<item>` elements in the document. Take care when using positional predicates: `//item[1]` does not select the first `<item>` in the document (for that, use `(//item)[1]`, but rather it selects every `<item>` element that is the first child of its parent element. This is because the predicate only applies to the final step in the expanded location path, which implicitly uses the child axis.

XPath Functions

We've used a number of XPath functions in examples: it's time now to give a complete list. Most of these functions are defined in the XPath specification itself. A few of them are added in the XSLT specification, which means that these functions are only available when you use XPath in the context of an XSLT stylesheet.

Vendors are allowed to add more functions of their own, or to provide mechanisms for users to implement their own functions, typically in an external language such as Java or JavaScript. These external functions will always use a namespace prefix to distinguish them from the built-in functions. For details of these extensions, see the vendor's documentation.

In the descriptions of the functions, I often say that a particular argument should be a string, or a number, or a Boolean. In nearly all cases this means that you can supply a value of any type, and it will be automatically converted to the type required: the conversion rules are those described under the functions `boolean()`, `number()`, and `string()`, which can be called directly if want to make the conversion explicit.

Because of space limitations, these descriptions of the functions are very brief. If you want a full explanation of the behavior, or more examples of how to make use of each function, you'll find it in the Wrox Press book *XSLT Programmer's Reference*.

boolean(arg1)

The `boolean()` function converts its argument to a Boolean value.

The argument may be of any data type. The rules for conversion are as follows:

Argument data type	Conversion rules
Boolean	No conversion
Number	0 is False, anything else is True
String	A zero length string is False, anything else is True
Node-set	An empty node-set is False, anything else is True
Tree	Always True

ceiling(arg1)

The argument `arg1` is a number. The `ceiling()` function returns the smallest integer that is greater than or equal to the numeric value of `arg1`. For example, `ceiling(1.2)` returns 2.

concat(arg1, arg2, ...)

The `concat()` function takes two or more arguments. Each of the arguments is converted to a string, and the resulting strings are concatenated.

contains(arg1, arg2)

The `contains()` function tests whether `arg1` contains `arg2` as a substring (in which case True is returned, otherwise False). Both arguments are strings. Like all other string comparisons in XPath, this is case-sensitive: `contains('Paris', 'A')` is False.

count(arg1)

The `count()` function takes a node-set as its argument, and returns the number of nodes present in the node-set. The argument must be a node-set. (Avoid using `count()` to test if a node-set is empty: you can do this more efficiently by converting the node-set to a Boolean, either explicitly using the `boolean()` function, or implicitly by using the node-set in a context where a Boolean is expected, such as a predicate.)

current()

The current() function has no arguments, and it returns a node-set containing a single node, the current node. This is the node currently being processed by the most recent <xsl:for-each> or <xsl:apply-templates> instruction. Usually this will be the same as the context node, which is referenced simply as ".". – but within a predicate the two are generally different. This allows you to write, for example:

```
//item[@code=current()/@code]
```

to find all <item> elements with the same code as the current element.

This is an XSLT function: it can only be used in XPath expressions contained in an XSLT stylesheet.

document(arg1 [, arg2])

The document() function finds an external XML document by resolving a URI reference, and returns its root node.

In the most common usage, arg1 is a string and arg2 is omitted. For example document("lookup.xml") finds the file called lookup.xml in the same directory as the stylesheet, parses it, and returns a node-set containing a single node, the root of the resulting tree. When arg1 is a string, relative URIs are resolved relative to the location of the stylesheet. As a special case, document("") retrieves the stylesheet itself.

It is also possible for arg1 to be a node-set. For example document(@href) finds an external XML file using the URI contained in the href attribute of the context node. Because the URI is now obtained from the source document, any relative URI is resolved relative to the source document rather than the stylesheet. If the node-set supplied as an argument contains more than one node, the document() function will load all the referenced documents and return a node-set containing the root node of each one.

The second argument is optional, and is rarely used. It can be used to provide a base URI other than the source document or the stylesheet URI for resolving relative URIs contained in the first argument.

A document loaded using the document() function can be processed by the stylesheet in just the same way as the original source document.

document() is an XSLT function: it can only be used in XPath expressions contained in an XSLT stylesheet.

element-available(arg1)

This function is used to test whether a particular XSLT instruction or extension element is available for use. Vendors are allowed to provide proprietary extensions to the XSLT language, provided they use their own namespace. Some vendors also allow users to implement their own extensions. This function allows the stylesheet author to test whether a particular vendor extension is available before using it.

The argument is a string containing the name of an element, and the result is True if the processor recognizes this as the name of an XSLT instruction or extension element.

This is an XSLT function: it can only be used in XPath expressions contained in an XSLT stylesheet.

631

false()

This function returns the Boolean value False. There are no arguments. This function is needed because XPath provides no literal constant for the value False.

floor(arg1)

The argument `arg1` is a number. The `floor()` function returns the largest integer that is less than or equal to the value of `arg1`. For example, `floor(3.6)` is 3.

format-number(arg1, arg2 [, arg3])

The `format-number()` function is used to convert numbers into formatted strings, usually for display to a human user, but also to meet the formatting requirements of legacy data standards, such as a need for a fixed number of leading zeroes. The format of the result is controlled using the `<xsl:decimal-format>` element. The first argument, `arg1`, is the number to be converted. The second argument is a string containing a format pattern that indicates the required output format.

The third argument `arg3` is optional, and if present it is a string containing the name of an `<xsl:decimal-format>` element in the stylesheet which defines the formatting rules. A summary of `<xsl:decimal-format>` is given on later in the section on *Top-Level elements*, but the details are outside the scope of this appendix. It allows you, for example, to change the characters that are used to represent a decimal point and the thousands separator. If `arg3` is omitted, the system looks for an unnamed `<xsl:decimal-format>` element in the stylesheet, and uses a built-in default otherwise.

The most commonly used characters in the format pattern are:

Character	Meaning
0	Always include a digit at this position, even if it isn't significant
#	Include a digit at this position if it is significant
. (period)	Marks the position of the decimal point
, (comma)	Marks the position of a thousands separator
%	Show the number as a percentage

For example, the following table shows how the number 1234.56 will be displayed using some different format patterns.

Format pattern	Output
#	1235
#.#	1234.6
#.#####	1234.56
#,###.000	1,234.560
0,000,000.###	0,001,234.56

`format-number()` is an XSLT function: it can only be used in XPath expressions contained in an XSLT stylesheet.

function-available(arg1)

This function is used to test whether a particular function is available for use. Vendors are allowed to add their own functions to those defined in the standard, provided they use their own namespace, and many vendors also allow users to define extension functions of their own. `function-available()` can be used to test the availability both of standard system functions and of extension functions. The argument is a string containing the function name. For an extension function this will always have a namespace prefix.

The result is the Boolean value True if the named function is available to be called, or False otherwise.

This is an XSLT function: it can only be used in XPath expressions contained in an XSLT stylesheet.

generate-id([arg1])

The `generate-id()` function generates a string, in the form of an XML name, that uniquely identifies a node. The argument is optional; if supplied, it must be a node-set. The ID returned is that of the node that comes first in the node-set, in document order. If the node-set is empty, `generate-id()` returns the empty string. If the argument is omitted, the context node is assumed.

Each XSLT processor will have its own way of generating unique identifiers for nodes. Different processors will return different answers. If you call the function twice for the same node during a particular transformation, you will get the same answer, but the next time you run the same stylesheet the answers may be different. The result is a made-up identifier; it bears no relationship to any ID values that might be present in the source document. The only constraints on the value are that the identifier must be syntactically a valid XML Name, and that it must be different for every node: this allows it to be used as the value of an ID attribute in the output document. This can be useful if you are generating an HTML document and want to generate internal cross references of the form `<a href="#n1234">`.

Testing `generate-id($A)` = `generate-id($B)` is a good way of testing whether $A and $B are the same node, assuming both node-sets contain singleton nodes. Don't use $A=$B to do this: that compares the string-values of the nodes, which might be the same even if $A and $B are different nodes.

`generate-id()` is an XSLT function: it can only be used in XPath expressions contained in an XSLT stylesheet.

id(arg1)

The `id()` function returns a node-set containing the node or nodes from the source document that have a given ID attribute. This relies on there being a DTD that identifies particular attributes as being of type ID. If the document contains such attributes, they must be unique (assuming the document is valid).

The argument may be a string, in which case it is treated as a whitespace-separated list of ID values. Alternatively, it may be a node-set, in which case the string-value of each node in the node-set is considered as a whitespace-separated list of ID values. All these ID values are assembled, and the result of the function is the set of elements having ID values that are present in this list. Of course, the most common case is that `arg1` is a single ID value, and the result will then contain exactly one node, if the ID value is present in the document or none if it is absent.

key(arg1, arg2)

The `key()` function is used to find the nodes with a given value for a named key. The first argument is a string containing the name of a key: this must match the name of an `<xsl:key>` element in the stylesheet, as described in the later section on *Top-Level elements*. The second argument supplies the key value or values you are looking for. It may be a string, containing a single key value, or a node-set, containing a set of key values, one in each node. The result of the function is a node-set containing all the nodes in the source document that have a key that is present in this list.

This is an XSLT function: it can only be used in XPath expressions contained in an XSLT stylesheet.

lang(arg1)

The `lang()` function tests whether the language of the context node, as defined by the `xml:lang` attribute, corresponds to the language supplied as an argument. `xml:lang` is one of the few attributes whose meaning is defined in the XML specification itself.

The argument is a string that identifies the required language, for example "en" for English, "de" for German, or "cy" for Welsh. The result is True if the context node is in a section of the source document that has an `xml:lang` attribute identifying the text as being in this language, and is False otherwise. The actual rules for testing the language code are quite complex (to cater for complexities such as US English versus British English) and are outside the scope of this appendix: you will find them in the Wrox Press book *XSLT Programmer's Reference*.

last()

The `last()` function returns the value of the context size. When processing a list of nodes, if the nodes are numbered from one, `last()` gives the number assigned to the last node in the list.

The test `position()=last()` is often used to test whether the context node is the last one in the list.

local-name([arg1])

The `local-name()` function returns the local part of the name of a node, that is, the part of the QName after the colon if there is one, or the full QName otherwise. For example, if the element name was written as `<para>` the local name will be `para`; if it was written as `<fo:block>` it will be `block`. If the argument is omitted, the function returns the local name of the context node. If the argument is supplied, it must be a node-set, and the result is the local-name of the first node in this node-set, taking them in document order. If the node-set is empty, the result is an empty string.

name([arg1])

The `name()` function returns a string containing the qualified name of a node, that is, the name as written in the XML source document, including any namespace prefix. If the argument is omitted, the function returns the name of the context node; if the argument is supplied, it must be a node-set, and the result is the name of the first node in this node-set, taking them in document order. If the node-set is empty, the result is an empty string.

The `name()` function is useful to display the name of a node. Try to avoid using it in a context such as `[name()='my:element']` to test the name of a node, because this won't work if a different namespace prefix has been used. Instead, test `[self::my:element]`, which actually tests the namespace URI corresponding to the prefix "my", rather than the prefix itself.

namespace-uri([arg1])

The namespace-uri() function returns a string that represents the URI of the namespace in the expanded name of a node. This will be a URI used in a namespace declaration, that is, the value of an xmlns or xmlns:* attribute.

If the argument is omitted, the function returns the namespace URI of the context node; if the argument is supplied, it must be a node-set, and the result is the namespace URI of the first node in this node-set, taking them in document order. If the node-set is empty, the result is an empty string.

normalize-space([arg1])

The argument arg1 is a string; if it is omitted, the string-value of the context node is used. The normalize-space() function removes leading and trailing whitespace from the argument, and replaces internal sequences of whitespace with a single space character. The result is a string.

not(arg1)

The argument arg1 is a Boolean. If the argument is True, the not() function returns False, and vice versa.

number([arg1])

The number() function converts its argument to a number. If the argument is omitted, it converts the string-value of the context node to a number.

The conversion rules are as follows:

Source data type	Conversion rules
Boolean	False converts to zero, True to one.
String	The string is parsed as a decimal number. Leading and trailing whitespace is allowed, as is a leading minus (or plus) sign. If the string cannot be parsed as a number, the result is NaN (Not a Number). The rules for converting a string to a number are essentially the same as the rules for writing a number in an XPath expression: conversion will fail, for example, if the number uses scientific notation or contains a leading "$" sign.
Node-set	Takes the string-value of the first node in the node-set, in document order, and converts this to a string using the rules for string-to-number conversion. If the node-set is empty, the result will be NaN.
Tree	Treats the tree as a node-set containing the root node of the tree, and converts this node-set to a number.

position()

The position() function returns the value of the context position. When processing a list of nodes, if the nodes are numbered from one, position() gives the number assigned to the current node in the list. There are no arguments.

round(arg1)

The argument arg1 is a number. The round() function returns the closest integer to the numeric value of arg1. For example, round(1.8) returns 2 and round(3.1) returns 3. A value midway between two integers will be rounded up.

starts-with(arg1, arg2)

The `starts-with()` function tests whether the string `arg1` starts with another string `arg2`. Both arguments are strings, and the result is a Boolean. Like all other string comparisons in XPath, this is case-sensitive: `starts-with('Paris', 'p')` is False.

string([arg1])

The `string()` function converts its argument to a string value. If the argument is omitted, it returns the string-value of the context node. This depends on the type of node: see the table in the earlier section on *The XPath Data Model* for more details.

The conversion rules are as follows:

Source data type	Conversion rules
Boolean	Returns the string "true" or "false".
Number	Returns a string representation of the number, to as many decimal places as are needed to capture its precision.
Node-set	If the node-set is empty, returns the empty string "". Otherwise, the function takes the first node in document order, and returns its string-value. Any other nodes in the node-set are ignored. The string-value of a node is defined for each type of node in the table under *The XPath Data Model* earlier in this appendix.
Tree	Returns the concatenation of all the text nodes in the tree.

string-length(arg1)

The argument `arg1` is a string. The `string-length()` function returns the number of characters in `arg1`.

substring(arg1, arg2 [, arg3])

The `substring()` function returns part of the string supplied as `arg1`, determined by character positions within the string.

`arg2` is a number giving the start position of the required sub-string. Character positions are counted from one. The supplied value is rounded, using the rules of the `round()` function. The function doesn't fail if the value is out of range; it will adjust the start position to either the beginning or end of the string.

`arg3` gives the number of characters to be included in the result string. The value is rounded in the same way as `arg2`. If `arg3` is omitted, you get all the characters up to the end of the string. If the value is outside the range, it is adjusted so you get either no characters, or all the characters up to the end of the string.

substring-after(arg1, arg2)

The arguments `arg1` and `arg2` are strings. The `substring-after()` function returns a string containing the characters from `arg1` that occur after the first occurrence of `arg2`. If `arg2` is not a substring of `arg1`, the function returns the empty string.

substring-before(arg1, arg2)

The arguments `arg1` and `arg2` are strings. The `substring-before()` function returns a string containing the characters from `arg1` that occur before the first occurrence of `arg2`. If `arg2` is not a substring of `arg1`, the function returns the empty string.

sum(arg1)

The argument, arg1, must be a node-set. The `sum()` function calculates the total of a set of numeric values contained in the nodes of this node-set. The function takes the string-value of each node in the node-set, converts this to a number using the rules of the `number()` function, and adds this value to the total. If any of the values cannot be converted to a number, the result of the `sum()` function will be NaN (Not a Number).

system-property(arg1)

The `system-property()` function returns information about the processing environment. The argument arg1 is a string containing a QName; a qualified name that identifies the system property required. Three system properties are defined in the XSLT standard, but others may be provided by individual vendors. The three standard properties are:

`xsl:version`	The version of the XSLT specification implemented by this processor, for example 1.0 or 1.1
`xsl:vendor`	Identifies the vendor of this XSLT processor
`xsl:vendor-url`	The URL of the vendor's web site

If you supply a property name that the processor doesn't recognize, the function returns an empty string.

This is an XSLT function: it can only be used in XPath expressions contained in an XSLT stylesheet.

translate(arg1, arg2, arg3)

The `translate()` function substitutes characters in a supplied string with nominated replacement characters. It can also be used to remove nominated characters from a string.

All three arguments are strings: `arg1` is the string to be translated, `arg2` gives a list of characters to be replaced, and `arg3` gives the replacement characters.

For each character in `arg1` the following processing is applied:

❏ If the character appears at position n in the list of characters in `arg2`, then if there is a character at position n in `arg3`, it is replaced with that character, otherwise it is removed from the string.

❏ If the character doesn't appear in `arg2`, then it is copied unchanged to the result string.

For example, `translate("ABC-123", "0123456789-", "9999999999")` returns `"ABC999"`, because the effect is to translate all digits to a `"9"`, remove all hyphens, and leave other characters unchanged.

true()

This function returns the Boolean True value. It takes no arguments. The function is needed because XPath provides no constant representing the value True.

unparsed-entity-uri(arg1)

The `unparsed-entity-uri()` function gives access to declarations of unparsed entities in the DTD of the source document. The argument is evaluated as a string containing the name of the unparsed entity required. The function returns a string containing the URI (the system identifier) of the unparsed entity with the given name, if there is one. Otherwise, an empty string.

This is an XSLT function: it can only be used in XPath expressions contained in an XSLT stylesheet.

Stylesheets, Templates, and Patterns

We've now finished our tour of XPath expressions. Let's return now to XSLT and look at the structure of a stylesheet and the templates it defines. We'll be using examples of XPath expressions throughout this section.

The <xsl:stylesheet> Element

A stylesheet is usually an XML document in its own right, and its outermost element will be an `<xsl:stylesheet>` element (you can also use `<xsl:transform>` as a synonym). The `<xsl:stylesheet>` element will usually look something like this:

```
<xsl:stylesheet
    xmlns:xsl="http://www.w3.org/1999/XSL/Transform"
    version="1.0">
</xsl:stylesheet>
```

The namespace URI must be exactly as written, or the processor won't recognize it as an XSLT stylesheet. You can use a different prefix if you like (some people prefer to use "xslt") but you must then use it consistently. The version attribute is mandatory, and indicates that this stylesheet is using facilities only from XSLT version 1.0.

If you see a stylesheet that uses the namespace `http://www.w3.org/TR/WD-xsl`, then it is not an XSLT stylesheet, but one that uses the old Microsoft dialect of the language shipped with IE 5 and IE 5.5. There are so many differences between these dialects that they are best regarded as separate languages: in this chapter, we are only describing XSLT. As part of the Microsoft XSLT processor, MSXML3 (currently available at http://msdn.Microsoft.com/xml), there is a tool to convert stylesheets from the old Microsoft dialect to XSLT.

The `<xsl:stylesheet>` element will often carry a number of other namespace declarations; for example, to define the namespaces for any extension functions you are using, or the namespaces of elements in your source document that you want to match. There are several other attributes you can have on this element:

Attribute name	Usage
id	An identifying name for the stylesheet. Not used by XSLT itself.
extension-element-prefixes	A list of namespace prefixes (separated by whitespace) that are being used for vendor-defined or user-defined stylesheet instructions (so-called extension elements).
exclude-result-prefixes	A list of namespace prefixes (separated by whitespace) that are not to be included in the result document unless they are actually referenced.

In a typical stylesheet, most of the elements immediately within the `<xsl:stylesheet>` element (which are known, rather inaccurately, as top-level elements) are likely to be `<xsl:template>` elements. We'll discuss these now, and return to the other kinds of top-level element in a later section.

The `<xsl:template>` Element

Templates are the building blocks of an XSLT stylesheet, like the procedures and functions in a conventional program. When a template is triggered (or "instantiated", in the jargon of the standard), it generally causes things to be written to the result tree. The contents of a template in the stylesheet consist of two kinds of node: instructions and data. When the template is triggered, any instructions are executed, and any data nodes (referred to as literal result elements and text nodes) are copied directly to the output.

For example, when the following template is triggered, it writes a `<para>` element to the result tree, containing the text of the current node in the source document:

```
<xsl:template match="author">
    <para>By: <xsl:value-of select="."/></para>
</xsl:template>
```

This little template contains a literal result element (the `<para>` element), literal result text `By:` , and an instruction (the `<xsl:value-of>` element).

There are two ways of triggering a template: it can be invoked explicitly, using the `<xsl:call-template>` instruction, or implicitly, using `<xsl:apply-templates>`.

The `<xsl:call-template>` instruction is very like a conventional subroutine call. It has a name attribute, which must match the name attribute of an `<xsl:template>` element somewhere in the stylesheet. When the instruction `<xsl:call-template name="table-of-contents"/>` is executed, the template declared as `<xsl:template name="table-of-contents">` springs into life.

The other mechanism, using `<xsl:apply-templates>`, is more subtle. This instruction has a `select` attribute whose value is an XPath expression that selects the set of nodes to be processed. The default is `select="child::node()"`, which selects all the children of the current node. For each of these nodes, the system searches all the templates in the stylesheet to find one that best matches that node. This search is based on the `match` attribute of the `<xsl:template>` element, which defines a pattern that the node must match in order to qualify.

We'll look in a moment at the detail of how match patterns work. First let's look at a complete stylesheet that uses template rules to define its processing.

Our example will be a very simple kind of transformation: subsetting of a file of records to include only those that satisfy certain criteria. The input will be a product file such as:

```
<?xml version="1.0"?>
<products>
    <product code="Z123-888" category="tools">
        <description>Large claw hammer</description>
        <weight units="gms">850</weight>
        <price>12.99</price>
    </product>
    <product code="X853-122" category="books">
        <title>Plumbing for beginners</title>
        <ISBN>0-123-456-9876</ISBN>
        <price>10.95</price>
    </product>
    <product code="S14-8532" category="tools">
        <description>Adjustable spanner</description>
        <weight units="gms">330</weight>
        <price>5.25</price>
    </product>
</products>
```

The requirement is to produce another product file, with the same structure, but selecting only those products whose price exceeds ten dollars, and omitting the price from the output.

The following stylesheet achieves this:

```
<?xml version="1.0"?>
<xsl:stylesheet xmlns:xsl="http://www.w3.org/1999/XSL/Transform" version="1.0">
    <xsl:template match="*">
        <xsl:copy>
            <xsl:copy-of select="@*" />
            <xsl:apply-templates />
        </xsl:copy>
    </xsl:template>
    <xsl:template match="product[price &lt; 10.00]" />
    <xsl:template match="price" />
</xsl:stylesheet>
```

How does it work?

There are three template rules. The first one matches all elements (match="*"). This template rule uses the <xsl:copy> instruction to copy the element node from the source tree to the result tree. It also copies the attributes of the element using <xsl:copy-of>: the expression select="@*" selects all the attribute nodes of the current element. It then calls <xsl:apply-templates/> to process the children of the current element, each one using the appropriate rule for that element.

The next two template rules are empty: they match an input element and produce no output, thus effectively removing that element and its contents from the file. The first of these two matches <product> elements that have a child <price> element, whose value is less than 10.00; the second matches <price> elements. Because these two rules have match patterns that are more specific than the first template rule, they take priority over it when the relevant conditions are satisfied.

The other nodes in the tree (for example the root node and text nodes) are handled by the built-in template rules used when no explicit rule is provided. For the root, this built-in template rule just calls `<xsl:apply-templates />` to process the children of the root node. For a text node, it copies the text to the result tree.

The output of the stylesheet looks like this (whitespace added for clarity).

```xml
<?xml version="1.0" encoding="utf-8"?>
<products>
    <product code="Z123-888" category="tools">
        <description>Large claw hammer</description>
        <weight units="gms">850</weight>
    </product>
    <product code="X853-122" category="books">
        <title>Plumbing for beginners</title>
        <ISBN>0-123-456-9876</ISBN>
    </product>
</products>
```

If you want to try this example out for yourself, follow the steps below:

❑   Download the sample files for this book from http://www.wrox.com

❑   Download Instant Saxon from http://users.iclway.co.uk/mhkay/saxon/

❑   Extract the executable `saxon.exe` into a suitable directory, say `c:\saxon`

❑   Open an MS-DOS console

❑   Change directory to the folder containing the Wrox examples, and then run the processor, as follows:

```
cd path-of-wrox-download
c:\saxon\saxon.exe products.xml products.xsl
```

Of course, if you already have another XSLT processor installed, such as Xalan or Oracle XSL, you can equally well run the example with that, changing the command line as required.

Patterns

The patterns that you can write in the `match` attribute of `<xsl:template>` are very similar to XPath expressions. In fact, they are a subset of XPath expressions and every pattern is a valid XPath expression. The converse is not true however.

By far the most common kind of pattern is a simple element name, for example `author` in the example above. This will match all `<author>` elements (but remember to include a namespace prefix if the element has a namespace URI).

Instead of a name, you can use any node test. The different kinds of node test were listed in an earlier section. For example, you can write `text()` to match all text nodes, or `svg:*` to match all elements in the `svg` namespace.

You can also add one or more predicates after the name. The predicate can be any XPath expression so long as it doesn't use variables or the current() function (which would be meaningless). For example, you could write section[@title='Introduction'] to match a <section> element having a title attribute with the value Introduction. Or you could use para[1] to match any <para> element that is the first <para> child of its parent element.

You can also qualify the pattern by specifying the names of parent or ancestor elements, using the same syntax as a location path in an XPath expression. For example, scene/title matches any <title> element whose parent is a <scene> element, and chap//note matches any <note> element provided it is a descendant of a <chap> element.

If you want to define a single template that matches several different patterns, you can use the union operator | to separate them. For example, the pattern scene | prologue | epilogue, matches <scene>, <prologue>, and <epilogue> elements.

The full rules for patterns are a bit more complex than this, but it's good practice to keep patterns reasonably simple, so the examples described here should be more than adequate for most stylesheets.

Selecting a Template Rule

When <xsl:apply-templates> is used to process a set of nodes, it won't necessarily happen that there's exactly one template rule that matches each node. There may be none, and there may be several.

It's possible to steer the process by using modes. If the <xsl:apply-templates> instruction has a mode attribute, the selected <xsl:template> element must have a matching mode attribute. If there's no mode attribute on the <xsl:apply-templates> element, it will only match <xsl:template> elements with no mode attribute. Modes are useful when there are several different ways of processing the same input nodes, for example you may want to process them one way while generating the body of the document, and another way when generating an index.

Here's an example that outputs all the sections in a chapter, preceded by a table of contents. The entries in the table of contents are hyperlinks to the relevant sections, with the identifiers for the links constructed using the XPath generate-id() function:

```
<xsl:template match="chapter">
  <h2>Table of Contents</h2>
  <xsl:apply-templates select="section" mode="toc"/>
  <xsl:apply-templates select="section" mode="body"/>
</xsl:template>
<xsl:template match="section" mode="toc">
  <p><a href="#{generate-id()}">
  <xsl:value-of select="title"/>
  </a></p>
</xsl:template>
<xsl:template match="section" mode="body">
  <h2><a name="{generate-id()}">
  <xsl:value-of select="title"/>
  </a></h2>
  <xsl:apply-templates select="para"/>
</xsl:template>
```

If there's no matching template rule for a node, a default rule is invoked. The default processing depends on the node type, as follows:

❑ For the root node and element nodes, it invokes `<xsl:apply-templates />` to process the children of this node. This may find explicit rules for these children, or it may again invoke the default rule.

❑ For text nodes and attribute nodes, it copies the string-value of the node to the result tree.

❑ For other nodes, it does nothing.

If there's more than one rule, a priority scheme comes into play. This works as follows:

❑ The processor must first see if the matching rules have different import precedence, and if so, reject any that have lower precedence than others. This will only happen if one template is in a separate stylesheet imported using `<xsl:import>`, which we'll describe in the later section on top-level elements within templates.

❑ Then the processor must look at the priorities of the rules. You can set a priority explicitly on a rule by using its `priority` attribute, for example a rule with `priority="2"` will be chosen in preference to one with `priority="1"`. If there's no explicit priority, the system allocates a default priority based on the syntax you use in the match pattern. This tries to ensure that highly selective patterns like `section[@title='Introduction']` get a higher priority than catch-all patterns like `node()`, but it's a hit-and-miss process, and it's safer to allocate priorities explicitly.

❑ If, after all this, there are still several possible candidates, the specification says it's an error. However, it gives the processor a choice of what to do about this. A strict processor is allowed to report the error and terminate processing. A more lenient processor is allowed to choose whichever rule comes last in the stylesheet, and use that. Some processors actually adopt a middle course, of continuing after a warning message.

Parameters

Whether a template rule is called using `<xsl:call-template>` or `<xsl:apply-templates>`, it's possible to supply parameters with the call. The calling instruction uses `<xsl:with-param>` to set a value for a parameter; the called template uses `<xsl:param>` to receive the value. If the caller sets a parameter that the called template isn't expecting, it is simply ignored; if the caller fails to set a parameter that's expected, it will take a default value, which can be specified in the `<xsl:param>` element.

The `<xsl:param>` and `<xsl:with-param>` elements have identical syntax: a `name` attribute to give the name of the parameter, and a `select` attribute containing an XPath expression to give its value. (In the case of `<xsl:param>`, this is the default value.) They can also have content, to express the value as a tree, in the same way as `<xsl:variable>`, which we'll describe later in this appendix.

Here's an example of a template that copies a node and its descendants, down to a specified depth. The template calls itself recursively: this is very much part of the programming style when you want to do anything complex with XSLT. Each time the template calls itself, it reduces the depth by one, until it reaches zero and the template does nothing, and returns immediately.

```
<xsl:template match="/ | * | text()" mode="shallow-copy">
    <xsl:param name="depth"/>
    <xsl:if test="$depth &gt; 0">
        <xsl:copy>
            <!-- copy all the attributes -->
            <xsl:copy-of select="@*"/>
            <!-- process all the children -->
            <xsl:apply-templates mode="shallow-copy">
                <xsl:with-param name="depth" select="$depth - 1"/>
            </xsl:apply-templates>
        </xsl:copy>
    </xsl:if>
</xsl:template>
```

You can call this to copy the root node to a depth of three with a call such as:

```
<xsl:apply-templates select="/" mode="shallow-copy">
    <xsl:with-param name="depth" select="3"/>
</xsl:apply-templates>
```

The match pattern on the template uses a union pattern to specify that the template will match the root node /, any element *, or any text node text(). If comments or processing instructions are encountered, the built-in template kicks in, which for these types of node causes them to be ignored.

The Contents of a Template

The contents of an <xsl:template> element (after any <xsl:param> elements, which must come first) form a template body.

A template body consists of a sequence of element and text nodes. The stylesheet may also contain comments and processing instructions, but these are ignored completely, so we won't consider them. Any text nodes that consist entirely of whitespace will also have been removed.

The element nodes in a template body can be further categorized:

❑ Elements in the XSLT namespace are instructions. These are conventionally prefixed "xsl:" but you can use any prefix you like.

❑ Elements in a namespace designated as an extension element namespace are instructions. The meaning of these instructions is vendor-dependant.

❑ Any other elements are literal result elements. These are copied to the result tree.

Text nodes appearing within a template body are also copied to the result tree.

Extension elements are outside the scope of this appendix: see the vendor's documentation if you want to use them. In this section, we'll review the XSLT-defined instructions, and then look more closely at literal result elements.

We've introduced the template body as the contents of an <xsl:template> element, but in fact many other elements, such as <xsl:if> and <xsl:element>, have content that follows the same rules and is handled the same way as a template body contained directly in an <xsl:template> element. So, the term template body is used generally to describe the content of all these elements.

Attribute Value Templates

Some attributes in an XSLT stylesheet are designated as attribute value templates. Examples are the name attribute of the `<xsl:attribute>` and `<xsl:element>` instructions. In these attributes, instead of writing a fixed value, such as «name="description"», you can parameterize the value by writing XPath expressions within curly brackets, for example name="{$prefix}:{$localname}". When the instruction is executed, these XPath expressions will be evaluated, and the resulting attribute value will be substituted into the attribute value in place of the expression.

If the XML source document uses curly braces within the attribute value and you don't want it to trigger this mechanism, write it twice, for example value="{{not an AVT}}".

The most common mistake with attribute value templates is to assume you can use them anywhere. You can't; they are allowed only in a few specific places. These are indicated in the descriptions of each XSLT element below. Don't attempt, for example, to write `<xsl:call-template name="{$tname}" />`: it won't work.

One particular point is that you never use curly brackets **inside** an XPath expression, only to surround an XPath expression within an attribute that would otherwise be interpreted as a text value.

XSLT Instructions

XSLT instructions are a subset of XSLT elements: essentially, those that can be used directly as part of a template body.
The instructions defined in XSLT 1.0 are as follows:

```
<xsl:apply-imports>          <xsl:fallback>
<xsl:apply-templates>        <xsl:for-each>
<xsl:attribute>              <xsl:if>
<xsl:call-template>          <xsl:message>
<xsl:choose>                 <xsl:number>
<xsl:comment>                <xsl:processing-instruction>
<xsl:copy>                   <xsl:text>
<xsl:copy-of>                <xsl:value-of>
<xsl:element>                <xsl:variable>
```

In the following sections, we'll look briefly at each one.

<xsl:apply-imports>

This is a very rarely used instruction. It has no attributes and is always empty. It is used while processing a particular node to invoke template rules from an imported stylesheet, overriding the normal rules for template selection based on import precedence.

<xsl:apply-templates>

We have already described this instruction earlier in the appendix. It causes a selected set of nodes to be processed, each one using the appropriate template rule based on match patterns and priorities.

The instruction takes two attributes, both optional. The `select` attribute is an XPath expression that defines the set of nodes to be processed: by default, the children of the current node are processed. The `mode` attribute gives the name of a processing mode: only those `<xsl:template>` elements with the same mode name are candidates for matching.

Within the invoked templates, any XPath expressions are evaluated with the context set by the `<xsl:apply-templates>` instruction. Specifically, the context node will be the node currently being processed, the context position (the result of the `position()` function) will be 1 for the first node processed, 2 for the second, and so on, and the context size (the result of the `last()` function) will be the total number of nodes to be processed.

The `<xsl:apply-templates>` instruction is often written as an empty element, but there are two other elements it may optionally contain: `<xsl:with-param>`, to define any parameters to be passed to the called template, and `<xsl:sort>`, which defines the sort order of the nodes to be processed. In the absence of `<xsl:sort>`, the nodes are processed in document order. `<xsl:sort>` is described later in the section titled *Sorting*.

<xsl:attribute>

The effect of `<xsl:attribute>` is to write an attribute node to the result tree. This is only possible if the last thing written was an element or another attribute. The `<xsl:attribute>` instruction has two attributes, name and namespace. The name attribute gives the name of the new attribute (this is mandatory), and the namespace attribute gives the namespace URI. If no namespace is specified, the namespace is taken from the prefix of the name, if this has one.

Both the name and namespace attributes are interpreted as Attribute Value Templates. The value of the new attribute is constructed from the content of the `<xsl:attribute>` element. This is another template body, but it should generate only text nodes. For example:

```
<xsl:attribute name="color">
    <xsl:value-of select="concat('#', $bgcolor)"/>
</xsl:attribute>
```

<xsl:call-template>

This instruction has already been discussed, in the earlier section on the `<xsl:template>` element. It takes a mandatory name attribute, which names the template to be called. There must be a template with this name in the stylesheet.

The only elements permitted in the content of `<xsl:call-template>` are `<xsl:with-param>` elements. These set the values of any parameters to be passed to the called template. The names used in the `<xsl:with-param>` elements should match the names used in the `<xsl:param>` elements of the called template.

<xsl:choose>

In a similar manner to If...else in Visual Basic, this instruction is used to perform conditional processing. The `<xsl:choose>` element itself has no attributes. It contains a sequence of one or more `<xsl:when>` elements, optionally followed by an `<xsl:otherwise>` element. Each `<xsl:when>` element specifies a condition, and the first one whose condition is satisfied is executed. If none of the conditions is satisfied, the `<xsl:otherwise>` element is used. For example:

```
<xsl:choose>
    <xsl:when test="lang('en')">Welcome</xsl:when>
    <xsl:when test="lang('de')">Willkommen</xsl:when>
    <xsl:when test="lang('fr')">Bienvenue</xsl:when>
    <xsl:otherwise>System error!</xsl:otherwise>
</xsl:choose>
```

The `test` attribute of `<xsl:when>` is an XPath expression, whose result is converted to a Boolean. The content of the `<xsl:when>` and `<xsl:otherwise>` elements need not be simple text as in this example; it can be any template body.

<xsl:comment>

This instruction is used to output a comment node to the result tree. It takes no attributes. The content of the `<xsl:comment>` element is a template body, but this should generate nothing other than text nodes. For example:

```
<xsl:comment>
    Generated with param1=<xsl:value-of select="$param1"/>
</xsl:comment>
```

<xsl:copy>

This instruction performs a shallow copy of the current node: that is, it copies the current node, but not its children. When the current node is a root or element node, the content of the `<xsl:copy>` instruction is taken as a template body, which is instantiated to create the content of the copied output node. When the current node is an attribute node, text node, comment, or processing instruction, the content of the `<xsl:copy>` element is ignored.

The `<xsl:copy>` instruction has an optional attribute `use-attribute-sets`. This is relevant only when copying an element. It has the same effect as the `use-attribute-sets` attribute of `<xsl:element>`, which is described later.

<xsl:copy-of>

This instruction performs a deep copy of all the nodes selected by the XPath expression in its `select` attribute. That is, it copies those nodes and all their descendants, as well as their attributes and namespaces, to the result tree.

If the result of evaluating the expression in the `select` attribute is a simple string, number, or Boolean, the `<xsl:copy-of>` instruction has the same effect as `<xsl:value-of>`: it converts the value to a string and writes it to the result tree as a text node. For example:

```
<xsl:copy-of select="@*" />
```

This copies all the attributes of the current node to the result tree.

The following instruction (which might be the only thing a stylesheet does) copies all the news items with a status of "current" to the result tree, together with all their content:

```
<xsl:copy-of select="/news/item[@status='current']" />
```

The `<xsl:copy-of>` instruction is always empty.

<xsl:element>

The `<xsl:element>` instruction writes an element node to the result tree. The content of the `<xsl:element>` instruction is a template body, which is instantiated to construct the content of the generated element.

647

The `<xsl:element>` instruction has attributes name and namespace. The name attribute gives the name of the new element (this is mandatory), and the namespace attribute gives the namespace URI. If no namespace is specified, it is taken from the prefix of the supplied element name, if this has one.

Both the name and namespace attributes are interpreted as Attribute Value Templates. The following example creates an `<html>` element using a namespace URI that is passed in as a parameter:

```
<xsl:element name="html" namespace="{$html-namespace}">
   <head>
      <title><xsl:value-of select="title"/></title>
   </head>
   <body>
      <xsl:call-template name="generate-body"/>
   </body>
</xsl:element>
```

The `<xsl:element>` instruction may also have an attribute use-attribute-sets. If present, this is a whitespace-separated list of names, each of which must be the name of an `<xsl:attribute-set>` element at the top level of the stylesheet. The effect is that the new element will be given all the attributes defined in these attribute sets.

<xsl:fallback>

This is a rarely encountered instruction. It is used within the content of a vendor extension element to define the processing that should take place if the extension element is not available. It can also be used if your stylesheet specifies version="2.0", say, (because it uses features defined in XSLT version 2.0), to define what should happen if the stylesheet is run using an XSLT processor that does not support version 2.0 features.

<xsl:for-each>

The `<xsl:for-each>` instruction is used to define processing that should be carried out for each member of a node-set. The node-set to be processed is defined by an XPath expression in the select attribute, which is mandatory. The processing itself is defined by the template body contained within the `<xsl:for-each>` element.

The following example creates one attribute node in the result tree corresponding to each child element of the current node in the source tree:

```
<xsl:for-each select="*">
   <xsl:attribute name="{name()}">
      <xsl:value-of select="."/>
   </xsl:attribute>
</xsl:for-each>
```

The node-set is normally processed in document order. To process the nodes in a different order, include one or more `<xsl:sort>` elements immediately within the `<xsl:for-each>` instruction. For more details, see the section on *Sorting*.

The `<xsl:for-each>` instruction changes the current node: each node in the node-set becomes the current node in turn, for as long as the template body is active. Sometimes `<xsl:for-each>` is used solely for this purpose, to set the current node for an instruction such as `<xsl:number>` or `<xsl:copy>` that only works on the current node. For example:

```
<xsl:for-each select="..">
  <xsl:number/>
</xsl:for-each>
```

This outputs the sequence number of the parent node. There is no iteration here: there is only one parent node, so the template body is only instantiated once.

While the `<xsl:for-each>` instruction is active, any XPath expressions are evaluated with the context set by the `<xsl:for-each>`. Specifically, the context node will be the node currently being processed, the context position will be 1 for the first node processed, 2 for the second, and so on, and the context size will be the total number of nodes to be processed. A common error is to write:

```
<xsl:for-each select="item">
  <xsl:value-of select="item" />
</xsl:for-each>
```

This fails (or rather, it produces no output) because the XPath expression in the `<xsl:value-of>` instruction is evaluated with an `<item>` as its context node, and the expression item is short for `child::item`, but the context `<item>` has no `<item>` elements as its children. Use `<xsl:value-of select="."/>` instead.

The two instructions `<xsl:apply-templates>` and `<xsl:for-each>` are the only instructions that change the current node in the source tree. They represent two different styles of processing, sometimes called **push** and **pull** respectively. Push processing (using `<xsl:apply-templates>`) relies on pattern matching, and it works best when the structure of the input is highly variable, for example where `<b>` elements may be found in many different contexts. Pull processing (using `<xsl:for-each>`) works better where the structure of the source is very rigid and predictable. It's a good idea to become familiar with both.

<xsl:if>

The `<xsl:if>` instruction performs an action if a condition is True. There is no else branch: if you need one, use `<xsl:choose>` instead. `<xsl:if>` has a mandatory test attribute, which defines the condition to be tested, as an XPath expression whose result is automatically converted to a Boolean. The `<xsl:if>` element contains a template body that is instantiated if and only if the condition is True.

This example outputs a message containing the word "errors" unless there was only one, when it uses the singular "error". It also uses an `<xsl:choose>`:

```
There <xsl:choose><xsl:when test="count($errors)=1">was
</xsl:when><xsl:otherwise>were </xsl:otherwise></xsl:choose>
</ <xsl:value-of select="count($errors)" />
error<xsl:if test="count($errors)!=1">s</xsl:if>
```

<xsl:message>

The `<xsl:message>` instruction is used to output a message. The specification isn't very precise about what happens to the message; this depends on the implementation. The `<xsl:message>` element contains a template body, which is instantiated to construct the message. This may contain any kind of XML markup, though text messages are likely to behave more predictably.

There is an optional attribute `terminate="yes"`, which causes execution of the stylesheet to terminate at once. For example:

```
<xsl:if test="not(/invoice)">
    <xsl:message terminate="yes">
        This stylesheet is only designed to handle invoice documents
    </xsl:message>
</xsl:if>
```

<xsl:number>

The `<xsl:number>` instruction is designed to perform sequential numbering of nodes. It calculates a number for the current node based on its position in the source tree, formats this number as required, and writes the result to the output tree as a text node.

This is a complex instruction with many attributes to control how the number is calculated and formatted. A detailed treatment is beyond the scope of this chapter: you can find full information in the Wrox book *XSLT Programmers Reference.* (ISBN 1-861003-12-9)

When used with no attributes, for example `<xsl:number />`, the result is obtained by counting the number of preceding siblings of the current node that have the same node type and name, adding one for the node itself, and formatting the result using the same rules as the `string()` function. Therefore, if the current node is the fifth `<para>` element within a `<section>`, the output will be 5.

The way nodes are counted may be modified using a number of attributes:

Attribute	Meaning
level	The default value is `"single"`, which counts preceding siblings of the current node. The value `"any"` counts preceding nodes anywhere in the document, which is useful for example to number figures or equations. The value `"multiple"` produces a multi-level number such as "10.1.3" or "17a(iv)".
count	This pattern defines which nodes are to be counted. For example `count="*"` causes all elements to be counted, not only those with the same name as the current node. For multi-level numbering, specify all the levels you want counted, for example `count="chapter	section	clause"`.
from	This is a pattern that indicates where counting is to start. For example, `count="p" from="h2"` counts the number of `<p>` elements since the last `<h2>` element.

The formatting of the result may also be modified using a number of attributes. The main one is `format`, which defines a format pattern (this is an attribute value template, so it can be constructed dynamically if you want). The following examples show how the number 4 might be formatted with various format patterns:

format pattern	output
1	4
(a)	(d)
-- i --	-- iv --

For multi-level numbering, you can use a format pattern such as "1.1(a)" to request an output sequence such as 1.1(a), 1.1(b), 1.1(c), 1.2(a), 1.2(b), 2.1(a).

The <xsl:number> instruction also has a value attribute. This can be used to supply the value directly, as a way of using the formatting capabilities of <xsl:number> without the node-counting features. It is often used in the form:

```
<xsl:number value="position()" format="(a)" />
```

The position() function gives the position of the current node in the sequence that the nodes are being processed, rather than its position in the source tree. This option is particularly useful when producing output in sorted order.

<xsl:processing-instruction>

This instruction is used to output a processing instruction node to the result tree. It takes a mandatory name attribute to define the name of the generated processing instruction. The data part of the processing instruction is obtained by instantiating the template body that the <xsl:processing-instruction> element contains.

<xsl:text>

The <xsl:text> instruction is used to output a text node to the result tree. This instruction may contain a text node but it must not contain any child elements.

Text contained directly in the stylesheet is written to the result tree automatically, whether or not it is contained in an <xsl:text> element. The reason for providing <xsl:text> is to give more control over whitespace handling. Text contained within an <xsl:text> element will be output exactly as written, even if it is all whitespace, whereas in other contexts whitespace that appears on its own between element tags will be removed from the stylesheet before processing.

For example, to output two names with a space between them, write:

```
<xsl:value-of select="given-name"/>
    <xsl:text> </xsl:text>
<xsl:value-of select="last-name"/>
```

The <xsl:text> element also has an optional attribute, disable-output-escaping="yes", which suppresses the normal action of the serializer to convert special characters such as < and > into < and >. This is a dirty feature that should be avoided, but it is sometimes useful if you want to generate not-quite-XML formats, such as ASP, PHP, or JSP pages.

<xsl:value-of>

The <xsl:value-of> instruction is used to write computed text to the result tree. It takes a select attribute whose value is an XPath expression. This expression is evaluated, the result is converted to a string (using the rules of the string() function), and written as a text node to the result tree. The most common usage is:

```
<xsl:value-of select="." />
```

This simply writes the string-value of the current node.

There is an optional attribute, `disable-output-escaping="yes"`, which has the same effect as with `<xsl:text>`.

<xsl:variable>

The `<xsl:variable>` element, when used as an instruction within a template body, declares a local variable. (It can also be used as a top-level element in the stylesheet, to declare a global variable.)

The name of the variable is given by its `name` attribute. This must different from any other local variable that is in scope at that point in the stylesheet, although it can override a global variable of the same name.

The scope of a local variable (that is, the part of the stylesheet where XPath expressions can refer to the variable) comprises those elements in the stylesheet that are following-siblings of the `<xsl:variable>` element, or descendants of those following-sibling elements. Using XPath notation, if the `<xsl:variable>` element is the context node, the scope of the variable is the node-set defined by:

```
following-sibling::*/descendant-or-self::*
```

This means, for example, that if you declare a local variable within an `<xsl:when>` branch of an `<xsl:choose>` instruction, you won't be able to access the variable outside the `<xsl:when>`.

The value of the variable can be determined in three ways:

❑ If the `<xsl:variable>` element has a `select` attribute, this attribute is an XPath expression, which is evaluated to give the variable's value.

❑ If the `<xsl:variable>` element has content, the content is a template body. This is instantiated to create a new tree (called a result tree fragment) and the value of the variable is the node-set containing the root of this tree.

❑ If the `<xsl:variable>` element has no `select` attribute and is empty, its value is the empty string.

Here's an example using the `select` attribute:

```
<xsl:variable name="number-of-items" select="count(//item)" />
```

Here's one that creates a result tree fragment:

```
<xsl:variable name="result-table">
<table>
   <xsl:for-each select="item">
   <tr>
      <td><xsl:value-of select="@description"/></td>
      <td><xsl:value-of select="@price"/></td>
   </tr>
   </xsl:for-each>
</table>
</xsl:variable>
```

With XSLT 1.0, there are restrictions on the way a result tree fragment can be used; in effect, the only things you can do with it are to convert it to a string, or to copy it (by using `<xsl:copy-of>`) to the final result tree. You can't actually process it using XPath queries. Many vendors have relaxed this restriction by providing facilities to convert the result tree fragment to a node-set, and a standard way of doing this is expected to come in the next version of the specification.

As we've already mentioned, variables can't be used in quite the same way as in ordinary programming languages, because they are "write-once" – they can't be updated, because there is no assignment statement. In effect, this means a variable is just a shorthand name for an expression that saves you from using the same expression repeatedly. Variables can also be useful to avoid problems with changing context. For example, if you write:

```
<xsl:variable name="this" select="."/>
```

Then as the first thing within an `<xsl:for-each>` loop, you will always be able to refer to the current node of this loop even from within nested loops.

Literal Result Elements

Any element found within a template body that is not recognized as an instruction is treated as a literal result element. The element is copied to the result tree, together with its attributes and namespaces. If the element is not empty, its content is a template body, and this is instantiated to create the content of the generated element in the result tree. For example:

```
<td valign="top"><xsl:value-of select="." /></td>
```

This is a literal `<td>` result element, whose template body causes the string value of the current node in the source document to be inserted into the `<td>` element generated on the result tree.

The attributes of the literal result element are interpreted as attribute value templates, so they can be generated using XPath expressions. For example:

```
<td valign="{$align}"><xsl:value-of select="." /></td>
```

There are two other ways of generating attributes for the result element:

❑ Use the `<xsl:attribute>` instruction within the template body.

❑ Use an `xsl:use-attribute-sets` attribute within the start tag of the literal result element. This has the same effect as the use-attribute-sets attribute of `<xsl:element>`. It is prefixed with "xsl" to distinguish it from attributes that you want to copy to the result.

A literal result element can also have attributes `xsl:version`, `xsl:extension-element-prefixes`, and `xsl:exclude-result-prefixes`. These override the similarly-named attributes on the `<xsl:stylesheet>` element for the region of the stylesheet enclosed by the literal result element. Again, the prefix "xsl" is used to distinguish them from attributes intended for the result tree.

Sorting

There are two instructions for processing a set of nodes, `<xsl:apply-templates>` and `<xsl:for-each>`, and they both allow the nodes to be sorted by specifying one or more `<xsl:sort>` elements. If you don't specify a sort order, the nodes will be processed in document order, that is, the order they appear in the source document.

Each `<xsl:sort>` element specifies a sort key. If there is more than one `<xsl:sort>` element, they specify the sort keys in major-to-minor order: for example if the first sort key is last-name, and the second is given-name, you will process the data in the order of ascending given-name within ascending last-name.

The `<xsl:sort>` element has a number of attributes to control sorting:

Attribute	Meaning
select	An XPath expression whose value represents the sort key. If omitted, the nodes are sorted by their string-value.
order	This can be "ascending" or "descending". Specifying descending reverses the sort order. The default is ascending.
data-type	This can be "text" or "number". Specifying number means that the sort keys are converted to numbers and sorted numerically. The default is text.
lang	A language code, for example "en" or "de". Allows the sort to use national collating conventions. The default is implementation-defined.
case-order	This can be "upper-first" or "lower-first". Indicates whether upper-case letters should precede their lower-case equivalents, or vice versa. The default is implementation-defined.

The expression giving the sort key is evaluated with the node being sorted as the context node. For example, to sort a set of `<book>` elements according to their author attribute, write:

```
<xsl:for-each select="book">
   <xsl:sort select="@author"/>
</xsl:for-each>
```

Or:

```
<xsl:apply-templates select="book">
   <xsl:sort select="@author"/>
</xsl:apply-templates>
```

Top-level Elements

We've looked at all the XSLT elements that can be used inside a template body. Let's now return to the top-level of the stylesheet and look at those elements that can be used as children of the `<xsl:stylesheet>` or `<xsl:transform>` element. Here is a list of them:

`<xsl:attribute-set>`	`<xsl:output>`
`<xsl:decimal-format>`	`<xsl:param>`
`<xsl:import>`	`<xsl:preserve-space>`
`<xsl:include>`	`<xsl:strip-space>`
`<xsl:key>`	`<xsl:template>`
`<xsl:namespace-alias>`	`<xsl:variable>`

We'll look at each one in turn, in alphabetical order. Within the stylesheet itself, the general principle is that top-level elements can appear in any order, except that `<xsl:import>` elements have to come before any others.

A stylesheet can also contain user-defined elements at the top level, provided they are in their own namespace. These will be ignored by the XSLT processor, but they can be useful for look-up tables and other constant data. Within an XPath expression you can access the stylesheet contents by writing `document("")` to refer to the root of the stylesheet tree.

`<xsl:attribute-set>`

This element defines a named set of attributes. This is useful where you want to create many result elements using the same attribute values, which sometimes happens when rendering documents for display.

The `<xsl:attribute-set>` element has a name attribute, which provides a unique name for this attribute set. Its content is a set of `<xsl:attribute>` instructions to generate the attribute values. To include this set of attributes in a result element, use the `use-attribute-sets` attribute on `<xsl:copy>` or `<xsl:element>`, or use the `xsl:use-attribute-sets` attribute on a literal result element.

`<xsl:decimal-format>`

This element defines a set of rules for formatting decimal numbers. These rules can be referenced from the `format-number()` function used in an XPath expression with the `format-number()` function elsewhere in the stylesheet. An `<xsl:decimal-format>` element may have a name attribute, in which case it is used when the third argument of `format-number()` uses this name, or it may be unnamed, in which case it is used when the `format-number()` function has no third attribute.

The `<xsl:decimal-format>` element allows characters and strings to be nominated for use in formatted numbers, and also in the format pattern used by the `format-number()` function. The ones that are most likely to be used are `decimal-separator`, which defines the character to be used as a decimal point, and `grouping-separator`, which defines the character used as a thousands separator. For example, if you want `format-number()` to use the continental European convention of using . as a thousands separator and , as a decimal point, write:

```
<xsl:decimal-format decimal-point="," grouping-separator="." />
```

The other attributes are outside the scope of this chapter, and are fully described in the Wrox book *XSLT Programmers Reference* (ISBN 1-861003-12-9).

<xsl:import>

The <xsl:import> element allows your stylesheet to incorporate definitions from another stylesheet. The element has an href attribute that contains the URI of the stylesheet to be imported. All the top-level definitions from the imported stylesheet are incorporated into the importing stylesheet, except that they have a lower precedence; which means that given a choice, the definitions in the importing stylesheet are preferred.

In many ways this is like sub-classing: the importing stylesheet inherits the definitions from the imported stylesheet, overriding them where necessary; this reflects the way the facility should be used. The imported stylesheet should contain general-purpose definitions for use in a wide range of circumstances, and the importing stylesheet should override these with definitions that are applicable in a narrower sphere.

The imported stylesheet may contain any top-level elements, but there are slight differences in the way the precedence mechanism works for different elements. In most cases, an object in the imported stylesheet is used only when there is no applicable object in the importing stylesheet. In some cases (<xsl:key> definitions, <xsl:output> definitions), the definitions in the two stylesheets are merged.

The imported stylesheet may contain further <xsl:import> elements, so there is a hierarchy just like a class hierarchy in object-oriented programming.

<xsl:include>

The <xsl:include> element is similar to <xsl:import>, except that it incorporates definitions from the included stylesheet with the same precedence as those in the including stylesheet. Again, the href attribute contains the URI of the stylesheet to be included. Whereas <xsl:import> allows the importing stylesheet to override definitions in the imported stylesheet, <xsl:include> is useful if the definitions are not to be overridden.

The effect is, for all practical purposes, to copy the top-level elements from the included stylesheet into the including stylesheet at the point where the <xsl:include> statement occurs. This must, of course, be at the top level, as an immediate child of the <xsl:stylesheet> element.

Note, however, that the attributes on the <xsl:stylesheet> element (such as exclude-result-prefixes) apply only to elements that are physically within that stylesheet, not to elements brought in using <xsl:include>.

<xsl:key>

The <xsl:key> element is used to create a named key definition, which is referenced when the key() function is used in an XPath expression.

The element has three attributes:

Attribute name	Meaning
Name	Defines the name of the key, corresponding to the first argument of the key() function
match	Defines a pattern that determines which nodes in the source document participate in this key
use	Defines an XPath expression that establishes the value that will be used to find these nodes, corresponding to the second argument of the key() function

It would be appropriate to explain keys in SQL terms. Effectively the system maintains a table, KEYTABLE, with four columns, DOC, KEY, NODE, and VALUE.

The effect of an <xsl:key> definition is that for each source document (that is, the original input document plus any document loaded using the document() function), entries are created in this table for each node that matches the match pattern in the <xsl:key> definition. These entries will have DOC set to the identifier of the document, KEY set to the name of the key, and NODE set to the identifier of the matching node. For each of these matching nodes, the use expression is evaluated. If the result is a string, this string is entered in the VALUE column. If the result is a node-set, one row is added to the table for each node in the node-set, with the VALUE column set to the string-value of that node.

The effect of the key() function is then to query this table as follows:

```
SELECT distinct NODE FROM KEYTABLE WHERE DOC = current_document AND
   KEY = argument1 AND VALUE = argument2
```

Here current_document is the document containing the context node.

The resulting set of NODE identifiers forms the node-set returned by the key() function. Note that there can be more than one <xsl:key> definition with the same name (they are additive); that there can be several nodes with the same value for a key; and one node can have several values for the same key.

A simple example: to index books by author, write:

```
<xsl:key name="author-key" match="book" use="author" />
```

To retrieve all the books whose author is Milton, use this XPath expression:

```
key('author-key', 'Milton')
```

Note that this works even if a book has multiple authors.

<xsl:namespace-alias>

This is a rarely used element; its main purpose is to enable you to write a stylesheet that generates another stylesheet as output.

There are two attributes, stylesheet-prefix and result-prefix. In both cases, the value is a namespace prefix, which must correspond to a namespace declaration that is in scope.

The effect of this is that any literal result element that appears in the stylesheet using the namespace URI corresponding to the stylesheet-prefix will be written to the output document under the namespace URI corresponding to the result-prefix.

This element is used to influence the way that the result tree is serialized. As we saw earlier in the chapter, serialization is not really part of the job of an XSLT processor, and for this reason processors are allowed to ignore this element entirely. However, in practice most processors do include a serializer and have done their best to honor the <xsl:output> element: it will be ignored only if you choose to handle the serialization yourself.

The main attribute is method, which may be set to xml, html, or text, or to a vendor-defined method distinguished by a namespace prefix. The value xml indicates that the output should be in XML 1.0 format, html that it should be an HTML document, and text that it should be a plain text file.

The meaning of the other attributes depends on which method is chosen, as shown in the following table:

Attribute	Applies to	Meaning
cdata-section-elements	xml	A whitespace separated list of elements whose content is to be encoded using CDATA sections.
doctype-public	xml, html	The public identifier to be used in the DOCTYPE declaration.
doctype-system	xml, html	The system identifier to be used in the DOCTYPE declaration.
encoding	xml, html, text	The character encoding to be used, for example ISO-8859-1. The default is the Unicode UTF-8 encoding.
indent	xml, html	Set to "yes" or "no" to indicate whether the output is to be indented for readability.
media-type	xml, html, text	The media (or MIME) type of the output.
omit-xml-declaration	xml	If set to "yes", indicates that the XML declaration at the start of the file should be omitted.
standalone	xml	Indicates the value for "standalone" in the XML declaration.
version	xml, html	The version of XML or HTML to be used (default is 1.0 for XML, 4.0 for HTML).

There are many aspects of the final serialization over which you have no control; for example you can't choose in HTML output whether accented letters will be output directly as themselves, or using numeric character references, or using standard entity names such as ä. Different processors will do this differently. It shouldn't matter, because it will look the same in the browser.

<xsl:param>

We have already met <xsl:param> as an element that can be used inside <xsl:template>, to indicate the parameters to a template that may be supplied when it is called. It is also possible to use <xsl:param> as a top-level element to define parameters that may be supplied when the stylesheet as a whole is invoked: the syntax is the same. The way parameters are supplied is not standardized: each vendor has its own API or command line syntax, but within the stylesheet, parameters can be accessed by means of a variable reference in an XPath expression, just like global variables.

If the <xsl:param> element specifies a value, this is used as a default when no explicit value is supplied when the stylesheet is invoked.

<xsl:preserve-space> and <xsl:strip-space>

These two top-level elements are used to control how whitespace in the source document is handled. In most data-oriented XML documents, whitespace between element tags is there for layout purposes only, and it is best to eliminate it before processing starts, by specifying <xsl:strip-space elements="*" />. For markup-oriented XML documents, spaces between tags may well be significant, and it is best to keep it in the document (which is the default).

Both <xsl:preserve-space> and <xsl:strip-space> have an elements attribute, which is a space-separated list of **NameTests**. A NameTest is either *, meaning all elements, or prefix:*, meaning all elements in a particular namespace, or an element name indicating a specific element. If you want spaces stripped from only a few elements, list these in <xsl:strip-space>. If you want spaces stripped from most elements, specify <xsl:strip-space="*" />, and list any exceptions using <xsl:preserve-space>.

Whitespace is only stripped from the source document when an entire text node consists of whitespace (that is, of the four characters space, tab, carriage return, and line feed). Whitespace that is adjacent to "real" text is never removed. So if you have a source file like this:

```
<president>
    <name>
    Bill Clinton
    </name>
    <address>
    The White House Washington DC
    </address>
</president>
```

The newline characters immediately before the <name> element, between the <name> and <address> elements, and after the <address> element will be eligible for removal by whitespace stripping. But the newline characters immediately before "Bill", immediately after "Clinton", and at the start and end of the address, will always be retained because they form part of text nodes that are not whitespace-only. If you want to remove these newline characters, you will have to do it during the course of the transformation, using the normalize-space() function.

> **Note for Microsoft users: when you invoke XSLT transformations using the MSXML3 processor, the normal procedure is first to construct a DOM representation of the input document using the Document.Load() method, and then to transform the DOM using the transformNode() method. By default, when you create the DOM, it is created without whitespace nodes. This process is carried out without regard to anything the stylesheet says about whitespace. If you want to preserve whitespace, set the preserveWhitespace property of the Document object to true.**

<xsl:template>

We've already seen the <xsl:template> element in action earlier in the chapter. Just to recap (because it is about the most important element in XSLT), the <xsl:template> element can have either a name attribute (to allow it to be called using <xsl:call-template>, or a match attribute (to allow it to be called using <xsl:apply-templates>, or both (in which case it can be called either way). In addition, it may have a mode attribute and a priority attribute.

It's an error to have two templates in the stylesheet with the same name and the same import precedence.

<xsl:variable>

We've seen <xsl:variable> used within a template body to define a local variable; it can also be used as a top-level element to define a global variable. A global variable can be referenced from anywhere in the stylesheet: unlike local variables, there is no ban on forwards references. Global variables can even refer to each other, so long as the definitions aren't circular.

Apart from this, global variable definitions look the same as local variables. They are always evaluated with the root node of the source document as the context node, and with the context position and size both set to 1.

It's an error to have two global variables with the same name and import precedence. If you have two with the same name and different precedence, the one with higher precedence (that is, the one in the importing stylesheet, or the one that was imported last) always wins.

Some Working Examples

This brings us to the end of the technical specifications in this chapter. To get a reasonably complete description of XSLT and XPath into limited space, we've included a lot of definitions and relatively few examples. So to compensate, here are a couple of examples of complete and (almost) realistic stylesheets.

Example: Displaying Soccer Results

We'll use an XML data file containing results of soccer fixtures, such as might be held in a database for a World Cup web site, and we'll show two stylesheets that format this data in different ways.

Source

The source file is soccer.xml. If you're interested, it contains the results of the matches played in Group A of the 1998 World Cup:

```
<?xml version="1.0"?>
<?xml-stylesheet type="text/xsl" href="soccer1.xsl" ?>

<results group="A">
<match>
    <date>1998-06-10</date>
    <team score="2">Brazil</team>
    <team score="1">Scotland</team>
</match>
```

```
<match>
    <date>1998-06-16</date>
    <team score="3">Brazil</team>
    <team score="0">Morocco</team>
</match>
<match>
    <date>1998-06-23</date>
    <team score="1">Brazil</team>
    <team score="2">Norway</team>
</match>
<match>
    <date>1998-06-10</date>
    <team score="2">Morocco</team>
    <team score="2">Norway</team>
</match>
<match>
    <date>1998-06-16</date>
    <team score="1">Scotland</team>
    <team score="1">Norway</team>
</match>
<match>
    <date>1998-06-23</date>
    <team score="0">Scotland</team>
    <team score="3">Morocco</team>
</match>
</results>
```

The First Stylesheet

The first stylesheet, `soccer1.xsl`, displays the results of the matches in a straightforward way.

First we'll give the standard stylesheet heading, and define a variable to hold the table heading that we'll use to display each result:

```
<xsl:stylesheet version="1.0"
    xmlns:xsl="http://www.w3.org/1999/XSL/Transform">

    <xsl:variable name="table-heading">
        <tr>
            <td><b>Date</b></td>
            <td><b>Home Team</b></td>
            <td><b>Away Team</b></td>
            <td><b>Result</b></td>
        </tr>
    </xsl:variable>
```

Now we'll define a named template to format dates. This takes an ISO-8601 date as a parameter (for example "2000-10-11") and formats it for display as "11 Oct 2000". This involves some simple use of the XPath string functions.

```
<xsl:template name="format-date">
    <xsl:param name="iso-date"/>
    <xsl:variable name="months"
        select="'JanFebMarAprMayJunJulAugSepOctNovDec'" />
    <xsl:value-of select="substring($iso-date, 9, 2)" />
    <xsl:text> </xsl:text>
    <xsl:variable name="month" select="substring($iso-date, 6, 2)" />
    <xsl:value-of select="substring($months, ($month - 1)*3 + 1, 3)" />
    <xsl:text> </xsl:text>
    <xsl:value-of select="substring($iso-date, 1, 4)" />
</xsl:template>
```

For the main part of the processing, we define a template rule for the root node, which calls
`<xsl:apply-templates>` to process all the `<match>` elements, sorting them by date, and within the
same date, by the name of the first team listed:

```
<xsl:template match="/">
<html><body>
   <h1>Matches in Group <xsl:value-of select="/*/@group"/></h1>
   <xsl:apply-templates select="/results/match">
      <xsl:sort select="date" />
      <xsl:sort select="team[1]" />
   </xsl:apply-templates>
</body></html>
</xsl:template>
```

Finally, we need to cover the logic to display details of a single soccer match. This first calls the named
template to format the date into a variable; then it constructs an HTML table, copying data into the
table either from the source documents or from variables, as required. (The `match="match"` attribute
may be confusing; it's a pure coincidence that one of the elements in our source document has the same
name as an XSLT-defined attribute).

```
<xsl:template match="match">
   <xsl:variable name="date-out">
      <xsl:call-template name="format-date">
         <xsl:with-param name="iso-date" select="date" />
      </xsl:call-template>
   </xsl:variable>

   <h2><xsl:value-of select="concat(team[1], ' versus ', team[2])"/></h2>

   <table bgcolor="#cccccc" border="1" cellpadding="5">
      <xsl:copy-of select="$table-heading"/>
      <tr>
         <td><xsl:value-of select="$date-out"/></td>
         <td><xsl:value-of select="team[1]"/></td>
         <td><xsl:value-of select="team[2]"/></td>
         <td><xsl:value-of select="concat(team[1]/@score, '-',
             team[2]/@score)"/></td>
      </tr>
   </table>

</xsl:template>
</xsl:stylesheet>
```

Running the Example

You can run this example using a processor such as Instant Saxon, as with the previous example, but
the simplest way to do it is directly in the browser.

Assuming you are using Internet Explorer 5 or 5.5, you can download and install MSXML3 from the
Microsoft web site at http://msdn.microsoft.com/xml. Be sure to download and run the utility
`xmlinst.exe`, which makes MSXML3 the default parser on your system. Don't try to run this example
with the old MSXML parser that came with IE5 or IE5.5: it won't work.

Once you have installed this software, just double-click on the file `soccer.xml` from Windows Explorer: it's as simple as that. This loads the XML file into Internet Explorer, and because it starts with an `<?xml-stylesheet?>` processing instruction, it invokes this stylesheet to convert the document to HTML for display.

Output

Here's what the output of the first stylesheet looks like in the browser (and yes, I do know that all the matches were actually played in France):

Stylesheet 2

Now let's write another stylesheet to display the same data a completely different way. One of the motivations behind XSLT, after all, was to make information reusable by separating the information from the logic for displaying it.

This stylesheet, `soccer2.xsl`, does some calculation to create a league table. We'll start it with `<xsl:transform>` this time, just to show that this works too, and we'll start by creating two global variables, one for the set of all teams, and the other for the set of all matches. If we select all the `<team>` elements in the document, we'll get duplicates: to eliminate these, we have to select only those `<team>` elements that are not the same as a previous team.

```
<xsl:transform
   xmlns:xsl="http://www.w3.org/1999/XSL/Transform"
   version="1.0">

<xsl:variable name="teams" select="//team[not(.=preceding::team)]" />
<xsl:variable name="matches" select="//match" />
```

The actual logic of the stylesheet will go in a single template rule, which we'll set up to be triggered when the `<results>` element is processed. This starts by outputting a standard header:

```
<xsl:template match="results">
<html><body>
    <h1>Results of Group <xsl:value-of select="@group"/></h1>
    <table cellpadding="5">
        <tr>
            <td>Team</td>
            <td>Played</td>
            <td>Won</td>
            <td>Drawn</td>
            <td>Lost</td>
            <td>For</td>
            <td>Against</td>
        </tr>
```

Now the template processes each team in turn. We're only interested in getting totals for the number of matches won and lost and the number of goals scored, so it doesn't matter what order we process them in.

We'll start, for convenience, by setting up a variable called `this` to refer to the current team.

```
<xsl:for-each select="$teams">
    <xsl:variable name="this" select="." />
```

The number of matches played is easy to work out: it's the number of nodes in the `$matches` node-set that have a team equal to this team:

```
<xsl:variable name="played"
    select="count($matches[team=$this])"/>
```

The number of matches won is a bit more difficult. It's the number of matches for which the score of this team is greater than the score of the other team, which we can write as:

```
<xsl:variable name="won"
    select="count($matches[team[.=$this]/@score &gt;
    team[.!=$this]/@score])"/>
```

The number of matches lost and drawn follows the same logic, just changing the test from greater-than to less-than in the first case, and equals in the second:

```
<xsl:variable name="lost"
    select="count($matches[team[.=$this]/@score &lt;
    team[.!=$this]/@score])"/>
<xsl:variable name="drawn"
    select="count($matches[team[.=$this]/@score =
    team[.!=$this]/@score])"/>
```

The number of goals scored by this team can be obtained using the `sum()` function, applied to the node-set consisting of all scores for this team in any match:

```
<xsl:variable name="for"
    select="sum($matches/team[.=$this]/@score)"/>
```

And the simplest way of finding the number of goals scored against this team is to total the scores of all teams in matches that this team participated in, and then subtract the previous total:

```
<xsl:variable name="against"
    select="sum($matches[team=$this]/team/@score) - $for" />
```

Having done the calculations, we can output the results:

```
<tr>
    <td><xsl:value-of select="."/></td>
    <td><xsl:value-of select="$played"/></td>
    <td><xsl:value-of select="$won"/></td>
    <td><xsl:value-of select="$drawn"/></td>
    <td><xsl:value-of select="$lost"/></td>
    <td><xsl:value-of select="$for"/></td>
    <td><xsl:value-of select="$against"/></td>
</tr>
</xsl:for-each>
</table>
</body></html>
</xsl:template>

</xsl:transform>
```

Running the example

You can run this stylesheet the same way as the previous one. Edit the `<?xml-stylesheet?>` processing instruction in `soccer.xml` to refer to `soccer2.xsl` instead of `soccer1.xsl`, and load `soccer.xml` into the browser again. (Or just click **Refresh** if IE 5 is still open).

Of course, this isn't the way you would actually do things in practice. The `<?xml-stylesheet?>` approach, which defines a default stylesheet for a particular XML document, only really works where you always process an XML document using the same stylesheet. If you want to select different stylesheets on different occasions, you'll have to create an HTML page that loads the source document and stylesheet explicitly. We'll explain how to do that next.

Output

This is what the result looks like in the browser:

Results of Group A

Team	Played	Won	Drawn	Lost	For	Against
Brazil	3	2	0	1	6	3
Scotland	3	0	1	2	2	6
Morocco	3	1	1	1	5	5
Norway	3	1	2	0	5	4

Selecting a Stylesheet Dynamically

You can do XSLT transformations either on the server or in the browser: in fact, you might be using XSLT as part of a batch application that is nothing to do with the Web at all. Therefore, the way in which you invoke the transformation will vary depending on the circumstances, as well as on your choice of XSLT processor.

However, converting XML to HTML in the browser is perhaps one of the most striking ways of using XSLT, so we'll concentrate on that in our next example. Here we will include some simple logic on an HTML page to invoke a transformation based on the user's selection.

The HTML page soccer.html reads like this:

```
<html>
<head>
    <title>Results of Group A</title>
    <script>
        var source = null;
        var style = null;
        var transformer = null;

        function init()
        {
            source = new ActiveXObject("MSXML2.FreeThreadedDOMDocument");
            source.async = false;
            source.load('soccer.xml');
        }

        function apply(stylesheet)
        {
            style = new ActiveXObject("MSXML2.FreeThreadedDOMDocument");
            style.async = false;
            style.load(stylesheet);

            transformer = new ActiveXObject("MSXML2.XSLTemplate");
            transformer.stylesheet = style.documentElement;

            var xslproc = transformer.createProcessor();
            xslproc.input = source;
            xslproc.transform();
            displayarea.innerHTML = xslproc.output;
        }
    </script>
    <script for="window" event="onload">
        init();
    </script>
</head>
<body>
    <button onclick="apply('soccer1.xsl')">Results</button>
    <button onclick="apply('soccer2.xsl')">League table</button>
    <div id="displayarea"></div>
</body>
</html>
```

What this does is to display two buttons on the screen, as shown below:

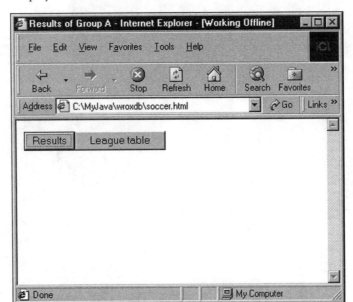

When you click on Results, the XML file is shown using stylesheet `soccer1.xsl`; when you click on League table, it is shown using `soccer2.xsl`.

For more details about the APIs used in this example, see the Microsoft product documentation, or the Wrox book *XSLT Programmers Reference* (ISBN1-861003-12-9).

Summary

In this appendix, we've looked at the role of XSLT as a transformation language for XML documents, and the role that XPath queries play within an XSLT stylesheet. We've given a lightning tour of XPath syntax, noting in particular the important role played by location paths as the way of navigating around the hierarchic structure of the source document.

Then we looked at how an XSLT stylesheet uses template rules and match patterns to define how each part of the source document should be processed. We looked at all the different instructions you can use inside a template body, and then came back to review the top-level elements you can use in a stylesheet to control processing options.

Then we relaxed by watching some soccer.

C

BizTalk Framework 2.0 Messages

We've mentioned the distinction between BizTalk Server, the software product, and BizTalk Framework, the messaging initiative. In Chapter 10 we gave an extended example of BizTalk Server's support for the BizTalk Framework initiative when we showed how the messaging service used the reliable envelope format. That format is the envelope structure provided as part of the BizTalk Framework. The sample we showed did not expose all of the envelope format. This appendix discussing the full syntax of the BizTalk Framework 2.0 XML vocabulary for message envelopes.

> *This appendix is based on the specification BizTalk Framework 2.0: Document and Message Specification (Microsoft, December 2000). An interesting sidelight of the specification is that it is the first tangible follow-through on Microsoft's pledge to migrate to W3C Schemas. The specifications are given in terms of both XML-DR and a draft of the as-yet unratified W3C schema format.*

BizTalk Envelope Structure

BizTalk Framework is all about the reliable and efficient routing of business messages. It makes no assumptions regarding the content of those messages except to assume that the core message is in XML format. The structure BizTalk Framework provides for routing is an envelope which is wrapped around the core business document and which carries information and requests related to the message interchange. With release 2.0 of the BizTalk Framework specification, the syntax of the vocabulary incorporates work done on envelope formats for the Simple Object Access Protocol (SOAP), an XML vocabulary currently enjoying a great deal of popularity among software developers.

Purpose and Origins

The BizTalk Framework message specification was first released shortly after the introduction of the BizTalk.org community site in 1999. Release 1.0 of the specification was developed largely by Microsoft with the advice and comment of selected industry third parties. The specification shared the current goals of providing an envelope for business-to-business messages that would facilitate their reliable and efficient routing, as well as being wholly self-contained.

Since that time, the SOAP specification has been released. While Microsoft is a major participant in the SOAP effort, SOAP has enjoyed wider support from the beginning, involving UserLand and DevelopMentor. Since then, IBM and others have joined in endorsing SOAP. SOAP is designed for a number of goals, but some of those overlap with BizTalk Framework. Most importantly, SOAP includes a message envelope format. That format includes the concept of a message consisting of an envelope that contains a header and a body. The header, in turn, includes some items which the message recipient must understand in order to process the message.

As the BizTalk Framework 2.0 effort proceeded, participants decided to alter the 1.0 structure to reflect the contributions of SOAP in order to avoid a proliferation of envelope formats for messaging schemes. Although BizTalk Framework 2.0 is very different from SOAP and addresses many needs not in SOAP's goals, it is definitely and explicitly influenced by that effort.

Structure

Every business message compliant with the BizTalk Framework 2.0 specification consists of an `Envelope` document element whose children are one `Header` and one `Body` element. That outer structure looks like this when namespace declarations are included:

```
<?xml version="1.0"?>
<SOAP-ENV:Envelope xmlns:SOAP-ENV="http://schemas.xmlsoap.org/soap/envelope/"
        xmlns:xsi="http://www.w3.org/1999/XMLSchema-instance">
  <SOAP-ENV:Header>
  . . . <!-- header child elements here -->
  </SOAP-ENV:Header>
  <SOAP-ENV:Body>
  . . . <!—business document here -->
  </SOAP-ENV:Body>
</SOAP-ENV:Envelope>
```

Note the two namespaces. The one whose prefix is `SOAP-ENV` refers to the core SOAP envelope schema. The URI which qualifies this namespace, incidentally, points to the schema for that envelope vocabulary, so you can readily follow it and compare the two schemas for yourself. The other namespace is taken from the W3C XML Schema effort and brings in that effort's extensible typing mechanism for complex, user-defined types.

The business document carries all the information needed to affect the business side of the document exchange. Our Site Service Description document from Chapter 3 and on is an example of one such business document. It concerns the business rules and state information which the messaging system is intended to implement. We will not consider that part of a BizTalk message further except to discuss the envelope's mechanism for conveying attachments. Suffice to say that the entire XML markup of the business document is inserted as an immediate child of the `SOAP-ENV:Body` element and no envelope information is to be found within that element. Our focus in this appendix, then, is on the contents of the `Header` element.

Header

The top level child elements reveal the function of the BizTalk envelope. All information needed to route messages to their proper destination, convey the contents of the business message, and indicate messaging services requested in conjunction with the transmission have a home in the `Header` element. Its children are also where BizTalk begins to diverge from the SOAP envelope structure. Here is a list of the child `SOAP-ENV:Header` element's child elements. Note that `SOAP-ENV:Header` has no attributes declared for it.

❑ `endpoints` – appears exactly once and describes the message sender and recipient

❑ `properties` – appears exactly once and conveys descriptive properties of the message interchange

❑ `services` – appears zero or once and indicates what functions may be desired from the receiving messaging service in the way of reliability

❑ `manifest` – appears zero or once and descibes the business document and any attachments

❑ `process` – appears zero or once and describes what step of a larger business process is served by this particular interchange

The BizTalk Framework specification declares separate namespaces for each child element. The child elements are different in terms of their purpose and do not overlap one another. We will therefore frame the rest of our discussion of the BizTalk Framework messaging specification in terms of these child elements.

Endpoints

The `endpoints` element conveys the source and destination of the interchange and is the closest analogy to a postal envelope in the BizTalk Framework. Because it is a critical piece of the BizTalk envelope structure, it bears the `SOAP-ENV:mustUnderstand` attribute with the value of 1. A receiver that gets a BizTalk envelope must understand the endpoints element or terminate processing with an error. It consists of mandatory `to` and `from` elements, each of which has a mandatory `address` element. The textual content of the `address` element, in turn, is an indicator that locates the entity to which the address refers. This is left open to the implementation.

The `address` element bears a single attribute, xsi:type. This attribute refers to a user-declared type from XML schemas as defined by the W3C. The particular types used with BizTalk envelopes are declared by the BizTalk Framework. The first thought, a URL, will work for those organizations that expose a unique protocol-specific message handler for each message type. For HTTP, that might take the form of an ASP that is confined to a particular message format, e.g., **Site Service Description**. As we saw in Chapter 10, however, BizTalk Server installations can use a single generic HTTP receive function for all message types, trusting the messaging service to sort messages out according to channels following submission. For that purpose, BizTalk defines the type **OrganizationName**. The reliable envelope handler in BizTalk Server sees this and passes the value to `IInterchange` through the appropriate parameter of the `Submit` call. Here is a sample `endpoints` element:

```
<eps:endpoints SOAP-ENV:mustUnderstand="1"
   xmlns:eps="http://schemas.biztalk.org/btf-2-0/endpoints"
   xmlns:biz="http://schemas.biztalk.org/btf-2-0/address/types">
   <eps:to>
```

```
      <eps:address xsi:type="biz:OrganizationName">BTFPartner</eps:address>
    </eps:to>
    <eps:from>
      <eps:address xsi:type="biz:OrganizationName">
        Wrox Site Managers
      </eps:address>
    </eps:from>
  </eps:endpoints>
```

Note the namespace declarations for the endpoints namespace and the type declarations namespace.

Properties

The `properties` element, for which BizTalk declares a namespace, carries informational properties that describe the document interchange. These are properties that would be expected to be processed by the messaging service or its equivalent. The `SOAP-ENV:mustUnderstand` attribute is required and defaults to the value 1. This element has four mandatory child elements which appear in the following sequence:

- ❑ `identity` – typed as a URI, the globally unique identifier used for message tracking and correlation of receipts and error responses with the original document

- ❑ `sentAt` – typed as a `dateTime.tz` value, this is the time at which the properties element was generated

- ❑ `expiresAt` – typed as a `dateTime.tz` value, this is the time after which the document must be declared invalid from the business standpoint and discarded

- ❑ `topic` – typed as a URI, denotes the content or business topic of the business document enclosed in the enevelope

The `identity` element will typically be a GUID, but the BizTalk Framework specification leaves this up to the specific messaging implementation. It could also, for example, be implemented as a hash on the enclosed business document. The only requirement is that the string uniquely identify the document. The BizTalk Server messaging service uses this for receipt correlation and to implement the reliability mechanism. If the sending messaging service has not received a receipt for a reliable interchange by the `expiresAt` time, derived from a setting in Messaging Manager provided by the BizTalk administrator, the interchange is moved to the suspended queue.

The `sentAt` and `expiresAt` elements are absolute times that include time zone designators to avoid confusion. It is important to consider transport protocol latency, time synchronization discrepancies between interchange partners, and the business case when setting the value of `expiresAt`.

The `topic` element has no requirement other than it be a token that is likely to be understood by both parties. The `mustUnderstand` attribute is not applicable to this element, so even that requirement is not absolute. Its purpose is to assist with routing in some implementations, e.g., topic-based routing within an application. The Framework anticipates that this value will be provided by the application that provides the business document. In BizTalk Server's case, the value of `topic` is provided by the reliable envelope component and consists of the name of the business document's document element. Here is a sample `properties` element:

```
<prop:properties SOAP-ENV:mustUnderstand="1"
    xmlns:prop="http://schemas.biztalk.org/btf-2-0/properties">
```

```
    <prop:identity>uuid:8FFBA256-34AC-4A61-BC5D-29FB49F28962</prop:identity>
    <prop:sentAt>2000-10-28T01:12:41+00:00</prop:sentAt>
    <prop:expiresAt>2000-10-28T01:22:41+00:00</prop:expiresAt>
    <prop:topic>root:MyBusinessDoc</prop:topic>
  </prop:properties>
```

Services

The `services` element is related less to the low-level mechanics of the messaging service than it is to the business process, yet it falls just short of the information that you would expect to find in the business document itself. The child elements of the `services` element request receipt services from the message recipient's messaging service implementation. There are two kinds of services that may be requested and they are represented by the `deliveryReceiptRequest` and `commitmentReceiptRequest` elements. Both elements are optional; either, both, or neither of the elements may appear. The `services` element itself has no attributes declared on it, although it will commonly bear a namespace declaration for the services namespace.

The `deliveryReceiptRequest` element tells the message recipient that the sender wants an acknowledgement when the message is received. This acknowledgement does not indicate anything about the business process. There are no guarantees that the message will be accepted or that action will be taken. The receipt simply tells the sender that the message was received. BizTalk Server 2000 will automatically create a `deliveryReceiptRequest` element when you specify the use of reliable envelopes. When it receives a BizTalk Framework envelope with such an element it will send a receipt (a BizTalk document containing a `deliveryReceipt` element) to the address specified within. The BizTalk Server messaging service uses this mechanism to add reliability to the interchange. As noted previously, when sending a message with a reliable envelope, the messaging service will leave the message on the scheduled queue until a receipt is received for it, all its retry attempts have been exhausted, or the deadline for receiving a receipt (discussed below) is passed.

The `commitmentReceiptRequest` element indicates that the sender desires notification of the recipients decision regarding processing of the sender's request. The recipient is expected to acknowledge with a BizTalk document containing a `commitmentReceipt` element. BizTalk Server 2000 does not automatically use this element at this time.

The `deliveryReceiptRequested` and `commitmentReceiptRequested` elements share a common structure. Neither has attributes defined. Both consist of two required elements, `sendTo` and `sendBy`. The `sendTo` element has a child address element such as we saw on the `to` and `from` elements under `endpoints`. The address is the destination to which the message recipient should send the receipt. BizTalk Server 2000 uses the URL configured by the BizTalk administrator for reliable receipts. The `sendBy` element is typed as `dateTime.tz` and is the absolute time by which the sender expects a receipt. In BizTalk Server 2000, this time is derived by adding the expected receipt interval from the Source Organization page of the channel wizard to the `sentAt` time. Here is a sample `services` element requesting both types of receipt services:

```
<services xmlns="http://schemas.biztalk.org/btf-2-0/services">
  <deliveryReceiptRequest>
   <sendTo>
     <address xsi:type="biz:httpURL">
      http://atropos/BTFPartner/BTFReceipts.asp
     </address>
   </sendTo>
   <sendBy>2000-10-28T02:22:41+00:00</sendBy>
  </deliveryReceiptRequest>
  <commitmentReceiptRequest>
```

```
   <sendTo>
     <address xsi:type="biz:httpURL">
      http://atropos/BTFPartner/BTFReceipts.asp
     </address>
   </sendTo>
   <sendBy>2000-10-28T08:22:41+00:00</sendBy>
  </commitmentReceiptRequest>
 </services>
```

Manifest

The optional `manifest` element serves to catalog all the contents of a multi-part document interchange. There are two ways you would use this. One is when you have multiple business documents you wish to transmit with a single interchange (the "boxcar" document of BizTalk Framework 1.0). The other is when the core business document requires attachments. These attachments need not be XML and, indeed, typically will not be of that format. You might, for example include image files or spreadsheets that support the business document. Since non-XML documents cannot conveniently travel within the bounds of an XML-format envelope, BizTalk Framework provides a mechanism compatible with multi-part MIME transmissions. The business document and its supporting documents are bundled into one HTTP transmission, each of whose parts receive a different encoding according to their content. Sorting this parts out on the receiving end is the purpose of the `manifest` element.

If the `manifest` element appears, it will contain one or more `reference` elements. There are no other elements or attributes declared for the `manifest` element's content model. Each `reference` element contains one or two child elements. The first, which must appear, is either a `document` element or an `attachment` element. The second, optional child, is a `description` element.

The `document` and `attachment` elements have the same structure. Neither have attributes, and both have a single required attribute named `href`. This is where things get a little tricky. The attribute is typed as `uri`. When the element is `document`, the value of `href` refers to an internal ID, specifically the `id` attribute of the document element of the business document. If the element is `attachment`, the URI begins with CID: and is the value of the `Content-ID` header. Here is a `manifest` element for a business document with one JPEG file attachment:

```
<manifest xmlns="http://schemas.biztalk.org/btf-2-0/manifest">
  <reference>
   <document href="#doc_id_1234"/>
   <description>Business document</description>
  </reference>
  <reference>
   <attachment href="CID:ref_image.jpg@btfpartner.com"/>
   <description>reference image file</description>
  </reference>
</manifest>
```

The HTTP headers (with partial contents) that go with that would look like this:

```
MIME-Version: 1.0
Content-Type: Multipart/Related;
    boundary=biztalk_2_0_boundary;
```

```
        type=text/xml;
        start="<businessdoc.xml@btfpartner.com>"

--biztalk_2_0_boundary--
Content-Type: text/xml; charset=UTF-8
Content-Transfer-Encoding: 8bit
Content-ID: <businessdoc.xml@btfpartner.com>

<?xml version="1.0"?>
<SOAP-ENV:Envelope xmlns:SOAP-ENV="http://schemas.xmlsoap.org/soap/envelope/"
         xmlns:xsi="http://www.w3.org/1999/XMLSchema-instance">
  <SOAP-ENV:Header>
   . . . <!-- header omitted for clarity -->
  </SOAP-ENV:Header>
  <SOAP-ENV:Body>
   <MyBusinessDoc id="doc_id_1234"
      xmlns="urn:schemas-btfpartner-com/busdoc">
      . . .<!-- omitted for clarity -->
   </MyBusinessDoc>
  </SOAP-ENV:Body>
</SOAP-ENV:Envelope>

--biztalk_2_0_boundary--
Content-Type: image/jpeg
Content-Transfer-Encoding: base64
Content-ID: <ref_image.jpg@btfpartnert.com>

. . . binary jpeg image here

--biztalk_2_0_boundary--
```

Notice that the URI in the manifest for the attached image file matches the `Content-ID` value of the jpeg portion of the transmission, while the URI for the document matches the value of the `id` attribute on the business document's document element. Note also that using attachments or boxcar transmissions in BizTalk Framework envelopes will require that you add an `id` field of attribute type to your business document's message specification.

Process

The optional `process` element contains information that helps the receiving messaging service relate this interchange with some ongoing business process. BizTalk Framework 2.0 is deliberately vague on this point. The purpose of the `process` element is to provide a container that lets individual partners relate messages according to some implementation-specific processing details. For example, a partner using BizTalk Server 2000 might want to reference a running instance of an orchestration schedule as well as a receive port in that schedule. Since these details can vary between implementations, BizTalk Framework cannot provide definitive structure. It is possible, however, to discern some broad areas that are likely to pertain to all implementations. It is these areas that the `process` element uses for its content model.

Consider the concept of a particular class of process. You might have a purchasing function, or a customer service function. A purchasing process might consist of multiple steps involving multiple messages. You would expect to go through a process of soliciting quotes, receiving bids, accepting or rejecting bids, and authorizing payment for each purchase. A BizTalk Server implementation could make this more specific by referring to a specific orchestration schedule that implements the business process. This concept is implemented in the `process` element as a required child element named `type`. It is a text-only element whose typed contents are a URI. The URI is resolved by the message recipient into a class of business process.

Of course, a production environment is probably going to be running multiple instances of the same process, e.g., several purchasing agents or multiple instances of a given schedule file. Certainly we would want to process purchase orders or bids concurrently. A means of determining which instance of a business process the incoming message pertains to is required. This is codified as the second required child element, instance. It, too, is a text-only element with a URI for its contents.

Finally, a business partner might wish to refine the process information by referring to a particular step in the process or by providing clarifying detail. Unlike the other two concepts, it is impossible to have a broadly useful implementation consisting solely of a name. If a URI were used, it would probably have to be a URL pointing to another XML document. Rather than require multiple round-trips or a multi-part transmission, the BizTalk Framework implements this notion as an open content, element-only element named detail. This element is optional, but if it appears, it may only appear once. If you were using BizTalk Server, you might use the port reference nomenclature discussed in Chapter 6 to implement this element's internal content. Note, however, that the internal content of the detail element is site implementation specific and is not specified in any way by either BizTalk Framework or BizTalk Server 2000.

Here is a sample process element with information regarding a BizTalk schedule instance:

```
<process xmlns="http://schemas.biztalk.org/btf-2-0/process">
  <type>sked://mymachine!XLANG Scheduler</type>
  <instance>
   {770C13A4-AB4C-4470-821F-D1FAE5235AE0}
  </instance>
  <detail xmlns:p="urn:schemas-btfpartner-com/schedules">
   <p:ToPort>
     NextStepPort
   </p:ToPort>
   < p:ResponsePort>
     ReplyPort
   </p:ResponsePort>
  </detail>
</process>
```

We're making the assumption that the partners in this exchange are both using BizTalk Server orchestration schedule to model their business process. They implicitly agree to exchange information regarding the name and instance of the schedule to use, and further agree to indicate which port on the schedule they wish to use. In particular, we are assuming they share a schedule in common. Each exchange, then, consists of sending a document and telling the recipient which port should receive the document. We need this information because conditional logic might cause us to change branches.

We've extended the detail element with two elements of our own: ToPort and ResponsePort. The name in ResponsePort becomes the name in ToPort in the message sent in response to the current message. In the above sample, the document is sent to NextStepPort. When the recipient replies to the above sample fragment, ReplyPort will be in p:ToPort, and some new port name will be in p:ResponsePort. The partner receiving the message strings the values together to obtain a valid BizTalk orchestration port reference and submits the document in the manner we explored in Chapter 6.

A Sample BizTalk Framework Message

For context, we've incorporated all the above samples into a complete message, shown below, complying with the BizTalk Framework envelope format. Optional elements are included.

```xml
<?xml version="1.0"?>
<SOAP-ENV:Envelope xmlns:SOAP-ENV="http://schemas.xmlsoap.org/soap/envelope/"
   xmlns:xsi="http://www.w3.org/1999/XMLSchema-instance">
  <SOAP-ENV:Header>
    <eps:endpoints SOAP-ENV:mustUnderstand="1"
       xmlns:eps="http://schemas.biztalk.org/btf-2-0/endpoints"
       xmlns:biz="http://schemas.biztalk.org/btf-2-0/address/types">
      <eps:to>
        <eps:address xsi:type="biz:OrganizationName">
          BTFPartner
        </eps:address>
      </eps:to>
      <eps:from>
        <eps:address xsi:type="biz:OrganizationName">
          Wrox Site Managers
        </eps:address>
      </eps:from>
    </eps:endpoints>
    <prop:properties SOAP-ENV:mustUnderstand="1"
       xmlns:prop="http://schemas.biztalk.org/btf-2-0/properties">
      <prop:identity>
        uuid:8FFBA256-34AC-4A61-BC5D-29FB49F28962
      </prop:identity>
      <prop:sentAt>2000-10-28T01:12:41+00:00</prop:sentAt>
      <prop:expiresAt>2000-10-28T01:22:41+00:00</prop:expiresAt>
      <prop:topic>root:MyBusinessDoc</prop:topic>
    </prop:properties>
    <services xmlns="http://schemas.biztalk.org/btf-2-0/services">
      <deliveryReceiptRequest>
        <sendTo>
          <address xsi:type="biz:httpURL">
            http://atropos/BTFPartner/BTFReceipts.asp
          </address>
        </sendTo>
        <sendBy>2000-10-28T02:22:41+00:00</sendBy>
      </deliveryReceiptRequest>
      <commitmentReceiptRequest>
        <sendTo>
          <address xsi:type="biz:httpURL">
            http://atropos/BTFPartner/BTFReceipts.asp
          </address>
        </sendTo>
        <sendBy>2000-10-28T08:22:41+00:00</sendBy>
      </commitmentReceiptRequest>
    </services>
    <manifest xmlns="http://schemas.biztalk.org/btf-2-0/manifest">
      <reference>
        <document href="#doc_id_1234"/>
        <description>Business document</description>
      </reference>
```

```
    <reference>
      <attachment href="CID:ref_image.jpg@btfpartner.com"/>
      <description>reference image file</description>
    </reference>
  </manifest>
  <process xmlns="http://schemas.biztalk.org/btf-2-0/process">
    <type>sked://mymachine!XLANG Scheduler</type>
    <instance>
      {770C13A4-AB4C-4470-821F-D1FAE5235AE0}
    </instance>
    <detail xmlns:p="urn:schemas-btfpartner-com/schedules">
    <p:ToPort>
      NextStepPort
    </p:ToPort>
    < p:ResponsePort>
      ReplyPort
    </p:ResponsePort>
    </detail>
  </process>
  </SOAP-ENV:Header>
  <SOAP-ENV:Body>
   <MyBusinessDoc id="doc_id_1234">
     . . . <!-- contents omitted for brevity -->
   </MyBusinessDoc>
  </SOAP-ENV:Body>
</SOAP-ENV:Envelope>
```

Receipt Documents

As noted earlier, BizTalk Framework may involve two kinds of receipts. The most common, which is implemented by BizTalk Server 2000, is the delivery receipt. The other is an acknowledgement or advisory of the recipient's business decision on the sender's request, termed a commitment receipt. Receipts are BizTalk documents, so they share a common top-level structure with the envelope structure shown above. That is, they consist of an `Envelope` document element bearing mandatory `endpoints` and `properties` elements. Unlike the business document element, the third child element of `Envelope` is either a `deliveryReceipt` or `commitmentReceipt` element. The `Body` element of a receipt is always empty.

Delivery Receipts

The `deliveryReceipt` element has a single required attribute, `SOAP-ENV:mustUnderstand`, and two required elements, `receivedAt` and `identity`. The `deliveryReceipt` element cannot contain textual content, and the `SOAP-ENV:mustUnderstand` attribute must always take on the value 1. The `receivedAt` element, typed as `dateTime.tz` in XDR schemas, is a timestamp referring to the instant the business document was received at the recipient's server. The identity element, typed as a `uri`, bears the identity value from the request document which the receipt acknowledges.

The `expiresAt` timestamp in the `properties` element of the receipt must coincide with the request document's deadline for receipts, i.e., the value of the `sendBy` element of the business document.

Here is a sample delivery receipt that acknowledges the sample request shown above:

```
<?xml version="1.0"?>
<SOAP-ENV:Envelope xmlns:SOAP-ENV="http://schemas.xmlsoap.org/soap/envelope/"
    xmlns:xsi="http://www.w3.org/1999/XMLSchema-instance">
  <SOAP-ENV:Header>
   <eps:endpoints SOAP-ENV:mustUnderstand="1"
       xmlns:eps="http://schemas.biztalk.org/btf-2-0/endpoints"
       xmlns:biz="http://schemas.biztalk.org/btf-2-0/address/types">
    <eps:to>
     <eps:address xsi:type="biz:httpURL">
       http://atropos/BTFPartner/BTFReceipts.asp
     </eps:address>
    </eps:to>
    <eps:from>
     <eps:address xsi:type="biz:OrganizationName">
       BTFPartner
     </eps:address>
    </eps:from>
   </eps:endpoints>
   <prop:properties SOAP-ENV:mustUnderstand="1"
       xmlns:prop="http://schemas.biztalk.org/btf-2-0/properties">
    <prop:identity>
     uuid:E54239E2-07D9-4e5d-ACCB-2F8B082169A8
    </prop:identity>
    <prop:sentAt>2000-10-28T01:13:00+00:00</prop:sentAt>
    <prop:expiresAt>2000-10-28T08:22:41+00:00</prop:expiresAt>
    <prop:topic>delivery_receipt</prop:topic>
   </prop:properties>
   <deliveryReceipt xmlns="http://schemas.biztalk.org/btf-2-0/receipts"
           SOAP-ENV:mustUnderstand="1">
    <receivedAt>2000-10-28T01:12:55+00:00</receivedAt>
    <identity> uuid:8FFBA256-34AC-4A61-BC5D-29FB49F28962</identity>
   </deliveryReceipt>
  </SOAP-ENV:Header>
  <SOAP-ENV:Body/>
</SOAP-ENV:Envelope>
```

Commitment Receipts

Like the delivery receipt, a commitment receipt is a basic BizTalk envelope with the addition of a commitmentReceipt element. Like its counterpart deliveryReceipt, commitmentReceipt must bear the SOAP-ENV:mustUnderstand attribute with the value 1. The element has only elements as its children, but its content model is slightly more complex than the delivery receipt.

The commitmentReceipt element begins with three required elements:

❑   identity – a uri which takes its textual content from the identity element of the request document

❑   decidedAt – the dateTime.tz typed timestamp denoting the time the decision was made

❑   decision – a value indicating the results of the decision

The BizTalk Framework 2.0 specification states that the possible values of decision are positive or negative, although the XDR schemas are not that restrictive, specifying only that the value must be a string value. The XSD schema for this, however, do specify this as an enumeration. We will assume the later as controlling.

This basic information is augmented by two optional elements:

- ❑ `commitmentCode` – an application-specific qualified name which further characterizes the decision

- ❑ `commitmentDetail` – application-specific open content providing details of the commitment decision

Here again there is a discrepancy between the two versions of the schemas. The XDR version states that `commitmentCode` is optional, while the XSD version says that it is required. The supporting narrative says that it is optional. This position makes sense given the open-ended nature of the information, so we will assume it is optional.

Both the optional elements are to be defined by the business partners and provide specific detail that helps make sense of the decision in the context of the transaction. For example, a request that is ordering some goods might receive a negative decision, with a value for `commitmentCode` that denoted an out-of-stock condition at the supplier and a `commitmentDetail` structure that indicated an expected resupply date and an indicator that the sender must resubmit the order on that date.

Here is a sample commitment receipt that might be sent in response to the sample request document above:

```xml
<?xml version="1.0"?>
<SOAP-ENV:Envelope xmlns:SOAP-ENV="http://schemas.xmlsoap.org/soap/envelope/"
    xmlns:xsi="http://www.w3.org/1999/XMLSchema-instance">
  <SOAP-ENV:Header>
   <eps:endpoints SOAP-ENV:mustUnderstand="1"
      xmlns:eps="http://schemas.biztalk.org/btf-2-0/endpoints"
      xmlns:biz="http://schemas.biztalk.org/btf-2-0/address/types">
    <eps:to>
     <eps:address xsi:type="biz:httpURL">
       http://atropos/BTFPartner/BTFReceipts.asp
     </eps:address>
    </eps:to>
    <eps:from>
     <eps:address xsi:type="biz:OrganizationName">
       BTFPartner
     </eps:address>
    </eps:from>
   </eps:endpoints>
   <prop:properties SOAP-ENV:mustUnderstand="1"
      xmlns:prop="http://schemas.biztalk.org/btf-2-0/properties">
    <prop:identity>
     uuid:E54239E2-07D9-4e5d-ACCB-2F8B082169A8
    </prop:identity>
    <prop:sentAt>2000-10-28T01:13:10+00:00</prop:sentAt>
    <prop:expiresAt>2000-10-28T08:22:41+00:00</prop:expiresAt>
    <prop:topic>delivery_receipt</prop:topic>
   </prop:properties>
```

```
      <deliveryReceipt xmlns="http://schemas.biztalk.org/btf-2-0/receipts"
             SOAP-ENV:mustUnderstand="1">
        <identity> uuid:5220C909-4D1B-48d8-818B-DDCEA227DF27</identity>
        <decidededAt>2000-10-28T01:12:55+00:00</decidedAt>
        <decision>positive</decision>
      </deliveryReceipt>
    </SOAP-ENV:Header>
    <SOAP-ENV:Body/>
  </SOAP-ENV:Envelope>
```

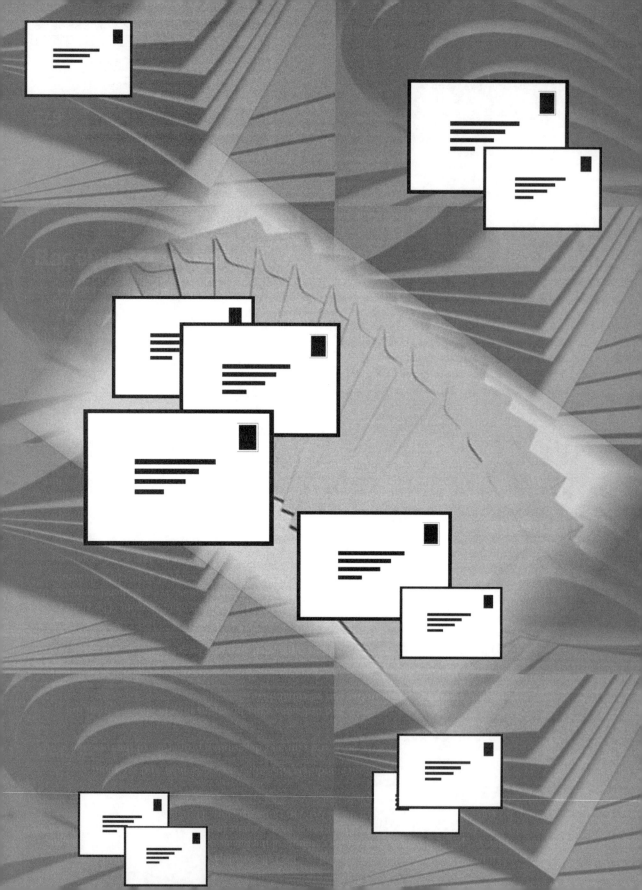

Index

A Guide to the Index

The index is arranged hierarchically, in alphabetical order, with symbols preceding the letter A. Most second-level entries and many third-level entries also occur as first-level entries. This is to ensure that users will find the information they require however they choose to search for it.

I

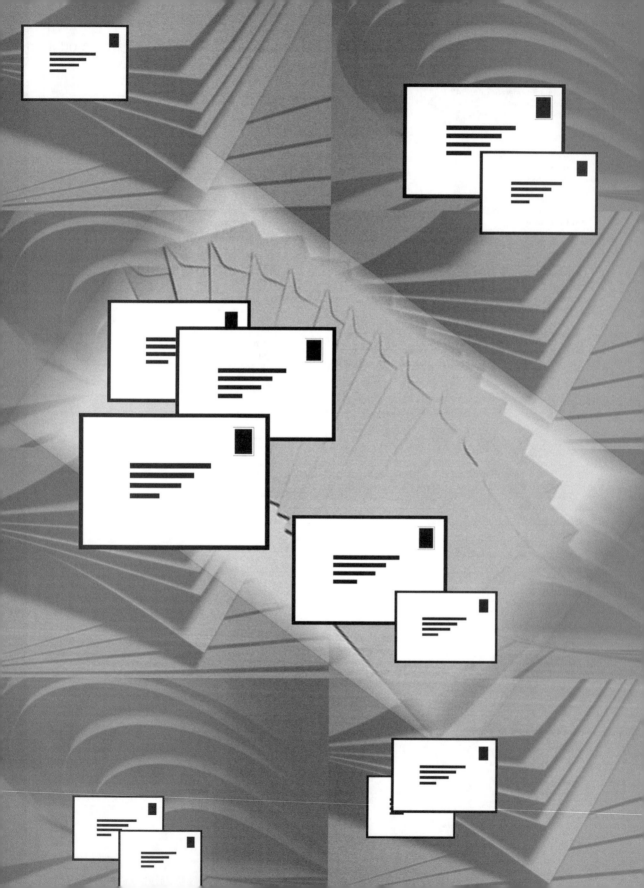

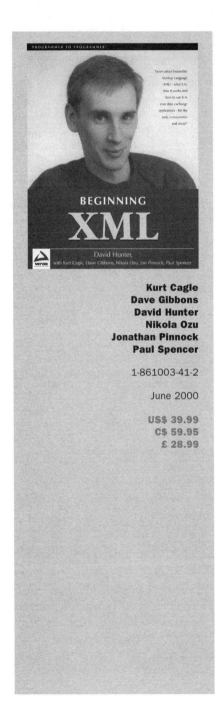

This book explains and demonstrates XML and related technologies. This is the exciting new way of marking up and manipulating data within your applications. XML is platform independent and versatile, meaning that it is rapidly becoming a major technology. Anywhere that data is exchanged between applications or tiers is a potential application for XML. This book will teach you how to use it in your data exchange applications – on the web, for e-commerce or in n-tier architectures – by explaining XML theory, reinforced with plenty of practical examples and real life solutions.

● XML syntax and writing well formed XML

● Using namespaces in XML

● Adding style with CSS and XSL

Summary of contents

Kurt Cagle
Dave Gibbons
David Hunter
Nikola Ozu
Jonathan Pinnock
Paul Spencer

1-861003-41-2

June 2000

US$ 39.99
C$ 59.95
£ 28.99

Kevin Williams
Michael Brundage
Patrick Dengler
Jeff Gabriel
Andy Hoskinson
Michael Kay
Thomas Maxwell
Marcelo Ochoa
Johnny Papa
Mohan Vanmane

1-861003-58-7

December 2000

US$ 49.99
C$ 74.95
£ 38.99

With the increasing amount of data stored in relational databases, and the importance of XML as a format for marking up data – whether it be for storage, display, interchange, or processing - you need to have command of four key skills: understanding how to structure, process, access, and store your data. By introducing guidelines for how to model your XML documents in relational databases and how to model relational database information as XML, we will establish structures that enable quick and efficient access, and make our data more flexible. We then look at the developer's XML toolbox, discussing associated technologies and strategies that will help us in describing, processing, and manipulating data. We also discuss common techniques for data access, data warehousing, transmission, and marshalling and presentation, giving working examples in every chapter.

- Guidelines for how to handle translating an XML structure to a relational database model
- Rules for modeling XML based upon a relational database structure
- Common techniques for storing, transmitting, and displaying your content

Summary of contents

Active Server Pages has developed over the last few years into the foremost technology for developing Internet and intranet applications. Central to any effective web application is data manipulation, and Professional ASP Data Access is a complete guide to creating ASP data-centric applications. This book will take you from database design principles, through building COM components for data access, to advanced topics such as data warehousing and data mining. Relational databases such as SQL Server, Oracle and DB2 are fully covered, as well as non-relational data stores such as Exchange 2000, directory services, legacy data, and XML. Wherever data is stored, this book will help you to write powerful ASP applications that make full use of all your vital information.

- Database fundamentals

- ADO, OLE DB and ODBC

- Building COM(+) components for data access

Summary of contents

PROFESSIONAL
ASP Data
Access

Dino Esposito, James R. De Carli, Jason Hales, Simon Robinson

Richard Anderson
James R De Carli
Dino Esposito
Charles Fairchild
Aaron Grady
John Granade
Jason Hales
Joshua Parkin
Rama Ramachandran
Matthew Reynolds
Simon Robinson
Ulrich Schwanitz
Julian Skinner
Kent Tegels
Thearon Willis

1-861003-92-7

October 2000

US$ 59.99
C$ 89.95
£ 43.99

Mark Chaffin
Brian Knight
Todd Robinson

1-861004-41-9

December 2000

US$ 49.99
C$ 74.95
£ 35.99

Professional SQL Server DTS provides a complete introduction to DTS fundamentals and architecture before exploring the more complex data transformations involved in moving data between different servers, applications, and providers. The book then focuses on DTS programming via the DTS object model, enabling developers to incorporate custom transformations and reporting capabilities into their applications. Advanced topics are explained including error handling, dynamic data loading, and data warehouses. With code and case studies this book gives the reader a complete picture of how to use DTS to its fullest potential. This book is principally aimed at database programmers and administrators who have a working knowledge of SQL Server, and who wish to take DTS beyond its most basic level and tailor it to their needs. It will also appeal to managers and project managers who want to gain an understanding of DTS and how it could benefit their businesses.

● A detailed explanation of the seventeen principal DTS tasks

● Connecting to, querying, and converting heterogeneous data

● Dynamic configuration of your DTS packages

Summary of contents

This book explores Application Center 2000, Microsoft's deployment and management tool for high-availability Web applications built on the Windows 2000 operating system. The book follows Wrox's Programmer to Programmer™ strategy, focusing on the product from the point of view of the developer rather than just the administrator. While it fully covers setup and administration issues, it is more than just a 'setting-up' book, addressing the issues involved in building and configuring applications on AC2K clusters - such as application design, component use, installation, session state management, and much more. This book is for any Web developer (Web sites or Web applications) that needs to achieve scalability through the use of a server farm or in a multi-server environment; this includes those looking for true 'enterprise-level' scalability.

- Simple-to-implement scalability, using multiple servers to 'scale-out'
- Automated high availability through load sharing and automatic fail-over
- Automatic synchronization of content and machine configuration across a cluster

Summary of contents

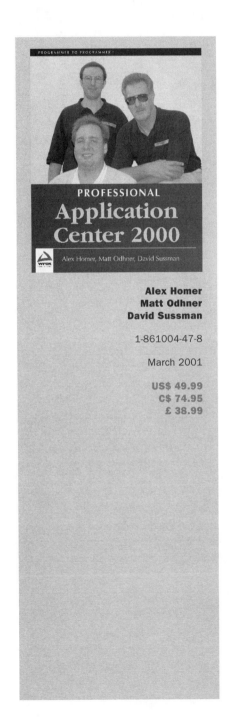

PROFESSIONAL

Application Center 2000

Alex Homer, Matt Odhner, David Sussman

Alex Homer
Matt Odhner
David Sussman

1-861004-47-8

March 2001

US$ 49.99
C$ 74.95
£ 38.99

Rob Vieira

1-861004-48-6

December 2000

US$ 59.99
C$ 89.95
£ 45.99

SQL Server 2000 is the latest and most powerful version of Microsoft's data warehousing and relational database management system. This new release is tightly integrated with Windows 2000 and offers more support for XML, as well as improved Analysis Services for OLAP and data mining. Professional SQL Server 2000 provides a comprehensive guide to programming with SQL Server 2000, from a complete tutorial on Transact-SQL to an in-depth discussion of new features, such as indexed views, user-defined functions, and the wealth of new SQL Server features to support XML. Whether you're coming to SQL Server 2000 from another relational database management system, upgrading your existing system, or perhaps wanting to add programming skills to your DBA knowledge, you'll find what you need in this book to get to grips with SQL Server 2000 development.

- A complete introduction to Transact-SQL
- Creating and using views, stored procedures, and user defined functions
- Querying a SQL Server database using English Query and Full-Text Search

Summary of contents

Beginning SQL Server 2000 for
Visual Basic Developers

SQL Server 2000 is a feature-rich and robust enterprise-level database application, which many VB programmers choose to provide the data layer in their n-tier applications. This book covers all you need to know to work with SQL Server 2000, to provide users of your VB and web-based applications with controlled access to your data. Starting with an introduction to designing and creating a database and working through creating increasingly complex T-SQL stored procedures, you'll learn how to incorporate data access (including ADO) into your VB applications, manage security, and make data available across the Web. Comprehensively explained step-by-step examples will guide you through creating an entire VB-based application to manage both the data itself and access to that data. Additionally, you will learn how to create and deploy web reports and an English Query application.

● Introduction to relational database design and theory

● Installing the Personal Edition of SQL Server 2000

● How to create and run stored procedures from VB applications and components

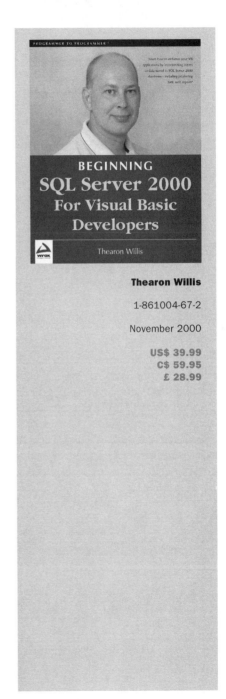

Thearon Willis

1-861004-67-2

November 2000

US$ 39.99
C$ 59.95
£ 28.99

Summary of contents

Professional SQL Server Development with Access 2000

Rick Dobson

1-861004-83-4

September 2000

US$ 49.99
C$ 74.95
£ 35.99

Access 2000 is the latest version of a product that has a proven record in providing powerful, cost effective, and convenient database solutions for small and medium businesses. Through the feature of Access projects, and the introduction of the Microsoft Data Engine (MSDE), Access 2000 now offers a way for Access developers to harness the power of the SQL Server range of database engines while working inside a familiar framework. This book concentrates on the use of Access 2000 projects with MSDE and SQL Server engines and will highlight the ease with which sophisticated, scalable database solutions may be constructed. Since the delivery of data over the Internet is becoming crucial, this book will also cover the approaches and technologies required to build database-driven Web pages.

● Full coverage of the use of Access 2000 projects with MSDE and SQL Server 7.0

● Introduces the use of Access 2000 with SQL Server 2000

● Programmatic database manipulation and querying using SQL, VBA, and ADO

Summary of contents